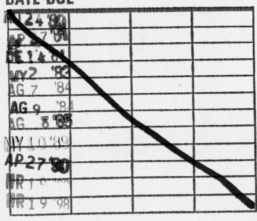

DATE DUE

MY 24 '81			
AP 7 '82			
SE 14 '82			
MY 2 '83			
AG 7 '84			
AG 9 '84			
AG 8 '85			
MY 10 '89			
AP 27 '90			
MR 19 '98			

LEADERSHIP IN CONGRESS

The
Study of
Congress
Series

LEADERSHIP IN CONGRESS

Stability, Succession, and Change

ROBERT L. PEABODY
Johns Hopkins University

LITTLE, BROWN AND COMPANY
BOSTON AND TORONTO

To my Mother and Father

Foreword

The Study of Congress is sponsored by the American Political Science Association with the support of a generous grant from the Carnegie Corporation. The project was first conceived by a small group of scholars and congressmen (the latter led by Chet Holifield, D-Calif., and Thomas B. Curtis, R-Mo.) who held a series of discussion meetings on Congress with financial aid from the Philip Stern Family Fund. These discussions led to an agreement to seek support for a comprehensive study of Congress. A formal proposal was prepared by Evron M. Kirkpatrick, Executive Director of the American Political Science Association, and Donald G. Tacheron, Associate Director, which resulted in the grant by the Carnegie Corporation.

The Study of Congress gave political scientists an opportunity to cover ground in one concerted thrust which they might individually inch over in a decade. Such an opportunity was unprecedented, and it increased the urgency and importance of the basic questions: What should be the target of the study? Who should do it? How should it be done?

Reform of Congress is always in the air. Congress is criticized, even by its own members, because, as a representative body, it mirrors the weaknesses as well as the strengths of the represented. Moreover, it is powerful; almost alone among the national legislatures, it has withstood domination by the Executive and has remained the coordinate branch the Founding Fathers meant it to be. What Congress does matters very much, here and abroad, and for that reason one is tempted to try to change it, to alter some procedure or structural arrangement in order to increase one's influence on the legislative product.

Nevertheless, reform is not the target of this research project. Congress does change, but slowly, adaptively in things that matter, and seldom according to blueprint. Structure and procedure are not neutral; they are used to work the will of those who control them. Moreover, alterations in them often have unforeseen consequences. This is more likely to be true when structure and rules, and to whose benefit they work, are imperfectly understood. The Study of Congress began, therefore, with a modest admission and an appropriate resolution: there are large gaps in what political scientists know about Congress and the Study would try to fill in as many as it could.

Each of the studies which make up the Study of Congress has been undertaken by a scholar already deeply immersed in the subject. The research in each case promises to produce a book, a monograph, or one or more scholarly articles. Each man is free to recommend changes in the organization and procedures of Congress, but there will be no "official" list of recommendations by the Study of Congress itself. The purpose of the Study is to produce original research studies of Congress. Like other research enterprises, the usefulness of this one will be determined by the people who use it.

The Study of Congress Series presents associated studies designed to tell interested people as much as possible about how Congress works. It provides analytical descriptions of Congress, its subsystems, and its relations with its environment. The series fills in research blanks and suggests relevant variables for future research. It provides some basis for stating the functions performed by Congress for the political system, evaluating the performance, and pointing out alternative structural arrangements and modes of action which realistically seem to be open to Congress. Until these tasks are completed, our lists of congressional reforms are little more than statements of personal preference.

Who are the party leaders of the United States Congress? How and why were these men chosen to lead the majority and minority parties in the House of Representatives and the Senate? In this seventh volume of the series, Robert L. Peabody examines the personalities of congressional leaders, their career backgrounds, the processes by which they are selected, and why most continue in office, but a few are removed from leadership by their partisan colleagues.

Beginning with an introduction to what House leaders do and how they are viewed by other members, the core of the book consists of a series of case studies of party leadership change — the selection of

House Democratic Majority Leaders in 1961, 1971, and 1973; and the overthrow of a House Republican Minority Leader in 1965. Generalizations flowing from these case studies, in turn, lead to a theoretical framework for exploring leadership selection processes in earlier and future Congresses. The latter parts of the book extend this analysis to a series of Senate contests — selections of a Democratic Majority Whip in 1965, 1969, and 1971; and the choice of a Republican Minority Leader in 1969 and 1971. The end product is an astute blending of materials gained from firsthand observation of the contests; extensive interviews with the participants; insightful comparisons of contests across positions, parties, and institutions; and more historical perspectives on congressional leadership selection.

Ralph K. Huitt

Preface and Acknowledgments

This book grew out of an isolated case study of congressional leadership change — then Representative (currently President) Gerald R. Ford's successful challenge to House Republican Minority Leader, Charles A. Halleck, on January 4, 1965. Analysis of additional party leadership contests led to speculation about broader and more historical problems of leadership succession in the United States House of Representatives, especially differing patterns of selection within and between the Democratic majority and the Republican minority parties. The next logical step was to extend the framework of analysis and techniques of research to cases of Senate leadership change. Overall, my strategies of research have been *empirical*: relying heavily upon observation and intensive, focused interviews; *inductive*: building toward generalizations from a series of case studies; *comparative*: analyzing contests across positions, parties, and institutions; and, *historical*: limiting studies, in the main, to leadership change in ten Congresses, the 84th to 93rd, and twenty years, 1955 to 1974.

To take a finite number of case studies and from them generalize about overall congressional party leadership change is not without its limitations and hazards. As a poet cautions:

> *no book of laws, short of unattainable reality itself,*
> *can anticipate every event,*
> *control every event: only the book of laws founded*
> *against itself,*
> *founded on freedom of each event to occur as itself,*
> *lasts into the inevitable balances events will take.**

* Reprinted with the permission of the author and publisher from A. R. Ammons, "One: Many," *Collected Poems, 1951–1971* (New York: Norton, 1972), p. 140.

Events in the form of leadership selection processes continue to unfold in the contemporary House of Representatives and Senate. This
book attempts to describe and analyze these processes.

For over a decade my greatest intellectual stimulus, support, and
encouragement has come from four students of collective decision
making and the legislative process: James S. Coleman, Heinz Eulau,
Richard F. Fenno, Jr., and Ralph K. Huitt. Each has become more
than a mentor; I consider them my friends. I am especially indebted
to Fenno and Huitt for their final reviews of the manuscript and their
suggestions for ordering, extending, and tightening the logic and presentation.

My indebtedness to many other congressional scholars is acknowl-
edged, in part, in footnotes to follow. Here, however, I single out
those who through personal conversations, written suggestions, or
both were most helpful in shaping my thinking: James D. Barber,
Milton C. Cummings, Jr., Lewis A. Dexter, J. Woodford Howard,
Charles O. Jones, Doris Kearns, John W. Kingdon, John F. Manley,
Donald R. Matthews, Nelson W. Polsby, Randall B. Ripley, Francis
E. Rourke, and David B. Truman. Norman J. Ornstein and David W.
Rohde, my colleagues on a forthcoming study of Senate decision mak-
ing, have provided numerous helpful comments and have saved me
from more than a few errors of omission.

This study could hardly have been undertaken without the cooperation, encouragement, and shared insights of many Representatives and
Senators, especially the principal incumbent leaders and candidates
for congressional party office since 1960. Beyond these actual or aspiring leaders, I would like to express my deep appreciation to those
members of Congress and their staffs who provided me with invalu-
able assistance over the past fourteen years: included are John B.
Anderson (R., Ill.), Hale Boggs (D., La.), Robert F. Drinan (D.,
Mass.), Thomas S. Foley (D., Wash.), President Gerald R. Ford
(then R., Mich.), Charles E. Goodell (R., N.Y.), Clarence D. Long
(D., Md.), James G. O'Hara (D., Mich.), Charles McC. Mathias,
Jr., (R., Md.), Dan Rostenkowski (D., Ill.), Paul S. Sarbanes (D.,
Md.), Hugh Scott (R., Pa.), Howard W. Smith (D., Va.), Joseph D.
Tydings (D., Md.), and Morris K. Udall (D., Ariz.).

Students of Congress would be hard pressed without the support
of congressional staff members willing to share their time, knowledge,
and insights with outside observers. My deepest obligation is to Gary
G. Hymel, a top assistant to several Democratic House leaders. What

began for me as a congressional internship in the office of the Majority Whip under Hymel's supervision in 1965 has developed into a continuing education on the workings of the House. Among others who have contributed to my understanding of congressional leadership change are House assistants, William Baroody, Jr., John E. Barriere, Terry Bracy, Margaret Culhane, Edythe Edwards, Verneil English, Mary Spencer Forrest, John Gabusi, William L. Gifford, D. B. Hardeman, Robert T. Hartmann, James C. Healey, Jr., Nancy Larson, Mary McInnis, John L. Monahan, William R. Pitts, William Prendergast, Michael L. Reed, Ranny Shuman, Irvine H. Sprague, David Stockman, Martin Sweig, and Josephine E. Wilson. I would also like to express my gratitude to a number of Senate staff members, especially, David Burke, Charles Dunn, Richard C. Drayne, Charles D. Ferris, John B. Fisher, John Gonella, Dorothy Herbert, John W. Hushen, Margaret Lynch, Betsy Moler, Wayne Owens (subsequently elected a member of the House of Representatives, 93d Congress, from Utah), Darrell St. Claire, Wayne Thevenot, Francis R. Valeo, and Nicholas Zapple.

Members of the parliamentary staffs of both the House and Senate, including Lewis Deschler, William Cochrane, William H. Brown, Charles W. Johnson, and Floyd M. Riddick, not only tried to answer my questions about caucus procedure and rules but also helped put recent contests in a more appropriate historical setting. I am further indebted to Robert Chartrand, Walter Kravitz, and Walter Oleszek of the Library of Congress, Congressional Research Service staff for background assistance and encouragement.

Many ideas that form the core of this book were discussed with other observers of or participants in the Washington, D.C. community, including David A. Bunn, Argyle Campbell, David Cohen, Mark Ferber, Russell D. Hemenway, Susan B. King, Sheila Koeppen, Larry Margolis, Graham T. T. Molitor, Richard W. Murphy, Richard P. Nathan, Neil Plimmer, Maurice Rosenblatt, Jack Talmaldge, Robert Vidaver, Richard D. Warden, Henry Hall Wilson, Jr., and Kenneth Young.

To political commentators and reporters, especially Don Bacon, John W. Beckler, Bruce Biossat, David Broder, James Deakin, Paul W. Duke, Shirley Elder, Frank Eleazer, Alan Ehrenhalt, Andrew J. Glass, Marjorie Hunter, Larry L. King, Richard L. Lyons, Arlen J. Large, Neil MacNeil, Mary McGrory, John D. Morris, Don Oberdorfer, Neal R. Peirce, David Secrest, Joseph W. Sullivan, III, Sally

Quinn, and Robert K. Walsh, I am indebted for sharing their knowledge and experiences.

My research was funded, most directly, by a grant from the Carnegie Corporation — the American Political Science Association Study of Congress Project. In addition, I would like to record my gratitude for support from a Social Science Research Council Research Fellowship, a Ford Foundation Faculty Fellowship, and assistance from the Russell Sage Foundation. Support for the Study of Congress, in general, and my own project, in particular, has been provided by the staff of the American Political Science Association, especially Evron Kirkpatrick, Walter Beach, Nancy Boland Edgerton, Thomas Mann, and Lois Ward.

My colleagues in the Department of Political Science at Johns Hopkins University continued to provide an intellectually stimulating and congenial environment within which to work. Successive waves of Hopkins' students, graduate and undergraduate, were subjected to early drafts of chapters more often, probably, than they cared to be. Many of them contributed to the research, analysis, and critiques of various case studies: included were Dan Beauchamp, Jeff Berry, Phillip Brenner, Curtis Cook, Jean Torcom Cronin, John Elliott, William Frasure, Maggie Gaines, John Glascock, Jerry Goldman, Susan Hammond, William Harader, Edward Heck, Joyce Rohr Lilie, David Lowe, Benetta Mansfield, Michael Nelson, Andy Savitz, Harvey Schantz, Burton Sheppard, Herbert Smith, Chris Steiner, and Steve Strickland. For inputs — psychological and intellectual — my thanks to all.

The original manuscript was typed and retyped with skill, understanding, and general good humor by Catherine Grover and Evelyn Scheulen in Baltimore, Maryland.

Final work on my manuscript was undertaken in the pleasant country setting and relative isolation of Oxford, England. I am indebted to the Warden and Fellows of Nuffield College, especially David Butler and Phillip M. Williams, not only for their hospitality but also for introducing to me the intricacies of British Parliamentary politics. At Nuffield, Lyn Yates and her staff of secretaries, especially Monique Backès, helped complete the typing of the manuscript.

Donald Hammonds and James Platt of Little, Brown and Company helped launch the Study of Congress Series, of which this book is a part. Richard Boyer, both as an editor and a friend, has been a continuing source of encouragement. My obligations to them, to

Betty Ann Tyson, to Jackie Sill, to Dixie Clark, and to others who assisted in the production process, surpass the traditional appreciation that most authors develop for highly competent practitioners of the publishing trade.

During the course of researching and writing this book, the patience and understanding of my wife, Judy, and my daughters, Susan, Lynn, and Jennifer, were sometimes put to unusual tests. Fortunately for the book and for me, they passed almost all of them. This book is dedicated to my mother and father — not the least for their sensitivity, idealism, and appreciation of politics.

Washington, D.C.   Robert L. Peabody
1975

Contents

PART IV   CONCLUSION

List of Tables

LEADERSHIP IN CONGRESS

President Richard M. Nixon meets with congressional leaders in more congenial times, early 1973. L. to r.: President Nixon, Senate Minority Leader Hugh Scott, House Majority Leader Thomas P. O'Neill, Jr., Speaker Carl Albert, Senate Majority Leader Mike Mansfield, and House Minority Leader Gerald Ford. Note the distinctive Oriental art motif of Senator Scott's leadership office located off the Senate floor in the Capitol.

(White House Photo)

PART I

Introduction

CHAPTER ONE

Congressional Leadership Change

Who are the party leaders of the United States Congress? How and why were these men chosen to lead the majority and minority parties in the Senate and in the House of Representatives? Once in office, what factors condition whether or not they succeed, simply drift along, or appear to be doing so poorly that other colleagues attempt to remove them from office? To what extent do the demands of leadership differ in the House as compared with the Senate? These are the primary questions this book will attempt to answer.

Leadership success in Congress can be evaluated by a number of criteria. A minimal definition of success would be election to one of a range of party leadership positions such as the whip or assistant floor leader, majority or minority leader, or Speaker. A somewhat more demanding criterion would be continuous reelection as a party leader. Advancement to higher office, for example, from whip to floor leader, would be a still more exacting criterion of success. Since this book primarily focuses upon the process of selecting congressional party leaders, our main definition of success is based on winning office, being reelected, and, more rarely, advancement to higher party office.

Of course, leadership success can also be evaluated in terms of broader criteria — the achievement of individual, group, party, or national objectives.[1] Are the needs of individual members *as they perceive them* being satisfied? Do various groups which make up the party — state delegations, regional groupings, and ideological factions — feel they have access to leaders? Are their goals being supported, ignored, or thwarted? Is the leadership maximizing votes on the floor? Are party platforms or presidential progress being implemented? Is Congress, through its leaders, meeting, let alone anticipating, the policy needs of the nation?

3

Obviously answers to questions such as these are increasingly difficult to assess as one moves from particular to more general and wide-
ranging criteria. Indeed, a study of such questions could provide the
focus for another book. Here, the problem of leadership effectiveness
is dealt with mainly as it affects the selection and survival of congressional leaders.

I

Of the 100 Senators and 435 members of the House of Representatives who serve in any given Congress, less than two dozen hold a
formal party leadership position — Speaker of the House, President
pro tempore of the Senate, floor leaders, whips, policy committee or
conference chairmen and the like. Most of these positions are elective:
party leaders are almost uniformly selected by their peers, voting by
secret ballot in House or Senate party conferences or caucuses. Although many Representatives or Senators may consider themselves
eligible, if not highly qualified, to serve as party leader, few actively
seek such positions during their legislative careers. Most members of
Congress seem content to cultivate their own constituencies and to
make their prime contributions through participation in committee
and floor activity.

Party leaders, committee leaders, and rank and file members in the
United States Congress while sometimes adversaries more often are
collaborators in the legislative process. Adversary relations are primarily, but by no means exclusively, partisan matters — majority versus minority, Democrats versus Republicans. Of course, few roll call
votes beyond the opening vote for Speaker of the House of Representatives are ever decided by strict partisan division. Both parties have
their dissident wings — southern Democrats and liberal Republicans,
in the main — and all parties have their mavericks. Moreover, conflict
can, and frequently does, occur along regional, ideological, urban-
rural, and other cleavages. Generational resentments flare up in both
the House and the Senate from time to time and may even spark
organized revolt and the removal of incumbent leaders. Still, all in all,
norms of accommodation and compromise are far stronger than those
that perpetuate conflict: "to get along, go along," "today's enemy may
be tomorrow's ally," "we are all compromisers in this body." These
norms are frequently voiced and, more importantly, practiced.

Few members of the House, fewer still in the Senate, consider
themselves followers — "we are all equal here" and "every member

starts off with one vote." But only a few in either body could be considered leaders in any general sense of the term. Members sometimes make estimates, such as "forty or fifty of us really run the House" or "there are only about twenty senators who really count." Regardless of the accuracy of these estimates, it is well to remember that leading or following are not independent concepts; they help to define one another.[2]

Four somewhat overlapping catogories of congressional leaders are (1) constitutionally designated leaders, such as the Speaker of the House and the President pro tempore of the Senate; (2) formal party leaders, such as majority and minority leaders and whips; (3) committee leaders, especially chairmen and ranking minority members; and (4) informal leaders, people whose intelligence, integrity, demonstrated experience, or active pursuit of higher office have earned them an added measure of esteem or respect from their peers. These categories are seldom pure for a variety of reasons. Customarily, Speakers perform in dual capacity, both as presiding officer of the House and as their party's principal leader. The Senate President pro tempore, traditionally the most senior member of the majority party, almost inevitably chairs one of the major Senate committees as well. Informal leaders, though they may not hold a committee chairmanship or position of ranking minority member, are quite likely to be high ranking on one or more committees. Thus, their influence is not unrelated to committee status. Seeking a Senate position from the House will not automatically accord higher prestige to a Representative, at least not until the aspirant is successful. The Senate's role as a presidential incubator in recent years has, however, enhanced the external prestige, if not always the internal influence, of certain of its members — like the Kennedys, Goldwater, Humphrey, and McGovern. Even the losers who return to the Senate occasionally can convert some of their increased visibility and stature into legislative payoffs.

Ralph K. Huitt and David B. Truman, among others, have emphasized the main obstacles to central party leadership in Congress: the members' independent constituency base, the system of decentralized standing committees, and the mediating and supplementary nature of American political parties.[3]

Unlike other large organizations — the Presidency, executive branch agencies, private business corporations, labor unions, universities, hospitals, and so on — legislatures do not maintain elaborate hierarchies, strict superior-subordinate relationships, or the right of top management to hire and fire almost at will. Leaders in parliamentary systems appear to have great control over the careers of individual members, but these influences are tenuous, indeed, in the United States Congress. Congressmen are rarely censured and almost never removed from office by actions of their party leaders, and they cannot be offered another constituency by their party when defeated by the electorate.

Members are fond of proclaiming their equal status: leader and non-leader alike have one vote. Each member is elected from an independent, decentralized constituency, a congressional district of between 400,000 and 500,000 people, or in the case of a Senator, from a state that may vary in population from Alaska's 300 thousand to the 18 to 20 millions of New York and California. Every Senator and Representative expends much time and effort to make his constituency more secure, mainly for himself, and only indirectly for his party. An enduring truism in American politics is that constituency demands, however perceived, are often at odds with the goals and objectives of national party leaders — from Presidents to congressional leaders, and downward. When in conflict, members are more likely to vote their constituency.

Given a paucity of formal powers, leaders, time and time again, must fall back upon the more subtle forms of influence, above all personal persuasion. The collegial nature of our national legislatures cannot be overstressed. Men (plus a handful of women) are thrown together day after day; they cultivate friendships (and not a few animosities) which sometimes last as long as an adult lifetime — 10, 20, 30, or more years. A successful congressional leader must be able not only to assess the personalities of his colleagues but also to cultivate an intimate knowledge of each state or congressional district and of how a given member relates to his constituency. Like a winning baseball manager, a congressional leader who expects to perform well and survive must know the strengths and weaknesses of his "players." The leader must build upon what has worked in the past, but remain flexible as conditions change. His decisions are almost always based upon increments of experience gained from observing votes and partaking in innumerable personal interactions with his colleagues.

Stemming from, and reinforcing, these political realities are members' expectations about what leaders can and cannot do for them and their sense of the strengths and limitations which grow up and around any given leadership position. From time to time strong legislative personalities — such as Thomas Reed, Joseph Cannon, and Sam Rayburn;

Robert Taft, Lyndon Johnson, and Everett Dirksen — enter into high office and infuse it with new vigor. Quite possibly, such a person may even succeed in altering the nature of the position. Legislative leaders, no matter how strong their personalities, can never fully escape the constraints placed upon them by the collaborative demands of their partisan positions and the fundamental autonomy of their followers which, in turn, flows from their independent constituencies.

II

If congressional party leaders have only limited power, can individual leaders have an impact? Put another way: What difference does it make whether or not the individual party leaders of the Senate and the House of Representatives are strong or weak, change-oriented or defenders of the status quo, liberal, moderate, or conservative? Initially, it would appear that most members of Congress seem to think leadership is important. They declare themselves most directly by the intensity of their competition for party leadership and the heavy commitment of resources — time, energy, and extent of membership involvement — that goes into most leadership contests.

The degree of difference that an individual leader can make is, of course, exceedingly difficult to evaluate, let alone measure with any precision. Is Senate Majority Leader Mike Mansfield a weaker leader than his predecessor, Lyndon Johnson? [4] Would Speaker Sam Rayburn have been able to move impeachment proceedings against President Richard M. Nixon with greater effectiveness than Speaker Carl Albert? Given changing personnel, varying political conditions, and different historical periods, definitive answers are elusive.

The effectiveness of congressional leaders regarding legislation is difficult to sort out from the influence of other participants such as committee chairmen, the president and his assistants, outside interest groups, and broader constituency pressures. Party leaders are only a more visible and vocal part of a complex web of influentials operating within and upon a legislative party. Thus, it is inevitable that their contributions are inextricably fused with, if not all but submerged among, the activities of their colleagues.

Perhaps the simplest and maybe the only answer to such questions are — "it all depends." It depends on who the leader is, what vitality and skills he possesses, what position he holds, under what institutional constraints he operates, how cohesive a majority of his party is behind him, his relationship to the President — in short, the impact of a wide range of fluctuating and interacting factors. Evaluation of the short-run or long-range effectiveness of any leader requires assessment of this wide range of conditions, only a few of which are tangible and discrete enough to lend themselves to precise measurement. In the final analysis, success or failure of a leader must be evaluated, like all significant political questions, in relative terms. The evaluation process always involves weighing imperfect and sometimes conflicting information, building on shaky assumptions, and making difficult judgments. Inevitably, even the most informed observers may find themselves in disagreement.

To answer "it all depends" may seem to beg the question. But demands on legislative leadership seem to differ from those placed on corporate executives, agency heads, or even the chief executive. The House and Senate are not bureaucracies with clear-cut goals and the members answer to no one constituency nor do they listen to the beat of any single drum. Collectively they form a representative institution, but individually they continue to pursue multiple and frequently conflicting goals. To quote a close student and practitioner of congressional leadership:[5]

> I happen to think that the House is messy, that the House will continue to be messy. It was messy under Cannon, under Clay, under Rayburn, under Albert, and it will be messy under whomever comes along.
>
> I think that there is a very good reason. It is a highly philosophical one but terribly practical. That is, that the democratic process is messy, thank God. It seems to me that if there is any hope that we have a clearly defined organizational chart, which will continue to work for more than a few years, that is illusory.
>
> Today's reform is tomorrow's disaster in a political situation, and I think that is very clear.

Further, it seems clear that changing climates over the past decade have acerbated the problems that contemporary leaders confront in both Houses. A third-term Senate Democrat comments:[6]

> The Senate itself is different. It is no longer an establishment kind of place. And every generation of young Senators who have come along have changed it a little bit. . . . The war and

other issues have changed the Senate. It is no longer made up of men who are willing to be part of a hierarchical arrangement with the leader at the top of the pyramid and everybody else in his proper place waiting to climb and all the rest of it. The institution just has been opened up too much. . . . Just as in all aspects of American life there is no such thing as blind followers any more in this country — blind acceptance of political leaders and institutions. And the same thing is true here. What came first the historians will have to sort out, but that is a fact. Senators no longer genuflect to committee chairmen. There isn't that kind of aura about the establishment.

The outputs of Congress, especially its legislative accomplishments, remain largely systemic. That is to say, a major proportion of its achievements, perhaps as much as 80 percent, is stimulated from outside — constituents, interest groups, the executive branch — processed through its decentralized committee structure, managed on the floor by committee leaders, modified and voted up or down by the full membership.

The party leadership's contribution to most of these legislative endeavors is marginal at best; they schedule legislation, work out appropriate floor strategy, and corral a few votes here and there. This is not to say that their contributions have no import. Indeed, the leaders' involvement or non-involvement may be critical to the success or failure of many important bills that are held or passed by a given Congress. A party leader may be instrumental in securing for a valued colleague a committee assignment or an appointment to a joint committee, which he, in turn, may parlay into national prominence. Party leaders may create or spur on a select committee to important legislative findings. Party leaders' support for opposition to an amendment or bill may mean its life or death.

Although leadership contributions may be marginal, most important political choices are made at the margins. The very closeness of a decision may indicate the significance and strength of the competing forces at work. Since no leadership, however resourceful and astute, can hope to effect all policy decisions, one clear measure of its success must be its willingness to assume risks. Inherently limited assets must be concentrated to bring about maximum benefits for resources invested.

If one may fault congressional leadership for their most consistent weakness, it would be their hesitancy to take risks, their lack of bold-

ness. Former Representative Clem Miller provides some of the underlying rationale for this dilemma:[7]

> They lead, but they lead only because they win. If they cannot
> be certain of winning, they don't want to go. Latent power,
> negative power, is so much better than power committed that
> lacks victory as a capstone. Hence, the legislative timidity of
> the Congress, both House and Senate. . . . Righteousness with
> victory is a fine thing. Righteousness with defeat is nothing
> much at all.

III

If we assume, as most observers both inside and outside Congress
seem to agree, that who the individual leaders are can be important,
then the study of their selection — how and why leaders are chosen —
needs little further justification.

Change in party leadership in modern industrial legislatures comes
about in three principal ways. *Inter-party turnover*, the wholesale replacement of a party's set of leaders by those of another party, occurs
when the results of a national election convert a minority into a
majority. Such change is rare. For example, in the United States
House of Representatives, party control has switched but twenty-four
times in the 94 Congresses elected every two years since 1788.[8] Indeed,
since 1930, the Republican party has only organized Congress twice,
the 80th (1947–1948) and 83rd (1953–1954) Congresses. Concentration in this book is on a more prevalent, if less dramatic type of
change, *intra-party change*, or the replacement of one or more incumbents within a party hierarchy by other members of the same
party. A third type of change, *institutional reform*, is characterized
not by the replacement of leaders but by alterations in party organization or in the rules of a legislature which modify the powers of an
existing office or create a new position. In the absence of inter-party
turnover and as an alternative to institutional reform, legislators frequently turn to intra-party change as a means to fill vacancies and as
a device to promote leadership more favorable to their own interests.

Throughout this study of intra-party leadership change, an attempt
is made to expose, if not always to answer, the following questions:

- Who are the congressional leaders? What manner of men are
  Speaker Carl Albert (D., Okla.), House Minority Leader John

Rhodes (R., Ariz.), Senate Majority Leader Mike Mansfield (D., Mont.), Minority Leader Hugh Scott (R., Pa.), their associates, their predecessors, and their possible successors?

- How and why did such individuals, not other Representatives or Senators, become the leading congressional spokesmen for their generations?

- By what means can congressional leaders persuade their colleagues to follow them? What resources, however limited, are available to them? What kinds of relationships and expectations do other members of Congress have with and about their leaders?

- What leads to congressional leadership change? Are there differential patterns of succession in the House and Senate? How do these patterns differ among Democrats and Republicans or between the majority and minority parties?

- What factors or conditions influence or help to explain rates of change and different patterns of leadership succession? Do these conditions vary among parties or from House to Senate?

IV

The core of this study consists of a series of narrative case histories of most of the critical leadership choices made by the House and Senate congressional parties over the past decade. Eight cases of contested change, four in each chamber, are presented in depth (see Table 1.1). These contemporary studies of individual intra-party leadership changes are set against a longer historical backdrop of party leadership selection in ten post-World War II Congresses, the 84th through the 93d (1955–1974). These Congresses follow the most recent election to bring about inter-party change in the organization of the House and Senate, that is, the midterm election of 1954.

Tables 1.2 and 1.3 present the principal cast of characters, the major party leaders in the House of Representatives and Senate since the beginning of the first Eisenhower Administration. As the case studies unfold, the personalities, backgrounds, and styles of these leaders will come into sharper focus. Still, several preliminary generalizations are in order. First, potential House leaders must begin their House careers at a relatively early age, averaging 36 years at the time they win their first election. Second, long House service is re-

Table 1.1
Case Studies in Congressional Party Leadership Change

		HOUSE OF REPRESENTATIVES	
Chapter	Office	Candidates*	Dates
3	Majority Leader	Carl Albert (D., Okla.) Richard Bolling (D., Mo.)	1961–1962
4	Minority Leader	Gerald Ford (R., Mich.) **Charles Halleck (R., Ind.)	1964–1965
5–7	Majority Leader	Hale Boggs (D., La.) Morris Udall (D., Ariz.) Bernard Sisk (D., Cal.) Wayne Hays (D., Ohio) James O'Hara (D., Mich.)	1970–1971
8	Majority Leader	Thomas O'Neill, Jr. (D., Mass.) Sam Gibbons (D., Fla.)	1972–1973
		SENATE	
12	Majority Whip	Russell Long (D., La.) John Pastore (D., R.I.) Michael Monroney (D., Okla.)	1964–1965
		Edward Kennedy (D., Mass.) **Russell Long (D., La.)	1968–1969
13	Majority Whip	Robert Byrd (D., W.Va.) **Edward Kennedy (D., Mass.)	1970–1971
14	Minority Leader	Hugh Scott (R., Pa.) Howard Baker (R., Tenn.)	1969, 1970–1971

* Winning candidate is listed first.   ** Incumbent.

quired before they become eligible for their party's highest ranking office of Speaker or minority leader, Democrats averaging 28 years of prior service, Republicans almost 18 years. One consequence is that both parties tend to elect leaders in their late 50's or older. Third, Democratic Speakers have been elevated traditionally to the top office of Speaker from the majority leadership position. Republicans have been advanced to Speaker (as in the case of Joseph Martin) from the office of minority floor leader. Typically, minority leaders have been selected from holders of another lesser leadership post, such as the chairmanship of the policy committee, campaign committee, or conference. Finally, up to the present time no Democratic leader has been removed from his position by contested means but two Repub-

Majority Party Leaders, House of Representatives, 1940–1974

| | Born | First Entered House | | First Elected Top Leader | | | Prior Position | Final Reason for Leaving Position |
		Year	Age	Year	Age	Years in House		
Democratic Speakers								
Sam Rayburn, Tex.[a]	1-6-1882	1913	31	1940	58	27	Majority Leader	Death
John McCormack, Mass.[b]	12-21-1891	1928	36	1962	70	34	Majority Leader	Retirement
Carl Albert, Okla.[c]	5-10-1908	1947	38	1971	62	24	Majority Leader	—
Republican Minority Leaders								
Joseph Martin, Mass.[d]	11-3-1884	1925	40	1939	54	14	Chairman, Campaign Comm.	Defeated by Halleck
Charles Halleck, Ind.[e]	8-22-1900	1935	34	1959	58	24	Majority Leader (1953–1954)	Defeated by Ford
Gerald Ford, Mich.[f]	7-14-1913	1949	35	1965	51	16	Chairman, Conference	Vice President
John Rhodes, Ariz.[g]	9-18-1916	1953	36	1973	57	21	Chairman, Policy Comm.	—

SOURCE: *Biographical Directory of the American Congress, 1774–1961* (Washington, D.C.: U.S. Government Printing Office, 1961).
[a] Rayburn was first elected Majority Leader in 1937; he also served as Minority Leader in the 80th (1947–1948) and 83d (1953–1954) Congresses.
[b] Although he never served as majority whip, McCormack dropped back to minority whip in the same two Republican-controlled Congresses (80th and 83d).
[c] Albert was first appointed majority whip in 1955, succeeding McCormack as Majority Leader in 1962.
[d] Martin also served as Speaker (alternating with Rayburn) in the 80th and 83d Congresses.
[e] Halleck was majority floor leader under Martin in these same two Congresses.
[f] Ford was ranking Republican on the House Appropriations Committee as well as Chairman of the Republican Conference when he successfully challenged Halleck in 1965.
[g] Rhodes was second ranking Republican on the House Appropriations Committee when he succeeded Ford as Minority Leader on December 7, 1973.

Table 1.3
Majority Party Leaders, Senate, 1953–1974

	Born	First Entered Senate		First Elected Floor Leader			Prior Position	Final Reason for Leaving Position
		Year	Age	Year	Age	Years in Senate		
Democratic Floor Leaders								
Lyndon Johnson, Tex.[a]	8-27-1908	1949	40	1953	44	4	Whip	Vice President
Mike Mansfield, Mont.[b]	3-16-1903	1953	49	1961	57	8	Whip	—
Republican Floor Leaders								
Robert Taft, Ohio[c]	9-8-1889	1939	49	1953	63	14	Chairman, Policy Comm.	Death
William Knowland, Calif.[d]	6-26-1908	1945	37	1953	45	8	Chairman, Policy Comm.	Retirement
Everett Dirksen, Ill.[e]	1-4-1896	1951	55	1959	63	8	Whip	Death
Hugh Scott, Pa.[f]	11-11-1900	1959	58	1969	68	11	Whip	—

SOURCE: *Biographical Directory of the American Congress, 1774–1961* (Washington, D.C.: U.S. Government Printing Office, 1961).
[a] Johnson was first elected majority whip in 1951; he became Minority Leader in 1953 and Majority Leader in 1955.
[b] Mansfield was first elected majority whip in 1957.
[c] Taft was elected Policy Committee Chairman in 1944.
[d] Knowland was first elected Policy Committee Chairman in 1953; he became Majority Leader upon Taft's death in August 1953.
[e] Dirksen was first elected minority whip in 1957.
[f] Hugh Scott was first elected whip in January 1969; he became Minority Leader following Dirksen's death in September 1969.

lican floor leaders, Martin and Charles Halleck, have been challenged and defeated in party conferences.

Compared with their House counterparts, potential leaders of the Senate enter it at a later age, on the average in their late 40s. All House leaders, save Robert A. Taft and William Knowland, had prior House service of five terms or more. In the Senate, long service before becoming a leader has not been as important a requirement as in the House: Senate leaders, six men, averaged about eight years of prior tenure. All but Lyndon Johnson and Knowland were in their late 50s or 60s by the time they assumed floor leadership. As in the House, Senate leaders had all served in lesser party leadership positions, usually as the whip, before becoming their party's principal spokesman. No Senate floor leader has been removed from office through contested means.

V

The methods of research relied upon in this study are primarily empirical, historical, and inductive. Nelson W. Polsby's intensive case study of the Albert-Bolling contest for the House majority leadership in 1961–1962 (reprinted here as Chapter 3) provided an initial stimulus.[9] My own case study of the Ford-Halleck contest for House Minority Leader in 1964–1965 (Chapter 4) led me into more historical research as a means of speculating about differences in leadership selection between the two parties and broader patterns of change.[10]

My principal research strategies have much in common with other empirically oriented congressional scholars.[11] Wherever possible I have attempted to gain access to the principal candidates, if not during the contest, then as soon as possible thereafter. I have made use of short, semi-focused interviews. Generally, I have also interviewed a rough cross-sample of other congressional party members and knowledgeable staff. My own first-hand observations have been supplemented by contemporary media accounts.[12]

Historical research on change in leadership was more frustrating. Newspaper accounts of all but the most recent contests were likely to be fragmentary and superficial. They were even less satisfactory in the exploration of a related problem — non-change, or why most leaders were continually reelected to party offices. Further, good biographies of House members were relatively rare compared with presidential, judicial, or even senatorial biographies.[13] Even the best of these seldom described leadership contests in detail; usually the accounts were anecdotal and one-sided.

Lack of knowledge about types of change, the conditions which promote one type of change rather than another, and possible party differences were further complicated by the hazards of generalizing from a limited number of cases. Still, the trends that have been induced rest not upon a sample, but a detailed analysis of a near-universe of cases, for some ten Congresses, the 84th to the 93d (1955–1974).

The plan of this book is rather straightforward. The next chapter provides an introduction to House party leadership, its organization, functions, and the expectations and relationships of the broader membership. A series of four case studies of contests for floor leadership, follow — three in the majority party (Chapters 3 and 5–8) and one in the minority (Chapter 4). Chapters 9 and 10 present a conceptual scheme for ordering these and some thirty additional cases of change in both parties, Democratic and Republican, over ten Congresses, the 84th to 93d (1955–1974).[14] Since Republicans have controlled the Congress only twice since 1930, the 80th (1947–1948) and 83d (1953–1954) Congresses, for practical as well as analytical reasons in analyses to follow I largely treat the Democratic party as the majority party and the Republican party as the minority party.

Part III focuses on the United States Senate and follows a similar organizational format. First a brief introduction to Senate leadership (Chapter 11) is presented, then a series of four case studies, three Democratic whip contests in 1965, 1969, and 1971 (Chapters 12 and 13), and the selection of a Republican Minority Leader in 1969 and 1971 (Chapter 14). Senate party leadership change is then examined in Chapter 15 over a comparable ten-Congress and twenty-year period (1955–1974).

Part IV consists of House-Senate comparisons and a detailed analysis of some twenty variables or conditions, briefly outlined below, which seem to influence or determine the degree and kind of congressional party leadership change.

VI

Intuitively at first, and then gradually over a series of case studies, I was aware of a number of conditions or variables which seem to facilitate, inhibit, or, in general, help to explain congressional leadership change. These twenty variables can be collapsed into four somewhat overlapping clusters: individual, positional, institutional, and external. Presented here, they serve as preliminary clues or guideposts to look for in the numerous case studies that follow. Some leadership contests bring into play almost all the variables, and many work at cross purposes. In other contests, one or two variables are so strongly operative they negate or minimize the effect of most others.

The first set of variables are *individual* in character and include (1) the personality and skill of the candidates, (2) their party identification, (3) their ideology, (4) their constituency and the region they represent, and (5) their seniority in Congress.

A second cluster of variables are *positional* in nature. These include (6) the level of positions sought by the candidates and (7) any established pattern of succession, as from floor leader to Speaker in the House.[15] Other positional variables are (8) the nature of accession to office, contested or otherwise, and (9) the stage of leadership development — beginning, mature, or stagnating. A final positional variable, (10) the degree of internal leadership involvement, is also closely related to the personality and background of the incumbent: Does he take an active or passive role in the selection of lesser party leaders?

The third cluster of variables, *institutional*, includes (11) a range of House-Senate differences, such as the size of the body, length of tenure, and expectations about leadership roles; (12) party strength and cohesion,[16] (13) majority or minority status, (14) differences in party hierarchy and structure, and (15) membership expectations about leadership roles. The impact of such variables upon party leadership selection become clearer after a number of House and Senate contests have been described.

A final set of conditions are mainly *external*: (16) aggregate elections results,[17] (17) the degree of presidential involvement, (18) interest group activity, (19) media influences, and (20) the temper of the times. Of these, only the last variable need receive more elaborate definition at this point in our explanation of conditions that affect leadership stability and change. Successive chapters, and especially the concluding chapter, provide illustrations in depth of many or all of these variables.[18]

The temper of the times as an explanatory variable has at least one gross limitation — it is something of a catchall category. Everything as yet unexplained can be attributed to, if not explained away by, broader political, social, and economic forces. Clearly, the expectations and activities of congressional leaders and the broader House and Senate membership are conditioned by major crises such as war, depression, or the threatened impeachment or resignation of a President. The direct impact of such forces on the *selection* of leaders is more difficult to establish.

A historical example may serve to demonstrate how one case of leadership change inevitably brings into play a number of additional variables. Just before the outbreak of the Civil War, House Republicans were deadlocked over who should become Speaker. Any candidate with experience or one who held a strong position on the slavery question was considered a liability. In Mary Parker Follett's words:[19]

> In the critical condition of political affairs in 1859 the Republicans were unable to elect their first candidate for Speaker, Mr. Sherman. They looked around then simply for a man who could be elected, for a man of whom the Republicans need not be ashamed, yet whose political opinions should not be pronounced enough to frighten those who it was necessary to attack. In Mr. Pennington, of New Jersey, they found a man just making his first appearance in the House, and without other experience in a legislative assembly than that gained by one term in the lower house of the New Jersey legislature. His qualifications for office were some legal attainments, dignity of manner, equanimity of temper, and an undoubted integrity and impartiality. While personally entirely unobjectionable, he had the advantage of being free from the weight of a career. This absence of a record in a time of such great political excitement gained for him the high position to which his mediocre talents would never have entitled him.

William Pennington, the last freshman ever to be elected Speaker of the House of Representatives, presided over the 36th Congress with impartiality, but he was defeated for reelection to the House after his single term.

Here, a combination of the temper of the times together with Pennington's personal attributes, variables (1)–(5), and the nature of the still undeveloped patterns of speakership selection, variables (6) and (7), seem to account for most of the reasons underlying his choice.

Chapter 2 introduces party leadership in the House of Representatives; the leaders are identified, and the limited resources available to them and the expectations which members hold about them are set forth. After a series of case studies of House and Senate leadership change, these analytical variables should become clearer and more meaningful. Some leadership contests offer clear-cut tests of ideology or seniority; in others, the personalities of the candidates loom large; others reinforce patterns of leadership succession.

VII

When changes in top leadership occur, for example, the overthrow of Minority Leader Charles Halleck by Republican Representative Gerald Ford in 1965 or the succession of majority whip Mike Mansfield to the office of Senate Majority Leader in 1961 following Lyndon Johnson's election as Vice President, the consequences are considerable. In the case of revolt, individual careers are made and broken. The organization and policy orientations of a party may undergo extensive moderation. Orderly succession, while it has less dramatic impact, also significantly affects "who gets what, when, and how." Some members move closer to the seats of power and others fall out of favor. Key committee assignments, both to legislative and party policy machinery, are likely to ride or fall on the outcomes of leadership contests. Even the patterns of leadership change may be considerably altered. Overall, the structure of a congressional party, its political outlook, the kinds of legislation it seeks to promote, its strategies of implementation, its relationship with the incumbent in the White House, are usually slow to change. But these outlooks, strategies, and relationships hinge in important ways upon the personalities, political backgrounds, seniority, ideology, and constituency and regional perspectives of principal party leaders in Congress. Only the periodic contest for the control of the White House, the occasional elections which convert one party from a minority into a majority within Congress, or an epic upheaval like the Civil War, the great depression, or the aftermath of Watergate are likely to have more significant consequences for party fortunes and public policies.

NOTES

1. Attempts to define and measure leadership effectiveness in terms of goal achievement and the satisfaction of membership needs have a long, if somewhat uneven history, in the literature of organizational theory that includes such theoretical classics as Chester I. Barnard, *The Functions of the Executive* (Cambridge: Harvard University Press, 1938) and Herbert A. Simon, *Administrative Behavior* (New York: Macmillan, 1948). For an overview of more re-

cent empirical studies, see James G. March, ed., *Handbook of Organizations* (Chicago: Rand McNally, 1965) and Ralph M. Stogdill, ed., *Handbook of Leadership* (New York: Free Press, 1974). For a more specific application to Congress, see Lewis A. Froman, Jr., and Randall B. Ripley, "Conditions for Party Leadership: The Case of the House Democrats," *Am. Pol. Sci. Rev.* **59** (1965), 52–63.

2. Cecil A. Gibb, "Leadership: Psychological Aspects," in *International Encyclopedia of the Social Sciences* **9** (New York: Macmillan, 1968), 92–93.

3. Ralph K. Huitt, "Democratic Party Leadership in the Senate," *Am. Pol. Sci. Rev.* **55** (1961), 334–335; David B. Truman, *The Congressional Party* (New York: Wiley, 1959), p. 95.

4. Cf. John Stewart, "Two Strategies of Leadership: Johnson and Mansfield," in Nelson W. Polsby, ed., *Congressional Behavior* (New York: Random House, 1971), pp. 61–92; and this author's independent assessment of the same two Senate Majority Leaders in Chapter 11 of this book.

5. Representative Richard Bolling, "Committee Organization in the House," *Hearings* before the Select Committee on Committees, U.S. House of Representatives, 93d Cong., 1st sess., Vol. 2, Pt. 1, June 14, 1973.

6. This quotation, as most of the interview excerpts used throughout the book, has not been attributed. This practice was followed in order to facilitate maximum candor and frankness among respondents. Given the heightened sensitivity of most leadership contests, I have also dispensed with the practice of indicating the dates of interviews. In too many instances it might further compromise the identity of the respondent, especially in the case of candidates for office of incumbent party leaders. For a further elaboration on interview techniques, see Note 12.

7. Clem Miller, *Member of the House*, edited by John W. Baker (New York: Scribner's, 1962), pp. 91–92.

8. U.S. Bureau of the Census, *Historical Statistics of the United States, Colonial Times to 1957* (Washington, D.C.: U.S. Government Printing Office, 1960), pp. 691–692.

9. "Two Strategies of Influence: Choosing a Majority Leader, 1962" in Robert L. Peabody and Nelson W. Polsby, eds., *New Perspectives on the House of Representatives* (Chicago: Rand McNally, 1963), pp. 237–270.

10. "The Ford-Halleck Minority Leadership Contest, 1965," Eagleton Institute Cases in Practical Politics, No. 40 (New York: McGraw-Hill, 1966).

11. See, for example, the works of Lewis A. Dexter, *The Sociology and Politics of Congress* (Chicago: Rand McNally, 1972); Ralph K. Huitt in Huitt and Peabody, *Congress: Two Decades of Analysis* (New York: Harper and Row, 1969); Donald R. Matthews, *U.S. Senators and Their World* (Chapel Hill: University of North Carolina Press, 1960); Richard F. Fenno, Jr., *The Power of the Purse: Appropriations Politics in Congress* (Boston: Little, Brown, 1966) and *Congressmen in Committees* (Boston: Little, Brown, 1973); Charles O. Jones, *The Minority Party in Congress* (Boston: Little, Brown, 1970); John F. Manley, *The Politics of Finance: The House Ways and Means Committee* (Boston: Little, Brown, 1970), and Randall B. Ripley, *Party Leaders in the House of Representatives* (Washington, D.C.: Brookings Institution, 1967) and *Majority Party Leadership in Congress* (Boston: Little, Brown, 1969).

12. These case studies are based, in the main, upon direct observation of the events; on contemporary journal, newspaper, and magazine accounts, especially those of *Congressional Quarterly*, and *The National Journal*; *The Washington Post*, *The Washington Evening Star*, *The Wall Street Journal*, and *The New*

York Times and *Time* and *Newsweek* magazines; and, above all, on focused interviews with key participants, especially members and congressional staff. Candidates were asked questions such as how they felt the campaigns were going, what they saw as their principal strengths and weaknesses as well as those of their opponents, and what strategies they were using to gain internal and external support. As the campaign developed I would try to interview a broader network of Representatives or Senators, varied by region, ideology, and seniority. In general, access was easier to obtain in the House and most of these cases were studied as they unfolded. In contrast, all but one Senate case were investigated after the contest had concluded, although the author had followed them informally at the time.

From 1961 through 1973 I have conducted or gained access to over 300 House interviews. My observations on the Senate are based upon about 60 interviews conducted from 1969 to 1973, plus 27 interviews of Republican Senators made available to me by Jean Torcom Cronin as part of her study of "Minority Leadership in the United States Senate: The Role and Style of Everett Dirksen" (Baltimore: Ph.D. dissertation, Johns Hopkins University, 1973). In addition, Norman J. Ornstein and David W. Rohde have made available transcripts from their more than 40 interviews conducted with incumbent or former Senators during the spring and summer of 1973. The interviews are part of our broader study of Senate decision making, funded in part by a Russell Sage Foundation grant. Beyond sharing of interview materials, all three have helped immeasurably to shape my thinking about the Senate.

My research on House Democratic leadership over the past decade was greatly facilitated by an opportunity to intern in the office of the late Hale Boggs of Louisiana, then majority whip, during the spring and summer of 1965. This experience included access to the House floor.

13. Treatment of Speakers has been something of an exception. See, for example, James A. Barnes, *John G. Carlisle* (New York: Dodd, Mead, 1931); James G. Blaine, *Twenty Years of Congress, from Lincoln to Garfield*, 2 vols. (Norwich, Conn.: Henry Bill, 1884); Samuel W. McCall, *The Life of Thomas B. Reed* (Boston: Houghton Mifflin, 1919); William A. Robinson, *Thomas B. Reed, Parliamentarian* (New York: Dodd, Mead, 1930); L. White Busby, *Uncle Joe Cannon* (New York: Henry Holt, 1927); Champ Clark, *My Quarter Century of American Politics* (New York: Harper, 1920); Bascom N. Timmons, *Garner of Texas* (New York: Harper, 1938); Joe Martin, *My First Fifty Years in Politics* (as told to Robert J. Donovan) (New York: McGraw-Hill, 1960). The only full-length biography of Sam Rayburn, C. Dwight Dorough, *Mr. Sam* (New York: Random House, 1962) is rich in family background and local lore, but relates little about Rayburn, the legislative leader and how he became Speaker.

14. This framework of analysis was originally set forth in Robert L. Peabody, "Party Leadership Change in the United States House of Representatives," *Am. Pol. Sci. Rev.* **61** (1967), 673–675. Portions of that article are presented in modified form in Chapters 9 and 10 by permission of the American Political Science Association.

15. Whether or not the pattern of succession is firmly established or merely emerging, is, of course, one of the research questions this study attempts to answer.

16. A simple majority of 51 Senators or 218 House members is enough to establish majority status. But what difference does it make for leadership survival or effectiveness if the strength of the party majority is large or small? Further, a party can be large in numbers but lack cohesion.

17. By aggregate election results I mean to focus upon the consequences of large

net gains or losses in biannual congressional elections in terms of party leadership stability or turnover.
18. Although Randall B. Ripley and Charles O. Jones concentrated upon the broader type of legislative success — the passage of party or administration programs — and not on leadership success in the sense of survival, their alternative sets of conditions make for useful comparisons. Ripley suggests four conditions which enhance legislative success if the majorities in Congress also control the White House: (1) larger majorities, (2) new and more enthusiastic majorities, (3) active presidential leadership, and (4) innovative congressional leadership. *Majority Party Leadership in Congress, op. cit.,* pp. 184–187.

Charles O. Jones identifies four external conditions — "temper of the times, relative political strength of the minority party, national party unity, and presidential power"; and six internal conditions — "procedure, size of the margin, majority party leadership, and organization [minority party leadership and organization], length of time in the minority, and relative strength of the party in the other House." *The Minority Party in Congress, op. cit.,* pp. 11–18. Of course, with all these conditions, including my own, it is the *combination* of variables that is crucial for determining whether or not a particular leader is successful in either sense.
19. M. P. Follett, *The Speaker of the House of Representatives* (New York: Longmans, Green, 1896), pp. 94–95.

At the White House to discuss the budget and his final State of the Union message, President Johnson meets with congressional leaders (1969): l. to r., Carl Albert, House Majority Leader, Leslie Arends, House Minority whip, Mike Mansfield, Senate Democratic Leader, Everett Dirksen, GOP Senate leader, John McCormack, House Speaker, Gerald Ford, House Minority Leader, Wilbur Mills, chairman of the House Ways and Means Committee, James W. Byrnes, ranking GOP member of the House Ways and Means Committee, and Hale Boggs, House Majority whip.

(UPI Photo)

PART II

The House of Representatives

The House of Representatives

CHAPTER TWO

Introduction to House Party Leadership

Congressional leaders have much in common with the leaders of other large, complex organizations; yet some characteristics of their jobs are unique. Leaders cannot be understood apart from their followers, but few leaders must interact with the diversity of party, region, ideology, and subject-matter specialization characteristic of the members of legislators of modern, industrial nations. All executives must attempt to manage with scarce resources, but legislative leaders seem to operate with an especially limited supply of rewards and sanctions. All leaders confront situational constraints, internal and external, but almost none rival the breadth and complexity of the environmental pressures imposed upon House and Senate leaders. Moreover, in common with other organizational spokesmen, the successes and failures of congressional leaders must be measured against the objectives which they and their followers set for themselves as well as the expectations of their publics, attentive and inactive.[1]

A number of further characteristics set congressional leaders apart from almost all other executives of large, complex organizations. First, they are politicians: they have to run for and be reelected to public office.[2] Second, they act as spokesmen for one or the other chamber of the national legislature. Their corporate jurisdictions may be as narrow as a question of elevator operator patronage or as broad as the possible impeachment of a President. Third, the breadth and complexity of the tasks they must coordinate also set them apart from all other leaders except their counterparts in other nations and the chief executive.

27

The highest priority tasks of any given Congress are twofold: (1) the representation of the diverse interests of their constituents and the reconciliation of these demands with national interests, and (2) policy making, in part through the checking and balancing of other branches of government, in part through use of their investigatory powers, but, most important, through the introduction, passage, and modification of bills and proposed constitutional amendments.[3] On rare occasions, a subsidiary function of Congress, such as the election of the President in the House of Representatives for lack of a majority in the electoral college or the launching of impeachment proceedings against a President may come to preoccupy its leaders and members.

THE ORGANIZATION OF THE HOUSE: SOME SITUATIONAL CONSTRAINTS

Members of any large organization are confronted with questions of divisions of authority and of how its leaders and followers should relate to one another.[4] In an organization of any duration such questions are seldom raised explicitly; offices are created, roles are established, traditions take hold. The near 200-year-old House of Representatives is not an exception, although, of course, its organizational complexity reflects its basic nature as a legislature: a body of people who represent diverse interests brought together to decide, and, if necessary, compromise on governmental policy.[5]

To begin, each of the House's 435 members represents a unique congressional district that on the average contains some 475,000 constituents.[6] Of course, only in idealistic terms can it be said that a Representative serves as a spokesman for all his constituents. About one-third of the House districts are consistently dominated by one party, mainly Democratic districts in the big cities and the South and Republican districts in the Midwest. In these places minority interests are likely to have little voice. But even in competitive two-party districts, most Representatives identify with only a portion of the electorate, sometimes barely a majority, but seldom more than two-thirds. That is to say, they are consistently returned to office by margins of from 51 to 70 percent of the two-party vote. It is to this subset of the electorate that a Representative is most alert in terms of access and services rendered. More importantly, Representatives are most closely identified with a cluster of interests in their districts, the people they grew up and went to school with, practiced their professions or worked with in other ways. From this pool come most of the people who work in their campaigns, make financial contributions to it, and who in the process develop or improve upon their access to congressmen. However, as David Truman has noted:[7]

> The politician-legislator is not equivalent to the steel ball in a pinball game, bumping passively from post to post down an inclined plane. He is a human being involved in a variety of relationships with other human beings. In his role as legislator his accessibility to various groups is affected by the whole series of relationships that define him as a person.

In the late 18th century, and throughout most of the 19th century, House members were relatively isolated from their home districts once they arrived in the nation's Capitol.[8] With technological developments of the late 19th and early 20th centuries — rail and air travel, the telephone, telegraph, mass media, and most recently, television, the nature of the representative process has undergone drastic alterations. Congressmen's offices today are in almost constant communication with their district constituents. Most members maintain at least one district office. They may make as many as 20 or more trips to their districts in any given session. The expanding population of their districts, the growing constituency casework, the increase in the range and complexity of their legislative burdens — all have produced a need for staff assistance.[9] A congressman is no longer a "one-man band." Each must now head a sizeable staff operation and each is supported by a much larger House bureaucracy. Still, a congressman is a part of a greatly decentralized community; like one of 435 separate fiefdoms, only loosely coordinated and tied together by personal, party, and committee ties.

Obviously, no organizational chart ever fully mirrors the actual lines of authority and responsibility it is supposed to show. The boxes are always too uniform in size, the lines too straight and unbroken. More important, no organizational chart begins to capture the informal lines of communication, the by-passing of formal chains of command, the stress and flux of people interacting. Such ongoing dynamics can never be mapped completely, but Figure 2.1 outlines some of the important relationships which characterize the contemporary House of Representatives.

THE SPEAKER. It is clear from Figure 2.1 that the Speakership in the House of Representatives is of central importance. This constitu-

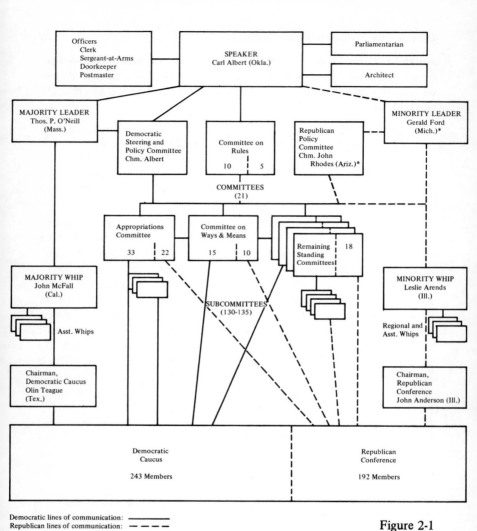

Democratic lines of communication: ————
Republican lines of communication: — — — —

Figure 2-1

* On December 6, 1973, Gerald Ford resigned from the House of Representatives to become the 40th Vice President of the United States, replacing Spiro T. Agnew. House Republicans unanimously elected John Rhodes of Arizona, their Policy Committee Chairman, to succeed Ford as Minority Leader. Barber Conable of New York became the new chairman of the House Republican Policy Committee. On August 9, 1974, following President Richard M. Nixon's resignation under the threat of impeachment, Ford was sworn in as the 38th President of the United States.

tionally designated officer has as one principal duty the task of presiding over the House. Throughout the decades, by rather steady increments of power at least until 1910, the Speaker has also emerged as the majority party's top leader. The Senate has no counterpart to the Speaker of the House. The closest approximation, the Senate Majority Leader, is not a constitutionally designated officer, is not even mentioned in the Senate Rules *Manual*, and never presides in his own chamber. The Speaker's stature is enhanced further by being second (behind the Vice President) to succeed to the presidency. Following Spiro T. Agnew's resignation from the vice presidency on October 10, 1973, and until Minority Leader Gerald R. Ford was confirmed as his successor on December 6, 1973, Speaker Carl Albert was only "one heartbeat away" from the presidency. But a most unusual set of events, the near simultaneous death, incapacity, or removal from office of both the Vice President and the President, is required before the Speaker succeeds to the presidency. (The President pro tempore of the Senate is third in succession, but his chances of becoming President are even more remote.)

Thirteen men, eight Democrats and five Republicans, have served as Speaker in the 20th century. As Table 2.1 demonstrates, lengthy service in the House, a minimum of eight to ten terms, is a basic prerequisite to election to this office. Further, ten of the thirteen 20th-century Speakers, and the nine most recent consecutively, have previously held the office of Majority or Minority Leader. No Speaker has come close to matching Sam Rayburn's record of 17 years' service in this high office. We shall return shortly to an in-depth analysis of the Speaker's pivotal role in the House leadership. But first, brief descriptions of the other principal party offices are in order.

FLOOR LEADERS. The House and Senate have always made use of floor *managers* for different pieces of legislation. Usually, the chairman and ranking minority member of the committee of original jurisdiction also oversee the floor debate, maintain control over time, and have considerable voice about who will speak for or against amendments. From time to time the prime responsibility for floor management is delegated to a subcommittee chairman and, perhaps, his minority party counterpart.

The modern conception of a floor leader as a separate and independent officer charged with overall responsibility for a party's legis-

Table 2.1
Speakers of the House of Representatives, 1903–1974

Name and State	Party	Dates of Service as Speaker	Years of Service	Years in House Before Election as Speaker	Age at Election as Speaker[a]	Prior Leadership Positions	Reasons for Vacating Office
David B. Henderson, Iowa	R	1899–1903	4	16	59	None	Retirement
Joseph G. Cannon, Ill.	R	1903–1911	8	28	67	None	Party became minority
Champ Clark, Mo.	D	1911–1919	8	16	60	Minority Leader, 1908–1911	Party became minority
Frederick H. Gillett, Mass.	R	1919–1925	6	26	71	None	Elected to Senate
Nicholas Longworth, Ohio	R	1925–1931	6	20	55	Majority Leader, 1923–1925	Death
John N. Garner, Tex.	D	1931–1933	2	28	62	Minority Leader, 1929–1931	Elected Vice President
Henry T. Rainey, Ill.	D	1933–1934	2	28	72	Majority Leader, 1931–1933	Death
Joseph W. Byrns, Tenn.	D	1935–1936	2	26	65	Majority Leader, 1933–1935	Death
William B. Bankhead, Ala.	D	1936–1940	4	20	62	Majority Leader, 1935–1936	Death

Name	Party	Years				Prior leadership	Reason
Sam Rayburn, Tex.	D	1940–1947 1949–1953 1955–1961	17	28	58	Majority Leader, 1937–1940	Party became minority (1947, 1953) Death (1961)
Joseph W. Martin, Mass.	R	1947–1949 1953–1955	4	22	62	Minority Leader, 1939–1947	Party became minority
John W. McCormack, Mass.	D	1962–1971	9	33	70	Majority Leader, 1940–1947, 1949–1953, 1955–1961; Min. whip 1947–1949, 1953–1955	Retirement
Carl Albert, Okla.	D	1971–	—	24	62	Majority Leader, 1962–1971; Maj. whip 1955–1961	
Average (Mean)			6.0	25.0	63.5		

Adapted from Randall B. Ripley, *Party Leaders in the House of Representatives* (Washington: Brookings Institution, 1967), pp. 14–15. Copyright © 1967 by the Brookings Institution, Washington, D.C. Reprinted by permission.

a Except in cases of mid-Congress selection, age is given as of the expiration date of the Congress prior to election as Speaker.

lative program can be traced back to the period just before World War I. The curbing of Speaker Joseph Cannon in 1910, the increasing importance of party loyalty in Congress, the needs of further organization brought on by the enhanced legislative burden of the war — all contributed to the institutionalization of the floor leader's role.

Prior to 1900, majority floor leaders had been appointed by Speakers.[10]

> In the House, the early titular floor leaders were at the same time the chairmen of the Ways and Means Committee. Before the division of work of that committee, the duties of its chairmen were so numerous that they automatically became the actual leaders, since as chairmen of that committee they had to direct the consideration of most of the legislation presented to the House. From 1865 until 1896 the burden of handling most of the legislation was shifted to the chairman of the Appropriations Committee, who then was designated most frequently as the leader. From 1896 until 1910 once again the chairmen of the Ways and Means Committee were usually sought as the floor leaders. During all of these years before the "Cannon revolution" of 1910, the Speaker, who appointed all members to committees, saw to it that his party opponent for the Speakership, some Representative with a large following, or one of his faithful lieutenants was made the floor leader.

In 1911, when the Democrats regained control of the House, Oscar Underwood of Alabama became the first Majority Leader to be elected by secret ballot in a party caucus. In 1919, when the Republicans returned to power, they elected Frank Mondell of Wyoming, a former chairman of the Ways and Means Committee, as floor leader and gave him additional party responsibilities, but kept him from membership on any of the standing committees of the House. After that date, regardless of which party organized the House, the Majority Leader no longer chaired Ways and Means or any other legislative committee. By 1925 the Majority Leader was firmly established as the Speaker's principal lieutenant and this practice has also been followed by both parties.[11]

The Minority Leader has a somewhat longer heritage as an independent officer. Prior to 1883 the identity and role of the Minority Leader remained rather obscure. Since that date, the candidate for Speaker nominated by the minority party has generally assumed the title and function of floor leader. Thomas Reed of Maine, who alternated between Minority Leader and Speaker between 1883 and 1899, did much to give the office stature and to prepare the way for its modern development.

Tables 2.2 and 2.3 provide some common background characteristics and career developments of the 22 men who have served as Majority and/or Minority Leader since the modern evolution of the office.[12] Both parties typically have turned to people in their middle 50s with an average record of 18 years in the House prior to their first selection. Of the fourteen Majority Leaders since 1910, seven became Speaker, four gave up the position because their party returned to the minority, two ran for the Senate, and one died.

The position of Minority Leader, reflecting the continuing frustrations of minority status, normally has proven less secure than its majority counterpart. Of the eleven Minority Leaders, two were ousted by their party and a third was denied the Speakership nomination. Only three Minority Leaders have advanced directly to the Speakership in this century — Clark, Garner, and Martin.

What preoccupies the time and interests of Majority and Minority Leaders? Their prime responsibility is marshalling their party's forces on the floor, working for majorities on key legislative votes. As is true of the Speaker, leaders seldom intervene in the drafting of legislation or interfere with a committee's initial deliberations. However, once a bill is scheduled for floor debate (agenda setting is closely coordinated through the Speaker), it is their job to see that committee-approved legislation is passed. Much depends, of course, on whether or not the party of the leader is in control of the White House. For Minority Leaders, this crucial fact determines whether their principal preoccupations are given over to bringing about the passage of the President's program, modifying it in part or more severely, or working to defeat the legislation of the opposing party.

All floor leaders, majority or minority, must deal with three broad areas of policy making: (1) internal organization, including relationships with other party and committee leaders and the supervision of their own staff; (2) legislative strategy, both the formulation of policy and its implementation, and (3) external coordination, particularly relationships with the White House and the executive branch, the national party committee, other party leaders, interest groups, the mass media, and in the broadest sense, the American electorate.[13]

Table 2.2

Majority Leaders of the House of Representatives, 1911–1974

Name and State	Party	Dates of Service as Leader	Years of Service	Years in House Before Election as Leader	Age at Election[a] as Leader	Reason for Vacating Job as Leader
Oscar Underwood, Ala.	D	1911–1915	4	16	48	Elected to Senate
Claude Kitchen, N.C.	D	1915–1919	4	14	45	Party became minority
Frank Mondell, Wyo.	R	1919–1923	4	22	58	Defeated for Senate
Nicholas Longworth, Ohio	R	1923–1925	2	18	53	Elected Speaker
John Tilson, Conn.	R	1925–1931	6	14	58	Party became minority; lost bid for Minority Leader
Henry Rainey, Ill.	D	1931–1933	2	28	70	Elected Speaker
Joseph Byrns, Tenn.	D	1933–1935	2	24	63	Elected Speaker
William Bankhead, Ala.	D	1935–1936	2	18	60	Elected Speaker
Sam Rayburn, Tex.	D	1937–1940	4	24	55	Elected Speaker
John McCormack, Mass.	D	1940–1947, 1949–1953, 1955–1961	17	12	48	Party became minority; elected Speaker
Charles Halleck, Ind.	R	1947–1949 1953–1955	4	12	46	Party became minority
Carl Albert, Okla.	D	1962–1971	9	15	53	Elected Speaker
Hale Boggs, La.	D	1971–1972	2	24	56	Death
Thomas O'Neill, Mass.	D	1973–	—	20	60	
Average (Mean)			4.8	18.6	55.1	

Adapted from Randall B. Ripley, *Party Leaders in the House of Representatives* (Washington: Brookings Institution, 1967), p. 26. Copyright © 1967 by the Brookings Institution, Washington, D.C. Reprinted by permission.
[a] Except in cases of mid-Congress selection, age is given as of the expiration date of the Congress prior to election as Majority Leader.

Table 2.3
Minority Leaders of the House of Representatives, 1908–1974

Name and State	Party	Dates of Service as Leader	Years of Service	Years in House Before Election as Leader	Age at Election[a] as Leader	Reason for Vacating Job as Leader
Champ Clark, Mo.	D	1908–1911, 1919–1921	5	13	58	Elected Speaker 1911; defeated in district, 1920
James Mann, Ill.	R	1911–1919	8	14	54	Defeated for Speakership nomination
Claude Kitchin, N.C.	D	1921–1923	2	20	51	Death
Finis Garrett, Tenn.	D	1923–1929	6	18	47	Defeated for Senate
John Garner, Tex.	D	1929–1931	2	26	60	Elected Speaker
Bertrand Snell, N.Y.	R	1931–1939	8	16	60	Retired
Joseph Martin, Mass.	R	1939–1947, 1949–1953, 1955–1959	16	14	54	Elected Speaker, 1947, 1953; defeated by Halleck, 1959
Sam Rayburn, Tex.	D	1947–1949, 1953–1955	4	[b]	[b]	Reelected Speaker, 1949, 1955
Charles Halleck, Ind.	R	1959–1965	6	24	58	Defeated by Ford, 1965
Gerald Ford, Mich.	R	1965–1973	9	16	51	Appointed Vice President, 1973
John Rhodes, Ariz.	R	1973–	—	21	57	
Average (Mean)			6.6	18.2	55.0	

Adapted from Randall B. Ripley, *Party Leaders in the House of Representatives* (Washington: Brookings Institution, 1967), pp. 30–31. Copyright © 1967 by the Brookings Institution, Washington, D.C. Reprinted by permission.
[a] Except in cases of mid-Congress selections, age is given as of the expiration date of the Congress prior to election as Minority Leader.
[b] Previously served as Majority Leader and Speaker.

The three broad areas are intertwined. A congressional leader may be more adept in one area than another; he may spend some days principally preoccupied by problems in one area to the detriment of pressing needs in the other two; but, he cannot afford to ignore any one of the three areas for very long without serious consequences to the effectiveness of his party and the strength of his own leadership.

PARTY WHIPS. The whip is third in the House majority party hierarchy, a nominal second in the minority party. Unlike the Speaker and the Majority Leader, however, the Democratic whip is appointive, not elective. Therefore, he is not free to represent his party or pressure its members in the same sense as the top party leaders or even his minority counterpart. The Republican whip is elective — Leslie Arends of Illinois, first selected in 1943, had all but institutionalized that position.[14]

The tasks of the whip, majority or minority, are essentially twofold: (1) communication by whip notices to members of the forthcoming legislative agenda; and (2) provision of information by which the party leadership decides whether to bring legislation to the floor, and/or what form amendments should take in order to ensure passage. The whips work through regional or assistant whips, each responsible for a zone of 10–20 members, on the average, in one or more states. When the leader requests, the whip conducts a poll to determine which members are for, leaning for, indifferent to, or against a proposed bill or section of a bill. By personal contact or telephone calls the whip makes a count so the leader has the best possible information to decide whether or not to move ahead, delay, or withdraw proposed legislation. A whip poll sometimes is jammed through in 24 hours or, more leisurely, in two or three days. The quality of the information gained is crucial to legislative floor strategy.[15]

OTHER PARTY OFFICES. Both Democrats and Republicans are organized, initially, in party caucuses or conferences held just before a new Congress convenes. (Fuller descriptions of these party caucuses will be provided in the chapters to follow since it is, generally, in these opening meetings that leadership contests are decided.) In recent years, both the Democratic Caucus and the Republican Conference have also played a much more regular and active role in hammering out questions of party and committee reorganization, including the reoccurring and vital issue of seniority and the election of committee chairmen and ranking minority members. The chairmen of both the Republican Conference and the Democratic Caucus have emerged as important leaders in their own right in the late 1960's and early 1970's, especially Republicans Gerald Ford (1963–1964), Melvin Laird (1965–1968), and John Anderson (1969–   ), and Democrats Dan Rostenkowski (1967–1970) and Olin Teague (1971–1974).

Both parties in recent years have also reactivated "policy committees" as a means of thrashing out partisan positions on legislative issues and attempting to develop greater party unity. The Republican Policy Committee had a rebirth in 1959 under the initial leadership of John Byrnes (Wisc.) and then of John Rhodes (Ariz.) after 1965. In December 1973, after Rhodes was elevated to the minority leadership, Barber Conable (N.Y.) was elected chairman. The Democratic Steering and Policy Committee, following years of inactivity, has undergone rather sporadic revitalization since 1973, under the Speaker's chairmanship. Both policy committees have between twenty and thirty members with the core membership elected regionally, but bolstered by other party leaders.

Although not shown in Figure 2.1, both parties also maintain active congressional campaign committees, called the Democratic National Congressional Committee and the Republican National Congressional Committee. Staffed by from three to ten professionals (Republicans have generally supported larger, better financed staff operations in attempts to overcome their minority status), the chairmen of these rather independently-run committees command considerable stature in their respective parties. It is not difficult to understand why. These senior party leaders oversee the raising of and disbursing of campaign contributions running in the several millions of dollars every two years. During the closing months of the campaign, in particular, they exercise considerable discretion about which members (and, even more important, which potentially incoming freshmen nominees) receive more than the token contributions of $3000 to $5000 dispensed to all incumbents. At least two former Republican campaign committee chairmen (Joseph Martin after 1938, Charles Halleck after 1946) utilized their success in those elections as a springboard to the floor leadership of their party.

THE COMMITTEE LEADERS. Although the focus of this book is primarily on party leaders, it is important to acknowledge other independent reservoirs of power in the House: the chairmen of committees, and to a lesser extent, the ranking minority leaders.[16] Usually, but not exclusively, the chairmen of the most powerful committees — men like Wilbur D. Mills of Arkansas (former chairman of the Ways and Means Committee);[17] Howard Worth Smith of Virginia (former chairman of the Rules Committee);[18] and to a lesser extent, George Mahon of Texas (Appropriations), have extended their power bases in the House beyond the jurisdictions of their own committees. The chairmen and ranking members of these three exclusive committees are almost always powerful men, especially when they work in tandem like former Appropriation Committee leaders Clarence Cannon (D., Mo.) and John Taber (R., N.Y.).[19]

The sources of committee chairmanship power stem from their control over committee organization resources, such as staff and space, and legislative outcomes. As one House veteran has observed:[20]

> The mortar that binds the system consists largely of what has been called inelegantly but properly "boodle" [the location of military installations, public works projects, the location of a post office, and the like].

> The boodle in itself is legitimate and productive. The hitch is in the way it is distributed ... The conservative ruling elders maintain their power by determining in large measure which House Members will get the larger portions. Generally, the stay-in-line orthodox Member will come away with the fuller plate.

Sometimes, committee leaders emerge as prospective candidates for top party leadership. Mills, in particular, had been mentioned as a candidate for Speaker in 1969, in 1971, and even in 1973, but for one reason or another he had never "gone to the wall," that is, openly declared his candidacy. We shall return to this generally cooperative, occasionally antagonistic relationship between party leaders and committee leaders in the chapters that follow.[21]

The committee structure of the House, like the leadership structure, is dual in nature. The party which controls the House chooses the chairmen, sets the ratios on committees (by negotiation with the minority party leadership) and generally dominates staffing, funds for investigations, and other housekeeping matters. On the three most prestigious committees of the House — Appropriations, Ways and Means, and Rules — the ratios have traditionally been kept at 3:2,

3:2, and 2:1. However, in times of large Democratic party majorities, such as those of the 89th (1965–1966) and 94th (1975–1976) Congresses, majority party advantages in terms of numbers have been increased. The higher ratio on Rules is dictated by its status as a "leadership committee," charged with scheduling legislation for floor debate. In general, the ratio of Democrats to Republicans on the remaining 18 standing committees fluctuates with the overall House ratio, currently better than 3:2.

THE RESOURCES OF THE SPEAKER
AND THE MAJORITY PARTY

"The Speakership is not only an institution, it is an opportunity, in which men of strong character have shown their leadership." [22] So wrote Mary Parker Follett just before the turn of the century as the Speakership was nearing the apex of its formal powers. Thomas B. Reed (R., Me.) was about to be reelected Speaker and shortly to pronounce his famous rulings against "disappearing quorums," and other dilatory tactics of the minority party.[23] The revolt against Speaker Joseph G. Cannon (R., Ill.), stripping him from his chairmanship of the Committee on Rules and his powers of committee assignments, lay less than two decades away.[24] Under Reed and Cannon the formal powers of the Speaker were immeasurably strengthened. Equally important, neither hesitated to use the powers. The arbitrariness of Cannon's personality eventually led to a situation in which for the first, and probably the last, time a heavy-handed rule of the Speaker emerged.

Since the revolution against Cannon in 1910 the problem has been almost the opposite. How can any Speaker make use of his much more limited formal powers to achieve his party's legislative objectives, let alone help Congress maintain a parity with an ever-expanding executive branch? That Speakers like Nicholas Longworth (R., Ohio) and Sam Rayburn (D., Tex.) from time to time have operated effectively has been attributed more to their strong personal characters and persuasive abilities rather than to the limited formal powers available to them. What seems to distinguish strong Speakers from the more mediocre ones has been a willingness to use their limited legislative powers to the hilt, at the same time exploiting other more personal forms of influence with skill and subtlety. They must initiate actions without getting too far out in front of a majority of their followers. They must operate with "controlled partisanship." A Speaker must function in two roles almost simultaneously — first, as the neutral presiding officer to protect the rights of *all* members, majority and minority alike, and second, as partisan leader of the majority party to seek ways to advance the party's policy objectives and continued control of the Congress.

PARLIAMENTARY POWERS. Despite the restrictions of 1910 the formal powers of a Speaker remain considerable. Rule I of the *Rules of the House of Representatives* sets forth most of the Speaker's parliamentary duties; to preside over the House, approve the journal, preserve order and decorum, maintain general control of the House side of the Capitol (including assignment of space), sign all acts and resolutions, put all questions, vote when it would be decisive,[25] and name members to perform the duties of the chair (Speakers pro tempore). Additional rules and precedents of the House provide for the Speaker to administer the oath of office to members, to grant or refuse floor recognition, to count for quorums, to pronounce adjournments, to appoint select committees and the House members of conference and joint committees, to appoint chairmen of the Committees of the Whole, to control admission to the floor and galleries, and to oversee the official reporters of the House (including committee stenographers and the preparation of the *Congressional Record*). If the House Judiciary Committee should report out a bill of impeachment against a President, the Speaker would preside over the floor debate and final vote.

LEGISLATIVE DISCRETION. Many of these powers require, of course, considerable discretion on the part of the Speaker. Although not a free agent in determining who shall have control of the floor (when a particular bill is under consideration, the members of the committee with jurisdiction have priority over non-committee members), the Speaker's right to inquire — "For what purpose does the member rise?" — gives him considerable latitude, especially since there is no appeal from the Speaker's recognition or non-recognition. Speakers have utilized this power on numerous occasions to favor certain individuals, their party's position, or to postpone or block proposals.

The power of recognition frequently enters into the series of discussions which the top leaders have with committee leaders before most major legislative floor debates. The central issues usually concern the compromises to be made, in the form of one or more amendments to different provisions of the pending bill if it is to carry a majority vote on final passage. Once the committee experts have had their say and the leaders have made their strategic judgments (often after the benefit of a whip poll), then the issue is to decide which member of the committee should offer the amendment. Is Southern Democratic support needed? Should Congressman A of Georgia be asked to offer the amendment? If Congressman A proposed the amendment, then the Speaker is alert to recognize him first. The leadership meeting then takes appropriate action to shore up wavering members or to convert those in opposition. The Speaker may immediately begin to telephone key people to gain support for the amendment and the Majority Leader and whips to align support on the floor.

INFORMATION. Strategy meetings provide another valuable resource over which the leadership maintains primary control — the House information network. Each congressman has sources of communication, internal and external, but no network is spread so extensively as that of the top leadership. If the White House is controlled by the leaders' party, much information from the executive branch to the Hill is received by the Speaker and the Majority Leader. If the opposing party controls the presidency, then Minority Leaders attend White House leadership briefings on a regular weekly basis. Still, most Presidents involve the majority leadership in at least once-a-month sessions as well as in special meetings called to discuss a particular foreign or domestic crisis. Regardless of who controls the White House, the Speaker and the Majority Leader have far more communication with the executive branch than most committee chairmen or the average senior party member.

Of course, most leadership communication is general rather than specific. Agricultural committee members are in closer and more frequent communication with the Department of Agriculture Assistant Secretaries and congressional liaison people, Education and Labor committee members with their downtown departmental policy makers, and so on. However, the less technical and more politicized the message, the more likely it will filter through the House leadership offices.

Information flows out as well as in. Unlike Senators, the typical House member seldom is asked to appear on the weekly televised talk shows, "Meet the Press," "Face the Nation," and similar network presentations. Such invitations usually are reserved for House leaders. In addition, the Speaker holds a daily five-minute press conference in his office just before the House convenes. Only infrequently are these conferences televised, but reporters from Associated Press, United Press International, and the leading metropolitan dailies attend to obtain further information on pending legislature or perhaps to tease a quotation from a generally taciturn Speaker.[26]

The information that dominates the Speaker's press conference — what's coming up on the floor and when — is eagerly sought by members of Congress since it affects the organization of their own work week. All, of course, on Fridays receive copies of their party's Whip's Notice which details the pending floor action for the coming week.[27] Such a schedule is notoriously unstable, and is likely to come unglued at the drop of a conference report. Only the leaders and their aides are likely to be cognizant of changes and postponements but even they cannot know that a vote scheduled for Wednesday will be delayed until Thursday. While information about scheduling is a lower-level resource compared to *control* over scheduling, it allows congressmen to plan ahead, to decide whether they are able to catch a plane home, make that fund-raising dinner in Dubuque, or meet with an important district businessman or labor leader.

SCHEDULING. Final control over scheduling is almost exclusively a top leadership function shared by the Speaker and Majority Leader, working in consultation with the minority leadership. Such control must be maintained to schedule the flow of legislation converging upon them from about twenty different directions — the standing committees of the House.

At the beginning of a session, even after an August recess, the majority leadership top aides systematically call the staff directors or chief counsels of committees to obtain legislation for floor consideration. Prior to vacation recess, before Easter or the 4th of July, and especially as the session comes to its usual frenetic wind-up, the situation is almost reversed. Committee chairmen will be hounding the Speaker, so their bills can be scheduled on the various calendars — Union, House, Consent, Private — or programmed for more extensive floor debate through a special order from the Rules Committee.[28] The ability to help members overcome the gap between the standing committees and the floor is one of the most important resources of power available to the majority leadership.

APPOINTMENTS. Another resource in the arsenal of a Speaker is his power of appointment. Prior to 1910, the Speaker had exclusive committee assignment powers; since then, control rests with the Committee on Committees of the respective parties. Before reforms initiated in 1973, majority leaders had only *ex officio* status on their own party's Committee on Committees. The 15 Democratic members of the House Ways and Means Committee had control over which committee assignments freshmen members would receive and who could be transferred from a lesser committee to a more prestigious one.[29] Upon the adoption of a resolution in the opening Democratic Caucus, the Speaker, Majority Leader, and chairman of the caucus were placed on the committee, each with a zone and a vote. In reforms consolidated just before the beginning of the 94th Congress, the Democratic Caucus took committee assignment powers away from Ways and Means Committee members and lodged them, instead, with the Democratic Steering and Policy Committee, headed by the Speaker. In addition to influence over regular committee assignments, the Speaker has exclusive power to appoint members of numerous joint, select, and special committees such as the prestigious Joint Economic Committee, the Select Committee on Crime, or one of the Boards of Visitors to West Point or the Naval Academy. By use of appointive power, a Speaker can reward the faithful or gain new supporters for legislative purposes.

EXCHANGE. Majority leaders may also make use of a wide range of personal and political favors as a means of further credit-building. Numerous examples illustrate the point:

— The Speaker drops in on a downtown Washington reception a member is holding for some important constituents;

— The Leader opens his office to and spends fifteen minutes conversing with a group of high school students from a member's home town;

— The Speaker makes himself available to advise and counsel a member with domestic problems or another who confronts a tough reelection campaign;

— The Leader sends a telegram to a fund-raising dinner, emphasizing why Congressman X should be returned to Washington; or, more emphatic still, the Leader attends the dinner and makes a speech.

Rarely does a Speaker say to a member, "I did X for you; now, I want you to do Y for me." The process is far more subtle; the emphasis is on general exchange over time rather than explicit *quid-pro-quos*.

Few sanctions are available to the majority leadership other than the *withholding* of such personal, political, and legislative assistance, the refusal to support a committee assignment, the lack of intervention when help is needed. Still, as one member observed, "No one likes to cross the Speaker needlessly. You may need his help the next day or the next week." [30]

Just as Speakers differ in their personal traits, they also vary in the ways they husband their scarce resources. Wright Patman of Texas is the only remaining member of Congress who served under the iron rule of John Nance Garner of Texas, the Democratic Speaker in the 72d Congress (1931–1932) and later Vice President under Roosevelt. Those who remember Garner have nothing but admiration for the way he controlled information and managed a closely divided House.[31] However, Garner could be mean and vindictive in his personal relationships — he thought nothing of bottling up the bills of enemies or of members on the fence. If members were not loyal to "Cactus Jack" Garner, their legislative bills were indefinitely shelved.

Rayburn, in contrast, generally believed that "the carrot was better than the stick." He would sometimes go out of his way to assist non-supporters. For example, when an appropriation for a dam in the district of an arch-conservative Democrat from Texas was in grave trouble, Rayburn stepped to the House floor and moved from member to member to personally convert enough votes to support the bill. Whether Rayburn was ever repaid in kind is not known, but the approval of that particular dam allegedly insured the reelection of that Texan for life. Representative Howard W. Smith, former Chairman of the House Committee on Rules, Rayburn's long-time friend but worthy antagonist, summed him up in the following way: "Sam was a good bookkeeper. He had an iron fist, but a glove of velvet."

For John McCormack, close disciple of Rayburn for twenty years and himself Speaker for nine years, "what [was] important about leadership in the House of Representatives [was] confidence and trust based upon personal friendship."

Carl Albert seems to have borrowed some from Rayburn, some from McCormack — he was one of the more popular leaders when he initially assumed the Speakership. Albert presided over the House in the early 1970s with intelligence, diligence, and geniality. But by mid-decade, the Democratic majority leadership was coming under increasingly severe criticism from their colleagues. An iron fist or even a little meanness seemed lacking.

THE RESOURCES OF THE MINORITY PARTY

Two obvious points about the resources of the minority party in the House of Representatives are that (1) the minority party is inherently disadvantaged as compared with the majority party in almost every conceivable resource, and (2) for more than four decades, it has been possible to equate the minority party with the Republican party in Congress.[32] Not since the 83d Congress (1953–1954), the first Eisenhower administration Congress, have the Republicans organized the House and Senate. The only other time since 1930 that the G.O.P. held majorities in either House was the famous 80th Congress (1947–1948), which Democratic President Harry S. Truman incorrectly but effectively labeled a "Do-nothing Congress." [33]

The major resource which a minority party lacks is, of course, votes. Over the past 46 years the Republican party has fallen as low as 89 members in the 75th Congress (1937–1938), averaging about 175 members or 40 percent of the House membership over the 23 Congresses.[34]

Committee chairmen, of course, are selected from the most senior ranks of the majority. The legislative influence of a ranking minority member is highly dependent upon the closeness of his relationship with the chairmen of his committee. By and large the ratios of Democrats to Republicans on the 21 standing committees of the House reflects the overall membership composition. The minority party also is disadvantaged in terms of staff, space, and control over investigatory funds.

At the opening roll call vote of a new Congress, the minority party candidate for Speaker inevitably loses on a party-line vote to the majority candidate, and subsequently serves as the minority floor leader. Almost never will party alignments be so pure throughout the more than 300 roll-call votes in each session of the two-year period. Still, the minority party continually faces an uphill challenge both in committees and on the floor — how can they win enough majority votes to convert their minority position into a winning one? Over the years the Republican minority has been somewhat successful in forging a series of legislative alliances with southern Democrats in what has come to be known as the "conservative coalition." As John Manley concludes:[35]

> . . . [The] Conservative Coalition, born in the 1930's, has persisted as a relatively common and potent voting alliance for forty years. In both chambers, the Coalition was less successful in the late 1950's and in the 1960's than it was earlier, but as the record of the Ninetieth Congress (1967–1968) shows the Coalition was anything but a paper tiger as the 1970's dawned. In that Congress, just prior to Richard Nixon's presidency, the Coalition won 65 percent of Coalition votes in the Senate, and 59 percent in the House. With a Republican in the White House, liberals in Congress feared the worst. And, with exceptions, they got it.

The shortcomings of continued minority status for Republicans in Congress has been partially offset by the election of two contemporary Republican Presidents, Dwight D. Eisenhower (1953–1960) and Richard M. Nixon (1969–1974). In Republican administrations the tasks of Republican Minority Leaders have fluctuated from trying to build majority coalitions for Republican programs or, short of those goals, to working to sustain presidential vetoes of Democratically sponsored legislation. With the strong Democratic gains of the 1974 congressional elections, these tasks were made more difficult, but not impossible. There is no such thing as a "veto-proof" Congress, a reality which President Ford was to exploit.

If the minority party does not enjoy the multiple benefits flowing from executive branch control, three basic alternatives are available: (1) cooperation with the presidential majority, (2) partisan opposition, or (3) promotion of constructive alternatives to administrative proposals. Of course, no party practices one alternative to the exclusion of the others, but through the years different House and Senate leaders have been predominantly identified with a certain policy stance. Among recent Republican congressional leaders, Senator Everett Dirksen and Representative Joseph Martin have most closely approximated a policy of cooperation with the majority; Senator William Knowland and Representative Charles Halleck, a policy of partisan opposition; and Senator Robert Taft and Representative Gerald Ford have come closest to a policy emphasizing constructive legislative alternatives to Democratic programs.[36]

RESOURCES OF THE MINORITY LEADER. A House Minority Leader has none of the parliamentary powers that accrue to the Speaker as presiding officer; the Minority Leader's activities are more comparable to those of the majority floor leader. The only occasion for which a Minority Leader presides over the House is to briefly congratulate his majority opponent who wins the Speakership at the opening of a Congress. Still, in common with the Speaker, a Minority Leader serves as his congressional party's prime external spokesman and principal legislative strategist. In general, similar resources to those of the Majority Leader are available, but are almost always restricted in scope and quality, even when the minority controls the presidency.

Relations, sometimes contentious, more often consultative, are always extensive between the House majority and minority leadership. At the opening of a Congress the two leaderships meet to decide upon the ratio of Democrats to Republicans on the 21 standing committees. This ratio — except in the cases of Appropriations, Rules, and Ways and Means — closely approximates the overall party division of the House of Representatives. The majority leadership retains control over the week-to-week scheduling of legislation, but frequently consults with the minority leadership. When a stalemate occurs or when a compromise is pending, the Minority Leader frequently is seen huddling with his majority counterpart on the floor or up at the Speaker's rostrum. Many parliamentary delaying tactics are available to the minority if the majority attempts to ride roughshod over its opposition. A principal responsibility of the minority leadership is to see that the rights of the minority members are continually protected.

In common with the majority leadership, a Minority Leader has command of an important information network. Some information derives from consultation with the majority leadership. When the President is of the minority party, then the Minority Leader's office becomes the central conduit for assembling and dispensing information about administration legislative programs. The House Minority Leader, accompanied by the whip, the chairmen of the conference and policy committees, and other party officials, attend weekly White House breakfasts to discuss legislative plans and other political matters. After the meetings, usually the floor leaders of the House and Senate appear before the television cameras to brief the waiting press.

A Minority Leader can easily summon a press conference of his own, or he may join with his Senate counterpart to hold monthly television programs, such as the famed "Ev and Charlie" and "Ev and Jerry" shows. These featured the colorful Senate Minority Leader, Everett Dirksen, first with Charles Halleck and later with Jerry Ford. Beyond appearances on such television shows as "Issues and Answers" or "Meet the Press," the Minority Leader has many opportunities to address party fund-raising dinners across the nation or to appear in behalf of his fellow congressmen in their home districts.

Technically, only the Speaker holds the power of appointment in the House. Routinely, however, he accepts those nominated by the Minority Leader for Republican appointments to the many special, select, and joint committees. Moreover, the Minority Leader serves *ex officio* as chairman of his party's Committee on Committees. Although the Leader has no vote on the committee, his influence often can be persuasive in obtaining a key committee appointment for a loyal supporter.

A Minority Leader can, like his majority party counterparts, avail himself of a wide range of personal and political favors in order to generate a broader base of support among his colleagues. John Rhodes, Jerry Ford, and to a lesser extent, Charles Halleck, earned reputations for keeping an "open door" policy, making themselves easily available for consultation with other Republican members. Ford, in particular, was an indefatigable campaigner in behalf of members running for reelection as well as for aspiring Republican candidates in the House. Minority Leaders must take every advantage of positive ways to build credit, since even fewer opportunities to exercise negative sanctions are available to them as compared with their majority counterparts.

MEMBERSHIP RELATIONS AND EXPECTATIONS OF LEADERS

The typical member comes to Congress, his ego inflated, ready to take on the world. He's just won out over all other competition in a district with over 400,000 people — so why shouldn't his ego be inflated?

As far as the leadership is concerned he figures he could do the job as well as anybody else. But everybody can't be Speaker, so he's willing to let McCormack or Albert or somebody else do it. You have to give up a little bit of power to get the House organized. He's willing to concede that as long as it's the bare minimum.

— Senior staff aide,
House Democratic leadership

Junior members of the House — those with fewer than three or four terms — probably hold the most ambivalent views about party leaders of any members of Congress. Almost by definition these members are the least accommodated, most frustrated and politically uneasy both about their roles in the House and about the uncertainty of their political futures. None of the majority members are likely to have a subcommittee chairmanship as yet (unlike Senate juniors). As a result of higher turnover, Republican members may soon find themselves a little higher in committee ranking, but the frustrations of minority status are hardly compensated by that mobility. Representatives into their second and third terms gain familiarity with committee and floor procedures — if they work at it. But they still lack the seniority that allows rewards in terms of legislative successes. Unless junior minority members inherit a safe seat, they must devote a great deal of time to constituency care with frequent travel to their districts.

It is particularly this junior group of members who are most likely to be critical of the workings of the House and its leadership. And why not? It is the seniority system, compounded by what is perceived primarily as a *status-quo*-oriented leadership, which continues to deny them stature or meaningful impact on the legislative process. Some resentment is captured in the comment of a second-term Plains States Democrat in the process of downgrading his party's 1971 majority leadership contest:

> Frankly, I don't give a crap for titles. This whip, Majority Leader crap doesn't interest me. The sooner everybody around here realizes that we're all part of the leadership, the better off we'll be. I don't like all this scheming to get to have some worthless title that isn't worth a damn, anyway.

Paradoxically, it is precisely at this point that the party leadership has greatest control over junior members' careers. Few decisions rival the importance of the committee assignment that a freshman receives in the opening month of a new Congress. Here, and probably with even greater weight on transfers to more prestigious committees, leadership influence can be decisive.

Freshmen members in particular, and early term members in general, seldom have their names linked to major or even secondary legislation — the operations of the seniority system insure against that. To obtain passage of minor legislation, a bill which may nevertheless be highly important to their district, leadership assistance may be crucial at almost every stage. As the late Representative Clem Miller comments:[37]

> ... This authority to refer bills, to sidetrack them or pigeon-hole them through the various calendar devices, is one of the principal power levers of the Speaker. Particularly for lesser legislation (which may be the life-blood of individual congressmen) the chasm between the standing committee and the House floor is bridged with the unchallenged power of the Speaker.

Finally, in the absence of drastic redistricting, a major election tide, or a personal scandal, the vast majority of congressmen are most vulnerable, electorally, at the beginning (and, by definition, the end) of their political careers. The value of a leader's campaign trip to the district ("The nation needs Congressman X"), the impact of a speech at an important fund-raising dinner ("Your contributions are vital to the election of Representative Y"), and even the willingness to spend a few minutes with the member and several of his constituents visiting Washington — all such political favors are likely to mean more to the younger member than the the more secure, seasoned veteran.

Which is not to say that the party leadership cannot have an impact on the careers of more experienced members as well. After four or five terms in office, Representatives are coming into some power of their own. If they have not yet transferred to the prestige committees of the House — Ways and Means, Appropriations, or Rules — they are likely to have enough seniority to have secured a subcommittee of their own on their committees of original assignment. Leadership, of course, has no direct control over who receives or who is passed over for an important subcommittee post. Here, the power of the chairman largely reigns supreme, although in recent years the various committees have adopted rules to protect their members from arbitrary or capricious actions of chairmen or ranking minority members.[38]

With a chairmanship (and to a lesser degree with a ranking minority position) comes control over legislation, increased opportunities to floor manage bills, enhanced stature and visibility, and in all likelihood, more space and staff. Attendant with some of these responsibilities is the chance for greater interaction with party leaders. By and large, however, the lives of these mid-career members continue to be district- and committee-centered.

What can leadership, majority or minority, do for these Representatives? With increasing frequency these members need leadership support in scheduling and implementing legislation. At this time in their careers (and in some cases even earlier) they have become eligible for the numerous joint committees, special boards, and commissions over which the Speaker (taking into consideration the recommendations of the Minority Leader) has exclusive power of appointment. Some will serve as assistant whips, others will represent their states or regions on campaign or policy committees. In short, many will be climbing the bottom steps of the "establishment" in their respective party hierarchies.

Those House members who make full use of the many advantages of incumbency are likely to carve out or maintain a fairly safe seat after two or three elections. Just about this time, as they reach their mid-40s or early 50s, many arrive at a turning point in their career. They decide whether they wish to try for a governorship, a Senate seat, or resign themselves to a full-time career in the House. (For some members, a higher proportion from the minority party, the choice may be between remaining in the House or seeking early retirement.)

For some promising younger House members — the Hathaways, Metcalfs, and Tunneys; the Goodells, Griffins, and Doles — the House may early become a frustrating environment. Broader horizons beckon. When opportunities to run for the Senate come (or in some cases an appointment is offered) members seldom hesitate to try to become one of 100 rather than just one of 435. In every election a few House members move precipitously to seek a Senate seat; less than half who attempt it succeed. Although the overwhelming majority of House members would welcome the opportunity to serve in the Senate, most are unable to try either because no Senate seat opens up at an opportune moment, because of a lack of visibility, or because of the high costs of running a statewide, as contrasted with a district, campaign. But the most direct route to the Senate is from the House. From 25 to 40 percent of the Senators in recent decades have been former Representatives.

In any given election about one-eighth of the House members retire or are defeated. Those who decide to seek reelection are overwhelming favorites to return — about 95 percent will win. Once reelected they settle into a slow but steady rise in their seniority. Seniority requires playing a waiting game — patience, good health, and electoral fortune are the necessary virtues. [39] Eventually, death, resignation, or defeat take their inevitable toll among senior members as well as those who wait. If members have maintained physical strength and political fortune has been kind, their late 50s or early 60s, after about eight or ten terms, may at last see them achieve a committee chairmanship. (A member of a minority party can expect to earn a ranking minority position a little earlier, say by age 50–55 and after as few as six or eight terms.)

Most mid-career House members have long since muted any strong feelings they may have about their party leaders. They can take them or leave them. [40] Except in cases of membership in the same delegation or a close friendship, party leaders can no longer effect their significant political choices. Few of these mid-career members will seek transfers to other committees. They usually can arrange for their own trips overseas. They generally are secure in their own districts. The great majority are locked into a career in the House and the long-range pursuit of a committee chairmanship. Only an active minority still explore means to other offices — a governorship, a career in the Senate, their own party leadership. Hopes of becoming a vice-presidential, let alone a presidential, candidate are all but quashed.

One small subset of this experienced, mid-seniority range of House members remains actively interested in House leadership. A few are protegés of the top leadership — Albert, Boggs, and Bolling under Rayburn; O'Neill under McCormack. (Albert was entering his ninth year of service in the House in 1955 when Rayburn appointed him whip instead of Boggs, thus ordering the pattern of leadership selection for nearly two decades. O'Neill had served nine terms when he was appointed majority whip by Majority Leader Hale Boggs and Speaker Carl Albert in 1971. Two years later, following Boggs' disappearance and presumed death in Alaska, O'Neill became the new Majority Leader.)

From among the ranks of other, more change-oriented congressmen of mid-seniority has come the impetus for most of the contests for House party leadership as well as the primary thrusts for reform of the Republican conferences in 1965 and 1971 and the Democratic caucuses in 1971 and 1973. Sometimes their successful actions have earned them places in their own party leadership (Bob Wilson [R., Cal.] after 1959; Charles Goodell [R., N.Y.] in 1965). Attempts to penetrate the established pattern of majority leadership succession by middle-ranking, change-oriented Democratic congressmen, as we shall soon see, have generally been frustrated (Morris K. Udall [D., Ariz.] in 1969 and 1971; Sam M. Gibbons [D., Fla.] and Phillip Burton [D., Cal.] in 1973, but not 1975).

Short of full committee chairmanship, much creative legislative and investigatory work must be done by subcommittee chairmen and ranking minority members. Much of the work is of a bipartisan nature. Under a weak or failing chairman, a collegial leadership of subcommittee chairmen frequently emerges. Usually the House leadership does not intervene in either committee leadership or legislative matters until the concern becomes exceedingly visible (as, for example, the Adam Clayton Powell affair) or their own presidential leadership asks them to intervene (as, for example, the Federal Elementary and Secondary Education Act of 1965).

COMMITTEE LEADERS AND PARTY LEADERS

> The leadership is supposed under ordinary circumstances to collaborate with the committees. After a committee has studied a bill, held hearings, processed a bill, and has spent months bringing in a report — other things being equal — the committees are entitled to the support of the leadership of the House . . .
>
> At the end of these long months, the longest peacetime session Congress has had — and with no visible reason — I honor the high office they hold but I cannot endorse the quality of leadership.
>
> I have sat under 10 Speakers — but I have never seen such biased and inept leadership.
>
> —Clarence Cannon, Chairman
> House Committee on Appropriations

Less than two hours after Chairman Cannon delivered his 1962 end-of-the-session tirade [41] against the new House Democratic leadership — Speaker McCormack, Majority Leader Albert, Majority Whip Boggs — Charles Halleck, the Republican floor leader, got up to offer the traditional resolution commending the Speaker: [42]

> *Resolved,* That the thanks of the House are presented to the Honorable John W. McCormack, Speaker of the House of Representatives, for the able, impartial and dignified manner

in which he has presided over the deliberations and performed the arduous duties of the Chair.

The resolution was unanimously agreed to (presumably the outspoken, 83-year-old Chairman of the Appropriations Committee had long since left the House floor).

Perhaps these two views can be seen as the anchor points between which the House leadership and their minority counterparts float in their delicate and fluctuating relationships with their some twenty-one committee chairmen and ranking minority members. The Cannon quotation is particularly revealing as it reaffirms a widely held view of committee leadership, namely that the leadership exists to support the committee product, that its job is to take a committee bill as a given and shepherd it through, protecting it from amendments from either side of the aisle.[43] Conversely, many ranking committee members seem to see that the job of their leadership is to help them substitute their own version of a bill, to modify unwise legislation or, indeed, to subvert it altogether through a motion to recommit.

The pro-forma nature of Halleck's end-of-the-session resolution should not hide another dimension of what ranking minority members and committee chairmen, alike, expect in their own leadership, namely, fairness, ease of access, and openness in dealing with members of their own party. And, of course, committee minority spokesmen were particularly dependent upon fair and impartial rulings from the Speaker and his selections of seasoned Democrats to preside over the legislative deliberations in the Committee of the Whole. As a former Speaker comments:

> The Speaker of the House has a dual role. He is both the parliamentary and presiding officer on the one hand and the leader of his party on the other. He has to be careful that he doesn't emphasize one aspect too strongly to the detriment of the other. It's a matter of balance, of harmony between the two.

Several additional factors should be kept in mind in analyzing the relationships of party leaders and committee leaders, majority and minority. First, committee leaders see themselves as the substantive and technical experts; they only begrudgingly acknowledge that party leaders might excel them in techniques of floor strategy or in a commitment to broader party and national objectives. They take pride in being considered as specialists; they are reluctant to accord too much of a legislative role for the prime generalists in the House, the party leaders. A former chairman of the House Rules Committee, himself a generalist, makes the criticism:

> The Speaker — he should be an administrative official. He doesn't have time to be a student of legislation . . . I felt that with [two former Speakers] I could go down to their office and say: "This is a bad bill, it shouldn't be passed." But they're just too busy; they don't have time to know what's in the bills. They're too bothered by other things — a member wants a post office in Squeedunk. He's got to see to it. He doesn't have time to read bills, to know whether they're good or bad.

A chairman, whose primary task is to bring but two or three major bills before the House in a given session, is naturally going to feel that only he and his closest committee associates are competent to know the contents of the bill and how to manage its progression through the Congress. A senior Southern Democrat talks about what is required to manage a bill on the floor (and, incidentally, the limited help one could expect from the leadership).

> [First] you have to know what you're doing . . . what the implications of given pieces of the legislation are.
>
> Second, you keep your promises . . . Other members have to know that if you say something, you mean it, that there will be a follow-up on the promises you make.
>
> Third, you have to put out for the House. You can't go in half-way. Personal persuasion can be important. You can't count on the whip system to count the votes for you or for the leadership. You have to know yourself where the votes are . . .
>
> Fourth, you have to have a feel or sense for what is going on at the moment . . . The only way to do this was to circulate, get behind the rail, pick up the complaints and feelings of the members.

This member was typically given a free reign by the leadership when he brought a bill from his subcommittee to the floor. His more conservative chairman was not always so generous with support. For example, he would refuse to relinquish control over debate time or strategy on acceptance or rejection of amendments. A former Speaker amplifies:

> What's critical for the Speaker is how you work with the committee chairman. Some of them are great and you don't have to worry about them — Wilbur Mills, for example. But some of the others are not so smart, and I have to help them out.

"Helping out" can take a variety of forms — scheduling the legislation on an appropriate day and week, assisting in the drafting and implementation of amendments, talking to other members on behalf of the bill, coming into the well to make the rare, partisan speech in favor of the legislation.

Party leaders and committee leaders are prone to share a number of common background characteristics. If Democratic, they are likely to come from one of the two power axes of the party — northern big-city districts or a southern and border base.[44] If Republican, the probability is high that both leaders and ranking members share a midwestern background.

Another common factor that tends to unite committee leaders and party leaders is the consistent "safeness" of their seats — longevity in office is essential to obtain both types of positions. Still, the relative length of service of committee chairmen as compared to the principal party leaders may ease or complicate the legislative tasks of the latter. The twenty-one chairmen in the 93d Congress averaged 66 years in age; collectively they represented more than 600 years of service or an average of 14.3 terms in office. Almost half had served longer than the Speaker's twenty-seven years in the House; all but five chairmen had been in Congress longer than the Majority Leader (first elected in 1952).[45] "The crucial factor," observed one aspiring leader, "is whether or not they were chairmen before the Speaker became elected. His relations are almost always easier with those who became chairmen after him." By these criteria, Albert, and to a lesser extent, McCormack, were bound to have greater difficulty getting their authority accepted than their predecessors. Rayburn, after all, had come to the majority leadership after several terms of distinguished service as Chairman of the Interstate and Foreign Commerce Committee. By comparison neither Albert (7th ranking on Agriculture) nor McCormack (3d ranking on Ways and Means) had much floor managing behind them when they became floor leaders. Their first few years were bound to be a testing ground; even Rayburn had his difficulties managing the unwieldy majorities in the 75th Congress (1937–1938).

The Republican House leaders in the early 1970's by contrast have a much more advantageous relationship with their ranking minority leaders, at least in terms of comparative length of service. As a result of the high turnover in ranking Republicans between the 92d and 93d Congresses, only one Republican outranked Minority Leader Gerald Ford in seniority; that member was Leslie Arends, the minority whip. Only four colleagues of John Rhodes of Arizona had greater seniority than he, the unanimous choice of the House Republican Conference to succeed Ford as Minority Leader in December 1973. Ranking minority members were both younger and far less senior than their Democratic counterparts. They averaged 59 years in age (as compared to 66) and had served about six fewer terms (8.4 as compared to 14.3) than Democratic chairmen.[46]

The relationship of ranking minority committee members to their leadership may be both more autonomous and less stressful than its counterpart in the majority party. Unlike the chairmen, ranking minority members do not have the prime responsibility for bringing bills to the floor. They may, however, play a stronger role as the sponsor of legislation which is being promoted by a President of their own party. If they wish to become effective legislators the main path lies through formation of a partnership with their chairman. Their satellite life is not without its frustrations:

> Our time is not our own. We're in the minority and the chairman of the committee makes the decision as to when the committee will meet. I can't go to [the chairman] and ask for a postponement when he calls one. It's a different kind of relationship, one you have to get used to.

For not a few ranking minority members their relationships with their chairmen may become more important than their ties with their own leadership — one thinks of Taber–Cannon (Appropriations), Byrnes–Mills (Ways and Means), McCulloch–Celler (Judiciary), Saylor–Aspinall (Interior), and other productive bipartisan teams.

What clearly distinguishes the relationships of majority party leaders and committee chairmen is that the latter regard the former as their *peers*, not their superiors. It is for this reason that even as powerful a Speaker as Rayburn would observe: "You cannot lead people by trying to drive them. Persuasion and reason are the only

ways to lead them. In that way the Speaker has influence and power
in the house." [47]

Party leaders in the House of Representatives, majority and minority, operate under considerable situational constraints, especially the
independence of members, the decentralized nature of the party and
committee structure, and the limited personal, positional, and political resources available to them. Still, some party leaders are more
successful than others both in terms of survival and the accomplishment of individual and collective objectives. With some understanding of who the leaders are and what they do, we can now turn
to the main objectives of this book — analysis of the process by which
party leaders are selected and evaluation of the question of why
some candidates win and others lose.

The next six chapters recount the selection of five House floor
leaders: Carl Albert (1962), Hale Boggs (1971), and Thomas O'Neill
(1973) in the Democratic majority party; Gerald Ford (1965) and
John Rhodes (1973) in the Republican minority party. Two of these
case studies warrant special attention if for no other reason than the
subsequent career advancement of the victors. Chapter 3 reprints Professor Nelson W. Polsby's analysis of the 1961–1962 contest for the
House Democratic floor leadership. He shows how Albert, pursuing a
largely internal or "inside strategy," was able to hold off the challenge
of another liberal, Richard Bolling of Missouri, despite the latter's
efforts to invoke an external or "outside strategy." Chapter 4 presents
a quite different kind of contest — a revolt against an incumbent
leader. In January 1965, Ford upset Charles Halleck of Indiana, the
Republican Minority Leader since 1959. Albert's elevation to the
Speakership in 1971 was not especially difficult to have foreseen in
the light of past precedents. But no one could have predicted the
series of events which brought Minority Leader Ford first to the vice
presidency in late 1973, and subsequently to the highest office in the
land following President Nixon's resignation. In retrospect, these
earlier leadership contests are most revealing of the men, their backgrounds, and their potential for national leadership.

Following the narrative histories of these and several subsequent
contests for party leadership, Democratic and Republican, Chapters
9 and 10 set forth an analytical framework for classifying and examining all instances of leadership change in the House of Representatives
since 1954, the last election bringing about a shift in the control of
Congress.

NOTES

1. This chapter takes as its organizing themes those outlined in Cecil Gibb's essay on "Leadership: Psychological Aspects" in the *International Encyclopedia of the Social Sciences*, Vol. 9 (New York: Macmillan, 1968), p. 91:

   > Definition of the simplest unit of analysis in leadership as the "act of leading" has led to the identification of our basic elements in the relationship: (1) the *leader*, with his "resources relevant to goal attainment" . . . ; (2) the *followers*, who also have relevant abilities, personality characteristics, and resources; (3) the *situation* within which the relationship occurs; and (4) the *task* with which the interacting individuals are confronted.

2. The President of the United States, of course, shares this risk and the unique perspective it provides. See Richard E. Neustadt's discussion of "The Common Stakes of Elective Politicians," in David B. Truman, ed., *The Congress and America's Future* (Englewood Cliffs, N.J.: Prentice-Hall, 1965), pp. 116–120.

3. In his definitive analysis of *The Growth of American Law*, James W. Hurst sets forth a fourfold classification of primary legislative functions: (1) the determination of general community policy, embodied in rules, principles, or standards to govern dealings among the people or between them and the government; (2) the creation of specific executive, administrative, and judicial machinery, and the scrutiny of its operation; (3) the performance of a middleman's role between particular constituents and the executive or administrative agencies; and (4) the investigation of facts of social interest. (Boston: Little, Brown, 1950), p. 70.

4. Harry Eckstein, "Authority Patterns: A Structural Basis for Political Inquiry," *Am. Pol. Sci. Rev.* **67** (1973), 1142–1161; Robert L. Peabody, *Organizational Authority* (New York: Atherton, 1964).

5. "For organizations which are composed of delegated representatives of conflicting interests, whether their basis be in ideal causes, in power, or in economic advantage, may at least in external form be collegial bodies. What goes on within the body is then a process of adjustment of these conflicts of interest by compromise." Max Weber, *The Theory of Social and Economic Organization*, ed. by Talcott Parsons (Glencoe, Ill.: Free Press, 1947), p. 396.

6. Under Article I, Section 2 and Amendment XIV, Section 2, Representatives are "apportioned among the several states . . . according to their respective numbers . . ." Following each decennial census Representatives are reapportioned among the several states. Thus, the size of a state delegation may range from one Representative (Alaska, Delaware, Nevada, North Dakota, Vermont, and Wyoming) to as large as California's 43 members.

7. David B. Truman, *The Governmental Process* (New York: Knopf, 1951), pp. 332–333.

8. James S. Young, *The Washington Community, 1800–1828* (New York: Columbia University Press, 1966).

9. Susan Webb Hammond, "Personal Staffs of Members of the U.S. House of Representatives," Ph.D. dissertation, Johns Hopkins University, 1973.

10. See Floyd M. Riddick, *The United States Congress: Organisation and Procedure* (Manassas, Va.: National Capital Publishers, 1949), p. 86, n. 1.

11. George B. Galloway, *History of the House of Representatives* (New York: Crowell, 1961), pp. 107–109; and Randall B. Ripley, *Party Leaders in the*

House of Representatives (Washington, D.C.: Brookings Institution, 1967), pp. 24–27.

12. Three Representatives — Claude Kitchen of North Carolina, Sam Rayburn of Texas, and John McCormack of Massachusetts — were elected as both majority and minority floor leaders during this period.

13. Randall B. Ripley discusses six major legislative functions performed by House leaders: "(1) organizing the party, (2) scheduling the business of the House, (3) promoting attendance of members for important votes on the floor, (4) distributing and collecting information, (5) persuading members to act in accord with wishes, and (6) maintaining liaison with the President and his top advisors." *Party Leaders in the House of Representatives* (Washington, D.C.: Brookings Institution, 1967), pp. 54–80 at p. 54.

14. First elected to the House in 1934, Arends served with diligence and loyalty under three successive Minority (or Majority) leaders. On four occasions, most notably a bid for the floor leadership in 1947, the Halleck–Martin contest of 1959, the Ford–Halleck challenge of 1965, and the choice of successor to Ford in December 1973, he was by-passed for a top leadership position. Hence, the nominalness of his "second-ranking" position, until his retirement from the House in 1974.

15. Randall B. Ripley, "The Party Whip Organizations in the United States House of Representatives," *Am. Pol. Sci. Rev.* **58** (1964), 561–576.

16. Richard Bolling, *House Out of Order* (New York: Dutton, 1965), esp. ch. 4: Neil MacNeil, *Forge of Democracy: The House of Representatives* (New York: McKay, 1963), esp. ch. 7.

17. John F. Manley, "Wilbur D. Mills: A Study in Congressional Influence," *Am. Pol. Sci. Rev.* **63** (1969), 442–464.

18. James A. Robinson, *The House Rules Committee* (Indianapolis: Bobbs-Merrill, 1963), pp. 81–88; Charles O. Jones, "Joseph G. Cannon and Howard W. Smith: An Essay on the Limits of Leadership in the House of Representatives," *Journal of Politics* **30** (1968), 617–46.

19. Richard F. Fenno, Jr., *The Power of the Purse: Appropriations Politics in Congress* (Boston: Little, Brown, 1966), esp. 136–160.

20. Bolling, *op. cit.*, p. 109.

21. As Barbara Hinckley has observed, "Party and committee leaders have 'grown up together' congressionally speaking. Their shared seniority and dependence on the stability of the leadership selection processes suggest common institutional loyalties and well-developed lines of communication and support." "Congressional Leadership Selection and Support: A Comparative Analysis," *J. of Politics,* **32** (May, 1970), pp. 268–287 at p. 285. For an understanding of the organization and operations of congressional committees, in general, see Richard F. Fenno, Jr., *Congressmen in Committees* (Boston: Little, Brown, 1973); and George Goodwin, *The Little Legislatures: Committees of Congress* (Amherst: University of Massachusetts Press, 1970).

22. M. P. Follett, *The Speaker of the House of Representatives* (New York: Longmans, Green, 1896), p. 64.

23. Samuel W. McCall, *The Life of Thomas Brackett Reed* (Boston: Houghton Mifflin, 1914), ch. 13.

24. L. White Busbey, *Uncle Joe Cannon* (New York: Holt, 1927), ch. 12; Charles R. Atkinson, *The Committee on Rules and the Overthrow of Speaker Cannon* (New York: Columbia University Press, 1911).

25. The Speaker may vote to make a tie and so decide a question in the negative or vote to break a tie and thus decide a question in the affirmative. Rule I, Section 6., *Constitution, Jefferson's Manual and Rules of the House of Rep-*

resentatives, Lewis Deschler, Parliamentarian, 91st Congress, 2d sess., House Document 439 (Washington, D.C.: U.S. Government Printing Office, 1971), p. 315.

26. Excerpts from Speaker John McCormack's late-in-the-session press conference of October 7, 1965 are not untypical:

> *Reporter:* What's the program for the day?
>
> *Speaker:* We have five items carried over under unfinished business, including the Kennedy film showing, tire taxes, Ryuku Island, a Nevada water project, and a presidential veto on H.R. 5902, a private bill. . .
>
> Then we get into the Highway Beautification Bill. It's scheduled for four hours of debate. . .
>
> *Reporter:* What about the balance of the week?
>
> *Speaker:* We will take up the farm bill conference report. It looks like the sugar bill will not come up until next week.
>
> *Reporter:* Have you got the members looking down the gun on these bills, Mr. Speaker?
>
> *Speaker:* No, I'm looking down the muzzle.
>
> *Reporter:* When do you expect to adjourn?
>
> *Speaker:* Ask Dirksen. Ask Mike Mansfield. The key to adjournment is in the Senate. The House can't adjourn without the consent of the other body. . . .
>
> *Speaker's aide:* Time, Mr. Speaker.

27. Somewhat paradoxically, the original Whip's Notice is *prepared* in the Office of the Majority Leader. The minority party essentially duplicates the majority version.

28. For discussion of the uses of the various House Calendars, see Lewis A. Froman, Jr., *The Congressional Process: Strategies, Rules, and Procedures* (Boston: Little, Brown, 1967), pp. 43–52.

29. The House Republican Committee on Committees, in contrast, is composed of one Representative from each state with Republican members in the House. Power is concentrated in the large states, since each member, save for recent class rpresentatives, has as many votes as there are members in his delegation. Nicholas A. Masters, "Committee Assignments in the House of Representatives," *Am..Pol. Sci. Rev.* **55** (1961), 345–357; David W. Rohde and Kenneth A. Shepsle, "Democratic Committee Assignments in the House of Representatives: Strategic Aspects of a Social Choice Prospect," *Am. Pol. Sci. Rev.* **67** (1973), 889–905.

30. During the first session of the 89th Congress, I was fortunate to serve as a congressional intern in the office of Majority Whip Hale Boggs of Louisiana. One June afternoon in 1965, while standing next to the Speaker in the well of the House and as a routine roll call was underway, I observed the following events during a five-minute period: (1) Congressman A from Pennsylvania approached the Speaker to complain about the harsh treatment he had received from Rules Committee Democrats while testifying on a _____ bill. The Speaker said he had already talked to Rules Committee member X about the difficulty he had given Congressman A; he hoped to see Rules Committee member Y that afternoon. (2) Congressman B from New Jersey asked the Speaker if he could secure a minor patronage appointment for a constituent. The Speaker replied that none were available at the moment, but he would see if one could be arranged. One of his aides went off to

make some inquiries. (3) Congressman C of Indiana asked for the Speaker's support on a bill that had recently passed the House Administration Committee nearly unanimously, but appeared destined for floor opposition. He needed the Speaker's assistance in scheduling the bill. The Speaker replied that while he, personally, was not very sympathetic, he was not against the bill and he would see what could be done to expedite its scheduling. (4) Congressman D of Ohio approached and said, "Mr. Speaker, I don't want to ask you for anything." Just then, the Speaker broke away to mount the rostrum in order to gavel the House to order before it went back into the Committee of the Whole. In the meantime, Congressman D could be seen in earnest conversation with the Majority Leader, presumably about the problem he had not taken up with the Speaker.

31. "On December 7, 1931, Garner was elected the thirty-ninth Speaker of the House of Representatives by three votes. One of his majority came into the House chamber on a stretcher. Two more came in wheelchairs. Never in modern times had there been so close a division between the two parties in the House." Bascom N. Timmons, *Garner of Texas* (New York: Harper, 1948), p. 134.

32. For the definitive treatment of these problems, see Charles O. Jones, *Party and Policy-Making: The House Republican Policy Committee* (New Brunswick, N.J.: Rutgers University Press, 1964); and Jones, *The Minority Party in Congress* (Boston: Little, Brown, 1970).

33. The 80th Congress was to pass such important measures as the Marshall Plan, the consolidation of the armed services into a single Defense Department, the Taft-Hartley Act, rent control, and tax reduction. Ripley, *Majority Party Leadership in Congress, op. cit.*, pp. 149–150.

34. *Congress and the Nation*, Vol. III (Washington, D.C.: Congressional Quarterly, 1973), p. 30.

35. John F. Manley, "The Conservative Coalition in Congress," *Am. Behav. Sci.* **17** (1973), pp. 223–247 at p. 239.

36. For development of these themes, see my "Political Parties: House Republican Leadership," in Allan P. Sindler, ed., *American Political Institutions and Public Policy* (Boston: Little, Brown, 1969), pp. 202–212.

37. Clem Miller, *Member of the House*, ed. by John W. Baker (New York: Scribner's, 1962), p. 44.

38. Norman J. Ornstein, "Causes and Consequences of Congressional Change: Subcommittee Reforms in the House of Representatives, 1970–73," paper prepared for delivery at the 1973 APSA annual meetings, New Orleans, September 7, 1973; David W. Rohde, "Committee Reform in the House of Representatives and the Subcommittee Bill of Rights," *The Annals of the Am. Acad. Pol. & Soc. Sci.*, ed. Norman J. Ornstein, **411** (1974), pp. 39–47.

39. I'm one of the few ranking members who doesn't consistently look to his committee chairman's health," candidly observed a senior Southern member. "I don't have his capabilities and it would be a far worse committee if he weren't here . . ."

Not every member is content to sit around and do nothing: a fifth-ranking member on another committee writes a letter to the President urging that he nominate a fourth-ranking member from another state to the Supreme Court. Another launches a presidential "boomlet" for his chairman. And so it goes.

40. A Western Democrat approaching high-ranking positions on two committees after five terms in the House comments: "You only want two things in a leader; first, someone who will see you, and second, understand your problems. Other than that there's not much they can do for you or against you."

41. *Congressional Record* (daily ed.), October 13, 1962, p. 22206.
42. *Ibid.*, p. 22250.
43. John W. Kingdon's research generally confirms the earlier findings of David B. Truman and Donald R. Matthews that party leadership tends to vote with their ranking members on the committee reporting the bill under consideration, *Congressmen's Voting Decisions* (New York: Harper & Row, 1973), ch. 4; Truman, *The Congressional Party* (New York: Wiley, 1959), pp. 237–244; Matthews, *U.S. Senators and Their World* (Chapel Hill: University of North Carolina Press, 1960), p. 126. Of course, there is always the problem of ascertaining who goes along with whom. The Democratic party leadership was clearly dominant in terms of floor strategy in most of the some dozen meetings held with committee leaders that I was privileged to attend during the summer of 1965.
44. The 92d Congress is fairly representative: The Democratic leaders came from Oklahoma; New Orleans, La.; Cambridge, Mass.; and Texas. Nine chairmen came from southern or border states; four more from big-city districts. Of the three Republican leaders one came from Michigan and two from Illinois. Eleven of the ranking minority members came from midwestern states, including six from Ohio alone.
45. Compiled from *Congressional Quarterly Weekly Reports* **31** (January 6, 1973, April 28, 1973), 16–26, 973–991.
46. *Ibid.*
47. *New York Times*, November 17, 1961, p. 28.

CHAPTER THREE

Two Strategies of Influence:
Choosing a Majority Leader, 1962

Political scientists seem to be fond of debating whether traditional political theory in America is dead or only sleeping.[1,2] Either way, there is no argument that the speculations which occupied thinkers of other days have been little used to illuminate current political behavior. The argument, when there is one, concerns whether it is even possible to use traditional political theory in this way. Regrettably, optimists on this point have not always demonstrated that they were right in supposing that traditional political theory could contribute to the understanding of present-day politics. But this does not mean that they are wrong.

A major obstacle to the use of traditional political theory in modern political science has been theory's long-standing concern with prescriptive statements. Prescriptions are not necessarily the best instruments for organizing information about the empirical world, since the preferences which they assert may not correspond to any observed (or even observable) events. However, prescriptions may in fact point to quite interesting and genuine dilemmas in the real world. In these circumstances, we have the option of converting the language of prescription to that of description if we desire to put traditional political theory to more modern uses.

The possibilities of this device have lately been explored by a group of students of the legislative process, using as their text the celebrated speech to the Electors of Bristol by Edmund Burke.[3] In

From Nelson W. Polsby, "Two Strategies of Influence: Choosing a Majority Leader, 1962," in Robert L. Peabody and Nelson W. Polsby, eds., *New Perspectives on the House of Representatives*, Second Edition, pp. 325–358. © 1969, 1963 by Rand McNally & Company, Chicago. Reprinted by permission of Rand McNally College Publishing Company.

this speech, on the occasion of his election as Member of Parliament from Bristol, it will be recalled that Burke undertook to state and resolve a recurring dilemma of the representative:[4]

> Certainly, gentlemen, it ought to be the happiness and glory of a representative to live in the strictest union, the closest correspondence, and the most unreserved communication with his constituents. Their wishes ought to have great weight with him; their opinion high respect; their business unremitted attention . . . But his unbiased opinion, his native judgment, his enlightened conscience he ought not to sacrifice to you . . . Your representative owes you, not his industry only, but his judgment . . . Government and legislation are matters of reason and judgment, and not of inclination; and what sort of reason is that, in which the determination precedes the discussion; in which one set of men deliberate and another decide . . . Parliament is not a *congress* of ambassadors from different and hostile interests . . . but . . . a *deliberative* assembly of *one* nation . . . We are now members for a rich commercial city; this city, however, is but part of a rich commercial nation, the interests of which are various, multiform, and intricate . . . All these widespread interests must be considered; must be compared; must be reconciled if possible.

Six years after Burke spoke these words, he stood for election once again, and on the same topic said:[5]

> I could wish undoubtedly . . . to make every part of my conduct agreeable to every one of my constituents . . . But . . . do you think, gentlemen, that every public act in six years since I stood in this place before you — that all the arduous things which have been done in this eventful period, which has crowded into a few years' space the revolutions of an age — can be opened to you on their fair grounds in half an hour's conversation? . . . Let me say with plainness . . . that if by a fair, by an indulgent, by a gentlemanly behavior to our representatives, we do not give confidence to their minds, and a liberal scope to their understandings; if we do not permit our members to act upon a *very* enlarged view of things, we shall at length infallibly degrade our national representation into a confused and scuffling bustle of local agency.

A brief historical detour will suggest certain empirical problems related to Burke's position. Shortly after the second speech quoted here, Burke withdrew his candidacy, feeling he could not win. He and his constituents had disagreed over several matters, in particular his vote to free Irish trade from restrictions operating in favor of Bristol. Burke remained in Parliament, however, representing a pocket borough thereafter.[6] Although acting on his principle of independence from constituent pressures was costly to him, Burke was clearly in a position to take a more luxurious stand on such a question than another member could who did not have the protection of a pocket borough and the party list.

This raises still a more general empirical point: Under what conditions will the representative be more likely to respond to the demands of "local agency"? When is he more likely to respond to a political situation as it appears to him in the light of his experience at the seat of government? Under what conditions will attempts to influence the representative through his constituency bring better results than attempts to influence him through the network of loyalties and affiliations he has built up through service in his deliberative body — and vice versa?

The United States House of Representatives is one laboratory for the exploration of questions such as these. Indeed, where the stakes are as high as they often are in House decision-making, it is not surprising that full-scale campaigns are mounted in order to sway sometimes no more than a handful of marginal votes. But are these votes swayed from the inside or the outside? Do constituencies matter more or less than colleagues? [7]

Sometimes the answer is reasonably clear and unequivocal. Here are examples of *inside* influences at work:

> Representative Cleveland Bailey is a genuinely dedicated opponent of reciprocal trade . . . [He] is unusual among members — probably unique — in that protection is *the* most important issue to him and that he creates the sense of having a deep felt conviction on the subject. In 1953–54 he went around and pled individually with a number of members to vote against reciprocal trade and for the West Virginia miners. One member put it, "He was rough, real rough . . . I had to be rough with him." Another said, "In the 1954 vote, Cleve Bailey was worth 15 votes to his side easily." [8]

> The morning of one of the key votes on reciprocal trade [1955], Speaker Sam Rayburn attended a breakfast of the freshman Democrats in the House. I asked one of the Congressmen who was there about it. He chuckled: "Oh, you

heard about that? . . . We'd just invited Mr. Sam to this breakfast. He turned it into a sort of speech and said he'd observed that *generally the new members got along better who went along,* but he didn't make any particular application — of course you could guess what he had in mind. . . ." [9]

On the other hand, it is sometimes possible to detect *outside* influences. The following example comes from the January, 1961, battle over the size of the House Rules Committee:

It was learned that Representative Howard Smith, Southern leader and Rules Committee Chairman, has held several meetings in his office in recent weeks with representatives of the most powerful conservative lobbies in the country, trying to shape a campaign to beat Rayburn by applying pressure on members from home. The groups included the National Association of Manufacturers, the United States Chamber of Commerce, the American Medical Association and the American Farm Bureau . . . Some members have reported heavy mail from business interests in their home districts . . . On the other side, Northern Democrats have sent out an appeal to organized labor for help. Yesterday, Andrew J. Biemiller, chief AFL–CIO lobbyist, was at the Capitol trying to line up votes . . . [10]

During the aid to education debate [a Roman Catholic congressman] threatened to kill the public school measure by tagging on to it a parochial school amendment. [Presidential Assistant Lawrence] O'Brien appealed to [the congressman's home district party leader] who immediately telephoned [the congressman]. "Who sent you there, me or the Bishop?" he growled. "And who's going to keep you there, me or the Bishop?" [11]

At other times strong inside and outside influences are blurred together quite inextricably:

A newspaper correspondent told me: "Oh yes, you know those two boys [congressmen] . . . well you know why Jack voted against the leadership? Just to oblige Joe to whom he's very close; Joe was afraid he'd be the only fellow from the state to vote against the leadership and he'd get into trouble with the leadership and the party organization so Jack went along with him to prevent his sticking his neck out all alone. . . ." [12]

The whip from the area told me . . . "Tom rather wanted to
go along with the leadership, but he found Dave and Don
and four other guys from surrounding districts were against
the leadership, and he decided he'd better go along with them,
because after all he's hearing a lot from his district against it,
and how could he explain his being for it and Dave and Don
and the rest being against it?" [13]

The [1961–1962] contest for the majority leadership of the House
provides, as it happens, a rather good contrast between the two strategies of influence. In turn, the close examination of this case may
begin to suggest answers to some of the questions posed above.

I

On January 10, 1962, the Democratic members of the House met
in caucus in the House chamber and nominated John McCormack
as their candidate for Speaker. Immediately following the conclusion
of this business, Richard Bolling of Missouri asked that the agenda
of the caucus be expanded by unanimous consent to include the
selection of a Majority Leader, and Carl Albert of Oklahoma, his
party's whip and the only congressman put in nomination, was
elected to that post. Thus ended a period of skirmishing for the
majority leadership that had principally engaged Bolling and Albert
from the time of Speaker Rayburn's death on November 16 of the
previous year.

Most newspaper coverage of this event gave the impression that
the battle between these two men was drawn on liberal-conservative
lines. In Bolling's press conference on January 3 announcing his
withdrawal from the race, newsmen repeatedly suggested that the
contrast between them was predominantly ideological. A newspaper-
woman asked, rhetorically, "Don't the liberals *ever* win around here,
Mr. Bolling?" Another widely quoted colloquy went:

Reporter: "Mr. Bolling, do you regard your withdrawal . . . as
a defeat for liberalism?"
Bolling: "Well, I consider myself a liberal, and at the moment
I certainly feel defeated." [14]

Close observation suggests that the liberal-conservative distinction
has only a limited kind of utility for understanding the Bolling-

Albert fight for the majority leadership.[15] It is not necessary to base this conclusion on a *Congressional Quarterly* tabulation showing that Albert supported the Kennedy program 91 percent of the time in the first session of the Eighty-seventh Congress and Bolling 94 percent — a fact continually cited by liberal supporters of Mr. Albert.[16] Equally significant are the facts, first, that Albert indeed had a great deal of support among members with impeccably liberal records of long standing and, second, that he was regarded at the White House as a genuine friend of the Kennedy program.[17]

If, then, the outcome of the Bolling-Albert contest cannot be explained by the usual ideological arithmetic one uses in analyzing the House, how can one explain what happened? In part, an explanation can be based on the strategies each of the main actors pursued. These strategies were in turn largely dictated by their respective positions and roles in the House during the final years of the Rayburn speakership.

Often great differences in resources between political actors are largely nullified by the fact that resources are generally employed at low levels of intensity and with indifferent skill. In this case, however, resources on both sides were employed with considerable skill and finesse, and hence the outcome comes closer to reflecting a common-sense notion of the logic of the situation than might otherwise have been the case. It makes sense to describe the "cards" that each man held because, in this instance, the man who held the better cards made no more mistakes than his opponent, and, in the end, he won.

It is worth stressing that only part of the explanation can be given by referring to the roles and strategies of the main participants and to the different ways in which their demands were communicated to other House members. Two other significant variables can be sketched in only very crudely. This battle took place in the very core of an institution about whose habits and practices precious little is known, and, second, it engaged the participation of a great many more facets of the human personality than political decisions in the House normally do. The mysteries of how men interact with one another, of what leads people into enmity, jealousy, friendship, all seem to me to have played a very significant part in this contest. Obviously, the extent to which the outside observer can detect and extract meaning from these relationships is extremely limited, and this must inevitably

weaken the plausibility and also the generality of the case I am about
to construct, using, for the most part, more readily accessible materials.

II

The realization that Speaker Rayburn's health was failing seriously
dawned on different members of the House at different times during
the summer of 1961. That summer happened to have been an extremely hot and humid one in Washington. The House stayed in
session continuously through the summer, one of the longest, bitter-
est, and most grueling sessions in the memory of veterans on Capitol
Hill.[18] Over the course of this period, many members and observers,
especially those who were close to the Speaker, could not help but
notice the wasting of Mr. Rayburn's solid, imposing figure, the
occasional, uncharacteristic wandering of his attention from the
business of the House, his increased susceptibility to bouts of fatigue
and irritability, the slowing of his gait.

The House is, in the words of one of its members, a "Council of
Elders." It honors age and places much power and trust in the hands
of its most senior and oldest men. One consequence of this fact is
the necessary, calm preoccupation of members — especially those just
below the top rungs of power — with the inevitable occurrence of
death. To that large fraction of members for whom the House is a
career and a vocation, the longevity of members above them in the
many hierarchies of the House — not the entirely predictable congressional election returns in their home districts — is the key to the
political future. This is not to say that members habitually rub their
hands ghoulishly or enjoy the prospect of losing valued friends, but
only that the norms and the rules of the House bring due rewards to
men who accept the world as it is, who prudently make their plans
and bide their time.

On the other hand, informal norms of the House also put constraints on members based on commonly accepted notions of decent
behavior, decorum, and good taste. Hence it is impossible for an
outsider to say when Mr. Albert and Mr. Bolling began thinking
in any concrete way about the next step in their careers within the
House. However, it seems safe to make two assumptions: First, that
they each had entertained some general thoughts on the question
of the majority leadership well in advance of the occurrence of an

actual vacancy (on January 9) or probable vacancy (on November 16) in the position. Second, both men knew Speaker Rayburn well, and both undoubtedly guessed earlier than most members that his health had permanently disintegrated.

III

On Saturday, November 18, Sam Rayburn was buried in Bonham, Texas. Mr. Albert reports that he had planned to wait until the following Wednesday to begin his campaign for Majority Leader. "I was in my office in McAlester on Sunday night," Mr. Albert said, "when Charlie Ward [his assistant] came in and said, 'Bolling has announced for Majority Leader.' I heard it on the radio that night and saw a copy of the press release from my hometown paper before I announced myself. It was an Associated Press report, and Bill Arbogast [who covers the House for AP] wrote the story."

As a result of this turn of events, Mr. Albert got into the race sooner than he had intended. Mr. Bolling had thrown down a challenge which he could ignore only at his peril. In addition, Mr. Bolling's action offered Mr. Albert an opportunity to run a campaign against him, rather than against any of the more popular or more senior members who had been mentioned for leadership positions.

To each side it appeared that the other had begun to make plans well before Mr. Rayburn's death. Observers partial to Mr. Albert noted that as long before as the previous spring, Mr. Bolling was being referred to in public as a prominent contender for a leadership post.[19] It was easy to infer that, at least in part, these references had been suggested or "inspired" by Mr. Bolling. On the other hand, observers partial to Mr. Bolling thought an alliance between Mr. Albert and the Speaker-to-be, John McCormack, was being announced when Mr. Albert, as his chief deputy, led the tributes on September 26, 1961, in honor of Mr. McCormack's twenty-one years as Majority Leader.[20]

It seems plausible to suggest that the signs and portents friends of both men were reading did not reflect conscious efforts by either man to organize a premature campaign for the majority leadership. Rather, each man appealed particularly to slightly different publics: Bolling to the press corps, Albert to various groups within the House itself. These groups may, without encouragement from either man, have initiated activity designed to facilitate their chances of advancement. "After Mr. Rayburn went home to Texas," Mr. Albert reported, "I had fifty or sixty members pull me aside and say to me, 'He's not coming back. Don't sit there and be done out of what you're entitled to.' But I refused to discuss the matter with them." Several members mentioned that they had volunteered their support to Mr. Albert, and some, apparently, had attempted to persuade him to run for Speaker. "I would never do that against John McCormack," Mr. Albert said. "Mr. Rayburn and Mr. McCormack picked me and made me whip, and to run against Mr. McCormack would have been the act of an ingrate."

Two groups were especially partial to Mr. Albert: his deputy whip organization and colleagues in the Oklahoma delegation. "We make a fetish of the fact that if you scratch one Okie you've scratched all of 'em," one member told me. As soon as Mr. Albert announced that he would run for Majority Leader, the members of the delegation did whatever they could to help his candidacy. The deputy whips gave Mr. Albert a party after Mr. Rayburn had gone to Texas, and attempted, without success, to induce Mr. Albert to begin work on his candidacy at that time.

Mr. Albert's announcement to the press followed the report of Mr. Bolling's by several hours. As soon as the announcement was made, Mr. Albert sent off a telegram to all members asking for their support and began telephoning each of them individually. "I bet you he was on the phone four days running," one member said.

Mr. Albert's intensive telephone campaign began with the west coast members. "James Roosevelt [congressman from Los Angeles] was the first man I called outside my own delegation," he said. By the end of the first day of telephoning, Mr. Albert thought he had all but five westerners committed to him. "If I wasn't sure of a senior man in a delegation," Mr. Albert said, "I started with the most junior men and asked them directly to support me. Then I'd work my way up the line so that when the senior man said, 'I'll have to check with my delegation,' I would have something to report to him. Of course on a thing like this, you call your friends first, but I had no set, written-out plan. I don't work that way."

The reasons members gave for supporting Mr. Albert are quite illuminating. They reflect two dominant themes, both of which illustrate the "inside" quality of his influence. On the one hand, Mr. Albert was his party's whip. Although there is no tradition which dictates that the whip shall be advanced to the majority leadership (as there is in promoting the Majority Leader to Speaker) many members felt that Mr. Albert nonetheless was "entitled" to the job by virtue of his six years' service in the leadership hierarchy of the House. Some of them said:

> [From a liberal leader:] I made a commitment to Carl based on his years of service as whip and the fact that he was in line for this job from the standpoint of his long service as whip.

> [From a southwesterner:] Because I feel that he was entitled to it by reason of his effective part in the leadership of the House along with the Speaker and Mr. McCormack, I promised him my support.

> [From the elderly dean of a large delegation:] I am a firm believer in the rule that has governed the House for over 100 years, and that is that of seniority. If Congressman McCormack is to be promoted to the Speakership of the House on the premise of his seniority and being in line position, then obviously the Majority Leader and whip should pursue the same course.[21] I have had the honor of being a member of this great body for [many years] . . . and while I would be reluctant to say that the seniority process does not have some imperfections, nevertheless if any other procedure were to be applied, I am inclined to believe that rather a chaotic situation would immediately be evident.

A second theme illustrates Mr. Albert's personal popularity in the House. Many members could cite warm personal ties they had developed with Mr. Albert. The late John Riley of South Carolina said, "Carl Albert married a girl from Columbia, you know, and so he is practically a constituent of mine."

A northern liberal: "I'm in something of a special situation with Carl, since we're the only two members of the House who [belong to an exclusive, honorary organization]."

A congressman from a border state said, "In all good conscience, I had to agree to support Carl because of his great help and encouragement to me [on a pet bill]."

A southwesterner said, "As one of his deputy whips, I feel committed to Carl Albert."

A southerner: "I committed myself to Carl Albert, who is my neighbor in the House Office Building."

Another southerner: "My association with Carl Albert has been extremely intimate."

Three men who served with Mr. Albert on committees:

"Carl and I have sat side by side on [our] committee for fifteen years."

"Carl has been very kind to me in the committee work and has done several things for me which have been very important for my people . . ."

"I sit right next to Carl Albert . . . We have been close personal friends due to our connection on the committee . . ."

Another member said, "Ordinarily I'm slow to make commitments, but due to a friendship with Carl which began when we were in the . . . Army together, I told him quite a while back that should he seek the position of Democratic leader, I would support him."

And some members, not unexpectedly, combined the themes. For example: "He is not only my neighbor but a member of my committee, and with it all a fine, able, conscientious man who has been doing the dirty work for the leadership for a long time . . ."

It was characteristic of Mr. Albert's "inside" strategy of influence that he used the telephone energetically and extensively himself to make personal contacts with members as quickly as possible. As whip, he was the custodian of a complete set of home, office, and district telephone numbers for each member.[22] One member said:

> Albert got on the phone and tracked me down in the frozen wastes of northern Rockystate the first day after the Speaker was buried. You wouldn't think politicians would fall for that, but many of them did. They were impressed by the fact that he'd called them first. As a result he was able to line up a lot of the members, including many northern bleeding-heart liberals, in the first few days.

The principal argument which Mr. Albert used in asking the support of almost all the members I spoke with was the fact that he had already received a large number of commitments. This is instructive, because it evokes the almost obsessive preoccupation of congressmen with "getting along" and not sticking their necks out unnecessarily. "This House gives out no medals for individual bravery," said one congressman, "except posthumously."

Mr. Albert had an important further asset — the apparent backing of John McCormack. "I have heard McCormack say again and again that we have got to have a team player," one congressman said. "I guess he means by that a member of his team, and I suppose he favors Carl Albert." I asked a newspaperman who was following the situation closely to tell me who the most important congressman on Mr. Albert's side was, and he replied, "John McCormack." However, I could find no evidence that Mr. McCormack gave Mr. Albert any public endorsement.

Describing his campaign, Mr. Albert said:

> I didn't want to hurt Mr. Bolling's feelings. I never once threw knives or wrote mean things, although plenty of knives got thrown at me. I never once got on television. The sum total of my national publicity was a release when I got into the race and a release when I got up to Washington saying I thought I had enough votes to win. I refused to go on television although I was invited to go on most of the news and panel shows. I never mentioned Bolling's name at all. I never mentioned issues or anything . . .

IV

Mr. Bolling's campaign, in contrast, followed an "outside" strategy of influence. As in the Rules Committee fight at the opening of the Eighty-seventh Congress and on numerous other occasions where he had planned legislative strategy and tactics, he held aloof from direct contact with most members. "I seldom try to persuade people directly," he said. "Our districts persuade us — if we are going to be persuaded at all."

Bolling had an uphill battle on his hands. He was severely handicapped at the start by his unwillingness to do anything in his own behalf until well after the Speaker had died. "It's a funny thing that Dick was so dilatory," a friend said. Although he leaked an announcement of his candidacy for the majority leadership to the press on November 19, the day after the Speaker's funeral, it was not until November 28 that he sent a strikingly diffident letter to each of the Democrats in the House. The letter said:

> Just a note to confirm that I am running for Democratic floor leader and am seeking the support of my Democratic col-

leagues for that position. Reports during the past week have been encouraging and I am in this contest all the way.

I am running on my legislative record and experience and hope that you will give my candidacy your consideration on that basis.

Several of his supporters expressed surprise at the mildness of this approach. The letter asked for "consideration," not support, and was not followed up by an energetic telephone campaign. Furthermore, Bolling had waited twelve precious days after the Speaker's death before making his move. Why?

Answers to a question of motive such as this one — even the answers given by Mr. Bolling himself — are bound to verge on speculation. My guess is that Mr. Bolling's hesitancy had something to do with the relationship he had had with Speaker Rayburn. According to the reports of numerous observers who had no axes to grind, Mr. Bolling and the Speaker had built a bond of affection between them that went well beyond the usual political alliance.[23] Mr. Sam, who had no immediate family, was well known for his habit of adopting political protégés with whom he could develop a relationship of warmth and trust similar to that found in the family situation. This was, apparently, Mr. Rayburn's way of overcoming the loneliness that otherwise might well have overtaken any elderly bachelor.

The need to overcome loneliness was strongly ingrained in Mr. Rayburn from childhood. Mr. Rayburn is quoted as saying:

> Many a time when I was a child and lived way out in the country, I'd sit on the fence and wish to God that somebody would ride by on a horse or drive by in a buggy — just anything to relieve my loneliness. Loneliness consumes people. It kills 'em eventually. God help the lonely . . . [24]

Mr. Rayburn's advice to Presidents Truman, Eisenhower, and Kennedy reflects the same theme. As he reported afterward, on a conversation with Mr. Truman just after the latter had become President:

> "You've got many hazards," I said. "One of your great hazards is in this White House," I said. "I've been watching things around here a long time, and I've seen people in the White House try to build a fence around the White House and keep the various people away from the President that he should see . . ." [25]

His biographer and research assistant, D. B. Hardeman says, "Mr. Sam was . . . annoyed by inactivity. When he could think of nothing else to do at home in Bonham he would get out all his shoes and polish them. He dreaded holidays and Sundays because visitors were few." [26]

Mr Rayburn found it particularly congenial to work with younger men. D. B. Hardeman says, "Lyndon Johnson once confessed, 'The Speaker and I have always been very close but if we are not as close as we were once, it is because I'm almost 50. If you notice, he never has older men around him.' " [27]

"I always liked the House the best," Mr. Rayburn said. "There're more people there, usually they're younger people, and as I've advanced in years, I've stepped back in my associations, boys, young people ten, twenty years younger than I. Their bodies are not only resilient but their minds are too. They can learn faster than the fellow advanced in years." [28]

One of the things which no doubt drew Mr. Rayburn to Mr. Bolling was the exceptional resiliency and quickness of the latter's mind. On this quality, friends and political enemies of Mr. Bolling agreed. He is an extremely "quick study," and had several other things in common with the Speaker:

"Bolling loves the House," a judicious, slow spoken southern congressman who knows him rather well told me. "He loves it and has studied it. He has read everything that has been written about the House and has studied its power structure. He has a brilliant mind."

Although nearly 35 years separated them, both Mr. Rayburn and Mr. Bolling were strongly committed emotionally to many liberal programs. Bolling refers to himself quite frankly as a "gut liberal;" *Time* magazine has aptly characterized Rayburn as a "liberal of the heart." [29] In addition, both men shared a high sense of rectitude in their work, treating the majority of their colleagues with reserve and judging them rather severely. This social distance which both men maintained was no doubt related in some complex way to the intensity of their feelings about political issues. It is instructive in this connection to note the tendency of both men to become laconic in public when dealing with problems with which they had great personal involvement. Compare Bolling's prepared statement of withdrawal from the majority leadership race in 1962 with Rayburn's statement of withdrawal in 1934 from an unsuccessful race for the speakership.[30]

In 1934 Rayburn said, "I am no longer a candidate for Speaker. There are no alibis. Under the circumstances, I cannot be elected." [31]

In 1962 Bolling said, "I am withdrawing from the race for leadership of the House. Developments of the last few days have convinced me that I don't have a chance to win." [32]

Bolling privately expressed an unwillingness amounting to an incapacity either to "do anything" until after a "decent" time had elapsed after the Speaker's death [33] or to canvass for votes in his own behalf. The major portion of this burden within the House was carried by Representative Frank Thompson of New Jersey and a group of four or five others. The brunt of Bolling's campaign was, however, carried on from outside the House.[34] Initially, he had to decide whether to run for Speaker or Majority Leader — which no doubt also contributed to the quality of hesitancy in his campaign.

Factors pointing to the speakership included the relative unpopularity of Mr. McCormack (1) with members, and (2) at the White House; but against this had to be weighed (1) Mr. McCormack's generally blameless voting record (from the standpoint of a pro-administration Democrat), (2) his long service in the second position, (3) the weight of a tradition which strongly favored the elevation of a Majority Leader, (4) Mr. Bolling's own relatively junior position, (5) the fact that Mr. McCormack, if he lost the Speakership, would remain as a Majority Leader not especially favorably disposed toward the program of an administration that had just done him in politically, and, (6) the fact that opposing Mr. McCormack would unavoidably exacerbate the religious cleavage in the House and the country which the fight over school aid in the last session had revealed.[35]

And so, Mr. Bolling decided to run for Majority Leader against the extremely popular Mr. Albert. In a straight popularity contest, Mr. Bolling knew he was "born dead." His role in the House had been quite unlike Mr. Albert's; indeed, several congressmen contrasted them starkly.

A close friend described Mr. Albert's approach to the job of whip:

> The whip is more the eyes and ears of the leadership than anything. On controversial matters, they like to know what the chances of success are ... So the deputy whips count noses, and the whip's job is to evaluate the count — especially to assess the doubtfuls ... Albert developed quite a genius for knowing what people would do ...

> Another service he performed endears him to people. Carl's the kind of a guy everybody could find. He would talk to the leadership for [rank-and-file congressmen].

> A lot of these eastern guys have a Tuesday through Thursday club. The whip takes the duty on of telling them if the signals change so they can get back here if they're needed.

> He's done so many things for people. They trust him. They think of him, "Here's a man I can talk to when I need help." When the members go about picking a leader, they want personal services, not intellectuals.[36]

> I dare you to find a member of Congress who said Bolling had lifted a finger for him.

A supporter of Mr. Bolling's (for whom Bolling had, according to this member's testimony, lifted many a finger) saw the roles of the two principals in much the same light, although his evaluation of their roles was quite different: [37]

> Albert's approach to legislative matters is, well, everybody ought to vote his own district . . . He brings his friends and his enemies in [to vote] both . . . Why the hell get [a certain southern congressman] out [to vote]? He doesn't vote with us on anything. And he's a deputy whip! It's ridiculous . . . The function of the whip [under Mr. Albert] is room service to members.

> Albert was the whip, but Bolling was doing the whipping . . . When the heat was being put on in the Rules Committee and all the other fights, it was Bolling putting it on, and he wasn't making any friends doing it.

Mr. Bolling was, as a friend of his described it, a "hatchet man" for Speaker Rayburn. This entailed a variety of activities on the Rules Committee, including monitoring the attendance of friends and foes, arranging for the disposition of bills, and keeping track of the intentions of the various (and numerous) factions in the House with respect to important legislation, in behalf of the Speaker. Occasionally, Mr. Bolling's job included putting the finger on members who were open to (or vulnerable to) persuasion, and he often had a crucial part in the process of persuading them — not always a pleasant task.[38]

Although Mr. Bolling is entirely in sympathy with policies espoused by liberals in the House, his position close to the Speaker precluded his joining in any formal way in the activities of the Democratic Study Group, the House liberal organization. As a friend of his put it, "Dick was aloof from the uprisings of the peasants."

"Bolling's got a sort of a chip on his shoulder," another member said.

"The thing you have to realize about Bolling," said an Albert backer, "is that he never bothers to speak to anyone else. I don't think Bolling understands politics."

Mr. Bolling's aloofness was, as I have suggested, probably something more than simply a reflection of his peculiar institutional position. A second friend of Bolling's said, "Despite a good deal of charm, Bolling just does not have a personality that inspires loyalty and friendship among men.[39] He's not a backslapping, how-the-hell-are-you type of guy. Bolling is personally quite pleasant, but reticent."

The late Clem Miller of California said, "Congress is a World War I rather than a World War II operation. You have to move huge bodies of men a few feet at a time . . . Dick's spent the last few years divorcing himself from a base of fire. His job was right-hand man to the Speaker. He came to Democratic Study Group meetings but always identified himself as an observer, not as a participant. He came in a sense to lecture us like small children rather than lead us in our councils. There was a good deal of hostility toward him in the Study Group as a result of that. The Study Group was set up as a foil for the leadership. You can't have your foot in both camps, and so Dick alienated the base of support that he needed in the House."

Another member, often allied with Mr. Bolling, characterized him as "totally unfriendly."

Mr. Bolling's personal situation within the House was further complicated by a common enough phenomenon. As a relative newcomer, as an extremely able member performing difficult tasks well, and as an intimate of the Speaker, Mr. Bolling was, in the opinion of several observers, the victim of a certain amount of jealous resentment.

"Jealousy is a big factor," one congressman said. "Liberals have several characteristics that tend to make them ineffective, and vanity is one of them. They tend to be prima donnas."[40] Another said, "Dick is not a popular man in the House, no doubt a surprise to newsmen. For one thing, he's resented because of his ability."

Liberals were clearly not the only group of congressmen susceptible to jealous feelings toward Mr. Bolling. His relative youth was offensive to some of his seniors. Mr. Bolling had risen very fast in the House and had been given many advantages by his friend, the Speaker. The record he had made thus far also suggested that, if elected, he would take many more initiatives than Mr. Albert and would more decisively challenge the powers of committee and subcommittee chairmen to control the flow and content of legislation — in behalf of programs for which many of these leaders had no particular liking.

Even to the superficial observer, Mr. Albert and Mr. Bolling are quite contrasting figures. Mr. Albert was 53 years old, exactly on the House median; Mr. Bolling was only 45. Albert is physically probably the shortest man in the House and looks nothing like the collegiate wrestler he once was. He has a softly lined, friendly, gentle face which, says a colleague, "always looks faintly worried." Bolling is a tall, husky, quite handsome and imposing-looking man who gives the appearance of great self-confidence and looks very much like the collegiate football player he was. Mr. Albert in conversation is homespun, soft-spoken, emotionally unengaged, and low-pressure. A colleague says, "You could vote impeachment of the President, and it wouldn't bother Carl." Mr. Bolling in conversation is articulate, expansive, sophisticated, intense; in short, one would surmise, a rather more threatening figure to someone of average inclinations than Mr. Albert.

Mr. Bolling has far greater acceptance in the higher echelons of the "downtown" bureaucracies and surely in the press corps than almost any other congressman, including Mr. Albert. Mr. Bolling is far more likely to spend his leisure hours among pundits, diplomats, and subcabinet officials than with congressmen, a pattern which Mr. Albert reverses. Mr. Albert prides himself, in fact, in spending a greater proportion of his time on the floor of the House than any other member, where he is continually accessible to his colleagues.[41]

To a great extent, Mr. Bolling understood that a variety of institutional and personal "inside" factors were working against him, and so he launched an "outside" campaign.

V

Bolling's task, as he saw it, was divided into several phases of activity. First, he had to stall the Albert bandwagon. Then he had to receive enough commitments to win himself. His primary targets were the big state delegations of New York, California, Illinois, and Pennsylvania. Secondary targets included getting a firm grip on his home state delegation and going after younger, liberal congressmen and congressmen who had substantial labor and civil-rights-minded constituencies.

His strategy for accomplishing these ends had two major features. First, he intended to draw as sharp a contrast as he could between himself and Mr. Albert on issues and sell the contrast as hard as he could through the mass media. Second, he set about "pulling strings" on members, a process which he had practiced before in legislative battles.[42] This entailed identifying the men and interest groups favorable to his candidacy who for various reasons could reach and persuade members of Congress. Naturally, the foremost among these would have been the President, but at no time was presidential aid offered, and none was requested by Mr. Bolling.

The position of the White House in this battle was a complex one. While the mass media, on the whole, bought Mr. Bolling's contention that substantial differences in public policy separated him and Mr. Albert, the White House never did. It regarded both men as good friends of the Kennedy program, each having personal and political strengths and weaknesses. To intervene in behalf of one friend would have meant sacrificing another. For the White House to intervene and lose would have been disastrous for its prestige and legislative program. To intervene and win would have been more satisfactory but still would have involved (aside from the making of enemies) great exertion, the distribution of indulgences and the "cashing in" on favors owed, all of which could otherwise be employed to improve the chances for passage of controversial reciprocal trade, medical aid, tax reform, and education bills. Several members of the President's official family were close to Mr. Bolling and were almost certainly partial to him, but none participated in the fight.

Mr. Bolling and his backers in the House concurred in the White House policy of non-intervention and in the reasoning behind it. The major inside advantage of their side, as they saw it, was a professional ability to predict outcomes accurately and to recommend appropriate strategies. They understood fully that the risks to the White House were great, the probabilities of success dubious. If they could come close to winning on their own, within perhaps five or ten votes, then their recommendation might change, since the

White House could then probably put them over the top. But it is not at all certain that even then the White House would have been ready to move.

If the administration was inactive, other keenly interested bystanders were not. The AFL–CIO backed Mr. Bolling strongly and performed several notable services in behalf of his candidacy. Labor lobbyists made a complete canvass of possible supporters in the House and, in several cases, made representations in Mr. Bolling's behalf with members. The NAACP was also active. Roy Wilkins, national chairman, telegraphed 153 selected branches of his organization, "Bolling right on 26 civil rights votes, Albert wrong. Wire, write or call your Congressman. This could affect civil rights legislation for years to come." The Democratic Reform Clubs of New York City were also interested in Bolling's candidacy, as were some local and national political leaders around the country and at least one farm organization.

An example of indirect influence in Mr. Bolling's behalf was described by an Albert supporter, "I heard that President Truman, a neighbor of Bolling's and a loyal Missourian, called Mayor Wagner of New York to try and get the New York delegation to support Bolling."

Mr. Bolling was especially successful in enlisting the aid of the mass media. Since the civil rights battle of 1957, when he anonymously kept newsmen briefed on the confusing tactical situation within the House, Mr. Bolling has been extremely popular with the Washington press corps.[43] He is asked to appear on broadcasts and telecasts much more often than the average member. He counts many Washington correspondents, including several famous ones, as close personal friends.

Hence, it is not altogether surprising that he was able to gain the endorsement of the *New York Times* as early as December 11. On Sunday, December 24, the *Times* reiterated its stand, saying, "The conservative coalition of Southern Democrats and Northern Republicans would find it much more difficult to exercise its suffocating veto over forward-looking legislation with the imaginative and hard-driving Mr. Bolling as majority floor chief." [44]

Five days previously, on December 19, James Wechsler, editor of the *New York Post*, gave a strong endorsement to Mr. Bolling, in which he printed a long verbatim extract of a letter endorsing Carl Albert which Bolling had received from Judge Howard W. Smith, leader of conservative southerners in the House.[45] Wechsler commented, "This is not to say Albert has faithfully followed Smith's gospel. He is a moderate, pleasant man whose voting record might be far more impressive if he came from a state more congenial to the advance of civil rights and less dominated by the natural gas interests. Despite their differences on a variety of matters, Smith is plainly confident that he can handle Albert; he is equally convinced that Bolling spells trouble . . ." [46]

On December 29, Marquis Childs[47] and Edward P. Morgan both urged the selection of Mr. Bolling, referring once again to the Smith letter and to issues separating the two candidates. Mr. Morgan was especially vigorous in his commentary: [48]

> . . . where Bolling has been consistently for them, Albert has been basically against civil rights legislation, federal aid to education, full foreign aid and regulation of the oil and gas industry. It is reliably reported that one Texas congressman told a southern colleague that "with Albert in there, oil will be safe for twenty years."

What of the outcomes of these activities? The relations between outside "pressures" and congressmen have been variously described in popular and academic literature. There is an old tradition which regards these relations as essentially nefarious.[49] Descriptively, the congressman is sometimes thought to be a relatively passive creature who is pulled and hauled about according to the play of pressures upon him and whose final decision is determined by the relative strength of outside forces.[50] More recently, political scientists have become preoccupied with the qualities of reciprocity in the relations of interest groups and politicians. This literature calls attention to mutually beneficial aspects of the relationship and lays stress on the ways in which politicians may act to govern the outside pressures placed on them.[51]

My information on the impact of Bolling's outside campaign is necessarily incomplete. It is apparent at a minimum that a sufficient number of congressmen were never reached by this campaign. One congressman said:

> Bolling's best hope was forces outside the House — labor and civil rights groups. But I received not one communication in his behalf from anybody. There was nobody campaigning for him. Nobody knew if he was serious or not. Where was the heat?

Another congressman, from a heavily populated area, said:

> Our delegation was never put on the spot. Bolling never tried
> to wage a campaign in our delegation. Apparently he tried to
> get labor leaders to pressure Cautious [the state party leader]
> to put pressure on our congressmen. This is OK, but you
> really have to put the pressure on because if you know Cau-
> tious, he won't ever move unless he's really in a box.

In other cases, congressmen were able quite easily to *resist* pressure. "The word got around," one liberal congressman said, "that
this wasn't like the Rules Committee fight, where there was a legitimate issue. Rather, it was all in the family, and any outside inter-
ference, even from the White House, would be resented."

Harlem's Representative Adam Clayton Powell, announcing his
support of Albert, charged that some organized labor representatives were putting pressure on some Democratic members of his
committee. He added, "I can't understand why labor union leaders
would do this. Frankly, this is Democratic party business, not labor
business." [52]

On the other hand, Bolling's campaign from the outside made
several converts. Representative Leonard Farbstein of New York
City, for example, announced that he would vote for Mr. Bolling on
the basis of Mr. Wechsler's column.[53]

Another congressman, a conservative veteran, wrote Bolling and
detailed the substantial political disagreements between them, concluding, "But Famous Farmer tells me he is supporting you, and
if he is supporting you, I am supporting you."

A leader of another interest group, in another part of the country,
wrote, "I have just been informed by Congressman Dean Delegation's home secretary that Dean will be supporting you for majority leader. If there are any particular targets in [this state], I'm
still available to apply whatever other pressures I can."

In aggregate, however, the impact of this campaign was not sufficient to accomplish Mr. Bolling's major goal. Edward Morgan commented with some asperity on the failure of Mr. Bolling to
consolidate his support on an ideological basis, and at the same time
he renewed the plea that the battle be defined in ideological terms:[54]

> If they voted . . . in support of their constituencies' needs for
> protection on gas prices, housing, civil rights and the like, the
> big city and industrial area representatives would have to

come down almost unanimously for Bolling over Albert on
their voting records alone and the man from Missouri would
have it cinched. But he doesn't have it cinched ... At least
one Massachusetts congressman has already committed himself to Albert in writing ... Adam Clayton Powell is looking
south ... So are a couple of New Jersey Representatives ...
Most surprisingly, perhaps, two leading California Congressmen, Holifield and Roosevelt, have not dashed to Bolling's
aid ...

Over the long New Year's weekend, Bolling, Thompson, and
Andrew Biemiller of the AFL–CIO met and assessed Bolling's "hard"
strength at between 65 and 70 votes. Perhaps 50 more would have
joined them if Bolling were going to win, but otherwise, they faded.
A Bolling lieutenant said, "Everybody wanted to know, 'What's
his chances?' The typical response was, 'I'll lie low. I'm with you if
you've got a chance; otherwise, nix.' "

By the most realistic calculations, however, Mr. Bolling fell short
of the 130 or more votes that he needed. He decided to withdraw
his candidacy rather than embarrass his supporters in their state
delegations and possibly jeopardize their future effectiveness in
Congress.

VI

It is possible to identify at least four reasons why Mr. Bolling's
attempt to win from the outside failed. The first two have already
been mentioned: Mr. Albert's extreme popularity and Bolling's
relative isolation provided little incentive for individual members
to seek outside excuses of their own accord to do what they could
more conveniently do for inside reasons. Second, the hands-off policy
of the White House deprived Mr. Bolling's campaign of what would
have been a major outside weapon had the President chosen to come
in on Mr. Bolling's side.

The third major obstacle to the success of the outside campaign
was the fact that, through no fault of Mr. Bolling's, a few of his
supporters unwittingly blunted one of his principal weapons, the
ideological contrast between himself and Mr. Albert. Just before the
opening of the second session of the Eighty-seventh Congress, and
at the same time the struggle over the majority leadership was going
on, a group of liberal congressmen proposed that a policy committee
be created in the Democratic party to be elected by the members

from each of the 18 whip zones. This committee was to advise and counsel with the leadership, and it was contemplated that it would be "more representative" (and presumably more liberal) than the leadership, unaided, would be.

Congressmen favoring this proposal circulated it among their Democratic colleagues in an attempt to get the fifty signatures necessary to place it on the agenda of the caucus which was to elect a new Speaker. Several liberals favoring Mr. Albert promptly signed, thus furnishing themselves with an excellent alibi, if they were challenged on ideological grounds by constituents and interest groups. They could claim that the fight over the majority leadership was not really significant since Bolling and Albert were, in their voting records, so close. But on the basic issue, on the institutional structure of leadership in the House, they were, as always, for liberalization.

This proposal went through several stages. At one point, it was seriously proposed that Mr. Bolling accept the chairmanship of this committee as the price for withdrawing his candidacy for the majority leadership. This proposal implied that the new Speaker had accepted the policy committee in principle.[55] Mr. Bolling was himself dubious about the chances that such a committee could perform the tasks its supporters envisaged for it. Counterproposals and negotiations buzzed back and forth about the possibility of putting "teeth" into the committee and about prior agreements as to its membership. At another level, Mr. Bolling and Mr. Thompson had to avoid being mousetrapped by the petition to put the policy committee on the agenda. To have signed the petition might have looked to Albert-McCormack forces like a proposal of terms and an acknowledgment of defeat. The fact that supporters of the Bolling candidacy were leading the fight for the policy committee was compromising enough as it was.

In the end, the whole idea came to nothing.[56] The proposal never received enough signatures to gain a place on the agenda, and at John McCormack's first press conference upon his nomination for the speakership, he said, "A policy committee is out." [57] But the policy committee plan served one significant purpose. It softened and blurred Bolling's attempt to define the issue between himself and Mr. Albert in such a way as to embarrass liberals who were not supporting him.

The fourth reason for the failure of the outside campaign is probably the most important. It has to do with the conditions under which the actual choice was going to be made. Normally, a congressman has considerable leeway in the casting of his vote because the issues are complex and technical, because the ways in which they are framed sometimes inspires no sharp cleavages of opinion, because interest groups are often disinterested and inattentive. But when an issue heats up and reaches the final stages of the legislative process, leeway dissipates. Interest groups become active. The mail begins to pour in.[58] Newsmen appear on the scene. Congressmen stick close to the Floor, listen to debate, mill around, stand ready to answer quorum calls or to vote on amendments.

There are four procedures for voting in the House: voices, standing, tellers, and roll call, in the order in which they expose members to public view. In the Committee on the Whole House, only the first three types of votes are taken. A diligent reporter or lobbyist can, however, even without benefit of a roll call, usually find out how a given member votes. The procedure is not foolproof, but, from the gallery, an outsider can always keep his eye fixed on one or a few congressmen whose votes are of interest to him. Corroboration, if any is needed, can be obtained by asking around among other congressmen.

The caucus at which voting for Majority Leader was to have taken place provided no such opportunities for outside surveillance. No spectators were admitted. Congressmen were even protected from the scrutiny of their colleagues; Representative Francis Walter, chairman of the caucus, sent word that the balloting for Majority Leader, when the time came, would be secret. The rules of the caucus say nothing about a secret ballot; rather, general parliamentary law governs the caucus meetings, and there is a special provision that "the yeas and nays on any question shall, at the desire of one fifth of those present, be entered on the journal" — all of which did not alter the fact that the balloting would be secret.

In spite of the interest which Mr. Bolling had stirred up among outside groups, these groups were operating under an insuperable handicap. The voting procedure maximized the chances that a congressman cross-pressured between the demands of "local agency" and his own personal feelings could vote his private preferences with impunity.

VII

What does this case suggest about the general relations between inside and outside influences in the decision making processes of the House? [59] Several things. First, it shows the extent to which inside and outside strategies tend to encourage different modes of communication among members and to evoke different definitions of the decision making situation. The inside strategy is likely to define situations as "family matters," and to feature face-to-face interaction among members. The outside strategy is likely to evoke a more ideological, issue-oriented definition of the situation. Interaction among members is more likely to take place through third persons, lobbyists, and the press. Second, this case suggests conditions tending to promote the success of each strategy of influence. Inside strategies are favored when: (1) the matter to be decided can be rationalized as in some sense procedural rather than substantive; (2) there are great differences in the inside strengths of the two sides, but their outside strengths approach equality; (3) members are protected from surveillance by outsiders. Outside strategies are favored, presumably, when these conditions are reversed.

Additional conditions bearing on the effectiveness of inside and outside strategies may be imagined. Presumably, the autonomy of a Representative from constituent pressures diminishes as his constituency approaches unanimity in its preferences *or* as the intensity of preference for a given alternative by any substantial portion of his constituency increases. We know that few decisions before Congress are likely to unite constituencies in this way or to inflame their passions to such a great extent. In addition, Congress takes routine steps to insulate its decision-making from certain kinds of outside influences.

One such device is the consideration of business in the Committee of the Whole, where substantial revisions of legislation can be made on the Floor without binding congressmen to a record vote. The committees — whose composition and behavior sometimes reflect outside interests[60] and sometimes inside distributions of influence[61] — mark up bills and vote on them in executive sessions only. A third device favoring inside distributions of influence in the House is the Rules Committee. One of the prerequisites for appointment to service on this committee is ability to "take the heat" and resist constituency pressures to report out bills which the House leadership wants killed.[62]

The enumeration of these devices hints at some of the problems facing two significant groups of outsiders: Presidents of the United States and political scientists. The President has a never-ending battle of converting decisions in the House choices from inside ones to

outside ones. Most of his attempts to influence decisions are direct,
but his efforts to dramatize issues before relevant publics may also
be interpreted as attempts to activate interest groups and unify
constituencies so as to make the employment of inside strategies of
influence in the House difficult.

For political scientists, the lesson is clear. In order to understand
the context within which decisions in the House are being made
sufficiently well so that we can identify the goals in terms of which
outcomes may be seen as "rational," it will be necessary to study the
House at close range. On the whole, political scientists have taken a
somewhat Olympian view of congressional behavior. We have tended
to organize our conceptions of rationality and legitimacy around
presidential goals and presidential party platforms.[63] This has operated to obscure the constraints on the behavior of those in the House
who share the policy preferences these political theories imply. It has
also, I think, bred a kind of impatience with the study of strategies
and tactics of house decision making, which study, I believe, is a
necessary step in understanding why the House operates as it does.

NOTES

1. This paper was originally presented at the annual meetings of The American
   Political Science Association, Washington, D.C., 1962. Several members of
   Congress, who I am sure would prefer to remain anonymous, read an early
   draft of this chapter and made many useful comments. I should also like to
   thank Lewis A. Dexter, H. Douglas Price, and Robert L. Peabody. Others
   who have been helpful include Aaron B. Wildavsky, Lewis A. Froman, Jr.,
   Norman O. Brown, Luigi Einaudi, Joseph Cooper, Alan L. Otten, and Neil
   MacNeil. Research assistance was provided by a Ford Foundation grant to
   Wesleyan University.
2. The phrase "traditional political theory" refers in this context to the history
   of political thinking rather than to any specific political doctrines. See, for
   example, David Easton, *The Political System* (New York: Knopf, 1953);
   Harry V. Jaffa, "The Case Against Political Theory," *Journal of Politics*, XXII
   (May, 1960), 259–75; Robert A. Dahl, "The Science of Politics, New and
   Old," *World Politics*, VII (April, 1955), 479–89; Dahl, "Political Theory,
   Truth and Consequences," *World Politics*, XI (October, 1958), 89–102;
   Norman Jacobson, "The Unity of Political Theory," in R. Young (ed.),
   Approaches to the Study of Politics (Evanston: Northwestern University
   Press, 1958), pp. 115–24.
3. Heinz Eulau, John C. Wahlke, Leroy C. Ferguson, and William Buchanan,
   "The Role of the Representative: Some Empirical Observations on the Theory
   of Edmund Burke," *Am. Pol. Sci. Rev.*, LIII (September 1959), 742–56.
4. "Speech to the Electors of Bristol," November 3, 1774, *Works* (London, etc.:
   Oxford University Press, 1906), II, 164–66.
5. "Speech at Bristol," September 6, 1780 in *ibid.*, III, 2, 3, 4.

6. *Ibid.*, and F. W. Raffety, "Preface" in *Works*, II, xiv–xv.
7. One approach to some of these questions was made by Julius Turner, who used the analysis of roll calls as his major source of data in *Party and Constituency: Pressures on Congress* (Baltimore: Johns Hopkins, 1951). See also David B. Truman, *The Congressional Party* (New York: Wiley, 1959).
8. Lewis Anthony Dexter, "Congressmen and the People They Listen To" (Cambridge: Center for International Studies, Massachusetts Institute of Technology, Ditto, 1955), chap. ii, p. 14, chap. viii, p. 7.
9. *Ibid.*, chap. v, pp. 4–5.
10. Richard L. Lyons, "Pressure Rises as House Moves to Vote on Rules," *Washington Post*, January 31, 1961.
11. *Time* (September 1, 1961), p. 14. The congressman is not identified here, as he was in the *Time* article, first, because he denies the conversation took place (*Congressional Record*, 87th Cong., 1st sess. [August 29, 1961], p. 16318) and second, because the *Time* reporter's source for the quote told me that he had deliberately left ambiguous the identity of the congressman, and, while the event really happened, the *Time* reporter was misled about whom it happened to.
12. Dexter, *op. cit.*, chap. viii, p. 4.
13. *Ibid.*, pp. 4–5.
14. The best news coverage by far of this press conference that I saw occurred in the *Baltimore Sun*, January 4, 1962. See Rodney Crowther, "House Race Dropped by Bolling."
15. Pursuit of this line of thinking at a McCormack-Albert press conference, January 9, visibly irked Mr. McCormack. "A reporter . . . caught [Mr. McCormack] at the door of the Speaker's lobby and asked him if he had asked for complete support of President Kennedy's program. The new Speaker drew back indignantly. 'I'm not trying to put words in your mouth,' said the reporter. 'Yes you are,' said Mr. McCormack, 'I've been voting for progressive legislation for 30 years. I'm not a one-year man. Why don't you wake up?' " Mary McGrory, "McCormack Speaks as His Own Master," *Washington Star*, January 10, 1962.
16. *Congressional Quarterly*, XIX (November 24, 1961), 1893–94. This tabulation also shows that throughout their careers in Congress, the voting records of these men were quite close by several criteria.
17. These statements, and many others throughout this paper, are based on interviews and observations gathered during the summer of 1961 and from December to February, 1961–62, in Washington. During these months I spoke on matters connected with the subject of this paper to over 100 congressmen, congressional aides, newspapermen, and others, and during the latter period, I conducted interviews with twenty-six Democratic congressmen from all sections of the country on the leadership selection process then going on. Quotations are from notes taken during these interviews, and are occasionally slightly altered so as to preserve the anonymity of the respondent. My work in the summer of 1961 was supported by a grant-in-aid from the Social Science Research Council, whose assistance is gratefully acknowledged.
18. The session lasted 277 days, the longest in ten years. Late one especially debilitating August afternoon, an elderly southern congressman shuffled over to where I was standing just outside the Speaker's lobby, and confided that he was going to sponsor a bill that would abolish the final month of each session of Congress.
19. For example, Mr. Bolling was introduced to a large public meeting at the Midwest Conference of Political Scientists on May 11, 1961, as "the next Speaker of the House of Representatives."

20. Mr. Albert's tribute on this occasion was much more elaborate than that tendered by any other member — save by Mr. McCormack's Massachusetts colleagues. See the *Congressional Record*, 87th Cong., 1st sess. (September 26, 1961), pp. 20084–96.

21. Mr. Albert entered the House in 1947, Mr. Bolling in 1949, making them thirtieth (tied with nine others) and thirty-ninth (tied with nineteen others) in seniority respectively in the Democratic party in the House — not a very great difference. Mr. McCormack, on the other hand, was the beneficiary of a long tradition of advancement from Majority Leader to Speaker, and, in addition, after the death of Speaker Rayburn, was third in seniority. He had never served as whip, incidentally, before his election as Majority Leader, nor had Speaker Rayburn. Both Mr. McCormack and Mr. Rayburn had held office for so many years it is highly probable that most members were unaware of the differences in the customs pertaining to the advancement of the Majority Leader and the whip.

22. Mr. Albert's administrative assistant said that this list happened to be in the Washington office while the telephoning was being done from McAlester, Oklahoma, where only the House telephone directory issued to all members was readily available.

23. Friends of Mr. Albert note that Mr. Albert was Speaker Rayburn's personal choice for whip in 1954 and further suggest that Mr. Albert was also a close personal friend of Mr. Rayburn's. One influential congressman said, "Mr. Sam thought the world of Carl Albert." But this same congressman indicated that he thought Mr. Bolling's relationship with the Speaker was unique. Without excluding the strong probability that Mr. Rayburn had a high personal regard for Mr. Albert (and, one supposes, several other members as well), the testimony of several knowledgeable and apparently unbiased observers was quite unanimous in indicating that for several years preceding his death Mr. Rayburn was particularly close to Mr. Bolling.

24. David Cohn, "Mr. Speaker: An Atlantic Portrait," *Atlantic Monthly* (October 1942), pp. 73–78. The quoted portion appears on p. 76. Mr. Cohn was a personal friend of the Speaker's. He comments on the quoted passage, "As he spoke, Rayburn relived the long, lean, lonely years of his childhood, and it was clear that he wished other children might be spared the bleakness of his youth."

25. CBS News, "Mr. Sam: A Personal and Political Biography," telecast, November 16, 1961.

26. D. B. Hardeman, "The Unseen Side of the Man They Called Mr. Speaker," *Life*, LI (December 1, 1961), 21.

27. *Ibid.*

28. CBS News, "Mr. Sam . . .," *op. cit.*

29. *Time*, LXXVII (February 10, 1961), p. 12. What is significant here, I think, is not the placement of either man on an ideological spectrum so much as the high degree of personal engagement which the references to parts of the body suggest.

30. I was a witness to the events surrounding the composition of Bolling's statement of withdrawal, and am quite convinced that Bolling had no knowledge of Rayburn's statement. Rather, the striking resemblance between the two seems to me to illustrate a remarkable similarity in the styles of the two men, not conscious imitation.

31. Bascom N. Timmons, "Rayburn" (ditto, n.d.), part 4, p. 1. This series was supplied to certain newspapers at the time of Speaker Rayburn's death. Mr. Timmons is a newspaperman accredited to the House Press Galleries from a

string of newspapers in the Southwest. He is a Texan and was a friend and contemporary of Mr. Rayburn's.

32. Rodney Crowther, *Baltimore Sun, loc. cit.* The psychologically minded would also no doubt find it relevant that Mr. Bolling's father died when he was in his early teens. However, anyone concluding from data such as have been presented here that either Mr. Bolling or Mr. Rayburn gave indications in their behavior of being emotionally crippled or lacking in control could not possibly be further from the mark. The point here is simply that certain easily verified events and patterns in the lives of each man may well have predisposed him to like the other.

33. Mr. Bolling's imputation of indecorousness (the news of which was communicated in such places as "Bitter Withdrawal," *Time*, LXXIX [January 12, 1962, 12]) was resented in the Albert camp. In their view, Mr. Bolling had himself precipitated the battle by first permitting word to leak to the newspapers that he was a candidate for Majority Leader.

34. One index of this is the apparent fact that Mr. Thompson is generally not too popular in the House (a fact of which both he and Mr. Bolling are aware). Mr. Thompson is an able and gifted man with extremely good political connections outside the House, both "downtown" and in his home state. (See Richard L. Lyons, "Thompson Decision to Retain Seat Gives House Liberals Needed Lift," *Washington Post*, January 31, 1961.) But inside the House, he has a reputation for being sharp-tongued, supercilious, and too witty for his own good. He has a way of hanging nicknames that "stick" on friend and foe alike — to the delight of the former, the great chagrin of the latter. One political ally of Mr. Thompson's said, "He has got the reputation that whenever he is in favor of a bill, it is bound to lose . . . Thompson is one of Bolling's major liabilities. I hear how the guys talk at the back of the room there [in the aisle behind the seats in the Hall of the House]. They say, 'Whose amendment is that? Thompson's? That guy? To hell with that!' And they vote it down." Another ally of Thompson's said, "Frank's always trying to talk silly with you when you're talking serious, and trying to talk serious when you're talking silly."

35. See H. Douglas Price, "Race, Religion and the Rules Committee" in Alan Westin (ed.), *The Uses of Power* (New York: Harcourt, Brace & World, 1962), pp. 1–71.

36. Mr. Albert's friend may, in reflecting unfavorably on Mr. Bolling, have done Mr. Albert a slight injustice. Mr. Albert was an honor graduate of the University of Oklahoma and a Rhodes Scholar — neither of which makes him an intellectual, but they clearly don't disqualify him either.

37. There are now several accounts of the 1961 battle over the Rules Committee in print, including a treatment of the episode in Price, *op. cit.*; the analysis of the vote by Milton C. Cummings, Jr. and Robert L. Peabody, in Peabody and Nelson W. Polsby, eds., *New Perspectives on the House of Representatives* (Chicago: Rand McNally, 1963), pp. 167–194; and a long chapter by Neil MacNeil in *Forge of Democracy* (New York: McKay, 1963), pp. 410–88.

38. See *Time*, LXXVII (February 10, 1961); William S. White, "The Invisible Gentleman from Kansas City," *Harper's* (May, 1961); Neil MacNeil, "The House Confronts Mr. Kennedy," *Fortune*, LXV (January 1962), 70–73.

39. Statements such as this one obviously are not intended to be taken with strict literalness. Most social scientists are agreed that the personal "qualities" of leaders vary according to the situation.

40. Cf. a similar comment on Senate liberals by Tristam Coffin, "The Well Tempered Politician," *Holiday* (April 1962), p. 107.

41. See John M. Virden, "Little Giant from Bug Tussle," *Saturday Evening Post,* CCXXXV (March 24, 1962), 94–97; Paul Duke, "Albert's Soft Sell," *Wall Street Journal,* March 6, 1962; "Carl Albert, Nose-Counter from Bug Tussle," *Time,* LXXIX (January 12, 1962), 13.

Certain other characteristics place Mr. Albert closer to the rank and file of congressmen than Mr. Bolling. Mr. Albert was a small town boy, the son of a farmer and laborer, educated in public schools, and is a Methodist. Mr. Bolling was born in New York City, the son of a well-to-do physician. He grew up in comfortable circumstances and socially prominent circles in Huntsville, Alabama, after his father's death went to Exeter and the University of the South, has a Master's degree from Sewanee, and did further graduate work at Vanderbilt, and is an Episcopalian. If the script for this contest had been written by C. Wright Mills or one of his followers, Mr. Albert would have been the more "liberal" candidate and wouldn't have had a chance. (See Mills, *The Power Elite* [New York: Oxford University Press, 1956]). Mr. Mills carefully excludes Congress from his discussion of "the power elite" for reasons which seem to this reader designed to protect his thesis from evidence which would reject it.

42. An example of this process was given in *Time,* Vol. LXXVII (February 10, 1961) at the time of the Rules Committee fight: "*Time* Correspondent Neil MacNeil listened as two Rayburn lieutenants were running down the list of doubtful members. On one: 'The General Services Administration ought to be able to get him.' On another: 'The Air Force can take care of him.' A third? 'If you can get the Post Office to issue that special stamp for him, you've got him.' And a fourth? 'The United Mine Workers can get him.' And a fifth? 'Hell, if we can't get him we might as well quit. Go talk to him.' A sixth? 'No, but I'll fix that bastard.' " *Time* gives the strong impression that the two lieutenants are Bolling and Thompson.

43. A Washington correspondent commented: "[Bolling] was a good news source and popular among newsmen from the time he first got on the House Banking Committee and became even more popular when he was moved to Rules as Rayburn's obvious protegé."

44. *New York Times,* December 24, 1961.

45. This letter was sent in response to Mr. Bolling's November 28 request for "consideration" from each Democrat. Supporters of Mr. Albert were dismayed by the fact that while they had not solicited Judge Smith's support and Mr. Bolling had, the Smith endorsement was being used by Mr. Bolling against Mr. Albert with the press.

46. James Wechsler, "Hill Battle," *New York Post,* December 19, 1961. Mr. Bolling's constituency is the Fifth District of Missouri, which includes most of Kansas City. Mr. Albert represents the 13 counties of Oklahoma's Third District, an area known as "Little Dixie." This district is predominantly rural and is somewhat depressed economically. Its major products are timber, peanuts, cotton, and livestock. Several Albert supporters suggested that a generally liberal record such as Mr. Albert had made in the House was in some ways a more creditable performance for a man from a district of this kind than for a man from a big city. Although this argument has some plausibility, it should also be noted that several of the most respected southern liberals and moderates in the House have come from districts very similar to Mr. Albert's. Sam Rayburn himself was one such example. Others would be Carl Elliott of Alabama, Frank Smith of Mississippi, and James Trimble of Arkansas. This argument may, in other words, be an attempt to appeal to a popular stereotype which automatically classifies big-city districts as "liberal" and rural

southern districts as "conservative." But it may be that on the vast majority of issues coming to a vote in Congress, representatives from southern, rural, economically depressed areas have constituencies as liberal as any in the country.

47. Marquis Childs, "The High Stakes in House Battle," *Washington Post*, December 29, 1961 — and elsewhere.

48. Edward P. Morgan and the News," American Broadcasting Company, December 29, 1961. The documentation of this case has never, to my knowledge, been made. I suggest that at the least the reference to Mr. Albert's position on federal aid to education would be difficult to defend.

49. See, for examples of this tradition, H. H. Wilson, *Congress: Corruption and Compromise* (New York: Rinehart, 1951), Karl Schriftgiesser, *The Lobbyists* (Boston: Little, Brown, 1951).

50. An excellent example of this mode of thinking is contained in Max Lerner, *America as a Civilization* (New York: Simon & Schuster, 1957), pp. 415 ff. and especially p. 424. More generally, see Arthur F. Bentley, *The Process of Government* (Evanston: Principia, 1949), Earl Latham, *The Group Basis of Politics* (Ithaca: Cornell University Press, 1952), Oliver Garceau, "Interest Group Theory in Political Research," *The Annals*, CCCXIX (September, 1958), and David B. Truman, *The Governmental Process* (New York: Knopf, 1955). Truman explicitly rejects the notion that congressmen are wholly passive.

51. Lewis A. Dexter, *op. cit.*, and Dexter, "The Representative and His District," *Human Organization*, XVI (Summer, 1947), 2–13; Dexter, "What Do Congressmen Hear: The Mail," *Public Opinion Quarterly*, XX (Spring, 1956), 16–26. See also Donald R. Matthews, *U.S. Senators and Their World* (Chapel Hill: University of North Carolina Press, 1960), esp. chaps. viii, ix.

52. Robert C. Albright, "Powell Backs Albert for House Post," *Washington Post*, December 1, 1961. Powell, unlike the congressman just quoted, checked with the White House before he made his announcement, obviously taking the position that the President had a legitimate interest in the outcome.

53. *New York Post*, December 21, 1961.

54. "Edward P. Morgan and the News," American Broadcasting Company, December 29, 1961. This account may be contrasted with a column put out by William S. White, a former Capitol Hill reporter. White's explanation of what happened is: "Whatever chance [Bolling] might have had, however, was sunk without a trace by the ultra-liberals themselves. They rushed forward to gather him into their arms, through zealous indorsements by such do-gooder groups as American for Democratic Action. No man in a House which — like the country itself — is essentially moderate could possibly have survived such embarrassing public embraces. So Mr. Bolling had to withdraw his candidacy. . . ." *Washington Star*, January 5, 1962 — and elsewhere. I could discover little evidence which would lend credibility to this analysis. Regrettably, Mr. White offers none.

55. The rate at which tentative proposals and counterproposals of this sort fly around Washington is perfectly phenomenal. Theodore H. White rhapsodizes about the kinds of people who often act in the capacity of carrier pigeon: "Washington holds perhaps fifty or a hundred . . . men, lawyers all, successful all, who in their dark-paneled law chambers nurse an amateur's love for politics and dabble in it whenever their practices permit. Where, in the regions, cities and states of the country, provincial lawyers love to counsel local politicians, promote names for the local judiciary, arrange the candidacies of lesser men, in Washington lawyers dabble in national politics, in appointments

to places of high political destiny. Their influence, collectively, can never be ignored, because, collectively, they possess a larger fund of wisdom, experience, contacts, memories, running back over thirty years of national politics, than most candidates on the national scene can ever hope to acquire on their own . . ." *The Making of the President, 1960* (New York: Atheneum, 1961), p. 33.

Newspaper people also quite often undertake this sort of activity, and occasionally lobbyists do, too.

Fortuitously, much of the activity described in this paper took place during the Christmas-Debutante-New Year's social season in Washington. As a result, many of the participants in these events kept running into each other at parties. Political science may some day catch up with the slick magazines and novels in comprehending the true significance of Washington parties. In this case, it appears that much of the negotiating on whether or not Mr. Bolling would join the leadership group as head of the policy committee took place on an informal basis, through intermediaries and without any soul-stirring confrontations of rivals such as are found in Allen Drury's *Advise and Consent*.

56. That is, it came to almost nothing. In mid-March, 1962, three months after the events described here took place, the Democrats reactivated a "steering" committee along the lines of the "policy" committee proposed at the opening of the session. Mr. Bolling did not become a member. A leading Democrat in the House observed to me that the members of this committee, including James Davis of Georgia, William Colmer of Mississippi, Paul Kitchin of North Carolina, Clarence Cannon of Missouri, were likely, if anything, to be *less* liberal than the leadership they were supposed to advise. This was an outcome exactly opposite to the one envisaged by proponents of the policy committee idea.

57. For the story at various stages, see: Robert C. Albright, "Drive is Begun for Democratic Steering Group," *Washington Post*, December 30, 1961; Mary McGrory, "McCormack Silent on Liberals Plan," *Washington Star*, December 31, 1961; Robert K. Walsh, "Party Harmony Setup Seen by House Liberals," *Washington Star*, January 5, 1962; Richard L. Lyons, "Liberal Democrats Defer Demands," *Washington Post*, January 9, 1962; Rowland Evans, Jr., "Democrats Unanimous," *New York Herald Tribune*, January 10, 1962.

58. Lewis Dexter makes the point that the mail usually comes too late to affect the substance of legislation. However mail is used here only as an index of attentiveness to issues on the part of publics. See Dexter, "What Do Congressmen Hear . . .," *op. cit.*

59. Obviously, no real-world case will fit a typology perfectly. It may be well to remind the reader that the predominant strategies of the major actors were as I have indicated, but that Mr. Albert had some support from outside the House (such as from Senators Kerr and Monroney and Governor Edmondson of Oklahoma), and many of Bolling's supporters within the House backed him for reasons other than outside "pressures" which he might have been able to bring to bear on them. These included some members from the South whose position on civil rights was more accurately reflected by Mr. Albert.

60. As, for example, the Agriculture Committee. See Charles O. Jones, "Representation in Congress: The Case of the House Agriculture Committee," *Am. Pol. Sci. Rev.* LV (June, 1961), 358–67.

61. There are numerous examples of this — e.g., the operation of the seniority system. See George Goodwin, "The Seniority System in Congress," *Am. Pol. Sci. Rev.* LIII (June 1959), 412–36. On the influence of state delegations on

committee assignments and the force of tradition in determining the allocation of seats, see, in general, Nicholas Masters, "Committee Assignments in the House of Representatives," *Am. Pol. Sci. Rev.* LV (June 1961), 345–57.

62. On the Rules Committee, see Robert L. Peabody, "The Enlarged Rules Committee," in Peabody and Nelson W. Polsby, eds. *New Perspectives on the House of Representatives* (Chicago: Rand McNally, 1963), ch. vii; and the following articles by James A. Robinson, "Organizational and Constituency Backgrounds of the House Rules Committee" in Joseph R. Fiszman (ed.), *The American Political Arena* (Boston: Little, Brown, 1962); "The Role of the Rules Committee in Regulating Debate in the U.S. House of Representatives," *Midwest Journal of Political Science,* V (February 1961), 59–69; "Decision Making in the House Rules Committee," *Administrative Science Quarterly,* III (June 1958), 73–86; "The Role of the Rules Committee in Arranging the Program of the U. S. House of Representatives," *Western Political Quarterly,* XII (September 1959), 653–69.

63. This comment may be anachronistic, judging from much of the recent work on the House. It agrees with Ralph K. Huitt's similar judgment in "Democratic Party Leadership in the Senate," *Am. Pol. Sci. Rev.* LV (June 1961), 333 f.

CHAPTER FOUR

The Ford-Halleck Minority Leadership Contest, 1965

On the morning of January 4, 1965, the House Republican Conference met in the Ways and Means Committee hearing room of the Longworth House Office Building to select a Republican candidate for Speaker of the United States House of Representatives during the 89th Congress.[1] The outcome of the Speakership contest, to be held two hours later on the House floor, was already a foregone conclusion. Thus, the 140 Republican Representatives-elect were actually meeting to choose their Minority Leader for the next two years. Since December 19, 1964, the challenger, Conference Chairman Gerald R. Ford, Jr., of Michigan, had been engaged in an open fight to overthrow the incumbent Minority Leader for the previous six years, Charles A. Halleck of Indiana. Halleck had countered the efforts of the Ford supporters with a lower-keyed campaign of his own to obtain votes from among the 120 returning congressmen and 20 freshmen who had survived the November 1964 election.

Ford won by a secret ballot vote of 73 to 67. After the balloting, Halleck, who took his defeat hard, but with courage and good grace, moved to make Ford's election unanimous.

The 1965 contest, at least on the surface, was not one of ideological contrasts. Both candidates had equally conservative voting records, but these records masked rather sharp differences in age, image, and the kind of strategy that the minority party should adopt in the months ahead. Ford, at 51, sandy-haired with the athlete's trim build, the symbol of a new generation of young, articulate, executive-

Reprinted with permission of the publisher and Eagleton Institute, *Cases in Practical Politics* (New York: McGraw-Hill, 1966), No. 40. A brief epilogue has been added. The original study was made possible by a grant from the Social Science Research Council's Committee on Political Behavior.

type politicians, urged the promotion of a "fighting, forward-looking party seeking responsible and constructive solutions to national problems." Halleck, at 64, the old pro of 30 years of service in the House, red-faced and heavy jowled, campaigned on a "record of solidarity in support of party principles," and near-unanimous opposition to the "costly, unwise and unnecessary proposals" put forward by Democratic administrations.

The contest for conference chairman, which took place immediately before the Ford-Halleck vote, involved both ideological and regional contrasts. Representative Melvin Laird of Wisconsin, a Midwest conservative, had aroused the enmity of the eastern moderates and liberals by his firm and unbending management of the Republican party platform prior to Senator Goldwater's nomination in July 1964. On the Sunday evening before the House Republican Conference, the Wednesday Club, a group of some 20 of the more moderate-to-liberal Republicans, had met and agreed to challenge Laird's candidacy with a candidate of their own, Peter H. B. Frelinghuysen, Jr. of New Jersey. Laird won by a vote of 77 to 62, but the surprising strength of Frelinghuysen's vote pushed him into prominence as a candidate to unify the party in a subsequent unsuccessful challenge to the incumbent whip.

During the next months, the new Minority Leader, Ford, was to undergo a series of challenges to his leadership, including a contest over minority personnel, a second defeat of Frelinghuysen as Ford's choice to replace Leslie Arends of Illinois as party whip, a failure to win a seat on the important Ways and Means Committee for one of his principal supporters, Charles Goodell of New York, and another challenge to Goodell as Ford's first choice for Policy Committee Chairman to replace the resigning chairman, John Byrnes of Wisconsin. Ford, Laird, and Arends subsequently resolved this challenge by creating a Committee on Planning and Research under the Republican Conference and appointing Goodell as its Chairman. On February 23, 1965, the same day that this appointment was approved, the Republican Conference elected John Rhodes of Arizona Chairman of the Republican Policy Committee without opposition.

Halleck, the defeated Minority Leader, was dropped from the top position in the Republican party hierarchy to eighth-ranking minority member on the Committee on Public Works.[2] Martin, the man he had defeated six years earlier in a bitter, behind-the-scenes struggle, 80 years old in 1965, had remained in the House to vote against

Halleck and for Ford. Ironically, both Martin and Halleck had been victims of election disasters for which neither could be held directly responsible, but which nevertheless served as the catalyst for revolution.

The seeds of unrest existed long before the election disaster of 1964. Dissatisfaction with Halleck's leadership goes back at least to the 1959 revolt; it came out into the open at the beginning of the 88th Congress when Ford defeated Charles Hoeven of Iowa in a secret ballot vote for Conference Chairman; and the agitation for leadership change continued to grow during the long and arduous legislative sessions of 1963 and 1964.

The 1959 revolt against Martin began with a different objective — getting the ailing Minority Leader to appoint some one other than himself as chairman of a dormant House Republican Policy Committee. Martin, underestimating the extent of the challenge, did not seriously consider this possible compromise until it was too late. The junior insurgents, led by Bob Wilson of California, settled on Halleck, the former Majority Leader in the 80th and 83d Congresses, as the heir apparent, even though he was not an overwhelming first choice. The insurgents thought the contest was all but over when they won by 96 to 50 the right to use a secret ballot. But many members who favored a secret ballot nevertheless ended up by voting for the incumbent. On the first ballot, Halleck received 73 votes, Martin 72, but neither had a majority because of one illegible ballot. Halleck emerged the winner on a second ballot by a vote of 74 to 70, with two members, presumably Halleck and Martin, voting present. While Halleck's election gave House Republicans more aggressive leadership, it was not interpreted as a complete victory by many of those advocating the change. For the time being these younger members, among them Thomas B. Curtis of Missouri, Ford and Laird, satisfied themselves with a revitalized Policy Committee under a separate Chairman, John W. Byrnes of Wisconsin.[3]

House Republicans had suffered a net loss of 47 seats in the election of 1958, just before Martin's defeat. Under Halleck's leadership Republicans reaped the benefits of a net gain of 20 seats in 1960, as John F. Kennedy ran behind three-fourths of the Democratic House candidates in his close victory over Richard M. Nixon. In 1962, the traditional pattern of midterm gains for the minority party was not realized. House Republicans picked up only two additional seats, increasing their membership in the 435-member House from 174 to 176 Representatives.

Just before the opening of the 88th Congress, two junior members, Robert P. Griffin of Michigan (first elected in 1956) and Charles E. Goodell of New York (first elected in a special election, May 26, 1959) met for lunch. What began as a discussion of forthcoming legislation in their House Education and Labor Committee shifted to matters of Republican party organization. Before the January 2, 1963 luncheon was over, it had been transformed into a planning session for a challenge to the established leadership. After considering and rejecting contests against either Halleck or Arends, Griffin and Goodell launched an over-the-weekend campaign aimed at capturing the Republican conference chairmanship. With the active support of most of the House members elected after 1958, and with the tacit approval of many of the same activists who had helped Halleck defeat Martin in 1959, the Young Turk candidate, the 49-year-old Ford, defeated the 67-year-old incumbent conference chairman, Charles B. Hoeven of Iowa, by a secret ballot vote of 86 to 78. As Hoeven left the 1963 conference, he described himself as the "scapegoat and fall-guy" of an effort by younger Republicans to take over the leadership. "I was picked as the lamb for the slaughter. This should serve as notice to Mr. Arends and Mr. Halleck that something is brewing." [4] Two years later, Mr. Hoeven's predictions were to prove quite accurate.

By 1964, at least four developments in House Republican party organization had given younger members more of an active role in policy making. The House Republican Policy Committee was operating under a separate chairman, John Byrnes, and with a wider base of membership. The House Republican conference had a new chairman, Jerry Ford, and presumably would meet more often and work more closely with the Policy Committee. A Subcommittee on Special Projects under the chairmanship of John Rhodes of Arizona was beginning to develop longer-range policy through a series of task forces. After 1961, at Halleck's suggestion, the subcommittee of the Committee on Committees charged with making committee assignments had included class representatives, including a spokesman for the freshman class. Despite these developments, the continued domination of these organizations by senior members and the continuing frustrations of minority status led to further unrest and dissatisfaction among the more junior members who made up well over a majority of the House Republican party.

With majority status comes not only control of the House, but the benefits which accrue from drafting and passing legislation which conforms to personal or party philosophy. On rare occasions a member of the minority party can take advantage of a situation which requires bipartisan action so as to play a major and constructive role in the legislative process. Thus, Griffin, as ranking minority member of the Education and Labor subcommittee which dealt with labor law reform, became the co-sponsor, with Halleck's support, of what was to become the Landrum-Griffin Act of 1959. Similarly, Goodell, with even less seniority than Griffin, was able to rework the proposals set forth by the Curtis Task Force on "Employment in a Dynamic American Economy" into Republican amendments which became the basis of the Manpower Development and Retraining Act of 1962. A number of young House Republicans, among them John V. Lindsay of New York, Clark MacGregor of Minnesota, and Charles McC. Mathias, Jr. of Maryland joined ranking Judiciary minority member William M. McCulloch in shaping what was to become the Civil Rights Act of 1964, again with Halleck's cooperation.

In the main, however, the minority's victories had come not from drafting constructive alternatives or modifying the administration's proposals, but from the defeat of the majority party's proposed legislation. It was at this endeavor that Halleck was particularly adept. He had served with the astute leader of the southern Democratic conservatives, Howard W. Smith of Virginia, on the Committee on Rules in the early 1940's. He knew most of the senior conservative southern Democrats on a first-name basis. He had gone hunting or fishing with many of them and shared the bourbon and branch-water conviviality of many a Rayburn "Board of Education" gathering.[5] Halleck's ability to rally Republicans in opposition to the Kennedy-Johnson programs was impressive. As he, himself, summed up his record as Minority Leader in his December 21, 1964 statement:

> ... In my first two years, being the last two years of the Eisenhower administration, practically all of his proposals were enacted into law, although we were much in the minority. During the past four years of the Kennedy-Johnson administration, most of the constructive legislation bears a very definite Republican imprint. Many costly, unwise and unnecessary proposals were either defeated or abandoned by virtue of almost solid Republican opposition.

But these efforts to secure unanimity had their costs. They were particularly distasteful to members of the moderate-to-liberal Wednesday Club, a group of younger House Republicans, who, by belief and the kinds of constituencies they represented, were most likely to bear the brunt of efforts to secure near-unanimity on issues which became tests of party loyalty. Two comments from members of this group illustrate this concern:

> Halleck wasn't a bad leader. The trouble was that when he was pushed, he submitted to a push from the right, rather than from the left. There has been too much negativism in the leadership, too much emphasis on saying "No" to everything ... We need to look for constructive alternatives, and be there first with some alternatives; not just listen to H. R. Gross and vote "No."

> We owe a great debt to Halleck. He's given us good leadership for the better part of six years. I still think he's the most capable leader we have. Our biggest complaint was that he didn't lead — he'd be absent or disinterested in what was going on on a day-to-day basis. And his attitude was apt to be — let's beat them just for the victory, not carefully choosing when to hold the line. And then it was likely to be a Pyrrhic victory — just being proud that we had lost only two or three Republicans. I'm tired of always painting ourselves into a corner. I don't like being there all the time.

Throughout the long and trying first session of the 88th Congress, Halleck was under attack from both the left and right. Conservatives, among them Richard Poff of Virginia, William Cramer of Florida, James Utt of California, and George Meader and August Johansen of Michigan, criticized Halleck for lending his support to the bipartisan coalition implementing civil rights legislation. On the day the civil rights bill was reported out of the House Judiciary Committee, a black furled umbrella, symbol of appeasement, was placed on the Minority Leader's table on the floor of the House. Halleck recouped some ground with conservatives on other issues, for example, his support of Illinois Representative Paul Findley's amendment restricting the sale of wheat to Russia in December 1963. But by making this and other issues a test of party loyalty, he further antagonized the more liberal wing of the party. As one senior House Republican summed up the squeeze that Halleck continually faced:

> A floor leader makes enemies. Halpern and Lindsay of New York — they are criticizing him for not moving fast enough. And on the other hand, Doc Hall and what's-his-name from Iowa — they are after him for moving too fast. So, he accumulates enemies no matter what he does.

If Halleck were more susceptible to "a push from the right," it was as much his own beliefs and the nature of his small town and rural Indiana district, as the recognition that the substantial base of the House Republican party was and is more conservative than moderate-to-liberal in its orientations.

Halleck's six-year reign as Minority Leader was subject to a further kind of limitation which his predecessor had been able to overcome in part. Under Martin, the Republican party had achieved majority status both in the 80th Congress (1947–1948) and the first two years of the Eisenhower administration (1953–1954). The limited patronage available to a Minority Leader had been augmented both by service under a Republican administration and Martin's friendship with Speaker Rayburn. But a Minority Leader, compared to the Speaker and the Majority Leader, inevitably suffers from fewer choice committee assignments to dispense to promising newcomers and party regulars. He has fewer positions on prestige boards and commissions with which to reward his friends and placate his enemies. Since the rewards are fewer and the competition usually keener, he more often ends up pleasing only one member or one state delegation, at the cost of antagonizing several.[6]

The kinds of irritations and personal animosities generated by conflicts over committee assignments or policy differences on legislation were, if anything, complicated still further by Halleck's temperament. He was a leader not afraid to lead, even if leading meant stepping on other people's toes. By his own definition, he ran "a damn tough shop." He was at his best on the floor of the House engaged in debate with his Democratic counterparts. His ability to make the quick retort, the caustic comment, while it won him admiration and respect when directed at the other side, did not endear him to his colleagues when this same testiness and abrasiveness was left unmodified in party councils. As a close supporter summed up Halleck's leadership style:

> His opponents were saying that Charlie had marshalled the Republicans too sternly . . . They were saying that he was to effective, too harsh a disciplinarian. The label "drill sergeant" was used. I think that argument back-fired. A leader, to be successful, has got to keep his flock in line. If you are going to be a leader, you have got to lead. It's as simple as that.

The unrest and dissatisfaction with minority status and the personal irritations stemming from frustrated committee assignments and differences over policy were heightened in 1964 by the pressures which inevitably mount in an election year. The rancorous contest for the Republican presidential nomination further increased frictions between the liberal and conservative wings of the G.O.P. In early July, the week preceding the Republican National Convention, liberals complained that a platform was being drawn up which would be "rammed down our throats." Republican Platform Chairman, Representative Melvin Laird of Wisconsin, together with his two principal assistants, Representatives Glenard Lipscomb of California and Charles Goodell of New York, worked effectively together to bring about a platform upon which the leading contender, Senator Goldwater and his eventual running-mate, Representative William Miller of New York, could campaign. At the same time, Laird and his associates tried to avoid planks which would needlessly irritate or drive liberals out of the party. Civil rights, control of nuclear policy, and the issue of extremism were focal points of conflict.

Halleck, a man who had promoted Wendell Willkie's candidacy in 1940, and who had helped to secure the nomination of Governor Thomas E. Dewey in 1948 only to be rejected by Dewey as a vice-presidential candidate, played a relatively minor role in the 1964 Republican Convention. He joined former Senator William Knowland, Mrs. Clare Booth Luce, and Senator John G. Tower of Texas in seconding Senate Minority Leader Everett M. Dirksen's speech nominating Goldwater. Ford, who received some attention as a possible vice-presidential nominee, supported his state's favorite-son candidate, Governor George Romney, and emerged relatively unscathed from the 1964 convention.

Congress, under continuing pressure from President Lyndon B. Johnson, remained in session until October 3, 1964. As tempers became more unruly and members champed to get back to their districts in order to campaign, personal animosities within and between parties flared. Halleck, put on notice that his leadership was under scrutiny, at least since Ford's 1963 defeat of Hoeven, was probably more ill-humored and quick to react with anger to the demands placed upon him by his colleagues. As one Ford supporter discoursed on the causes of friction that led to the challenge to Halleck's leadership:

> It had been a long, hot summer, as long as any I can remember. There were several sources of irritation which crystallized around Halleck. If I had to put it in one word, and this is a great oversimplification, it would be arrogance. Not a case of being stuck on himself, not that, but rather a detachment,

seemingly purposively — he wouldn't consult with others. It
seemed as if he saw himself as the fountainhead of wisdom. He
became a little impatient and short-tempered . . .

I think a contest would have come, sooner or later, if we had
won. Sure, the elections were clearly a factor, not a motivating
factor, but a convenient excuse.

On November 3, 1964, President Lyndon B. Johnson led the
Democratic party to its greatest national election victory since 1936.
The impact of Senator Barry M. Goldwater's candidacy was particularly disastrous for Republican House candidates. The Democrats
picked up 48 seats previously held by Republicans. Republican candidates won only ten seats previously held by Democrats, for a net loss
of 38 seats.

Conservative House Republican incumbents as identified by low
federal role support scores in the 86th Congress, were particularly hard
hit (Figure 4-1). Of the 40 Republican incumbents who ran for reelection and were defeated, 28 or 70 percent, had voted seven times
or fewer for a larger federal role on eighteen key roll call votes selected
by *Congressional Quarterly* in 1963 and 1964. Twenty of these defeated incumbents had been among the 62 Republican Representatives
who had endorsed Senator Goldwater's candidacy prior to the Republican party nominating convention in July, 1964.[7] In contrast, only a
scattering of liberal House Republicans, including one Wednesday
Club member, Abner Sibal of Connecticut, were defeated. Figure 4-1
also demonstrates the predominantly conservative base of the House
Republican party. While Republicans averaged seven votes or fewer
on these eighteen selected roll calls, House Democrats averaged thirteen votes or more in favor of maintaining or increasing the federal
government's role in our society. The leadership of the House Republican party has generally come from the right-center of the party,
as the voting records of Halleck, Arends, Laird, and Ford clearly
illustrate. On these eighteen votes, all four voted against a larger
federal role on all but four or five votes, two of which were votes for
the first and final passage of the Civil Rights Act of 1964. The most
conservative voting records in terms of this index are those of John
M. Ashbrook of Ohio, and two defeated candidates for re-election,
Bruce Alger of Texas and Ralph F. Beerman of Nebraska. None of
these members cast a vote among the eighteen which could be interpreted as support of a larger federal role. At the other extreme, Sey-

No. of
Members

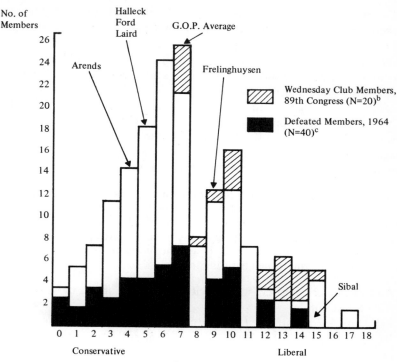

Figure 4-1

mour Halpern of Queens County, New York City, voted in favor of maintaining existing programs or increasing the federal role on seventeen of the eighteen votes. The voting records of Wednesday Club members range from the moderate scores (7 of 18) of Howard Robison of New York, Herman T. Schneebeli of Pennsylvania, and Robert Ellsworth and Garner Shriver of Kansas to the liberal voting record of John V. Lindsay of New York (15 of 18).

What is more significant in terms of the Halleck-Ford contest is that a substantial proportion of these 40 defeated Republican incumbents were older and more senior members, and hence, more likely to support the established leadership. Nineteen of the 40 had served 10 years or more in Congress, including such senior members as Ben Jensen of Iowa and Walt Horan of Washington, the ranking minority members on Appropriations with 13 and 11 terms in Congress, respectively. New York, the hardest-hit Republican delegation in

Congress, lost six senior members, including Katharine St. George, second-ranking on Rules, Walter Riehlman, ranking minority member on Government Operations, and J. Ernest Wharton, second-ranking Republican on Interior and Insular Affairs. These losses, coupled with the retirement of such senior members as Clarence Kilburn, Harold Ostertag, and the Republican vice-presidential candidate, William Miller, drastically reduced the strength of the New York delegation within the party hierarchy. At the same time, the election results radically improved the opportunities for revolt against Halleck, the incumbent Minority Leader. As one of his supporters assessed the impact of the 1964 election:

> There was a general feeling of dismay at the results. If the election had gone the other way, no doubt Charlie would have remained . . . Many of the people defeated would have been Halleck supporters. In general, the more seasoned members of the House favored Halleck. It was the newer and less seasoned members who turned basically to Ford.

And as Halleck himself summed it up: "Many of my most stalwart friends lost out."

Figure 4–2 illustrates this bottom-heavy structure of the House Republican party in the 89th Congress. It also illustrates the relatively heavy losses suffered among the more senior ranks of the party as a result of deaths, retirements, and the heavy election losses of 1964. For example, of the fifteen House Republicans in the 88th Congress first elected in 1942 or earlier, four were defeated for re-election, three had retired, and one had died. Only seven of these members remained at the opening of the 89th Congress, among them Martin, Arends, and Halleck. Relatively large classes of incoming members, compared to the decimated ranks of senior members, had resulted in a substantial majority of the party, almost 58 percent, having been elected in 1958 and subsequent elections. The five least-senior classes, or members elected in 1956 and later, made up two-thirds of the total House Republican party membership in 1965. It was this fertile ground for revolt which led younger activists to contemplate seriously the possibilities of a leadership change following the election disaster.

Open speculation about a direct challenge to Halleck's leadership at the opening of the 89th Congress apparently dates from a story first appearing in the Scripps-Howard newspaper chain on October 28, 1964, six days before the election.[8] As Marshall McNeil surveyed

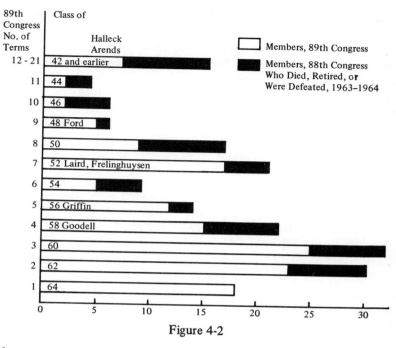

Figure 4-2

the scene: "The candidate of the 'rebels' is Representative Melvin Laird (R., Wis.), a rising star on the GOP side of the House." Among Laird's backers, McNeil listed his two close associates on the Republican Platform Committee, Goodell of New York and Lipscomb of California, and conservative New York Representative Steven B. Derounian (subsequently upset by the Johnson landslide). The same day that the Scripps-Howard story appeared, Ford was campaigning for Halleck and the Republican ticket in Warsaw, Indiana. In response to a reporter's inquiry, Ford issued a press statement reiterating his support of Halleck and praising House Republican leadership as "constructive and effective." Ford concluded that "no case thus far has been made for a change in either our principles or leadership." [9]

In the aftermath of election disaster, while Goldwater called for rebuilding the Republican party along conservative principles and urged consideration of a realignment of the national parties, G.O.P. liberals and moderates were challenging his control over the party organization. Republican National Chairman Dean Burch, a young

Arizonian hand-picked by Goldwater, became the symbol of this struggle.

While the fight for control of the national party organization continued, a number of junior Republican congressmen, among them Griffin and Goodell, were assessing the implications of the November election for their own legislative leadership. As members returned to Washington and met for lunch, talked by telephone, rehashed the election at social gatherings, and pondered on the directions that party policy should take, it was inevitable that Halleck's leadership and possible challengers would be discussed. As one Representative summed up the state of affairs in November:

> If you took a general poll right after the election, I think that most of the Republican members would have been ready for a change. The whole thing was sort of chaotic after that period. Sentiment for a change subsided and then got to a point where there didn't seem to be much of a consensus at all.

Ford had flown back to Washington the day after the election in order to put himself into isolation to fulfill two prior publishing commitments. He had promised to write an article for the January *Fortune* analyzing the state of the Republican party. He had also agreed to collaborate on a book on the Warren Commission. Both drafts were due by late November. As a matter of routine, with Halleck's assent, he had sent out a call for a Republican Conference to be held on the morning of January 4, the day the new Congress would convene. While working in his office, Ford talked with an occasional member and received several telephone calls which raised the general question of leadership change. He also discussed party affairs and the leadership question in a general and preliminary way with several close friends, including Laird and Griffin. As of early November, and indeed, as late as the December 16 conference, Ford did not consider himself to be an active contestant for Minority Leader.

During this same period, the Wednesday Club was holding several meetings to discuss ways to "rebuild the party in the tradition of Lincoln" and to expand their membership so as to be able to be more influential in the coming Congress. In the main, the Wednesday Club had adopted a "wait-and-see" attitude on the question of leadership change. Attitudes ranged from those members who feared a Laird-Ford conspiracy to several leaning toward Ford, and a few who were advocating running one of their own members as a third candidate, should a leadership fight take place.[10]

A number of other Republican Representatives, who felt more strongly about the need for a change, had in the meantime been meeting informally or holding telephone conversations. One of them was Donald Rumsfeld of Evanston, Illinois, first elected to Congress in 1962. Rumsfeld had previously served on the staffs of two congressmen, including an interval on Griffin's staff in 1959. Dismayed by the election results, and unhappy with the prospect of becoming a majority party without more constructive leadership, Rumsfeld telephoned a respected senior colleague, Missouri Representative Thomas B. Curtis, the week after the election. Curtis, second-ranking minority member on the Ways and Means Committee, ranking minority member on the Joint Economic Committee, and long an intellectual gadfly of the House Republican party, was concerned about problems of minority staffing, needs for long-range policy research, and the general state of the House Republican party. Spurred on by several Republicans, Curtis sent out on November 18, a remarkable eight-page, single-spaced typewritten letter to all of his colleagues.[11] He began:

> Like most of the rest of you, I suppose, I have been reading in the newspapers what is supposed to be going on in respect to the Republican leadership in the coming Congress.

> Frankly, I am a little tired of behind the scenes maneuverings when it comes to establishing party machinery and policies which deeply concern all 140 Republican Congressmen and should concern our entire Party.

> Why not have these matters out in the open so all 140 of us can get our two bits worth in? I received a notice from Jerry Ford with Charlie Halleck's blessing that, on January 4, 1965, we will meet in Republican caucus. Well, that is entirely too late to get moving, unless again it is the plan for a few self-appointed members of our waning group to make the decisions for the rest of us ahead of time in the hopes they can get the majority of us to go along.

> Let's get our leadership established on one basic premise, if no other, that major decisions on party organization and policy matters be made on as broad a base as possible. It may take a little more time and a bit more patience, but the net result will be, I am certain, a better organization, better policies, and better politics. In order to do this, I suggest that we have a Party caucus within the next two or three weeks.

Curtis then proceeded to outline in detail some of the changes in minority staffing, House rules, and the Republican House organization, which he felt warranted the calling of a Republican conference in mid-December. As he concluded toward the end of his letter:

> Yes, I am dissatisfied with our leadership in the House, not necessarily our leaders, however . . . I'm not arguing for a change of leaders, but I am arguing for a change in the techniques of leadership. Regrettably, what happened after 1958 was a mere change of leaders, with only a few minor changes in the techniques of leadership.

In Washington, D.C., Griffin and Goodell reacted to the Curtis letter in the same way. Together, and in conversations with other members, they had discussed the desirability of holding a mid-December meeting as a testing ground for the leadership. It also seemed appropriate to use the meeting as a means of capitalizing on essentially dead-news space for promoting Republican alternatives to the Johnson administration proposals on such subjects as medicare and federal aid to education. Finally, like Curtis, they felt a genuine need to meet, consider and plan Republican alternatives to the substantial House rules changes which would be put forward by the House Democratic leadership under pressure from the reform-oriented Democratic Study Group. As they later recalled, "the Curtis letter opened up possibilities."

On November 25, the day before Thanksgiving, five young moderate conservatives met in Griffin's office with Curtis, who had flown in from St. Louis just for this meeting. In addition to Griffin, Goodell, and Curtis, the group included Albert H. Quie of Minnesota, Donald Rumsfeld, and John Anderson of Illinois.[12] In agreement on the need for a mid-December meeting, they made plans to generate the necessary requests from fifty members to call the conference. Among other proposals for party organizational change, they discussed one with far-reaching implications — that members in top leadership positions not hold ranking minority positions on legislative committees at the same time. If adopted, three of the top four leaders — Arends, Ford, and Byrnes — would have to choose between their leadership positions and serving as ranking minority members on Armed Services, Appropriations, and Ways and Means, respectively.[13]

Over the Thanksgiving holidays, Ford had flown with his wife to Puerto Rico for a vacation. While he had discussed the leadership question with several members, his attitude as he later recalled it "was one of keeping at arm's distance." He and Griffin discussed the calling of a conference by telephone just before he flew back to

Washington for one day, December 1. By this time, Ford had heard from a "substantial number" of House Republicans, either by letter, telephone or conversation, most of whom had reacted favorably to the Curtis proposal. Ford took a letter calling for a December 16 conference to the Minority Leader. Knowing full well that the calling of a conference was within Ford's discretion, Halleck gave his reluctant endorsement. Neither felt sufficiently concerned about a possible contest to cancel out-of-town vacation plans. On December 2, Ford flew to California to fulfill several speaking engagements and to enjoy three days of golf while vacationing in Palm Springs. Halleck flew back to Lake Wales, Florida.

On December 10, 1964, dismayed that the leadership had not yet circulated a conference agenda, Curtis sent out a five-page proposal of his own. That same day, Ford returned to Washington and discussed the conference agenda with Griffin and Goodell.

Friday, December 11, was a full day for Ford. In the morning he met with Representative Laird, a good friend and close associate on the Defense subcommittee of the House Committee on Appropriations. He also conferred with Governor George Romney, in town to meet with the Michigan delegation. Ford lunched with the three other principal leaders of the House Republican party, Halleck, Arends, and John Byrnes, the Policy Committee Chairman. The subject was the conference agenda. At the end of the lunch, as Ford later recalled:

> Mr. Halleck went around the room and asked the various members if they planned to run again for the leadership. Mr. Arends said, "Yes," he planned to run for whip. John Byrnes said that while he agreed in principle with the suggestion that the ranking member of a committee should step down and not hold a leadership position at the same time, he thought that with that exception, he would probably be a candidate, again, for Policy Committee Chairman.
>
> Then Charlie asked me what my plans were. I said, "I don't intend to run again for Conference Chairman, but I can't tell you if I'm going to be a candidate for the leadership or not. I haven't made up my mind. There are some people who are promoting me and talking to me about it. But I will say this. If I decide to be a candidate I will tell you before I go ahead." This was the first time, I think, he felt that I was seriously considering running. It was a little tense.

The calling of the House Republican conference was widely interpreted in the press as both a warning to Halleck and a preliminary
victory for the younger members. By the time the conference convened on Wednesday, December 16, it was being described as a testing ground for Halleck's strength. One hundred and nineteen Republicans were present for the morning session, including 16 of the 20
newly-elected members and 18 "lame-duck" members of the 88th
Congress. Attendance fell off sharply for the afternoon session. By
the time the Conference broke up about 5 P.M., less than 50 members remained on the House floor. Those who stayed had largely
concerned themselves with party organizational structure, forthcoming legislative issues, and anticipated House rules changes — matters
not calculated to bring on a clash of personalities, at least not out in
the open. Perhaps the most important action taken by the conference
was the creation of an 11-member committee on House Republican
organizational structure, a group which became known as the Quie
Committee. To newspapermen and television commentators waiting
on the outside it appeared as if most of the steam had gone out of the
"dump Halleck" movement.

In retrospect, these almost universal misreadings were easy to understand. What had gone on within the conference was something quite
different than what had been conveyed by the joint appearances of
Halleck and Ford at informal press conferences held after both the
morning and afternoon sessions. Television film taken at noon for
evening viewing was equally misleading. On all of these occasions
Halleck had been affable, relaxed, and seemingly in control of the
situation. As he replied when asked about a leadership contest: "I
haven't gotten out a seatbelt, yet." Ford, in contrast, had appeared
bland, deferential and rather uneasy. To all questions regarding a
possible contest he had replied: "It was not the purpose of the conference to get into questions of leadership or personalities." Although
Halleck had been aggreeable and conciliatory during the morning
session, as the afternoon wore on he had become more argumentative
and irritable.

After the Republican conference adjourned, another, much smaller
meeting got underway in the office of Representative Goodell of New
York. From the point of view of most of the members who gathered
in Goodell's office, the conference had more than lived up to expectations:

> The conference was a great success. For seven hours we met.
> There was good discussion and good ideas put forth. About

30 to 40 members participated — only one guy was negative. Whenever anybody would propose anything, Charlie would get up and he would try to say why he wasn't at fault. No one was trying to pin the tail on Charlie. At that meeting he could have picked up the ball and run with it . . . Charlie was at bat, but he struck out.

Ford was no shining light at the conference, but most of us realized the difficult and delicate restraint with which he played his role. It enhanced his image. By the same token, Charlie Halleck's efforts to be dynamic fizzled. The result was it put guts into Goodell and Griffin and others of us who played a part.

Insurgents who wish to challenge an incumbent House leader face four interrelated problems: (1) Is a contest justified? (2) Can they win? (3) What *single* candidate can they coalesce behind? (4) How do they secure commitments or otherwise adopt a strategy which will discourage other strong potential candidates from entering the race? Thus, the broad problems faced by House Republican activists in 1964, if not the particular details, were quite similar to those confronting Republican members concerned about Martin's leadership in 1958. They were also related to those problems encountered by Democratic House members who considered a challenge to Majority Leader John McCormack, the heir-apparent to the Speakership upon Rayburn's death in 1961.

In 1964, the first question — whether or not a challenge to Halleck was justified — was quickly resolved. Most of the 15 members who gathered in Goodell's office the evening of the December 16 conference readily agreed that Halleck had not assumed positive leadership. Instead, he had reacted negatively or merely tolerated their proposals for change. These younger members, frustrated by continued minority status and dismayed by the election results of 1964, were looking for something more than business as usual. Given their restricted number, they were convinced that their appeal had to be directed to a wider audience than just the House itself. As one of the more junior members summed up the reasons for going after Halleck: "The decision to run was made on the grounds that certain things had to be done. It was not made on the conviction that victory was possible, that Ford could win."

But no matter how strong the grievances, real or imagined, as a more seasoned insurgent put it — "you don't go, unless you think you can win." Running a campaign against an incumbent leader is hazardous. It inevitably generates antagonisms which are long-lasting and potentially damaging to the minority party's chances of becoming a majority party. If their challenge were unsuccessful, the incumbent would have a great deal to say about the way in which future benefits, particularly committee assignments, would be handed out. Many of the Young Turks were still at a career stage where they were giving serious consideration to transfers to more prestigious committees. Almost all were ambitious enough to want to play a more important role in party organization and policy determination.

But if the risks were high, the rewards of winning would also be high. They would, they felt, have taken a long step forward towards the achievement of their eventual goal — majority status. They would have built up a sense of obligation on the part of the man they had helped put into office. They would be in a position to play an active role in decisions subsequently made by him.

In the main, these were conservative Republicans, if a younger generation of "pragmatic" conservatives. They were united in the need for new and vigorous leadership, although they disagreed among themselves as to which of several candidates was best equipped to project this more constructive, positive, forward-looking image. While most were moderate conservatives, others ranged in outlook from far-right to unorthodox liberal. They represented districts from California to Massachusetts. The characteristics, if any, which distinguished them from other House Republicans were summed up by one of the key participants:

> We picked activists and those who could stand the heat. When you hold one of these meetings, pretty soon the word gets around. Halleck knew who was there. We didn't want those who would be embarrassed if Halleck found out — those who have a particular legislative interest and just want to pursue it or those who need Halleck's support to get the committee assignment they require.

Above all, they had among them a range of diversity of outlook which would enable them to make a reasonably accurate estimate of the strengths and weaknesses of any of the possible opposing candidates.

Only two potential challengers — the 42-year-old Laird, first elected to the House in 1952 and 51-year-old Ford, first elected in 1948 — were seriously considered. Laird had been tapped for the important Appropriations Committee as a freshman; Ford in his second term. Ford had gone on to become the principal Republican spokesman on defense appropriations. Laird had specialized in health matters and HEW appropriations as well as defense. Both had impressive records of party service. Ford had served as Chairman of the Republican conference since 1963. Both were key members of the Republican Policy Committee. Laird, in addition, was a member of the Republican Congressional Compaign Committee. He had helped put together the Republican party platform since 1952, serving as Vice-Chairman in 1960, as Chairman of the Joint Committee on Republican Principles in 1962, and as Chairman of the Platform Committee in 1964.

In terms of television presence and potential for making more effective use of the press, both candidates were considered superior to Halleck. Each of the potential challengers had other strengths, which were at the same time perhaps their greatest liabilities.

The forthright and likeable Ford was respected by his colleagues. Yet some of them felt he lacked initiative and had failed to exploit the potential of the Republican conference. As two members explained the problem:

> There is a problem with any leadership position — a lack of time, the pressure of just so much to do and so little time to do it.

> That was the problem with Jerry, last year. He took over the conference from Hoeven and everybody had high hopes, but Jerry spent a lot of his time on Appropriations. He's a dedicated technician. The Defense Subcommittee took up most of his time. He did a hell of a job on that committee working from 10:00 in the morning until 5:00 at night, or later. And then Johnson put him on the Warren Commission and that was important, but time-consuming. He just couldn't do all that and as a result, the conference suffered. He tried to recognize it, to take this dead body — not a dead body, but an ineffective body — and make it work, but he was spread too thin.

> *   *   *

> Laird has some characteristics which make him better suited for the conference chairman than Ford. He's not afraid to step on people's toes, to push people. Ford was too good-natured, too affable.

Laird, on the other hand, was considered both more vigorous as a leader and more controversial as a candidate, particularly among the Wednesday Club members. Two comments — the first from a strong

Laird lieutenant, the second from a key Ford supporter — illustrate the play of these factors in the final choice of Ford over Laird:

> From my point of view, Mel Laird has the most prospects for leadership. He has the knowledge; he listens to other people, and he makes decisions . . .

> I don't think resentment from San Francisco amounted to much . . . If Laird had decided to go, the Wednesday group was not enough to block him from winning. That's not the point at all. The reason Laird did not go was that he was convinced that it was not the time to have a major upheaval.

*   *   *

> I felt strongly all along that Ford was the only one who had a chance to win. There wasn't any other person seriously considered other than Mel Laird. Criticism of Mel came mainly from the convention, his role as platform chairman. That criticism hasn't affected me. I just read the liberals, the Wednesday group, as pretty solidly opposed. If you split up the moderates and conservatives between Halleck and Laird, and the Wednesday group voted solidly for Halleck, that would be decisive.

> Laird is more controversial. He's more dynamic. He's got more leadership. At the same time, he's irritated and antagonized some people, made enemies along the line. Ford has not. I don't know how you measure these things. It's a feeling, a reading you get. There were fewer people mad at Ford and some people who were quite opposed to Laird. You end with the conclusion that Ford could command more support than anybody else. The members respect him and they like him.

Ford emerged as the stronger candidate, if not the more aggressive leader. His position as chairman of the conference gave him an initial advantage. His age and his 16 years of congressional service compared with Laird's 12, took some of the sting away from a "youth versus age" issue which might have driven some of the more senior members, who were critical of the incumbent, back into the Halleck camp. If Laird possessed more inherent political acumen, he had also antagonized more members than Ford. As another conservative colleague commented: "Laird had several strikes against him, and not just with the Wednesday crowd . . . Mel is damned able; he's ambitious, and that's not necessarily a fault; but he's also a maneuverer — and a lot of people have this feeling."

The most critical problem of all was keeping the number of challengers restricted to a single candidate. Here, the group which met in Goodell's office was, in a sense, only ratifying an agreement which Ford and Laird had tentatively arrived at before the conference. Should one of them decide to enter the race, the other had agreed that he would not run. Laird went even further. On at least two occasions the week before the conference, he had suggested to newspapermen that a contest might take place and that Ford was the likely choice.

Ford did not want to run unless he had a good chance of winning. At the same time he recognized that it might be then or never. The 1964 election defeats provided more impetus for change than would probable midterm gain in 1966. His position as conference chairman was a more likely springboard than the ranking minority position on Appropriations. He recognized that he could not effectively discharge the demanding obligations of both positions in the 89th Congress.

Laird's opportunities to seek higher office were more restricted than Ford's. Both Laird and Halleck were more closely identified than Ford with the Goldwater candidacy — Laird because of his role as Platform Chairman, Halleck as a result of his seconding speech. A further complication faced by Laird was the presence of another member of the Wisconsin delegation, John Byrnes, in one of the top four leadership positions.[14] Byrnes, sympathetic to the Quie Committee proposals which would limit the number of positions which could be held by any one member, was seriously considering resigning from his chairmanship of the Republican Policy Committee in order to devote his full-time efforts to Ways and Means. But until Byrnes submitted his resignation, or let it be known that he was willing to step down, Laird's freedom to seek higher office was further limited. Finally, and probably most important, Laird recognized an obligation to side with Ford should he seek the opportunity to run. They were good friends. Both belonged to the influential Chowder and Marching Society, one of several informal House Republican social groups. They had developed a mutual trust and admiration through long association on the Appropriations Committee and a parallel devotion to conservative Republican party principles. As a close associate of both men reviewed the situation in mid-December:

> The newspapers have been wrong about this thing. If we decide to go, the difficulty won't be in deciding between Laird and Ford. It will be up to them . . . Both are big men. They are

good personal friends. They both have a great deal of admiration for each other. Once the decision is made, they will
see to it that it does not become a three-man race.

Following the Wednesday evening meeting, Griffin tried to reach
Ford at home but was unsuccessful. The next morning, Griffin, Goodell, and Quie met with Ford to report the consensus of the meeting
— that there should be a challenge, that Ford was the first choice of
most of the participants, and that preliminary assessments seemed to
indicate that Ford had a good chance of winning. Ford withheld a
final decision until he could discuss his plans with his family that
evening. However, the Young Turks were sufficiently encouraged by
Ford's response that they held a second and smaller meeting that
afternoon with other Republican members in order to take further
readings. In the meantime, Ford conferred with several friends who
were high-ranking officials of national business associations and was
not discouraged by their reactions. As he later recalled the reasons that
convinced him that he should run: "I think it was the fact that some
very good people felt I should be a candidate and that there should
be a contest for the minority leadership. I finally concluded that these
people ought to have an opportunity for a vote." [15]

Perhaps the key decision in a campaign against an incumbent leader
is the choice of an opposing candidate. Once that choice is made,
subsequent decisions of strategy and tactics are heavily influenced by
it. For example, the Ford supporters had no choice as to whether or
not the campaign would be conducted out in the open or as in 1959
behind the scenes. Even before the December 16 conference, Ford
had advised Halleck that if he decided to run, he would notify him
in advance. In any event, press reaction to the conference made an
open contest almost mandatory. Television and newspaper accounts
had so dampened the idea of a contest, that Ford's supporters felt
they had to move rapidly in order to generate momentum for a challenge. Other key decisions such as the timing of the announcement,
the content of the campaign, the decision to run independent from
other contests, the kinds of individual commitments which were
sought, and the degree of emphasis on "outside versus inside" influence, were all affected by the personality of the challenger and his
working relationships with his principal supporters.

On Friday, December 18, Ford went ahead with a planned meeting
of the incumbent minority members of the Appropriations Committee in his office. One of these members who stayed behind to discuss

the problem of leadership change was Silvio Conte of Massachusetts, an outspoken Wednesday Club member. Ford and Conte were still talking when a small delegation headed by Griffin, Goodell, and Quie arrived to get Ford's answer. Together with Donald Rumsfeld of Illinois and Robert Ellsworth of Kansas, this group formed the nucleus of the Ford campaign organization. Ellsworth, one of the more conservative members of the Wednesday Club, had gone to Ford on his own immediately following the election. They had held several conversations about party leadership before Ellsworth was invited by Griffin to attend the smaller Thursday afternoon meeting. In the two weeks which followed, Quie became less involved in the Ford campaign in order to concentrate on the ad hoc committee on party organization. Conte became less active as the need to keep the Ford campaign divorced from the Wednesday Club became more acute. In addition to this organizational core, as many as thirty additional members were to play a crucial role in the Ford campaign working primarily with their state, regional, or class delegations.

By Friday morning, December 18, it was assumed that the campaign was on. No debate ever took place as to whether Ford should run or not. Other members joined the group, and the questions became when and how should Ford announce his candidacy. Some members urged withholding the announcement until Monday, December 21, in order to gain maximum television exposure. Others argued for holding a press conference as early as possible, even though this would bring the incumbent Minority Leader back from his Florida vacation that much sooner. These members argued that it was imperative to seize the initiative and to get Ford on the telephone calling other members as soon as and as often as possible. Persuaded as much by pressure from newspapermen as by any logical arguments, Ford scheduled a press conference for Saturday, December 19, at 11 A.M. After several unsuccessful attempts to reach Halleck by telephone in Florida, Ford ended up notifying him by telegram. On Saturday morning, Ford sent a telegram to the remainder of his colleagues:

> Today I am announcing my candidacy for the minority leadership of the House. During the next two years our performance as Republican Congressmen will have a great impact on the future of our party. I am convinced that our House Republican talent, energy and dedication can and must be utilized fully if we as a party are to better represent and promote the best

hopes of the American people and if we are to become a majority party. I hope I have your support. I look forward to a personal visit with you in the near future.

My best wishes for a happy holiday season.

Jerry Ford

More than one member, and certainly Minority Leader Halleck, would find his holiday season cut short.

Ford formally launched his campaign at a press conference held in the hearing rooms of the Committee on Veterans Affairs across from his third-floor office in the Cannon House Office Building. After noting that the Republican party had controlled both the White House and Congress for only two years at the same time in the past 33, Ford called for "new ideas, new spirit, and new leadership."

> We have within our Republican ranks a great wealth of talent, energy, and dedication. When properly channeled and utilized to the fullest, this talent will promote and communicate the image of a fighting, forward-looking party seeking responsible and constructive solutions to national problems.

> By finding ways to better utilize these impressive talents through new techniques and bold leadership, by a willingness to try new ideas, by leading rather than simply reacting, we can and we must develop the respect and the support of the American people.

In the question period following, Ford promised to make 60-minute ball-players out of all 140 members of the House Republican party. The *Washington Sunday Star* featured a three-column AP wirephoto of the University of Michigan's most valuable player in 1934, football center Gerald R. Ford, Jr. Except for his receding hairline, Ford in 1964 did not look much the worse for wear.

During the question period which followed the reading of his formal statement, Ford made clear that his campaign was in no way related to the movement to replace Dean Burch as Republican National Chairman. When asked if Mr. Laird had indicated his views about the contest for Minority Leader, Ford replied:

> My candidacy is on my own. I am not a part of any slate or ticket. There will be a vacancy for the House Republican conference chairman in January. Any one of the 140 members can be a candidate at that time, Mr. Laird included.

Ford and his supporters had considered, but abandoned, the idea of running a slate headed by Ford and Laird. They had concluded that any such slate would run the risk of antagonizing other influential members who would not be a part of the slate but who might otherwise support Ford running independently. Above all, Ford wanted to run a campaign which would be non-ideological and would appeal to both the conservative and liberal wings of the party. If, for example, Ford had suggested a Wednesday Club candidate for either whip or Policy Committee chairman, he ran the risk of losing the support of those members who felt an obligation to the incumbents or those southern members who resented the role played by the liberals in the civil rights fight. If just Ford and Laird ran as a team, Ford feared the further alienation of the Wednesday Club members, who were still resentful of Laird's role as Platform Committee Chairman in San Francisco. While relatively unimportant in the House in terms of numbers, their ties to the national press and to governors such as Nelson Rockefeller of New York, and William Scranton of Pennsylvania could not be discounted. It was as much the difficulty in putting together such a slate, as the problem of maintaining party harmony afterwards, which led Ford to his decision to run independent of any other candidate.

The main thrust of the Ford campaign was based upon obtaining as many solid commitments to his candidacy as early as possible. It was hoped that then they would be able to hang on or increase their majority up through the day of the vote on January 4. These members were aware that the forces behind Halleck had estimated that they would win by 20 votes in 1959, only to barely edge Martin by four votes on a second ballot. The Ford strategy called for the candidate and his supporters to contact as many members as possible by telephone and in person before Halleck could return and begin his counterattack. Since many members were in their home districts or on vacations, one of the first steps taken by his supporters was the preparation of a master list indicating the current location and telephone number of each member. Before the campaign was over three up-dated lists had been prepared. Some 30 to 35 members used these lists or telephone numbers from them to urge members to vote for Ford.

Vote counting is an intricate process. At his press conference Ford properly avoided giving a premature answer to the question of just how many members were committed to his candidacy. Given the tendency for each side to overestimate its strength, particularly the incumbent, only the most cautious interpretation of what constitutes a commitment is justified under conditions of a secret ballot vote. At the beginning, both sides operate under conditions of imperfect information:

> You start with the boys you know are with you. Those are the ones you know best. Then, you take the boys who you know are with Halleck. You talk with other members and you build up the lists on both sides. At the beginning the bulk are in the middle and those are the ones you concentrate on. You go down the lists with other members, members who know them, who are in the same delegation, those who know who is mad at Halleck and who is close to Ford. You find out who are the people who are likely to be influential with the members.

> Without counting the new members, I would say as of now that Ford has a 3 to 1 ratio of those who are definitely for Ford or Halleck. Of course, we know our own side better. We don't know those who are definitely for Halleck. And if they are, if Ford calls, they won't tell him. So the ratio could be 3 to 2 or 3 to 3 or even 3 to 4 for Halleck. The big group right now is in the middle — the undecided. Leaving out the new members, it's god-damn close.

The 20 freshmen members presented a particularly difficult problem for the insurgents. Too much was at stake in the way of committee assignments to ask these incoming members to make formal commitments. However, a number of contacts were made to inform them on the nature of Ford's challenge and to obtain a sense of how they were leaning. In the main, freshmen members were heavily dependent upon the advice given to them by senior members from their region or state. For example, several southern members close to Ford worked at obtaining a sympathetic response from among the nine new southern and border state Republican members.

From the beginning, the Ford forces emphasized an inside strategy.[16] That is to say, the bulk of their time and effort was concentrated on member-to-member contacts. But they did not neglect "outside" or indirect pressures. They had worked until midnight Friday night, December 18, and for several hours on Saturday morning drafting Ford's press release and preparing him for the kinds of questions he might expect at the press conference. They hoped to capitalize upon front-page Sunday headlines as evidence of how Ford's favorable image would help the Republican cause in the months ahead. Other indirect pressures were utilized when and where they were thought to be effective, but the main objective of this aspect of the Ford campaign was to neutralize the efforts of outsiders. National party leaders, interest group representatives, state and local party officials and fund-raisers, who might otherwise have been active in Halleck's behalf, were told that this was an internal affair, a decision which should be left up to House members. The word was passed that "Jerry was a sound guy, that he had a good chance of winning, and it would be a good thing not to be active against Ford." Ford's position on the Defense Appropriations subcommittee, his contacts with the Michigan automotive industry, U. S. Steel, the National Association of Manufacturers, the Chamber of Commerce and other national business leaders stood him in good stead. As another member commented: "It was mostly Jerry's reputation — he had sold himself over the years." Ford also made a point of calling national political leaders, including Goldwater, Miller, Nixon, and a number of important state governors, as soon as he announced. Ford's supporters felt that it was particularly important that his efforts to oust Halleck not be associated in any way with movements to remove or keep Dean Burch as National Chairman.

As the campaign entered its second and final week, Ford flew to Michigan to join his family in a planned skiing vacation over the Christmas holidays. Ford's supporters were convinced that they had the votes to win, but they began to worry, more and more, about how to maintain their lead. The absence of a vigorous counterattack from the Halleck camp made them all the more uneasy. Griffin, Goodell, and Rumsfeld began to reach out for ways to keep alive the momentum of the campaign. Outside strategies began to occupy more of their time. Every related column and newspaper story was scrutinized for its implications and the kinds of reactions it might engender among the various wings of the party. Reprints from Ford's January *Fortune* article, "What Can Save the G.O.P.?," were mailed to as many members as possible, despite the advice of one Ford supporter who feared the moderate tone of the article might lead to right-wing defections. In the hopes of generating a bandwagon effect vote estimates were released to the AP and UP wire services on Thursday, December 31, 1964. Five days before the vote, just prior to New Year's

Day, the wire services carried stories containing the following break-downs:

Solid for Ford 61
Leaning toward Ford 20
Unknown sentiments 29
Solid for Halleck 25
Leaning for Halleck 5

Halleck aides responded by announcing their own total of 85 votes, committed and leaning to Halleck, but unlike the Ford supporters, they did not offer a breakdown of votes.[17]

Ford flew back from Michigan on Saturday, January 2. On Sunday, his supporters learned of a mid-day meeting of 10 or 12 members, mainly conservatives, to which Halleck had been invited. Three members who had been active in Ford's behalf were among those who attended. By mid-afternoon the "solid" count for Ford began to drop. Counter-efforts by Halleck and his supporters were beginning to cut into the Ford lead.

Charles Halleck had flown back from Lake Wales, Florida, the day after Ford's December 19 announcement, upset and irritated by the challenge, but confident that he could campaign and win on his record. He had several times been disappointed in his quest for higher national office, but he had never lost an election. For five times running, the citizens of the Jasper-Newton circuit in Indiana had elected him prosecuting attorney. His first success had come in 1924, following his graduation from the Indiana University Law School. In 1935 he had entered a special election and won the first of 16 campaigns for election to the House of Representatives. With the behind-the-scenes support of presidential aspirant, Governor Thomas E. Dewey of New York, Halleck emerged as Majority Leader from a field of candidates at the beginning of the 80th Congress (1947–1948).[18] He was reelected as Majority Leader for the 83d Congress (1953–1954) without opposition. As incumbent Minority Leader from 1959 to 1964, Halleck had a number of advantages. Chief among these were: (1) his demonstrated record as a party leader; (2) his position at the center of communications for House Republicans; (3) his past and present influence over committee assignments and other appointments; (4) credits built up from past favors rendered to members, particularly campaign and fund-raising speeches; (5) strong ties with outside party officials and interest group representatives; (6) extensive contacts with the national press, particularly syndicated columnists; and (7) a general reluctance to change on the part of many members.

Halleck's initial steps were calculated to utilize these assets. His first decision was to campaign on his record as Minority Leader under Eisenhower, and particularly his record of successful opposition to the Kennedy-Johnson programs. On Monday, December 21, he scheduled a press conference. The text of a statement, which had been sent to all House Republicans, was released to the press. It began:

> I expect to continue as Republican Minority Leader in the House of Representatives and will do all that I properly and reasonably can to that end. In this endeavor I sincerely hope for the support of my friends.
>
> After all, the decision is for the Republican members of the House to make. In making that decision I would assume that my record as Minority Leader over the past six years would be an important consideration.

After summarizing a number of organizational changes he had helped to implement, Halleck stressed the Republican record of solidarity in support of party principles:

> On vote after vote Republicans from North, South, East, and West — from urban and rural areas — have stood shoulder to shoulder on issues of vital importance to America. On six major issues over the past two years, our roll call votes averaged 162 to 3, an amazing example of teamwork. A study of Republican votes in the House from January 1961 to mid-1964 shows that where we had a policy position, the Republicans averaged 150 to 14 on 51 House roll calls.
>
> With our numbers reduced it is more important than ever that we continue this sort of teamwork.
>
> This would be my purpose as Republican Leader.

As the party's principal floor leader for 18 years, Halleck was in the position to know more about what kinds of influences moved men and the members' strengths and weaknesses than any other Republican in the House.

Halleck spent most of that first week activating the communication network which had been effective in the past. His first calls were to personal friends, including other members of the Indiana delegation and Les Arends, the Minority Whip. Other members, such as James

Utt and Bob Wilson of California, John Rhodes of Arizona, and Paul Findley of Illinois, called in or dropped by Halleck's office to offer assistance. Later, Halleck expanded his contacts to the deans of large state delegations and to other members for whom he had rendered favors in the past. He seldom asked for outright commitments. When he talked to freshmen members, he inquired about their committee preferences but made few, if any, outright promises. As a close associate commented on the reasons for Halleck's approach:

> Charlie feels that you cannot seek a commitment for yourself without committing yourself to repay that commitment. If you get a commitment there would be some obligation, and maybe the leader wouldn't be able to live up to his side of the agreement . . .
>
> As a leader you must be careful what you promise and to whom. It's damn practical politics not to overcommit yourself — not promise something you can't follow through on. You don't know if you can keep your promises.

Halleck did not appear to capitalize fully on his credits outstanding. If "he had money in the bank," as one close associate put it, "he wasn't able to cash in." In part, it was because Halleck was reluctant to ask others to help him. In part, his problem was complicated by the fact that many of his closest supporters had been defeated. He was aware that the contest would be decided by secret ballot, a precedent established by his own victory over Martin. Thus, commitments would be difficult to enforce. Toward the end of the campaign, Halleck began to press more strongly the claims that had been accumulated over the years.

From the beginning, Halleck's strategy in terms of inside versus outside influence had been mixed. Probably no challenger could match his ties with state and local party leaders that fund-raising dinners and appearances had helped to strengthen. Halleck's contacts with interest group representatives, enhanced by favors rendered on legislation over the years, were equally pervasive. As a Ford supporter commented:

> We knew that Charlie would make use of lobbyists. He knows most of them. A lot owe their positions in the companies they represent to their close associations with Halleck. So he has many contacts and many good friends, among them . . . And, of course, Halleck has done favors in the past for others. So these people have a vested interest in maintaining Halleck in the position of Minority Leader.

While some lobbyists would hesitate to interfere with an internal matter like a vote on party leadership, most would proceed with caution so as not to antagonize whoever might win. In some cases, veiled and more direct inquiries from district newspaper publishers and financial contributors about how members intended to vote generated more resentment than support for Halleck. Again, the secret ballot would largely render such pressures ineffective.

Halleck's national press support had probably been hurt by his performances at the Joint Republican Congressional Press Conferences. Almost any man would have been overshadowed by the mellifluous Senate Minority Leader, Everett M. Dirkson of Illinois. Quickly dubbed the "Ev and Charlie show," the straight-man, Halleck, more often than not got only a profile shot in subsequent television spots on national news programs. However, the contacts he had cultivated with newspapermen over the years were an undeniable asset. For example, during December, a number of national columnists, including William S. White, Arthur Krock, Richard Wilson, and Raymond Moley, wrote columns sympathetic to Halleck and critical of efforts being made to depose him.[19] Editorial comment was generally supportive of Halleck. Even the *New York Times* warned against the dangers of playing musical chairs with the leadership.

A final advantage possessed by any incumbent leader, one which proved particularly effective in Halleck's case as the contest drew to a close, was a general resistance to change. House members, particularly the senior Republicans, had become familiar with the ways in which Halleck operated. Any new leader would bring about a change in these working arrangements. If the new relationship might be an improvement, it was as likely as not to be less satisfactory. A number of the proposals being discussed by the Quie committee, including those aimed at limiting the number of positions which could be held by ranking minority members, were threatening to some senior members. Others, such as the second-ranking members on Appropriations and Armed Services, stood to gain. Probably no member could look forward to the vote, and the bitterness it would probably engender, without mixed feelings. These cross-pressures helped to generate further support for the status quo.

Halleck faced a series of complications as the campaign entered the final week. His efforts to reconvert members committed to Ford were inhibited by the Christmas and the New Year's holidays. Most of his supporters — and their numbers were far fewer than those working for Ford — did not get active in their telephone contacts until after Christmas. Over the weekend before the January 4 vote, as members began to reassemble in Washington, D.C., both sides launched final intensive drives to capture wavering members.

While the pace of the Halleck-Ford contest was quickening, several members close to Representative Laird of Wisconsin had quietly, but effectively, been engaged in a low-keyed operation to line up votes for their candidate for conference chairman. Laird made no formal announcement until the Tuesday after Christmas, December 29.[20] However, Representative Lipscomb of California, a close friend and long-time associate on the Appropriations Committee, had circulated a letter on December 22, 1964, urging support for Laird. His letter read in part:

> With Jerry Ford having announced that he will seek the position of Minority Leader in the 89th Congress, we will need to give attention to the task of filling the position of Chairman of the Republican Conference.
>
> I strongly believe that Mel Laird has the ability and experience to make him a very effective Chairman of the Conference and hope you feel the same.
>
> We are all aware of Mel's fine record in the House and as a member of the Appropriations Committee. In addition, he has served the Party brilliantly in positions of highest responsibility. His service as Chairman of the Committee on Republican Principles and Policies in 1962 and as Chairman of the Platform Committee for the 1964 Convention are two outstanding examples.

Several other able young conservatives, among them Robert Michel of Illinois, first elected in 1956, and James Battin of Montana, first elected in 1960, joined Lipscomb in rounding up votes for Laird's candidacy. All were in agreement that his campaign should be kept separate from the Ford-Halleck contest.

Laird's announcement for conference chairman was like a red flag to east-coast liberals. It reinforced their belief that Ford and Laird were linked in a conservative conspiracy to take over the party leadership, a leadership team which they feared Laird would dominate. Furthermore, they believed the position of conference chairman to be one possessing much greater potential for innovation than either the Policy Committee chairmanship or the position of whip, a view shared by the Laird supporters.

Later that week, the new dean of the New York Republican delegation, Paul A. Fino of the Bronx, New York, announced his support of Halleck's leadership and his candidacy for conference chairman. Laird supporters estimated that almost any liberal eastern candidate would receive as many as 50 votes. As a result of other developments, and lack of unanimous support within the New York delegation, Fino's campaign got no further than brief discussion at the New York delegation breakfast caucus the morning of the conference.

On Sunday evening, the night before the vote, Wednesday Club members, meeting at the Washington home of New York Representative Ogden Reid, decided to field a last-minute candidate of their own against Laird. After considering several possibilities, they finally settled on Peter H. B. Frelinghuysen of New Jersey, one of the few moderate members in their ranks with seniority equivalent to Laird's. Probably only a scattering of members outside the Wednesday Club were aware that Frelinghuysen had accepted an invitation to join that group after the November election.

In that same hectic atmosphere of the final weekend, the fears of the Ford supporters about their campaign peaking too early began to materialize. The swing of votes back toward Halleck continued at an increased pace through Sunday afternoon. Earlier that day, Halleck had met with a group of mainly midwestern conservatives, who put forth their demands about the kinds of changes they would like to see in the leadership if Halleck were retained. Among this group were several members who had worked actively for Ford. Griffin, Goodell, and Rumsfeld, the key counters for Ford, had been keeping their estimates as conservative as possible, changing members from solid to leaning, or leaning Ford to leaning Halleck, as more information came in. By 4 p.m., Sunday, their count had dropped to 56 solid votes for Ford. As they later commented on the arguments that were winning votes for Halleck:

> These Republicans liked Charlie and they respected him. He's been a hard-working Republican. He's spoken in many of their districts. Many of these felt they had a personal obligation to Charlie Halleck. Almost every Republican in the House is indebted to him in some way.

The challengers intensified their efforts. Ford, who at one point was considering going home for dinner, stayed on to continue his telephoning until 11 p.m. By 6 p.m., the tide for Halleck appeared to have ebbed. Several of the members who had been considered doubtful called in with reassurances or dropped by Ford's House office to report on new converts.

Attention then shifted to keeping wavering large state delegations in line. Members of the Pennsylvania delegation, which caucused at 6 P.M., were reassured that no decisions had as yet been made about House minority employees. They were upset because of rumors that one of their patronage appointees was in danger of demotion. The Ohio delegation was also a center of intense activity. One of Halleck's chief supporters in that delegation was arguing "why blame Halleck for the election outcome" and seemed to be making some inroads among other Ohio members previously leaning toward Ford. Telephone calls were made to shore up support in these and other large delegations.

Throughout the final drive every effort was made to prevent the Ford campaign from being labeled either pro-conservative or pro-liberal. In order to avoid alienating the liberals, Ford refused to meet with the conservatives who had earlier approached Halleck. Sunday evening, the Wednesday Club met to evaluate its position. As one Ford campaigner commented: "God help us if they endorse Ford as a bloc — we'll lose conservatives all over the place." Calls were made to several sympathetic members to prevent such a possibility from maturing.

A whole range of last-minute concerns kept the Ford supporters working until midnight. A respected senior member of a wavering large-state delegation was approached about nominating Ford. In part because of his past relations with Halleck and in part because of the unrest within his delegation, this member declined the opportunity. Ford turned to Michigan Representative Elford A. Cederberg, the member who had successfully nominated him for conference chairman in 1963. When Ford left about 11 P.M., he took home with him a copy of the opening day's *Congressional Record* from 1963. If he won, he would have little time to familiarize himself with procedures or to prepare his introduction of the Speaker-elect.

The Halleck supporters worked neither as intensively nor as late. In retrospect, however, most believed that their final weekend efforts had been successful. Their Sunday evening count, while not as "hard" as the Ford estimates, showed more than eighty members committed or leaning to the incumbent Minority Leader. Several of his close supporters were not as optimistic: "I thought we had a fifty-fifty chance . . . I think there was probably a greater reluctance to level with

Charlie than with Ford." And another recalled: "On the Sunday before the vote, I knew it was going to be close. I thought we would win by about two votes."

The Ford supporters spent the last hour Sunday evening going over the conference agenda and discussing various contingencies that might arise from last-minute maneuvers by the Halleck forces. Ground rules had been worked out by Clarence Brown, ranking member of Rules and agreed to by both sides. Plans were made to counteract any changes, as, for example, attempts to do away with the secret ballot agreement or to postpone the vote on the minority leadership.

As the small group of Ford supporters broke up their meeting at midnight, some 10 hours before the vote, they were cautiously optimistic. Their final estimate read:

Solid for Ford	67
Leaning Ford	22
Undecided	7
Solid for Halleck	36
Leaning Halleck	8

They reminded each other that Halleck was supposed to have at least a 20-vote edge going into the conference in 1959, and that Martin had been confident that he was going to win, too. But, they reasoned, neither side in 1959 had been engaged in anything like the organizational effort that they had gone through in the past two weeks. Compared to 1963, they felt much more confident. Again, that contest had been a much more spontaneous and short-term effort. Except for some pre-conference telephoning by Ford and endorsements at state delegation breakfast meetings the following morning, the challengers had done about all they could do to ensure Ford's success.

The first Republican conference of the 89th Congress was gaveled to order promptly at 9:30 A.M. on Monday, January 4, 1965 by its outgoing Conference Chairman, Gerald R. Ford, Jr. Since Ford was a candidate for higher office, he turned the gavel over to the past Vice Chairman, William Cramer of Florida, who was subsequently elected temporary chairman by acclamation. Another southern Republican, Richard Poff of Virginia, was elected temporary secretary, and the first roll was called to ascertain a quorum.[21] All but one of the 140 Republican Representatives-elect were present for the first call. The last Republican member came in after the vote on the permanent conference chairman, but in time to participate in the Ford-Halleck contest. Thus, every Republican member was present to vote in 1965 as compared to the 146 votes cast out of a possible 153 in 1959.

The next order of business was especially critical — the adoption of rules, including provisions for secret ballot elections for contested offices. Both Halleck and Ford had accepted this provision in advance following the precedent set in the Martin-Halleck contest of 1959 and ratified by the procedures governing the Ford-Hoeven contest in 1963. It had also been decided that nominating speeches would be limited to a single spokesman for each candidate. The Ford forces suffered several anxious moments brought on by an earlier comment in the Illinois delegation breakfast caucus that Arends, who had fought for an open ballot for Martin in 1959, might make a similar appeal this time. However, Brown offered the rules resolution as agreed upon, and it passed without a dissent.

The next item on the agenda was the election of a permanent conference chairman. Lipscomb nominated Laird. Frelinghuysen, who had not been put forward as a candidate until 8 P.M. the previous evening, did not arrange for someone to nominate him until he talked with fellow New Jersey Representative William T. Cahill on the way to the conference that morning. Frelinghuysen was, perhaps, as surprised as anyone by the strength of his showing, 62 votes against 77 for Laird. He had reaped the benefit of what anti-Laird sentiment existed, together with most of the east-coast regional vote. In addition, it appeared that a late Sunday evening telephone call to Halleck by John Lindsay of New York had generated a scattering of votes from among Halleck and Arends supporters for the Wednesday group candidate.[22] Some of these Halleck people felt that Laird had worked behind the scenes for Ford, if not pushed him into the campaign. Lindsay, Bradford Morse of Massachusetts, and several other liberals, apprehensive about Laird dominating Ford and believing that there was little to choose between the conservatism of Ford as compared with Halleck, were to respond by casting their votes for Halleck for Minority Leader.

Ford was nominated by Elford Cederberg of Michigan; Halleck by Ross Adair of Indiana. Both members took the highroad in their nominating speeches and talked mainly of the virtues of their respective candidates. The mechanisms of the vote were simple. No formal roll was called. Members merely wrote the name of one or the other candidate on white slips which had been provided and dropped their ballots into a closed box placed on a table sitting in front of Representative Catherine May of Washington, the chief teller. To the consternation of Representative May and her fellow congressmen, no matter how many times they counted the ballots, the tally came out 72 votes for Ford, 68 for Halleck, and one ballot marked "present." This totalled 141 votes, or one more than the full quorum of Representatives-elect. In order to prevent any possible charge of misconduct, the newly-elected Conference Chairman, Melvin Laird, ordered a second roll call. This time members brought forward their ballots as their names were called alphabetically. Despite some last-minute efforts to change the outcome, the lines held firm, and Ford was elected the new Minority Leader by a vote of 73 to 67. The former incumbent moved to make the vote unanimous. In the few minutes remaining before the new Congress convened, the Republican members re-elected John Byrnes as Policy Committee Chairman. They also listened to a brief explanation from Brown on the Republican position on proposed changes in House Rules.

Approximately one-half hour later on the House floor, all of the Republicans joined ranks to vote for Ford for Speaker of the House of Representatives for the 89th Congress. To no one's surprise his Democratic opponent, John W. McCormack of Massachusetts, was overwhelmingly reelected. Ford was to find himself a Minority Leader in more ways than this, even within his own ranks, in the months ahead.

Why did Ford win and Halleck lose? As with all close leadership contests, a range of factors combined to decide the outcome. Halleck's own cryptic explanation masks as much as it reveals. "It's the only election I've ever lost," Halleck said, "and it was because I got myself involved in a beauty contest." Much more was at stake than contrasts in age and physical appearance, as the respective statements of the two candidates on December 19 and December 21 clearly demonstrate. While ideology in terms of their voting records was not directly at issue, the activists were able to convince a majority of their colleagues that Ford would project a more positive image to the nation and work toward more constructive alternative programs within the House of Representatives.

Personal factors — "the mysteries of how men interact with one another, of what leads people into enmity, jealousy, friendship" — played an important part in the outcome.[23] Some members were so dominated by strong friendship, a long-held grudge, or intense personal ambition that they made up their minds early for one of the two candidates and were not budged. The vast majority of the members approached the vote with considerable ambivalence. As a key Ford lieutenant commented:

> Most members were trying to make an assessment on the merits of the two candidates and most were torn between. They were, themselves, in conflict. They were moving in different directions, struggling to decide which way to go. These were guys really trying to think about what was best for the party, not just what was best for themselves.

A Halleck supporter echoed these remarks: "I doubt if any person who voted did not have mixed feelings at the time." Since close leadership contests inevitably involve a high degree of personal indecision, the search for an underlying rationale for change, and the ability to seize the initiative and maintain the momentum of the campaign became all the more important.

The necessary, but not sufficient, cause for revolt was the Republican election disaster of November 1964. The Goldwater defeat and the net loss of 38 Republican House seats created the psychological climate within which revolt flourished. Some of the same pressures which eventually led Dean Burch to tender his resignation as Republican National Chairman in mid-January 1965 were at work in the overthrow of Halleck. The Goldwater nomination and the election results created more internal dissension and unrest in the Republican party than any event since the split between the Taft and Roosevelt wings of the Republican party in 1912. But Halleck, unlike Burch, was not primarily a scapegoat. The dissatisfaction with Halleck extended back to bitterness engendered by Halleck's defeat of Martin in 1959. This irritation and unrest was compounded by the continuing frustrations of the minority status of the Republican party. Agitation for change, only temporarily dampened by Ford's defeat of Hoeven in 1963, intensified throughout the long and trying sessions of the 88th Congress. Halleck could not be directly blamed for the election debacle, but it provided an excuse for promoting a revolt that had been long fermenting. It was not so much the psychological climate created but the kinds of House Republicans who were defeated that ultimately made a change in leadership possible. The activists, led by Griffin and Goodell, would not have challenged Halleck's leadership unless they thought they had a good chance of winning. In the main, it was the more senior and conservative members who were defeated in the 1964 election. It was the older survivors who subsequently rallied behind Halleck in his contest with Ford. Without the heavy election losses of 1964 it was extremely unlikely that a challenge would have been initiated. The continued frustrations of minority status and increasing dissatisfaction with Halleck's leadership probably made an eventual challenge inevitable.

By late November, however, sentiment in favor of a leadership change had largely abated. Only a scattering of members had returned to Washington. Many had gone south for vacations or were out of the country. While a few members were still debating ways to improve party leadership, perhaps a majority of the members had by that time decided to go along with Halleck and Arends for at least another two years. It was at this point that the Curtis letter was circulated to the membership. As a key participant later recalled: "It was like throwing a match into some tinder that was dry." The Republican Conference in mid-December was called for purposes other than leadership change. Its most important consequence, however, was to put Halleck on test and bring back to Washington a widely diversified group of younger activists, convinced that the first step toward achieving majority status was new and more vigorous leadership. Of the two most likely challengers, Gerald R. Ford, Jr. of Michigan and Melvin R. Laird of Wisconsin, Ford emerged as the candidate with the better chance of winning. By dint of superior organization and hard campaigning the Young Turks were able to establish an early lead for their candidate which was never relinquished. Ford was successful because some 30 to 35 members worked actively in his behalf to obtain commitments from a majority of the 140 Republican Representatives.

Halleck's counterattack was a classic illustration of "too little and too late." His first decision was to campaign on his record. From the beginning, he underestimated the strength of his opposition. He did most of his own telephoning. He had far fewer members working actively in his behalf. He seldom asked for commitments and he failed to press home the natural advantages accruing to the incumbent. Not until the last days of the campaign did he begin to go all out in calling in the obligations owed to him for past favors rendered. As a close associate reviewed the Halleck campaign:

> Ours was a low-key operation. The other side was cranked up. Halleck felt he had made his record as best he could, and if that wasn't good enough, OK. It was not a great production over here. There were no panic buttons pushed as far as he was concerned.

Halleck did not even make full use of the potential influence he could exercise on committee assignments, particularly with freshmen. While the Ford supporters were able to contact every member at least once, a number of Republicans never heard from the Halleck camp, including at least two freshmen. As one of these commented:

> One thing that impressed me about the Ford people were the statistics. They apparently had the votes to back them up. Halleck was claiming he had 85 votes, but he hadn't even bothered to contact me. If Halleck was that much out of touch with his troops, he wasn't doing a good job as far as a leader. Frankly, this had as much to do with my vote as anything. That impressed me very unfavorably.

As Halleck concluded: "The vote was 73 to 67. I didn't go all out. I could have put a lot of heat on in a lot of places and, I think, changed the outcome. It was my decision to campaign on my record."

Despite Halleck's slow start and his tendency to go it alone, the tide was turning in his favor in the final stages of the campaign. The many advantages possessed by an incumbent began to have their effect. An observation by one member, who was listed as "solid" by the Ford supporters until just before the vote, is revealing:

> A lot of people just didn't know how they were going to vote up until the end . . . I waited myself until the morning of the vote to make up my mind. I finally decided to vote for Halleck. There were so many reasons to vote for Ford, but not enough reasons to vote against Halleck.

And as a member of the Indiana delegation commented:

> Charlie was better known. He came into the districts; he met the party workers. He was one of the best campaign fundraisers there was. I'm sure this bothered a lot of people who had made commitments to vote against Charlie. Their consciences hurt them, because they had been the people who had said, "Gee, Charlie, I'm having a fund-raising dinner in my district. Will you come and help me?" And Charlie would say, "Well, I'm tied up and awfully busy, but I'll come out and do it for you anyway." And out he'd come. This helped us particularly as the lines began to narrow, as we began to know where people stood. I think it began to affect the outcome. If we had had a few more days here on the spot, Charlie could not have been tipped.

The secret ballot prevents any definitive assessment of the final vote. It is possible, however, to reconstruct from newspaper accounts and interviews a reasonably accurate estimate of the breakdown of votes by state delegations. Halleck's chief sources of strength came from his own Indiana delegation, a substantial majority of the Illinois delegation headed by Arends, and near stand-offs in the large California and Ohio delegations. Halleck probably retained a majority of Ohio's fifteen votes; Ford won a somewhat higher proportion of California's fourteen votes. In addition to these votes, Ford's winning coalition was composed of his own Michigan delegation, the preponderance of votes in New York, Pennsylvania, New Jersey, and the New England states, and an unexpectedly high proportion of southern Republican votes. When a shift of four votes will make a difference in the outcome, all votes are crucial. However, Ford's ability to enlist the support of several senior southern Republicans in his behalf including Poff and Cramer was among the most central factors in his victory. In addition, Ford held an edge in most of the middle-sized state delegations such as Wisconsin, Kansas, Minnesota, and New Jersey. With the possible exceptions of these two states, no medium-to-large state delegation, save for the candidate's own states, lined up solidly for either member. Many of the smaller state delegations split their votes as well. In terms of ideological support, Ford received a substantial majority of the Wednesday Club members' vote, more than held his own with the moderate conservatives, and picked up most of the south and a scattering of hard-core conservatives elsewhere. Halleck, in contrast, did somewhat better among the most conservative members outside the south, almost held his own with the moderates, and picked up as many as six or eight liberal votes. Ideology was not directly at issue, but differences in outlook were reflected in the "Young Turk versus Old Guard" division which developed. In the final analysis, it was the bottom-heavy structure of the House Republican party which made victory possible for Ford. The bulk of his support, and certainly the organizational nucleus of his campaign, came from members elected since 1956.

Whether Halleck could have reversed the outcome if he had gone all out, or if he had put on "a lot of heat in a lot of places," is, of course, a moot question. It does seem probable that if the campaign had continued for a week into the session or if the secret ballot mechanism had not been operating, Halleck would have retained his position. But these are academic speculations. For want of a reversal of four votes on the morning of January 4, 1965, Halleck's long career of party leadership in the House of Representatives was ended.

EPILOGUE

If the events culminating in the January 4, 1965 Republican conference vote ended the leadership career of Charles Halleck, they also thrust Gerald R. Ford into a position of major responsibility. Over the next nine years he was to build a reputation, first as an effective opposition leader to President Johnson and, later, as a loyal supporter of President Richard M. Nixon's legislative programs. The size of the House Republican minority was to increase by 50 seats, but never expand beyond a high-water mark of 192 members in the 91st and 93d Congresses.

Most of his colleagues found Ford to be a man of his convictions, eminently fair, and willing to keep the door open to Republican colleagues of all ideological persuasions. Conservatives and moderates found him easy to work with, a leader willing to share power. Even Representative Donald W. Riegle, a liberal Michigan Republican who switched to the Democratic party in February 1973 would assess Ford's record as minority leader in generally positive terms:[24]

> Ford's sense for the issues and his leadership ability are probably best measured by his performance as House Minority Leader from 1965 through 1968 rather than by the past five years [1969–1973]. For Ford's behavior has varied dramatically, depending on the party in the White House.
>
> With Lyndon Johnson as President, Ford was an activist, creative Minority Leader. When the Republicans gained the presidency, Ford seemed to see his role as limited essentially to that of advancing and defending Nixon positions.

Richard M. Nixon had begun 1973, his fifth year in office, in triumph. He could claim credit for ending American military involvement in Vietnam. Visits to the Peoples Republic of China and the Soviet Union seemed to have significantly improved our international relations and the cause of world peace. The economy of the United States, while continuing to show signs of inflation, nevertheless seemed prosperous. Nixon had won a second term in the White House by an impressive margin — 60.7 percent of the two-party vote.

Gallup polls in early February 1973 showed 68 percent of the American public approving Nixon's handling of the job of President.

But his triumph was short-lived. The attempted Watergate cover-up, the resignations of high-level White House officials, murkiness as to the extent of the President's involvement, the threatened indictment of Vice President Spiro T. Agnew and his subsequent resignation — all contributed to the plummeting esteem of the Nixon Administration. Through the balance of 1973, Nixon's relationships with Congress continued to deteriorate. His public opinion ratings dropped to a low of 25 percent approval.

On October 12, 1973, a beleagured President turned to Congress to nominate House Republican Leader Gerald R. Ford of Michigan to succeed Spiro T. Agnew as Vice President of the United States. Mr. Nixon set forth three criteria he followed in choosing Ford:[25] (1) He should be an individual who is "qualified to be President." (2) He should be one "who shares the views of the President on foreign policy and national defense." (3) He should be able to work with both parties in Congress. Seven weeks after his nomination, following extensive congressional hearings, and overwhelmingly favorable confirming votes in the Senate and the House, the 25-year House veteran was sworn in as the 40th Vice President of the United States.[26] Admitting that he was a "Ford, not a Lincoln," his confirmation nevertheless enhanced speculation that if Nixon were impeached or resigned, Republicans might well have a strong standard bearer in Ford for the presidential election of 1976.

The Selection of a New Minority Leader. Even as Ford was being nominated for the vice presidency, speculation was put forth about who the House Republicans would choose as their new Minority Leader. On October 15, 1973, 57-year-old John J. Rhodes of Arizona, the chairman of the House Republican Policy Committee, became the first candidate to announce. In a letter sent to his 191 colleagues, Rhodes promised that he would "work with all Republican members in order to make this Congress one of solid legislative accomplishments." A 21-year House veteran and the second-ranking minority member on the powerful House Appropriations Committee, Rhodes was to prove to be so strong a candidate as to force all other contenders to either withdraw or not announce at all. Personally popular and respected, ideologically close to Ford,[27] Rhodes had the further advantage of a number of close friendships inside and outside the House. Chief among these were fellow members of the class of 1952, Bob Wilson of California, the former chairman of the Republican Congressional Campaign Committee; and Melvin Laird, no longer a member of the House but still a powerful influence as White House counselor in charge of domestic programs. Three weeks after he announced his candidacy, on December 7, 1973, Rhodes became the first unanimously elected Republican Minority Leader since the selection of Joseph Martin of Massachusetts in 1939.

For a brief period it appeared that Rhodes would not get by without a full-scale contest. On the same day that Rhodes letter was circulated, two other conservative Republicans — Leslie C. Arends of Illinois and Samuel L. Devine of Ohio — announced their candidacies. The 78-year-old Arends had served as party whip for 30 years under three successive Republican floor leaders — Martin, Halleck, and Ford. Devine, a member of the House since 1958, was elected Vice Chairman of the Republican conference in 1971. (At that same opening day conference he had come close to upsetting the current Chairman, John B. Anderson of Illinois, but lost by a vote of 81 to 89.) Devine, an informal leader of the "Republican Regulars," a group of mostly senior conservative G.O.P. members, was to withdraw from the minority leadership contest the following day pledging support to Rhodes "in the interest of party unity." [28]

Most close observers of the House considered John Anderson, a moderate, to be Rhodes' strongest possible opposition. First elected in 1960, the 51-year-old Anderson had won the conference chairmanship in 1969 after Laird left that post and the House to become Secretary of Defense. The most liberal of the House G.O.P. leadership, Anderson had often been at odds with the White House and conservatives in the House. His problems were further complicated by the already announced candidacy of Arends, the dean of his delegation. It would be unprecedented for a congressional party to bestow the two top leadership positions upon Representatives from the same state. Finally, Anderson was seriously considering a possible challenge to incumbent Democratic Senator Adlai E. Stephenson III in 1974. Conceding that at best his chances would be "uphill," Anderson reluctantly announced on October 16, 1973 that he too would not be a candidate for the minority leadership.

By Wednesday, October 17, Arends remained the sole challenger to Rhodes; however, the contest was all but over.[29] It mattered little, save perhaps to Arends, that he had received the unanimous endorsement of his 14-member Illinois delegation. Over the weekend of October 20–21 came the Saturday night massacre — the firing of Special Watergate Prosecutor Archibald Cox and the resignation of Attorney General Elliot Richardson. A staunch supporter of Nixon, Arends was apparently deeply affected by these events. Making little headway against Rhodes, Arends finally decided to withdraw from the contest on October 24. Twenty-two days later, on November 15, 1973, Arends would announce his plans to retire from the House at the end of the 93d Congress.[30] His career would encompass 40 years of congressional service.

From the outset Rhodes had enjoyed wide support. On the day of his announcement he had told reporters, "It looks so good it scares me. I wish the vote could be tomorrow." [31] His initial lead discouraged Anderson from entering; it forced Devine and Arends to withdraw weeks before the Republican conference finally met to choose its new Minority Leader. No other candidate had the following that Rhodes had built up over 21 years in the House, the last nine as Chairman of the Republican Policy Committee. Anderson had little hope of overcoming his moderate voting stance, the lack of enthusiasm for his candidacy from the White House, and a delegation already splintered by Arends' candidacy. The 78-year-old Minority Whip had just been around too long; few Republicans wanted to provide him with the minority leadership as a consolation prize for the remainder of the 93d Congress.

On December 6, 1973, the House of Representatives approved the nomination of Gerald R. Ford as Vice President of the United States. The following morning, the House Republican conference unanimously endorsed John Rhodes as its new Minority Leader.

NOTES

1. This chapter is based on observation of these events from early December 1964 to January 1965, and interviews with over forty Republican Representatives and ten key staff members during and after the Ford-Halleck contest. I would like to acknowledge my indebtedness to these members and also to numerous readers of an earlier draft. While I have tried to avoid excessive footnoting, I have made extensive use of newspaper accounts from the *Washington Post*, the *Washington Star*, the *New York Times*, and *The Wall Street Journal*.
2. Halleck was given his choice of several high-ranking positions on committees on which he had previously served, including Rules, Government Operations, and House Administration. He selected Public Works in order to continue his fight for a deep water harbor in his district near the Burns Waterway site,

a project which has come in conflict with the Indiana Dunes National Lake-shore Park bill.

3. Charles O. Jones, *Party and Policy-Making: The House Republican Policy Committee* (New Brunswick, N.J.: Rutgers University Press, 1964), pp. 32–38; Joe Martin, *My First Fifty Years in Politics* (as told to Robert J. Donovan) (New York: McGraw-Hill, 1960), pp. 3–19.

4. "Ford Election Sparks Shifts in GOP House Strategy," *Congressional Quarterly Weekly Report*, XXI (February 8, 1963), pp. 149–156. From Ford's point of view his candidacy was not a planned step on the road to the minority leadership. As he recalled these events in 1965: "There was no design, no specific plan to go after the minority leadership, at least in my mind, when we made that campaign. But it enabled me to establish a rapport with this group — these young fellows like Charlie Goodell and Bob Griffin. It showed us what could be done if you were organized and were able to carry through your plans. Of course, then, we didn't have as much time. It was kind of a spontaneous candidacy. But we got our feet wet, and we learned how and what we had to do in order to be successful."

5. For a description of the usefulness of this device for inter-party cooperation and a similar operation, referred to as Halleck's "clinic," see Neil MacNeil, *Forge of Democracy: The House of Representatives* (New York: David McKay, 1963), pp. 81–84.

6. Halleck's choice of George Goodling of Pennsylvania over Silvio Conte of Massachusetts for a minority vacancy on the Migratory Bird Conservation Commission, and his appointment of Jack Westland of Washington instead of John Saylor of Pennsylvania for a vacancy on the National Forest Reservation Commission, illustrates the problem. Both Westland and Goodling were among those Republican incumbents who were defeated in 1964. Conte and Saylor were early and active Ford supporters. Victory brings its rewards, however. Late in January Ford appointed Conte to the Migratory Bird Conservation Commission and Saylor to the National Forest Reservation Commission, *Congressional Record* (daily ed.) *Digest* (February 1, 1965), p. D57.

7. A full page advertisement in the *New York Times* listing the 62 House members who endorsed Goldwater prior to the convention concluded: "We are convinced that the nomination of Senator Barry Goldwater by the Republican party will result in substantial increases in Republican membership in both Houses of Congress." (*New York Times*, July 7, 1964, p. 21.)

8. Marshall McNeil, "Halleck Meets Opposition," *Washington Daily News*, October 28, 1964, p. 28.

9. Ronald Sharp, "Michigan Congressman Praises Halleck as U.S. Minority Leader," *Warsaw* (Indiana) *Times-Union*, October 29, 1964, p. 1.

10. For the origins of the Wednesday Club, its subsequent enlargement, and the role its members played in the Ford-Halleck contest and its aftermath, see Paul Duke and Stanley Meisler, "Republicans After the Debacle: 1. The Frustrated Moderates," *The Reporter*, February 11, 1965, pp. 26–28.

11. Excerpts from the Curtis letter are reprinted in *Congressional Quarterly Weekly Report*, XXII (December 4, 1964), pp. 2766, 2789. The quotations are taken from a copy of the original letter.

12. Rowland Evans and Robert Novak, "Inside Report: The December Caucus," *Washington Post*, November 30, 1964, p. A17. In addition to the independent and respected Curtis, this group included able young members from four important state delegations — Michigan, New York, Minnesota, and Illinois — and at least one Representative from each of the classes elected since 1956 with the exception of the freshman class.

13. On January 14, 1965, just prior to the vote which reelected Arends as Republican whip, the Republican conference adopted an amended version of this proposal. Ford, as Minority Leader, had already given up his position on Appropriations; Byrnes had indicated his intentions to resign as Policy Committee Chairman; and Arends had decided to step down to second-ranking minority member on Armed Services. If a party leader resigns or is deposed in the future, he will resume the position on the committee to which his previous seniority entitles him.

14. A possible candidate for higher office before 1964, Byrnes had all but been eliminated from consideration because of unfavorable publicity arising from his relations with the Mortgage Guaranty Insurance Corporation of Milwaukee, Wisconsin, a company which had also figured in the Bobby Baker hearings. For background, and Mr. Byrnes' subsequent denial of any "wrongdoing or intention of wrongdoing," see *The Wall Street Journal*, November 22, 1963, p. 26; 109 *Congressional Record*, pp. 226–34–22642.

15. Another Republican member compared Ford's decision to run with the drafting of Eisenhower in 1952 — a response to a call for public duty: "My impressions of Ford are that he is not personally ambitious, but rather desirous of filling whatever role that he could and should fulfill. He was not a guy dying to become Minority Leader." Several of his more cynical colleagues, however, pointed out that Ford began his political career by defeating an incumbent Republican congressman, the late Bartel J. Jonkman, in 1948; that he did not discourage discussion of his possible candidacy for the vice-presidential nomination in 1960 and 1964; and that Ford has not abandoned consideration of higher national office.

16. "The inside strategy is likely to define situations as 'family matters,' and to feature face-to-face interaction among members. The outside strategy is likely to evoke a more ideological, issue-oriented definition of the situation. Interaction among members is more likely to take place through third persons, lobbyists, and the press." Nelson W. Polsby, "The Strategies of Influence: Choosing a Majority Leader, 1962," ch. 3 of this book.

17. Robert K. Walsh, "Two House Factions Ask Open Caucus Voting," *Washington Star*, December 31, 1964, p. B3; "Halleck, Ford Both Claim Leadership Victory," *Washington Post*, January 1, 1965, p. A2. The Ford forces went so far as to allow the AP and UPI representatives to examine the lists which they had compiled in order to authenticate their counts.

18. Halleck, as Republican Congressional Campaign Committee Chairman, rode the crest of a net gain of 56 House seats in the 1946 election. A fellow Rules Committee member, Clarence J. Brown of Ohio, was one of several major contenders. Another was Senate Minority Leader, then Representative, Everett Dirksen of Illinois. (*New York Times*, January 3, 1947, p. 1.)

19. White's first column, "Unrest in Congress: Knives Drawn in Both Parties," *Washington Post*, December 9, 1964, p. A20, illustrates the hazards of premature prediction: "But that the vari-colored rebellions in the House — whether against the Halleck Republican orthodoxy or the Williams-Watson Democratic heterodoxy — will come to nothing whatever is a sure bet already." Events subsequently proved him wrong on both counts. White's later columns are more cautious, but as strongly pro-Halleck, "Verdict on Halleck: Purge of G.O.P. Leader Opposed," *Washington Post*, December 23, 1964, p. A22; and "New Congress: Senseless Bloodletting Abounds," *Washington Post*, December 30, 1964, p. A20. For examples of other columns sympathetic to Halleck, see Arthur Krock, "In the Nation: Ancient Ritual Impending in the G.O.P.," *New York Times*, December 22, 1964, p. 28; Richard Wilson,

"Halleck Has Impressive Record for Action on Major Legislation," *Minneapolis Tribune*, December 24, 1964, p. 4; and Raymond Moley, "Halleck vs. Ford," *New York Herald Tribune*, January 3, 1965, p. 13. Several of these columns were clipped, photocopied, and sent to House Republicans by a member of the Indiana delegation.

20. "Laird Seeks to Head House G.O.P. Conference," *Washington Post*, December 30, 1964, p. A2. The strategic advantages enjoyed by Laird are summarized in a column by Rowland Evans and Robert Novak, "Laird is Sitting Pretty: Wisconsin Congressman Will Win Whether Halleck or Ford Gets G.O.P. Leadership," *Washington Post*, December 27, 1964, p. E7.

21. Cramer and Poff were subsequently elected to the positions of Vice Chairman and Secretary of the conference for the 89th Congress. In early January both positions were accorded higher status as part of the formal leadership as the result of Quie Committee recommendations and conference approval.

22. One of the more enjoyable stories which circulated the corridors of Capitol Hill after the vote was a comment attributed to the Senate Minority Leader, Everett M. Dirksen, allegedly made in the Senate minority caucus, Monday morning, before the House conference results were known: "Charlie is in good shape — that New York fellow made a deal with Halleck and he will win by 30 votes." This apparently true story helps to illustrate the vast informational gulf which separates the two sides of the Capitol.

23. Polsby, *op. cit.*, p. 75.

24. Donald W. Riegle, Jr., "Ford: Nixon's Better Idea," *Washington Post Outlook*, December 9, 1973, pp. B-1, B-6.

25. Carroll Kilpatrick, "Rep. Ford Picked for Vice President," *Washington Post*, October 13, 1973, p. A-1. Democratic Speaker Carl Albert appears to have had more to do with the selection of Ford than anyone except the President himself. It was Albert who advised Nixon that Ford would have the least difficulty being confirmed of any possible nominee. "A Voice in Naming Ford: Carl Albert," *New York Times*, October 15, 1973, p. 10.

26. Ford was confirmed by a vote of 92 to 3 in the Senate on November 27, 1973. The House vote of 387 to 35 took place on the late afternoon of December 6, 1973. He was sworn in at a joint meeting of the two Houses an hour later.

27. "Whenever I have to leave town," Rhodes told reporters, "I tell them to pair me the way Ford votes." Richard L. Lyons, "Rhodes Moves to Cinch Ford's House G.O.P. Post," *Washington Post*, October 16, 1973, p. A-2.

28. *New York Times*, Oct. 17, 1973, p. 30.

29. "Rhodes Seems Certain to Take Ford's Place," proclaimed the *Washington Post*, October 17, 1973, p. A-2; the *New York Times* was predictably more cautious, "Rhodes of Arizona is Leading Race for Post of Minority Leader," October 17, 1973, p. 30.

30. Forced to run from an almost entirely new congressional district in 1972, Arends had encountered primary opposition for the first time since 1960.

31. *New York Times*, October 16, 1973, p. 32.

CHAPTER FIVE

The Selection of a House Majority Leader, 1971: The Candidates

At the opening of the 92d Congress in January 1971, House Democrats elevated three senior party leaders to higher office. On January 21, 1971, Carl Albert of Oklahoma, majority leader since 1962, was elected the 46th Speaker of the United States House of Representatives. Two days earlier, a majority of his Democratic colleagues had advanced incumbent whip, Hale Boggs of Louisiana, to the position of majority leader. The strong and spirited challenge of Representative Morris K. Udall of Arizona and three other contenders had come to little avail. In a final triumph for the establishment, the two top Democratic leaders turned to a veteran Rules Committee member Thomas P. "Tip" O'Neill, Jr. of Massachusetts, a co-chairman of the Democratic Congressional Campaign Committee, and appointed him as majority whip. Opportunities for advancement up the ladder of leadership succession in the House had come about when the 78-year-old former Speaker, John W. McCormack of Massachusetts, retired at the end of the 91st Congress (1969–1970).

When do such campaigns for major leadership posts in the United States Congress begin? In the immediate sense, of course, a campaign may be said to date from the period when vacancy is first revealed, or challengers decide to revolt against the existing leadership. Thus, to the outside public and not a few journalists, May 20, 1970, the date that Speaker McCormack had held a press conference announcing his retirement plans, would appear to be a logical beginning. In a second and more fundamental sense, leadership contests begin in the minds of the major candidates much earlier. As their legislative careers unfold, crucial turning points occur, opportunities which advance them toward or close forever their chances to step upon the lower rungs of a leadership ladder.

Who are these leaders and challengers? How did their legislative careers develop? When did they first begin to see themselves as potential leadership material? Questions such as these preoccupy an active minority of the membership of all organizations, but especially the seasoned incumbents of freely-elected national legislatures such as the U.S. House of Representatives.

Only a few — perhaps as low as 10 percent — of the 435 members who serve in the House each Congress, some for many terms, ever come to be considered potential elective leadership material. Many, of course, get siphoned off for important legislative leadership roles culminating in committee chairmanships. If past experience is relevant, and it appears to be, then the one man who has most to say about grooming future leaders is the Speaker of the House. Without his help the lowest rungs of the ladder — whip or caucus chairmen — are difficult to attain.

Twice, in 1962 and 1971, candidates had tried to grasp the middle rung of the ladder, the office of majority leader, in a lateral fashion. Both times these attempts failed. Instead appointive whips were elevated to elective majority leadership positions. In 1962, as we have seen, Majority Whip Carl Albert overcame the challenge of Richard Bolling of Missouri, and was elected without need to resort to a contested caucus vote.[1] The present case study relates how Hale Boggs moved from whip to majority leader, disposing of four opponents, in a contest which took two caucus ballots before he received a majority. Because of its complexity, this study is divided into three chapters. This chapter introduces the major contenders and explores the initial strengths and weaknesses of their campaigns. Chapter 6 develops the campaign chronology in detail from May 1970, until the eve of the Democratic Caucus on January 19, 1971. Chapter 7 presents the details of the caucus vote, and discusses the aftermath of the election, including the appointment of a whip.

I

From a short-run perspective then, this hard-fought majority leadership contest began with John W. McCormack's decision to step down as Speaker at the end of the 91st Congress. Carl Albert, the incumbent Majority Leader, had long since spread the word that he would be a candidate for Speaker when and only when McCormack retired or died.

Why did Speaker McCormack decide to retire at the end of 1970? The most immediate reason seems clear. More than a dozen possible contenders were waiting to file for his 9th District, South Boston seat, should it become vacant. At least one was threatening to run against the 42-year House veteran, admittedly with no hope of success. McCormack might have announced his plans earlier were it not for indictments against Dr. Martin Sweig, his long-time legislative aide, and Nathan M. Voloshen, a lobbyist and friend, involving the alleged use of the Speaker's name and office for unauthorized purposes. After asserting his own innocence and suspending Sweig pending future investigations, the Speaker declared his intentions to seek reelection in 1970 and serve as Speaker in the 92d Congress.

Throughout 1969 and early 1970, moreover, McCormack was under increasing attack from younger, more reform-oriented members of his party. Just before the opening of the 91st Congress, four-term Representative Morris K. Udall of Arizona challenged the aging Speaker. (Udall was six years old when McCormack won his first House seat.) On January 2, 1969, McCormack easily won the nomination to a fifth term as Speaker by a Democratic Caucus vote of 178–58. However, the Democratic Study Group won the concession of regularly scheduled monthly caucus meetings. In February 1970 California Representative Jerome R. Waldie's resolution of "no confidence" in the Speaker's leadership was tabled by a vote of 192–23. Still the mounting criticisms took a toll.

Probably the principal reasons the Speaker decided to step down were personal. Although 78 years old, he was still in good health. But Eugene T. Kinnaly, his administrative assistant for over 25 years, had died in 1969. McCormack's wife, Harriet, at 85, was in increasingly poor health and soon to be hospitalized. The love and devotion of the McCormacks to one another was legendary — he claims never to have missed a dinner with her. Even before 1968, the Speaker had talked about looking forward to a time of "rest and relaxation." His sense of loyalty to his country and party made him reluctant to retire in the same year that President Lyndon B. Johnson decided not to run for reelection. By the end of 1970, McCormack would have served for nine years, longer than any other Speaker except his predecessor, Sam Rayburn, who served for 17 years. All these reasons, public and personal, affected McCormack's May 20th decision.

II

In the process of announcing his retirement decision Speaker McCormack went out of his way to endorse and praise warmly the man he
felt should succeed him. Carl Albert, said McCormack, is "an ad-
mirable man who performed his duties diligently. I was blessed to
have him as my majority leader." Albert, who had been given little
notice of the Speaker's impending decision, nevertheless wasted no
time sending a personal letter to the offices of all of his Democratic
colleagues:

> As you know, our beloved Speaker, John McCormack, today
> announced his decision to retire at the end of this session of
> Congress. This will advise I am a candidate for Speaker in the
> 92nd Congress. I will sincerely appreciate your signing up in
> support of my candidacy.

Endorsements were quick to come — from Richard Bolling of
Missouri, Albert's opponent in his campaign for majority leader in
1961–1962; from Morris Udall, who simultaneously announced his
candidacy for the majority leadership; and, perhaps most important
of all, from Wilbur Mills of Arkansas. As chairman of the Ways and
Means Committee, Mills was probably the one member of the House
who had the requisite skills and prestige to run Albert a close race
in a head-to-head contest. Unlike Albert's support, most of Mills'
strength was southern, big-city, and conservative. Had such a race
materialized, members of the moderate-to-liberal Democratic Study
Group might well have swung the balance of power to Albert. Although many northern issue-oriented congressmen remained fearful
that Albert might prove too cautious, they nevertheless preferred
Albert over Mills. No such challenge developed, however, and before
the month was out Albert had received favorable responses to his letter from more than 100 members. Albert spent little time personally
requesting support from members. Instead, he was content to work
through senior members of his own state and the deans of other delegations.

The personal endorsements of two House leaders — incumbent
Whip Hale Boggs and Caucus Chairman Dan Rostenkowski — never
were given to Albert. Why were these two men, both of whom were
prominently mentioned in speculation about the majority leadership,
reluctant to indicate their support? Decisions to not routinely endorse
the candidate almost certain to be the next Speaker reveal a great

deal about the personalities, strengths, and shortcomings of three prime actors in the making of a Speaker, a majority leader and the unmaking of a potential whip.

It was nearly certain that Majority Leader Albert would be elected the next Speaker of the House for three basic reasons: tradition, personality, and geography. To begin with, Albert benefited from a clear-cut tradition of succession from the majority leader to the Speaker. Of 13 Speakers who have served in the twentieth century, Albert was the tenth to advance directly either from majority leadership or from minority leadership following a congressional election turnover in party control. Indeed, Udall's challenge to McCormack at the opening of the 91st Congress was the first contested election for nomination to the Speakership since 1923.[2]

A former Rhodes Scholar, Phi Beta Kappa member, and national oratorical champion, Albert first entered the House in 1946. His class of freshmen members was particularly distinguished, including future Presidents John F. Kennedy and Richard M. Nixon. Albert was born in McAlester, Oklahoma in 1908. From the age of six he expressed an interest in Congress, an ambition that was realized at the age of 38. At 5 ft. 4 in., Albert came to be known as the "little giant from Little Dixie." Effective floor debate and hard work on the Committee on Agriculture soon brought the young Oklahoman to the attention of then Democratic Speaker Sam Rayburn of Texas. Representing adjacent districts across the Red River, the two men had much in common, and a warm friendship developed. When a vacancy occurred in the appointive position of whip in 1955, Albert was selected over several other likely candidates, chief among them Hale Boggs.[3] As a partial compensation to Boggs, a new position of deputy whip was created for the equally ambitious Louisiana congressman.

Boggs had more seniority than Albert (first elected to the House in 1940, but then defeated after his first term and not reelected until 1946), but he was by-passed for several reasons. Speaker Rayburn was intensely loyal to members who considered, as he did, the House as a career. Perhaps he resented Boggs competing for the Louisiana gubernatorial nomination in 1952. Albert, in contrast, never openly considered abandoning the House for a possible alternative political office. Second, because Albert was from Oklahoma, a border state, he might have been a somewhat more acceptable appointment to other House Democrats than that of a straight southerner, even a liberal, reform-oriented, urban Democrat like Boggs. Finally, and probably most detrimental to his appointment, Boggs was a Roman Catholic. Rayburn could hardly have been considered anti-Catholic, but he may well have been reluctant to have both his majority leader (McCormack) and the whip of the same faith. (As developed later at length, the Catholic issue proved to be an important underlying factor in the 1970–1971 majority leadership contest, only that time it worked in Boggs' behalf.)

In 1962, following Speaker Rayburn's death at the end of the first session of the 87th Congress, McCormack, Albert, and Boggs all advanced up the leadership ladder with only a limited challenge to Albert from Richard Bolling of Missouri (Chapter 3). McCormack was nominated for Speaker without opposition. Albert was unanimously elected majority leader and they turned to Boggs as their choice for majority whip.

Throughout his 24 years in the House Albert had practiced a code of personal and party loyalty — first to Speaker Rayburn, and later to Speaker McCormack — with a voting record generally consistent with the principles of the national Democratic party. "I look upon myself as a down-the-road Democrat," he declared. "Speaker Rayburn often described himself as a 'Democrat without any prefixes or suffixes.' I look upon myself as being that kind of Democrat, plain and unvarnished." [4]

On the floor Albert's early skills at oratory stood him in good stead. He could be partisan without resorting to demagogy. As a presiding officer his gavel was firm, his grasp of the parliamentary situation acute. He was also seen as an extremely dedicated worker and a perennial worrier — both factors may have contributed to his heart attack in September 1966. If by 1970 he was moderating his pace more, it was not reflected by an almost continuous frown and frequently wrinkled forehead as he strolled the corridors or sat on the House floor. Yet, Albert could also turn on one of the widest and friendliest grins in Washington, and he was noted for the interest he took in the welfare of his colleagues. [5]

> I guess you could say that the main element in my climb to the leadership is the fact that I've heard more speeches than anyone else and called more people by their first names. I've always been fascinated by them. There are so many variances and eccentricities. I got so that I could guess within a few votes how they vote on any given issue.

Here, of course, Albert was not only stating how he got to be a leader, but reaffirming what is basic to successful legislative leadership, that is, knowledge of the members and their constituencies. This was one of Rayburn's supreme strengths. And Albert seemed intent on patterning his Speakership after Rayburn's, with suitable modifications to take into consideration the expanding role of the Democratic Caucus and the changing issues of the 1970's.

Albert's interest in other congressmen seems to have been reciprocated by his colleagues. One reason he easily advanced to the Speakership was summed up in a widely affirmed statement — "Nobody's mad at Carl." His critics might complain that he sometimes vacillated, that he was too apprehensive about antagonizing other members to take the right action and move vigorously to enforce it, but almost no one would deny his popularity. In a *National Journal* poll of House Democrats taken in early May 1970, Albert came across as the "most popular" Democratic congressman in the House.[6]

Moreover, nearly every member assumed that Albert routinely would succeed McCormack; nearly all members, that is, except Albert. Taking no chances, he not only set in motion machinery designed to secure every Democratic member's vote, he also declared himself neutral in the contest as to who should become the majority leader. His simple explanation — "I can't get involved; these men are my friends" — masked several benefits of his position but also created one major potential liability. Admittedly, neutrality was the best way to insure his own election. Further, it can be conceded that it would make his job as Speaker relatively easier. Staying above the battle, he would be in a position to help heal any wounds that a bitter internecine fight might engender. It could be argued, however, that his endorsement of one strong candidate could have prevented such a fight from developing. And his neutrality also meant that whoever was elected majority leader would come on board with little or no obligation to Albert as Speaker. Why did Albert take the stance he did, especially since it ran counter to the quiet but effective support which acting Speaker McCormack gave his own campaign against Bolling in late 1961? Why wasn't 1970–1971 merely a replay of what happened nine years earlier, that is, a mere token challenge to the appointive whip as he sought to move up to an elective position?

To answer these questions it is necessary to explore the personality and background of the man who eventually succeeded to the majority leadership, Hale Boggs of Louisiana. Why was his reputation at such a low ebb when McCormack announced his decision to retire? How did Boggs overcome his initial disadvantage and go on to win quite handily?

III

Well, at the beginning there were about 10 or 12 contenders. For a time there I could walk around the floor and look at any fella and say, "Well, he's one of my opponents."

— Hale Boggs, *CBS Morning News*,
January 20, 1971

By his early 50s Hale Boggs had established the most impressive House career of any of his contemporaries. First elected to Congress at the age of 26, he served as the youngest member of the 77th Congress (1941–1942). Defeated in 1942, he returned to Congress in 1946 after service with the U.S. Maritime Commission and the Naval Reserve. Two years later, Speaker Sam Rayburn singled him out for appointment to the powerful Ways and Means Committee. By 1969 he had risen to the position of ranking majority member, second only to its prestigious chairman, Wilbur Mills of Arkansas. And, of course, membership on this committee simultaneously brought with it membership on the Democratic Committee on Committees, which was charged with making committee assignments and transfers. Since 1962 he had been serving as whip, or the number three man in the Democratic party hierarchy.

If any one trait could have been said to characterize Boggs, it was forcefulness. His six-foot frame carried some 200 pounds. By the early 1970's a heavy shock of black wavy hair had taken on salt-and-pepper coloring. He remained one of few who could preside over the House and obtain almost instant attention with a quiet rap of the gavel. Boggs' stock-in-trade were intensive personal relationships with members of the House built up over 26 years in Congress, 16 of which had been in a leadership capacity, first as deputy whip and later as whip. Over the years he has earned a reputation as an expert on trade and economic policy. Almost every member conceded that Boggs made a vigorous floor presentation and projected well on national television shows such as "Meet the Press." Aggressive, intelligent, as charming as nearly any House member when he wanted to be, Boggs was nevertheless in deep trouble with his colleagues when the majority leadership vacancy occurred.

From the characteristic of "forcefulness" to charges of arrogance and aloofness was an all too easy step. Many of Boggs' critics were quick to single out these traits. Complained one fourth-term member from the West: "He seems to hold many members in contempt and they resent it. Boggs is much like Lyndon Johnson — very arrogant." A more senior midwestern member coupled Boggs' apparent aloofness with a lack of availability on the floor. "He comes in, stands around the floor with that damn *New York Times* folded under his arm. Then, before you can talk to him, he's ducked out the back door and headed for that hideaway of his. You can't get to him." [7] Others close to Boggs defended him:

> His was not the intellectual and moral arrogance of a Morris or Stewart Udall; it was a different kind. Boggs felt that once you were elected to the House you were a politician in your own right and past the stage where you needed to be coddled. He just got impatient with other members from time to time.

Criticisms of Boggs' unapproachability or disdain might have led to a challenge to Boggs in any event, but it was a more deep-seated concern about alleged "emotional instability" which brought most of the candidates who ran against him into the fray. In 1968 and 1969 the majority whip seemed to be under considerable stress and tension. Two non-candidates, one from his own Ways and Means Committee, another, a closely concerned friend, described several of the incidents which contributed to the charges:

> We had this mark-up session in committee — Hale came in, his face flushed; he was coherent, but arrogant as hell — he wanted to monopolize the session. The Chairman just kept quiet and let him run along. It finally seemed to work itself out.

> Boggs came on to the floor — his face was flushed. It was as if he had taken a couple of amphetamines, or a couple of "belts." His arms were pumping up and down. He was speaking loudly, but not making much sense.

Opposing candidates were, if anything, more critical. Here are interview comments from his four announced opponents, all dated from interviews held several months before the January 19, 1971 caucus.

Hale Boggs — I still can't believe that he's a serious contender. But he's come back some from June. At that time an awful lot of people were very leery of Boggs ... I'm against Boggs becoming majority leader because he doesn't have sufficient emotional stability to undertake the job.

My normal inclination would have been to support Boggs, but his performance the last year or two — drinking or some sort of carrying on — convinced me he shouldn't be majority leader. I did a little checking around and I decided he couldn't win. He had no solid support, not even in the South. I looked over the other candidates and decided to become one myself.

Boggs had to come out strong, but very early I became convinced he did not have the votes, not even in the South ... My honest impression is that Hale Boggs is the least popular of the candidates — he has stepped on the toes of too many members, he's arrogant, and last year he must have flipped his lid. Now, he's desperately trying to recoup.

If it wasn't for personal weaknesses of Boggs, his succession to the majority leader would be a foregone conclusion. And that pattern is still his greatest asset. I had a liberal tell me today that it was a serious question in his mind as to whether or not we should upset the pattern of moving up from whip to majority leader.

With such intensely held feelings prevalent among at least a strong minority of the Democratic membership in the House, it was not surprising to find references to an alleged problem of instability appearing in the press. For example, *The Nation*, on February 9, 1970, carried a long article critical of the Democratic leadership and reporting stories of Boggs "abusing his authority" and rambling in debate on the House floor. One most potentially damaging story about House leadership change was written by former *Harper's* editor, John Fischer. Fischer was an old Oklahoma friend and Rhodes Scholar classmate of Carl Albert's. Writing for the October 1970 *Harper's*, Fischer singled out Morris K. Udall of Arizona and Dan Rostenkowski of Illinois as the two leading candidates to succeed Albert as majority leader. Boggs was written off in one brutal paragraph:

One might suppose that Hale Boggs, the present whip, would be a natural candidate for promotion to the leadership, as Albert was before him. Ordinarily that would be the case —

but in handling his whip's duties Boggs has offended too many people. "Supercilious" and "overbearing" are some of the kinder terms other congressmen used in characterizing him. In addition, many regard him as emotionally unstable and prone to crack under pressure.

Ordinarily, such an essay, even in as widely read a magazine as *Harper's*, would not have aroused undue concern in the Boggs camp. But this article was given added credibility by the author's long association with Albert. Matters were not helped by the actions of national editor, Willie Morris, who arranged for reprints to be sent to every Democratic member of the House. Just how many members read, let alone gave credence to, the article, is another question. Probably the article served to reinforce biases already held by congressmen.

Did Boggs show some signs of emotional instability in 1968 and 1969? More important, if elected to majority leader, would he be "prone to crack under pressure?" There is little question but that Boggs had been under severe stress prior to the majority leadership contest. First, so long as Mills continued to serve in the House, Boggs was effectively blocked from assuming the chairmanship of the Ways and Means Committee. Second, he held an appointive position of leadership — he had never been put to a test of his peers' support. Boggs knew, however, that it was merely a matter of time until the test came, perhaps as early as January 1969 if McCormack followed his original intentions to retire at the end of the 90th Congress. Third, Boggs took on an extremely stressful assignment in August 1968, the chairmanship of the Democratic platform committee at Chicago. He had been able to work out accommodations on most of the issues confronting a badly divided Democratic party, save for the plank on Vietnam. Agreement on that controversy was ultimately hammered out in floor debate, probably to the satisfaction of almost no one. Finally, and perhaps most crucially, Boggs encountered in 1968 the most difficult election campaign of his last 24 years in the House — a campaign he won by a bare 51 percent of the vote. Two close elections back-to-back would almost certainly have eliminated him from further consideration for higher leadership positions in the House. All these stresses, coupled with Boggs' strong drive to become Speaker, must have led to fierce tensions. To these were added the common occupational hazard among some congressmen, an urge for a drink or two to relieve the pressures, and this might account for the temperament and behavior attributed to Boggs during 1968–1969.

Supporters of Boggs seemed tolerant of whatever had transpired and they turned out to be a majority in the House. A midwestern congressman, who accompanied Boggs to Europe after his arduous 1968 campaign, observed, "We're lucky, we don't have to run for re-election in New Orleans." Said another, "Sure he might have had some problems, but who doesn't, and look how he pulled himself together, once the campaign (for majority leader) began."

Even taking into account the low number of returns and the possible bias of respondents (only 74 replies from 245 House Democrats), evidence of the low ebb of Boggs' reputation in the House was provided also by an early May 1970 poll sent out by *National Journal* just before McCormack's decision to step down. When asked, "Regardless of your personal feelings toward the individuals, who would you say are the three Democratic congressmen with the strongest leadership ability?", the results were as follows: (composite score: 3 pts., first choice; 2 pts., second choice; 1 pt., third choice):

Mills, Ark.	104
Albert, Okla.	68
Udall, Ariz.	57
Bolling, Mo.	18
O'Hara, Mich.	17
Fraser, Minn.	15
Boggs, La.	11
Edmondson, Okla.	9
Rostenkowski, Ill.	8

Quite likely personal antagonisms may have contributed to these assessments of reputation and performance.

The most difficult blows were to come from Boggs' fellow leaders, McCormack and Albert. Boggs was never officially notified of Speaker McCormack's press conference on May 20, 1970. Instead, he heard about it from reporters and had to elbow his way into the Speaker's rooms to get his customary chair near the right side of the Speaker's desk. Contrasted to his strong endorsement of Albert's candidacy, all that the Speaker could come up with when asked about Boggs' possible candidacy was that he had been an "able and loyal" whip. Some stories that covered the Speaker's conference dropped the first adjective. Although McCormack was later to become one of Boggs' strongest supporters, Albert, for reasons already advanced, maintained his neutrality up to the very end of the majority leadership contest.

May and June of 1970 were low points in Boggs' campaign. In assessing various candidates for the majority leadership, the *Washington Post* found Boggs "too liberal for the South, yet (with) little support in the North." The lead *New York Times* story covering McCormack's decision to retire did not even mention the majority whip as a leading contender. Perturbed, if not discouraged, Boggs never bothered to announce his candidacy, except by word of mouth, until after the November elections. Reasoning that the race was to be won or lost on the House floor, he quietly set about to convert the senior members of southern and other state delegations. He also made a personal call upon George Meany, the President of the AFL–CIO. Boggs advised Meany that he would run and reminded Meany of his past and continuing friendship to labor.

If his campaign was low-keyed, even listless at times, it was because Boggs, too, was not totally optimistic about his chances.

IV

Once Speaker McCormack announced his decision to retire, two younger moderate-to-liberal candidates — Morris K. Udall of Arizona and James G. O'Hara of Michigan — declared their candidacies immediately. Wayne L. Hays, a more conservative, "establishment" Democrat entered the race a week later. The last candidate to challenge the incumbent whip, B. F. Sisk of California, entered the race on November 19, 1970 only after the campaign of another Californian, Deputy Whip John Moss, appeared to be making no headway. The ages, committee assignments, and House service of the principal candidates for majority leader are summarized in Table 5.1.

V

"Mo" Udall was dreaming of a pot at the end of a rainbow. You don't get to the end of a rainbow very often in this town.

— Washington lobbyist

Morris K. "Mo" Udall of Arizona was the second youngest candidate in the race (48), the one with the least seniority (nine years), had served on two of the least prestigious committees in the House (Post Office and Civil Service, and Interior and Insular Affairs), and

Table 5.1
Profiles of Announced Candidates for the Majority Leadership Contest, 1970–1971 [a]

	Hale Boggs	Wayne Hays	B. F. Sisk	James O'Hara	Morris Udall
District	La.(2)	Ohio(18)	Cal.(16)	Mich.(12)	Ariz.(2)
Democratic Members in State Delegation	8	7	20	7	1
Years in Congress	26	22	16	12	9
Number of Members with more Seniority [b]	20	32	59	82	118
Committee(s) and Rank (Chairman = 1)	Ways and Means(2)	House Admin.(1) Foreign Affairs(3)	Rules(6) Agric.(13)	Educ. and Labor(8) Interior(13)	P.O. and Civil Service(4) Interior(8)
Leadership positions	Whip			Asst. Whip	
Vote ratings [c]					
ADA	48	32	44	92	76
COPE	86	83	80	86	83
ACA	16	17	7	17	0
Date announced candidacy, 1970	Dec. 2[d]	May 27	Nov. 19	May 21	May 20

[a] All rankings and ratings are for the end of the 91st Congress unless otherwise noted.
[b] Seniority rankings as of the beginning of 92d Congress, *Congressional Quarterly Weekly Report* 29 (January 15, 1971).
[c] *Congressional Quarterly Weekly Report* 29 (April 16, 1971), pp. 866–867. The three groups making ratings are: Americans for Democratic Action, AFL–CIO Committee on Political Education, and Americans for Constitutional Action.
[d] Boggs did not formally request the support of his returning colleagues until a letter was circulated on December 2, 1970. Informally, he was active only after late May.

began with one of the smallest House delegations supporting him (only his own vote). As Udall was quick to quip: "My delegation caucuses in my bathtub." Yet, despite these initial handicaps, from the beginning of his formal announcement on May 20, 1970 until his defeat by Boggs on January 19, 1971, Udall was either out front or running a close second.[9]

Udall first came to Congress following a special election on May 2, 1961. His oldest brother, Representative Stewart Udall, had accepted an appointment as Secretary of Interior in the newly formed Kennedy administration, thus creating a vacancy in the Second District, the most southern Arizona congressional district. The second of three sons of the late Levi S. Udall, Chief Justice of the Arizona Supreme Court, Morris was born in St. Johns, Arizona on June 15, 1922. He was elected president of the student body in 1947 at the University of Arizona, where he earned a law degree in 1949. A childhood accident that resulted in the loss of an eye did not deter Udall from a prominent athletic career in college. Indeed, at 6 ft. 5 ins., Udall went on to play professional basketball for the Denver Nuggets.[10] He then returned home to practice law and serve first as deputy and later as Pima County (Tucson) Attorney. When in 1954 a congressional vacancy occurred in the southern Arizona district dominated by Tucson, both Morris and Stewart considered running. Family considerations detained Morris from entering the contest and Stewart was to serve three full House terms, and part of a fourth, before moving on to the Kennedy Cabinet.

When the younger Udall, Morris, arrived in Washington in 1961, he better understood the duties and complexities of a congressman's life than most entering freshmen. Almost from the beginning, he hoped to become a leader in the House. At that time, he would sit on the floor of the House with his *Congressional Pictorial Directory* putting the faces and pictures of the members together, so that he eventually knew the names of all his colleagues on both sides of the aisle. Following in his brother's footsteps, he soon became active in the Democratic Study Group, a loose affiliation of more than 100, mostly northern and western moderate-to-liberal members. In 1963, he helped to revive a bipartisan set of seminars for freshmen congressmen, in cooperation with the American Political Science Association. These meetings served as catalyst for a book entitled *The Job of the Congressman*, by Udall and Donald Tacheron.[11]

To write a book is one task, but to begin to make a name for himself as an accomplished legislator was something much more complicated. Udall did well also in this arena. Drawing on oratorical skills developed in his days as County Attorney, Udall sponsored a series of interior and postal bills. One crowning achievement was the passage of a federal pay raise that included a salary increase for his fellow congressmen from $30,000 to $42,500 per year.

Udall appeared likely as a candidate for future House leadership in other respects. His district had become increasingly "safe." Winning reelection in 1962 by 58 percent, the young Arizona congressman had increased his margin to nearly 70 percent in his last two elections, 1968 and 1970. Moreover, he was widely regarded as one of the most articulate speakers in the House. Udall combined technical mastery of legislation with a quick mind and a wry, engaging sense of humor.[12] All these qualities were prime requisites for a successful floor leader.

What finally made Udall stand above other possible contenders was his audacious challenge to the incumbent Speaker at the opening of the 91st Congress in 1969. Udall realized, of course, that he would have little chance of winning — his was a symbolic challenge. He stated in advance that even if he should receive more votes than McCormack, he would request that a second vote open to all contenders be held. After a feverish two-week campaign Udall went into the January 2, 1969 caucus with what he felt were 85 firm commitments. He found then, as he was painfully reminded once again in 1971, that "firm" commitments give way under natural pressures to side with a winner. The 1969 result was Speaker McCormack, 178, and Udall, 58. (Four votes were cast for Wilbur Mills, a man who was not even nominated.)

Udall emerged from his 1969 defeat with a major attribute, a hard core of dedicated supporters who were firmly committed to Udall's candidacy should he decide to run again. Most were junior members — four terms or less. Their ideology was predominantly liberal. When Speaker McCormack announced his intention to retire, Udall could and did take an immediate lead in the search for vote commitments. However, Udall's forced confrontation with the Speaker was not without liabilities. Not only did he earn the ire of McCormack, Udall also made it difficult for himself to gain subsequent support from older colleagues, especially along the heavily Catholic Northeast urban corridor.

VI

> I don't think I will have much trouble with outside groups.
> They have worked well with me on legislation as compared
> with the other candidates, and for that matter, anybody else
> in Congress.

— James G. O'Hara
October 5, 1970

The second candidate to enter the race was competitive, hard-working
James G. O'Hara of Michigan. A past chairman of the Democratic
Study Group, O'Hara was viewed by almost all his colleagues as a
vigorous and effective spokesman for labor, educational and civil
rights causes, and, ideologically, slightly to the left of Udall. Wasting
little time once he had heard of McCormack's decision, O'Hara sent
a telegram to his colleagues on Thursday morning, May 21, advising
them that he was holding a press conference at 10:00 A.M. that same
day. The purpose, as stated, was to announce "my support for Carl
Albert for Speaker and my own candidacy for majority leader in the
next Congress." A member of Congress since 1958, the 45-year-old
O'Hara represented the southeastern Twelfth District of Michigan,
suburban Macomb County, plus several precincts in northern Detroit.
On his initial appointment to the Education and Labor Committee,
O'Hara quickly established a reputation as one of its brightest and
most indefatigable workers. By 1970, though he still lacked the necessary seniority to command a subcommittee, O'Hara was widely regarded as one of the two or three most competent legislators in the
fields of labor, education, and civil rights policy in the House.[13] Sometimes his caustic tongue and no-holds-barred tactics earned enemies;
despite this, most of his adversaries seemed to respect him. Along with
Richard Bolling's, O'Hara's advice on legislative tactics and parliamentary procedure was sought by other Democratic Study Group
members.

Not all of O'Hara's assets, however, were readily transferable into
leadership support. First, he had to compete with Udall for most of
the change-oriented votes in the House. As the long summer extended
into the fall, O'Hara discovered that many of the votes he hoped for
had been preempted by his Arizona colleague. Second, O'Hara's
strong positions on labor and civil rights issues made him an anathema

to most southerners. Further, many conservatives, including some big-city-machine congressmen, resented O'Hara's liberal stance on education, social welfare, and issues of party reform. Finally, the outside interest group pressures that O'Hara could bring to bear proved to be rather ineffective in a contest decided by secret ballot voting.

O'Hara's personality and family-oriented style of living made his candidacy, if anything, more difficult. He was far from the classic old-style Irish politician of the big-city machine. Late afternoons and evenings did not find him ensconced at the Democratic Club in the Congressional Hotel or the Rotunda, sipping drinks with colleagues or lobbyists. Nor did he spend much time at the congressional gym or steam room unwinding after long legislative days. Instead, his idea of "getting away from it all" was to climb into the cockpit of one of his two small sailboats along with one of his sons and engage in some competitive racing. (He and his wife, Susan, who helped nurse him back to health in a Veteran's Hospital after the war, have seven teen-age children.) O'Hara's socializing with his congressional friends is confined mainly to weekdays. He prefers to spend evenings and weekends with his family.

For these and other reasons O'Hara was probably the most ambivalent of all of the candidates about staying in the race, once entered. He found fulfillment not alone from close family life and his sailing, but also from being at a point in his legislative career where he could "pick his own spots," that is, to choose the kind of legislation with which he wished to become actively involved. The life of a majority leader, observed O'Hara in mid-campaign, might not be all that enjoyable. "You would have to take up every [legislative] cat and dog that came along." Instead of working with chairmen with whom you share mutual respect, "you deal with guys you don't always care to deal with." But O'Hara could not quite persuade himself to drop out, though his campaign did not shift into high gear until the final two weeks of the contest.

VII

Either way I couldn't lose.

— Wayne L. Hays
December 1, 1970

Wayne L. Hays of Ohio entered the contest for majority leadership on May 27, 1970, for two basic reasons, one negative and one positive.

As he looked over the several announced candidates — Udall and O'Hara, and other likely contenders, Boggs, John Moss of California, and perhaps Rostenkowski — Hays found himself unimpressed. More important, as a tough-minded, mainstream Ohio congressman, Hays felt he could reach and hold a broad spectrum of House Democrats:

> Members don't want extremes on either end — right wing or left. I felt I could appeal to the moderate members in both groups, the non-extremists in the South and the non-extremists among the liberals ... The ultra-liberals don't like me and neither do a few reactionaries like that guy in (a southern state), the guy who beat (former member). I can't think of his name at the moment, but he'd be against me and others like him.

Beginning with a solid majority of Ohio's seven Democratic members, Hays hoped to extend his support into the neighboring states of West Virginia, Pennsylvania, and throughout the Midwest. Unlike most northern and western candidates, Hays' tough foreign policy stance and "hawkish outlook" on Vietnam, gave him a solid bridge to southern support. He was confident that a close friendship with Mendel Rivers (Chairman of the Armed Services Committee until his death in late December 1970), could be parlayed into a majority of votes in the South Carolina delegation, plus support from other southern militants as well.[14]

Possessor of one of the most caustic wits and sharpest tongues in the House, Hays' style of floor debating had yielded several converts and not a few enemies. A Hays supporter relates the following story about himself. As a freshman he had given a one-minute speech critical of the Republican leadership, after which he was quickly gaveled to silence by Speaker McCormack. Then Gerald Ford, the Republican minority leader took the floor and lambasted him for what seemed like three or four minutes. No Democratic leader rose to defend the freshman member, but then, in his words:

> Some guy stood up and began defending me and shredding the hide right off the Republicans. It made me feel "right" again. The guy walked off and never said a thing to me. I had to ask somebody else to find out who he was — it was Wayne Hays.

Not all of Hays' caustic one-minute speeches on the floor earned admirers. More than one Democrat, with scars hardly healed, would remember and put Hays near the bottom of his own list of preferred candidates for majority leader.

Hays, a life-long resident of Belmont County, Ohio, had served the constituents of the east-central Eighteenth District of Ohio since 1948. As an undergraduate Hays majored in history and political science at Ohio State University. He has held public office at all levels of government — mayor of Flushing, Ohio, state senator, county commissioner, and congressman. By 1970, the former speech writer and history teacher had enough seniority to hold a third-ranking position on the Committee on Foreign Affairs and ranking membership on House Administration. Following the 1970 primary defeat of House Administration Chairman Sam Friedel of Maryland, Hays was in line to assume that top position in the 92d Congress. As Hays later summed up his activities: "I didn't put on much of a campaign. I felt pretty relaxed about it. I knew I'd end up majority leader or Chairman of House Administration — either way I couldn't lose."

VIII

The outlooks of these four candidates, Boggs, Hays, Udall, and O'Hara, and a fifth candidate, B. F. Sisk of California, who waited until after the fall congressional elections before launching his campaign, suggest several observations. None were ideologues; all candidates came from within the broad middle spectrum of the party, with Udall and O'Hara somewhat left of center. What the various candidates stood for, how they had voted on the many issues, was a factor in determining who eventually was acceptable to a majority of House Democrats.

On roll call votes when a majority of Democrats voted against a majority of Republicans in the 91st Congress, all five candidates for majority leader were with their party more than 60 percent of the time. As Table 5.2 suggests, Hays and Boggs were both somewhat more inclined than the other three candidates to stray from closed partisan ranks and vote with Republicans. Yet Boggs was only half as likely as the average southern Democrat to vote in opposition to a majority of House Democrats.

More revealing, yet, are conservative coalition scores for the second session of the 91st Congress (1970). Using then Majority Leader Albert's record for comparison, Boggs and Sisk have nearly identical patterns of voting — supporting the conservative coalition about two-

Table 5.2
Candidates for House Majority Leadership,
1971: Ideological Comparisons

	PARTY UNITY SCORES 91ST CONGRESS 1969–1970		CONSERVATIVE COALITION SCORES[a] 1970	
	Unity	*Opposition*	*Support*	*Opposition*
Albert, Okla.	79	14	36	57
Boggs, La.	71	19	36	59
Hays, Ohio	60	13	25	43
O'Hara, Mich.	82	12	7	93
Sisk, Cal.	62	19	34	52
Udall, Ariz.	80	13	11	77
Average				
North Democrats	66	15	15	63
South Democrats	43	40	64	17
All Democrats	59	24	—	—

SOURCE: *Congressional Quarterly Weekly Report*, XXIX (January 29, 1971), No. 5, pp. 237–247.
[a] See Note 15 for a CQ definition of conservative coalition scores.

fifths of the time, opposing it about three-fifths of the time.[15] Hays places slightly lower on both conservative coalition support and opposition scores than Boggs, Sisk, or Albert. This largely reflects missed votes, which lower the scores. In contrast, both Udall and especially O'Hara have much lower conservative coalition support scores, 11 and 7 percent, respectively, for the 44 roll call votes so categorized in 1970. In other words, Udall was somewhat left and O'Hara more so on this major measure of a right-to-left voting continuum in the Congress. Northern Democrats, on the average, opposed the conservative coalition some 63 percent of the time and joined it about 15 percent of the time.

Members of the House put only limited faith, if any, in such academic measures as party unity or conservative coalition scores. In close association with each other day after day, all faced with making decisions on over 300 roll call votes per session, most members can predict with considerable accuracy their party brethren's ideological responses to and feelings about a given bill. Their impressions of other members quite naturally are heightened when it comes to judging prospective candidates for leadership.

For the great majority of members the ideological viewpoints of the candidates were fairly set — Boggs, Hays, and Sisk were establishment candidates, the Louisiana member seen as a little more progressive, if not liberal, than the transplanted Texan or the rural Ohioan. (One of Boggs' image problems through the early stages of the campaign involved overcoming a cliché — "too liberal for the South and too southern for the North" — which seemed to flow from one newspaper rewrite desk to another, up and down the eastern seaboard.) In contrast most members viewed Udall and O'Hara as change-oriented, left-of-center, reform candidates. Udall had begun to downplay his role in the Democratic Study Group several years before his 1969 challenge to McCormack. He was never able to make a clean break, even if he thought it strategically wise, since the broad base of his support had to come from these same moderate-to-liberal members. O'Hara's strong and effective advocacy of education, civil rights, and labor causes and his past chairmanship of the Democratic Study Group had stamped him as the most liberal of the five candidates.

Democratic members would not choose a Majority Leader solely on ideological grounds. Clearly, however, only a broad middle-range voting pattern was acceptable, as witnessed by the ideological moderatism of the three most recent men who had made it to majority leader and Speaker, Rayburn of Texas, McCormack of Massachusetts, and Albert of Oklahoma.

Probably only the candidates themselves paid attention to CQ, AFL–CIO, and ADA vote ratings. Here, too, the moderate-to-liberal candidates, Udall and O'Hara, seemed to place the most emphasis on analysis of voting records. As early as January 1970, Udall commissioned a memorandum in which his voting records in the 90th Congress and the first session of the 91st were compared to those of other possible candidates, Mills, Rostenkowski, Boggs, Boland, O'Hara, Bolling, and Albert. O'Hara's staff mimeographed a number of vote ratings for the five publicly announced candidates for distribution to selected members and the press. One key vote haunted Udall — on repeal of Section 14b of the Taft-Hartley Act in 1965, the Arizona congressman voted for recommittal and against final passage. Despite the fact that Arizona had already enacted its own right-to-work law, labor unions used this vote against Udall even though his overall voting record was generally supportive of labor. The establishment candidates — Boggs, Hays, and Sisk — seemed to feel less need to justify their voting performances. Further, their staffs were less likely to include anyone with a political science background.

Nuances about a candidate's position in the past or in the future could be important. The new majority leader, whoever he was, would play a central role in future legislative decisions on tactics and strategy. In turn, these day-to-day leadership decisions — when to offer an amendment, what form it should take, who should offer it — would mount in importance. Indeed, over time such decisions can crucially affect whether or not the rank-and-file members, especially the freshmen, returned to Congress or went down to election defeat.

IX

Given the hesitancy of most members to commit themselves to anyone but a front-runner at such an early stage in the contest, it was not surprising to find other possible contenders considering the plunge. Most held off until they could take private soundings on the degree of enthusiasm which their candidacy might engender. The national press was, of course, not hesitant in its speculations. At least five members — John E. Moss of California, Richard Bolling of Missouri, Edward P. Boland 2nd, Thomas P. O'Neill, Jr. of Massachusetts, and Dan Rostenkowski of Illinois — were frequently mentioned as possible contenders following Speaker McCormack's announcement of his retirement plans.

Austere John Moss, a highly respected member of the Government Operations and Interstate and Foreign Commerce Committees, had served as deputy whip since 1962. Moss' campaign never really got untracked, in part because of a rather constrained personality, in part because of the ideologically schizoid nature of the 20-member California delegation. By the time Moss formally announced his candidacy, Boggs and Udall had already tapped as many as three to five votes each in this prime hunting ground. Not until late November was a showdown finally held in the delegation when B. F. Sisk of Fresno entered the race.

With few intellectual peers in the House and an acknowledged reputation as a skillful floor strategist, Richard Bolling of Missouri again was mentioned in the press as a possible candidate for the majority leader. However, the 22-year veteran and third-ranking member of the Committee on Rules made no effort to become a candidate or even get involved on behalf of another candidate. Still, he was quick to endorse Carl Albert for Speaker. The two men had made a rapprochement since Bolling's uphill, last-ditch effort to upset Albert's bid for the majority leadership in 1961–1962.[16] Few House members seemed to take Bolling's "availability" very seriously in the 1970–1971 contest for Majority Leader. His caustically written books on House operations, procedures, and reform had enhanced his national reputation but had hardly endeared him to his senior colleagues.[17] His own role in the majority leadership contest remained marginal and behind the scenes. "I'm for someone and against someone else," appeared to be the extent of his involvement.

Long-time roommates, "Eddie" Boland and "Tip" O'Neill of Massachusetts seemed to engage in a classic case of Alphonse and Gaston throughout the summer and fall of 1970. Both first elected to the House of Representatives in 1952, the two men shared a northwest Washington, D.C. apartment when they did not commute to their home districts. Boland represented Springfield; O'Neill, Cambridge and part of Boston. Initially, both men were hindered by their Massachusetts base and a feeling among other members that after McCormack's long reign, the leadership should be spread to other regions. Boland, most frequently discussed as a dark-horse liberal candidate, waited in the wings for awareness to materialize among the members that neither Udall nor O'Hara could make it. Eighth-ranking on Appropriations, Boland at 59 years of age, had solid rapport with big-city politicians and an ease of access to many southerners which other liberals lacked. But leadership seldom seeks out a member — if he wants it, he must woo it actively. Big, congenial Tip O'Neill, an Irishman of the old school yet with a grasp of the changing times, appeared to have as many supporters as Boland. O'Neill had a reputation for being a shrewd vote-counter but this was offset somewhat by a complacency that sometimes bordered on laziness. Both Boland and O'Neill seriously considered the possibility of becoming active candidates in the late fall, but neither seemed able to reach an agreement with the other as to which should be candidate and which the campaign manager. In the closing week of the campaign, both men played active roles: Boland worked for Udall and O'Neill applied the clincher for the Boggs campaign.

Perhaps no member in the House, with the exception of Morris Udall, better illustrates the frustrations of being young, competent, and blocked for higher leadership than does Dan Rostenkowski of Illinois. Big (6 ft. 3 in., 210 lbs.), ruggedly handsome, and of Polish descent, Rostenkowski was first elected to Congress in 1958. A handpicked protegé of Mayor Richard Daley, his career demonstrated both the benefits and frustrations of being a rising lieutenant in what is perhaps the last strong big-city party machine in the country. Rostenkowski could never be sure just how much his selection and rapid promotion to the leadership of the Chicago delegation was his own doing. Ability he has, however, and his rise in the House was relatively swift — freshman Representative at age 31, member of the House Ways and Means Committee at age 37, Chairman of the Democratic Caucus, the number four position in the Democratic hierarchy, at age 39.

Few members were surprised to hear Rostenkowski being discussed as a contender for the majority leader or, more remotely, the Speakership, when the announcement came that John McCormack would step down. Mayor Daley would be a strong supporter if Rostenkowski decided to enter either contest. When first informed that the Democratic House in all of its wisdom was prepared to nominate for Speaker "that little guy who couldn't control the convention," Daley was surprised and disappointed. Since the Democratic Convention of 1968 and Albert's difficulties in controlling the delegates, the Mayor had not been one of his admirers. Rostenkowski's reluctance to endorse Albert for Speaker flowed partly from a parallel uneasiness; he also preferred to keep his options open on the outside chance the Speakership might be within his own reach.

Rostenkowski was even more pressed regarding what he should do about the contest for majority leader. He was closer to Hale Boggs than most House members, one of several assistant whips that the Louisianian most depended upon. Finally, both Hale Boggs and, later, Carl Albert had asked him to run for an unprecedented third term as chairman of the caucus. One of Rostenkowski's strong suits was his ability to preside over a controversial caucus with integrity and order. Not nearly as adept at floor speaking as Albert, Boggs, or Udall, he nevertheless was quite skilled at making short statements and rulings from the chair. Both a firm gavel and an ability to react quickly to fluctuating parliamentary situations were needed at the opening caucus. The agenda would include not only the election of the top two Democratic leadership positions but also important questions of seniority and other party reforms. Throughout the summer and fall Rostenkowski, consulting his experienced administrative assistant, James C. Healey, gave much thought to becoming a contender. If Boggs' campaign had not begun to gain momentum, there is little doubt that Rostenkowski would have announced his candidacy. His solid establishment credentials, his ability to draw enthusiastic support in a number of big-city delegations beyond Chicago, his acceptability to many southerners would have made him a formidable candidate.

By mid-December, however, Rostenkowski had all but removed himself from consideration for either top position. Instead, he launched into the fullest possible preparation for the two- or three-day caucus in January. He decided that with Albert's and Boggs' blessing, he would run for an unprecedented third term as caucus chairman. If Hale Boggs, Rostenkowski's preferred candidate for majority leader, won, there was strong likelihood that Rostenkowski would be appointed as whip. The two men had discussed the possibility several times but had not yet reached a firm agreement.

X

What can be said, by way of generalization, about the ten men who became candidates or were seen as likely contenders for the House majority leadership? They ranged in age from 42 (Rostenkowski) to 60 (Sisk); in seniority from Udall (9 years) to Boggs (26 years). But, on the average, these contenders were men in their middle 50s who had been in the House about nine terms (18 years). They had gravitated to the major committees: Rules (three contenders), Ways and Means (two), and Appropriations (one). Almost without exception, they were first elected to the House of Representatives by age 40. Once elected, the House became a career, one at which they had each been singularly successful. Only Boggs of all the candidates had ever suffered a House election defeat. In that isolated event, Boggs was upset at age 28 by the former incumbent he had first defeated in 1940.

Another generalization seems warranted: The contenders, like the larger body of which they were a part, were "locals." [18] With some exceptions (Sisk was born in Texas and migrated to California in the 1930's; O'Hara was born in Washington, D.C. but went to high school in Detroit), typical contenders were born, went to elementary and secondary school, and began work in the same district they represented in Congress. More often than not, they also attended college in their home states. Only three of the ten Representatives were lawyers as contrasted with about five out of ten for the House as a whole. What generally set these actual or likely candidates apart from their colleagues was that they arrived at the House earlier, adapted more readily, and seemed to demonstrate immediately to House leaders and their contemporaries that they possessed "leadership potential."

NOTES

1. Nelson W. Polsby, "Two Strategies of Influence: Choosing a Majority Leader, 1962," in Robert L. Peabody and Nelson W. Polsby (eds.), *New Perspectives on the House of Representatives*, 2d ed. (Chicago: Rand McNally, 1969), pp. 325–358. (Reprinted here as Chapter 3.)
2. The last attempt to depose an incumbent Speaker was made in December 1923, when a group of insurgent Republican progressives nominated Representatives Henry A. Cooper (R., Wisc.) against Speaker Frederick H. Gillett (R., Mass.). Democrats nominated Finis Garrett of Tennessee. A two-day deadlock was broken by the then Majority Leader, later Speaker, Nicholas Longworth, and Gillett was finally relected Speaker.
3. Representative Percy Priest of Tennessee chose to be Chairman of the Interstate and Foreign Commerce Committee rather than return to his position as Majority Whip when the Democrats regained control of the House in 1955.
4. Robert K. Walsh, "Quiet Carl Albert Approaches the Top," *The Sunday Washington Star*, January 17, 1971, p. E-3.
5. William Chapman, "Carl Albert: Winning With a Waiting Game," *The Washington Post*, January 10, 1971, p. B-3.
6. Unpublished worksheets of poll compiled by the *National Journal*'s Center for Political Research. Results must be interpreted with some caution since only 74 of the 245 House Democrats chose to return the anonymous mail ballot.
7. These and other quotations from members are not attributed in order to protect the anonymity of the source. Occasionally, I have slightly modified a quotation so as not to violate a confidence.
   In addition to from two to six interviews with each publicly announced candidate, I personally interviewed more than 30 Democratic members and kept in weekly communication with more than 20 strategically placed staff assistants. This narrative case study could not have been written without their cooperation and candid assistance. I was also able to make use of almost 70 interviews (50 congressional, 20 staff), usually of a shorter duration (10–15 minutes), compiled by a team of six Johns Hopkins University graduate and undergraduate students during the week before and after the January 21, 1971 caucus vote. To these students, Jeffrey Berry, Samuel Katz, Burton Sheppard, Gary St. Peter, Robert Sufit, and Frances Wersells, I express my appreciation.
8. John Fischer, "The Easy Chair: The Coming Upheaval in Congress," *Harper's*, October 1970, pp. 21–40, at p. 36.
9. Larry L. King, "The Road to Power in Congress: The Education of Mo Udall — and What It Cost," *Harper's*, **242** (June 1971), 39–63. Reprinted

in Morris K. Udall, *Education of a Congressman*, ed. by Robert L. Peabody (Indianapolis: Bobbs-Merrill, 1972), pp. 291–328.

10. Udall's athletic ability stood him in good stead with the gym crowd, a group of about 100 congressmen, Democrats and Republicans, who regularly use the paddle-ball courts, steam room, and swimming pool in the Rayburn House Office Building.

11. Morris K. Udall and Donald G. Tacheron, *The Job of the Congressman*, 2d ed. (Indianapolis: Bobbs-Merrill, 1970). Udall sent hand-inscribed copies of the book to all 435 members of the House of Representatives in the 91st Congress, as well as to the 140 Democratic candidates running for the House for the first time in 1970.

12. The *National Journal* poll, cited earlier, selected Udall as the most articulate Democrat in the House. It also ranked him third behind Mills and Albert in overall leadership ability.

13. O'Hara was the last of five freshmen appointed to the Education and Labor Committee in 1958, an unfortunate twist of fate that kept him from a subcommittee chairmanship until 1971. Even then, a new subcommittee on Agricultural Labor had to be created for him.

14. Rivers died on December 28, 1970. Both Hays and Boggs found good hunting grounds on the Air Force jets which conveyed senior colleagues to and from the funeral in Charleston, South Carolina.

15. According to the criteria in *Congressional Quarterly*, such a roll call occurs when a majority of voting southern Democrats and a majority of voting Republicans oppose the stand taken by a majority of voting northern Democrats. During 1970, such a coalition occurred on 17 percent of the House roll calls, winning 70 percent of the time. *Congressional Quarterly Weekly Report*, Vol. XXIX (January 29, 1971), No. 5, pp. 242–247.

16. Polsby, *op. cit.*

17. *House Out of Order* (New York: Dutton, 1965), and *Power in the House* (New York: Dutton, 1968).

18. Roger H. Davidson, *The Role of the Congressman* (New York: Pegasus, 1969), ch. 2.

CHAPTER SIX

The Campaigns for House Majority Leader, 1970–1971

In the 91st Congress (1969–1970), the House of Representatives consisted of 246 Democrats and 189 Republicans. Democrats made a net gain of nine congressional seats in the November 1970 elections. The task, then, of each announced candidate for majority leader — O'Hara, Hays, Udall, and, later, Boggs and Sisk — was to secure a majority of committed votes (128 would be needed) from the 255 Democrats who would assemble at the opening Democratic Caucus of the 92d Congress on January 19, 1971. Each candidate followed a similar "inside" strategy at the beginning. They sought support from within their state delegations, regions, committee associates, and close friends. In the last three months of the campaign, November and December 1970 and January 1971, three candidates added an "outside" strategy, albeit with considerable variation in style and success.[1] Hays and Sisk seemed largely to limit their campaigns to the use of internal contacts and resources.

It is more and more apparent that pinning down members on a leadership vote is exceedingly difficult. When the election result is a foregone conclusion as, for example, when Carl Albert was elevated to Speaker, a majority is easily secured. Few members are hesitant to commit their votes. Indeed, it is likely there will be a rush to get on the bandwagon early. But if, as in the majority leadership contest under study, no sure winner can be determined, then most members are more reluctant to make a pledge.[2] What adds to the complexity, of course, is that the final vote is cast by secret ballot. Given the relatively large size of the electorate, no one, save the member, himself, will know just how he voted. And this opens up the possibility of a member making two or more commitments, and thus, seemingly, having the best of both worlds.

"A member's word is his bond." Few norms of the House, or for that matter, most legislative bodies, are so widely quoted and seemingly observed. Why is this so? — partly because the majority of members are persons of integrity, but also because most legislative issues are resolved by open, that is to say, public, roll call votes. When an explicit agreement is made — "I'll vote for your amendment, if you'll vote for mine" — both partners to the arrangement are able to observe whether or not compliance is forthcoming. Failure to comply for one or more extenuating reasons may be overlooked once, or even twice, especially if reneging is telegraphed in advance. But members who go back on their word with any degree of regularity are soon exposed and isolated. Their votes are devalued and other members will not enter into exchange relationships with them. Since exchange of trust, information . . . votes, underlies the entire legislative process, members of the House can ill afford not to honor their word.[3] In short, personal integrity is reinforced by the most powerful kind of exchange sanction.

But what happens when the secret ballot is substituted for the open roll call? First, of course, members gain the anonymity so essential to free choice in leadership selection. If a member votes with discretion he cannot be "punished" by the winning side or a ruling clique attempting to perpetuate itself. The benefits of a secret ballot vote in questions of leadership selection would seem to outweigh its limitations. The principal candidates in our study, however, were to encounter great frustration in the months ahead trying to determine just what constituted a genuine commitment and how to be sure a "commitment" was transferable into a caucus vote.

I

Probably no candidate was more successful in obtaining early commitments in late May and early June of 1970 than Morris K. Udall. He formed a cadre of supporters from his January 1969 challenge to McCormack — Representatives Frank Thompson of New Jersey, Lee Hamilton and Andrew Jacobs of Indiana, Bob Leggett of California, Thomas Foley of Washington, and Patsy Mink of Hawaii. Other members who continued to support the Speaker in 1969, like Dante Fascell of Florida and Abner Mikva of Illinois, came to play especially active roles in the Udall campaign. Udall also received several firm, but silent, commitments from younger southerners. They agreed to vote for him, but felt they could not afford to support him openly for fear of retribution from Boggs, their delegations, or their constituents back home. Within a month Udall had more than 10 members working actively in his behalf and some 40 firm commitments. His problem from the beginning was just how to broaden his base beyond the West and Midwest into the Northeast and the South. Moreover, he somehow had to break away from an almost exclusive reliance upon support from members junior to him (four terms or less).

Unlike Udall's campaign which was characterized by an early surge, Boggs began much more hesitantly. True, he had the initial advantage of a unanimous eight-member Louisiana delegation behind him. The same day it met to endorse Albert it also agreed to support Boggs for majority leader. One key member, Joe Waggonner, was given an additional incentive to back Boggs. Boggs' election to majority leader would open up a vacancy on the House Ways and Means Committee, an assignment Waggonner had long coveted. More than one Louisiana member might dislike Boggs personally, or resent his liberal voting pattern, but they recognized the tangible and intangible benefits likely to accrue to their state if one of their own Representatives moved up in the leadership.

Unlike Udall, Boggs relied on no group meetings. Instead he concentrated on seeking individual commitments from a few senior members: Waggonner, Edward Hébert (the dean of the Louisiana delegation), George Andrews of Alabama, Mendel Rivers of South Carolina, Bob Sikes of Florida, George Mahon and Omar Burleson of Texas, Philip Landrum and John Flynt of Georgia, Jamie Whitten and William Colmer of Mississippi, and above all, Wilbur Mills of Arkansas. Alignment of these senior members, it was felt, would be followed by the balance of the southern delegations.

Several of these southern leaders abandoned Boggs for the late-blooming candidacy of B. F. Sisk. Some felt Boggs was just too liberal and others disliked him for personal reasons. But the majority whip had to have most of the southerners behind him — some 88 votes in all — or his candidacy would come to nought.

Equally important, Boggs had to win and hold a majority of the northern, mostly big-city establishment members. Here the roles of several of his assistant whips would be important — Hugh Carey and Sam Stratton of New York, John McFall of California, and most important, Dan Rostenkowski of Illinois. If Rostenkowski were to enter the race, clearly Boggs would lose his chance for a first or second ballot victory. More than most opponents, Rostenkowski could hurt him in the Midwest and even in the South. On the other hand, as a supporter, Rostenkowski would probably bring along votes that Boggs otherwise could not attract.

The majority whip's campaign began to gather momentum in July and August at which time a series of garden parties were held at his home in Bethesda, Maryland. For a number of years the Boggs' annual spring garden party, co-hosted by Charles Davis, a Chicago lobbyist and former Ways and Means Committee staff member, had captivated congressmen, staffers, interest group representatives, newspaper reporters, and their wives. Attendance had numbered 1000 or more people. The cocktail parties held during the late summer of 1970 were much smaller affairs, built initially around invitations to a set of committee members from, for example, Ways and Means, Appropriations, and Rules. After the first gathering of 50–60 people, other members were invited more or less at random. The parties were seldom so intimate that pressure could be brought to bear on a recalcitrant colleague.

Many members looked upon the Boggs' parties with rather wry amusement. But other colleagues (and their spouses), came away perhaps with the impression that Hale was a polished host, his wife, Lindy, a warm and gracious hostess, and "wouldn't it be a shame" if such pleasant parties were curbed instead of expanded next year.

Hays, only moderately less active on the floor and in the cloakrooms than Udall and Boggs, from the beginning adopted a variant in soliciting members:

> I'm not asking commitments from any members. I say to them
> — "I'd like to have your vote, but I don't expect anything in
> writing or in blood." On the basis of that, quite a few people
> have said they'll support me.

Later in his campaign, Hays would voice a meaner threat. Noting that he was about to become chairman of the Committee on House Administration with its jurisdiction over committee budgets, he would ask the only half-facetious question, "Would you rather have me as a happy majority leader or an unhappy chairman of House Administration?"

The Ohioan also tried to gain more support by inviting actual and potential supporters to several small luncheons which were usually held in his Rayburn suite. After good food, wine, and cigars, a member might find it difficult not to declare his support or at least indicate that he was leaning toward Hays.

O'Hara made his initial contacts with "Michiganders," members of the Education and Labor Committee, and such close liberal associates as James Corman of California and John Brademas of Indiana. His only hope for a bridge to southern votes seemed to lie in a marriage of convenience with another assistant whip, Jack Brooks of Texas. For personal and geographical reasons Brooks could not see himself being appointed whip by any of the other candidates, except, possibly, Wayne Hays of Ohio. Once O'Hara had aligned his closest support, he returned to his usual deep legislative involvement, including a heavy workload on two conference committees. He did not really become active again on his own behalf until late December as the "lame-duck" session came to a close.

II

In October 1970, Congress recessed for its mid-term elections. It seemed almost certain that a lame-duck session would be necessary, the first in two decades. It also became increasingly clear that the majority leadership contest was boiling down to a two-man race between Boggs, the establishment candidate, and Udall, the spokesman for change and reform. With the congressional elections only a month away, all the candidates, but especially these two, looked for more supporters among the incoming freshmen.

On October 2, 1970, Boggs sent a letter to the 140 freshmen candidates for office, most of them in districts currently held by Republicans. Along with his letter, the Democratic whip sent a copy of the 1968 Democratic party platform with a reminder that he had served as chairman. He offered his assistance in their campaigns, an offer which subsequently led to at least four speeches. (It appears that three of these winning freshmen backed Boggs.) Boggs concluded his letter with what was his first formal declaration of candidacy:

> As you probably know, I am a candidate for Majority Leader in the House, and I welcome your support. I believe I have the experience in the party as Assistant Majority Leader and Chairman of the Platform Committee to provide the leadership necessary to keep our Party in the majority.

Although Udall could not send a letter on stationery of the Office of the Democratic Whip, or send copies of the official party platform, he could offer his campaign assistance and he did. Six candidates accepted, three of whom were subsequently elected and all three of whom ultimately supported Udall's candidacy. In addition, Udall helped organize two pre-election meetings sponsored by the Democratic Study Group for non-incumbent candidates.

All the majority leadership candidates, except Wayne Hays, took further action on election night. Boggs and O'Hara both sent telegrams to all 255 Democrats elected on November 3, 1970. Udall and Sisk sent letters to their current and prospective colleagues. Udall's letter was the most candid — he stated that he was running for majority leader and asked directly for support. Sisk, who still had to clear his candidacy with his California colleagues, said nothing about his future ambitions. He merely offered his congratulations and looked forward to working with his colleagues in the new Congress. Hays, maintaining his low profile, neither wrote, telegrammed, nor telephoned. He planned to meet and work on the new members in Washington.

Congressional leaders, as well as would-be candidates for the leadership, must come from safe districts, preferably from districts where they win regularly by 60 percent of the two-party vote or better. Leaders need to maintain flexibility on the diverse issues that come before them. They cannot afford to worry about whether they are going to be returned or not. They seldom can afford to go back home with any frequency or duration when the legislative push is on at the close of a session.

In 1970 all the candidates for majority leader met the criteria of representing safe districts with votes to spare. Boggs had recouped most of the ground lost in his near-upset in 1968. Benefiting from redistricting engineered by a friendly legislature and Governor, Boggs won by 73 percent in 1970. Running from his part Detroit, part suburban district, O'Hara amassed the highest percentage victory of all the candidates for majority leader, 76 percent. Udall won with better than 69 percent in Arizona. Wayne Hays in Ohio had his usual comfortable margin of better than two-to-one. And B. F. Sisk in California, about to declare his candidacy, had been reelected by the strong margin of 68 percent.

House Democrats found cause for modest rejoicing as a result of the November 3, 1970 elections. A net gain of nine seats would result in a 255–180 Democratic advantage over the Republicans in the forthcoming 92d Congress. Of the four announced candidates for majority leader it appeared initially that Udall had gained the most. Of the 33 new Democratic members-elect, 6 had defeated older, more establishment-oriented Democrats in primaries. O'Hara or Udall could expect to reap the benefit of most of the votes of these change-oriented members — freshmen such as, Bella Abzug of New York, Father Robert Drinan of Massachusetts, Paul Sarbanes of Maryland, and Ron Dellums of California. On balance, at least 20 of the 33 incoming freshmen Democrats appeared to be potential moderate or liberal votes.

III

Two weeks after the election, as the reconvened 91st Congress got underway, a fifth candidate entered the race, B. F. Sisk of California. Cooperating closely with Sisk, Chet Holifield, the dean of the California delegation, called a meeting on November 19, 1970. Both Sisk and John Moss were present. After some discussion it was agreed that the man who could command a majority would become the California candidate for majority leader. Further, it was agreed that the losing candidate would withdraw and support the winning candidate. Since early summer, Sisk had deferred to Moss' efforts to align support, in part because the House deputy whip had two more years of seniority. When Moss first called him, Sisk said, "Sure, go ahead and get your feet wet — see how you do." However, the candidacy of John Moss had not gone very far; it was time to see whether or not Sisk could do better. Both men left the Speaker's dining room in the Capitol and walked across the hall to have coffee in the Members' dining room. Fifteen minutes later, when the two men returned, Sisk had eased out Moss by a vote of 9 to 7.

On the surface, "Bernie" Sisk would not appear to be one of the likeliest men to enter the contest for majority leader. At 60, the oldest of all candidates, he was also the most casual and unassuming. Yet Sisk had several assets that for a time made it seem that he was going to effectively undercut the establishment candidacy of Hale Boggs. Even starting as late as he did, he could count on a dozen or more votes of the 20-member delegation. California Democratic members felt quite strongly that their delegation was entitled to one of the top three positions in the House leadership. Following the 1970 census and redistricting, they could be expected to add another three or four seats, thus making California the largest Democratic delegation in Congress. A native of Texas who had not moved to the San Joaquin Valley of California until 1937, Sisk had exceptionally strong ties with members of the Texas and other southern delegations. He had been encouraged to run against Boggs by such southern stalwarts as Bob Sikes of Florida and William Colmer of Mississippi, the chairman of his own Committee on Rules. As a member of the powerful scheduling group, Sisk had been in a position to do favors for members, sometimes by voting for a rule, other times by helping to bottle up legislation which a majority of members did not wish to see come to the floor. Finally, Sisk had done a commendable job of floor managing the controversial Legislative Reorganization Act of 1970 through to its final passage. Dealing with many of the most complicated internal matters of the House, methods of voting, staffing, and possible changes in seniority, the calm, slow-talking Californian placated the senior power-wielders in the House, and at the same time brought about enough changes to satisfy all but the most reform-oriented younger members.

Yet Sisk, like all the other candidates, also had drawbacks. Some members felt he could not sustain a strong floor presence on legislation, issue after issue. These critics were joined by others who felt that Sisk would be the weakest of the five announced candidates as an external spokesman charged with taking the position of the Democratic party to the country. In an election year, particularly with the presidency controlled by the opposing party, the majority leader would need to appear more often on television. Nor was Sisk seen by many members as the kind of majority leader who would be effective at fund-raising dinners or campaigning for them in their districts. From one of his opponents came perhaps the unkindest criticism of all: "Sisk — what the hell has he ever done to be suddenly injected in as a Great White Hope?"

The next three weeks were critical for Sisk and, indirectly, for Boggs. On Sunday, November 29, 1970, the highly influential "Evans and Novak" column in the *Washington Post* reported Sisk cutting into Boggs' vital southern strength, especially in North Carolina. According to these columnists, Sisk had been encouraged to run not only by Sikes of Florida, but also by Boggs' own colleague, Joe Waggonner of Louisiana. Most damaging of all, if true, they suggested that "Sisk all along has been the personal favorite of the most powerful of all southerners, Wilbur Mills of Arkansas." [4]

The next day at a meeting of the House Ways and Means Committee, Mills told Boggs he denied the *Washington Post* report. Instead, Mills maintained, he continued to support Boggs. Pressing the opening, Boggs called back later that day and asked his chairman if he would consider giving a nominating speech. Mills tentatively agreed. That same day, first by telephone and later on the floor, Waggonner also denied the story. Boggs had survived a major threat.

What seems clear, in retrospect, is that Sisk failed to make the inroads in the South that his major sponsors hoped he would. North Carolina had not agreed to switch to Sisk, for the simple reason that most of its members were as yet uncommitted to any candidate. The Georgia delegation, headed by Boggs' fellow Ways and Means Committee member, Phil Landrum, and Assistant Whip John Flynt, met hastily and unanimously endorsed Boggs. This action helped to stem any tide that might have moved toward the Californian. Sisk picked up some commitments in Texas, Florida, and elsewhere, but not enough to bring about wholesale defection from the Boggs following.

Equally important, Sisk had rough going in the Midwest and Northeast. Here and there, he picked up isolated support — Mel Price of Illinois, Richard Ichord of Missouri — but the Californian found it especially difficult to crack the heavily Catholic northeastern corridor. He made overtures to Hugh Carey of New York and Edward Boland of Massachusetts as whip possibilities, but both men ended up in other camps. He also approached Fernand St. Germain of Rhode Island. By mid-December, for all practical purposes, the Sisk bid was dormant. His only hope lay as a compromise choice if neither Boggs nor Udall were able to secure majorities in the caucus.

One of the front-runners, Morris Udall, reached a plateau of 60–70 votes, and had difficulty gaining more than his obvious initial strength among moderate-to-liberal northerners and westerners. Most of his southern support, with the exception of Gibbons and Fascell in Florida, was hesitant to openly endorse him. More conservative midwestern Democrats had flocked to Hays, Sisk, or Boggs. Many of the uncommitted votes, still estimated as high as 50–60 in December, were concentrated in the Northeast and big cities. Apparently most of the holdouts simply "wanted to be with a winner" and waited to see who the winner would be.

Following strategy gleaned from case studies of the Albert-Bolling majority leader contest in 1962 and the Ford-Halleck minority leadership contest in 1965, Udall made use of an expanding group of members to gain support, validate vote counts, and generate enthusiasm.[5] By December, more than 30 members were campaigning actively in his behalf. Claiming "more intelligence than anybody else — let's see how good a forecaster I am," Udall disclosed his hardcore and projected first ballot estimates as of December 4:

	Hard core	First ballot
Udall	42	85
O'Hara	31	55
Boggs	29	55
Sisk	16	45
Hays	10	15

Admitting that his projections for O'Hara "might be a little high," Udall at this stage of the contest felt moderately confident. But, he cautioned, "it will take two, three, or four ballots to settle it."

IV

Boggs' strong election victory on November 3, 1970, following his slender election vote of two years before, provided him with a major psychological boost. He and Gary Hymel, his administrative assistant, returned to Washington, D. C. and spent three days making long-distance telephone calls to members over the Veteran's Day weekend. The election had provided an easy opening gambit. After congratulations were offered, Boggs could slide effortlessly into a request for support of his candidacy. Some calls were made to reinforce standing commitments, but altogether more than 20 new pledges were obtained. By mid-November, Hymel revealed in confidence that Boggs had "68 firm votes and another 40 that we haven't yet asked." Most of the latter were southerners whom Boggs had not yet personally contacted, but whom he felt would finally give their support. Even by the most optimistic of his tallies, though, Boggs was 20–30 votes short of a majority. He also had no way to estimate how much slippage there might be between mid-November and the caucus on January 19.

After Boggs' initial shock and worry over Sisk's entry into the campaign wore off, Boggs seemed to become more active. Most of late November and early December, he was closeted with southern colleagues to shore up wavering support. Boggs stressed three themes:

1. He was a southerner, with a southern constituency. The South could not claim a blood relationship with any other candidate (Sisk, after all, had left Texas; now he owed his allegiance to California).

2. If Boggs was not elected majority leader, then for the first time in decades, the states of the old Confederacy would not have a representative in the elected leadership of either body.

3. In the House, the absence of a southerner in the leadership could open the door to a renewed assault on the last bastion of Southern power — committee chairmanships and the seniority system.

The latter argument was particularly telling with the "old bull elephants," senior chairmen like Mendel Rivers of South Carolina, his successor, Edward Hébert of Louisiana, and George Mahon and Wright Patman of Texas.

Further evidence of candidate tendencies to inflate their strength while discounting the vote commitments of their opponents can be seen from Boggs' early December estimate of first ballot strength:

Boggs	100–105
Udall	60
Sisk	20
O'Hara	12
Hays	10
Boland	15
Undecided	33
	255

In mid-December, Boggs had the opportunity to meet the charges of "emotional instability" head on. In a pre-taped *CBS News* interview Boggs was confronted with the "prone to crack under pressure" quotation from the *Harper's* magazine article. His first response was laughter, then the comment that "only the record speaks for itself. I've been in public office for 30 years," Boggs continued, "under the most difficult and trying circumstances. I've never seen any, I've never felt that there's been any, great emotional strain." [6]

Television seemed to have little or no impact on this campaign, in any event. Boggs could not recall a single member who commented on these taped interviews with all five candidates. Yet the film was featured for about 10 minutes on both the morning and evening CBS

News program on December 8, 1970. Probably most of the incumbent members already knew each other intimately and many of the arriving freshmen saw little more than brief news film clips on any of the House leadership candidates before they arrived in Washington, D. C.

In the end, Boggs disposed of the instability issue more directly — by his performance on the floor, interacting with his colleagues, coping with the pressures of running for majority leader. During the days just before the November election and especially through the long, testing hours of the lame-duck session, when Boggs was not pounding the corridors in search of votes he could be found on the floor. He missed few opportunities to support Democratic measures, to chide his opponents across the aisle, and to criticize the Nixon administration. Speaker McCormack, no friend to Udall, made certain that Boggs had multiple opportunities to display his considerable talents as a presiding officer. Time seemed to be operating in Boggs' behalf.

When the Democratic party and his many Washington friends gave McCormack a farewell party on December 9, 1970, the Speaker went out of his way to pull Majority Leader Albert into the receiving line and salute him as his successor. Later, he brought Boggs into the line, too.

December 29, 1970 may be seen as the turning point in Boggs' quest for the majority leadership. Boggs presided most of that Tuesday as the House membership, back from the holidays, entered into the last week of the 91st Congress. In the course of the day's events, the majority leader-to-be heard the following kinds of reports:

- Speaker McCormack said he thought Boggs was going to win.

- Majority Leader Albert, in one of the first direct comments he made about the race, spontaneously remarked that he thought things were jelling for Boggs.

- Later that afternoon a senior member from the majority leader's Oklahoma delegation offered his commitment to Boggs.

Finally, as if to make a full day complete, the *Washington Star* carried a column by Charles Bartlett playing up the role of the Speaker "trying specifically to wrap up the majority leader's post for an old associate, Hale Boggs of Louisiana." [7]

V

During October and November, O'Hara had difficulty making up his mind whether or not to continue as a serious candidate. But after he finished managing the manpower bill in late December, the competitive "juices started to flow." Civil rights, education and, above all, labor lobbyists began to sound out members on his behalf. Generally, O'Hara instructed them to "low-key it," not to lean heavily on any members. When asked in early December if he had as many as 35 to 40 votes, he candidly replied, "No, not that many, but I do expect to have 50 to 55 votes on the first ballot." It was O'Hara's theory from beginning to end that only he could beat Boggs in a head-to-head contest. He was convinced that the northeastern establishment members — the O'Neills, the Cellers, the Rooneys — just could not tolerate Udall. Conversely, even though he had a more liberal voting record than Udall, O'Hara felt he was viewed more sympathetically by these party regulars. Therefore, O'Hara's strategy became one of trying to gain as much first ballot strength as possible, hoping to hold out to a fourth or fifth ballot showdown.

Hays was regarded as low man in just about everybody's book except his own. Quietly garnering support from other members like himself, the party regulars, conservative-to-moderate in their voting patterns, the sharp-tongued Ohioan surprised everyone with his first ballot showing. All along, he offered to put his money where his mouth was. On December 22, Caucus Chairman Dan Rostenkowski called the five announced candidates together for a luncheon to see if they couldn't agree on the voting decision rules in caucus. Wayne Hays, pulling several $100 bills from his wallet, offered to bet any other candidate that he would not be low man on the first ballot. He got no takers.

Room H-128 is a medium-sized room located on the first floor, south-side, of the Capitol, and made famous as the site of Speaker Rayburn's "Board of Education" meetings. Since Speaker McCormack was not a bachelor and didn't drink, the room fell into relative disuse as a place where the Speaker's key advisers gathered to plot strategy and unwind from a legislative day. Nevertheless, the room's use was controlled by the Speaker and it was a fitting place for a group of would-be majority leaders to meet and plan the ground rules for caucus nominations and voting procedures.

Caucus Chairman Rostenkowski presided and used the occasion to announce that he would not be a candidate for majority leader, although he did plan to run again for chairman of the caucus. After some discussion Boggs, Hays, O'Hara, Sisk, and Udall agreed on a voting procedure in which nominations would be closed before the first ballot commenced, and the low man would be dropped after the second and each successive ballot. A majority of those present and voting would be required for election of the majority leader. The complete language of the agreement (drafted by Udall) was circulated to each candidate, modified slightly, and later ratified by the full Democratic Caucus membership without a murmur.[8] For all practical purposes the announced candidates had effectively lessened the chances that a dark horse might enter the field at the last moment. Moreover, they had prevented the selection of a compromise candidate from outside the field should a stalemate occur in the balloting.[9]

According to all accounts the luncheon conversation, if not amiable, was at least reasonably good-natured. These men had studied each other's strengths and foibles at first hand, for a minimum of a decade and, in several instances, for much longer. The room's dark rose drapes and subdued lighting almost seemed necessary as a backdrop for the intense ambitions which were under check but never dimmed. One candidate remarked:

> Every guy in there knows he's a winner. If you could harness all the ego-power in that room — what a source of energy you would have. Why, you could light up New York City for the next ten years!

As the 91st Congress droned to a close on January 2, 1971, the five announced candidates for majority leader once again took inventory of their chances. Boggs had been viewed in June as much more vulnerable than he was proving to be. Indeed, by the end of December, a Boggs majority on the first ballot was within striking distance. He claimed 118 first ballot commitments. His chairman, Wilbur Mills, quietly advised others that he would make a seconding speech for his top-ranking colleague on Ways and Means. Both Speaker McCormack and Majority Leader Albert seemed to think Boggs was close to home.

Still, Morris Udall did not concede defeat. He believed he had at least a 50/50 chance. The lanky Arizonan numbered his first ballot strength at around 85, enough, he believed, to lead Boggs on this first crucial test of strength.

Although Tony Coelho, Bernie Sisk's bright young administrative assistant, talked about a first ballot strength for Sisk in the neighborhood of 80–85 votes, his boss was no longer so optimistic. At least one southern committee chairman speculated that "Wayne Hays will lead them all on the first ballot." The Ohio candidate was more realistic — he doubted if any candidate, with the possible exception of Boggs, would come in with more than 60–65 votes. A labor lobbyist predicted that "when the dust settled, O'Hara would be the winner." O'Hara, himself, had "some self-doubts, but not strong enough to get out." Depending upon who you talked to, the contest was generally seen as coming down to Hale Boggs vs. Mo Udall, with a possible stalemate leading to Sisk or O'Hara.

As Congress closed, most congressmen headed for home or flew South to vacation resorts. About 10 days remained for the final efforts candidates cared to make until the January 19, 1971 caucus.

VI

For the five announced candidates for majority leader, vacations were brief or not at all. Hale Boggs flew to New Orleans for several days of Gulf fishing aboard a Freeport Sulphur charter fishing boat. The majority whip flew back to Washington, D. C. the weekend of January 9; he was prepared to make an all-out effort to secure a first ballot victory. Wayne Hays and Bernie Sisk had repaired to their home districts even before final adjournment. The deaths of close relatives kept both men away from Washington longer than they had anticipated. Sisk returned to the Capitol on Tuesday, January 12; Hays did not arrive until the weekend before the Democratic Caucus. The two younger candidates, Morris Udall and James O'Hara, never left town. Instead, they telephoned newly arriving freshmen members and sought personal visits with them.

With most members out of town and difficult to reach even by telephone, the importance of outside forces, press and interest groups took on more importance. Favorable newspaper accounts and columns could be and were photocopied and distributed by inside mail to members' offices to be available when they returned. The interest group pressures that remained to be mobilized would be concentrated either in the home district or in Washington during the last one or two days preceding the caucus. For the most part external pressures seemed surprisingly light or were played out behind the scenes. As one fourth-term member observed in mid-December:

> So far there's been almost no pressure from interest groups, save labor on a low-keyed basis — and that's because, I think, O'Hara has told them to keep it that way . . .

> It will mount, though, the week before the caucus. I won't be able to walk through the hall, here [outside the House chambers] without 15 or 20 descending upon me. Then it will be more like major legislation on the floor.

Such wholesale lobbying failed to materialize in Washington, even on the day of the caucus. What direct interest group pressure was applied, and there did appear to be a surge at the end, was largely focused in the home districts of wavering members.

VII

The "power of the press" may be greatly exaggerated from time to time, by both its admirers and its detractors.[10] Nevertheless, one observation seems true — newspapers have great power to help or hurt individual men. All the candidates gave some credence to these alleged powers. That is, they assumed that their colleagues occasionally read accounts of the progress of the campaign for majority leader and put some stock in how the leading columnists of the land assessed the various candidates. But it was Boggs, Udall, and their principal staff assistants, who went out of their way to cultivate the press. In contrast, the three trailing candidates made only moderate efforts and met with little success in gaining sustained favorable press, except for home-town coverage.

The rise and fall of Sisk's candidacy is a case in point. His entry into the race on November 19 received considerable California publicity, especially in his home-town *Fresno Bee* and other California McClatchy chain newspapers. The *Washington Post* carried the story on page 2, but the *New York Times* Sunday edition relegated Marjorie Hunter's story to page 48. In her interpretation, Sisk's bid was "generally regarded as a severe, perhaps fatal blow to Mr. Boggs' hopes of moving up from his post as Majority Whip into the leadership slot now held by Representative Carl Albert of Oklahoma . . ."[11]

Rowland Evans and Robert Novak gave the Sisk candidacy an additional boost in their *Washington Post* column the following Sunday:[12]

> ... Representative Hale Boggs of Louisiana has been ravaged by the sudden new candidacy of a rival certain to cut into his vital southern strength — middle-road Representative B. F. (Bernie) Sisk of California.

Their widely-read "insiders" column went on to label Representative Sikes of Florida and Representative Waggonner of Louisiana as strong encouragers, and concluded that Sisk even had the support of Wilbur Mills. Three weeks later, Evans and Novak wrote a retraction in all but name. Sisk had "slipped." Mills was in the Boggs camp, after all. "The upshot: Boggs, though hurt by Sisk, is now back in strong contention." [13] Just how high the Sisk balloon rose is a matter of some speculation; clearly some writers and columnists read more into the flight than was warranted.

No candidate made more skillful use of columnists than Boggs. In part, his success was based on an intimate acquaintance with these men, in some cases going back several decades. Here, his garden parties, smaller dinners, and intimate luncheons in his office all played a part. As one newspaperman, not close to Boggs, observed: "How can they help not writing favorable columns? They've been lulled by the good whiskey and fine wine."

Some columns were largely spontaneous. For example, a telephone call from the dean of national political columnists, William S. White, led to a December 12 *Washington Post* column, "They're Shaking Boggs' Ladder." Directed largely against Sisk (the other candidates were not even mentioned), White made the strongest possible case for elevating Boggs from whip to majority leader. Copies were reproduced by Boggs' office, and sent to all 246 Democratic incumbents by Representative Samuel Stratton of New York, an assistant whip.

Other favorable columns came out of routine telephone inquiries from reporters. For example, after Robert Novak was dutifully informed of some errors in a previous column, he cross-checked them, and wrote a later Sunday column, noting that Mills supported Boggs, not Sisk. All candidates were well aware that it's not what the general public gleans that matters, but what members talk about in the cloakroom. Here, a negative column can start a rumor; a favorable column can help soften up a possible convert.

Still additional columns evolved from closely coordinated luncheons or conferences with columnists:

- Charles Bartlett, "Democrats' Unity Faces Two Tests," *Washington Star*, December 29, 1970, made the case for Speaker McCormack's support for Boggs.

- Frank Mankiewicz and Tom Braden provided a balanced interpretation of "Boggs vs. Udall in the House," *Chicago Sun-Times*, January 4, 1971. (It's as important to neutralize what might have been a hostile column, as to gain a favorable one.)

- Joseph Alsop chipped in with some strong propaganda, "Boggs: The Favorite," *Washington Post*, January 6, 1971.

- Joseph Kraft provided one of the most balanced and informed pieces, "Scramble in the House," *Washington Post*, January 10, 1971.

In this arena, Gary Hymel's prior background as a New Orleans newspaper reporter proved to be a special benefit for Boggs. The net result: at least four highly favorable pieces; several others which tended to balance or neutralize criticism, and only one or two columns which were at all hostile or critical of Boggs.

Morris Udall was not without his own resources in a war of slanted news accounts, favorable columns, and editorial endorsements. Liberal weeklies such as the *New Republic* and *The Progressive* were quick to promote the candidacies of Udall and O'Hara.[14] In the cloakrooms of the House, however, their readers could probably caucus in a telephone booth. The *St. Louis Post Dispatch* wrote a strong editorial in Udall's behalf, but neither the *Washington Post* nor the *New York Times* could be prevailed upon for positive endorsements.[15] Reporters such as Dan Thomasson of the Scripps-Howard chain might provide some positive coverage, but it hardly offset the numerous columns slanted in Boggs' favor. Thomasson's story in the *Washington Daily News*, published just a week before the vote, often read more like a press release than a news analysis:[16]

Representative Morris K. Udall, Arizona, appeared today to have a substantial lead in the race for House Democratic Leader that many observers had all but conceded to Democratic Whip Hale Boggs, Louisiana . . .

And top Democratic Party officials see a now-possible Udall victory as a big boost to their party's congressional image for the 1972 elections. These party figures regard Representative Udall as a vigorous, articulate spokesman who could campaign effectively for Democratic candidates in any section of the country.

Adding substance to such a story were the results of a *Congressional Quarterly* straw poll released on January 11, 1971.[17] With barely one-half (129) of the 255 Democratic Representatives-elect returning their mail ballots, the CQ poll showed Udall the first choice of 46 members, Boggs with 30 votes, and the remaining candidates trailing: Sisk, 18; O'Hara, 11; and Hays, 6. When first and second choices were lumped together Udall led Boggs by 67 to 46. Newspaper headlines played up the Arizona Representative's "enhanced" chances: "Udall Leads Race for Majority Leader," "Poll Finds Udall Ahead in Party Leader Race."[18] Only in the body of the story were the disclaimers found: "the results are admittedly inconclusive"; "all of the candidates are far short of the votes needed to win." And the Boggs forces immediately claimed that Udall supporters had "tried to flood the results of an otherwise sagging poll" in order to generate more favorable results. In the process, of course, they downplayed their own efforts to do the same. Both sides conceded privately that younger, more liberal members were more likely to respond than were old-guard southern and big-city establishment types. Hence, the poll had to be interpreted with caution.

Nevertheless the results of this poll, and the newspaper headlines accompanying it, added fresh fuel to a Udall bandwagon effort. Groups of 20 or more of his some 40 hard-core supporters, most of them junior to Udall, met several times during the final week of the campaign. In general, they fed on one another's enthusiasm. No one contended that a majority was yet within grasp. But hopes were high that their candidate could lead on the first ballot with 80 to 85 votes and hold Boggs to a lesser count, say 70 votes. Once it was revealed that Boggs did not have the first ballot strength he claimed (115 to 125 votes), the Udall forces could win on a second or third ballot. A master list of some 96 "soft or undecided" names was assembled for the "final push." Udall supporters then divided these names among themselves for additional contact.

VIII

About six days before the caucus, one key mover on Udall's behalf
decided to spike once and for all the incredulity with which most
of the Washington press corps continued to assess the strength of
Udall's committed votes. The congressman asked AP's John Beckler
— "a friend and straight-shooting newspaperman" — to his office.
The Udall supporter then proceeded to go over the counts, state by
state and member by member. That might have been sufficient to
achieve his objective, convincing the press of the authenticity of
their claims, but the congressman decided to go still further. He gave
the tally sheets to Beckler with two provisos: (1) he would not use
individual names and (2) he would not show the list to any other
candidate. Beckler agreed. His Thursday AP wire story carried the
following leads:

> Washington (AP) 1-14-71 — With the race for House Demo-
> cratic leader nearing its end, supporters of Representative
> Morris K. Udall of Arizona say they have the votes for an ulti-
> mate victory — and are showing a score sheet to prove it.

> The claim is denied vehemently by Representative Hale Boggs
> of Louisiana, Udall's chief opponent, who sees the possibility
> of a first-ballot victory for himself in next Tuesday's election.

> But so confident is the Udall camp it has made available a
> tally sheet showing where each of the 254 Democrats stands in
> the five-way race, something no other candidate has been will-
> ing to do.

> The Udall tally shows no one will have the 128 votes needed
> to win on the first ballot, but on a final ballot with all candi-
> dates eliminated except Boggs and Udall, the Arizonan would
> win handily.

> The tally gives Udall 131 votes in a Boggs-Udall showdown,
> with 55 for Boggs and 70 undecided.

> The Udall tally shows him with 93 first-ballot votes to 43 for
> Boggs, with 21 going to Representative B. F. Sisk of California,
> 18 to Representative James G. O'Hara of Michigan, 15 to
> Representative Wayne Hays of Ohio, and 63 undecided.

Later that day, Beckler confronted the Boggs camp with the Udall
claims:

> Boggs' count, listing only figures, gives him 125 first-ballot
> votes — only three short of victory with 47 for Udall, 14 for

Sisk, 10 for Hays, 8 for O'Hara, 6 for Representative Edward P. Boland of Mass., and 37 undecided.

There are some surprises on the Udall list, especially in the South, where he is claiming four first-ballot votes in North Carolina, three in Texas, two in Florida, and one each in Alabama, Arkansas, Georgia and Mississippi.

Although Boggs' forces say he has a rock-bottom 50 southern votes, the Udall list gives Boggs only 24 on the first ballot and 31 on the final ballot.

These claims, at great variance with one another, illustrate several themes common to most closely contested congressional leadership races. First, any contest to be decided by secret ballot is bound to lead to considerable "slackness" in count. Members have great flexibility in what they say to the candidates, and the candidates have a tendency to hear what they want to hear.[19] A Representative might respond, "You know where I'll be on this one," intending to convey some ambivalence about his final position; the candidate is prone to accept it as bordering on a commitment, that is, he interprets, "He'll be in my camp." Second and third ballot commitments provide still more flexibility — "I've already given a first ballot commitment to Candidate A (he got to me early or in a moment of weakness), but I'll be for you on the second ballot." Even the point at which a member might change his support from one candidate to another was open to considerable mixed perception. A "second ballot vote" might range from a strict literal interpretation — "I'll be with Candidate X on the first ballot only, and with you from that point on" to "You'll have my 'second' ballot, only at the point my original candidate wavers or drops out of contention" — which might not occur until the third or fourth ballot, if at all. No doubt some members pledged to one candidate and remained committed to their first choice throughout the eight months of campaigning. Many other members, as many as one-third of the 255 Democratic Representatives-elect, found it difficult to say "no." This minority seemed to place few, if any, limits on permissible dissimulation. A freshman member, who sought eagerly an essential (to him) Interior Committee assignment, put something of a reverse twist on the tallying process: "So far three candidates have contacted me; I've told them all the same thing, that I'm not committing myself, but (eyes gleaming) they *all* think I'm for them." Expected first ballot strengths

Table 6.1
Candidate Vote Predictions for House Majority Leadership, 1971

	CANDIDATES PREDICTIONS OF FIRST BALLOT VOTES ON THE EVE OF THE CAUCUS					
	Boggs	Hays	Sisk	O'Hara	Udall	Undecided
Boggs, La.	125	10	14	8	47	37
Hays, Ohio	60–75	40	40	25	60–75	50
Sisk, Cal.	75	20	50+	20	75	13
O'Hara, Mich.	70–80	←35→		42	50–60	40+
Udall, Ariz.	43	15	21	18	93	63
Actual first ballot votes	95	28	31	25	69	—

of the five candidates on the eve of the caucus totaled about 350 votes, almost 100 more than could theoretically or actually be cast (see Table 6.1).

Another point that needs to be stressed is that all candidates tend to magnify their first ballot strength for public consumption, for the maintenance of *esprit de corps* among their campaign supporters, and/or their own psychological well-being. If campaign organizations remain uncertain about the outcome of a contest, they are kept mobilized. If a candidate is not among the front-runners, he faces a further decision: should he pull out in advance or run the risk of further loss of face among his colleagues. It is not so much his own ego-deflation that he endangers as the "unnecessary" costs he may inflict upon his supporters, especially those who are prepared to give his seconding speeches. Committee transfers and assignments have not yet been made. Should the candidate subject his supporters to the wrath of the potential winner and his aides if his own cause is clearly lost? All the trailing candidates — Hays, O'Hara, and Sisk — considered not submitting their names for nomination, but all decided that the situation was uncertain enough that a later ballot victory was still possible, if no longer probable.

IX

Several factors combined to keep the situation relatively fluid as late as the weekend before the caucus on January 19. The various vote tallies being circulated lacked credibility. O'Hara, hearing the Udall vote claims, immediately called John Beckler and asked him to cross-check several members of a large East Coast delegation. Beckler's calls turned up at least one member who admitted being committed to both O'Hara and Udall. "I told both of them I was for them because I am. I'll vote for whichever one stays in the running," this member rationalized.

Boggs was publicly acknowledged as the front-runner by all candidates, save Udall (and even by him on the eve of the vote), but no one could be sure of Boggs' count. With important assists from key congressmen — Hébert and Waggonner in his own delegation, Mills as the chairman of his committee and the most respected southern congressman, and a small coterie of his friends, many of them assistant whips — Boggs had largely run his own campaign. His counts were primarily his own, ably tallied and cross-checked by Gary Hymel.

Another key operator in Boggs' campaign was Tommy Boggs, the 30-year-old son of the congressman, and a close personal friend of several younger southern members. A defeated candidate for the House in 1970, running in the Republican-leaning Eighth District of Maryland, the younger Boggs had met and befriended a number of the incoming freshman members.

As the caucus drew close, the majority whip intensified his efforts to win on the first ballot. Throughout the week of January 11 to 15, Boggs was in touch personally or by long-distance telephone with 84 different members. Of 19 freshman members — some of whom came to see him about committee assignments — a few purposely avoided talking about the forthcoming caucus. Said Paul Sarbanes of Baltimore, Maryland, upset primary victor over the incumbent chairman of Public Works, "It would be like mixing oil and water." Others were not so hesitant to make known their desires for committee assignments in the context of party leadership choice. For it was clear, even to the novitiate, that Boggs as a member of the Democratic Committee on Committees would have more to say about a favorable committee assignment than any other candidate whether he won or lost.[20]

Boggs maintained an intense pace through the weekend before the caucus. Occasionally he took advantage of the misguided release of the tally sheet by the Udall camp. He told wavering members: "Look, this is a secret ballot vote, but what the Udall people are doing is telling everybody how you're supposed to be leaning."

The majority whip also activated the many political ties and interest group contacts he had built up during 20 years on the Ways and Means Committee and his service as a party leader. The AFL–CIO, the UAW, and other large unions considered Boggs a known quality, generally sympathetic to their interests. During the last two weeks of the campaign, they "covered their bets" — "If O'Hara isn't going to make it, then Boggs is our second choice." The Seafarers' Union, through its principal Washington lobbyist, Phillip Carlip, contacted several members on Boggs' behalf, concentrating upon those who served on the Committee on Merchant Marine and Fisheries. Several oil company representatives talked to members of the Texas delegation. The mayor of an East Coast city was prevailed upon to telephone his Democratic delegation. Tobacco and textile interests in the Carolinas actively supported the majority whip. And so it went, with some positive reinforcement results but only rare "turnaround" decisions.

Sometimes an indirect contact from candidate to interest group representative, campaign contributor, or from party figure to another member, would fizzle or backfire. A southern committee chairman was heard to complain: "I resent the way Hale campaigns; he talks to people in your district. Mo Udall; he comes straight out and asks you for your vote." This chairman subsequently voted for Sisk. A young East Coast big-city member, who was considering running for mayor, was called by his leading campaign contributor and urged to vote for Boggs. He backed Udall. But the pull and haul was evident, especially in the final 10 days before the caucus.

At that time, the O'Hara campaign could only be described as "low-key," although the young Michigan law-maker became highly charged and intensely active. Working closely with Ken Young of the AFL–CIO and other labor, education, and civil rights lobbyists, his campaign began to have some impact. The Boggs camp admitted losing "at least two members," but claimed O'Hara was hurting Udall more. On Friday, January 15, a memorandum went out to the O'Hara floor group summarizing "where we stand."

> The battle is not yet won — by anybody. Our count shows no one having more than Boggs' 70–80 first ballot votes. Udall still stands at about 50–60. O'Hara has 42 hard commitments on the first ballot without counting the probables. Sisk and Hays have about 35 votes between them. The 40 or more who haven't yet made a decision are mostly in the northern, big-city delegations.

The O'Hara strategy was to hold on until the third or fourth ballot: "By hanging tough, it boils down to Boggs vs. O'Hara. At that point, O'Hara will win."

Sisk and Hays each had a somewhat comparable third-or-fourth ballot strategy. Both were dependent upon Boggs crumbling and the other establishment candidate dropping out. Meanwhile, Boggs continued his drive for a strong first ballot showing.

The weekend before the caucus saw the tide begin to recede from Udall and flow toward Boggs. A young East Coast member ideologically in tune with Udall called in to report with regret that he no longer was free to vote for the Arizona member. Within 24 hours he had received a pro-Boggs telephone call from a senior member of his region whose judgment he greatly respected; he had been urged by a staff contemporary and good friend not to waste his vote on Udall; perhaps most importantly, he had been advised by a representative of the union that had made major contributions to his campaign that Boggs was their preferred choice. On Monday afternoon he let Boggs know of his reconsideration — this commitment pushed Boggs over the 125 mark. Later, the same junior member called Udall to apologize. Udall couldn't help admiring his friend's honesty, even as he saw his own chances for victory slipping away. Few members were as obliging and candid.

The Udall forces got a temporary uplift toward the end of the week when Edward Boland of Massachusetts indicated he was firmly in the Arizonan's camp and ready to go to work. Boland was given a list of about 40 northeastern and Appropriations Committee members who were considered to be undecided. A personal letter was sent on January 18 from Boland to these and other members urging them to join with him in "a strong vote of confidence for our new Majority Leader."

> I will not only vote for Mo, but he has asked me to put his name in nomination; I will do so. I believe he will make an outstanding floor leader — reasonable, sensible, fair, thoughtful, and always available.

Meanwhile, another Massachusetts senior spokesman, Tip O'Neill, Boland's Washington, D. C. roommate since 1952, was working many of the same New England and East Coast Democratic members on behalf of Boggs. Massachusetts would have a strong lead-in for the appointive position of party whip, no matter which way the contest turned.

X

Hays returned to town only the day before the caucus. He talked on the telephone to both Sisk and Boggs that day. Sisk and Hays, competing for many of the same votes, had each tried, half seriously and half kidding, to convince the other to withdraw, but neither prevailed. Later, Hays' analysis of the votes led him to phone Boggs, then to take an early evening walk from his Rayburn office to the majority whip's offices in the Capitol. As the Ohioan later recalled this meeting with Boggs:

> He offered to come over here. There was no prestige involved. But I had a dinner over on the Senate side, and I had to pick up a key in the House Administration Committee rooms in the Capitol, so I went over there. Knowing Hale's habits, I knew if I waited in my office it might be 8:00 or 8:30 before he arrived . . .

> He showed me his list of votes. I knew there were 20 people he didn't have — some in Pennsylvania that were committed to me, and elsewhere.

> We talked before a number of times, but Monday evening we shook hands on this agreement. If Boggs was in danger, I'd pull out to support him and he said he would do the same for me if I were close to winning. It was pretty clear to me by then that if Boggs went down, then Udall would win.

About an hour after Hays left Boggs, a tired Udall, sitting in his Cannon 119 office, was discouraged, but by no means a resigned candidate.[21] Unaware, of course, of the Boggs-Hays agreement, he commented several times that all along he had underestimated the weight of the establishment in the House. In contrast to previous evenings, his telephones were more silent. His entire staff, save for a Johns Hopkins University–SAIS graduate intern, had gone home. Udall talked about several members who had recently phoned:

> I lost _____. He's a good friend, and you have to admire his honesty in telling me.

> _____ of Ohio. He's a good liberal. How can he end up voting for Boggs?

Then, he bemoaned O'Hara's candidacy. "On Wednesday, the press is going to say the liberals have fouled up again, and they'll be right." Finally, Udall turned to pick up the telephone again. Before he began to call the few "undecideds" he assumed he still had a chance for, he offered his own prediction of what would happen the following afternoon in caucus:

> Boggs is claiming 140 votes tonight, or 125 or 117 (last week) — he doesn't have those but he'll have to be below 100 or I'll have to be ahead of him on the first ballot . . .

> O'Hara's votes cut into mine. If I get only 70 and trail Boggs, then it will be mighty difficult to get back momentum.

Much later, about 1:30 A.M., as Udall sat before a dying fire in his den at home, he again reviewed his chances to become the first liberal, change-oriented majority leader in decades. His final thought to himself as he headed for bed was, "I'm dead."

NOTES

1. Polsby, Chapter 3 of this book.
2. The fencing that took place in the fall when some members began work on behalf of the leading candidates sometimes reached the point of ludicrousness. A Udall supporter relates that he was approached by another member whom he believed to be a behind-the-scenes supporter of Boggs. The scenario, with several variations, follows:
   Boggs supporter: "How do you think Hale is doing?"
   Udall supporter (not yet publicly committed): "I think he's doing fine" (because he thinks Boggs may well be leading).
   Boggs supporter: "Do you think you could be for him?"
   Udall supporter: "Why, are you working for him?"
   Boggs supporter: "Yes" (or possibly, "No," depending upon how well he knew his contact).
   Udall supporter: "Well, I've already committed myself to Udall" (or, "I haven't yet made up my mind," again depending upon the character of their past relationship) or even, "I'm thinking of running myself."
   Boggs supporter: (Laughter)
   Udall supporter: "Do you think that's funny?" (Breaks off conversation in mock anger).
3. James S. Coleman, "Political Money," *Am. Pol. Sci. Rev.* **64** (December 1970), 1074–1087; Peter M. Blau, *Exchange and Power in Social Life* (New York: Wiley, 1964); Robert L. Peabody, "Organization Theory and Legislative Behavior: Bargaining, Hierarchy, and Change in the U.S. House of Representatives," paper delivered before the Annual Meeting of the American Political Science Association, New York City, September 1963.
4. Rowland Evans and Robert Novak, "Boggs Bopped," *Washington Post*, November 29, 1970, p. B-7.
5. Polsby, Chapter 3 and Peabody, Chapter 4 of this book.
6. Transcript of *CBS Morning News*, Bernard Kalb, Interviewer, December 18, 1970, pp. 9–10.
7. Charles Bartlett, "Democratic Unity Faces Two Tests," *Washington Star*, December 29, 1970, p. A-9.

8. The most pertinent paragraph of the resolution provided that "After nominating and seconding speeches, balloting shall proceed without interruption or recess from ballot to ballot until one candidate shall have received the votes of a majority of those present and voting and then be declared elected; providing that following any ballot a candidate wishing to withdraw shall be entitled to recognition for one minute for the purpose of advising the caucus."

9. For example, the caucus would not be able to turn to someone like Wilbur Mills, who had not campaigned or been nominated. "Low man out" had not been used as a decision strategy in previous House races. On January 2, 1935, William B. Bankhead of Alabama came within 15 votes of securing a necessary majority of votes for majority leader for the 75th Congress. All eight candidates (including John W. McCormack of Massachusetts) remained in the running, but Bankhead picked up 26 more votes and won with 5 votes to spare on the second ballot. Legislative Reference Service, memorandum, researched by Walter J. Oleszek, May 27, 1970, p. 2.

10. Richard Harwood, "Power of the Press: Myth or Reality," *Washington Post*, January 28, 1971, p. A-14; Michael Green, "Nobody Covers the House," *Washington Monthly* 2 (June 1970).

11. Marjorie Hunter, "House Democrats Vie for Top Post," *New York Times*, November 22, 1970, p. 48.

12. Evans and Novak, *op. cit.*

13. Rowland Evans and Robert Novak, "Slipped Sisk," *Washington Post*, December 20, 1970, p. B-7.

14. "House Battle," *New Republic*, December 5, 1970; "Udall and O'Hara," *New Republic*, January 16, 1971; Erwin Knoll, "The House Afire," *The Progressive*, January 1971.

15. One of Udall's close supporters from Missouri had helped to generate the *St. Louis Post Dispatch* endorsement. The *Washington Post* was never cracked, despite a close friend or two on the editorial desk. The day after the contest, the *New York Times* complained about a continuation of the *status quo* in the leadership. "Where were they when we needed them?" complained a Udall staff member.

16. Dan Thomasson, "Udall Leading for House Post," *Washington Daily News*, January 12, 1971, p. 10.

17. *Congressional Quarterly Weekly Report* 29 (January 15, 1971), 141–146.

18. *Washington Post*, January 12, 1971, p. A-2; *Washington Evening Star*, January 12, 1971, p. A-1.

19. Midway in the campaign, Udall and O'Hara attended several strategy meetings in Frank Thompson's office where a list of the state delegations was reviewed member by member to determine their leanings. The Mississippi delegation was being discussed and its members were being routinely assigned to Boggs, or Sisk, when Udall broke in: "I think Sonny Montgomery will vote for me; he continues to be open and friendly." O'Hara retorted caustically, "Yes, and Jamie Whitten said 'Hello' to me in the corridor today." Motivations are seldom simple and clear-cut, but Udall apparently received at least one southern vote because of a friendship and mutual respect developed during common attendance at congressional prayer breakfasts.

20. Boggs retained his seat on the Democratic Committee on Committees (the 15 majority members of the Ways and Means Committee) until after committee assignments for the 92d Congress were completed. On February 3, 1971 the Democratic Caucus chose his fellow Louisianan, Joe Waggonner, as his successor. Waggonner defeated the Democratic Study Group chairman, Donald Fraser of Minnesota, by a vote of 119 to 104.

21. Cf. Larry L. King, "The Road to Power in Congress," *Harper's* 242 (June 1971), pp. 39–63 at p. 57.

CHAPTER SEVEN

The 1971 House Democratic Caucus
and Its Aftermath

I'm sitting here just like the man in the fork of a tree. Won't know which way to jump, until I jump.

— Senior southern congressman
on the eve of the caucus

In January, I'll sit there on the floor and watch the wheels within wheels turn.

— Fourth-term western Representative

As the 254 Democratic Representatives-elect straggled to the floor of the House for their party caucus the morning of Tuesday, January 19, 1971, they wended their way through a crowd of spectators that included newspaper reporters, TV and radio commentators, lobbyists, congressional staff, college professors, and students. Most spectators were more prompt for the 10:00 A.M. opening than the congressmen, even though the members, with the possible exception of the personal staff of the candidates, had much more at stake. For these Democratic members would choose not only a new Speaker, but a new majority leader, someone who, in all probability, would succeed to the Speakership within the next decade. Thus, barring death, election upset, or rare party revolt, the Democrats were selecting their principal leaders for the next two decades or more.

I

Before the caucus selected the majority leader, it had to proceed through a mixed order of business, some routine and some potentially explosive. Since early December the chairman of the caucus, Dan Rostenkowski of Illinois, had made plans, conferred with the leadership, consulted with the House parliamentarians, and listened to dissident liberals about the proposed agenda and possible rules changes. Among other important items, this caucus would discuss and vote on a number of recommendations put forward by the Committee on Organization, Study, and Review, the so-called Hansen Committee after its chairman, Representative Julia Butler Hansen of Washington. This 11-member committee had met during the preceding summer more than a dozen times to consider questions of seniority and committee organization. Hand-picked by Rostenkowski and McCormack to provide geographical and ideological balance, the committee's membership included both O'Hara and Hays.

Finally, the caucus would consider what had become almost a biennial matter, a challenge to the seniority of southern members, in this case, the seating of the entire Mississippi delegation.

Rostenkowski, who had seriously considered becoming a candidate for majority leadership, had seen his friend and senior colleague on the Ways and Means Committee, Hale Boggs, come back as a leading contender in the closing months of the 91st Congress. An assistant whip since 1965, Rostenkowski had discussed the leadership race with Boggs at length through the summer and fall. The likelihood that Boggs might turn to Rostenkowski as his choice for majority whip had been discussed a number of times.[1] Both men agreed that their understanding, whatever it might be, should not be publicly acknowledged or widely disseminated among the House membership. The first and most obvious reason was that it would inhibit Boggs' ability to negotiate and secure the support of several other leading Democrats who might covet the appointment. A second reason for wanting to discourage talk of a "deal" was that it could be played upon by opposition candidates as an example of "crass, political manipulation," "smacking of Mayor Daley's bossism," and "wheeling and dealing." Finally, of course, Rostenkowski wanted to avoid criticism that would inhibit his presiding with integrity and fairness during the trying and controversial caucus yet to come. His task was difficult enough without further complications.

Did the two men have an arrangement preceding the caucus? In the last analysis, perhaps only they and their closest staff associates would know for certain. All evidence seems to point in the direction of a general understanding — Rostenkowski would work to align his Chicago colleagues and friends in other delegations behind Boggs' candidacy.[2] In turn, there was the strong presumption that should the Louisianan win, his first recommendation for whip would be his younger friend from Chicago.[3]

Although both congressmen might deny it, it seems clear in retrospect that Udall and Boland had a similar understanding; that O'Hara probably would have rewarded the support he received from Jack Brooks of Texas had he won; and that Sisk looked long, hard, and unsuccessfully for a northeastern Catholic whip choice to balance his candidacy. Only Wayne Hays seems not to have seriously negotiated with other members to strengthen his own candidacy for majority leader. More likely, he continued to entertain some hopes of becoming Boggs' choice for whip.

II

Behind closed doors, with the press and public excluded as is customary, the Democratic membership routinely adopted an order of business which called first for the election of the chairman of the caucus. To Rostenkowski's great surprise his efforts to win an unprecedented third term without opposition were challenged. Frozen from other positions of leadership since the death of Speaker Rayburn, the 20-member Texas delegation nominated 60-year-old Representative Olin E. "Tiger" Teague as its candidate for caucus chairman. First elected to the House in 1946, Teague was a much-decorated combat veteran. (He originally earned his nickname from aggressive play on a high school football team.) At the caucus, despite the absence of nearly half of the delegation including the proposed candidate, Omar Burleson quickly persuaded his colleagues to back Teague. Accepting the nomination without much enthusiasm, Teague marked his ballot "Rostenkowski" when the time came to vote. When his turn came to march down the aisle and deposit his ballot, he held it high to show it to his opponent. The final vote went the other way: Teague, 155; Rostenkowski, 91. The defeated candidate had heard rumors the previous evening that Teague might be a candidate but had not taken them seriously. Indeed, even during the nominating speeches, he fully expected his opponent to withdraw.[4]

In this, as in every contest in the House, a number of factors decided the final outcome. Chief among them were Teague's personal popularity, his strong southern base, and the fact that no prior caucus chairman had ever served for more than two terms.[5] Enthusiasm for Teague, generated by Burleson, Bob Sikes of Florida, and the behind-the-scenes activity of several northern members, spread too quickly to be a strictly spontaneous ouster.

Admittedly, Rostenkowski's own personality and his close ties to the Daley political organization did little to offset some of the Texan's initial advantages. Big, aggressive, tough-minded, the Chicagoan had probably bruised more than one colleague's ego in his rapid rise to House leadership. Members of the New Jersey delegation were still doing a slow burn because Rostenkowski, from his vantage point on the Democratic Committee on Committees, did not fill a vacancy on the Interstate and Foreign Commerce Committee for more than a year. He reserved this choice assignment for an incoming Chicago freshman. Meanwhile several New Jersey members were kept from advantageous committee assignments. For some House liberals the vote against Rostenkowski was a cheap rap at Mayor Daley and the Chicago machine image. Finally, some Udall and O'Hara supporters, knowing of the closeness between Rostenkowski and Boggs, probably took advantage of the vote as a means of frustrating the one and possibly throwing the other's bid for leadership off stride.

As news of the Rostenkowski upset penetrated to the corridor outside the Speaker's office, spectators wondered whether it meant a decisive setback for Boggs. Three hours went by before a negative answer was made known. Meanwhile, the remaining officers of the caucus were selected and nominations for the Democratic candidate for Speaker were under way.

In this year of Democratic internecine warfare, even Albert suffered a challenge. Representative John Conyers, a four-term black congressman from Detroit, decided to use the Speaker's contest as a forum to protest the way in which the challenge to the seating of the Mississippi delegation was being frustrated. Only 19 of his Democratic colleagues seemed to agree with him that this was the proper vehicle for such a protest. To no one's surprise, the genial Oklahoma Representative easily won the Democratic nomination for Speaker by a vote of 220 to 20. Not even all of his 11 black colleagues voted for Conyers, but later they unanimously supported a Conyers resolution to strip seniority from the five Mississippi Democrats. Still, the motion failed decisively, 111 to 55.

III

Finally, about 2:00 P.M. nominations were opened for the majority leader. Teague was in the chair, his predecessor sitting beside him advising on parliamentary procedure. There were no surprises this time — each of the five publicly announced candidates was nominated; no last-minute dark-horse contenders entered the race. Each candidate had submitted in advance a list of his nominator (a five-minute speech) and four seconders (two-minute talks each) to the caucus chairman. The candidates drew lots for the order in which their nominations and seconding speeches would be presented (see Table 7.1).

Speeches in party caucuses probably change about as many votes as speeches on the floor of the House, that is to say, very few indeed. Still, all candidates gave considerable attention to the selection of nominators and seconders and the order in which they spoke. For it was not the content of the speech that was important, but rather what that speaker symbolized by way of personal reputation and regional backing.

Typically, the nominating speech was delivered by the senior member of the candidate's own state delegation (Holifield of California, Hébert of Louisiana, and Diggs of Michigan). In Hays' case, since he was the senior member in Ohio, he turned to his friend and chairman of the Foreign Affairs Committee, "Doc" Morgan of Pennsylvania. Udall, as the lone Democratic member from Arizona, could choose from the entire country. Edward Boland of Massachusetts was a calculated choice to break through to Catholic New England. The three establishment candidates, at least, found it propitious to call upon one of the nine Democratic congresswomen (Green of Oregon, Sullivan of Missouri, and Hansen of Washington) for a seconding speech. Udall seriously considered asking Patsy Mink of Hawaii to speak in his behalf, but finally opted for another attractive "comer" from the West, Tom Foley of Washington. Every candidate felt compelled to have at least one supporter from the South or Southwest — Sisk and Boggs each had two. Texans spoke on behalf of every candidate except Boggs. Every candidate went out of his way to demonstrate broad regional support by his choice of spokesmen: O'Hara revealed the narrowest base — he had no seconder from the West or the Rocky Mountain states. He had hoped for a seconding speech by Carl Perkins of Kentucky, the chairman of the House Education and Labor Committee, but at the last moment Perkins was unavailable.

If any speech changed votes, or more important, kept errant votes from straying, it was the closing seconding speech for Boggs delivered by Wilbur Mills. The powerful chairman of the Ways and Means Committee emphasized his candidate's party loyalty, intellect, and

Table 7.1
Nominators and Seconders of Majority Leadership Candidates, 1971

Candidates	Sisk, Cal.	Boggs, La.	Hays, Ohio	O'Hara, Mich.	Udall, Ariz.
Nominators	Holifield, Cal.	Hébert, La.	Morgan, Pa.	Diggs, Mich.	Boland, Mass.
Seconders	Sikes, Fla. E. Green, Ore. Ichord, Mo. Casey, Tex.	Sullivan, Mo. Matsunaga, Ha. Carey, N.Y. Mills, Ark.	Hansen, Wash. Kazen, Tex. Gray, Ill. Podell, N.Y.	Brooks, Tex. Scheuer, N.Y. Fraser, Minn.	Dulski, N.Y. W. Green, Pa. Foley, Wash. Purcell, Tex.

courage. Mills questioned whether he, or another member, would have had the courage Boggs showed in taking on the oil industry and working for reduction of the depletion allowance in 1969. Mills stressed that he and Boggs shared a close working relationship on the Ways and Means Committee for 22 years (leaving unvoiced any preference he might have had for wanting Boggs off the committee). This speech probably went a long way toward anchoring in the senior members of the South and convincing wavering freshmen that here, after all, were the two people who would decide on their committee assignments.

Balloting for the majority leadership got under way about 3:00 P.M. on small, green slips of paper handed out by "Fishbait" Miller, the House Doorkeeper. After considerable confusion over balloting in the Rostenkowski-Teague and Albert-Conyers contests, the new Caucus Chairman Teague now insisted that members walk down the aisle toward the Speaker's chair. At that point they were held until recognized by the Reading Clerk. As his name was called, the member deposited his ballot in a metal wastepaper basket placed on the dais before the Speaker's rostrum. After all balloting was finished, the basket was carried to a table in the Speaker's lobby where the nominators for each candidate served as tellers in counting ballots. Each ballot was unfolded, read aloud by the Doorkeeper's assistant, and placed in five separate stacks that represented the five candidates. Tellers recorded them in five columns, Boggs, 1, 2, 3, 4, tally; 1, 2, . . . , and so on.[6]

Boggs took an early lead and never lost it. At the end of the first ballot the count was as follows:

Boggs	95
Udall	69
Sisk	31
Hays	28
O'Hara	25
	248

With 248 ballots cast, the majority whip was but 30 votes short of the 125 vote majority he needed to move up to majority leader.[7] Could Boggs be stopped?

The answer was quickly forthcoming. As soon as the results were announced, two of the trailing candidates, Hays and O'Hara, were on their feet to seek recognition from the chair. Teague recognized Hays first, and the senior Ohioan withdrew, endorsing Boggs in the process. When O'Hara's turn came, he too dropped out, but he failed to endorse his friend and fellow-liberal, Morris Udall, as some members hoped and expected him to do.[8] Sisk gave serious consideration to withdrawing at that stage of the contest, too. However, Holifield and Sikes of Florida prevailed upon him to stay through one more ballot on the long shot that there might still be a stalemate.[9]

Under the rules adopted at the December 23 candidates' meeting, the second round of balloting was to begin just as soon as the first ballot results were announced and candidates who desired had withdrawn. This time pink paper ballots were used, members once again milled around, then walked down the center aisle to vote as their names were acknowledged. The counting procedures were the same as for the first ballot.

By 4:17 P.M. Boggs arrived at a majority of 125 favorable votes and the Democrats had a new majority leader. Boggs had 15 votes more than required when the second ballot count was concluded:

Boggs	140
Udall	88
Sisk	17
	245

More than half of the 45 votes Boggs picked up between the first and second ballots came from the Hays camp. By the Ohioan's own reckoning, 26 of his 28 first ballot votes went to Boggs. "I know of two that did not — they told me they had a second ballot commitment to Udall." Later, he explained his motivations for withdrawing to a *National Journal* reporter:[10]

> I dropped out because I was afraid I would destroy his [Boggs'] momentum and destroy him. I had a lot of commitments from Boggs' people on the second ballot.

Not all observers would agree. Some members thought it was just a case of Hays sensing the way the wind was blowing and hurrying to gain credit for helping to put Boggs over the top.

Clearly, Sisk had little reason to stay in contention, as his sharp decline from 31 to 17 votes confirmed. Again, most of his lost votes probably went to the winner.

Udall picked up only 19 votes between the first and second ballots. It seems clear, in retrospect, that most of these votes were original O'Hara ballots, although some of O'Hara's support from union-dominated districts would have gone to Boggs rather than to Udall. Udall's failure to support labor's drive to repeal Section 14b of the Taft-Hartley Act in 1965 had returned to haunt him. In the final analysis, Udall's overall strength may have been as high as 100 votes. But when members sensed, after the first ballot, that the Arizonan could not win, some of his marginal support flocked to Boggs.[11]

In sum, Udall's worst fears on the eve of the election were realized. He did not hold Boggs much below 100 votes; his own first ballot strength was too far behind the front-runner to make a rally feasible.

IV

Interpretations of the election outcome were as varied as the candidates themselves. O'Hara described it as "a vote of confidence for the *status quo.*" Boggs denied this: "I would characterize that as a rather exaggerated statement of a very dear friend of mine who had been defeated . . . I'm not *status quo* — I never have been." [12] The new floor leader went on to insist that the new leadership team would be "innovative" and "susceptible to change."

Hays reacted philosophically to his defeat. All along he had felt "pretty relaxed" about it. He knew from the beginning he would become either majority leader or chairman of the House Administration Committee. Within the week the new leadership was turning to him with requests for assistance on Capitol personnel and operations.

Sisk, too, took his loss in stride; he was "relaxed, relieved, and just glad it's over." [13] Few members of Congress could claim to have come so far — from depression-day poverty and thinning nectarines in California orchards to the halls of Congress, membership on the powerful Rules Committee, and a third-place finish in a contest for Democratic majority leader. Tony Coelho, Sisk's administrative assistant, took it harder than his "boss." Generally true throughout the Capitol, the personal staffs of the losing candidates could not immediately bounce back. For more than one, life took on an added cynicism.[14]

Udall's concession speech in the well of the House, with its blend of humor, candor, and good grace, was well received. As he moved to make Boggs' election unanimous, he complimented Boggs as a "national Democrat," one who could serve as a spokesman for all groups in the Democratic House — conservatives, moderates, liberals, southerners, northerners, and westerners. Later, as he left the hall and stood in the crowded corridor near the Speaker's chambers, Udall was pressed by reporters to reveal his innermost feelings. Outwardly composed but inwardly churning, he recalled a cemetery marker in Tombstone, Arizona which said simply, "Johnson — done his damndest." That, Udall said, seemed a fitting epitaph for his own campaign. Later, back in his office among staff and friends, he was less sanguine and no longer above the battle. A touch of bitterness and disappointment was evident as he reflected upon members who had said one thing and done another.[15]

Boggs, of course, was elated. After his election he searched for Carl Albert on the House floor, so the two leaders could hold a joint press conference. The caucus plunged back into its business, which included the question of seating the Mississippi members. Boggs and Albert never did get together. Meanwhile, the whip and Boggs' personal office staff opened a bar in his ground-floor offices on the east front of the Capitol. Mrs. Albert came by about 6:15 P.M. to congratulate a beaming Mrs. Boggs. When the new majority leader arrived at 6:25 P.M., accompanied by his administrative assistant, they were met with applause and cheers by the some 30 to 35 friends, newspaper and magazine reporters, former congressmen, and staff. Boggs had been busy making the first of many TV tapes in his new capacity — this one for the following morning's CBS News. Then Boggs turned to Jimmy Nickens, his young friend and staff assistant, and asked him to fix a drink. The new majority leader moved slowly through the room, kissed the ladies, shook hands, and chatted with friends. Several times he shook his head, indicating to himself and others: "I can't believe it — I just can't believe it." As if to put away all final doubt, President Richard Nixon telephoned to offer his personal congratulations. Earlier in the day, former President Lyndon Johnson and former Speaker McCormack had telephoned to offer their encouragement and any final assistance they might provide.

V

Two days later, January 21, 1971, the 92d Congress convened. Carl Albert was nominated Speaker by the new chairman of the Democratic Caucus, Representative Olin Teague of Texas. His Republican counterpart, John Anderson of Illinois, then nominated the minority leader of six years, Gerald R. Ford, Jr. of Michigan. True to form, all Democrats called "Albert," and all Republicans shouted "Ford," when names were read by the Reading Clerk. The vote counted 250 for Albert, 176 for Ford. A few minutes later, while hundreds of Oklahoma visitors watched on six large closed-circuit colored television sets in Statuary Hall in the Capitol, "the little giant from Little Dixie" was sworn in as the 46th Speaker of the House of Representatives.

There was little time for basking in glory. Almost immediately, Albert and Boggs were preoccupied with a series of disappearing quorums as Republicans fought to protest a proposed 21-day rule change. The next day, by a vote of 133 to 254, the new leadership would suffer its first floor defeat. The conservative coalition — a majority of Republicans combined with mostly southern Democrats — had refused to adopt a 21-day rule change previously endorsed in the Democratic Caucus.

Other questions of internal organization continued to preoccupy the House Democrats. The caucus had selected a new Speaker, majority leader, and caucus chairman, but the number three position in the Democratic hierarchy, the majority whip position, remained to be filled.

By tradition the majority leadership usually announces its choice for whip on the opening day of the new Congress. But, in this instance, a successor was not chosen or announced until Friday, the second day of the 92d Congress. The previous Wednesday, those most responsible for the second day's caucus activities, Carl Albert, Hale Boggs, and Olin Teague, had met for breakfast in the whip's office in the Capitol. Dan Rostenkowski, also invited, had arrived late. Two others also present were Pat Jennings, the clerk of the House and former Congressman from Virginia, and Gary Hymel, Boggs' assistant. Before Rostenkowski arrived the new Speaker and majority leader had their first hurried opportunity to discuss the appointment of a whip.

During the previous afternoon and evening, Albert had been bombarded by requests to convert the traditionally appointive position into an elective one. Many calls came from Udall supporters, but Albert found himself initially sympathetic to the idea for other reasons. First, the position of whip was increasing in stature. Second, there was a strong undercurrent of opposition to placing a person on the ladder of succession by appointment, particularly since such a pattern to positions of higher leadership seemed to be developing. Third, Albert was aware that Boggs would select Rostenkowski, an appointment Albert unalterably opposed for reasons already intimated. Finally, Albert would have been happy with Udall as whip, not only because they regarded each other highly but also because Udall could attract certain dissident liberals back into the fold. Should the caucus favor the idea, the Arizonan's proven base of 90–100 votes, plus a quiet word from Albert, quite likely would put him over.

It remains unclear whether Udall's name was ever mentioned, or if Boggs voiced his position on the question. However, shortly after the breakfast meeting, Albert ran into several reporters on the way back to his first-floor Capitol office. They asked him if he were opposed to electing a whip. Albert replied that he wasn't opposed; indeed, he was sympathetic to the idea.

For public consumption, Boggs neither favored nor opposed electing a whip in the party caucus. As he told a reporter shortly after his own election, "You could easily argue that question from both sides." [16] Privately, he wished the position to remain appointive, in part, because he wanted a whip who would be loyal to himself (and to the Speaker) and, in part, because he recognized that to achieve geographical balance someone from the Midwest or Northeast should be chosen. Three of the top four leaders represented the adjacent states of Oklahoma, Louisiana, and Texas. Both the Midwest and Northeast had far larger regional delegations than the West. Finally, on personal and geographical grounds and questions of loyalty, he was opposed to Morris Udall as either an elected or appointed whip.

As the word spread among Democratic congressmen that the new Speaker leaned toward electing a whip, members opposed to Udall, the elective mechanism, or both, began to confront Albert in the Democratic cloakroom. Finally, a small group of senior members, Albert and Boggs among them, walked out the back door of the cloakroom and down the hall to the more quiet Ways and Means Committee room. There, Tip O'Neill of Massachusetts and Hugh Carey of New York presented two principal reasons for keeping the position appointive. One was geographical: If the whip were elected, what was to prevent the fourth leadership position from going to the South or the Southwest? The other reason concerned the need for loyalty and close cooperation among the top three positions. "If you make that position elective," said a participant, "it could be like putting a viper in the hen house." Before the end of the meeting, Wilbur Mills strolled in and added his voice to the arguments against making the position elective. Under the weight of the arguments of mainstream members, Albert apparently reconsidered and backed off from his initial stand about making the whip an elective position.

In the caucus about an hour later, Wayne Hays of Ohio and Ken Gray of Illinois jointly offered a resolution to make the whip position an elective one. But it was not to be. The tip-off came when both Albert and Boggs spoke against the resolution on grounds of geographical and loyalty concerns. Respected members of the change-oriented side chimed in, among them Bolling and even Udall. If the motion had carried, Udall was prepared to make a contest of it, but when Albert changed his mind, "that was the ball game." By the time John Conyers offered a tabling motion, only a voice vote was needed to defeat the resolution. Still, a substantial, and probably increasing, number of members seemed to resent the use of the whip's position as a stepping-stone to higher office. Representative Dante Fascell's motion that would have restricted the as-yet-unappointed whip to two successive terms, or four years, was barely defeated, 71–68.

Who would Boggs and Albert appoint? Boggs preferred Dan Rostenkowski, his colleague on the Ways and Means Committee who easily met the twin requirements of loyalty and geographical balance. But Albert had other ideas. He said a main reason for rejecting Rostenkowski was that his loss in the caucus indicated a lack of confidence on the part of many Democratic members. There were other factors as well — at least one member of Rostenkowski's own Illinois delegation. had gone to Albert to protest Rostenkowski's selection. Apparently this member felt that the young Chicago leader had sometimes dealt rather arbitrarily with the downstate members in the Illinois delegation. Finally, Albert had not overlooked Rostenkowski's reluctance to endorse his own candidacy for Speaker the previous summer.

The two leaders each had exercised a veto of sorts: Albert had eliminated Rostenkowski; Boggs refused to entertain the choice of Udall. Boggs next asked his administrative assistant to draw up a list of possible candidates who would meet the twin geographic and loyalty requirements. Hymel, working systematically through a whip's tally book, came up with a list of eight names, three from the East, three from the Midwest, and two from the West.

On Friday morning, Boggs took that list to a meeting in Albert's office. The Speaker glanced at the list, crossed out three names, and told Boggs that any of the remaining five people would be acceptable to him. Boggs' first choice was Thomas P. "Tip" O'Neil of Massachusetts.

The 58-year-old O'Neill, still smarting from Udall's challenge to his close friend, Speaker McCormack in 1969, helped to put Boggs over the top in 1971. In a head-to-head battle with his roommate, Eddie Boland, it seems clear that O'Neill got more than his share of the New England votes for Boggs. When Boggs had called the genial Irishman about a week before the caucus vote to see how he was leaning, O'Neill replied with a story: When he, at age 21, entered his first race as a candidate for the Cambridge City Council, a neighbor, Mrs. O'Brien, confronted him on the street:

> "Tip, I'm going to vote for you even though you never asked me to."
>
> I said: "Mrs. O'Brien, I've been shoveling your walk and mowing your grass ever since I can remember, I didn't think I had to ask you to vote for me."
>
> "Tip," she told me, "I always like to be asked just like everybody else."

Boggs was quick to grasp the message, and he asked O'Neill if he would vote for him for majority leader. O'Neill replied that he would, but only if his fellow Massachusetts Representative, Edward P. Boland, decided not to run. This proved to be the case.

After Boggs' victory, O'Neill came by his whip's office to remind him of the parable of Mrs. O'Brien. The new majority leader acknowledged that he still remembered, which led O'Neill to continue:[17]

> Well, you know that I wasn't going to support you originally, and you owe me no obligations, but I'd like to be whip, and I'm asking you for it.

The evening before the announcement on the House floor, O'Neill was convinced that he was out of contention. Though he was only two years older than Boggs and four years younger than Albert, he thought the new leadership would turn to a younger man, possibly Hugh Carey of New York. Unbeknownst to O'Neill, the 52-year-old Carey had run into opposition within his own delegation. One of the senior New York Democrats apparently resented the pace at which Carey was moving up in the House and spreading his influence throughout the delegation.

O'Neill was notified that he was the choice for whip by a 12:25 P.M. telephone call on Friday, January 22, 1971. "Tip," said the Speaker, "this is Carl. Here's Hale and he has something to tell you."

To provide somewhat broader geographical balance and better floor support, the leadership decided to abandon the position of deputy whip and create two new positions called "floor whips." John Brademas of Indiana, an O'Hara supporter, and John McFall, a Californian who had remained loyal to Boggs, were chosen to fill the new positions. Meanwhile, John Moss, who had made an abortive run at the majority leadership before Sisk replaced him as the California candidate, had quietly resigned as deputy whip. He would, he said, be preoccupied with heavy committee duties.

VI

In the House of Representatives six months is a generation.

— Speaker Rayburn

Why did Hale Boggs win and Morris Udall and the other contenders lose? At first glance the answer to this question would seem perfectly straightforward and simple. The incumbent whip was supported by senior, establishment members, only a few of whom broke away to back Hays and Sisk. Udall and O'Hara, on the other hand, split up the more junior, change-oriented members with the Arizonan receiving most of their votes. Throughout most of the 1960's and early 1970's, House Democrats of the former type tend to outnumber those of the latter type by a rough ratio of three to two.

Evidence for this proposition comes from taking an alphabetic roster of House Democrats in the 92d Congress, listed alphabetically by states, and allocating members into two categories: establishment (or *status-quo*-oriented) and change-oriented (especially in the institutional reform sense).[18] Most members fall rather neatly into one of the two extremes. (A residual or in-between column can be used for those members difficult to classify.) George Andrews of Alabama, first on such a roster, is clearly classified as "establishment." So too would be Harold T. Johnson of California, John C. Kluczynski of Illinois, or James A. Burke of Massachusetts. These members, used to working by the rules of the game in the House, tend to represent safe districts, they have served for a decade or more; and, by and large, the system has been good to them (and their districts).

Change-oriented members, fewer in number and more junior, by definition are motivated toward reform if not radical alteration of the system. David Pryor of Arkansas tends to fit this classification. More clear-cut examples would be Phillip Burton of California, Abner Mikva of Illinois, and Michael Harrington of Massachusetts.

Classification does not follow strict ideological lines. Men in both camps could have closely approximated roll call voting records. Some establishment types vote quite liberally, for example. Still, conservatives-to-moderates tend to be establishment types; liberals are more likely to be change-oriented.

A few members are difficult to classify in either camp. In what category would one place Richard Bolling of Missouri or Ed Edmondson of Oklahoma, for example? Both have worked well within the system, but both have been open to change. On the strength of his writings, Bolling clearly belongs in the change-oriented group. Further, a number of freshmen have yet to align themselves with either classification. Finally, some members seem to move from the change-oriented group toward the establishment sector as they grow older or gain seniority.

Table 7.2 lists the 45 states with one or more Democratic House

Table 7.2
Establishment and Change-Oriented House Democrats, 92d Congress, Classified by State Delegations

State	Establishment	Mixed or Unclassifiable	Change-Oriented
Alabama	4	1	
Alaska		1	
Arizona			1
Arkansas	2		1
California	10	2	8
Colorado	1		1
Connecticut	2	1	1
Florida	6	1	2
Georgia	6	2	

Table 7.2   (continued)

State	Establishment	Mixed or Unclassifiable	Change-Oriented
Hawaii	1		1
Illinois	8	2	2
Indiana	1	1	3
Iowa	1		1
Kansas		1	
Kentucky	4	1	
Louisiana	7	1	
Maine			2
Maryland	3		2
Massachusetts	4	2	2
Michigan	2	1	4
Minnesota	3		1
Mississippi	4	1	
Missouri	5	1	3
Montana		1	
Nevada	1		
New Jersey	5	2	2
New Mexico		1	
New York	9	4	11
North Carolina	4	3	
North Dakota		1	
Ohio	5		2
Oklahoma	3	1	
Oregon	1	1	
Pennsylvania	9	3	2
Rhode Island	1	1	
South Carolina	5		
South Dakota		2	
Tennessee	4		1
Texas	15	2	3
Utah		1	
Virginia	4		
Washington	1	1	4
West Virginia	4	1	
Wisconsin	1		4
Wyoming		1	
TOTALS	146	45	64

members. Each delegation has been more or less arbitrarily divided into the three categories: establishment, mixed or difficult to classify, and change-oriented. Establishment members outnumber change-oriented members two to one. Even if mixed and unclassifiable members are grouped together with change-oriented members, the establishment members enjoy a favorable ratio of about three to two. The point of the table is not its member-by-member or even state-by-state accuracy but rather its demonstration of a basic theme — an establishment candidate like Boggs, and for that matter, Wayne Hays and B. F. Sisk, starts off with an impressive advantage over any candidate inclined toward reform or change of the institution — at least for the 92nd and similar Congresses.

What themes seemed to appeal to most of these establishment members? First, Boggs stressed again and again his demonstrated party loyalty. He reminded members that he had rendered years of faithful party service as whip and also had served as chairman of the National Platform Committee. Moreover, he was the only candidate with something to lose. Admittedly, the other candidates put their prestige on the line, but nothing like the personal setback that Boggs could have suffered in Washington and back home had he been defeated. Finally, the senior Louisianan selectively emphasized his southern ties. A defeat for Boggs, it was claimed, would mean a defeat for the South, seniority, and the whole process of decentralized, committee-centered legislating. Not all these arguments were persuasive. Still, they found the receptive ears of many members who were fond of emphasizing geographical ties, preferred the seniority system, and appreciated the benefits of a logical and orderly pattern of leadership succession.[19] In short, with Boggs you would know where you stood. Udall, in contrast, was viewed with uncertainty and by some considered as a direct threat to some of these cherished traditions.

Basic establishment themes were reinforced by the respective seniority of the two principal contestants. Boggs, beginning his 27th year of congressional service, was in the top 10 percent of House Democratic members in terms of seniority. Only 20 people, 13 of them chairmen of congressional committees, were more senior than he. In contrast, Udall was a rank upstart. He had only nine years of service, and some 118 members, or almost half of the House Democrats in the 92d Congress, had more seniority than the Arizona challenger. The other three candidates fell midway between Boggs and Udall — Hays had 32 members more senior than he, Sisk had 59, and O'Hara had 82.[20]

Put another way, Udall would have had to convert and hold all but a half-dozen of the House Democrats with less seniority than he had, were the issue to be decided on grounds of seniority alone. The evidence from candidate polls and interviews strongly supports the interpretation that House Democrats were, in fact, divided largely along senior-junior lines in the preliminary and final caucus votes. For example, of the 41 members who worked actively in Udall's behalf, only six had served six terms or more — Sidney Yates of Illinois (ten terms), Frank Thompson of New Jersey, Dante Fascell of Florida, and Henry Reuss of Wisconsin (eight terms), and Robert Kastenmeier of Wisconsin and Thaddeus J. Dulski of New York (six terms). Twenty-two, or just over half of his most active supporters, were members of the classes of 1962 and 1964. Udall had the support and backing of only one committee chairman, Dulski, who presided over one of Udall's two committees, Post Office and Civil Service. Dulski was not only the youngest committee chairman in the House at 55, but also the most junior, having first been elected to Congress in 1958. Udall's other chairman, the competent, if acerbic, Wayne Aspinall of Colorado, who presided over Interior and Insular Affairs, never responded to Udall's pleas for support.

One important exception to this general demarcation along senior-junior lines was the strong showing Boggs made among the 33 freshmen. For Udall to win, he would have to hold these freshmen by at least a two-to-one margin. Instead, it appears that Boggs actually got more freshman votes than Udall on both the first and second ballots. An overly simple explanation would attribute this shift to Boggs' influential position as ranking member of the Ways and Means Committee, and hence, his image as "a man who could take you where you wanted to go" in terms of committee assignments. Certainly more than one freshman desperately sought "Agriculture" or "Interior" as a necessary assignment, if he were to hope to return two years later. But, by and large, the matter of committee assignments as an inducement surely was bolstered by other and broader bases of support. Boggs gained at least one freshman vote because of a friendship that developed when he worked on the Democratic Platform Committee in 1968. Another freshman went along with Boggs as the "establishment candidate," because, he argued, the seniority system had been beneficial to his part of the country. Gary Hymel, Boggs' administrative assistant, counted 13 freshman votes for Boggs on the first ballot, and probably nineteen all told. Though other candidates contested individual votes, they all seemed to agree that the new majority leader had more than held his own among the entering House members.

Regional and state delegation forces also contributed to a tendency for freshman members to break toward establishment candidates.[21] To begin with, few freshmen come to Washington, D.C. completely isolated from state delegation and regional influences. An occasional small state member might escape the former, but seldom the latter. Personal contacts with more senior members, plus what the freshman member could pick up in his home-town newspapers might be about all he could rely on for information until he met the candidates. Boggs and Udall campaigned for freshmen members more than the other candidates, but even their personal contacts were limited to a single appearance in perhaps, at most, a half-dozen districts.

When freshman Mike McCormack from the state of Washington found all but one of his senior colleagues committed to Udall, it was not surprising to find him leaning strongly in that direction, too. Conversely, a first-termer from New York City was left pretty much to reach his own decision, since in his delegation, members were not consistent in support of any one candidate.

As Table 7.3 suggests, regional influences had a still broader impact. Both Udall, and later Sisk, were initially disadvantaged by their small base, Udall with only his own vote to begin with and Sisk, with a state delegation already invaded and fragmented. More important, perhaps, they were competing for votes among the smallest regional base in the country, a mere 39 votes. Similarly, O'Hara and Hays, while they began with relatively small and nearly unanimous state delegations of seven members each, soon found themselves in contention for the balance of the Midwest's 55 votes.

Boggs, providing he could convince the great majority of southern colleagues that he was not too "liberal," had the best of both worlds — a unanimous Louisiana delegation behind him and the largest regional base within which to seek out votes of any candidate. Perhaps only the Northeast, if it could have agreed upon backing a *single* candidate, could have given the South a close contest for an overall majority. Boggs, with the highly critical support of O'Neill, Carey and other northeasteners, put the two largest regions together. In short, he maintained the southern–big-city leadership axis which has dominated the House Democratic party for decades.

Table 7.3
Democratic Members and Candidates for Majority Leader
by Major Geographical Regions, 92d Congress

West		*Midwest*		*South*		*East*	
Alaska	1	Ill.	12	Ala.	5	Conn.	4
Ariz.	1	Ind.	5	Ark.	3	Del.	0
Cal.	20	Iowa	2	Fla.	9	Me.	2
Colo.	2	Kan.	1	Ga.	8	Md.	5
Ha.	2	Mich.	7	Ky.	5	Mass.	8
Ida.	0	Minn.	4	La.	8	N.H.	0
Mont.	1	Mo.	9	Miss.	5	N.J.	9
Nev.	1	Neb.	0	N.C.	7	N.Y.	24
N.M.	1	N.D.	1	Okla.	4	Pa.	14
Ore.	2	Ohio	7	S.C.	5*	R.I.	2
Utah	1	S.D.	2	Tenn.	5	Vt.	0
Wash.	6	Wisc.	5	Texas	20	W.Va.	5
Wyo.	1			Va.	4		
	39		55		88		73

Candidates:

Sisk	Hays	Boggs	None
Udall	O'Hara		

Total House Democrats: 255

* One South Carolina seat became vacant following the death of Mendel Rivers on December 28, 1970.

Still other factors, religion and social mores, worked to Udall's disadvantage and Boggs' ultimate victory. Most members would probably deny that Boggs' Roman Catholicism and Udall's Mormonism played any part. Still, it is hard to ignore the simple arithmetic. One hundred and thirteen Catholics served in the 92d Congress; 77 were House Democrats. Together they constituted the largest single religious denomination as well as the largest number of Catholics ever to serve in a Congress. The great majority of these House Democrats represented big-city districts, mostly concentrated along the northeastern corridor.

Udall was one of four members of the Latter-Day Saints among House Democrats. If Udall might be labeled a "Jack-Mormon" (no longer a practitioner of all of the LDS prohibitions), then Boggs was probably a more pragmatic Catholic than many.

Such religious affiliations were not, in themselves, enough to elect Boggs or defeat Udall, but their impact was enhanced by other events. Although he was divorced in 1965, Udall remained close to his six children. In 1968 he married again, this time to Ella Royston Ward, a secretary for the Post Office and Civil Service Committee. The divorce and remarriage were probably overlooked by most congressmen, but Udall's advocacy of population control legislation did not endear him to some conservative Catholics in the House. Coupled with Udall's challenge to still another venerable Catholic institution, the Honorable John W. McCormack, some of the 77 House Democratic Catholics had a further excuse for not supporting Udall. Edward Boland's endorsement of Udall on the eve of the caucus vote came far too late to offset the underlying northeastern apprehension about Udall. The positive gains that might have been achieved by Boland's efforts were effectively offset by O'Neill's support of Boggs.

VII

Despite the ease with which the outcome can be explained, it might have been possible to turn it all around. What would it have taken to make Udall a winner? Perhaps some combination of four possible developments could have made him the new majority leader: (1) greater seniority, (2) a broader, diversified base of support, (3) O'Hara's assistance in neutralizing anti-Udall sentiment among labor leaders, and (4) some action or shortcoming of Boggs which would have reawakened earlier misgivings about his judgment and performance.

A central reason for Udall's defeat was his junior standing in an institution which not only places a high premium on seniority, but more important, invests most power in its senior incumbents. The Arizona Representative was at least two terms short of his maximum potential by this criterion. His chances if he, rather than his brother, had first come to Congress in the mid-1950's, or the leadership position had opened up two or four years later, remain, of course, purely speculative.

Some scattered evidence exists for a thesis which has the "old bulls," the chairmen and other high-ranking members, entering the fray in concert at the last moment for the sole purpose of defeating Udall. Fearful not so much of Udall, but of the "Jerome Waldies and Brock Adamses" behind him, these senior committee leaders, so the argument runs, mobilized their forces behind Boggs. Boggs was a known quantity. But who could tell how far Udall's cohorts might go in radically revising the Hansen committee report? Perhaps three or four chairmen might be stripped of their seniority, with the liberals not content to limit themselves to a challenge to District of Columbia Committee Chairman John McMillan of South Carolina? [22] Boggs was endorsed as a southerner and the strongest of the three establishment candidates. At least one of the losing candidates advanced such an interpretation:

> A lot of people, who were for me, said they had to vote for Boggs on the first ballot because they feared Udall. Then, if Boggs stumbled, they would come back to me. The object was to stop Udall, either on one ballot or another.

Isolated senior members may have been active in Boggs' behalf in the closing week of the campaign, but there is little evidence of any *concerted* drive on the part of the committee chairmen to block Udall.

That is not to say that Udall's candidacy would not have been substantially aided by the presence of two or three powerful chairmen in his camp. His campaign was highly organized, his strategy imaginative, but his base of support lacked diversity. Consciously modeled after the Ford-Griffin-Goodell group which overthrew Republican Minority Leader Charles Halleck in 1965, the Udall team remained far too homogeneous — not so much in age or regional diversification, but in its lack of participation by senior establishment and conservative types.[23] Overall, the Udall strategy meetings tended to be dominated by youthful liberals who feed upon one another's optimistic reports. Udall was not unaware of the problem and tried desperately to broaden his base. He reviewed his overall support following his defeat as follows:

> I had great strengths and great weaknesses and my organizational base was both. These great "shock troops" would say, "What can we do?" You can't tell them not to get involved. So we tried to keep them quietly busy. There were some great workers among them, and some not so good.
>
> Others like _____, _____, _____ [three southern members], we couldn't get surfaced . . .
>
> Boland's delay in making up his mind hurt. If he could have come my way in December, then we might have put together

a little team of more conservative members: people like Boland, Clarence Long (Md.), and Dante Fascell (Fla.). Then add some guys from Texas, Tennessee, and Kentucky, and it might have taken off.

Among liberal members a few still argue that if O'Hara had withdrawn from the race early, the outcome would have been different. Perhaps, but quite likely not. Throughout 1970 and into early January, Udall benefitted from having another candidate in the race who was perceived as more liberal. For Udall to make inroads into Texas, Tennessee, and other southern and border states, he could not afford to be painted as *the* liberal, Democratic Study Group candidate. O'Hara's source of strength lay with three groups: Michiganders, black congressmen, and a score of issue-oriented members like himself. Not all these members were easily transferable to a mountain-state, Mormon moderate, especially the more labor-oriented congressmen. Several days after the caucus, O'Hara elaborated on both points:

> My votes? . . . A few were close personal friends mainly from Michigan — Ford, Dingell, Nedzi, and Brademas — people like that. Then, there are others whose gut reactions to issues are the same as mine — Don Fraser, Jim Corman. And finally, the blacks; I think I got the lion's share of that group: Bill Clay, Lou Stokes, Parren Mitchell, and so on.

> You add up the blacks, the Michigan guys, and the true believers and that's about it.

Could he have helped Udall by pulling out earlier? "No, I don't think so." O'Hara felt from the beginning that Udall couldn't win. A majority of his votes did go to Udall on the second ballot, but the combination clearly fell far short of victory. O'Hara was asked if, in retrospect, any liberal candidate could have won, or were they all "born dead"? For several minutes, O'Hara considered various combinations of events and people. He concluded, "No, I'm afraid it couldn't have been done."

One can argue, however, that change-oriented congressmen in the House are open to criticism for not uniting behind a single candidate. Certainly, intense efforts were made by Representatives William Ford of Michigan, Sam Gibbons of Florida, and others. But just who that candidate should have been meets with varying judgments, at the beginning of the race in May, 1970, on the eve of the vote in January, 1971 and beyond. With the benefit of hindsight, Udall appears to

Representative Hale Boggs, newly elected House majority leader in 1971 receives congratulations from two senior colleagues from Louisiana: F. Edward Hébert, Chairman of the House Armed Services Committee (center), and Joe D. Waggonner, Jr., about to replace Boggs on the powerful House Ways and Means Committee.

(Dev O'Neill)

Defeated House majority leader candidate Morris K. Udall meets the press outside the Democratic Caucus, January 1971. The campaign button on his lapel has been turned upside down so that it reads "oW" instead of "Mo."

(Dev O'Neill)

have been stronger than O'Hara; and one can speculate about the drawing power of Edward Boland. But what *if* (one of the most expansive words in the English language) several candidates had stayed in through November or December, and then all had withdrawn in favor of the clear frontrunner, probably Udall? Perhaps, only then, would the first ballot strength of the change-oriented candidate have rivaled Boggs. Further, it would also have been necessary for O'Hara, Thompson, Bolling, and others with impeccable labor credentials to have neutralized or turned around labor union opposition to Udall. Of course, this type of speculation is open-ended.

The fourth, and most decisive, change that could have effected a different outcome in the 1970–1971 majority leader contest would have been if Boggs' behavior could have been criticized. Probably each candidate thought to himself at one time or another — it's not so much a question of my winning, but will Boggs lose it? Will he say or do something to raise again criticisms of aloofness and "instability"? But under Boggs' steady performance, such issues faded into the background. From the beginning, the majority whip refused to listen to his critics or to take his detractors seriously. Instead, he slowly and effectively dispelled the rumors that circulated. He did it in the most impressive way possible, by the quality of his conduct in person, his behavior in committee, and his speeches and floor leadership. Others helped: the Speaker, for example, provided multiple opportunities for Boggs to preside over the House. By November and December 1970, his measured conduct began to pay off in an increasing number of vote commitments — his own tally showed 50–60 by September, 70–80 after Veteran's Day, over 100 by the end of the 91st Congress, and near 130 on the eve of the caucus. Not all congressmen would honor their original commitments, but enough did to give Boggs 95 votes on the first ballot and a substantial majority on the second.

Unquestionably time worked in Boggs' behalf. In the words of the late Speaker Rayburn, "In the House of Representatives six months is a generation." So many issues are confronted, so much legislation is disposed of, estimates of leadership ebb and flow. But it was more than time. Over the long summer, fall, and into the lame-duck session in January, Boggs was able to demonstrate repeatedly that he could operate under pressure with great skill and style. Two observations from defeated opponents reinforce this:

> At the beginning, I think a good many people were antagonistic to Boggs — those peccadilloes of his. But the longer you got away from these, opposition to him tended to diminish.

Boggs did a remarkable turn-about — one of the best jobs I've seen in the ____years I've known him. He was working — god-damn, he was a tiger! If he'd been that kind of a whip all along, he would have been foreordained as majority leader.

In January 1971 House Democrats completed a major, if incremental, change in their party leadership. Majority Leader Albert advanced routinely to Speaker, Majority Whip Boggs won the most intensive and critical contest of his lengthy political career as he succeeded to the majority leadership, and two additional veteran members of the House establishment, O'Neill of Massachusetts and Teague of Texas, regained leadership positions for state delegations which had long dominated their party's leadership.[24] While Albert, O'Neill, and Teague would continue to figure prominently in House Democratic politics for Congresses to come, fate would intervene within two years to make Boggs' triumph short-lived.

NOTES

1. Speculation about such a combination occurred frequently in the press, for example, as early as Roland Evans and Robert Novak, "McCormack Aims to Thwart Liberals by Supporting Boggs, Rostenkowski," *Washington Post,* July 20, 1970, p. A-23; and as late as William V. Shannon, "New Leadership in the House," *New York Times,* January 4, 1971, p. 31.
2. Few members in the House rivaled Rostenkowski's reputation for being able to "deliver" a dozen or more votes to one candidate or another. On legislative issues, he and his Chicago delegation members could usually find common ground and his influence also extended to friends and big-city colleagues across the Midwest and into New England. In a leadership contest these ties would inevitably be more fragile, especially since Rostenkowski was not the candidate himself.
3. To put it more bluntly, one man's "understanding" is another man's "deal."
4. New York, the largest delegation in the House, with 24 members, was also caught by surprise. Their probable candidate, Hugh Carey (later to be elected Governor of New York), had just been elected to the Ways and Means Committee at the final caucus of the 91st Congress. A supporter of Boggs and a friend of Rostenkowski, Carey was in no position to make a challenge at the opening caucus. The weekend before the vote, the Udall forces had half-expected Boggs to announce a slate composed of himself, Rostenkowski for whip, and Carey for chairman of the caucus. "Too many Catholics, too much Ways and Means," grumbled one seasoned House veteran, dismissing the rumor.
5. "As soon as I heard 'Jake' Pickle (a Texas member who seconded Teague's candidacy) say, 'We ought to spread this position around', I knew Dan was in trouble," commented a friend of Rostenkowski.
6. The nominator of one of the candidates, whose eyesight was failing, was shored up by several of the seconders. Actually, the entire counting process was collective and remarkably informal. Still, the House Democrats managed to avoid the embarrassment of their Republican counterparts, who six years earlier had

uncovered one-too-many ballots in the Ford-Halleck contest, forcing the need for re-balloting.

7. One vacant seat had been created by the death of Rivers (S.C.). In addition, each of the six absentees, Abernathy of Mississippi, Andrews of Alabama, Celler of New York, Dowdy of Texas, Jarman of Oklahoma, and Long of Louisiana, was a probable vote for Boggs.

8. The expectation was based on false assumptions. In a December meeting of O'Hara-Udall supporters the question had been raised, and O'Hara had replied, "Whenever I see I can't win, I'll get out. But I won't tell anyone else how to vote — the people that support me are intelligent enough to make up their own minds." About a week before the caucus he had told both Holifield and Boggs, on separate occasions, that he did not intend to endorse any other candidate if he withdrew. Finally, he reacted to the events and personalities of the moment. After Hays endorsed Boggs, O'Hara's immediate reaction was "not to respond the same way, . . . not to be a cheap shill."

   Few votes are transferable in leadership contests, in part because of the secret ballot and, more important, because there is likely to be but minimal return, tangible or otherwise, for the member who is asked to switch allegiance. In O'Hara's own words: "I want you to vote for candidate Glutz because I'm for him is just not terribly persuasive to a guy who was for you because you best reflected his views and interests. And that's especially true in an arena where everybody knows everybody else so intimately."

9. Such a possibility appeared even more dubious after Hays and O'Hara pulled out, since Sisk, unless he achieved prodigious gains, would have remained low man and been forced to drop out after the second ballot.

10. Andrew J. Glass, "Congress Report: House Democrats Back Establishment in Electing Boggs Floor Leader," *National Journal* 3 (January 23, 1971), pp. 186–190, at 187.

11. The tendency for members to flock to the winning side is probably as old as contest for legislative leadership. As Mary Parker Follett observed in her classic study of the House Speakership (*The Speakership of the House of Representatives* [New York: Longmans, Green, 1896], p. 38):

    Another important factor in the Speaker's election is the relative probability of success: who will win in the caucus? is what everyone asks himself with the greatest eagerness, for it is well to be on that man's side as early as possible. Each candidate tries to make the waverers believe that he will win, and the waverers stand out as long as possible without committing themselves.

12. Transcript of *CBS Morning News*, January 20, 1970, p. 2.

13. Mike Green, "At 60, and with Perspective, Bernie Sisk Lacks Rancor," *Fresno Bee*, January 20, 1971, p. 4.

14. Having glimpsed the possibilities of victory, the relatively youthful, tight-knit staff of Morris K. Udall — Terry Bracy, John Gabusi, Dee Jackson, Bonnie Kell, Roger Lewis, Fred Palmer, and others — probably paid a heavier personal cost, initially. Within a week or so, however, they were looking for new legislative challenges for their boss, and considering alternative career prospects, such as a 1974 Senate bid.

15. Two days later, after Udall heard of the upset of Senate Majority Whip Edward Kennedy by conservative Robert Byrd (see Chapter 13), he sent him a note of personal condolence:

    As soon as I pick all the liberal buck shot out of my rear, I'll come over and help pull those liberal knives out of your back. If you pull them straight, it doesn't hurt as much.

Kennedy was quick to reply:

> It so happens I have four knives of unknown origin which I have extracted from my back. I'm happy to send them to you, if you need them.

16. Glass, *op. cit.*, p. 190.

17. David E. Rosenbaum, "House Majority Whip: Thomas Philip O'Neill, Jr.," *New York Times*, January 25, 1971, p. 10.

18. This classification, admittedly impressionistic, was made on the basis of a decade of close observation of the House of Representatives and its members. My original list was cross-checked informally with several experienced House staff members.

19. The counter-argument of the opposing candidates, that Albert was the first appointive whip since Oscar Underwood of Alabama to move up to majority leader, appeared to be less persuasive.

20. Compiled from *Congressional Quarterly Weekly Report* **29** (January 15, 1971), 138–139.

21. As a defeated candidate observed somewhat bitterly, "You can't count on the freshmen. They come in scared; anyone in authority can manipulate them."

22. With the support of Albert and Boggs, McMillan survived the threat by a Democratic caucus vote of 126 to 96. Still, a pattern was set for utilizing the new procedure first recommended as part of the Hansen Committee report.

23. Chapter 4, "The Ford-Halleck Minority Leadership Contest, 1965."

24. Not only had Rayburn of Texas and McCormack of Massachusetts led the House for 30 years, but the last two Democratic Presidents, Kennedy and Johnson, had launched their political careers as House members of these two state delegations.

CHAPTER EIGHT

The Choice of a House Majority Leader and Whip, 1973

At 8:59 A.M. on the morning of October 16, 1972, a small, twin-engined Cessna 310C took off from Anchorage International Airport, its planned destination, Juneau, Alaska, southeast by about 560 miles. Four men were on board: Don E. Jonz, 38, a seasoned Alaskan pilot;[1] Nicholas J. "Nick" Begich, 40, one-term U.S. House Representative from Alaska, who was campaigning for reelection; Russell L. Brown, 37, his district office aide; and Representative Hale Boggs of Louisiana, 58, completing his fourteenth term in the House and his second year as Democratic majority leader. Boggs had interrupted his end-of-the-session congressional duties to fly to Alaska to address two campaign fund-raising dinners for Begich, one in Anchorage the night before, the other scheduled in Juneau that evening.

The pilot had filed a visual flight rules plan, although some unfavorable weather conditions — rain, moderate to severe turbulence — could be expected along the proposed route.[2] The aircraft disappeared into overcast skies when it was heading south toward the 2500-foot Portage Bay Pass on its ascent out of Anchorage toward Whittier. Beyond lay rugged, snow-covered mountains, glaciers, and for a part of the journey, the storm-tossed seas of the Gulf of Alaska. No radio contact was ever established with the pilot. When the Cessna 310C failed to arrive in Juneau, the most extensive search ever made for a missing aircraft was launched. Some 35 to 40 military and more than 50 civilian planes spent 3600 hours covering about 325,000 square miles — but to no avail. After 39 days of searching, much of it conducted in the face of fog, icy rain, and heavy snow, the Air Force Rescue Coordination Center at Elmendorf Air Force Base finally called off the attempt.[3]

Despite the disappearance and presumed death of Boggs and Begich, 22 days after the aircraft disappeared, on November 7, 1972 both congressmen were reelected to the 93d Congress. Boggs had only token primary opposition in Louisiana's Second District, and no Republican had filed for the general election. Thus he won, unopposed. The missing Begich was elected by 56 percent of the vote over his Republican State Senate opponent, Don Young of Fort Yukon.

Probably the last people to give up hope for the missing men were their wives, Lindy Boggs and Pegge Begich. Mrs. Begich had gone through a parallel experience, although of much shorter duration, in 1970. On a campaign trip the entire Alaskan Democratic ticket, and the candidates for governor and U.S. Senator, had been lost for nine hours when their light seaplane had had to put down on water when confronted by impenetrable fog. This time, as hope faded, Mrs. Begich, mother of six children (ages 15 to 4), and Mrs. Boggs, mother of three married children, faced another dilemma. Should they attempt to carry on the tradition and philosophies of their husbands and run for their vacated House seats? [4]

State laws differ as to the procedures for determining when and how a congressional seat is declared vacant. A certificate of presumptive death was rendered following a jury verdict by Alaska District Court Judge Dorothy D. Tyner on December 29, 1972. A special election in Alaska was announced by Governor William A. Egan for March 6, 1973. Mrs. Begich lost a three-way convention battle to the chairman of the state's Democratic Central Committee, Emil Notti, the son of an Italian gold-rush prospector and an Athabascan Indian woman. Notti's native background and his militant stance on land claims, however, were to fall short of winning him the general election. Begich's original opponent, Republican Don Young, won the seat in early March by better than 3000 votes in an election generally characterized by low voter turnout.

Lindy Boggs was to fare much better in New Orleans. She had been active in politics, and had managed many of her husband's campaigns. She knew the party leaders and they were well aware of her political talents. Although Republicans were increasing in force in Louisiana politics, it could be assumed that if Lindy Boggs won the Democratic primary her election was all but assured.

At his family's request, Hale Boggs had not been included in the Alaskan presumptive death proceedings. On January 3, 1973, the House of Representatives passed H. Res. 1 declaring his seat vacant.

Louisiana Governor Edwin Edwards announced a special election to be held March 20, 1973. On February 3, 1973, Lindy Boggs easily defeated four other Democratic primary opponents, winning better than 73 percent of the vote. In the general election on March 20, Lindy Boggs defeated her Republican opponent by better than a four-to-one margin.

How would she do in the House? Those who came to know Lindy during Hale's 31 years of active politics had few doubts. She had been more of a partner than an understudy to her husband. At 56 she became the most knowledgeable freshman to enter the House in many a term. From the beginning she was on a first-name basis with almost all of the committee chairmen. But that was to come later.

First, House Democrats had to decide on a successor to their missing majority leader.

I

Who would succeed Hale Boggs as the next majority leader? As the likelihood of Boggs' survival dimmed, talk in the Democratic cloakroom turned to speculation about his successor. The odds-on favorite in almost everybody's book was 59-year-old Thomas P. "Tip" O'Neill, Jr. of Cambridge, Massachusetts.[5] This popular Irishman was already serving as the majority whip, the number three man in the Democratic party hierarchy. Thus, O'Neill, under Speaker Carl Albert's direction, announced to his House colleagues on October 17, 1972 that Boggs, Begich, and their fellow travelers were missing in Alaska. For the remainder of the session O'Neill served as acting majority leader.

A serious illness, disappearance, or death of a member while Congress is in session almost invariably reinforces existing leadership patterns of succession; O'Neill was to be the beneficiary.

Boggs had been in Alaska principally to help a young colleague but, secondarily, to secure a supporter in his own drive for reelection as majority leader, and eventually, his quest for the Speakership.[6] After his disappearance his heavy schedule of speechmaking and appearances on behalf of other Democrats throughout the United States was picked up by his leadership colleagues, Speaker Carl Albert and Majority Whip O'Neill.[7]

O'Neill had a further reason for already being heavily involved in the campaign fates of his colleagues. Since 1970 he had served first as co-chairman and later chairman of the Democratic National Congressional (Campaign) Committee, the body charged with the responsibility of reelecting incumbent House Democrats and helping freshmen candidates.[8] In addition to raising and distributing campaign funds, the nine-member DNCC staff coordinates a speaker's bureau, conducts research on issues, and distributes a wide variety of photographic and written news media releases. Nominally made up of a Representative from each state with a Democratic delegation, most of its operations are coordinated by the chairman, who works closely with the staff director (Ken Harding until late 1972, succeeded by his assistant, Ted Henshaw).

Money is what makes the committee run and control over campaign contributions is its principal source of power. The rule of thumb — all incumbents begin with a similar amount, $3000–5000, and promising freshman candidates are helped, but by lesser amounts — is sometimes honored in the breach. In other words, it is up to the chairman, working closely with the staff director, to decide whether or not a particular campaign can be salvaged by having money made available or whether the money could be better used elsewhere. The candidate's requests are listened to, but usually he is the last one to assess his chances with any objectivity. From July until November, it had largely been up to O'Neill to decide who received money and who didn't.[9]

Even before it began to look as if Boggs would not be found, O'Neill was like a man playing five-card stud poker with a near-unbeatable hand. After three cards had been dealt, he was way out in front — a high pair showing with a like-card in the hole. He was the incumbent majority whip, the position from which the last two majority leaders, Albert and Boggs, had moved upward on the leadership ladder. He was the chairman of the Democratic National Congressional (Campaign) Committee with considerable power over funds that could be significant in the closing stages of 50 or more tight congressional races.

O'Neill's hole-card, to pursue the analogy, was his personal popularity, deep-seated and widespread. Big and heavy-set, 6 ft. 2 in., and about 260 pounds, with a shock of greying hair brushing over his eyes, O'Neill had many friends and few visible enemies in the House. One congressman would call him the person "most unaffected" by Washington's power and social structure, as much at home talking with Presidents (he was extremely close to John F. Kennedy and on good terms with Lyndon B. Johnson) as with his north-side Boston and Cambridge constituents on the weekends.[10] In common with many successful politicians, O'Neill delighted in telling anecdotes and he told them well. In addition, he had the uncommon ability to make the story fit the occasion or relate to a particular colleague or person. Firmly entrenched as part of the northeastern, Catholic, big-city establishment, O'Neill also related well to all but the most conservative southerners. O'Neill was one of the first of his kind to take a strong anti-Vietnam war stand, a position which served him in good stead with many liberal, change-oriented, younger members.

A gregarious, Boston-Irish politician who prefers to downplay the stereotype, O'Neill represents a district with a varied ethnic base (about 6 percent Irish, 10 percent Italian), and more colleges and universities than any other in the country, 36, including Harvard, Massachusetts Institute of Technology, and his own alma mater, Boston College.

O'Neill had lost only one election, his first, when he ran for a city council seat in Cambridge. He ran a successful campaign for the Massachusetts State House the same year he graduated from Boston College in 1936, and served first as minority leader, and then as the first Democratic Speaker ever elected in the Massachusetts House of Representatives (1948–1952).[11]

Perhaps O'Neill's toughest political campaign came in 1952 when he made his first bid for the U.S. House of Representatives. John F. Kennedy was vacating the seat to make a (successful) bid for the U.S. Senate. O'Neill beat his primary opponent, State Senator Michael LoPresti, by 3000 votes and went on to win the general election by nearly 60 percent of the vote. Since 1956 he has not received less than 73 percent of the vote in a general election and in five elections he has had no Republican opposition. O'Neill has continued to keep a hand in state politics. In 1962 he almost single-handedly converted a struggling campaign for the governorship by Endicott "Chub" Peabody into a last-minute victory over Republican John Volpe. Operating from the 22d floor of the John F. Kennedy Federal Building in Boston, O'Neill is widely recognized as the Massachusetts State Legislature's unofficial lobbyist in Washington.

Placed on the House Rules Committee in 1955 by his close friend and mentor, then Majority Leader John F. McCormack of Massachusetts, by 1972 O'Neill had risen to fifth-ranking member. After McCormack became Speaker in 1962, O'Neill served for about three months as the principal leadership spokesman. His constituency demands and a pattern of living which found him as often in Boston as in Washington finally led him to turn most of the Rules Committee leadership chores back to his colleague, Richard Bolling of Missouri. Still, throughout the 1960's and early 1970's, O'Neill was a loyal, stabilizing influence on the committee, first for McCormack and subsequently for Albert.

In 1970–1971, both O'Neill and a close friend, Edward Boland of Massachusetts, seriously considered running for the majority leadership. Unable to resolve the question of which should be the candidate and which the campaign manager, the two 10-term veterans ended up backing different horses. Boland declared for Morris K. Udall; O'Neill opted for Boggs and in the process delivered or insured most of New England's Democratic votes for the eventual winner. When Boggs' first choice for whip was vetoed by Speaker Albert, O'Neill became his compromise choice.

By late October of 1972 O'Neill, although the front-runner for Boggs' position, nevertheless began to hear cloakroom rumblings about challenges from several directions. Inhibited from announcing his own candidacy until it was certain that the majority leader could not be found, O'Neill chafed with uncertainty brought about by his personal sympathy for Mrs. Boggs, his desire to avoid antagonizing the missing majority leader's supporters, and the question of how long he should delay declaring his own candidacy.

The transition from front-runner to active candidate was facilitated on election night, November 7, 1972. O'Neill watched election returns in his Washington whip's office, from time to time picking up the telephone to congratulate winning colleagues. During the evening, he was joined by Thomas Hale Boggs, Jr., son of the missing congressman and a former candidate for Congress from Maryland, and Gary Hymel, administrative assistant to Hale Boggs since 1965. They had known O'Neill for better than six years and both were keenly aware of the dilemma O'Neill confronted.

The following morning, an arranged telephone call took place between O'Neill and Lindy Boggs. In her gracious and politically sensitive way, Lindy Boggs gave O'Neill the "go ahead." She told him that "one had to be practical" and that if Hale were around and in a similar situation, he would want to get started. Tommy Boggs sat beside O'Neill, and O'Neill referred to his presence, during telephone conversations that were to throw O'Neill's campaign into full gear. With three secretaries lining up congressmen across the country, and Leo Diehl, O'Neill's administrative assistant coordinating the calls, by that evening the majority whip was well on his way. When he stopped to have dinner with his wife, Milly, and two daughters, O'Neill already claimed 63 firm commitments. This count included at least eight votes from such as Edward Boland, James Burke, and Michael Harrington from Massachusetts, Robert Tiernan from Rhode Island, and others, close associates who had volunteered their support even before O'Neill actively solicited pledges.

In that first day of telephone calls O'Neill mainly concentrated on "regulars," members in the mainstream of the party, primarily big-city, eastern and midwestern Democrats. He took few chances on a soft count. After congratulating the members on their own reelection, he would declare his own candidacy, assure the member that he had conferred with the Boggs family, and finally ask for support. Unless the member wavered or seemed evasive, O'Neill would conclude: "I'm marking you down as a hard, firm commitment — O.K.?" Not until the member answered "Yes," "No question," or words to that effect, would O'Neill or Diehl mark a dark X beside the member's name on a House whip checklist, broken down state by state.

Forty-six more supporters were added on Thursday and 11 on Friday, bringing the running total to 120, as O'Neill took a 7:40 P.M. shuttle from Washington to Boston's Logan Airport. As O'Neill's telephoning shifted to southern conservatives and ultra-liberals, commitments were increasingly hard to come by — still the majority whip felt confident. In three days of intensive telephone calls he had run his total up to within one vote of an absolute majority of the Democratic Caucus.[12]

The winning vote — a critical vote in several ways — was locked up Saturday night. It was a commitment from F. Edward Hébert, dean of the Louisiana delegation and chairman of the Armed Services Committee. Hébert had been approached in New Orleans by Gary Hymel at a reception being held for Lindy Boggs at the home of Hale Boggs' brother. With Hébert's vote and Lindy's encouragement, O'Neill had little difficulty aligning the balance of the Louisiana delegation. Hébert's conversion, despite strong philosophical differences between the two men, practically assured that no southern coalition was likely to form around any other major candidate.

With more calls coming in over the weekend O'Neill's November 13 press release announcing his candidacy was little more than a formality. It read in part:

> Everyone is aware of the apparent tragedy which has befallen our present Majority Leader, Hale Boggs. Having worked with Hale for many years on both legislative and party matters, I feel a deep sense of personal grief over his disappearance. While we are all still hopeful concerning Hale's whereabouts, it is important that our party continue to fulfill its leadership role during the 93d Congress. I therefore believe that it is time for me to step forward and formally declare my candidacy for the position of Majority Leader.

Citing his record as whip, chairman of the Democratic National Congressional (Campaign) Committee, and a high-ranking member on the Rules Committee, O'Neill concluded:

> I believe that my experience in every aspect of House affairs, legislative as well as parliamentary, stands me in good stead to assume the responsibilities of Majority Leader. The key to the success of the 93d Congress is strong, effective, and consistent leadership. I believe that I can meet the challenge.

Although O'Neill decreased his telephone campaign somewhat, he was up to 150 hard commitments by his own count on Thanksgiving Eve. He then stopped telephoning in any systematic way, but through mid-December still received calls from members out of the country or anxious to be recorded. His last tally showed 171 commitments of the 241 expected votes.[13]

II

O'Neill was not to have an uncontested ride to the majority leadership. Only one other candidate, 52-year old Sam Gibbons, a southern liberal from Tampa, Florida, formally challenged O'Neill. But several other members, including Wayne Hays of Ohio, B. F. "Bernie" Sisk of California, and Joe Waggonner of Louisiana, considered entering the fight for the vacated post. All except Gibbons were to back out for one reason or another as it became increasingly clear that O'Neill was likely to be a sure winner.

Both Hays and Sisk had run against Boggs two years earlier as alternative establishment candidates. The other two candidates in that race, Udall of Arizona, who had run second to Boggs, and O'Hara of Michigan, both liberals, had given the possibility of challenging O'Neill little or no consideration. For Udall, "O'Neill had most of Boggs' strengths with few of his liabilities." Questioned by newsmen, Udall indicated early that he was "strongly inclined not to run." [14]

Instead, Udall quietly set about putting himself in a position either to be appointed or elected to the number three position of majority whip.[15] O'Hara, who had found himself whiplashed by a combination of school busing and redistricting problems back home, had been returned to the House with only 50.8 percent of the vote. The pragmatic Michigan liberal felt that most of his next two years would best be spent in fence-mending.

Within two years, tough, conservative Wayne Hays of Ohio had built himself such a power base as chairman of the Committee on House Administration and the Foreign Affairs Subcommittee on State Department Organization and Foreign Operations that he was being referred to by his colleagues as "the other Speaker." Most of his power stemmed from his control over such mundane, but nevertheless important, matters to members as accounts, travel and stationery allowances, the House restaurants, and office equipment. The "overriding" reason Hays gave for not wishing to be considered for a leadership post was that tradition called for the majority leader to give up any committee chairmanships he held. Hays added that he wanted to finish the task of computerizing certain operations of the House, including a newly installed electronic voting mechanism.[16] What Hays did not add was that he had already been in touch with individual members of the Democratic National Congressional (Campaign) Committee in a bid to succeed O'Neill as chairman of that powerful group.[17]

Bernie Sisk of California, a 10-term veteran, only one step below O'Neill on the House Committee on Rules, also did not give the race a great deal of consideration. A native of Texas, with close personal ties to members of a number of southern delegations including Florida and North Carolina, Sisk made a few telephone calls to see if a western-southern coalition could be put together. After Gibbons and O'Neill became active, Sisk told a reporter in mid-November that he was going away for a few weeks to think about his candidacy. Nothing ever developed.

Nothing developed either for the only other two candidates mentioned as possible opposition for O'Neill, outgoing, conservative Joe E. Waggonner, Jr. of Louisiana and Democratic Caucus Chairman Olin E. "Tiger" Teague of Texas. Both leaders of the informal bloc of conservatives, who continue to "think southern" along with others like Omar Burleson of Texas and Robert L. F. Sikes of Florida, Waggonner and Teague assessed the caucus as being more liberal than previously, despite the overall loss of 11 Democratic seats in the November election. Waggonner had succeeded Boggs on the Ways and Means Committee two years before — he could live with O'Neill. Teague, about to take over the chairmanship of the Science and Astronautics Committee, was preoccupied with moderating prospective reforms coming up in the January caucus. As O'Neill began to make inroads in the south, most notably through Hébert's commitment, any possibility of a challenge from a southern conservative was laid aside, if it had ever seriously been considered.

LEADERSHIP FOR A CHANGE. What contest there was for majority leader in 1973 was left up to change-oriented, hard-driving, 52-year old Sam Gibbons of Florida. A southern liberal with solid labor credentials, Gibbons was elected to the House of Representatives in 1962 after 10 years in the Florida state legislature. Promising service on the Education and Labor Committee led to floor management of the controversial antipoverty bills in 1966 and 1967, even though he was not yet a subcommittee chairman. In 1969 he won appointment to the Ways and Means Committee, despite the fact that his own delegation had nominated another candidate from Florida.[18] A strong advocate of congressional reform, Gibbons chaired a special bipartisan task force on House reorganization, which eventually provided the main thrust behind the passage of the Legislative Reorganization Act of 1970. He also played a major role in support of Udall's unsuccessful bid for the House majority leadership in 1970–1971.

What compelled this competent politician to make such an uphill effort for party leadership? In Gibbons' own words:

> A number of people asked me to run, both in and around Congress. I had been discouraged about our party leadership, the way things were going.
>
> And frankly, there was my own ambition. I had been looking for an opportunity to run.
>
> I really think the Democratic party needs stronger leadership ... We don't select our leaders on the issues. Most of our leaders are anointed — there's no real contest ...
>
> I decided I would try to run an issue-oriented campaign.

When Gibbons first considered running for a party office his initial inclination was to bid for the chairmanship of the Democratic Caucus.

When Hale Boggs disappeared, Gibbons and his administrative assistant, Hector Alcalde, thought "Why not go for broke?"

Gibbons recognized a number of factors in the way of his candidacy. Unlike O'Neill and some other prospective candidates he had no claim to office; he had not served as whip or even as a committee chairman. Campaigning on the theme of "leadership for a change," with the double entendre intended, Gibbons formally announced his candidacy for House majority leader at a press conference held in his Rayburn Office Building suite on Friday, November 10, 1972.[19]

His campaign, he said, would offer "youth, vigor, determination, and geography." Viewing himself as a national Democrat, but one who had maintained strong ties to the South, he felt he could appeal to all three wings of the party — southern conservatives, "regulars from northern cities and elsewhere, and younger, change-oriented liberals." [20] In private, Gibbons conceded most of the "regulars" to O'Neill, but he hoped to combine the 80–90 moderate-to-liberal change-oriented members of the House with enough southerners to offset O'Neill's initial advantages.

By the time Gibbons held his press conference, he and O'Neill had already been talking on the telephone for better than two days. Working initially with members already strongly predisposed, O'Neill had got an early jump. Gibbons would complain later of running into O'Neill's "tracks all over the place." He was able to escape defeat in the first week, but "I never could get any momentum going." [21]

O'Neill was aware of a challenge by Gibbons as early as the Wednesday evening following the election. A Florida member had advised O'Neill he thought "Sam was going to go, that he would have most of the Florida delegation behind him, even though some of us tried to talk him out of it." By O'Neill's own tally, Gibbons began with nine Florida votes or all but two of that state's Democratic delegation. As the two men tracked each other by telephone across the country, the majority whip was to encounter only one member outside the Florida delegation, a Texan, who announced outright he was for Gibbons. Of course, Gibbons was getting more commitments, but most members were reluctant to tell the odds-on favorite for majority leader that they might have other leanings.

Gibbons received mixed treatment in the press in his campaign. Some of his issue-oriented letters to colleagues were distributed to the press and received favorable reaction. In late November, the *Washington Post*'s Richard L. Lyons wrote a sympathetic column, "House

Reined by Status Quo." Although he commented favorably on some of Gibbons' proposed changes, Lyons also noted that[22]

> House Democrats have made it pretty clear in recent years that one thing they don't want in a party leader is someone who is going to push them too hard, to innovate, change the system, open it up.

By continually referring to his underdog role, however accurately, the press made it more difficult for Gibbons to obtain converts among a widely dispersed electorate.

In a campaign variously described by even sympathetic members as "tough," "uphill," or "doomed from the beginning," Gibbons nevertheless succeeded in contributing three innovations to House leadership contests. The first, a series of two- to three-page letters outlining various leadership needs and possible congressional reforms, had a measure of success.[23] His discussions of such subjects as secrecy, scheduling, seniority, and the appropriations process probably reinforced his support by change-inclined colleagues without affecting his chances with the more *status-quo*-minded members, many of whom were probably disinclined to read them anyway.[24]

Gibbons' second innovation, attempting to meet with state delegations during November and December in order to air his views, might have met with greater success if it hadn't been for scheduling difficulties. This strategy was modelled somewhat after those employed by presidential candidates at national nominating conventions. Gibbons even had hopes of luring O'Neill into appearing with him. In calls to the deans of state delegations, Gibbons promised that no commitments were to be sought at the meetings. He merely wanted a chance to discuss his views about the need for stronger leadership. The Florida candidate was prepared to fly wherever a delegation or several smaller state delegations could be assembled, including as far away as the Pacific Northwest. At least one gathering was scheduled, a December 12 meeting of the Illinois delegation, but this was cancelled at the last minute because of the death in a plane crash of Representative George Collins of Chicago. The main problem Gibbons encountered was in the timing of meetings; members were scattered far and wide. A few deans promised to assemble their delegations in Washington before the caucus met, but by then the contest was all over.

The third innovation by Gibbons was an inside mail, secret ballot poll of the members, prepared for delivery to the Capitol offices of each member on December 12. Sent to the member or his chief assistant, and accompanied by an explanatory letter and a pre-addressed but otherwise unmarked envelope, the ballot read as follows:

> PLEASE RETURN IN ATTACHED ENVELOPE BY
> INSIDE MAIL SO THAT SENDER IS <u>NOT</u>
> IDENTIFIED.

> QUESTION: Should Sam Gibbons continue in race for
> Majority Leader?
>
> Yes_____
>
> No_____

As late as early December, Gibbons said for hometown press consumption that he had "blunted the bandwagon" of front-runner O'Neill and argued that it was still an "open race." However, Gibbons was too experienced a counter from both his own Ways and Means effort and the Boggs-Udall contest not to realize that the race was nearly over. He heard too many declarations of support for O'Neill from members he needed in his own camp to leave any chance for an upset.

Over the Christmas holidays, Gibbons returned to Tampa and assessed his chances. His own poll, by the low rate and inconclusiveness of the returns,[25] confirmed most of his worst fears:

> They trickled in so slowly. Sometimes ten in one day, but the next day there would only be two.

> Sometimes it was "even-steven," sometimes I was ahead or behind. But so many just didn't come in at all.

Gibbons concluded he had no recourse but to withdraw. Naturally he was reluctant to reveal his final count, but it is difficult to conceive that Gibbons ever got as high as 60 firm commitments.[26] On December 28, 1972 Gibbons sent personal telegrams to all of his supporters, plus the Speaker and the majority whip advising them of his decision. Once the wire services picked up the story (it took only an hour), Gibbons issued a formal news release on December 29:

> After long deliberation and based upon the best evidence available I have decided not to continue in the Majority Leader race.

I do wish to signify that I would like to serve in a leadership position. I wish to make clear that I am interested in working to develop a strong and positive Democratic program for the Congress and to make the necessary changes in the caucus and House procedures so that Congress may function more effectively.

As his news release reveals, Gibbons had by no means given up on his ambition for leadership. In short, he was still available for the whip's position, should it become elective. Gibbons had no illusions that a gracious victor would turn to him and *appoint* him to the number three slot. Still, by late December the likelihood of an *elective* whip appeared more and more possible.

III

The momentum for changing the appointive whip position to an elective one was largely instigated by one man, Representative Phillip Burton of California. He may rightfully claim that without his nearly single-handed efforts this reform would not have come as close to succeeding as it did. But, ironically, it was the coupling of this effort with his own bid to become the first elective whip that ultimately led to the rejection of this reform.

When the Democrats control the House, the Speaker and the majority leader choose the whip, usually in close consultation with each other. On occasion the Speaker may make the appointment unilaterally, as Rayburn apparently did in 1955, or he may, in essence, exercise a veto power, as Albert seemed to limit his involvement in 1971. The primary arguments that favor keeping the position appointive are: (1) The position is primarily a supportive one — seeking information, covering the floor, assisting the Speaker and the majority leader. (2) The top leaders need to retain the power to select their number three man, a member who must remain loyal to them and their legislative objectives. (3) Appointment provides a better means of bringing about regional and ideological balance in the leadership.

In the fall of 1972, however, an increasing number of members were growing restless with a leadership selection process which seemed to them to result in an "automatic escalator." True, only Carl Albert had made it all the way from appointive whip to majority leader to Speaker. But Boggs seemed to be on his way before his tragic accident, and here was O'Neill, only two years as whip, now advancing almost uncontested up the ladder.

Two years before, in the January 1971 caucuses some of this uneasiness about the pattern of leadership succession had broken out into the open. The day following the elections of Albert and Boggs, an attempt had been made to make the whip's position an elective one. Although the new Speaker initially seemed sympathetic to the change, other senior establishment members, among them Boggs and O'Neill, were opposed. After heated debate a motion to table had been shouted through and the elective whip resolution was laid aside.

Even earlier there had been some discussion of the elected whip in the Hansen Committee on Organization, Study, and Review, first established in March 1970 as an arm of the Democratic Caucus. But it had not become one of the reform committee's recommendations to the full caucus in 1971. Burton and Hays had spoken in its favor, but there were others who felt the choice of the whip should be left to the leadership.[27]

Few members gave much thought to whether or not the whip should be appointed or elected until after Boggs' disappearance. With O'Neill doing a reasonably effective job as whip, the question could hardly be more academic. But the vacancy in the number two party position, together with the ease with which O'Neill moved up, dramatized as never before how critical the choice of whip could be. Ordinarily, a whip would serve for three or four terms before an opening might occur. By then, he would generally be viewed as part of the leadership.

BURTON LAUNCHES HIS CAMPAIGN. One member quick to seize upon the implications of the disappearance of Majority Leader Boggs was the ambitious, aggressive, and politically astute chairman of the Democratic Study Group, Phil Burton of California. Since the DSG represented more than 150 of the more moderate-to-liberal Democrats in the House, its chairman would inevitably play a major role in caucus deliberations. As a member of the Hansen Committee, Burton also was strategically placed to influence its recommendations to the caucus.

Burton was already engaged in evaluating proposed reforms: seniority, the closed rule, changes in the Democratic steering committee, leadership powers. In November and December, Burton would meet first with the DSG executive committee, and later with the broader membership to thrash out the priorities and exact language of the resolutions the DSG would present to the Democratic Caucus.

Opportunities for significant reform looked even more promising than two years before. The Democratic Party was to suffer a net loss of 11 seats in the November 1972 elections. But losses of older, more conservative Democrats through retirement, and primary upsets, plus the election of more youthful liberal members, meant that the caucus meeting in January 1973 should be more open to reform.

In addition to major responsibility for coordinating overall DSG reform proposals in the months ahead, Burton had a pet project of his own.[28] He announced his scheme at a $10 cocktail fund-raising party in San Francisco on Friday, November 2, 1972, four days before the election. First, he planned to introduce a resolution in January to convert the appointive whip to an elective position; second, he would become a candidate for this about-to-be created position.

One commonly accepted truism in politics is that you cannot be "horse and jockey," candidate and campaign manager, at one and the same time. Burton was not only going to be both, he was first committed to building the racetrack.

If the plan sounded audacious, running his own campaign for a position he hoped to create, it was not out of character with Burton's personality and style. A loud, boisterous legislator, given to punctuating about every third sentence with an expletive, Burton at 47 was used to taking on giants (and windmills) and, more often than not, slaying them.

Born in Cincinnati, Ohio on June 1, 1926, but raised and educated in California, Burton was elected to the California State Assembly in 1956 as its youngest member. Brash and outspoken even then, but possessing a talent for legislative compromise, the young legislator quickly made a name for himself in social welfare reform. In 1964, after the incumbent Democratic congressman resigned to become Mayor of San Francisco, Burton was elected to the 88th Congress in a special election. Burton's Fifth District is heavily Democratic (he won by 82 percent in 1972), contains a large Oriental population, many blacks (about one-fifth), and most of San Francisco's poor people.

Burton applied his skills first on the Interior Committee, and later on Education and Labor as well. By the late 1960's he was well known, if not always well liked; respected, if considered abrasive by many of his colleagues.

DSG CHAIRMAN. In 1971, after just seven years in Congress, he took on most of the past chairmen of the DSG and their chosen successor, James Corman, a Representative first elected in 1960 and a fellow Californian.[29] Few members, and certainly not the DSG's own establishment members like Don Fraser of Minnesota, James O'Hara of Michigan, and Frank Thompson of New Jersey, thought "Crazy Phil" had a chance.[30] Burton put on a whirlwind personal and telephone campaign which brought together the "new left" wing of the DSG with its older, labor-identified and more urban-machine wing. The final vote was Burton, 72, Corman, 48.

Even Burton's enemies, and he has his share, begrudgingly give him credit for energizing the Democratic Study Group and providing it with a continued sense of purpose and momentum. The DSG consisted of about 145 dues-paying members (at $100 per year) when Burton was elected chairman. He extended his efforts to recruit a swing group of members — mostly border state, conservatives, and older members. His efforts and the quality of the staff's output brought the DSG up to about 160 members after the first year and around 165 by 1972.[31] The object of the recruitment was clear. In Burton's terms: "If we don't have a majority of the caucus, how can we be effective?"

In retrospect, Burton was to see the DSG chairmanship as "definitely a plus" in his efforts to make the whip's post an elective one. "It gave me visibility. It provided a measure of me as a leader. I think that the way I performed over the last two years helped me a lot."

The early stages of Burton's campaign for the elective whip differed little from those of O'Neill and Gibbons in their bids for the majority leadership. On election night, Burton called other members around the country, mainly to congratulate them on winning. In these early telephone calls, it would depend upon how well he knew them as to whether or not he indicated that he was running.[32] During the first weeks, Burton said, "I put much more emphasis on the issue of the elective whip rather than my own candidacy." Burton never did issue a press release or a formal announcement of his candidacy. From the beginning he was determined to run an "inside" campaign.

Burton's arguments in favor of the elective whip were the standard ones: "It would break the ascension to leadership by way of appointment at the beginning . . . Appointing the whip almost precludes any meaningful contest later on . . . We should have a choice at the beginning." From election night until the Democratic Caucus on January 2, 1973, Burton estimates he contacted 85 percent of the members.

> I didn't do a count until very late. I never sat down with
> cards or a yellow tablet and kept track over time as such. A

count in the early stages would have been idle to do. After the first several weeks it was more of getting a feeling as to the potential.

Almost from the beginning, but particularly in the last week to 10 days, a set of efforts that he had tried to keep separate — whether or not to elect the whip, and his own candidacy — became more and more interrelated. Other candidates, sensing the possibility that the whip might be elected, began to surface. Among them were John Brademas, John McFall, Sam Gibbons, and possibly, Morris K. Udall. Burton was forced to shift his own efforts. "When it became more possible that the elective whip resolution would carry, during the last week to 10 days I gave more weight to my own candidacy, attempting to obtain personal commitments to me."

On the eve of the caucus, Burton, by his own counts at least, seemed to be doing surprisingly well. Later he would tell reporters (which probably indicates some calculated inflation) that as many as 150 members appeared to be committed, or leaning, to the elected whip. Burton's tighter count on his own personal candidacy reached 109, a count that included some second, as well as first, ballot strength.

IV

Two members more than any others favored retention of the appointive whip. They were, not surprisingly, the two people who had most to gain from maintaining the *status quo* — the two incumbent floor whips, 54-year-old John McFall of California and 44-year-old John Brademas of Indiana. Appointed by Albert and Boggs from the same list from which O'Neill had been selected two years ago, their duties had been largely left undefined except in the general sense of assisting the majority whip. Coming from the Far West and the Midwest, they provided further regional balance to the top leadership.

McFall, a tall, lanky Irishman, had represented an essentially agricultural district in California's San Joaquin Valley since 1956. By 1972 he had enough seniority to earn him the chairmanship of the Subcommittee on Transportation of the House Appropriations Committee. Easy to get along with, a kind of member's member,[33] McFall had early become active in the House whip hierarchy. In 1962, he succeeded John Moss as the assistant whip for California, one of 18 similar whips from zones around the country. Moss had been promoted to deputy whip, succeeding Hale Boggs as the rest of the party leadership had moved a step up the leadership ladder following Speaker Sam Rayburn's death in late 1961.

Somehow John Moss never fit in as a "team player," to use former Speaker John McCormack's words. In 1971, when the Democratic leaders advanced once again, John Moss failed to grab a chair. He and Hale Boggs had never gotten along well and friction was compounded when Moss made an early but abortive declaration of his own candidacy for majority leader in mid-1970. When it came time to appoint a whip, Boggs turned to O'Neill of Massachusetts rather than to a member of the large California Democratic delegation.

Throughout the 1960's, McFall stepped in as needed when Moss and Albert had suffered illnesses, for a time as acting deputy whip and once as acting majority leader. A close ally of Boggs, McFall was one of few Californians who had remained loyal during his bid for the majority leadership in 1970–1971. Thus, his appointment to floor whip was hardly surprising, once Boggs was elected.

John Brademas of Indiana, the other appointed floor whip, was something of a long shot. First elected to Congress in 1958, a former Rhodes Scholar and political science professor, Brademas had demonstrated his capacity for floor leadership mainly through education legislation. Active in the Democratic Study Group, indeed, seen as its prospective new chairman, Brademas had made a point of maintaining his friendships with Albert (also a former Rhodes Scholar) and Boggs. (In the 1971 contest for majority leader he had privately committed himself to James O'Hara of Michigan, but expressed sympathy for Udall and avoided any antagonism toward Boggs.) With both Rostenkowski of Illinois and O'Hara out of the picture, the 44-year-old Indiana member seemed to be a good midwestern selection for Albert and Boggs. Brademas was young, intelligent, could represent his region, and be seen as a symbolic gesture toward bringing DSG-type liberals back into the fold.

Brademas and McFall worked well together in their new job of floor whip. In the early days of a session when McFall would be preoccupied with Appropriation Subcommittee responsibilities, Brademas would cover the floor. Later, when Brademas became intensively involved in education legislation, especially on the highly controversial school busing sections, McFall would assist O'Neill in most of the day-to-day floor routine. McFall recommended to the leadership that his younger colleague join him as a co-chairman of the Congressional Campaign Committee's Research Committee, a group that formulated materials for Democratic incumbents and new Democratic candidates running for House seats. If Brademas tended to concentrate more of his energies on campaign research, McFall probably spent more time on the floor working, as he put it, on "the nuts and bolts of the legislation process." [34]

Neither man knew the other very well before their appointments. They developed a mutual respect for each other, if not a friendship, because of almost daily interaction attending the Speaker's pre-noon press conferences, shared floor responsibilities, and other leadership activities.

After Boggs' disappearance it was patently clear to both Brademas and McFall that one of them stood a strong chance to become the next appointive whip. They both realized, of course, that while their chief opposition was likely to be the other floor whip, it was possible that the Speaker and new majority leader might go beyond the "ladder" and appoint another member. As they came to hear of Burton's proposal to make the post elective, however, they decided to pool their efforts and work together to keep the position appointive.

Neither man was motivated by personal ambition, alone. Both felt there were strong arguments in favor of keeping the position appointive. By and large their telephone and personal contacts emphasized the standard arguments: the nature of the job, the need for loyalty to the leadership, regional balance, and the like. As the January caucus approached and it appeared that the elective whip might carry, both men shifted their strategy somewhat — they worked less in tandem and placed more emphasis on securing individual commitments.

Of the two men, Brademas put on a more extensive campaign, personally and by telephone. Two years junior and 10 years younger than McFall, with less floor exposure and not as much personal popularity, his campaign was going to be more uphill, regardless of whether the job was appointive or elective.

McFall got started later, made fewer telephone calls, focused more on maintaining a majority of the California delegation behind the appointive position and his own candidacy. Here, he was greatly aided by Chet Holifield, the dean of his delegation, chairman of the Committee on Government Operations, and a past chairman and early leader of the DSG. If Holifield lost some of his reformist zeal as he grew older, his ties with other senior members from around the country continued strong.

Since both Burton and McFall were from California, competition for votes in this delegation was especially keen. Members seeking committee assignments or transfers had to keep in mind that the shortest path toward success lay through McFall, Holifield, the dean of the delegation, and Corman, the state's representative on the Committee on Committees. On the other hand, Burton, with strong ties to the California Assembly, could intimate that the way to maintain a safe seat in the face of future congressional redistrictings, was to back his own candidacy and the elective whip resolution. Burton would end up claiming 15 votes for the elective whip, seven against with one vote undecided. McFall figured the California delegation was split down the middle, about 12 votes for elective and 11 against.

McFall also got unexpected assistance from another influential House member, Richard Bolling of Missouri. A decade before, Bolling had run against Carl Albert in a bid for the majority leadership, but had withdrawn before a caucus vote. In a sense a partial victim of the "ladder mentality," his arguments in favor of retention of the appointive whip would be listened to with perhaps even greater weight. Spokesman for the leadership on the Committee on Rules first for Rayburn, then for McCormack, then for Albert, since about 1965 Bolling had become increasingly valuable to Albert as a political adviser. By the early 1970's his relationship to the Speaker was almost as close as it had been with Rayburn.

Two years earlier Bolling had spoken out against the elective whip in the Democratic Caucus; he was to do so again in 1973. In addition to counseling McFall, he made a number of telephone calls on his behalf.[35] Close to Andrew Biemiller, a former congressman and the Legislative Director for the AFL–CIO, Bolling also helped confirm that labor favored the retention of the appointive whip and would find McFall an acceptable choice.

By and large, interest groups remained on the sidelines on this question. One other labor organization, the United Auto Workers, let it be known that they too favored keeping the position appointive. But neither the AFL–CIO nor the UAW went out of their way to bring any pressure to bear on labor-sympathetic members. If the position did become elective, then would be the time for labor activity to insure the choice of one of their own.

About the only group working actively in behalf of the elective whip was Common Cause. Even this effort was sporadic — most of the group's public appeal and congressional lobbying was focused upon the questions of seniority, the closed rule, and "opening up" committees.

V

Crucial to the success of the drive to obtain an elective whip was leadership "neutrality." Burton had held conversations in the late fall with both Albert and O'Neill and had come away believing, rightly or wrongly, that while neither leader especially favored an elective whip, they were willing to have the issue played out in the January caucus and abide by its decision.[36] Albert had told another prospective candidate for an elective whip that he liked the logic of an elective whip position, that it would be "more democratic that way." Although maintaining a public stance of neutrality up to and through the caucus, Albert told other members in private that he preferred the whip to be an appointive position. He also gave his blessing to the McFall-Brademas drive to align support for the retention of an appointive whip.

O'Neill's position was somewhat more open. He would tell the press that he favored the appointive whip. He would counsel several possible contenders for both the appointive and elective method of selecting a whip that he "preferred the appointive, but could live with the elective." In his own drive for the majority leadership, O'Neill was to receive more than 20 direct solicitations from other members who wished to be appointed whip. Playing this hand close to his vest, O'Neill made no commitments. Instead, he encouraged most members who talked to him, or at least did not discourage their hopes. O'Neill told most of them that he appreciated their interest and would certainly take their regional and personal contributions into consideration. Of course, first of all he had to be elected majority leader.

About the same time that Burton arrived back in Washington, D.C. in mid-December, and McFall and Brademas were cranking up their opposition, other prospective candidates for elective whip began to surface. Gibbons, already resigned to losing his contest for majority leader, considered seriously making a bid for elective whip. Morris K. Udall of Arizona explored the possibility that Albert and O'Neill might appoint him whip. He perceived himself as the candidate most likely to bring younger and more reform-oriented liberals back into the fold. If the position were to be elective, he was prepared to wage a multiple-ballot candidacy.

All these moderate-to-liberal prospective candidates faced the possible threat of a "southern candidate" as well as what had come to be labeled the "O'Hara-Udall" dilemma. If two or more liberals were running for the same office, what kind of a mechanism could be devised to prevent like-minded reformers from knocking one another out, while a more conservative member walked away with the prize? [37]

Just who that southern conservative or midwestern regular was, who might have run to defeat Burton, McFall, or any other of the leading contenders, was never to be resolved. The drive for an elective whip was to be stalled in the January 2, 1973 afternoon session of the House Democratic Caucus.

VI

The opening caucus of the 93d House Democratic Caucus was called to order shortly after 10 A.M. on Tuesday, January 2, 1973. Before all newly elected and returning House Democratic members could dispose of the elective whip question, the caucus would first have to deal with its more traditional concerns — organizing the caucus, nominating its candidates for Speaker, majority leader, and the officers of the House of Representatives (clerk, sergeant-at-arms, and so on), and selecting its Committee on Committees. Only later in the afternoon would the caucus arrive at the questions of party and congressional reform and the overriding issue of the time, the Vietnam War.

The some 240 Democrats who assembled on the House floor in the Capitol included only 27 new members. Still, its membership was probably more introspective than past caucuses, more defiant and more anxious to get moving.[38] One reason for its preoccupation with internal structure was a strong feeling among most members that the relative prestige of the legislative branch had reached a new low in the eyes of the electorate. Only Congress, and especially the majority party, could bring about the necessary internal reforms to stem the growth in executive powers. Much anger was directed at Republican President Richard M. Nixon who, in winning his second term, had defeated the Democratic nominee, Senator George McGovern, with nearly 61 percent of the popular vote.

On the eve of the election it had appeared that a peace in Vietnam was almost at hand. Yet, the war was still going on and the President had resumed wholesale bombing of North Vietnam with scarcely an effort to involve congressional leaders in his decisions. Questions of the President and his war powers, spending and the impoundment of funds — the priorities of the nation — were the questions that were to preoccupy the 93d Congress.

The Democratic Caucus began rather routinely. Congresswoman Leonor Sullivan of Missouri, the caucus secretary, called the meeting to order and presided until the unopposed nomination and reelection of Caucus Chairman Olin Teague of Texas. Once its agenda was adopted, the caucus turned to its first order of business, nomination of its candidates for Speaker and majority leader.

THE NOMINATION OF THE SPEAKER AND MAJORITY LEADER. Following election to his fourteenth term on November 7, 1972, Speaker Carl Albert had returned to Washington, D.C. determined to improve upon his leadership in the previous Congress, to seize more initiative, and to work toward becoming a strong Speaker. He had spoken in behalf of 17 Democrats in the past election, some of these engagements having been taken over from the missing Majority Leader Hale Boggs.

Throughout November and into December he heard of possible challenges to his Speakership, first from Wilbur Mills of Arkansas, the chairman of the House's most powerful committee, Ways and Means, and later from other potential candidates of the right and left wings of the party. Already uneasy about forthcoming reforms, Albert felt more apprehensive about a possible challenge in 1973 than he had in 1970. None of his senior staff were allowed to take vacations in December. However, if Mills, who had been talked of as a possible candidate for the Speakership in the past two Congresses, had any intention of running, he quietly abandoned such plans. He would not, he told his intimates, "run against my friend, Carl Albert." [39]

Another member of the Ways and Means Committee, Phil Landrum, 63, and the dean of the Georgia delegation, apparently toyed with the idea of opposing the Speaker, but backed off short of any formal announcement.[40] Landrum, disgruntled about pressures from the left in general, and rumors about a Black Caucus member being appointed whip, in particular, preferred Mills as his first choice.

Representative John Conyers, Jr. of Michigan, the Speaker's only formal challenger two years before, again became his only declared opponent in 1973. The four-term liberal Detroit congressman and Black Caucus member launched his campaign on December 8, 1973. "We need," he said, "a leadership of innovation, not stagnation — of anticipation, not reaction." A second "Dear Colleague" letter, sent out the following week, outlined the 43-year-old black congressman's views on congressional reform. By and large, his criticisms of Albert remained unanswered.

The observation of a second-term member from the Midwest sums up these threats to Albert as well as any:

> Sure, there's dissatisfaction with Albert. But John Conyers, who wrote some letters that I thought were terrific, only got 25 votes. And Phil Landrum, who was making all sorts of noises, didn't even have enough support to run. So the liberals and the conservatives never could get together on their own, much less with each other against Albert. Both want him to be more assertive, but in different directions. The only thing they agree on is Congress' power against the executive and Carl says he will be more assertive now.

On January 2, 1973, the 93d House Democratic caucus nominated Carl Albert as its candidate for Speaker by a vote of 202 to 25.[41] Conyers could take some credit, if not much solace, for a five-vote increase over 1971 (220–20).

A few minutes later, Thomas P. O'Neill, Jr. won election to the office of majority leader even more handily. No one opposed him. His earlier challenger, Sam Gibbons of Florida, stood up at the end of the nominating speeches and announced:

> Tip, I can tell you something that nobody else in this room can. You haven't got an enemy in the place.

DEFEAT OF THE ELECTED WHIP RESOLUTION. It was getting along toward 2 P.M. when Representative Bob Eckhardt of Houston, Texas offered his simple resolution calling for an elective whip: "Resolved, that the position of whip be elective same as the majority leader and the vote to be held at the following meeting of the caucus." A three-term House member, far more liberal than the average Texan, Eckhardt had a reputation for fairness and ability. Though he was not the southerner most calculated to bring other members of his region in behind him, Burton preferred Eckhardt to other possible sponsors because, as he later recalled, "He would make a well prepared, thoughtful statement . . . and he was a Texan. He had it worked out with Teague." Eckhardt's main argument was that now, as never before, House Democrats needed the strongest possible leadership in order to assert power against the executive branch.

When Richard Bolling rose to speak against the motion he made a similar argument but came to the opposite conclusion — elective whips could be divisive. After Bolling developed his arguments in favor of retaining the appointive whip, he paused, looked around, saw no others rising, and quickly moved to table the motion.

Normally such a motion is non-debatable, but John Dent, an eight-term Representative from Pennsylvania, rose and asked unanimous consent to speak out of order. No one objected and Dent proceeded with his usual fiery, if somewhat rambling, oratory to speak in favor of the elective whip resolution. Such a procedure had worked in the Pennsylvania legislature (Dent had served as a Democratic Senate floor leader for 17 years), so why wouldn't it work in the House of Representatives?

Just before the vote James Stanton of Cleveland, Ohio, beginning his second term, moved that the vote be by secret ballot. Bolling's motion to table was narrowly beaten, 115 to 110.

Chairman Teague was about to bring the original resolution to a vote when newly elected Majority Leader Tip O'Neill rose and asked for unanimous consent to speak. No one could object and O'Neill proceeded to deliver the death blow to the notion of an elective whip, at least for the 93d Congress. Although O'Neill gave a rather hazy historical account of why the elective whip had proven to be an unfortunate method for selecting past Republican leaders, his main point was quite convincing. In effect, O'Neill argued — Why deny me what my predecessors have had, the power to appoint the whip?

The consensus among most House Democrats who were interviewed, including Phil Burton, was that O'Neill's speech turned around at least five votes. Although several speakers followed, Wayne Hays in favor of the change, Jake Pickle of Texas against, the final vote went against the elective whip resolution, 123 to 114.

If O'Neill's speech, making clear where at least one leader stood, was decisive, others saw it as a major gamble. Commented one activist:

> What could he say if he lost? It would have demonstrated much less confidence in the new majority leader. He had to gamble to turn around the prior vote ... But not to win? ... Sure, only three shifts were required, but it was a real crap shoot.

Those who worked to keep the position appointive, especially Mc-Fall and Brademas, felt that O'Neill had little choice but to make his position known. They had urged him to do so while the first vote was being tabulated.

Where did the additional 12 votes on the second ballot come from? Those who favor conspiratorial theories may argue that O'Neill kept votes back, or even that the ballot box was stuffed. The most simple and plausible interpretation is that these votes came from members who returned from late-lunch activities. Most observers also agree little effort was made by either side to actively work the floor.

Several other factors had an impact on the outcome. One was Burton's attempt to convert the position from appointive to elective and at the same time to promote his own candidacy. In the early stages many House members tended to discount Burton's chances. As the possibility of an elective whip became more feasible, other possible contenders began to promote the idea.[42] As Burton's candidacy edged to the fore, a different group of House members began to fear that he might win. J. J. Pickle of Texas had characterized the whole movement as an attempt by the DSG to elect one of its own. Burton's own interpretation of the resolution's defeat places considerable weight on southern defections:

> There was more than a majority for the elective whip in the South until sometime today. Some of the southerners voted "Yes," but a clear majority voted "No."

Burton's assessment is confirmed by more than one southerner. A second-termer from a rural district offered the following interpretation:

> We approached the elective/appointive argument purely from a pragmatic standpoint. We conservative "redneck" types [this with a smile and a flip of his shirt collar] were in a much weaker position than we were in the last session. We knew that Tip as a liberal northeasterner would pick someone with recognized and ideological balance . . . We couldn't take any chances with the possibility of a Phil Burton or a Mo Udall.

One of Burton's closest friends was to sum up the whole effort — "the issue got Burtonized."

Three days later the hurt of the loss for Burton seemingly had vanished, although undoubtedly the scars would remain. He looked ahead to forthcoming caucuses and attempts to implement further DSG reforms. Had it been difficult trying to ride the two horses at one time? "Yes, I was able to keep almost perfect balance, but not quite." Was the concept of an elective whip dead for the time being? "Its time will come again, perhaps as early as the 94th Congress."

VII

All but one of the four congressional parties — Senate majority and minority, House majority and minority — elect their party whips. A case can be and was made for the exception, the House Democratic majority, on the grounds that the *third* man in the party hierarchy should be chosen by and directly accountable to the top leaders of the party. At the opening caucus, newly elected Majority Leader O'Neill, with Speaker Albert's quiescent support, argued for and helped to keep the whip's position appointive. The power to appoint obviously enhances the strengths of the top leadership as well as minimizes potential conflict over the implementation of legislative programs. Still, pressures to convert the position into an elective one continued, not least because of younger member dissatisfaction with an "automatic escalator" pattern in the leadership hierarchy — from whip to majority leader to Speaker.

If anything, these tensions were reinforced a week after the caucus, when O'Neill and Albert appointed John McFall (Cal.) and John Brademas (Ind.), floor whips under O'Neill in the previous Congress, as whip and chief deputy whip, respectively. McFall was selected over Brademas for four prime reasons: his age (54 to Brademas' 46), seniority (nine terms to Brademas' eight), an edge in personal popularity, and the size of the California delegation. In addition, the leadership created still another tier in the whip hierarchy by appointing three deputy whips: Richard Fulton of Tennessee, Spark M. Matsunaga of Hawaii, and James Wright of Texas. Only time would tell whether or not at least some of these men were destined for higher leadership positions in the future.

NOTES

1. Ironically, Don Jonz, the pilot, had written a rather "machismo"-styled article for *Flying* entitled "Ice: Without Fear," which appeared in the October 1972 issue, pp. 67–68, 123.
2. Transcript of Presumptive Death Proceedings, District Court for the State of Alaska, December 11, 16, 1972.
3. George Lardner, "Boggs Search Is Halted," *Washington Post*, November 25, 1972, p. A-1. The longest previous Alaskan air search in which missing persons were found alive was in May 1972, when a couple were rescued 13 days after their plane disappeared.
4. Although the tradition of a surviving wife succeeding her husband in Congress is no longer as prevalent as it once was, about 40 percent (31 of 78 as of 1971) of all women who served in Congress initially entered by this route.

"Who Gets Elected," *Guide to the Congress of the United States* (Washington, D.C.: Congressional Quarterly Service, 1971), pp. 467–68.
5. Elected to his eleventh term in the House in 1972, the nickname "Tip" has several possible derivatives. The most popular story is that he was named after an old-time baseball player, James Edward O'Neill, whose stock-in-trade had been fouling off pitches, hence "Tip," until the pitcher walked him. Another close associate of O'Neill attributes the nickname to the close affinity of his initials, T and P. The ultimate "in-group," which included former Speaker John McCormack, more frequently called O'Neill, "Tommy."
6. Gary Hymel, Boggs' administrative assistant, later recalled: "He was doing what a majority leader has to do. There's a maxim that you can't turn down any colleague who asks you to campaign for him, even a 'safe seat' colleague."
7. Paradoxically, one of the Speaker's first assignments was to fly from Washington, D.C. to Pennsylvania in a Cessna 310, the same type of aircraft in which Boggs, Begich, Russell, and Jonz had disappeared over Alaska.
8. O'Neill succeeded to the co-chairmanship on the committee with Ed Edmondson of Oklahoma in 1970 following the death of Mike Kirwan of Ohio, chairman since 1948. Edmondson resigned in March 1972 to spend full time on an unsuccessful bid for the U.S. Senate.
9. More than one House Democrat tended to discount the power, if not the discretion, that O'Neill wielded. "In the first place, incumbents usually get the same amount, initially. But the chairman has to watch it that he doesn't end up antagonizing more incumbents than he pleases. Some guy may say, 'Jeez, I only got $3000, and Jones got $4000 — how come?' I suppose the main benefit is being able to put money into or withhold it from non-incumbent races. A freshman might have difficulty overlooking a candidate for party leadership who appears to have just put $5000 into his campaign."
   Freshmen members who were interviewed tended to confirm this impression. A West Coast freshman: "O'Neill really did a hell of a job. He, representing the Democratic National Congressional (Campaign) Committee, raised dough and he came around. He was out working for our election; he signed the checks we got from the DNCC. We had contact with him all during the general election, so he had a head start with us."
10. Neil MacNeil, "The Impeachment Congress: House Leader 'Tip' O'Neill," *Time*, February 4, 1974, pp. 14–22.
11. Thomas H. Mullen, the long-time administrative assistant of O'Neill's Boston district office, grew up with O'Neill and played high school basketball with him. He recalls observing to O'Neill, after he had just obtained the Massachusetts House Speakership, "We've come a long way from Barry's corner." It was the neighborhood hangout for friends who planned and worked in O'Neill's first campaigns and still surround him at birthday parties or festive occasions like his annual St. Patrick's Day parties in Washington (complete with green beer). As a perceptive Washington social commentator notes: "To know O'Neill for 20 years is to be a newcomer." Myra MacPherson, "Tip O'Neill: Bridging the Last Hurrah and the New Breed," *Washington Post*, December 31, 1972, p. E-2.
12. Two hundred forty-three Democrats, plus Independent John J. Moakley of Massachusetts (upset victor over Louise Day Hicks) were elected on November 7, 1972. The loss of Boggs, Begich, and George Collins of Illinois, who also died in an airplane crash, would reduce the total to 240 votes in the caucus — hence, a majority of 121 would be needed to win. (On January 2, 1973, delegates from District of Columbia, Puerto Rico, the Virgin Islands,

and Guam were also allotted caucus votes; Moakley would also vote, bringing the total potential vote to 245.)

13. When queried about whether or not there was any pattern in the some 60–70 Democratic members or incoming freshmen who refused to make a pledge to him, O'Neill divided them into three groups: (1) some committee chairmen, who by past practice or present leanings preferred not to take a position; (2) some members, as many as 20 he never reached, either because they were out of the country, or never called back after repeated telephone calls (five or six were members-elect who couldn't be tracked down); (3) the balance were either southern conservatives or "way-out liberals." The latter, he said, "told me they 'were 99 percent for me,' but they were never with me."

14. Richard L. Lyons, "Fight for Boggs Post Looms in House," *Washington Post*, November 10, 1972, p. A-12.

15. The question of whether to appoint or elect a majority whip was again emerging as a possible caucus issue. (A later section of this chapter details these events.)

16. Under the Legislative Reorganization Act of 1970 and the Electronic Voting Act of 1972 the House of Representatives had installed electronic voting (first mentioned as a proposed reform in 1913) and was moving toward more effective information retrieval and other computer services.

17. On March 20, 1973, almost three months after the selection of the new majority leader, the House Democratic National Congressional (Campaign) Committee elected Wayne Hays as its chairman. He was unopposed. The leadership, however, maintained a strong voice on the committee — O'Neill, the former chairman, was elected deputy chairman.

18. Ways and Means seats, in part because of the committee's broad legislative jurisdiction, in part because its members serve on the Committee on Committees for their party, are highly coveted. They are the only committee assignments formally decided by Democratic Caucus votes. Although spirited regional contests are frequently conducted, Gibbons' victory was unprecedented, in that a seat previously held by Florida's A. Sidney Herlong, Jr. was vacant and the state delegation had nominated another conservative Florida member, Don Fuqua, to succeed him. Gibbons mounted an intensive member-to-member campaign outside Florida for caucus support that eventually forced Fuqua to step aside before the caucus vote.

19. No campaign for congressional leadership ever begins with a formal press conference. Both O'Neill and Gibbons had taken preliminary soundings with their closest associates at least as soon as it became apparent that Boggs was not likely to be found. Human nature being what it is, probably few House Democrats, if any, had not mentally calculated the meaning of the disappearance of the majority leader to their own careers, almost simultaneously with the grief and sorrow they may have felt.

20. Richard L. Lyons, "Leadership Up For Grabs," *Washington Post*, November 11, 1972, p. A-1.

21. The impressions of two contemporaries, both sympathetically inclined toward Gibbons by age, ideology, and friendship, suggest some of the difficulties. A junior midwesterner commented: "The game was over before the teams got on the field." And a westerner, with several more terms of experience, observed: "It was like charging into a machine gun nest."

22. *Washington Post*, November 30, 1972, p. A-23.

23. In an effort to get a head-start in his campaign, Gibbons had his initial "Dear Colleague" letters typed even before the election; these included a slightly different letter for incoming freshmen. Dated the day after the election, it was

a simple matter to cull out those candidates who had lost and send out the balance in quadruplicate, the original to the member's home, carbon copies to his D.C. home, his Capitol office, and his district office.

24. One colleague later told Gibbons: "Sam, you sent out so much mail during the holidays, that I'd have been kept busy just reading it."

25. Besides the problem of limited returns, not many more than 100, Gibbons could never be sure exactly of the kind of reading he was getting. Some of O'Neill's supporters apparently checked "Yes" to the question "Should Sam Gibbons continue in the race?" Once O'Neill knew he would defeat Gibbons, he preferred that Gibbons run instead of a last-minute unknown with clout entering the contest. And, of course, O'Neill's backers stood to gain more credit for their support from a "contest" in contrast to an unopposed victory.

26. Leo Diehl, O'Neill's administrative assistant, would revise this estimate sharply downward. He strongly believed that if the challenge had come to a vote Gibbons would have received "at most 25 votes and that's giving him everything."

27. The extent of support for the elective whip proposal within the Hansen Committee in 1970–1971 depends largely upon whether or not a proponent or an opponent is quoted. One member talked about "near unanimity" for the change. Another member had difficulty recalling any discussion, let alone a consensus: "It (the Hansen Committee) operates like the building of the Tower of Babel . . . It's a free flow of conversation, skipping from one subject to another . . . The elective whip may have been discussed, but no one took it seriously."

28. One member would later complain: "Phil Burton was a stumbling bloc to reform. He had a single issue — the elective whip. As a result December was a bad, bad month [for the DSG]."

29. John Brademas of Indiana had planned to run for the DSG chairmanship, but decided that his January 1971 appointment as Democratic floor whip (under O'Neill), together with his Education Subcommittee responsibilities, already spread him too thin.

30. It's not clear who first gave Burton this label but it seems to be widely, if affectionately, applied by his colleagues and not a few staff. "Crazy" he is not, but Burton comes on so strong and with such enthusiasm that it's almost as if he were on a continuous "high."

31. Not every DSG member is as sanguine about the advantages of enlarged membership. Several stress the danger of dilution of organization purpose. Others point out that "so-and-so may be 'members,' but that doesn't mean they come to meetings, let alone vote with us in caucus."

32. As Burton recalled: "If it was somebody I was close to, I'd say right off that I was proposing the elective whip and that I'd like to have it . . . If I knew him to be the kind of congressman who was precise, who would say how he felt and he didn't indicate that, if he spoke in broader terms, I'd ease off. I'd back off and tell him I'd be back to him later. It all depended on the individual . . ."

33. One reason for McFall's popularity with some House members is that he minimized any impression of getting one step ahead of any other member. A confirming piece of evidence was his relative obscurity. Once, at a Washington interest group luncheon three mid-career Senators independently approached a more visible House member to inquire: "Who is this fellow, McFall?" "And this, after 16 years in the House," his more visible colleague was to complain.

34. This division of labors would eventually work to McFall's benefit in the appointment of a whip to succeed O'Neill. He was to become, in Albert's terms, "a man who was on the floor, covering the job as I used to do."

35. As Bolling summarized his reasons for supporting an appointive whip and backing McFall: "I believe in one, dominant, legislative leader . . . You can't have a Speaker, a junior Speaker, and a junior-junior Speaker and that's what you would have if the whip were elected. The whip has to play a subordinate function . . . McFall is a guy who has proven his capacity. He was the one who was there, on the floor, last year. He's part of the system, he's in the party, and in the center, ideologically. Thus, the available person and the theory impelled me to speak out in favor of the appointive whip."

36. In a further attempt to provide legitimacy to the effort, Burton appealed in late December to Chairman Hansen to reconstitute her reform committee. His objective, to generate a favorable report on the elective whip resolution, was thwarted when the chairman refused to call the committee together. One member reports that she backed off when she heard the leadership was not "neutral" but continued to favor an appointive whip.

37. As made clear in Chapter 7, this is more a "liberal," if not an "academic," problem among contemporary House Democrats, since the combined votes of Udall and O'Hara in 1971 still fell far short of a winning majority. In 1973, however, it appeared as if a liberal candidate might be able "to put it all together."

38. The 93d Congress was also characterized by a relatively high turnover in House committee chairmen (six) and ranking minority members (nine). Overall turnover (42 new Republican and 27 new Democratic members) was only slightly above normal.

39. What appeared to give Mills' candidacy greater credence in 1972 than in the past was his own intensive involvement in the campaigns of other House members, especially in the form of contributions, many of them funneled through a group called "The Committee for a Democratic Congress," run in collaboration with former Democratic party Treasurer (now Chairman) of the Democratic National Committee, Robert Strauss of Texas.

According to one ripe rumor that passed through the corridors of the House, Mills and Albert had made a "deal" — Albert would serve for no more than one term, then step aside to allow Mills to become Speaker. The alleged meeting place — half-time at the Oklahoma–Arkansas football game — wipes out the credibility the rumor might have had. Oklahoma University (the Speaker's alma mater) did not play Arkansas in 1972.

40. Mary Russell, "Georgia's Landrum Thinking of Making Run for Speaker," *Washington Post*, November 16, 1972, p. A-4.

41. The next day, to no one's surprise, Carl Albert defeated Jerry Ford, the Republican nominee for Speaker, by a party-line vote of 236–188. *Congressional Record* (daily ed.), January 3, 1973, pp. H-2-3.

42. One California colleague of Burton was to sardonically observe to the press immediately following the tabling vote, "Since a majority in there [pointing to the House floor] want to be whip, I figure it will be an elected whip."

CHAPTER NINE

House Party Leadership Selection: 1955–1974

Four questions continue to provide the primary focus of this book: (1) Who are the principal congressional party leaders? (2) How are they selected? (3) What patterns of leadership change characterize the four congressional parties — House Democrats and Republicans, Senate Democrats and Republicans? and (4) What factors or conditions account for differences in types and variable rates of change among the congressional parties over time? Obviously, even the closest examination of five selections of House floor leaders over a decade, three by the majority party, two by the minority party, can only partially answer some of these questions. More cases of leadership change must be analyzed, although all cannot be examined in the same depth and detail as in Chapters 3–8.

This chapter begins by outlining a scheme for classifying types of intra-party leadership change. This scheme is illustrated with 36 cases of change or attempted change that took place in the U.S. House of Representatives in the 84th to 93d Congresses (1955–1974).[1] This era was characterized by Democratically controlled Congresses and also encompassed the end of Rayburn-Martin leadership in the House. It included the administrations of four Presidents — Eisenhower, Kennedy, Johnson, and Nixon — and the initial months of a fifth, former House Minority Leader Gerald Ford.

Some rather striking differences in the degree to which the House Republican minority party resorts to contested change as compared with the relatively harmonious patterns of leadership selection characteristic of the Democratic majority party throughout most of this period are examined here. Then in Chapter 10 some of the conditions which seem to facilitate one type of change rather than another are explored. Finally, several of the consequences of leadership change for individual careers, legislative goals, party fortunes, institutional strengths, and representative processes are suggested.

Three variables have been selected to classify types of intra-party leadership change: (1) whether or not a vacancy existed in a leadership position, (2) the presence or absence of an established pattern of succession, and (3) the extent to which the change was contested. When dichotomized these variables lead to a sixfold classification scheme, as outlined in Table 9.1. The first variable is discrete: either a vacancy existed in a given position such as the Speakership, or it did not. The vacancy could come about for a variety of reasons, including death, resignation, retirement, or election defeat. The remaining two variables are not as easily dichotomized. Patterns of succession may be quite firmly established as with elevation from the minority or majority leader to the office of Speaker in the House of Representatives. Other patterns, such as succession to the majority leader from the position of party whip, are only tentative and emerging.

The final variable, the extent to which a given change was contested, is even more difficult to define in operational terms. For purposes of this analysis, a "contest" takes place when two or more legislators announced their candidacies and worked actively to align support. For simplicity of classification the "contest–no contest" variable has been dichotomized, although as with most variables in the social sciences, it may be viewed as continuous rather than discrete.[2] That is to say, there are a number of finer gradations along a continuum which a more fully developed scheme would have to take into account. For example, the "no contest" classification may include situations where a contest was considered but abandoned short of announcement because the dissident party faction decided it did not have the necessary votes to make a successful challenge.[3] Contests may range from (a) situations in which two or more candidates announced but all but one withdrew before the final vote, to (b) controversies which forced concessions, although the leaders remained in office, or (c) instances of successful revolt.[4]

These distinctions will become more meaningful after discussion and illustration of the types of intra-party leadership change suggested by this classification scheme: (1) routine advancement, (2) appointment or emergence of a consensus choice, (3) open competition, (4) challenge to the heir apparent, and (5) revolt or its aftermath.

These types are ordered in terms of the amount of credit expendi-

Table 9.1
Types of Intra-Party Leadership Change

	NO CONTEST	CONTEST
NO VACANCY	*Status quo*	(5) Revolt or its aftermath
VACANCY Established pattern of succession	(1) Routine advancement	(4) Challenge to the heir apparent
No established pattern of succession	(2) Appointment or emergence of a consensus choice	(3) Open competition

ture (time, energy, number of members involved, and so on) which each is likely to engender.[5] Routine advancement involves little or no expenditure of resources. One member is seen as the likely successor. Dissident members may invest some time conducting an informal poll of the membership to see if a contest has any chance of succeeding. Typically, no commitments are sought, and the campaign is never launched for lack of a single candidate behind whom all opposing factions might rally. The second and third types usually involve lower party positions for which the stakes are not as high. Leadership appointments may be challenged in a party conference or caucus, but only at considerable risk. If no consensus choice emerges, several candidates may run. Friends, committee associates, and state or regional delegations are brought in on either side. When the leadership position is important for the resources it controls, such as the campaign committee chairmanship, or because it is seen as a stepping stone to higher office, then more members are recruited to work actively in behalf of the candidates. If the contest goes to a formal vote, the pressures to align uncommitted members become intense. The greatest credit expenditure is likely to occur in challenges to an heir apparent, or in contests to remove incumbent party leaders. Revolts may involve the full time and energy of as many as a third of the party membership over a period of several weeks or longer.

The upper left-hand cell of Table 9.1, or the *status quo* is, of course, the customary situation. No vacancy in a leadership position exists and no contest takes place. Continuity in office is the general practice in the House of Representatives, as in most organizations. For example, Representative Joseph Martin, Jr. of Massachusetts was first elected to Congress in 1924. He became Republican minority leader in 1939. He was reelected minority leader seven times and Speaker twice before his one defeat in 1959 by his former majority leader in the 80th and 83d Congresses, Charles Halleck of Indiana. Halleck was twice reelected minority leader before being overthrown by Gerald Ford in 1965. Ford was reelected four times before he was appointed Vice President by Richard M. Nixon in December 1973. John Rhodes of Arizona took Ford's place as Republican minority leader in 1973 and was reelected without opposition in 1975. Republican Whip Leslie Arends, first elected whip in 1943, maintained his position under four different minority leaders — Martin, Halleck, Ford and Rhodes — until his retirement at the end of the 93d Congress.

The late Speaker Sam Rayburn of Texas was first elected to Congress in 1912. He became chairman of the Interstate and Foreign Commerce Committee in 1931. In 1934 he briefly challenged Joseph W. Byrns of Tennessee, the incumbent majority leader, for the nomination for Speaker. However, Rayburn withdrew from the race before a vote in the Democratic Caucus. Rayburn went on to defeat Rules Committee Chairman John J. O'Connor of New York in a contest for majority leader in 1937. He was elevated to the Speakership in 1940. His occupancy of the top Democratic leadership position during the next 21 years was never challenged. John W. McCormack of Massachusetts, who served as a loyal lieutenant to Rayburn from 1940 until 1961, was first elected Speaker in 1962. He was reelected four consecutive times until he retired at the end of the 91st Congress (1969–1970). His successor, Carl Albert of Oklahoma, was first elected in 1971 and reelected in 1973 and 1975.

The ability of incumbents to retain office is not difficult to explain. Party leaders, particularly Speakers, have multiple opportunities to grant favors, create obligations, and build credit, all of which they can use to maintain a network of continuing support. A Speaker or floor leader has available, in addition, a lesser number of sanctions, including the withholding of patronage and the vetoing of committee assignments, the threat of which can act as deterrents to contested change. In addition, a number of benefits are to be gained from continuity of party leadership, not the least of which is experienced floor management. Contests, and particularly revolts against incumbent leadership, are likely to generate high costs in terms of subsequent party harmony. For all these reasons, the predominant pattern in congressional parties is the retention of incumbents rather than frequent leadership turnover.

II

Initial evidence of the relative infrequency of change in five major party-wide positions in both the Democratic and Republican parties for a 20-year period, 1955–1974, is presented in Tables 9.2 and 9.3. This period was selected because it encompassed the ten complete Congresses since the last election bringing about inter-party change in the organization of the House, the mid-term election of 1954.

For the Democratic party, the majority party in the House of Representatives throughout this period, the five major party-wide leadership positions are the Speaker, the majority leader, the majority whip, the chairman of the Democratic Caucus, and the chairman of the Democratic National Congressional Campaign Committee.[6] With the exception of the whip, all these positions are elective. The Democratic whip is appointed by the majority leader who consults with the Speaker. Nominations to lesser party positions are influenced considerably by the Speaker and majority leader, but their choices must be ratified by the Democratic Caucus which is composed of all Democratic House members. Table 9.2 lists the incumbents for these five positions since 1955.

For the Republican party, the minority party throughout this period, the five major party positions are minority leader, minority whip, chairman of the Republican Conference, chairman of the Republican Policy Committee and chairman of the Republican National Congressional Campaign Committee. All these positions are elective in the sense that the nominees must ultimately be acceptable to the Republican Conference, counterpart to the Democratic Caucus. For two offices during most of this period — the whip and the chairman of the Congressional Campaign Committee — the selection process was made by separate committees. From 1919 until 1963 the choice of the whip was formally made by the Republican Committee on Committees, acting on the recommendation of the Speaker or minority leader. Since 1965, the whip has been directly elected by the Republican Conference. The chairman of the Republican National Congressional (Campaign) Committee, the counterpart to the Democratic National Congressional (Campaign) Committee, is elected by that committee. As with the Republican Committee on Committees, each state with Republican members is entitled to one Representative with as many votes as there are Republican House members in his state delegation. Table 9.3 lists the incumbents for these five Republican leadership positions for the 84th–93d Congresses.

As Tables 9.2 and 9.3 suggest, the prevailing practice is continuity in office rather than leadership change. At first glance, Republicans appear somewhat less susceptible to change than Democrats. Of the 50 hypothetical changes which the leadership in each party could undergo (a change in each position with each Congress) the House Democratic party had made 19 changes, the Republican party but 13.[7] At least seven of the Democratic changes were directly attributable to the death of an incumbent (Sam Rayburn, Hale Boggs, Francis Walter, and Michael Kirwan) as compared with only one among Republican leaders (Richard Simpson). Moreover, 5 of the 19

Table 9.2
Democratic (Majority) Party Leaders, House of Representatives,
1955–1974

Congress	Speaker	Majority Leader	Majority Whip	Caucus Chairman	Congressional Campaign Committee Chairman
84th: 1955 1956	Rayburn, Texas(9-16-40)[a]	McCormack, Mass.(9-25-40)	Albert, Okla.(1-55)	Rooney, N.Y.(1-55)	Kirwan, Ohio (1948)
85th: 1957 1958	"	"	"	Price, Ill.(1-57)	"
86th: 1959 1960	"	"	"	"	"
87th: 1961 1962	Rayburn McCormack	McCormack Albert	Albert Boggs, La.	Walter, Pa.(1-61)	"
88th: 1963 1964	"	"	"	Thomas, Texas(1964)	"
89th: 1965 1966	"	"	"	Keogh, N.Y.(1-65)	"
90th: 1967 1968	"	"	"	Rostenkowski, Ill.(1-67)	"

Table 9.2   (continued)

Congress	Speaker	Majority Leader	Majority Whip	Caucus Chairman	Congressional Campaign Committee Chairman
91st: 1969	"	"	"	"	O'Neill, Mass.
1970					Edmondson, Okla.(1970)
92nd: 1971	Albert (1-21-71)	Boggs (1-21-71)	O'Neill, Mass.(1-23-71)	Teague, Texas(1-21-71)	"
1972	"	O'Neill (1-3-71)		"	O'Neill(1972)
93rd: 1973			McFall, Cal.(1-3-73)		Hays, Ohio(3-20-73)
1974					

SOURCES: George Galloway, *History of the House of Representatives* (New York: Crowell, 1961); Randall B. Ripley, "The Party Whip Organizations in the United States House of Representatives," *Am. Pol. Sci. Rev.* **58** (1964), 561–576; *Biographical Directory of the American Congress, 1774–1961* (Washington, D.C.: U.S. Government Printing Office, 1962); *Congressional Record*; *Congressional Quarterly Almanacs*; *New York Times*.

a Dates in parentheses indicate when the Representative was first elected to his party leadership position by the Democratic Caucus or Congressional Campaign Committee.

Table 9.3
Republican (Minority) Party Leaders, House of Representatives,
1955–1974

Congress	Minority Leader	Whip	Policy Committee Chairman	Conference Chairman	Congressional Campaign Committee Chairman
84th: 1955 1956	Martin, Mass.(1-3-39)[a]	Arends, Ill.(1943)	Martin, Mass.(1-49)	Hope, Kan.(1-51)	Simpson, Pa.(1-53)
85th: 1957 1958	"	"	"	Hoeven, Iowa(1-57)	"
86th: 1959 1960	Halleck, Ind.(1-7-59)	"	Byrnes, Wisc.(1-7-59)	"	Miller, N.Y.(1-60)
87th: 1961 1962	"	"	"	"	Wilson, Cal.(6-61)
88th: 1963 1964	"	"	"	Ford, Mich.(1-9-63)	"
89th: 1965 1966	Ford, Mich.(1-3-65)	"	Rhodes, Ariz.(2-23-65)	Laird, Wisc.(1-3-65)	"
90th: 1967 1968	"	"	"	"	"

Table 9.3 (continued)

Congress	Minority Leader	Whip	Policy	Committee Chairman	Conference Chairman	Congressional Campaign Committee Chairman
91st: 1969 1970	"	"	"	"	Anderson, Ill. (1-10-67)	"
92nd: 1971 1972	"	"	"	"	"	"
93rd: 1973 1974	Ford; Rhodes, Ariz. (12-7-73)	"		Rhodes; Conable, N.Y. (12-13-73)	"	Michel, Ill. (2-73)

SOURCES: George Galloway, *History of the House of Representatives* (New York: Crowell, 1961); Randall B. Ripley, "The Party Whip Organizations in the United States House of Representatives," *Am. Pol. Sci. Rev.* **58** (1964), 561–576; *Biographical Directory of the American Congress, 1774–1961* (Washington, D.C.: U.S. Government Printing Office, 1962); *Congressional Record*; *Congressional Quarterly Almanacs*; *New York Times*.

[a] Dates in parentheses indicate when the Representative was first elected to his party leadership position by the Republican Conference or Congressional Campaign Committee.

Table 9.4
Types of Intra-Party Leadership Change,
House of Representatives 84th-93d Congresses (1955–1974)

	NO CONTEST		CONTEST [a]	
	Democratic Majority	Republican Minority	Democratic Majority	Republican Minority
NO VACANCY	*Status quo*		*(5) Revolt or its aftermath*	
			Speaker McCormack vs. Udall, 1969 [b] Albert vs. Conyers, 1973 [b] Caucus Chairman Teague vs. Rostenkowski, 1971	Minority Leader Halleck vs. Martin, 1959 Ford vs. Halleck, 1965 Conference Chairman Ford vs. Hoeven, 1963 Anderson vs. Devine, 1971 [b] Minority Whip Arends vs. Frelinghuysen, 1965 [b]
VACANCY Established pattern of succession	*(1) Routine advancement* Floor leader to Speaker McCormack, 1962 Albert, 1971		*(4) Challenge to an heir apparent*	

Table 9.4 (continued)

	NO CONTEST		CONTEST [a]	
	Democratic Majority	Republican Minority	Democratic Majority	Republican Minority
No established pattern of succession	*(2) Appointment or emergence of a consensus choice*		*(3) Open competition*	
	Majority Whip Albert, 1955 Boggs, 1962 O'Neill, 1971 McFall, 1973 Caucus Chairman Rooney, 1955 Price, 1957 Walter, 1961 Thomas, 1964 Keogh, 1965 Rostenkowski, 1967 Congressional Campaign Committee Chairman O'Neill-Edmondson, 1970 O'Neill, 1972 Hays, 1973	Conference Chairman Hoeven, 1957 Policy Committee Chairman Byrnes, 1959 Rhodes, 1965	Majority Leader Albert vs. Bolling, 1962 Boggs vs. Udall, Hays, Sisk, O'Hara, 1971 O'Neill vs. Gibbons, 1973	Minority Leader Rhodes vs. Arends, Devine, 1973 Conference Chairman Laird vs. Frelinghuysen, 1965 Anderson vs. Betts, Quie, 1969 Policy Committee Chairman Conable vs. Clawson, 1973 Congressional Campaign Committee Chairman Miller vs. McCulloch, 1960 Wilson vs. McCulloch, 1961
Total number of changes	15	3	6	12

[a] In cases of contest, the winning candidate is listed first.

[b] Strictly speaking, four of these contests — McCormack vs. Udall (1969), Albert vs. Conyers (1973), Arends vs. Frelinghuysen (1965), and Anderson vs. Devine (1971) — do not illustrate a change in leadership since all four incumbent leaders withstood the challenges.

Democratic cases were accounted for by the practice of rotating the heretofore largely honorific position of caucus chairman among senior Democrats who had not yet attained the chairmanship of a standing committee.[8]

In addition, two leaders in each party have withstood challenges to their incumbency within the past decade — Speaker John McCormack in 1969, Speaker Carl Albert in 1973, Minority Whip Leslie Arends in 1965, and Republican Conference Chairman John Anderson in 1971.

Even if one lumps these attempted changes in with all cases of actual leadership change, the totals for the five positions for each party over a two-decade period — 21 for Democrats and 15 for Republicans — remain quite small. As will soon become apparent, the way in which change comes about has far more important consequences than the number of cases of changes or attempted change, per se.

III

The utility of a classification scheme is demonstrated both by its ability to order phenomena as well as by the fruitfulness of the hypotheses it generates. Before suggesting why one party resorts to conflict as a means of change more frequently than the other party, each of the five types of intra-party leadership change needs further elaboration. Four of the five types are illustrated by 36 cases of change or attempted change which took place during the 84th–93d Congresses (Table 9.4). Two earlier contests for the nomination for Speaker within the Republican Party in 1919 and 1931 provide more clear-cut cases of the remaining type, challenge to an heir apparent.

(1) ROUTINE ADVANCEMENT. This first type of intra-party leadership change takes place when a vacancy occurs in a top leadership position, a clear pattern of succession exists, and the next-ranking member in the party hierarchy is elevated without challenge. One index of the increasing institutionalization of the House has been the development of patterns of succession to top leadership. Almost all 13 Speakers in the twentieth century have been elevated from either the majority leadership or from the minority leadership following congressional election victories. The major exception to this established pattern was Frederick H. Gillett's defeat of Minority Leader James R. Mann for the Republican nomination for Speaker after Republicans regained control of the House in 1919.

McCormack's accession to the Speakership in January 1962, following the death of Rayburn, illustrates the prevailing practice of routine advancement. Rayburn and McCormack had served together in the principal Democratic leadership positions in the House since September 1940. When Speaker William B. Bankhead of Alabama died in 1940, Majority Leader Rayburn was elevated without contest. McCormack, with White House backing, defeated Clifton Woodrum of Virginia for the office of majority leader by a vote of 141 to 67. Prior to his selection, McCormack was chairman of the Democratic Caucus and fourth-ranking member on the Ways and Means Committee. His northern background, which complemented Rayburn's, was a strong factor in his election. The two men served in tandem throughout the 1940's and 1950's, dropping down to minority leader and minority whip, respectively, during the two Republican-controlled Congresses, the 80th and 83d.

Rayburn's health began to fail in the summer of 1961. Before he left for his home in Bonham, Texas in late August he designated Majority Leader McCormack as Speaker pro tempore. Rayburn died on November 16, 1961.

None of McCormack's possible liabilities — his age, religion, or lack of popularity with some elements of the House, particularly Democratic Study Group members — proved serious enough to bring on a challenge. As Polsby details in Chapter 3, some members feared that McCormack, at 71, was slowing down and could not provide the strong leadership necessary to get the Kennedy legislative program enacted. Others were hostile to the elevation of another Roman Catholic to another position of national leadership along with President Kennedy and Senate Majority Leader Mansfield. Although not particularly popular with northern liberals and some southern members, McCormack had the support and respect of a number of the senior oligarchs of the House, especially Carl Vinson of Georgia and Howard W. Smith of Virginia. The inability of his opponents to rally around one of several other possible candidates, and the hands-off policy adopted by President Kennedy and his White House assistants, made McCormack's election inevitable. On January 10, 1962, he became the 45th Speaker of the House.

Albert's advancement to the Speakership in January 1971, detailed in Chapters 5–7, was another case of routine advancement. Albert's succession, however, was slightly marred by the last-minute symbolic challenge of John Conyers, Jr., a three-term, black congressman from Detroit, Michigan. Since a "contest" has been defined as a situation in which "two or more legislators announce their candidacies and *work actively to align support*," this case more nearly fits as an instance of routine advancement rather than a challenge to the heir apparent.[9]

(2) APPOINTMENT OR EMERGENCE OF A CONSENSUS CHOICE. This second type of change is illustrated by a number of appointments or unchallenged elections at the lower levels of the party hierarchy where patterns of succession are not yet established. The appointments of Majority Whips Carl Albert in 1955, Hale Boggs in 1962, Thomas O'Neill in 1971, and John McFall in 1973 are illustrative. The factors that influenced these appointments have been described in some detail in Chapters 3 and 5–8, but can be briefly recapitulated here.

When the Democrats regained control of the House in the 84th Congress (1955–1956), a vacancy had been created in the whip position by Tennessee Representative Percy Priest's elevation to the chairmanship of the Committee on Interstate and Foreign Commerce. Albert, beginning his fifth term, had come to Rayburn's attention because he was the Representative of the Oklahoma district adjacent to Rayburn's own Texas district and because of his parliamentary skills displayed in floor debate. At the same time that Rayburn and McCormack appointed Albert as majority whip, they created a new position of deputy whip for another talented young Representative, Hale Boggs of Louisiana. In January 1962, after Albert was elected majority leader, he appointed Boggs as majority whip. John Moss of California advanced from a regional whip position to deputy whip at the same time. However, eight years later, Moss removed himself as a possible whip candidate in the 92d Congress by briefly challenging Boggs for majority leader.

After Boggs withstood the challenge of four other opponents, he and Albert appointed O'Neill as whip. O'Neill, a nine-term veteran who had been instrumental in Boggs' victory, readily advanced to majority leader following the disappearance of Boggs in Alaska in October 1972. Elected by unanimous consent, O'Neill appointed as whip his deputy, John McFall of California. More than other characteristics, these appointive whips shared mainstream, national Democratic party voting records and demonstrated personal loyalty to the existing party leadership.

The selection of the chairmen of the Democratic Caucus for all but the last two or three of these ten Congresses also illustrates this second type. For most of the two decades, the position was mainly a ceremonial one. Nominated by the leadership and selected from a pool of loyal, senior members, the principal responsibility of the chairman was to preside over the party caucus just before the opening session. Under Speaker Rayburn and throughout most of McCormack's reign, the caucus was seldom convened during the balance of the Congress. Under strong pressure from the Democratic Study Group,[10] a coalition of mainly moderate-to-liberal northern and western members, Speaker McCormack agreed at the opening of the 91st Congress (1969–1970) to allow monthly meetings of the caucus.

By tradition, incumbent caucus chairmen serve for one or, at the most, two terms. When, in 1971, Dan Rostenkowski, at the urging of both Albert and Boggs, ran for an unprecedented third term, he was upset by the last-minute bid of Olin Teague of Texas.

Until 1963 the chairman of the Republican Conference was also mainly an honorary title with few duties beyond presiding over infrequent meetings of House Republicans. Unlike the Democrats, the Republicans have not followed the practice of rotating the position. Thus, Clifford Hope of Kansas served in this capacity from 1951 until his retirement in 1956. Charles Hoeven of Iowa, first selected in 1957, served until his defeat by Gerald Ford at the opening of the 88th Congress. Since Ford's election in 1963, and particularly since Melvin Laird's election in 1965, the responsibility of the Republican Conference chairman has undergone considerable reorganization and upgrading. With increased importance has come enhanced competition for the position.

Two uncontested choices for chairman of the Republican Policy Committee also illustrate emergence of a consensus choice. In response to the disastrous 1948 election, Republicans who sought to improve their organizational structure converted a defunct steering committee into a policy committee. Little was made of it, however. Republican Minority Leader Martin served as chairman of a largely inoperative committee for the next 10 years. In 1959, following Charles Halleck's overthrow of Martin, the chairmanship was given independent status. John W. Byrnes of Wisconsin, the most senior available member save for Halleck among several members considered as possible challengers to Martin, was elected without opposition.

The selection of John Rhodes of Arizona as Byrnes' successor in 1965 is a less clear-cut case of a consensus choice. Byrnes resigned from the chairmanship of the Republican Policy Committee in late

January 1965 to devote full time to serving as ranking minority member on the Ways and Means Committee. With Byrnes' endorsement, on January 14, 1965, the Republican Conference adopted a resolution which prohibited its five principal party leaders from serving as chairman of or ranking minority member on standing committees. Byrnes' intention to resign had cleared the way for another Wisconsin Republican, Melvin Laird, to be elected chairman of the Republican Conference. The selection of Rhodes was not challenged, even though he was not the new Minority Leader Ford's first choice. Rhodes, first elected to Congress in 1952, had served as chairman of the Policy Committee's subcommittee on special projects since 1961. A friend of Ford's, he had nevertheless stayed with the incumbent leader in the 1965 contest. After Rhodes announced his candidacy, Ford considered putting up a candidate of his own choice, but because of the potential costs to his own prestige and to party harmony, he decided to avoid a direct confrontation. With the support of Laird and Arends, he created a separate Committee on Planning and Research to coordinate the task forces. Ford's first choice to head the Republican Policy Committee was four-term Representative Charles Goodell of New York. Goodell, co-manager of Ford's successful challenge to Halleck, was appointed chairman of the newly created Committee on Planning and Research. His appointment was confirmed on February 23, 1965, and on the same day Rhodes was unanimously elected chairman of a restructured Republican Policy Committee.

Selections for the position of chairman of the Democratic Congressional Campaign Committee have remained uncontested throughout this 20-year period. When the health of venerable Michael Kirwan of Ohio, chairman since 1948, began to fail, Democratic members of the committee chose two respected senior members, Thomas O'Neill of Massachusetts and Edward Edmondson of Oklahoma, to serve as deputy chairmen. O'Neill was sponsored by Speaker McCormack, Edmondson by Majority Leader Albert. After Kirwan's death in 1970, O'Neill and Edmondson were elected co-chairmen. When Edmondson resigned to run for the Senate in 1972, O'Neill, even though he was now the party whip, assumed the full chairmanship. As majority leader, however, O'Neill had to give way to the uncontested candidacy of Wayne Hays of Ohio (see Chapter 8).

(3) OPEN COMPETITION. When a vacancy occurs in a party leadership position which is not appointive and for which no pattern of

succession has been established, open competition between two or more candidates may take place. The three contests for Democratic floor leader already reported in depth — Albert vs. Bolling in 1961–1962 (Chapter 3), Boggs vs. Udall, Hays, Sisk, and O'Hara in 1970–1971 (Chapters 5–7), and O'Neill vs. Gibbons in 1972–1973 (Chapter 8) — satisfy these conditions with one important qualification. To the extent that a pattern of advancement from whip to majority leader is emerging, then these cases might better be classified as a challenge to an heir apparent.[11]

In the absence of any such pattern in 1962, Richard Bolling's abortive effort to prevent Carl Albert's advancement from Democratic whip to majority leader at the opening of the second session of the 87th Congress must still be categorized as an example of open competition. Following Rayburn's death in 1961, Bolling at first considered challenging McCormack. He finally concluded he would have a better chance to defeat Albert, although he realized that in both cases the odds were severely stacked against him. Strong support for Bolling's candidacy failed to materialize, however, so Bolling announced his withdrawal on January 3, 1962. One week later, at the opening caucus, Carl Albert unanimously was elected majority leader.

Speaker McCormack's May 1970 announcement that he intended to retire at the end of the 91st Congress brought about a chain of events that led to the most extensive contest preoccupying House Democrats in more than three decades. With five candidates competing for the floor leadership, as much or more time, energy, wind-scale membership involvement, and credit expenditure went into this contest as in either of the two major House Republican contests of the past 20 years, the minority leadership revolts of 1959 and 1965.

With Hale Boggs' lengthy leadership experience, his ranking majority position on the Ways and Means Committee, his oratorical and parliamentary skills, the question was not so much why he won but why he was challenged at all. After eight months of campaigning, Boggs emerged as the front-runner and ultimate victor. Building upon a first ballot lead of 95 votes to Udall's 69 with the remaining candidates trailing, Boggs won a substantial majority on the second ballot. Once again, a combination of southerners and big-city regulars prevailed. The Democratic leadership's choice for whip was Thomas P. O'Neill, Jr. of Massachusetts.

Following Boggs' disappearance and presumed death in Alaska in October 1972, O'Neill had little difficulty in his elevation to the majority leadership. Briefly challenged by Sam Gibbons, a five-term, moderate liberal from Florida, this junior Ways and Means Committee maverick withdrew his candidacy in late December when it became apparent that he did not have the votes to upset O'Neill. Helping to defeat a challenge to the principle of the appointive whip at the opening caucus in 1973, the new majority leader chose John McFall of California to succeed him as whip.

Is the Democratic majority developing a further pattern of succession from whip to majority leader, in addition to the firmly established practice of elevating floor leaders to Speaker? Although the trend seems apparent — Albert, Boggs, O'Neill — three cases cannot yet be said to have solidified the pattern. A crucial test for the emerging pattern will come with the next vacancy in the Democratic party hierarchy. A strong minority, although not yet a majority, of House Democrats continue to be unhappy about this "automatic escalator," especially since the bottom man on the ladder is appointed by the top leadership and not elected by the entire Democratic Caucus.

John Rhodes' unanimous election as minority leader on December 7, 1973 represented both an example of open competition, not unlike the predominant Democratic pattern of selecting their floor leaders, and a sharp departure from recent Republican practices for selecting their top leader. Although Rhodes was challenged, his 21 years of seniority, his solid conservative record as second-ranking minority member on the powerful Appropriations Committee, his demonstrated leadership as chairman of the Republican Policy Committee, and his personal popularity resulted in a relatively easy win. As such it compared to the Albert and O'Neill victories of 1962 and 1973. In all three contests the announced opposition withdrew before the final vote.

Both regional and ideological differences were at issue in another example of open competition, the contest between Laird of Wisconsin and Peter Frelinghuysen of New Jersey for chairman of the Republican Conference in 1965. Ford, the chairman in the previous Congress, had announced his intention to resign regardless of the outcome of his open challenge to Minority Leader Halleck. Laird, sympathetic to Ford's candidacy, announced his own independent bid for the conference chairmanship on December 29, 1964, the week before the 89th Congress convened. First elected to Congress in 1952, Laird had risen to fourth-ranking Republican on Appropriations and had served as chairman of the Republican Platform Committee at San Francisco in 1964. His firm management of the drafting of the platform, which Senator Barry Goldwater and Representative William Miller later campaigned on, led to intensified criticism of Laird from eastern seaboard liberals such as John Lindsay of New York and Bradford Morse and Silvio Conte of Massachusetts. Joining with 20 House colleagues, organized as the Wednesday Club, they decided to field a last-minute candidate of their own. Meeting on Sunday night before the January 4, 1965 vote, the Wednesday Club selected Frelinghuysen as their choice. He had only recently joined the group but he was one of few members with seniority equivalent to Laird. Despite Frelinghuysen's late announcement he received 62 votes to 77 cast for Laird.

Laird resigned from the House in January 1969 to become Secretary for Defense in President Nixon's newly formed administration. His successor as chairman of the Republican Conference was John Anderson of Illinois, a Republican moderate beginning his fifth term. Anderson ended up winning decisively with 116 votes to 46 for Ohio conservative Jackson Betts, while Minnesota moderate Albert Quie trailed with 18 votes. The 1973 contest to determine a successor for Policy Committee Chairman John Rhodes also represents a clear-cut case of open competition. Less than a week after Ford became Vice President and Rhodes succeeded him as minority leader, Rhodes' place was taken by Barber Conable, a five-term conservative from upstate New York. He defeated Del Clawson, a six-term, fellow conservative from southern California, by a vote of 88 to 77. Conable, fourth-ranking Republican on Ways and Means, became the first New York Representative elected to a top House Republican leadership position in 35 years.[12] Finally, the three contests for chairmanship of the Republican Congressional Campaign Committee in 1960, 1961, and 1973 also illustrate this type. Richard Simpson of Pennsylvania, chairman from 1953 to 1960, died on January 7, 1960. Many of the Republican members who had backed Martin against Halleck in 1959, aligned themselves behind William McCulloch of Ohio. On January 20, 1960 the Halleck forces won another victory when their candidate, William E. Miller of New York, was elected chairman. Miller had behind-the-scenes support from Vice President Richard M. Nixon, and was also acceptable to another prospective presidential candidate, Governor Nelson Rockefeller of New York.

When Miller became chairman of the Republican National Committee in June 1961, another non-midwesterner, Bob Wilson of California, became chairman of the Republican Congressional Campaign Committee, emerging from a field of potential candidates which included Laird of Wisconsin, Rhodes of Arizona, and Ford of Michigan, in addition to McCulloch. While the selection of Miller and Wilson cannot be divorced from prior House contests and political maneuvering on the national scene, they also reflected successful efforts to expand geographical and suburban representation within the House Republican leadership.

After more than 11 years of mainly frustrated efforts to change his party from a minority into a majority in the House, Wilson decided to resign his chairmanship in 1973. Disappointed by the congressional results of the 1972 election (Republicans had picked up but 12 House seats despite Nixon's overwhelming reelection), Wilson was also embittered by the reluctance of the White House and the Committee to Reelect the President to divert surplus campaign funds into House and Senate races. Two midwestern moderate conservatives, nine-term veteran Robert Michel of Illinois and five-term member Clarence Brown, Jr. of Ohio, emerged as the principal contenders. Michel's personal popularity and seniority prevailed, despite the presence of two other Illinois members, Arends and Anderson, in the Republican party leadership. The actual vote within the Republican Congressional Campaign Committee was termed "close," but was not released.

(4) CHALLENGE TO THE HEIR APPARENT. This type of contest takes place when a vacancy occurs due to death, defeat, or retirement, but the apparent successor's claim is contested. No clear-cut case took place in the House during the 84th–93d Congresses. Several earlier contests in this century, the Gillett-Mann struggle over the nomination for Speakership in 1919, and the upset of former Majority Leader John Q. Tilson by Republican Rules Committee Chairman Bertrand H. Snell in 1931 just prior to the organization of the 72d Congress, are illustrative examples.

The Republican Party had endured minority status and the rather arbitrary rule of Minority Leader Mann of Illinois, successor to Speaker Cannon, for eight years before they regained control of the House in the election of 1918. Favorable election results did not inhibit national party leaders and House opponents of Mann from putting together enough support within the Republican conference to win the nomination, and ultimately, the Speakership, for Frederick

H. Gillett of Massachusetts. Gillett, first elected to the House in 1892, was one of two Republicans who had served longer than any other member, save for ex-Speaker Cannon. Gillett, the ranking Republican member on the Committee on Appropriations, had few personal enemies. Mann, in contrast, had antagonized many members in both parties with his relentless and caustic criticism of legislation. In addition to his strong identification with the Cannon regime, his opponents accused him of conflict of interest in his relations with the Chicago meat-packing industry. On February 27, 1919, Gillett defeated Mann by 138 votes to 69 with three other candidates receiving 18 votes.[13] Gillett served as a rather ineffective Speaker from 1919 to 1924, when he resigned to run for the Senate.

In 1931 Halleck's predecessor, Joseph Martin of Massachusetts, backed Bertrand H. Snell of New York in a bitter conference struggle that resulted in the overthrow of Republican Speaker Nicholas Longworth's apparent successor, 73-year-old John Q. Tilson of Connecticut.[14] Longworth died on April 9, 1931 before the 72d Congress convened. Tilson had served as Republican Majority Leader under Longworth since 1925, the year in which Martin was first elected to the House. This contest followed a 48-seat election setback for the Republicans in 1930. The deaths of several Republican incumbents before December 1931 allowed the Democrats to gain control of the House and frustrated Snell's ambitions to be Speaker. Snell voluntarily retired from the House in 1938. Martin, the eastern assistant whip and the Republican campaign chairman in a year in which the Republicans won back 80 seats, was elected minority leader in 1939, without any serious challenge.[15]

(5) REVOLT OR ITS AFTERMATH. This last type, usually the most extensive in terms of the investment of resources required, takes place when: (1) no vacancy in a leadership position exists, (2) the incumbent cannot be persuaded to step aside, and (3) an intra-party contest ensues. The Halleck-Martin struggle for the minority leadership in 1959, the Ford-Hoeven fight over the chairmanship of the Republican Conference in 1963, and the Ford-Halleck contest for the minority leadership in 1965, all clearly illustrate this type of intra-party change. Ford's attempt to remove incumbent Minority Whip Arends in 1965 and a challenge to Conference Chairman John Anderson's bid for reelection in 1971 represent somewhat different forms of revolt.

Neither was successful, but the former involved an effort to bring new blood into the leadership as an aftermath of revolt, while the latter was more characteristic of several protest challenges to incumbent Democratic leaders.

In the late 1950's, when Martin's health began to fail, a number of young Republicans sought more vigorous party leadership. The election disaster of 1958 provided a further impetus for change. In mid-December, more than a dozen Republicans met in the office of Representative Bob Wilson of California to discuss what could be done to improve party fortunes. They agreed that new leadership was needed, but they were divided in a choice among Halleck of Indiana, Byrnes of Wisconsin, Ford of Michigan, and Simpson of Pennsylvania. In an informal poll of members, they found widespread sentiment for change, but only one active candidate, former Majority Leader Halleck. After determining that the White House would remain neutral, Halleck announced his candidacy. On the eve of the vote, his backers estimated they had more than 80 votes of the 154 Republican Representatives-elect. Martin, like Halleck six years later, did not take the challenge seriously until it was too late.

At the afternoon conference on Tuesday, January 6, 1959, the Martin forces led by Richard Simpson of Pennsylvania, Leo Allen and Leslie Arends of Illinois, and Clarence Brown of Ohio, lost a move to avoid a secret ballot by a vote of 96 to 50. Halleck edged Martin on the first ballot by a vote of 73 to 72 with one ballot rejected as illegible. Since neither candidate received a majority, another ballot was necessary. Halleck won on the second ballot by a vote of 74 to 70.[16]

The Ford-Hoeven contest of 1963 was an important precursor of the 1965 minority leadership struggle. It was initiated at the opening of the 88th Congress by two junior members of the House Education and Labor Committee, Robert P. Griffin of Michigan (first elected in 1956) and Charles E. Goodell of New York (first elected in a special election on May 26, 1959). After considering and rejecting challenges to either Halleck or Arends, Griffin and Goodell decided to go after the Republican Conference chairmanship as a further step toward revitalizing party machinery. With the active support of most of the House members elected in 1958, 1960, and 1962, and the tacit approval of many of the same activists who had promoted the Halleck upset of Martin, they launched an over-the-weekend campaign against Hoeven, the incumbent conference chairman since 1957. On January

8, 1963, their candidate, the 49-year-old Ford, defeated the 67-year-old Hoeven, by a secret ballot vote of 86 to 78.[17]

A necessary, but not sufficient, cause of the 1965 revolt was the Republican election disaster of November 1964. The Goldwater defeat and the net loss of 38 Republican House seats created a psychological climate within which revolt flourished. But the seeds of dissatisfaction with Halleck's leadership extended back to bitterness engendered by Halleck's defeat of Martin in 1959. This irritation and unrest was compounded by the continuing frustrations of minority status. Agitation for change, only temporarily dampened by Ford's defeat of Hoeven in 1963, intensified throughout the long and trying sessions of the 88th Congress.

A post-election House Republican Conference held on December 16, 1964 put Halleck to test. Although called to evaluate Republican party organization and policy positions, its principal consequence was to bring back to Washington a diversified group of younger activists who were convinced that the first step toward achieving majority status was new leadership. Two likely challengers emerged, Gerald R. Ford, Jr. of Michigan and Melvin R. Laird of Wisconsin. Ford, with four more years of seniority, was selected as the candidate with the best chance of defeating Halleck.

On January 4, 1965, at the opening of the 89th Congress, Ford defeated Halleck by a secret ballot vote of 73 to 67. In the final analysis, it was the two-thirds of the House Republican party in the five most junior classes which made victory possible for Ford.[18]

A fourth contest, New Jersey Representative Frelinghuysen's unsuccessful challenge to incumbent Minority Whip Leslie Arends of Illinois 10 days after Ford's defeat of Halleck in 1965 came about as an aftermath of revolt. In this instance the challenger ran with the new minority leader's endorsement in a losing effort to consolidate the revolt and provide wider geographical and ideological representation within the minority leadership. Arend's early start in the defense of his incumbency, his more than 20 years of service as a party whip, and his widespread personal popularity proved to be too strong. He won by 70 votes to 59. Frelinghuysen's personal reserve and rather aristocratic background cost him some support. So did his identification with the Wednesday Club. Conservatives, already smarting under National Chairman Burch's resignation, found Frelinghuysen's stand on the nuclear policy plank at San Francisco and his general liberal voting record on foreign affairs further reasons for opposing Ford's choice. In any event, Ford, like Martin and Halleck before him, came to understand more fully that members are more hesitant to reveal their true preferences to an incumbent minority leader.

The last example of revolt among House Republicans during these 10 Congresses came in 1971 when conservative Sam Devine of Ohio, launched an attack against incumbent Conference Chairman John B. Anderson of Illinois. He and a number of his supporters accused Anderson of moving too far left-of-center both in terms of his voting record in the Rules Committee and on the floor. Anderson, who had won the position rather easily two years before, found himself hard pressed but still the victor by a secret ballot vote of 89 to 81.

Democratic party leaders encountered no parallel challenges to their authority until near the end of this 20-year period. Two of the three contests — Morris K. Udall's bid for the Speakership against the 77-year-old John McCormack in 1969, John Conyers' protest challenge to Speaker Albert's reelection in 1973 — were more symbolic than sustained and realistic efforts to upset incumbent party leaders. Indeed, Udall announced, in a late December 1968 "Dear Colleague" letter, that should he defeat McCormack, he would immediately call for a new election for Speaker open to all candidates. Still, McCormack had little difficulty winning a fifth term as Speaker at the January 2, 1969 Democratic Caucus by a secret ballot vote of 178 to 58.

Several characteristics distinguish Michigan Representative Conyers' 1973 protest candidacy against the reelection of Speaker Albert from his 1971 opening-day caucus challenge. Conyers announced his second effort several weeks in advance instead of just before the caucus, and he worked actively to obtain pledges of support from his colleagues in 1972. Thus, his latter effort more appropriately qualifies as a "contest" even though Albert scored one-sided victories in both contests (220 to 20 in 1971; 202 to 25 in 1973).

Several features of Olin Teague's upset of incumbent Democratic Caucus Chairman Dan Rostenkowski in January 1971 were quite unusual. First, Rostenkowski, at the urging of Albert and Boggs, sought an unprecedented third term. Second, this was the first caucus vote to be held over this position in at least two decades. Finally, Teague's victory represented the first successful revolt against an incumbent Democratic party leader in more than three decades. Several factors help to explain the immediate outcome — Teague's personal popularity, the membership's hesitancy to break with a two-term tradition, and the inability of a leadership in transition to enforce its preferences. Neither Albert nor Boggs had as yet been elevated to Speaker or majority leader when Rostenkowski went down to defeat.

IV

The differences between the dominant types of change adopted by House Democrats as compared with House Republicans over this 20-year period are considerable. As Table 9.4 illustrates, 15 of the 21 instances (71.4 percent) of leadership selection by Democrats were uncontested. In contrast, only 3 of 15 cases (20.0 percent) of Republican leadership selection occurred without a contest.[19] Moreover, 5 of the 12 Republican contests involved challenges to incumbents, including two successful revolts against minority floor leaders.

House Democrats, building upon and reinforcing their majority status, have taken advantage of a well established pattern of harmonious succession from floor leader to Speaker and seem to be developing a supporting practice of elevating their whips to the position of floor leader. The House Republican party, relegated to minority status for most of the past four decades, have instituted no clear patterns of leadership succession. Open competition and even revolt against established leadership have been much more prevalent.

Before an examination of several factors or conditions which might help to explain these overall party differences, several aberrations in the data and possible qualifications of these trends should be made more explicit. As the late V.O. Key, Jr. once warned, "our analytical schemes must, to be sure, make provisions for the accidental, the erratic, the unique, and we must be forever alert to the possibilities that the verified general proposition of one era may not hold at a later time." [20]

Differences in frequencies and types of leadership change between the two House congressional parties reflect, in part, several rather "accidental" or "unique" factors. First, as already noted, the Democratic whip is appointed. This method of selection accounts for four instances of uncontested change. Somewhat offsetting the possible distortion of this analysis has been the unusually long tenure of Republican Whip Arends — over 30 years.

Second, attention should also be called to the Democratic tradition of rotating their caucus chairmen every two or four years, a practice that contributes to the high ratio of harmonious vs. contested cases of change within the House Democratic party. From a broader perspective, it can be argued that both historical "accidents," the appointive whip and the rotating caucus chairmanship, are merely additional mechanisms by which the Democratic party has seen fit to avoid leadership contests and perpetrate harmonious change. More about this interpretation will follow a discussion of Democratic and Republican differences in hierarchy and party structure in the next chapter.

Key's second point, "that the verified general proposition of one era may not hold at a later time," suggests the need for a closer examination of possible shifts in trends which might not be easily revealed by the data summarized in Table 9.4.

A shift within the Democratic party toward more extensive competition since 1968, which was not revealed by my earlier six-Congress analysis,[21] is brought into clearer focus in Table 9.5. The 36 cases of leadership change and attempted change have been condensed into three categories, C = contest; © = contest, but with the incumbent retaining his position, and NC = no contest. The differences between the House Democratic majority and the Republican minority were most pronounced in the initial six Congresses. (Eight of nine changes were uncontested by the Democrats, but only three of ten were unchallenged by Republicans.) In contrast, over the latter four Congresses, House Democrats contested almost half of their leadership selections, or five out of twelve, while House Republicans continued their predominant mode of contested leadership change in all five cases. However, as already noted above, three of the five Democratic contests over these eight years — Udall's challenge to Speaker John McCormack in 1969, Gibbons' brief bid for the majority leadership post against O'Neill in 1973, and Conyers' abortive efforts to unseat Speaker Albert in 1973 — were essentially symbolic and launched with little or no hope of success.

Why has the House Democratic majority developed patterns of succession and utilized relatively peaceful means of leadership change for most of these 10 Congresses? What new factors seem to account for the flurry of contests among Democrats in the late 1960's and early 1970's? What caused the Republican minority to resort so infrequently to uncontested leadership change throughout the 20-year period? In the next chapter some of the most important factors or conditions which seem to explain these marked differences in pat-

Table 9.5

Contested and Non-Contested Change in House Party Leaders, Democratic and Republican, 84th–93d Congresses (1955–1974)

	84th 1955–56	85th 1957–58	86th 1959–60	87th 1961–62	88th 1963–64	89th 1965–66	90th 1967–68	91st 1969–70	92d 1971–72	93d 1973–74
Speaker[a]										
Dem.				NC				©	NC	©
Rep.										
Floor leader										
Dem.				C					C	C
Rep.			C			C				C
Whip										
Dem.	NC			NC		©			NC	NC
Rep.										
Caucus (Conference) Chm.										
Dem.	NC	NC		NC	NC	NC			C	
Rep.		NC			C	C	NC	C	©	
Policy Committee Chm.[a]										
Dem.										
Rep.			NC			NC				
Congressional Campaign Chm.										
Dem.								NC	NC	NC
Rep.			C	C						C

C = contested; © = contested, but incumbent retains position; NC = non-contested.
[a] The top and fifth rows apply only to *Democratic* Speakers and *Republican* Policy Committee Chairmen, respectively.

terns of leadership among the two House congressional parties will be explored.

NOTES

1. The principal framework of analysis for this chapter was initially set forth in Robert L. Peabody's "Party Leadership Change in the United States House of Representatives," *Am. Pol. Sci. Rev.* **61** (1967), 675–693. Reprinted by permission. Copyright © 1967, the American Political Science Association. The original data base consisted of 19 cases of intra-party leadership change occurring in the 85th to 89th Congresses (1955 to 1966). Seventeen additional cases from the 90th to 93d Congresses (1967 to 1974) have been added for further analysis.
2. For discussion of this problem in the determination of causality, see Hubert M. Blalock, Jr., *Causal Inferences in Nonexperimental Research* (Chapel Hill: University of North Carolina Press, 1964), pp. 32–38.
3. The attention of journalists and political scientists is naturally drawn to instances of organized revolt. For newspapermen, it is conflict, of course, which makes news. But political scientists also need to explore situations where the threatened change does not get beyond the discussion stage, as for example, threats to replace Thomas Kuchel, the incumbent minority whip in the United States Senate, at the opening of the 89th Congress, and disgruntlement with Speaker McCormack's leadership at the beginning of the 90th Congress.
4. In the Republican party, type (a) is illustrated by the Miller-McCulloch contest of 1960, (b) by the unsuccessful challenge against Minority Whip Arends in 1965 as well as the famed "revolt" against Speaker Cannon in 1910, and (c) by the minority leadership contests of 1959 and 1965.
5. For general discussion of exchange theory, see Talcott Parsons, "On the Concept of Influence," and James S. Coleman, "Comment on 'On the Concept of Influence'," *Public Opinion Quarterly* **27** (1963), 37–62, 63–82; George C. Homans, "Social Behaviour as Exchange," *Am. Jour. of Sociology* **63** (1958), 597–606; and Peter M. Blau, *Exchange and Power in Social Life* (New York: Wiley 1964). For more specific applications of exchange theory to legislatures, see Robert L. Peabody, "Organization Theory and Legislative Behavior: Bargaining, Hierarchy and Change in the U.S. House of Representatives" (paper delivered before the American Political Science Association, New York City, September 7, 1963); James S. Coleman, "Collective Decisions," *Sociological Inquiry* **34** (1964), 166–181; and James D. Barber, "Leadership Strategies for Legislative Party Cohesion," *Journal of Politics* **28** (1966), 347–367.
6. One should note that specific positions across party, and even within the same party over time, may vary in responsibility and the manner in which they are selected. For example, the Republican whip is an elective position; the Democratic whip is appointive. The stature and resources of the chairmanships of both the Republican Conference and the Democratic Caucus have undergone considerable growth beginning about the mid-1960's. Nevertheless, in the aggregate and over time, it seems justifiable to contrast and compare rates and kinds of changes in the two party leaderships.

   Two additional leadership positions, the chairman of the Democratic Steering Committee and the chairman of the Republican Committee on Planning and Research, have been omitted from this analysis. The Democratic Steering Committee, allegedly the counterpart of the Republican Policy Committee, was largely dormant throughout this period. It was, however, revitalized somewhat under McCormack and more extensively in 1973 with Speaker Albert serving as chairman. The chairmanship of the Republican Planning and Research Committee was not created until 1965 and made elective only after 1967. Robert L. Peabody, "Political Parties: House Republican Leadership," in Allan P. Sindler, ed., *American Political Institutions and Public Policy* (Boston: Little, Brown, 1969), pp. 181–229.

7. For the Democrats these 19 leadership changes include two for Speaker: McCormack (1962) and Albert (1971); three for majority leaders: Albert (1962), Boggs (1971), and O'Neill (1973); four for whip: Albert (1955), Boggs (1962), O'Neill (1971), and McFall (1973); seven for chairman of the Democratic Caucus: Rooney (1955), Price (1957), Walter (1961), Thomas (1964), Keogh (1965), Rostenkowski (1967), and Teague (1971); and three for campaign committee chairman: co-chairmen O'Neill and Edmondson (1970), O'Neill (1972) (after Edmondson resigned to run for the Senate), and Hays (1973). Two cases of *attempted* leadership change, Udall's challenge to Speaker McCormack in 1969 and Conyers' bid against Speaker Albert in 1973, have been added for purposes of analysis in the following section.

   The 13 Republican changes in leadership include three for minority leader: Halleck (1959), Ford (1965), and Rhodes (1973); none for whip; three for policy committee chairman: Byrnes (1949), Rhodes (1965), and Conable (1973); four for conference chairman: Hoeven (1957), Ford (1963), Laird (1965), and Anderson (1969); and three for campaign committee chairman: Miller (1960), Wilson (1961), and Michel (1973). In the following section two more instances of attempted change have been added: Frelinghuysen's unsuccessful attempt to defeat incumbent Whip Arends in 1965 and Devine's challenge to Conference Chairman Anderson in 1971.

8. The position of chairman of the Democratic Caucus began to develop independence and an identity of its own in the late 1960's, especially after regular monthly meetings were inaugurated in 1969. See Walter Oleszek, "Party Caucuses in the United States House of Representatives," (Washington, D.C.: mimeograph, 1973) and Robert L. Peabody, "House Leadership, Party Caucuses and the Committee Structure," *Working Papers on House Committee Organization and Operation*, Select Committee on Committees, U.S. House of Representatives, 93d Cong., 1st sess. (Washington, D.C.: U.S. Government Printing Office, 1973).

9. As outlined in Chapter 8, Conyers mounted another, largely symbolic, challenge to Speaker Albert's reelection in late 1972. This time his efforts were more organized and directly aimed at Albert's alleged ineffectiveness as a leader. Hence, the latter challenge has been classified as an instance of "revolt."

10. For background on the organization, development, and effectiveness of the Democratic Study Group, see Kenneth Kofmehl, "The Institutionalization of a Voting Bloc," *Western Political Quarterly* **17** (1964), 256–272; Mark F. Ferber, "The Democratic Study Group: A Study of Intra-Party Organization in the House," Ph.D. Dissertation, University of California, Los Angeles, 1964; and Arthur G. Stevens, Jr., Arthur H. Miller, and Thomas E. Mann, "Mobilization of Liberal Strength in The House, 1955–1970: The Democratic Study Group," *Am. Pol. Sci. Rev.* **68** (1974), 667–681.

11. These contests, especially the last instance, come close to qualifying as the fourth type, *challenge to an heir apparent* for the following reasons. Ex-

cerpts from the interviews reported in Polsby's detailed study of the 1962 contest clearly reveal the extent to which members perceived Albert as " 'entitled' to the job by virtue of his six years' service in the leadership hierarchy of the House" (Chapter 3, p. 75). But while the pattern of succession from floor leader to Speaker has been firmly established, there is only an emerging precedent for elevating the party whip to floor leader. Oscar Underwood of Alabama served briefly as minority whip in 1900–1901, but 10 years intervened before he became majority floor leader in 1911. With the possible exception of John Garner of Texas, no other floor leader until Albert had served as whip prior to his first selection as floor leader — Randall B. Ripley, "The Party Whip Organizations in the United States House of Representatives," *Am. Pol. Sci. Rev.* 58 (1964), p. 563, p. 564, n. 19. Albert, however, was able to capitalize on McCormack's two related experiences of serving as minority whip and then moving back up to majority leader following the 80th and 83d Congresses.

Similarly, Boggs, in his 1970–1971 quest for the majority leadership was able to capitalize upon his 16 years of leadership experience, seven as deputy whip and nine as whip. Further evidence that the whip is perceived as "heir apparent" was provided by O'Neill's unanimous choice for elevation to majority leader after but two years' service as whip.

12. Conable, a House member since 1965, had held the chairmanship of the House Republican Research Committee since 1970. That position had been especially created by newly elected Minority Leader Gerald Ford in 1965 for another New Yorker, Charles Goodell. The last New York Republican Representative to serve in a major leadership position was Bertrand H. Snell, minority leader from 1931 to 1938.

13. *New York Times,* February 28, 1919, p. 1; Chang-wei Chiu, *The Speaker of the House of Representatives Since 1896* (New York: Columbia University Press, 1927), pp. 25–27.

14. Snell moved from 55 votes on the first ballot to a 96 to 64 lead over Tilson on the seventh ballot but still one short of a majority. Before the eighth ballot began, Tilson moved to make the nomination unanimous. *New York Times,* December 1, 1931, pp. 1, 4; December 8, 1931, pp. 1, 16.

15. Joe Martin, *My First Fifty Years in Politics* (as told to Robert J. Donovan) (New York: McGraw-Hill, 1960), pp. 81–82.

16. The best single review of this contest is Charles O. Jones, *Party and Policy-Making: The House Republican Policy Committee* (New Brunswick: Rutgers University Press, 1964), pp. 29–38. His summary contains one questionable statement: "A poll of members showed that John W. Byrnes of Wisconsin had the most support, Gerald R. Ford, Jr. of Michigan was second, and Halleck was third." (p. 35). A more plausible interpretation is that the informal polls taken in late December and early January were too indefinite to do more than suggest that there were several possible candidates with Halleck and Byrnes the front-runners. The insurgents discussed going with Byrnes, but found him reluctant to step out in front of Halleck, an experienced floor leader. When one of their group, former Representative Jack Westland of Washington, discussed with Halleck in Florida the possibilities of a revolt, Halleck insisted on his right as the former majority leader to make the challenge. Other contemporary accounts seem to support this interpretation. See, for example, Richard Fryklund, "Story of G.O.P. Revolt Has Varied Chapters," *Washington Star,* January 11, 1959, p. A-1; John L. Steele, "G.O.P. Tactics That Toppled a Veteran Leader," *Life,* January 19, 1959; and Martin's own version, *op. cit.,* pp. 3–19. I am indebted to Representa-

tive Bob Wilson for making available a scrapbook of clippings and other materials which he kept on this contest.

17. "Ford's Election Sparks Shifts in GOP House Strategy," *Congressional Quarterly Weekly Report* **21** (February 8, 1963), 140–156.

18. Peabody, "The Ford-Halleck Minority Leadership Contest, 1965," Chapter 4 in this book.

19. The contrasts between the two House parties for the initial six Congresses under study, the 84th–89th (1955–1966) were even more stark. Eight out of nine instances of Democratic leadership change (or all but the Albert-Bolling case) were uncontested. Seven out of ten cases of Republican leadership selection were decided by intra-party combat. Peabody, "Party Leadership Change in the House of Representatives," *op. cit.*, p. 686. Two sets of findings emerged from the initial analysis of these cases (p. 693):

1. Democratic majority:

a. The Democratic majority is much more likely than the Republican minority to resolve questions of leadership change through non-contested elections or appointments.

b. The longer the period of majority status, the more likely the majority party is to develop established patterns of succession.

c. When contests take place in the Democratic majority, they will most likely occur at the middle or lower levels of the party hierarchy.

2. Republican minority:

a. The Republican minority is more prone to intra-party leadership change through contested means.

b. The longer the period of minority status, the more prone the minority party is to leadership change through revolt.

c. Revolts are most likely to occur following congressional election disasters (the net loss of 30 or more seats).

Although, on balance, the tentative conclusions from this first study held up rather well over the extended 20-year period, several modifications were also called for (see especially Table 9.5 and the discussion of its implications).

20. "The State of the Discipline," *Am. Pol. Sci. Rev.* **52** (1958), 961–971 at 966.

21. See, n. 19, *supra*.

CHAPTER TEN

Factors Influencing House Leadership Stability and Change

Long periods of one-party dominance, increased average tenure in office for Representatives, and the institutionalization of patterns of succession to the Speakership have contributed to a trend toward leadership stability in the mid-twentieth century House of Representatives. The election of Sam Rayburn (D., Texas) and John McCormack (D., Mass.) to the offices of Speaker and majority leader in 1940, of Joseph Martin (R., Mass.) to the office of minority leader in 1939, and of Leslie Arends (R., Ill.) to the position of minority whip in 1943, marked the beginnings of the longest tenures in these four positions for any incumbents in the history of Congress.[1] For a variety of reasons — the expanding workload of Congress, heavier burdens on leaders, lowered tolerance for lengthy leadership incumbency, and enhanced retirement benefits — these records of sustained leadership service are not likely to be approached, let alone surpassed in the years to come.

Although the revolt against Minority Leader Martin in 1959 and the death of Speaker Rayburn in 1961 may have marked the end of an era, moderately lengthy tenure in leadership offices continues to prevail. For the past two decades, at least, it has been common for leaders to be reelected for three or four terms or more, especially within the majority party. Incumbent stability, not change, has been the dominant pattern of intra-party leadership selection in the House of Representatives.

It is exceedingly rare for a principal party leader to suffer an election defeat; invariably, the representation of a safe district and a resulting long tenure are prerequisites to high office. Death, retirement, or resignation are usually the events that create leadership vacancies.

When vacancies have occurred in top leadership positions, the prevailing practice for Democrats has been to elevate the next officer on a leadership ladder extending from whip to majority leader to Speaker. Moreover, most of these selections were relatively peaceful and only infrequently resulted in a contest between two or more members seeking higher office. Competition has been much keener among the Republican minority especially at the lower and middle level of leadership positions. At the extreme range of intra-party leadership contests, in terms of resources expended, have come revolts against established leaders. As already noted, Republicans have engaged in several revolts against incumbents from 1955–1974.

What factors or conditions promote contested change as contrasted with more orderly succession? Why has the House Republican minority party generally resorted to contested change, while the Democratic majority party has been more prone to patterns of peaceful, strife-free succession?

I

Among the most important factors or underlying conditions which combine to facilitate or inhibit one type of leadership change rather than another are (1) the personality and skill of the incumbent, (2) the level of position and pattern of succession, (3) the nature of accession to office, (4) majority-minority status, (5) election results, and (6) differences in party hierarchy and structure.

PERSONALITY AND SKILL OF THE INCUMBENT. The comparative age, health, personality, and skill of the incumbent and of actual or potential challengers clearly are among the most crucial factors that affect patterns of leadership change. In contrast to their Democratic counterparts, first Martin, and later, Halleck seemed to have lost touch with their colleagues, particularly junior Republicans. In the 1959 minority leadership contest Halleck and his supporters leveled this criticism to telling advantage against the aging and ailing Martin. Similar charges were to be leveled at Halleck in 1965. As one of his supporters admitted: "I don't know anyone who was really close to him. That was one of Charlie's problems, communication. I presume he ate by himself. He didn't show up at the Republican luncheon in the Capitol. He shielded himself from other members. He was out of touch with the team to an unnecessary degree." Truman's analysis of voting patterns in an earlier Congress, the 81st, provides some corroborating evidence. Neither Martin nor Halleck appeared to be very influential with the more junior members of the Republican minority; Democratic junior members were much more likely to vote in accordance with their administration and their party floor leader, McCormack.[2]

One characteristic of successful leadership is an ability to recruit and develop younger talent for positions of future leadership. Rayburn reputedly had this quality. One of Ford's principal campaign themes was the promise he made to be available and to make 60-minute ball players out of all 140 House Republicans. Ford maintained his reputation for fairness and kept his promise to be accessible to all factions of his party, especially junior members, throughout his nine years as minority leader.

Assessments of personality played a prominent role in the outcome of other contests, for example, Albert's popularity and Bolling's relative estrangement in 1962. But Morris K. Udall's personal popularity was not enough to offset Boggs' strength among southerners and northern party regulars in the 1971 majority leadership contest. In short, personality is likely to be decisive only when other factors such as ideology and regional strength are neutralized.

THE LEVEL OF POSITION AND PATTERN OF SUCCESSION. Clearly, the level of a position and the pattern of succession which has come to characterize it can have substantial impact on rates of contested change. Thus, Democrats have built upon a tradition of elevating their majority leader to the Speakership, usually without a contest. By creating an appointive instead of an elective whip, further contests have been avoided. Moreover, Democrats seem to follow an established pattern of promoting whips to majority leaders. Until recent years the chairman of the caucus was largely seen as an honorary title to be rotated among loyal senior members.

The rate of contested change in the Democratic majority has, however, increased in the late 1960's and early 1970's as a result of a number of challenges to these institutional arrangements: most notably were Udall's bid for the Speakership against McCormack in 1969; Rostenkowski's quest of a third term as caucus chairman and his subsequent defeat by Teague in 1971; and the attempt to convert the appointive whip into an elected position in 1973.

House Republicans have been unable or unwilling to take advantage of similar positional characteristics which might have dampened the number and intensity of their leadership contests. With no opportunity to organize the House since the 83d Congress, they have been unable to elect a Speaker of their own with the subsequent opening up of lesser leadership positions. Moreover, they have developed no clear pattern of succession to the minority leadership. Instead, they have either revolted against the incumbent leader or resorted to open competition with leading candidates drawn from among a pool of middle-level leaders — the chairmen of the conference, the policy committee, and the campaign committee, or the whip. In contrast to the Democratic party, the G.O.P. whip has been an elective, not an appointive, position, and other party offices have seldom fallen within the minority leader's influence or patronage control. Both the absence of clear-cut levels among party positions and few entrenched patterns of succession have contributed to the relatively high rates of contested change characteristic of the selection of House Republican leaders.

THE NATURE OF ACCESSION TO OFFICE. Leaders who come to power through a relatively peaceful transition (as Albert moved from whip to majority leader to Speaker) confront a different set of predispositions on the part of their followers than those who arrive through strenuous contests or open challenges to incumbent leaders. Following the intensely competitive 1971 contest, it took Hale Boggs the better part of two years before he exercised his role as majority leader with some confidence and security. Charles Halleck and Gerald Ford both came to realize that one cost of their successful revolts was a split in their party. For a session or two, at least, embittered minority members overlooked few opportunities to criticize or undermine their new leadership. One contest was likely to beget another, especially within a minority party whose electoral fortunes were turning downward.

MAJORITY–MINORITY STATUS. Leadership contests are generally won by those who can mobilize the greatest number of members willing to work long and intensively in an effort to convert their fellow congressmen. Here, more than in typical battles over legislative issues, personal loyalties and animosities developed during a series of Congresses are crucial. Respect, trust, and affection play at least as important a role as explicit bargaining based on such tangible objects of exchange as committee assignments or the promise of additional patronage. Over the long run, however, the majority leadership enjoys greater stability, in part, because of its superior resources, both tangible and intangible.

Congressional leaders have many opportunities to help colleagues achieve their personal and legislative objectives. A leader's endorsement may decide among several candidates who receives a preferred committee assignment. A floor leader may interrupt a member's speech to argue in favor of his public works project and, in the process, convert enough wavering members to make the difference. Party leaders appear at fund-raising dinners. They provide the personal endorsement that enhances a member's chances for reelection. Both majority and minority party leaders are constantly involved in such credit-building endeavors. But majority party leaders enjoy superior resources. They work within a climate of expanding rather than contracting credit.

Credit expands because of the multiple benefits which accrue with majority status. There are more committee assignments and appointments to prestige boards and commissions to be distributed. It is the majority which receives most of the credit when legislation is passed. Their projects receive higher priority. Majority members chair the committees and subcommittees. With position comes staff, superior access to executive officialdom, and greater influence on legislative outcomes. Since there are more benefits to go around, majority members are more satisfied and less critical of their leadership. Majority status promotes a search for compromise, accommodation, and the acceptance of the established patterns of succession.

In contrast, the minority party operates in an environment of continuing frustration and increasing discord. There are fewer choice committee assignments to go around. The majority controls most of the prestige appointments. Political patronage and staff assistance are not as abundant. Opportunities for constructive participation in drafting and implementing major legislation are more limited. Limited resources, contracting credit, inability to adequately reward the party faithful, prospects of continuing defeat in floor struggles — all foster internal dissension and tend to undermine the leadership. If election results continue to run against the minority party, as they have with

House Republicans in recent times, then party juniors are motivated to take their frustrations out by making changes in leadership.

ELECTION RESULTS. Party structure and leadership change in the House of Representatives are closely related to congressional election results. In the first place, the party which wins a majority of the 435 seats earns the right to organize the House, choose a Speaker, and select the committee chairmen. What has not been so clearly understood is the relationship between the aggregate size of the net gain or loss and its implications for intra-party leadership change. Strong victories promote good will and greatly reflect to the benefit of party leaders. Conversely, defeat results in pessimism, hostility, and a search for scapegoats, especially within a minority party. If the net losses are particularly severe, as many as 30 to 50 seats, then the possibilities of minority leadership change through revolt are greatly enhanced.

Table 10.1 summarizes the congressional election results and party line-ups from 1954 to 1974. This period was particularly trying for House Republicans. Eisenhower was in the White House from 1952 to 1960, but Republicans lost control of Congress after 1954. They continued as a minority party through the mid-1960's and early 1970's even though Nixon won in 1968 and 1972.

At least three, and perhaps all five cases of revolt were preceded by election disappointments. Halleck apparently considered the possibility of a contest against Martin after the elections of 1954 and 1956, but did not make a bid because White House neutrality was not forthcoming. In the 1958 election, House Republicans suffered a net loss of 47 seats. Halleck's defeat of Martin followed. Under Halleck's leadership and with Nixon at the head of the ticket, House Republicans made moderate gains in 1960. When traditional mid-term gains were not forthcoming in 1962, junior Republicans led by Goodell and Griffin took out their frustrations on Republican Conference Chairman Hoeven. In 1964, with Goldwater at the head of the Republican ticket, House Republicans lost 48 House seats and picked up only 10 seats previously held by Democrats. Ford's defeat of Halleck and the attempt to remove Arends followed. A senior Republican, who played a prominent role in both the 1959 and 1965 minority leadership contests, summed up the climate created by election defeats:

Table 10.1
Party Line-Ups, House of Representatives and President,
1954–1974

Election Year	Congress	Representatives Elected		Gains/Losses [a]		President
		Dem.	Rep.	Dem.	Rep.	
1954	84th	232	203	+19	−18	Eisenhower (R)
1956	85th	234	201	+ 2	− 2	
1958	86th	283	154	+49	−47	
1960	87th	263	174	−20	+20	Kennedy (D)
1962	88th	259	176	− 4	+ 2	
1964	89th	295	140	+38	−38	Johnson (D)
1966	90th	248	187	−47	+47	
1968	91st	243	192	− 5	+ 5	Nixon (R)
1970	92nd	255	180	+12	−12	
1972	93rd	243	192	−12	+12	
1974	94th	291	144	+48	−48	Ford (R)

From *Congress and the Nation*, Vol. III, 1969–1972 (Washington, D.C.: Congressional Quarterly Service, 1973), p. 30; *Congressional Quarterly Weekly Report* 33 (January 18, 1975), p. 111. Reprinted by permission.

[a] Net gains or losses are calculated on the basis of the total shift in party strength from one election to the next. They do not reflect minor changes within a Congress due to deaths, resignations or special election outcomes. Further, gains and losses may not always balance because of independent candidates or increases and decreases in the size of the House as a result of the admission of Hawaii and Alaska and reapportionment.

Such elections normally make minorities anxious. A climate is created. Members are seeking some way to make a change. It is in the nature of things. If the results are downhill, you make the change. If you hold your own or win, you don't. The election defeat creates an environment which makes members look for some change. It's a sense of unrest, a sub-conscious searching for something to ease individual consciences. The result is often "let's change our leadership."

Following Ford's victory over Halleck, Republicans staged their largest electoral comeback of these two decades — a net increase of 47 seats in the 1966 mid-term election. As Table 10.1 indicates, Republicans were to remain at between 180 and 192 seats for the next eight years. Unlike his immediate predecessors, Ford never had to undergo the threat of a substantial House Republican electoral set-back. Moreover, the frustration of minority status in the House was partially eased, at least for a time, by the election of Republican administrations in 1968 and 1972.

The Democratic majority fared far better throughout this period, a factor which contributed to stable leadership. After regaining control of the House in 1954, Speaker Rayburn and Majority Leader McCormack picked Albert as whip and created the new position of deputy whip for Boggs. In the face of Eisenhower's overwhelming victory in 1956, the Democratic leadership was content to hold its own. Inability to capitalize on large Democratic majorities achieved in 1958 led to the formation of the Democratic Study Group. Composed of mostly northern moderates and liberals, the DSG played a crucial role in the 1961 fight to enlarge the principal scheduling body of the House, the Committee on Rules. But Rayburn also needed Republican votes to offset 1960 election losses in his narrow 217–212 win.[3] After Rayburn's death, McCormack, Albert, and Boggs each advanced one step in the party hierarchy. Following decisive election gains in 1964, the DSG promoted caucus action which stripped two southern Democrats of their committee seniority and brought about further liberalization of the House rules.

A net loss of 47 seats in the House Democratic party in 1966, while it might have wrought havoc within the minority party, only served to entrench the majority leadership. The Democrats who lost were generally junior, northern, and western liberals representing marginal districts. Those who returned were likely to be more senior, southern conservatives and big-city party regular.[4] For the balance of the decade and into the early 1970's the net gain or loss between the two House parties never exceeded a dozen seats. The aftermath of Watergate coupled with economic hardships led to extensive Republican House losses in 1974. Although election defeat tends to produce party leadership conflict within the Republican minority, such was not the case following 1974. Rhodes, the new minority leader, maintained his popularity since he could not really be blamed for the Republican setbacks. Both election losses and successes have generally enhanced leadership in the House Democratic majority. However, it is not just the climate created by the election, but its impact on hierarchy and party structure within the two House parties which promotes or deters change.

DIFFERENCES IN PARTY HIERARCHY AND STRUCTURE. The Republican minority has been more prone to leadership change through contested means for another two reasons. First, unlike the Democratic majority, Republicans in recent Congresses have suffered from a disproportionate ratio between junior and senior members. This problem becomes particularly acute after major election defeats, such as in 1958 and 1964. For example, following the Goldwater disaster, 93 of the 140 House Republicans (66.4 percent) were members of the five most junior classes (1956, 1958, 1960, 1962, and 1964). Even with the large class of entering freshmen, the comparable figure for Democrats was 169 members out of 295 (57.3 percent). What was more striking, however, was not the relatively greater average seniority among Democrats, but the comparative depth among its senior members. Of 72 members in the 89th Congress who had served 10 terms or more, only 11 (15.6 percent) were Republicans. Just as Martin before him, it was Halleck who suffered most from the loss of loyal senior supporters in 1964.

Conversely, the very existence of this pool of senior Democrats, many of them committee chairmen and heads of state delegations, helps to explain the development of hierarchical patterns of leadership succession and the reluctance to challenge incumbents characteristic of the Democratic majority. A Representative must have substantial service, a minimum of five terms, before he can be considered a candidate for leadership. Seniority is not the only factor. The dissident factions must settle on a candidate capable of winning. When a vacancy occurs there are likely to be two or three equally plausible prospects, no one of which is preferable to all factions within the party. Hierarchical balance is bolstered by traditions of the majority party which foster moderation and acceptance of the existing leadership. "Above all, in the House, one must *last*. If one does last, influence will accrue, but this power is diluted with any defeat. So a congressman, however strong or senior, does not commit himself carelessly. He waits." [5]

Differences in party structure also contribute to the variations in types of leadership change characteristic of the two House parties. At the risk of oversimplification and ignoring variations from Congress to Congress, the Democratic majority is composed of more than two northern moderates and liberals for every southern conservative. Urban-machine Democrats and border-state congressmen, epitomized by Speaker McCormack and Majority Leader Albert, have traditionally formed a moderating nucleus between the ideological extremes of the party. Neither wing can organize the House nor reap the benefits of majority status without the other. Although this dominant cleavage makes House Democrats less cohesive than Republicans in their voting patterns, majority status and the need to promote a presidential program often lead to greater accommodation among elective leaders and seniority leaders than is the case among minority Republicans.[6]

In contrast, the Republican minority, although characterized by greater voting cohesiveness, is less susceptible to compromise and accommodation. Its rather monolithic voting structure is skewed heavily in the conservative direction. Little attempt seems to be made by conservatives, who outnumber liberals by six, or seven, to one, to tolerate dissent or elect liberals to the party leadership. If the activities of the Wednesday Club in a series of contests taking place at the opening of the 89th Congress were at all characteristic, liberals have seldom been cohesive enough to form a balance of power between personal or sectional interests within the predominantly conservative Republican ranks.

Lacking a longer historical perspective the full import of party structure for leadership change must remain speculative. But it would appear that the basic bimodal distribution within the Democratic majority is a strength as well as a weakness, since it promotes compromise and a trading off of major leadership positions between North and South. The relatively monolithic structure of the House

Republican party may lend itself to party harmony and centralization of leadership when the G.O.P. controls Congress, but this same structure seems to discourage accommodation and the selection of its leaders short of contests in times of minority status.

II

What difference does it make when a Halleck upsets a Martin or a McCormack succeeds a Rayburn? More broadly, what are the consequences when one party, the Democratic majority, develops patterns of succession to top leadership, while the other, the Republican minority, seldom stops short of contests in the selection of its party leaders? As Truman, Huitt, and others have pointed out, the discretionary aspects of congressional leadership are considerable.[7] Leaders' personalities and backgrounds not only shape the positions they occupy, but also have important influences on the careers of their supporters and the success or failures of legislation. The predominant mode of change adopted by the two House parties has additional consequences for national elections, the two-party system, and representative government.

Within the confines of this book it is impossible to assess fully the impact of even the most important leadership choices made by the two House parties during this 20-year period. It is possible, however, to use two examples, Halleck's defeat of Martin in 1959 and McCormack's elevation to the Speakership in 1962, to briefly illustrate some of the most important kinds of consequences of replacing one incumbent leader by another.[8]

Revolt, by its very nature, results in more wholesale change than in orderly succession. Following his defeat of Martin, Halleck brought new vigor to the Republican party leadership. A canny, aggressive "gut-fighter," he was at his best in the give-and-take of floor debate and behind-the-scenes maneuvering. In contrast to Martin, he seldom cooperated with Rayburn, McCormack, and the more liberal wing of the Democratic majority, but instead actively cultivated ties with conservative southern Democrats. Moderate Republicans on the Committee on Rules, who retired or advanced to the Senate, were replaced with solid conservatives. The dormant Republican Policy Committee was reinstituted, John Byrnes of Wisconsin was elected chairman, and arrangements were made to provide professional staff. Under Byrnes and John Rhodes of Arizona, task forces were created to investigate problems which cut across committee lines or which might serve as the basis for campaign issues. Freshman members were given representation on the executive subcommittee of the Republican Committee on Committees.

When Halleck took over as minority leader in 1959, House Republicans consisted of 154 members. At one time during the 88th Congress, the number increased to 178. For a majority of 140 Republicans-elect at the beginning of the 89th Congress, however, Halleck's ability to promote party solidarity and to administer defeat to Democratic proposals was not enough. Ford's promise to "promote and communicate the image of a fighting, forward-looking party seeking responsible and constructive solutions to national problems" struck a receptive chord. The intensive efforts of some 30 members who worked in Ford's behalf led to Halleck's defeat only six years after his own coup.

Peaceful succession brings on more incremental change, but the impact of such different personalities as Rayburn and McCormack on the office of the Speaker was considerable. McCormack's style was both more institutional and partisan than Rayburn's. He called more meetings to discuss legislative strategy and involved the majority leader and whip to a much greater extent than Rayburn did. Under his leadership, the Democratic Steering Committee was temporarily revived and the caucus came into somewhat greater use. In 1969, the Speaker, responding to Democratic Study Group pressures and Udall's insurgency, acquiesced to regular monthly meetings of the caucus.

The telephone was one of McCormack's most effective weapons — "I'd call the devil if I thought it would do any good." In contrast, Rayburn operated on a more independent and personal basis. He preferred the intimacy and informality of after-the-session gatherings of the "Board of Education." [9] The whip organization was used less frequently and Rayburn almost never called a party caucus beyond the opening meeting.

McCormack's shift from partisan majority leader to impartial presiding officer was not an easy transition. His strong partisan identifications reflected his South Boston organizational ties. Rayburn's rural Texas background and more conservative political outlook made him more acceptable to most southern Democrats. He was more inclined to cooperate with Republicans, a relationship facilitated by his close friendship with Martin.

When a new Speaker or minority leader is selected, some congressmen exercise greater influence and others fall out of favor. The relationship of members of the Committee on Rules to Speaker McCormack provided an illustration. The influence of Bolling of Missouri and Thornberry of Texas declined; O'Neill of Massachusetts and, to a lesser extent, Madden of Indiana, gained influence. Committee assignments in 1963 also reflected the composition of the new leadership. For example, McCormack was instrumental in packing the Committee on Appropriations with five northern liberals over the objections of its conservative chairman, Clarence Cannon of Missouri.

Leadership change also has a direct impact on legislation. Certainly, a bill to enlarge the House of Representatives to 438 members by adding one additional member from Massachusetts, Missouri, and Pennsylvania would not have advanced as far as it did without the new Speaker's support.[10] McCormack's Catholicism made it even more mandatory that any federal-aid-to-education bill be accompanied by some resolution of the church-state issue. The possibilities of strong civil rights, medicare, and mass transit legislation improved as a more sympathetic leader advanced to the Speakership. Since ideological differences among Martin, Halleck, and Ford were less pronounced and the minority has far less control over scheduling, the impact of leadership change on Republican legislative goals is more difficult to trace. However, Ford made a more intensive effort to launch constructive Republican alternatives to Democratic administration programs than either of his two predecessors.[11]

The relatively peaceful modes of leadership change practiced by House Democrats in recent years have promoted party harmony, facilitated the passage of legislation, and thus aided the reelection of Democrats. But the development of patterns of succession is by no means universally endorsed by House Democrats. A junior member, a potential candidate for leadership, summed up some of the disenchantment:

> A man shouldn't become a leader just because 15 or 20 years
> ago somebody made an obscure decision to put someone in as
> whip or deputy whip, and then he advances up the hierarchy.
> There's a real problem in the House. It's a kind of hardening

of the arteries, too much bureaucracy. We're beginning to be more like the people we criticize downtown. Leadership should come from a man's proven ability, not just because he got started on the ladder . . .

I think what the Republicans have done is a healthy development. If Joe Martin were a Democrat, we'd still have him as our leader.

Change through contested means has a number of different consequences. Few House Republicans have complained about bureaucratized patterns of succession since few exist. House Republicans can take some consolation from one by-product of overwhelming election defeats — able younger members are moved into positions of high rank far quicker than by any other means. The overall costs to internal party harmony from frequent contests are more difficult to estimate. More latent than manifest, they may seldom reveal themselves overtly in legislative voting patterns. But the animosities and bitterness resulting from leadership contests remain an underlying source of tension and distrust.

To an extent not adequately stressed, congressional leadership change has important consequences for national politics and the strength of the two-party system. The House provides a pool of talent for nominations to the Senate or state-wide offices. The Senate has always produced more presidential candidates, but the House is frequently an early or mid-career stage for aspiring national leaders. House members continue to participate intensively in the selection of candidates, the writing of party platforms, and the management of national conventions.

The party which does not control the White House turns to its congressional leaders for the nucleus of opposition party leadership. As leaders of the congressional majority, Rayburn and Johnson, McCormack, Albert and Mansfield, have had more resources at their command, including better press coverage, than Republican minority leaders like Dirksen and Scott or Halleck and Ford. When their party does not control the White House, the Joint Senate-House Republican Leadership and the Republican Coordinating Committee play dominant roles in the selection of domestic campaign issues and the structuring of debate on foreign policy. For all these reasons, changes in House leadership have implications far beyond the internal activities of Congress.

III

Intra-party leadership change may also be viewed as an important immediate stage of the governing process. Every two years the electorates of 435 House districts make critical judgments about the individuals who will represent them in Congress. These collective decisions have a number of further consequences for representative government in the United States. First, the election results advance or limit the careers of some 800 promising politicians, not a few of whom are destined for national leadership as party spokesmen, committee chairmen, future Senators, and presidential aspirants. Second, the aggregate outcome of seats won and lost determines the congressional party that will be the majority and have the right to organize the House of Representatives. Third, the size of the majority sets the limits for success or failure of the President's legislative program. If Congress is controlled by the opposition party, or if the President's party does not have a working majority, then the President's expectations as to what is politically feasible must be lowered. He may even have to shift from a policy largely oriented toward passing legislation to one primarily designed to promote campaign issues two or four years hence. Finally, as the findings of Chapters 9 and 10 suggest, the size of the net gain or loss sets the climate for continuity or change in House party leadership. These aggregate election results provide the clearest instruction offered by the electorate in what is at best a generalized and largely uninformed evaluation of administration and congressional performance.[12] Congressmen appear to translate these collective instructions into mandates for continuing support or opportunities for change in congressional party leadership.

IV

This analysis began by distinguishing three basic kinds of leadership change in legislatures, inter-party turnover, intra-party change, and institutional reform. After noting that continuity rather than change is the predominant pattern of congressional leadership, five types of intra-party leadership change were set forth: (1) routine succession, (2) appointment, or the emergence of a consensus choice, (3) open competition, (4) challenge to an heir apparent, and (5) revolt, or its aftermath. All but one of these types were illustrated by 36 instances of leadership change or attempted change which took place in the five top party-wide leadership positions in both House parties during the 84th to 93d Congresses (1955–1974). The remaining type, challenge to an heir apparent, was illustrated by two earlier contests in 1919 and 1931.

Some rather striking differences were revealed in the predominant mode of change practiced by the two House parties over the past two decades. For most of these ten Congresses, the Democratic majority party was able to resolve its problems of leadership change by relatively peaceful means. Indeed, 15 out of 21 cases of leadership change between 1955 and 1974 were decided short of contests. However, over the last several Congresses, open competition and even challenges to Democratic incumbent leaders were occurring with greater frequency. In contrast, the Republican minority party throughout 84th–93d Congresses was much more likely to resort to contests — 12 out of 15 instances of leadership selection were characterized by two or more candidates actively working to align membership support. Almost all these contests went to a conference vote. In five instances, most notably the minority leadership contests of 1959 and 1965, change in Republican party leadership was sought through organized revolt against incumbent leaders.

One question has remained largely unanswered to this point. Given the House Democratic party's dominant pattern of selecting leaders by relatively harmonious means for most of these two decades, what factors led to the flurry of contests in the late 1960's and early 1970's? Among the most important reasons would seem to be (1) the change-oriented beliefs and actions of an attractive candidate for leadership, Arizona Democrat Morris K. Udall, (2) the caucus reforms instigated by the Democratic Study Group, and (3) the shifting composition and modified outlooks of House Democrats, especially through a large influx of freshmen members in the 89th and subsequent Congresses.

Several pages earlier we quoted a "potential candidate for leadership," strongly disenchanted with his own party's selection patterns. Not surprisingly, these were the remarks of Morris Udall, just entering his third term in the House in 1965. Less than four years later he put his beliefs and those of a number of other change-oriented Democratic Representatives to test in his 1969 challenge to Speaker McCormack. Two years later he fought a hard campaign for majority leader against Hale Boggs and three other candidates. Udall lost both races but his efforts helped to generate further contests. Sam Gibbons, who provided O'Neill with most of the limited opposition he encountered in 1973, was a principal Udall lieutenant in 1971. Even the symbolic challenges of John Conyers to Speaker Albert in 1971 and 1973 appear to have derived at least partial inspiration from Udall's 1969 bid.

The upsurge of internal reform efforts led by the Democratic Study Group in the late 1960's and early 1970's, successful as they were in bringing about caucus change, probably hampered efforts by Udall, O'Hara, Gibbons, and Burton to break apart the more established patterns of leadership succession. To the extent they became labelled as "DSG candidates," it seemed to hurt them more than it helped.[13] Under the successive chairmanships of Frank Thompson of New Jersey, James O'Hara of Michigan, Donald Fraser of Minnesota, and Phillip Burton of California, the DSG did succeed over the 91st–93d Congress in pushing through a number of important caucus reforms, including regular monthly meetings, biannual elections of committee chairmen, open committee hearings, revitalization of the Democratic Steering and Policy Committee, and revised procedures for caucus instruction of the standing committees on legislative policy.[14] To talk of a revival of "King Caucus" would be premature,[15] but the Democratic Study Group efforts contributed greatly to a climate of change within which challenges to establish patterns of leadership selection could be raised if seldom implemented.

A necessary, but insufficient cause, alone, for internal reform and the increasing number of contested leadership cases within the House Democratic party has been the shift in compensation and outlook of the more junior Democratic Representatives in the last four to five Congresses. The 89th Congress (1965–1966) brought in the second largest class of Democratic freshmen throughout these two decades — more than 50 new members.[16] Although only 23 of these members survived through 1973, by the 93d Congress nearly half of the Democratic majority (47.4 percent) were men and women who had come to Washington, D.C. since 1964. Moreover, the 91st and 92d Congresses were also marked by increased retirement rates and primary defeats among its senior members. For example, the 92d Congress saw 6 chairmen, 20 subcommittee chairmen, and 9 ranking Republican members on the 21 standing committees leaving the House of Representatives. Still, the hierarchy of the House Democratic party, as compared to the Republican party, remained much more dominated by its senior members. Of 76 members in the 93d Congress who had served 10 terms or more, only 15 (19.7 percent) were Republicans.[17]

If the numbers of junior Democrats, alone, were insufficient to reverse established patterns of leadership, they nevertheless appeared to be more sympathetic to contested change. Regardless of philosophy, age, and regional base, most junior members entered the House with a more critical attitude toward seniority. As *Washington Post* correspondent David Broder observed following the 1972 elections:[18]

> Like those entering other trades and professions, the House newcomers tend to be men and women impatient with the old ways of doing business; less willing to "move up the chairs," waiting silently for years for their turn at a subcommittee chairmanship; less deferential to their elders; and more insistent on grabbing a piece of the action now.

Even though the views of these change-oriented members had largely been frustrated in those contests which occurred between 1969 and 1973, there remains hope for future success. A minimum requirement would be an able and popular candidate with a broader basis of support than just his own region and those of similar ideological persuasions. Most of his own delegation and classmates and many of those from more junior ranks would have to rally to a need for more aggressive leadership. All would then have to seek out and recruit substantial numbers of the incoming freshman Democrats in order to attain their objectives. The difficulties in achieving all these requirements suggest that established patterns of leadership selection in the House Democratic party may likely prevail for the immediate future — but the winds of change are in the air.

NOTES

1. Rayburn served for 17 years as Speaker and four years as minority leader (the 80th and 83d Congresses) before his death in 1961; McCormack capped 17 years as majority leader with nine years as Speaker before his retirement in 1971. Martin has served 16 years as minority leader, four years as Speaker (the 80th and 83d Congresses) before his defeat in a party primary in 1966. Arends completed more than 30 years as whip before his retirement at the end of the 93d Congress. These four party leaders averaged nearly 80 years of age and more than 46 years of service at the time of their death, defeat, or retirement from the House of Representatives.

 2. David B. Truman, *The Congressional Party* (New York: Wiley, 1959), pp. 212–227.
 3. Milton C. Cummings, Jr. and Robert L. Peabody, "The Decision to Enlarge the Committee on Rules: An Analysis of the 1961 Vote," in R. L. Peabody and Nelson W. Polsby, eds. *New Perspectives on the House of Representatives* (Chicago: Rand McNally, 1963), pp. 167–194.
 4. Jeff Fishel, *Party and Opposition* (New York: McKay, 1973), pp. 169–191.
 5. Excerpt from an unpublished newsletter of the late Representative Clem Miller (D., Cal.), January-February 1962, p. 3.
 6. For evidence of such effects in an earlier Congress, the 81st, see Truman, *op. cit.*, pp. 231–246; more generally, see David R. Mayhew's discussion of the House Democratic party as one of "inclusive" compromise, the Republican party as one of "exclusive" compromise, *Party Loyalty Among Congressmen* (Cambridge: Harvard University Press, 1966), ch. 6.
 7. Truman, *op. cit.*, p. 245; Ralph K. Huitt, "Democratic Party Leadership in the Senate," *Am. Pol. Sci. Rev.* **55** (1961), 336–337.
 8. For a more detailed analysis of the consequences of Ford's defeat of Halleck, see Robert L. Peabody, "Political Parties: House Republican Leadership," in Allan P. Sindler, ed., *American Political Institutions and Public Policy* (Boston: Little, Brown, 1969), pp. 181–229.
 9. For a discussion of Rayburn's use of this informal steering committee, see Neil MacNeil, *Forge of Democracy: The House of Representatives* (New York: David McKay, 1963), pp. 82–84.
10. McCormack finally disavowed his support of H.R. 10264 after an uneasy partisan coalition came unglued on the floor of the House of Representatives during the amendment stage — *Congressional Quarterly Weekly Report* **20** (March 16, 1962), p. 429.
11. Peabody in Sindler, *op. cit.*, pp. 181–229.
12. "In Detroit in January 1957 only 18 percent of the people could correctly name the Congressman from their own district, and only 13 percent knew the names of both United States Senators from Michigan ... The world of the political activists and the newspapers which report political events is much more remote from the world of the average citizen than is generally realized." Daniel Katz and Samuel J. Eldersveld, "The Impact of Local Party Activity Upon the Electorate," *Public Opinion Quarterly* **25** (1961), pp. 1–24, 20. "The electorate sees very little altogether of what goes on in the national legislature. Few judgments of legislative performance are associated with the parties, and much of the public is unaware even of which party has control of Congress. As a result, the absence of party discipline or legislative results is unlikely to bring down electoral sanctions on the ineffective party or the errant Congressman." Donald E. Stokes and Warren E. Miller, "Party Government and the Saliency of Congress," *Public Opinion Quarterly* **26** (1962), pp. 531–546, 545. For a summary of studies examining the limits of the public's information about politics and the representative process, see John Wahlke's paper: "Public Policy and Representative Government: The Role of the Represented," Department of Political Science, University of Iowa, 1967, pp. 6–10.
    It seems clear that the electorate does not bring down electoral sanctions upon the ineffective party in the sense of the responsible party doctrine. However, members of Congress, particularly Representatives in the minority party, seem to interpret large-scale shifts in seats won or lost as a judgment on their party image and the caliber of its leadership.
13. If the DSG claimed a membership of 140–160 members during the late

1960's and early 1970's, one might well ask why they were unable to elect one of their own to the regular Democratic party leadership. Neither a commitment to liberal programs, a willingness to support internal reform, nor a pledge to back particular leadership candidates binds the members of the Democratic Study Group. Although the great majority of its membership is made up of northern and western moderate-to-liberals, they range from militant leftists to rather conservative party regulars, who generally vote more liberally than they feel. Not a few of its members pay annual dues of $100 almost solely to take advantage of DSG-prepared weekly summaries of legislation and more comprehensive research reports.

14. Although the language of these and other specific reforms was sponsored by a range of members, both inside and outside the DSG, the modern idea of reviving the Democratic Caucus as a means of party and House reform can be traced to Representative Richard Bolling's books, *House Out of Order* (New York: Dutton, 1965), esp. ch. 11; and *Power in the House* (New York: Dutton, 1968), esp. ch. 7.

15. See the criticisms of a number of House Republicans warning of the revival of the Democratic Caucus as an "ominous herd." *Congressional Record* (daily ed.), June 27, 1974, pp. H-5841–5844; July 29, 1974, pp. H-7292–7293; Mary Russell, "G.O.P. Fears Return of King Caucus in House Next Year," *Washington Post*, July 29, 1974, p. A-2.

16. The largest incoming Democratic groups of freshmen prior to the 94th Congress were the class of 1958 with 60 members and the class of 1964 with 65 members. Frustrations with the regular party leadership led to the establishment of the Democratic Study Group in the 86th Congress. Reform pressures by the DSG have been on the increase since 1965 and especially over the past four Congresses, 91st–94th.

17. "Terms of Service," *Congressional Directory*, 93d Congress, 1st sess. (Washington, D.C.: U.S. Government Printing Office, 1973).

18. "The Changing House," *Washington Post*, November 26, 1972, p. B-7.

PART III

The Senate

Senate Majority Leader Mike Mansfield of Montana confers with his close working associate, Democratic Majority Whip Robert Byrd of West Virginia.

(Al Muto)

CHAPTER ELEVEN

Introduction to Senate Party Leadership

In a body of 100 ambitious people — almost all of them, by definition, skilled and astute politicians — why do so few Senators gravitate toward elected party leadership, while the vast majority choose to make their mark on public policy primarily through legislative specialization? Put another way — why are most Senators seemingly content with the slow, step-by-step advancement up two or more committee ladders, each step by and large enhancing their control over the drafting and the implementation of legislation? Striving to become a party leader would seem to be a qualitatively different kind of choice than a decision to work toward a given committee chairmanship or to attempt to excel as the nation's leading authority on tax reform or atomic energy legislation. It would appear to more closely parallel the increasingly frequent career decision of as many as a tenth of the Senate to use their public visibility as a springboard to still higher office, namely, the vice presidency or presidency of the United States.

Whether a Senator decides to run for the presidency, pursues a career as a party leader, or strives to make a mark as a legislative policy-maker need not necessarily be an exclusive choice. On rare occasions politicans of superior intellect, rare political skills, and consuming ambition have pursued all three — Robert Taft of Ohio, Alben Barkley of Kentucky, and Lyndon Johnson of Texas are cases in point. Still, the great majority of Senators remain content to make their mark through legislative specialization, or so it would seem.

In the beginning years of a Senator's career, of course, no firm commitment to one line of advancement or another is necessary. Every freshman member of the Senate routinely receives two or more

321

committee assignments. Since 1953 for Democrats and 1959 for Republicans, at least one of these assignments has been to a major committee.[1] Moreover, only the rare member of either party does not immediately assume at least one subcommittee chairmanship or ranking minority position. Thus, the paths to legislative specialization are quickly launched even for those freshman members who do not arrive with a prior legislative background or other governmental experience.

The organizational structure of the Senate is not unlike that of the House of Representatives with its dual party hierarchy and approximately parallel committee structure (17 standing committees as compared to 21 in the House). Of course, as a result of the smaller size of the Senate its committees are smaller, and Senators typically serve on two, three or even more committees as compared to one, or at most two, for the average House member.

Few Democratic Senators can expect to obtain a committee chairmanship until after they have been reelected to a third term or more. Reflecting their more limited numbers and somewhat higher turnover, Republican Senators might expect to advance to a ranking minority position on one of the less prestigious committees after eight or ten years of seniority.

In the Senate, much less often than in the House of Representatives, party leaders seldom are forced to abandon their legislative specialties even after they achieve top leadership. Unlike their House counterparts, Senate leaders continue to serve on committees and hold, on the average, four or five subcommittee chairmanships or ranking minority positions in any given Congress. Still, their broad responsibilities for legislative programming and the constraints of time force party leaders to serve mainly as policy generalists rather than legislative specialists.

Questions about what motivates a few Senators to seek party leadership, the great majority to concentrate on making legislative contributions, and still a third group to put substantial energies into seeking the presidency are not easy to answer. It seems clear that most Senators are content, or their abilities or the nature of their constituencies constrain them, to pursue but one or, at most, two such objectives. The necessary, but not sufficient, cause for becoming a party leader, a leading presidential aspirant, or an important legislative spokesman would seem to be sustained service in the Senate, usually two terms or more. Thus, any Senator who wishes to survive must be so fortunate as to represent a one-party state and continue to avoid primary upsets or, over time, be able to convert a competitive two-party state into a relatively safe constituency. The advantages of incumbency are such that many Senators are able to build just such a strong electoral base.

Beyond the necessity of reelection, the question remains largely unexplored of why some Senators opt for the role of a behind-the-scenes senior oligarch such as the late Richard Russell (D., Ga.) or Eugene Millikan (R., Colo.), rather than seeking the alternative of formal floor leadership — the pattern of Lyndon Johnson, Everett Dirksen and others. For Robert A. Taft, the predominant Republican oligarch of the World War II era and its aftermath, it was his party's succession to majority status in 1953 that caused him to assume the position of floor leader. Prior to that occasion he had been content to remain chairman of his party's policy committee. For most of these Senate influentials, personal style, geography, ideology, and not a little luck move them toward or away from positions of formal leadership. One Senator may prefer to operate in the corridors and back rooms of the Capitol because he neither debates well nor seeks the public limelight. Still another may be eliminated from strong consideration for assistant floor leader or some other party role which might lead to top leadership because his candidacy would not properly balance the geographical or ideological blend thought desirable in the combined leadership.

Richard Russell, who apparently rejected the floor leadership of his party, or at least never aggressively sought it, seemed to prefer, instead, to hand pick and direct others from behind the scenes. It was Russell who summarized Lyndon Johnson's potential for the floor leader's role: "He doesn't have the best mind on the Democratic side of the Senate; he isn't the best orator; he isn't the best parliamentarian. But he's the best combination of all of these qualities." [2] Johnson's meteoric climb to top Senate leadership — minority floor leader after but four years of service — was made possible by a combination of fortuitous events, including the back-to-back defeats of two of his predecessors, the generally low esteem in which the position was then held, and Russell's continued preference for the chairmanship of the Armed Services Committee rather than the floor leader's job.

Why did Johnson seek the whip's position and, later, the floor leadership? Perhaps not alone for the prestige of the office or even the contributions he might make to achieve Democratic party leadership objectives. He launched his political career in the House of Representatives where two of his strongest Texas mentors, Speaker Sam Rayburn and former Speaker and Vice President John Nance Garner, had made their marks. Garner, in particular, had been struck with presidential ambition only to be blocked by President Franklin D. Roosevelt's quest for an unprecedented third term in 1940. It was Roosevelt who exerted the other strong influence in Johnson's early political career. Long before his election to the Senate in 1948, Johnson appeared to have his heart set on the nation's highest office. A party leadership role in the Senate would provide him with the testing ground and national exposure by which he might overcome the liability of being a southerner. With the sole exception of a transplanted Woodrow Wilson, neither party had turned to the son of a state of the Old Confederacy as its presidential nominee since the Civil War. And, of course, Johnson might never have achieved his objective except for the assassination of President John F. Kennedy in 1963.

Other Senate party leaders have clearly shared and even acted upon similar presidential ambitions, for example, Barkley, Taft, Knowland, and Edward Kennedy. Presumably these leaders were also motivated by the importance of becoming Senate party officers and what might be accomplished while serving as an incumbent. Rising to the floor leadership in the United States Senate is a political achievement unrivaled by any office save the presidency and perhaps the vice presidency or Speakership. Senate leaders, like those of all national legislatures, can take great pride in being selected for high office by their peers. Other motivations for seeking party office are as diverse and complex as those which compel people to run for political office in the first place — personal drive, the need for recognition, the pursuit of material benefits, career advancement, the emulation of significant others, sheer fascination with politics and the legislative game, the love of power, the desire to do good, the desire to ameliorate injustice, patriotism on behalf of one's country and its institutions — the list seems endless.

The focus of this chapter is largely upon party leaders, Democrats and Republicans, who have sought and won office over the past two decades no matter what their dominant motivations. As the importance of formal leadership positions has grown, incumbents has been almost continuously involved in the leading political and legislative questions of the day. Only the responsibilities of the Speaker and floor leaders of the House of Representatives rival and only those of the President of the United States exceed the scope of those of Senate party leaders. In the most ordinary times the questions of who these Senate leaders are, how they achieve their offices, what they do and with what success are important ones. When the country operates under divided government as it did under President Eisenhower from 1955 to 1960 or under President Nixon from 1969 to 1974, then the answers to these questions — who the Senate floor leaders are, the effectiveness of their styles, the range of their philosophical leanings, the implications of their geographical base, and the extent of their political ambitions — become all the more critical.

I

Top party leadership in the Senate is, almost without exception, collegial in nature. Even the strongest floor leader surrounds himself with loyal lieutenants. He must, of necessity, cooperate closely with the majority of his committee leaders. The majority leader usually has to co-opt the support of the minority leader if the scheduling of legislation and other business of the Senate is to go forward smoothly. Of course, some floor leaders develop a stronger, more independent, more partisan style of leadership than others. Nevertheless, though leadership style remains only a matter of degree, leadership itself is more or less collegial from one set of leaders to the next.

Unlike the Speaker of the House, who came to be recognized as the dominant leader of that body by the time of the Civil War, party leadership in the Senate remained rather sporadic and decentralized until World War I.

Why did the office of floor leader take so long to become institutionalized? Definitive historical accounts of the growth of party leadership during the late nineteenth and early twentieth centuries are lacking,[3] but the answer would seem to be dependent on a combination of factors, including constitutional grounds, the slow growth of party identification as a bond in the Senate, and the continuing independence which continues to characterize most Senators, representing as they do, complex and differing economic and political interests and separate geographical entities. It took the direct election of Senators as a result of the ratification of the Seventeenth Amendment in 1913, the pressures on Congress brought about by World War I, the increasing industrialization of our nation, and an expanding legislative and constituency workload to break down some of these strong inhibitions against the formation of an enduring party leadership.

The United States Constitution specifically provides for only three congressional offices: the Speaker of the House, the Vice President (who serves as President of the Senate), and a President pro tempore to preside in the Senate in the absence of the Vice President. Article I, Sections 2 and 3, further provided for each House to "choose . . . other officers" although nothing was specified about the form of the offices, the selection of officers or their duties.

Unlike the office of Speaker which gradually evolved into the dominant position of House party leadership, the President pro tempore of the Senate has seldom been other than a figurehead. Neither he nor the Vice President ever spends much time presiding. (That chore is handed over, for the most part, to freshman Senators.) Until the late nineteenth century the appointment or election of the President pro tempore was held to be "for the occasion only." Thus, more than one Senator occupied this office in numerous sessions, and in others, none were selected. In 1890 Presidents pro tempore began to serve until "the Senate otherwise ordered." The tradition that the position be filled by the majority member with the greatest seniority did not fully take hold until the second decade of the twentieth century.

FLOOR LEADERS. The closest equivalent office in the Senate to the Speaker of the House is the position of majority floor leader. But this position is extra-constitutional and of relatively recent vintage; at no time does the incumbent preside over the Senate. The historical roots of the position can be traced back to the practice of both parties electing caucus (now called conference) chairmen in the 1880's and 1890's. As the offiial Senate history puts it: "It is difficult, if not impossible, to point to anyone who functioned as the 'majority leader of the Senate' until the end of the 19th century." [4]

Of course, individual members from time to time have assumed leading roles in deciding what the Senate would or would not do from 1789 until the present. The practice of floor management of legislation by committee chairmen is as old as the Senate itself. With the adoption of standing committees in 1816 and the abandonment of rotating chairmanships after 1833, floor management by chairmen or a designated ranking majority member and the ranking minority member became the standard practice. This pattern, made more explicit and orderly by the use of unanimous consent agreements, continues in the contemporary Senate.[5]

Throughout most of the eighteenth and nineteenth centuries, there was no one leader to "give way" to other legislatures. Partisan floor leadership was fragmented, decentralized, and occasional. Beginning in the middle 1880's, three developments toward the evolution of the modern office of floor leader were (1) regular and repeated elections of caucus chairmen by both parties; (2) consolidation of leadership in the hands of a clique of Republican chairmen led by Nelson Aldrich of Rhode Island and William B. Allison of Iowa; (3) a similar consolidation of power among the Democrats, led by Arthur Pue Gorman of Maryland.[6]

> Party caucuses are also as old as the Senate:[7] Caucuses of Senators of a particular party, of a common interest, of a geographical area, or of some 'blocs' have been called from time to time from the beginning of the first Senate for all kinds of purposes, including the determination of the position to be taken on certain proposed legislation, or such things as to determine the names and sizes of committees. These meetings, however, were not invoked to perform as organized political caucuses for the purpose of selecting persons to serve as floor leaders for the parties during the sessions of the Senate until the latter part of the 19th century.

Conferences and caucuses occasionally served as instruments for hammering out party policy, but for the most part these "Democratic and Republican organizations rarely attempted to schedule legislation or enforce unity in voting. In brief, Senators were free to go about their business more or less as they pleased." [8] Before the 1800's, caucus chairmen, when they were elected at all, seldom served for more than one Congress.

By the end of the nineteenth century it was clear who the chairmen of the party caucuses were, but it was by no means clear that these same men would provide floor leadership. Neither party elected "leaders" as we know them today. As Randall B. Ripley concludes:[9]

> The practice of electing a single majority leader or minority leader who would serve during an entire Congress and presumably would be reelected did not become established until the period between 1911 and 1913 . . .

Table 11.1
Senate Floor Leaders, Democrats and Republicans, 1911–1974

Name and State	Dates of Service as Floor Leader	Years of Service	Years in Senate Before Election as Floor Leader	Reason for Vacating Office
DEMOCRATS				
Thomas Martin, Va.	1911–1913, 1917–1919	4	16	Death
John Kern, Ind.	1913–1917	4	2	Defeat
Gilbert Hitchcock, Neb.[a]	1919	1	8	—
Oscar Underwood, Ala.[b]	1920–1923	3	5	—
Joseph Robinson, Ark.	1923–1937	14	10	Death
Alben Barkley, Ky.	1937–1949	12	10	Vice Pres.
Scott Lucas, Ill.	1949–1951	2	10	Defeat
Ernest McFarland, Ariz.	1951–1953	2	10	Defeat
Lyndon Johnson, Texas	1953–1961	8	4	Vice Pres.
Michael Mansfield, Mont.	1961–	—	8	—
	Average (Mean)	5.6	8.3	
REPUBLICANS				
Shelby Cullom, Ill.	1910–1913	3	27	Resignation
Jacob Gallinger, N.H.	1913–1918	6	22	Death
Henry Cabot Lodge, Mass.	1919–1924	6	26	Death
Charles Curtis, Kan.	1925–1929	4	16	Vice Pres.
James Watson, Ind.	1929–1933	4	12	Defeat
Charles McNary, Ore.	1933–1944	11	16	Death
Wallace White, Me.	1944–1949	5	13	Resignation
Kenneth Wherry, Neb.	1949–1951	3	6	Death
Styles Bridges, N.H.[c]	1952–1953	1	15	—
Robert Taft, Ohio	1953	1	14	Death
William Knowland, Cal.	1953–1959	5	8	Resignation
Everett Dirksen, Ill.	1959–1969	10	8	Death
Hugh Scott, Pa.	1969–	—	11	—
	Average (Mean)	4.9	15.7	

Adapted from Floyd M. Riddick, *Majority and Minority Leaders of the Senate*, 91st Cong., 1st Sess., Sen. Doc. 91–20, 1969, and Randall B. Ripley, *Power in the Senate* (New York: St. Martin's Press, 1969), p. 30. Reprinted by permission.

[a] Hitchcock served as acting leader for a brief period until Underwood was elected on April 27, 1920.

[b] Underwood declined to run for floor leader at the beginning of the first session of the 68th Congress, Dec. 3, 1923.

[c] Bridges became President pro tempore of the Senate when Taft opted for floor leader at the beginning of the 83rd Congress, January 3, 1953.

Thus, until roughly 1911–1913, the real party leaders were not necessarily the formal floor leaders or caucus chairmen. Only since 1911–1913 has it become customary for actual and potential power to reside in the titled majority leader or minority leader.

Even after 1911–1913 there would be floor leaders who would defer to other powerful members of the Senate on many matters of legislative policy making.

Democratic Senator John Kern of Indiana is assumed to be the first caucus chairman to combine formal title with effective floor leadership, especially during the first two years of the Wilson administration.[10] Since 1911, 10 Democrats and 13 Republicans have served as "floor leaders" of their respective parties.[11] Table 11.1 lists these men, their years of leadership services, the amount of time they served in the Senate prior to their election as leader, and their reasons for vacating office.

PARTY WHIPS OR ASSISTANT FLOOR LEADERS. Congress has followed numerous legislative practices of the English Parliament, even to the extent of adopting the titles of some of its party leadership positions. Some Senators at one time probably performed tasks similar to the contemporary whips, but the institutionalization of the office of whip did not occur until the twentieth century. In his official Senate history, Walter J. Oleszek dates the first Democratic whip from 1913 — J. Hamilton Lewis of Illinois.[12] Lewis served in that capacity from 1913 to 1919, and again, from 1933 to 1939. His job — to see that Democratic colleagues would be present or paired on roll call votes — still remains a core activity of contemporary whips. Republicans were quick to adopt this innovation. James Wadsworth of New York was appointed whip in 1915, only to be succeeded one week later by Charles Curtis of Kansas. Curtis, who served in this capacity from 1915 until 1924, was the first whip to be elevated to floor leader, in 1925. All told, some 14 Democrats and 11 Republicans have served as whips over the past half century (see Table 11.2).

For most of the pre-World War II period the whip's job was held by members who represented the heartlands of their respective parties and seldom had to worry much about their own reelections. As the issues confronting the Senate became more complicated — what to do about post-war economy, cold-war tension, the emerging civil rights legislation — the question of who assisted in the leadership of the Senate took on greater significance. Thus the whip began to take on more

Table 11.2
Senate Whips, Democrats and Republicans, 1913–1974

Name and State	Dates of Service as Whip	Years of Service	Years in Senate Before Election as Whip	Advancement to Floor Leader[a]
DEMOCRATS				
J. Hamilton Lewis, Ill.	1913–1919, 1933–1939	12	0	no (twice)
Peter Gerry, R.I.	1919–1929	10	2	no
Morris Sheppard, Texas	1929–1933	4	16	—
Sherman Minton, Ind.	1939–1941	2	4	—
Lister Hill, Ala.	1941–1947	6	3	—
Scott Lucas, Ill.	1947–1949	2	8	yes
Francis Myers, Pa.	1949–1951	2	4	—
Lyndon Johnson, Texas	1951–1953	2	2	yes
Earle Clements, Ky.	1953–1957	4	2	—
Michael Mansfield, Mont.	1957–1961	4	4	yes
Hubert Humphrey, Minn.	1961–1965	4	12	—
Russell Long, La.	1965–1969	4	16	—
Edward Kennedy, Mass.	1969–1971	2	6	—
Robert Byrd, W. Va.	1971–	—	12	—
	Average (mean)	4.5	6.5	
REPUBLICANS				
J. W. Wadsworth, N.Y.	1915	0 [c]	1	—
Charles Curtis, Kan.	1915–1924	10	6	yes
Wesley L. Jones, Wash.	1924–1929	4	16	no
Simeon Fess, Ohio	1929–1933	4	6	no
Felix Hebert, R.I.	1933–1935	2	4	—
Kenneth Wherry, Neb.[b]	1944–1949	5	1	yes
Leverett Saltonstall, Mass.	1949–1957	8	4	no[d]
Everett Dirksen, Ill.	1957–1959	2	6	yes
Thomas Kuchel, Cal.	1959–1969	10	6	—
Hugh Scott, Pa.	1969	1	10	yes
Robert Griffin, Mich.	1969–	—	4	—
	Average (mean)	4.2	5.8	

Adapted from Walter J. Oleszek, *Majority and Minority Whips of the Senate,* 92nd Cong., 2d Sess., Sen. Doc. 92–86, 1972, and Randall B. Ripley, *Power in the Senate* (New York: St. Martin's Press, 1969), p. 34. Reprinted by permission.

[a] This column indicates whether the whip became floor leader if that position became vacant during his tenure.

[b] The Republicans appointed no whip between 1935 and 1944.

[c] Wadsworth served as whip for only a week.

[d] Saltonstall did, however, become chairman of the Republican Conference.

sustained duties and to benefit from enhanced exposure — trips to the White House, expanded relations with the press, more responsibility for legislation. The whip also emerged as a likely successor to the majority leader.

Prior to 1947, five incumbent whips (one of them twice) were in a position to succeed to a vacancy in the floor leadership, but only one of these, Charles Curtis of Kansas, advanced. Since 1947, all three Democrats who had that opportunity — Scott Lucas in 1949, Lyndon B. Johnson in 1953, and Michael J. "Mike" Mansfield in 1961 — did, in fact, become floor leaders. Three of the last four Republican whips with that opportunity — Kenneth Wherry in 1949, Everett Dirksen in 1959, and Hugh Scott in September, 1969 — made similar advancements. Only Leverett Saltonstall of Massachusetts was passed over, although in 1957 he became chairman of the Republican Conference. A majority of his Republican colleagues apparently considered him too liberal for the floor leadership position.

Some indication of the limited importance of the office up to the late 1940's can be gleaned from two facts. From 1935 until 1944, Republican Senators did not even bother to select a party whip, probably because of their reduced numbers during the New Deal period. Some whips, including Lister Hill of Alabama, Democratic whip from 1941–1947, voluntarily gave up the job because they did not feel the position was worth the effort.

Different from the House of Representatives, where the large number of members dictates the need for elaborate whip organizations, in the Senate whips usually have utilized staff to do any necessary minimum polling. As one whip describes the process:

> We usually delegate it to [Secretary to the Minority] to do the actual contacting. There are some [polls] where he can get a reading easier than we can. There are others where we can get it better than he can — it's just a personal situation . . . You have to know each [Senator] personally — how they react.

Whip notices have come into increasing prominence in recent years to alert members to pending floor action, the nature of unanimous consent agreements, and exactly when roll call votes can be expected.

Two further signs of the increasing institutionalization of Senate leadership came about in 1965 when Majority Leader Mansfield felt it necessary to appoint four assistant whips. The appointments stemmed from his concern over what he felt to be lack of adequate floor coverage from his assistant leader, Russell Long of Louisiana (see Chapter 12). Hugh Scott followed suit in 1969–1970 by designating six regional whips to assist the G.O.P. leadership in floor coverage. Aside from exposure to parliamentary practices probably the prime benefit gained from holding these positions is the modicum of prestige achieved back home rather than any vastly improved communication, added legislative strength, or a sense of enhanced party loyalty.

OTHER PARTY LEADERSHIP POSITIONS. Among other party positions, the chairmanship of the Republican Policy Committee and the secretary of the Democratic Conference have occasionally assumed enough importance over the years to warrant some separate discussion. Steering committees have waxed and waned in both parties since the 1880's, with most of their power until recent times dependent upon the personal prestige of their chairman. Thus, Robert A. Taft, chairman from 1944 until he assumed the position of majority floor leader at the opening of the 83d Congress in 1953, had more to say about overall Republican legislative policy than any of the interim floor leaders who followed Charles McNary of Oregon. Taft's effectiveness stemmed not only from his intellectual command of legislative problems, but also his prominence as a likely G.O.P. presidential candidate from 1940 until 1952. In 1947, following passage of the Legislative Reorganization Act of 1946, steering committees were renamed Policy Committees and allotted public funds.[13] Appropriations gradually were increased over the years from $64,670 each in 1947 to better than $280,000 in 1972.

The secretary of the Democratic Conference has rarely risen above the status of a party functionary except as a geographical or ideological balance to the two main leadership positions. From 1967 until his elevation to whip in 1971, Robert C. Byrd of West Virginia represented the border and southern states in the leadership; he also spent long hours on and around the Senate floor making himself invaluable to his colleagues. More so than in the House, the power of Senate leadership positions fluctuates to a large extent based on the drive, skill, and personal influence of the incumbent.

Over the past three decades leadership in the Senate G.O.P. has tended to be both more formal and decentralized than it has been in the Democratic party.[14] Both parties elect a floor leader and assistant floor leader, or whip, and a conference secretary. The Democratic floor leader also presides over meetings of all Democratic Senators in their conference, directs the formulation of party strategy and the scheduling of legislation as chairman of the Policy Committee. In addition, he guides the appointment of Democrats to Senate committees as chairman of his party's Steering Committee or committee on committees. In contrast, in the Republican party, the counterparts of these positions are held by four different Senators (see Figure 11.1). Thus, in terms of structural advantages, at least, the potential for strong, concentrated leadership remains much higher for Senate Democrats than for Senate Republicans.

Since World War II the office of the floor leader has gradually acquired stature, staff support, and institutionalized power. Some of the money to build staff came as an aftermath to the passage of the Legislative Reorganization Act of 1946. Other benefits are the direct result of *quid pro quos* arranged by strong leaders like Johnson and Dirksen. In their drive to consolidate power, they capitalized upon the importance attached to office space, funds, and staff in the legislative exchange process. Still, less aggressive leaders who succeeded them, men like Mansfield and Scott, have also reaped the benefit of these leadership emoluments. In 1970 the majority and minority leaders each received an annual salary of $49,500, or $7,000 more than other congressmen. Each enjoys the use of an impressive suite of offices located just off the Senate floor and has access to a chauffeur-driven limousine. Both offices are allotted four additional staff positions and annual appropriations of over $100,000. In the capacity as chairman of his party's policy committee, the Democratic leader also oversees a further allocation of more than a quarter of a million dollars annually.

Of course, floor leaders in the Senate are still heavily dependent upon personal persuasion — as distinct from formal powers — and external factors largely beyond their control: whether or not their party is that of the President, the size of their majority or minority, and the general climate for stability or change in the country. Perhaps the best illustration of the wide range of latitude allowed Senate majority leaders is provided by the contrasting styles of Lyndon B. Johnson, Democratic floor leader from 1953 to 1960 and Mike Mansfield of Montana, majority leader since 1961.

III

For the past two decades two Democratic floor leaders — Johnson of Texas and Mansfield of Montana — led Senate Democrats. Johnson took office as his party's minority leader in 1953, just four years after

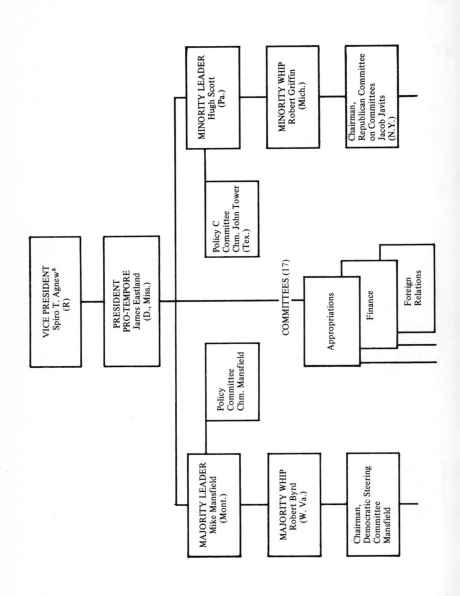

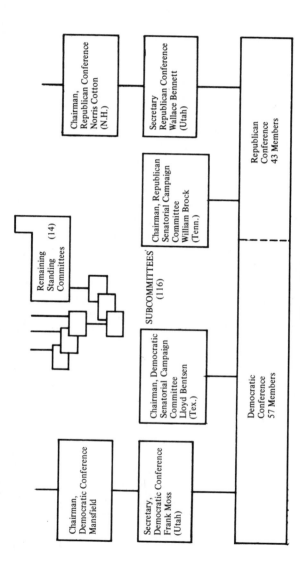

Figure 11-1

ᵃ Agnew resigned from the vice presidency on October 10, 1973 after pleading "no contest" to a charge of tax evasion. On October 12, 1973, President Richard M. Nixon nominated House Republican Leader Gerald R. Ford as a successor. Following Ford's confirmation and swearing-in on December 6, 1973, he served as Vice President until Nixon's resignation on August 9, 1974. After Ford was sworn in as President, he nominated former New York Governor Nelson Rockefeller to be Vice President on August 20, 1974. Four months later, after extensive Senate and House hearings, Rockefeller became the nation's 41st Vice President on December 19, 1974.

his first election to the Senate. He served as majority leader for six additional years (1955–1960) until his selection as the Democratic vice presidential nominee in 1960. After John F. Kennedy and Johnson were elected in November 1960, they supported the elevation of incumbent Democratic whip, Mike Mansfield, to floor leader in January, 1961. By 1975, the mild-mannered Montana Senator was serving his fifteenth consecutive year as Senate majority leader, a length of tenure exceeding by more than five years that of any previous incumbent.[15]

No definitive attempt to analyze the role of the Senate majority leader will be undertaken here.[16] An analysis would have to take into consideration the initial institutionalization of the office under John W. Kern of Indiana, the contributions of other acknowledged "strong" leaders such as Joseph T. Robinson of Arkansas and Alben Barkley of Kentucky, as well as the difficulties encountered by still other, less able leaders. Fortunately, Ralph K. Huitt has already provided the definitive treatment of the floor leader's job, especially as carried out by Lyndon B. Johnson from 1953 to 1960.[17] What follows is mainly an overview of Johnson's efforts as compared with the style of his successor, Mike Mansfield. While their contrasting leadership styles by no means exhaust the range of alternatives available to floor leaders, they do serve to highlight the considerable variations which appear to be both acceptable to and effective for the Senate majority party.

Despite its increasing institutionalization, the growth of staff, and its enhanced stature, the primary role of the majority leader remains similar to that at its inception, namely, to program and to expedite the flow of his party's legislation. The extent and relative success of the leader's role varies, of course, from one Congress to the next.

Bills are introduced by individual Senators with or without co-sponsorship. When the Administration and the Senate are controlled by the same party, most of the legislative program will be introduced by the relevant committee or subcommittee chairmen. Most bills are routinely referred to an appropriate committee by the parliamentarian, but from time to time the majority leader may intervene — for example, a civil rights bill may be sent first to a relatively friendly Commerce Committee in order to avoid its defeat at the hands of an unfriendly Judiciary Committee. Unlike procedures in the House of Representatives prior to 1975, bills may be referred to two or more committees for serial deliberation and modification. The sheer volume of legislation and jealously guarded committee prerogatives generally prevents party leaders from intervening in committee deliberations to any great extent. Thus, subcommittees almost without exception and full committees in most cases maintain unlimited control over legislation until it is reported out for floor consideration. About the best that any leader can do with a recalcitrant committee is to meet with its chairman and ask for cooperation. The floor leader, working closely with the Democratic Policy Committee, the Democratic whip, committee leaders, and the Republican leadership, decides when bills will come to the floor and under what conditions. As Lyndon Johnson summed up the process:[18]

> The Majority Leader is more than a leader of the majority. He is actually the leader of the Senate. As chairman of the Policy Committee, perhaps his most important function is programming the bills that come out of committee and ultimately become law.

In the case of most bills, those of a minor, technical, or noncontroversial nature, the majority leader merely assigns them to a calendar and routinely schedules them for floor deliberation. On Mondays, a call of the calendar is privileged business after the morning hour.[19] More controversial legislation is taken up in the Democratic Policy Committee and subsequently considered under unanimous consent agreements.

Policy committees were created for both parties by the Legislative Reorganization Act of 1946. Republicans, under the leadership of Robert Taft, quickly took advantage of the new funding. The Democratic Policy Committee largely remained inoperative, however, until Johnson assumed the minority leadership in 1953. He viewed the Policy Committee as "a potentially powerful instrument, a top strategy board of Senators with staff guidance from outside experts that would compete for ideas and policies with the executive branch of government."[20] Through shrewd appointments, including Earle Clements of Kentucky, minority whip, Johnson expanded his influence over the nine-member committee that already included his close associates, Russell of Georgia and Kerr of Oklahoma. Although the committee never quite attained the elevation Johnson hoped for, it did seem to become a personal Johnson appendage, and a center of new ideas. Its activities were often vital in helping Johnson seek and find essential legislative compromises.

Under Mansfield the Democratic Policy Committee underwent expansion in size and assumed a broader role in adopting positions on policy issues. It came to include the four formal leaders (the majority leader, majority whip, the President pro tempore of the Senate, and the secretary of the Democratic Conference), six members at large, and the four members of the Legislative Review Committee. In addition to giving Mansfield advice about legislation and floor scheduling, the Democratic Policy Committee met twice a month to debate policy and to issue statements on matters ranging from tax reform to the withdrawal of forces from Vietnam. The group's activities took on a new emphasis since 1969 after the Nixon Administration came to power. As Mansfield commented, "When the Democrats were in charge, we bowed to the President. Under Nixon, we function primarily as a policy determining committee." [21]

The Democratic Policy Committee is sometimes described as the counterpart to the House Committee on Rules, but this comparison is misleading. The Senate committee has no authority to issue rules governing floor debate, imposes no limits on time, and seldom delays a bill from being scheduled. Further, the Senate committee is a partisan committee and as such excludes minority members.

Bills of some controversy — that is to say, most legislation of import — once reported from committee, are placed on a Senate calendar. The majority leader, following consultation with his whip and the Policy Committee, confers with the minority leader and other interested Senators as to when the bill should be scheduled for floor action and how much time is anticipated for debate.

Increasingly, the Senate has come to rely heavily on unanimous consent agreements to close debate and bring amendments and the final bill to a vote. The ability of any Senator to speak for as long as he chooses is, of course, one of the most sacred traditions of the Senate. Hence, the need for the majority leadership to confer widely and extensively with other Senators who have an interest in a particular amendment or in the bill as a whole. On the other hand, all Senators jealously husband their time. They like to know from day to day when votes will be forthcoming and at what hour. Once the majority leader feels he has arrived at a consensus he will obtain the floor and ask for unanimous consent to close debate and vote at "a time certain," perhaps the following day or a day later. If no Senator objects then the unanimous consent agreement is entered into, and the business of the Senate is expedited.

A second, more extreme way to close debate in the Senate is by invoking Rule XXII, the filing of a cloture petition. Prior to a 1975 rules change, two-thirds of the Senators present and voting were required to vote in favor of limiting debate, and thus, achieve cloture. The present rule calls for a three-fifths or constitutional majority, that is, 60 or more Senators (out of 100) must favor cloture. Under both the old and the new cloture provisions no new amendments can be introduced and each Senator is limited to one hour on the bill or amendments already at the Senate clerk's desk. Leaders hesitate to invoke this mechanism because of the obvious difficulties in obtaining two-thirds (now three-fifths) support. From 1917, when the cloture rule was first adopted, through 1971, only 9 of 58 cloture votes passed. Nevertheless, two major civil rights bills, the Civil Rights Act of 1964 and the Voting Rights Act of 1965, were enacted into law after the successful invoking of cloture by Majority Leader Mansfield, strongly supported by President Johnson.[22]

Once legislation reaches the floor, the only formal power available to the majority leader is his right of recognition. The Vice President or the presiding officer must recognize the majority leader first. He then has the opportunity to express his viewpoint, to explain his reasons why he is for or against the particular amendment or bill, to yield to whom he chooses. An effective leader can exploit this right to initiate a legislative battle when he wants it and on the most favorable terms obtainable. Other than his formal prerogative to initiate legislation and to move to adjourn the Senate, a majority leader, like all other Senators, is left to rely on his style, his personality, and his powers of persuasion.

IV

The only real power available to the leader is the power of persuasion. There is no patronage; no power to discipline; no authority to fire Senators like a President can fire his members of Cabinet . . .

It's persuasion with colleagues on both sides of the aisle. Anything the Senate may do requires a majority vote. About all the leader can do is to recommend.

— Majority Leader Lyndon B. Johnson, 1960

What power do the leaders have to force these committees, to twist their arms, to wheel and deal, and so forth and so on, to get them to rush things up or to speed their procedure?

The leaders in the Senate, at least, have no power delegated
to them except on the basis of courtesy, accommodation, and
a sense of responsibility.

— Majority Leader Mike Mansfield, 1963

If both Majority Leaders Johnson[23] and Mansfield[24] are in agreement as to their limited powers, probably no two men ever brought
more contrasting personalities and styles of leadership to a common
leadership position. By all contemporary observations and accounts
the two men appeared to be nearly polar opposites in terms of such
personal qualities as aggressiveness, dominance, and power-seeking.
The adjectives most often used by his fellow Senators to describe
Johnson's style were "domineering," "ruthless," "shrewd," "forceful."
In contrast, Mansfield's personality is described with words like "gentle," "mild-mannered," "professorial," "fair." Such assessments must
be tempered with the awareness that Mansfield is also a political
leader of considerable effectiveness and thus is unable to avoid resorting to some forcefulness and aggression in his dealings with other
Senators. But, whereas Johnson seemed to thrive on the positive asser-
tion of leadership, Mansfield goes out of his way to avoid the open
exercise of power.

Mansfield did not seek a leadership position. Both the whip's job
in 1957 and the majority leadership position in 1961 were thrust upon
him, first by Johnson and later by Kennedy and Johnson. In contrast,
Johnson aggressively sought his leadership positions, actively cultivating the support of Richard Russell of Georgia, the Senate's dominant
oligarch in the post-World War II period.

Once in office Johnson expanded his powers through staff additions,
a revitalized Policy Committee, control over committee assignments,
involvement in leadership selection, and an enhanced legislative role.
Under the tight leadership reins of Lyndon Johnson, the selection of a
party whip was only a formality. Johnson conferred with other senior
Democratic influentials, such as the late Richard B. Russell of Georgia and Robert Kerr of Oklahoma, about the choice. Occasionally, a
preferred possibility, such as former Senator George Smathers of Florida in 1956, encountered too much opposition, and the choice de-
volved upon a less controversial Senator, in this instance, Mike Mansfield of Montana.[25] Both the selection of Mansfield and Johnson's
earlier choice of Earle Clements of Kentucky in 1953 were approved
routinely by a unanimous vote of the Senate Democratic Conference.

Again, Mansfield provides a contrast. He regularly returned about $150,000 a year in unspent Policy Committee funds to the Treasury, preferring to work with a "tight staff." [26] He expanded the size of the Democratic Policy Committee, added more junior members, and generally "democratized" its activities. Although he continued the "Johnson rule" of insuring that each freshman Senator received at least one major committee assignment, Mansfield appears to have preferred operating as but one member of the 17-member Democratic Steering Committee. Unlike Johnson, who took an active role in selecting his Democratic whips, Mansfield remained completely neutral in the whip contests of 1965, 1969, and 1971. "It's been my policy not to take a stand ahead of time, to let the caucus decide, and to lean toward those who have been in office — that's been my consistent practice."

A succinct and sympathetic description of Johnson's style of legislative leadership comes from Ralph Huitt:[27]

> Persuasion was, in Johnson's case, overwhelmingly a matter of personal influence. By all accounts, Johnson was the most personal among recent leaders in his approach. For years it was said that he talked to every Senator every day. Persuasion ranged from awesome pyrotechnics known as "Treatment A" to the apparently casual but always purposeful exchange as he roamed the floor and the cloakroom. He learned what a man wanted and would take, and he asked for help. He did not hesitate to "cross the aisle"; Republican votes saved him more than once, sometimes to the surprise and chagrin of *their* leadership.

Johnson could be tough, assertive, and even belligerent if the occasion demanded it. Evans and Novak assert that "the extra, indeed the dominant ingredient" in Johnson's success as a majority leader was his "overwhelming personality," best reflected in what came to be described as "The Treatment." [28]

> The Treatment could last ten minutes or four hours. It came, enveloping its target, at the LBJ Ranch swimming pool, in one of LBJ's offices, in the Senate cloakroom, on the floor of the Senate, itself — wherever Johnson might find a fellow Senator within his reach. Its tone could be supplication, accusation, cajolery, exuberance, scorn, tears, complaint, the hint of threat. It was all of these together. It ran the gamut of human emotions. Its velocity was breathtaking, and it was all

in one direction. Interjections from the target were rare. Johnson anticipated them before they could be spoken. He moved in close, his face a scant millimeter from his target, his eyes widening and narrowing, his eyebrows rising and falling. From his pockets poured clippings, memos, statistics. Mimicry, humor, and the genius of analogy made The Treatment an almost hypnotic experience and rendered the target stunned and helpless.

Despite his central position as majority leader, accompanied by an almost inevitable control over scheduling and the flow of legisla-tion on the floor, Mansfield goes out of his way to promote a climate in which every Senator is perceived and treated as equal to every other Senator. When Mansfield set a new record of continuous service as majority leader in 1970, Senator Robert Byrd of West Virginia, then the secretary of the Democratic conference, had this to say:[29]

> Mike Mansfield treats every Senator alike; and with respect to the use of his great power as majority leader, he is very, very careful in exercising that power.

Both the formal tributes paid to him in the *Congressional Record* over the years and the more candid remarks of his colleagues in off-the-record, focused interviews, stress his impartiality, fairness, and funda-mental decency as a human being.

The not-for-attribution comments of his colleagues were apt to be more critical of Mansfield while almost never neglecting to stress his fairness and quite competence. Observed one former Senator who served closely under both Johnson and Mansfield:

> I haven't seen my friend Mansfield, whom I like very much, do anything differently than [Johnson], except that he's much more patient and he doesn't run it [the Senate] nearly as harshly as Lyndon Johnson ran it. And Mansfield is a sweet fellow that lets everybody have his say. Johnson would cut 'em off, boy ... If he figured you were not going to say the right thing as far as he was concerned he'd figure out a way to ad-journ the Senate. And you could go out and make your speech on the Capitol steps ... Now, Mansfield doesn't do that. Mansfield is very, very fair, objective. He doesn't have any real close friends, he's just, he's just what he is — I don't guess there's ever been a fairer, really sweet fellow all the way around to everybody than Mansfield.

Mansfield's own characterization of his personal style as contrasted to Johnson's clearly bears out these striking personality differences. His response was as direct and short-hand as his reputation for laconic replies might have predicted:[30]

> There is a night and day difference. He was an outgoing person. My personality is somewhat retiring. He brought a vim, vigor, a desire to do the job, which I did not. He got votes by different methods than I do. He developed wounds which I have not. He won victories in the short run. I think I have worked toward victory over the long run.

Given their contrasting personalities and styles of leadership, can it be said that Johnson was more effective than Mansfield? With Robinson and Barkley, these men are the only majority leaders who have held that position for an extended period. Writing in 1960, Huitt could quite correctly observe that Johnson "was by general agreement the most skillful and successful in the memory of living observers." [31] That judgment could be extended to today, but Mansfield has nevertheless become an effective majority leader in his own right.[32]

Johnson had the advantage of serving his six years as majority leader with a relatively passive President of the opposing party.[33] In contrast, for his first eight years as floor leader, Mansfield served under Presidents of his own party. Harry McPherson, a staff assistant to both men, compares their respective strengths:[34]

> Now, in 1961, Mansfield was the obvious choice for Democratic leader. The initiative of government had shifted to the White House, to a President who promised forward motion instead of retrenchment, progress instead of vetoes. [Kennedy] needed a leader in the Senate who would serve as a conduit for his programs — not an independent source of power who wished to write his own. Johnson was the ideal opposition leader; Mansfield would be the perfect team player.

Both Kennedy and Johnson were relatively aggressive in terms of presenting legislative programs to Congress, although Kennedy was to find his programs thwarted throughout most of the 87th and part of the 88th Congresses. President Johnson, capitalizing upon the wave of sympathy that followed Kennedy's assassination, was to prove extremely effective as a domestic legislative leader, especially in the landmark first session of the 89th Congress (1965).[35] Johnson's troubles with Congress began with the escalation of the Vietnam War, not the least difficulty stemming from the strongly held opposing views of the Senate majority leader. After 1969, Mansfield resumed the role of a majority opposition leader, but this time against a legislatively aggressive Republican administration. As during the last six years of the Eisenhower Administration, President Nixon had to confront opposition majorities in both Houses of Congress from 1969 through 1974. Johnson had been able to cooperate with the President throughout most of Eisenhower's Administration. Nixon's more aggressive stance and the playing out of Watergate, however, caused the 92d and especially the 93d Congresses to become attempted veto-conversion sessions. Democratically controlled Congresses passed their own legislation, only to confront Nixon vetoes which proved extremely difficult to override, especially in the House.

Perhaps in terms of overall responsibility, no factor is more crucial than the nature of a Senate majority leader's relationship to the White House. Is his party in control of the presidency or is he a principal leader of the opposition? Mansfield may not have been as effective as Johnson in the latter role, but his contributions to the landmark legislation of the 89th Congress were impressive. Since Johnson never served in the capacity of a majority leader working with a President of his own party — and indeed may have accepted the vice presidential nomination in large part because he sensed the reduction in status that he probably would have encountered — no comparison between his potential effectiveness and Mansfield's actual accomplishments is possible.

Another reason comparisons are difficult is the size of the Democratic majorities available to the two leaders. Johnson began as a minority leader, but one vote away from assuming majority control. He commanded slender one- or two-vote majorities in the 84th and 85th Congresses. Not until after the landslide election of 1958, when Democrats increased their Senate margin to 66 to 34, did Johnson ever enjoy a strong legislative majority. Ironically, the infusion of the predominantly liberal class of 1958 not only produced a new cohesion and *esprit de corps* in Republican ranks, it also resulted in Johnson's most frustrating years as his party's legislative leader. With the liberal wing of his party in open revolt, the drab 86th Congress closed with a completely frustrating August rump session following the nominating conventions of the two parties.

Mansfield assumed control of two-to-one majorities throughout most of the Kennedy-Johnson Administrations. Not until the Nixon Administration did the size of the Democratic majority drop into the fifties — 58 to 42 in the 91st, 55 to 45 in the 92d, 57 to 43 in the 93d Congresses.

It can be argued that the more *laissez-faire*, permissive leadership of a Mansfield works better with larger, more unwieldy majorities and that, conversely, Johnson's tight, driving style of control was all but necessitated by narrower majorities where every vote counted. As already noted, Mansfield's skills seemed particularly suited for the role of majority leader shepherding the programs of activist Presidents of his own party; Johnson's skills as an opposition leader were unparalleled. In the final analysis, greater historical perspective is needed to evaluate fully the relative effectiveness of these two men, but they clearly illustrate the wide range of style allowable in effective Senate leadership.[36]

V

Although the United States Senate is characterized by much greater membership autonomy, less "distance" between freshmen and senior members and a much flatter hierarchy than the House, differences in status, seniority, and resources still exist. These constrasts naturally affect the attitudes and expectations which members hold vis-à-vis their leadership. Just as no one Senator is average, no one Senate can be said to be typical. Each includes a changing ratio of majority to minority party members; its exceptional and not so exceptional Senators; its critical issues, its legislative breakthroughs; its series of accommodations with the House, played out through conference committees; its separation of powers confrontations. The 93d Senate with its Watergate investigations, the resignation of the Vice President, its attempt to regain control over war powers, its many efforts to override presidential vetoes, and the threat of impeachment culminating in the President's resignation was certainly more politicized and involved more stark confrontations than any other recent Congress.

The stratification of the Senate of the 93d Congress was quite parallel to its predecessor. The 93d Senate consisted of 57 Democrats and 43 Republicans. The 92d Senate with 55 Democrats and 45 Republicans was more closely divided along party lines than any Senate since the 85th (1957–1958) with 49 Democrats and 47 Republicans.[37] In terms of seniority, the bottom one-third of the 92d Senate had not yet served a full term of six years; the middle one-third were in their second terms or had barely launched a third term (mainly Democratic members of the bench-mark class of 1958 which had broken apart the close partisan division of the Senate); the top one-third of the Senate hierarchy included all of its committee chairmen except four — Labor and Public Welfare, Post Office and Civil Service, District of Columbia, and Veterans' Affairs.

These divisions roughly approximate the threefold breakdown of the House into newcomers, middle-range experienced members, and senior members, many of them occupying positions as chairmen or ranking minority members. What clearly differentiates Senators from House members is not only their relative proportion of the total amount of congressional power (however loosely defined or measured), but also their visibility and relatively quick absorption into the power structure. In the Senate, even the most recently arrived freshman is not all that distant from the highest ranking committee chairman or party leader; the House freshmen are much more junior and isolated. No Senator is ever unimportant or totally ineffective, even the most aged, ailing, or alcoholic. Senators inherently are more visible than their House counterparts. Senators' individual activities are covered closely by the national press corps and they have many opportunities to make the evening news or to appear on national talk shows. For these reasons, their probability of becoming household names statewide, if not throughout the nation, is greatly enhanced. A former lower-echelon House leader who became a Senator indicated one manifestation of this visibility:

> A Senator is far more powerful as an individual, even than [most] of the . . . leaders in the House. He is far more able to pronounce, able to influence, public opinion. No media programs came to me in the House and asked me to appear, whereas they were all interested in me as the Senator from
>
> ———————.

Moreover, most freshman Senators move almost immediately into formal positions of committee leadership. Fully 55 of the 57 Democratic Senators in the 93d Congress (1973–1974) took advantage of the staff assistance and other benefits flowing from the incumbency of at least one subcommittee chairmanship.[38] Only one Republican Senator, William V. Roth, Jr. of Delaware, did not hold at least one ranking minority position on either of his committees (Finance and Government Operations). In contrast to House members, who wait six or eight years to achieve similar positions, this rapid rise in stature is striking.

Given a Senator's relative autonomy, abundant opportunities for media exposure, and quick immersion in legislative matters, there is little reason to wonder at the lack of deference which even the lowliest freshman seems to accord his party leaders. Respect, trust, and even accommodation are readily demonstrated, but very little awe or excessive veneration is apparent.

A freshman Democrat contrasted the differing leadership styles of Mike Mansfield and Lyndon Johnson and related why he preferred the more relaxed, decentralized style of Majority Leader Mansfield:

> Mike is an easygoing leader. He seldom communicates with other Senators — he's like a sphinx.
>
> I don't know in the long run whether a loose or tight-running leadership is better. It was tight under LBJ; now it's loose. I'm not sure which is a better adversary to the executive . . . I prefer a loose ship because I've become a maverick.

Another maverick, a liberal Republican, told of a direct challenge to his Republican floor leader during his first year in office. The younger Senator was attempting to "resuscitate" the nomination of a controversial executive branch appointee which was being held up by the minority leader.

> In Senate fashion, I spent five pages eulogizing [Senate leader] — round phrases, "great statesman" — then on the last page, the knife came out.
>
> Just before the speech he was standing in the cloakroom. I walked over and gave him a copy of the speech. He said, "I won't read that." I said, "It's a courtesy." And he looked at me and said, "Courtesy? You just remember this, I've got some political clout and you're going to hear from me."

A conservative freshman Republican was quick to affirm the kind of freedom which would allow such a speech to be made in the first place. In the process he noted his independence not only from his leadership but also from a Republican White House:

> I don't know that anybody influences Senators very much. I've read reports of how the President had people down and

twisted their arms, but I don't think it happens. In most cases
the people who claim to have had their arms twisted vote
against the President anyway . . . And as to whether or not the
floor leader could influence votes, I think he does it by virtue
of his personality or his ability to persuade. So far as having
any force to use, I don't think it's in the cards. I don't think
Senators are put together that way.

A southern Democratic freshman reports his view of a changing
Senate:

Before, younger members felt that you didn't speak in your
first term and that you waited until you had something to say.
There used to be a big thing of the maiden speech. People
would be notified and they'd come over. I don't even know
anybody who makes a maiden speech now — that's all
changed . . .

And of course many of us come from Congress or from legislative experience in your state. There wasn't anything intimidat-
ing to me about the U.S. Senate after 12 years of legislative
work.

What seems to be occurring in the Senate of the late 1960's and
early 1970's is a general abandonment of the norm of apprenticeship
— that freshman Senators are expected to assume a quiescent, subordinate and deferential role to senior Senators, including their
leaders.[39] Instead, incoming members are seldom hesitant about speaking out; they play an immediate and active role in legislation; they are
out to establish a visible and public record from the start.

A number of observers, journalists, political scientists, and Senators
themselves began to call attention to this dispersal of power in the
early and middle 1960's. As *New York Times* correspondent Tom
Wicker commented in 1965:[40]

The Senate of the United States is today a mildly progressive
legislative body in which the Old South has lost its grip, in
which junior members are playing increasingly important roles,
in which the fabled power of the committee chairman has been
scattered, and in which the dominant influences are those of
urban, industrialized America and the President of the United
States.

Not all observers were as quick to notice the "winds of change"
blowing in the Senate. The myth of an "inner club" dominated by

"Senate types," as propounded most notably in William S. White's *Citadel: The Story of the U.S. Senate*,[41] continued to survive into the late 1960's. In a May 1967 *Harper's* essay, Clayton Fritchey labored mightily to list the men "who really run the Upper House — how they are chosen, what they do, and how they hold on to their power." [42]

However, as Nelson W. Polsby persuasively pointed out in his 1969 essay, "Goodbye to the Inner Club," White's idea of an inner club

> vastly underplayed the extent to which *formal* position — committee chairmanships, great seniority, and official party leadership — conferred power and status on individual Senators almost regardless of their clubability. Second, it understated the extent to which power was spread by specialization and the need for cooperative effort. Fritchey's list bears this out: of 92 nonfreshman Senators in 1967, he listed 53 as members or provisional members of the Inner Club.[43]

As Polsby was to conclude, elsewhere: [44]

> We can think of the internal politics of the Senate not as a small group of powerful men surrounded by everybody else, but as a group which divides labor and power — unequally to be sure, but still significantly — among almost all of its members.

A further reason why freshman Senators appear to enjoy greater independence compared to their predecessors of two decades before, let alone their contemporary House counterparts, is because their leaders have little or no control over committee assignments. Mike Mansfield, the Democratic majority leader, continues to appoint the members and preside over the Democratic Steering Committee. At his direction both the Democratic whip and the secretary of the conference have become members with full voting rights. But in keeping with his quiet, accommodating style of leadership, Mansfield seldom takes an active role in the trading and bargaining which characterizes this committee's deliberations. The Johnson rule — that every freshman Senator should receive at least one important committee assignment before the seniority system takes over — continues in force. Most assignments are not heavily contested. But when a seat opens up on a prestige committee like Finance or Appropriations, the leadership seldom acts with one voice and almost never is the major beneficiary in terms of political credits. The winning candidate is not necessarily the most senior member but the one who can align a majority of commitments from the members of the Steering Committee.

The Republican leadership has even less direct influence on committee assignments. Neither Minority Leader Scott nor Assistant Leader Griffin is a member of the 18-member Republican Committee on Committees. Save for a modified version of the Johnson rule adopted in 1971, all Republican assignments are awarded strictly on the basis of seniority. James L. Buckley, a freshman Senator from New York, describes the process as "mechanical." [45]

> Once the minority vacancies on the various committees become known, the Republican members of the incoming class line up in order of seniority, and take their pick. Each Senator is appointed to two major committees, and often to one or more minor ones. My own initial assignments were to Public Works, Space, and the District of Columbia.

On rare occasions an "undesirable" member can be kept off a committee through the process of persuading another, more senior, member to apply for the post, but that is only the extension of a strict seniority principle.

Another significant development enhancing the relative independence of incoming freshmen, Democrats and Republicans alike, has been the formation of class clubs, differing from their House counterparts in that they are bipartisan in membership. Both the Senate classes of 1970 and 1972 have held meetings and collectively lobbied their more senior colleagues on various housekeeping matters (size of staff allowances, space allocations, information capabilities) and rule changes. As one of the principal activists in the class of 1970 observed:

> I think they had some class clubs before but I don't think they leaned on people like we are. I think they were a little more leery of what they would do. They didn't want to rock the boat as much.

> We went to the last Legislative Appropriations Committee meeting. Seventeen members showed up and argued for an increase in clerk-hire provisions.

Although the focus of these class clubs is necessarily limited — substantive issues with any partisan or ideological aspects would drive them apart — they compose nearly 40 percent of the Senate member-ship and thus represent a strong potential force for change.

Senators in the middle range of seniority, a term or two already behind them, seem less likely than their House counterparts to un-dergo an agonizing slow-down or frustration of their career develop-ment. Since every Senator serves on two and often three or four committees, the assignment process seldom takes on the career im-portance that it does in the House. If things go badly on one com-mittee, a Senator can shift his legislative efforts to another issue area. Amendments during floor debate from non-committee members are not discouraged as they are in the House. Since committees are smaller (an average of 13 to 17 members as compared with 35 or more mem-bers in the House), upward movement is both more visible and actual.

Not unlike upwardly mobile House members looking toward a Senate career, the transitional Senator (no longer a freshman, but not yet a committee chairman) is not infrequently tempted to bid for his party's presidential nomination. The ten Democratic Senators who either announced or were frequently mentioned as possible presiden-tial aspirants in 1971–1972 — Bayh, Harris, Hughes, Humphrey, Hartke, Jackson, McGovern, Kennedy, Muskie, and Proxmire — averaged about 12 years of Senate experience. Only Senator Jackson had been elected to more than three consecutive terms. George McGovern, the eventual Democratic presidential nominee, was serv-ing out his tenth year in the Senate. John F. Kennedy had two fewer years in the Senate when he successfully ran for the presidency in 1960. Although Majority Leader Johnson had 23 years of congressional service behind him in 1960, only the last 12 had been in the Senate. Republican Senator Barry Goldwater was completing his twelfth year of Senate service with only 11 Republicans more senior to him when he sought the presidency in 1964. .

Of course, opportunities to run for the presidency are not restricted to Senators of the middle range in seniority. Interior Chairman Jack-son is a case in point. Richard Russell of Georgia, the de facto Demo-cratic power in the Senate for many years, was said to have broken down in tears when he failed to win his party's presidential nomina-tion in 1952. Then only 54 years of age, Russell was already second-ranking to Carl Hayden of Arizona in terms of service (Hayden had begun his Senate career in 1927, Russell in 1933).

Democratic chairmen, Republican ranking minority members, and other high-ranking committee members are, for the most part, too deeply enamored of their Senate careers, too intensely involved in the areas of their legislative specialization, and too old in age and service to seriously consider a quest for their party's presidential nomination.[46]

Like the most prestigious committee chairmen in the House, most Senate senior members consider themselves at least the peers of their party leaders and sometimes a bit superior to them. Part of their independent stance comes from length of service; they have seen party leaders come and go. Part stems from the history of the position; floor leaders were not formally recognized as such until after World War I.[47] For most of the 1920's through the 1940's, these offices were seen more as a necessary appendage rather than a central mechanism in the scheduling and implementation of legislation.

When asked early in 1963 why the Kennedy-Johnson legislative program seemed to be going nowhere, the former majority leader, then Vice President, Johnson told one of his former Senate aides: "We've got all of the minnows; we've got none of the whales." This staff member, Harry McPherson, later described some of the characteristics of the "whales" who have dominated the Senate in past years — Russell, Anderson, Kerr, Taft, and more recently, Magnuson, Stennis, Long, and Williams.[48]

> Whales were chairmen, but not all chairmen were whales. Whales had the negative power to stop legislation, either because they opposed it or were indifferent to it. A controversial proposal could not pass without their friendly intervention. Not that all of them had to support it; the consent of only one or two was required to give the rest of the Senate confidence that a bill — like a stock issue backed by a respected underwriter — was all right to support.

Although McPherson mainly limits his analysis to Democratic Senators, the minority party also had its share of influentials — for example, Aiken, Bridges, Cooper, and Millikin. An illustration provided by a Republican Senator, even if it is somewhat self-serving, suggests how crucial an amendment's sponsor can be:

> A man got up in the Senate and offered an amendment about three years ago, for which he got some seven votes, one of which was mine. The minority secretary came over and said to me: "I agree with you, I think that's not a bad amendment and if you'll offer it, you'll get 35 votes."

> And that's true, I would have. The reason was that others didn't like him. They don't have an anti-feeling as far as I'm concerned, even though I do scrap with a lot of people on the floor.

The personality of a member and the trust and confidence that his colleagues place in him remain central features of legislative success in both Houses of Congress. Not surprisingly, personal relationships seem to take different forms in the two bodies. Some House members can develop close, long-lasting friendships with a few members, usually from their own delegation and committees. Close Senate friendships are probably more rare in part because members are more "star-struck" and cross-pressured for time. Still, Senators are thrown together more intensively on the floor, inevitably gaining a much more thorough sense of the strengths and weaknesses of *all* of their colleagues. Leaders, intensively involved in almost all legislative matters and extensively on their feet during debate, are subject to especially intense scrutiny and continuous reevaluation by their colleagues.

In both bodies each member has one vote, and is thus constitutionally and theoretically equal to every other member. Clearly, personal skills and technical competence as well as the inevitable workings of the seniority system and the acquisition of positional power make some members "more equal than others." The range of that inequality, especially for leaders, appears to be more disparate in the larger body than in the smaller. Furthermore, as David Truman has observed, formal leaders are more likely to be actual leaders in the larger body.[49] On the other hand, Senate leaders, operating with fewer constraints and greater flexibility, may have more opportunity for unusually strong influence over legislation and national public policy. Overall, the most important situational constraints affecting the success of Senate party leaders are the basic, if not increasing, independence of individual Senators, the size and cohesion of the majority or minority he works with, and whether or not the White House is occupied by an activist President of his own party.

Now that we have some indication of the major party positions in the Senate, how these positions became institutionalized, and what the modern conception of leadership votes is, it is possible to explore Senate leadership selection processes in greater depth. Chapters 12 and 13 treat three Democratic majority whip contests: Russell Long's victory over several contenders at the opening of the 89th Congress (January 1965); Edward Kennedy's surprising upset of the incumbent whip, Long, at the opening of the 91st Congress (1969); and Robert Byrd's defeat of Kennedy at the opening of the 92d Congress (1971). With the death of Minority Leader Everett M. Dirksen in September 1969, Republicans were faced with the problem of selecting a new floor leader (Chapter 14). Hugh Scott, the incumbent whip, was able to win out over several conservatives, especially newcomer Howard Baker of Tennessee. Two years later, Scott withstood another challenge from Baker by an almost identical vote. Chapter 15 takes a longer and more analytical look at Senate leadership selection patterns over 10 Congresses, the 84th to 93d (1955–1974).

NOTES

1. Rowland Evans and Robert Novak, *Lyndon B. Johnson: The Exercise of Power* (New York: New American Library, 1966), pp. 63–64.
2. "Democrats: The General Manager," *Time*, June 22, 1953, p. 20. For background on Russell's unusual role as de facto leader in the Senate, see Evans and Novak, *op. cit.*, esp. pp. 39–40, 63–64; Frederick W. Collins, "Senator Russell in the Last Ditch," *New York Times Magazine*, October 20, 1963, pp. 16ff; Douglas Kiker, "Russell of Georgia: The Old Guard at its Shrewdest," *Harper's*, September 1966, pp. 101–106; and Harry McPherson, *A Political Education* (Boston: Little, Brown, 1972), esp. pp. 54–56.
3. But see Floyd M. Riddick, "Majority and Minority Leaders of the Senate: History and Development of the Offices of the Floor Leaders," Senate Doc. 92-42, 92d Cong., 1st Sess. (Washington, D.C.: U.S. Government Printing Office, 1971); Walter J. Oleszek, "Majority and Minority Whips of the Senate: History and Development of the Party Whip System in the United States Senate," Senate Doc. 92-86, 92d Cong., 2d Sess. (Washington, D.C.: U.S. Government Printing Office, 1972); David J. Rothman, *Politics and Power: The United States Senate, 1869–1901* (Cambridge: Harvard University Press, 1966); Randall B. Ripley, *Power in the Senate* (New York: St. Martin's Press, 1969); and Margaret R. Munk, "Origin and Development of the Party Floor Leadership in the United States Senate," Ph.D. dissertation, Harvard University, 1970.
4. Riddick, *op. cit.*, p. 2.
5. As Mike Mansfield comments on the common practice: " . . . we try to treat other Senators as we would like to be treated. We don't step on their prerogatives or interfere with their responsibilities. When the Senate is acting on a bill, I make way for the chairman of the committee that handled that bill, let him sit in the Leader's chair while I take my place as a Senator." "A Size-up of President Nixon: Interview with Mike Mansfield, Senate Democratic Leader," *U.S. News and World Report*, December 6, 1971, p. 60.
6. Rothman, *op. cit.*, pp. 43–72; Ripley, *op. cit.*, pp. 26–29; Nathaniel W. Stephenson, *Nelson W. Aldrich: A Leader in American Politics* (New York: Scribners, 1930); Leland L. Sage, *William Boyd Allison* (Iowa City: University of Iowa Press, 1956); John R. Lambert, *Arthur Pue Gorman* (Baton Rouge: Louisiana State University Press, 1963).

7. Riddick, *op. cit.*, p. 1.
8. Rothman, *op. cit.*, p. 4.
9. Ripley, *op. cit.*, p. 26.
10. Claude G. Bowers, *The Life of John Worth Kern* (Indianapolis: Hollenbeck, 1918); Randall B. Ripley, *Majority Party Leadership in Congress* (Boston: Little, Brown, 1969), ch. 3.
11. Floor "leaders" were not formally designated as such in the minutes of the two party conferences until 1920 for the Democrats and 1925 for the Republicans. The Democratic floor leader continues to serve as ex-officio chairman of the Democratic Conference; the Republican Conference formally separated the two positions in 1945.
12. Oleszek, *op. cit.*, p. 4.
13. Hugh A. Bone, *Party Committees and National Politics* (Seattle: University of Washington Press, 1958); Bone, "An Introduction to the Senate Policy Committee," *Am. Pol. Sci. Rev.* **50** (1956), 339–359.
14. From the vantage point of the 1950's, Donald R. Matthews would conclude: "Democratic party leadership is highly personalized, informal, centralized in the hands of the floor leader [p. 123] ... Even when compared with the Democratic party under a relatively weak leader, the Republican leadership is more formalized, institutionalized, and decentralized" (p. 124). *U. S. Senators and Their World* (Chapel Hill: University of North Carolina Press, 1960). The decentralized leadership style of Mike Mansfield, majority leader since 1961, and the drive toward centralization of Everett Dirksen, minority leader from 1959 to 1969, only partially compromise these generalizations.
15. Senator Alben Barkley (D., Ky.) held the previous record of 9 years and 165 days, having been first elected as majority floor leader on July 22, 1937 and serving in that capacity until January 3, 1947. Upon reelection to the position of floor leader in January 1975, Mansfield surpassed the record of 14 consecutive years of floor leadership (majority and minority) held by Joseph Robinson (D., Ark.). *Congressional Record* (daily ed.), June 23, 1970, pp. S 9560–9564.
16. The focus here is not upon "what *should* be the role of the Senate majority leader?" but rather "what *is* the range of alternative styles open to contemporary majority leaders?" Unfortunately, the two kinds of questions have not always been kept distinct in the literature of role theory. The first in inherently an "ought" or value-laden concern; the second an empirical question. In the analysis which follows, I have attempted to use *role* as the generic term for the range of expectations and activities accompanying a given position, such as the majority leader, and to refer to *style* as the particular traits, mannerisms, and techniques with which any incumbent infuses a particular role. Empirically, of course, role and style are inextricably mixed. However, for analytical purposes they can be isolated and discussed separately.
17. Ralph K. Huitt, "Democratic Party Leadership in the Senate," *Am. Pol. Sci. Rev.* **55** (1961), 333–344. Reprinted in R. K. Huitt and Robert L. Peabody, *Congress: Two Decades of Analysis* (New York: Harper & Row, 1969), pp. 136–158.
18. "Leadership: An Interview with Senate Leader Lyndon Johnson," *U.S. News and World Report*, June 27, 1960, pp. 88–93, at 88.
19. For a more extensive discussion of the various Senate calendars and ways of bringing bills to the floor, see Lewis A. Froman, Jr., *The Congressional Process* (Boston: Little, Brown, 1967), ch. 7.
20. Evans and Novak, *op. cit.*, p. 61.

21. Andrew J. Glass, "Congressional Report: Mansfield Reforms Spark 'Quiet Revolution' in Senate," *National Journal*, Reprint No. 16 (Minneapolis: Winston Press, 1972), p. 9.
22. Raymond E. Wolfinger, "Filibusters: Majority Rules, Presidential Leadership and Senate Norms," in Wolfinger, ed., *Readings on Congress* (Englewood Cliffs, N.J.: Prentice-Hall, 1970); John G. Stewart, "Independence and Control: The Challenge of Senatorial Party Leadership," Ph.D. dissertation, University of Chicago, 1968).
23. "Leadership: An Interview with Senate Leader Lyndon Johnson," *op. cit.*, p. 89.
24. *Congressional Record* (daily ed.), November 18, 1963, pp. 20972–75, at 73.
25. As one Senator describes the process, "LBJ would try to influence the selection of whip. He would see or call influential Senators — 'how about so and so?' He'd be in a position of suggestion. Most of us would wind up saying to the majority leader, 'Well, who do you think it should be?' . . . At one time Smathers was all but cleared. But then, the liberals and labor objected, and then there was the problem of two leaders from the South. So then Johnson went back to the Senate influentials. 'How about Mansfield?' By the time it got to the conference, it was cut and dried."
26. Glass, *op. cit.*, p. 9. In contrast, the Republican Policy Committee customarily spends nearly all of its annual appropriation.
27. Huitt, *op. cit.*, p. 338.
28. Evans and Novak, *op. cit.*, p. 104.
29. *Congressional Record* (daily ed.), June 23, 1970, p. S 9563.
30. Interview with Mansfield, August 8, 1972. Unfortunately, I was never able to ask President Johnson the same question, or have I been able to uncover any in-depth assessment of how he viewed his successor's style and personality. Mansfield was not Johnson's first choice for whip and the two men didn't work as closely together in the leadership as Johnson and Earle Clements, Mansfield's predecessor. Their relationship after Johnson succeeded to the presidency appeared to be one of mutual respect, but the relationship became increasingly estranged in the middle and late 1960's because of Mansfield's opposition to Johnson's Vietnam policies.
31. Huitt, *op. cit.*, p. 144. The rhetoric of Evans and Novak was even stronger: ". . . Lyndon B. Johnson had tamed the Senate within an eight-year span unmatched in accomplishment or mastery." *Op. cit.*, p. 224.
32. Glass. *op cit.*; Julius Duscha, "Mike Mansfield: Straight Shooter in the Senate," *The Washingtonian* 5 (September 1970), pp. 37–44.
33. As Huitt argues, the situation of a majority leader who controls Senate programming responsibilities while working with a President of the opposite party (Johnson's situation) is perhaps the most advantageous relationship. On the other hand, being majority leader under a legislatively aggressive President operating without adequate popular support is probably the most difficult situation (a Lucas or McFarland under President Truman). *Op. cit.*, p. 336.
34. McPherson, *op. cit.*, p. 183.
35. Tom Wicker, *JFK and LBJ: The Influence of Personality Upon Politics* (Baltimore: Penguin Books, 1969).
36. After completion of this section, I discovered that John G. Stewart had already undertaken and published a comparable analysis, "Two Strategies of Leadership: Johnson and Mansfield," in Nelson W. Polsby, ed., *Congressional Behavior* (New York: Random House, 1971), pp. 61–92. Stewart's essay, distilled from his 1968 University of Chicago dissertation (cited in

n. 22), is based, in part, upon close personal observation as a staff assistant for Senator Humphrey while he was majority whip. Stewart's essay is especially useful in its attempt to analyze the impact of the Johnson and Mansfield leadership strategies, pp. 78–87. Our independently arrived-at conclusions are quite parallel.

37. Both Congresses included two Senators nominally affiliated with the major parties, Harry F. Byrd, Jr. (Indep.-Dem., Va.) and James L. Buckley (Conserv.-Rep., N.Y.).

38. Norman J. Ornstein and David W. Rhode, "Seniority and Future Power in Congress," in N. Ornstein, ed., *Congress in Change* (New York: Praeger, 1975).

39. "The first rule of Senate behavior, and the one most widely recognized off the Hill, is that new members are expected to serve a proper apprenticeship." Matthews, *op. cit.*, p. 92. The abandonment of this norm shows up in my leadership change interviews and is also consistently rejected in a series of interviews on Senate internal decision-making processes conducted in 1973–1974 by Rohde, Ornstein, and Peabody. See "Political Change and Legislative Norms in the United States Senate," paper delivered before the meetings of the American Political Science Association, Chicago, September 2, 1974.

40. "Winds of Change in the Senate," *New York Times Magazine*, September 12, 1965, p. 52.

41. Published by Harper & Row, New York, 1956.

42. *Harper's*, May 1967, pp. 104–110.

43. *Washington Monthly* (August 1969), pp. 30–34; reprinted in Nelson W. Polsby, ed., *Congressional Behavior* (New York: Random House, 1971), pp. 105–110, at 107.

44. *Congress and the Presidency* (Englewood Cliffs, N.J.: Prentice-Hall, 1964), p. 45.

45. James L. Buckley, "On Becoming a United States Senator," *National Review*, February 2, 1973, p. 142. Prior service as a Senator, member of the House, or governor (in that order) enhances an incoming member's seniority. Remaining ties are resolved in favor of Senators from states with larger population sizes.

46. To take only members of the top third of the 92d Congress in terms of seniority, the 20 Democrats averaged 66 years of age and 20 years of service; the 13 Republicans averaged 70 years of age and 19 years of service. (By way of comparison, Dwight D. Eisenhower, the oldest candidate to succeed to the presidency, was 62 when he ran for his first term in 1952.)

47. Riddick, *Majority and Minority Leaders of the Senate, op. cit.*, pp. 1–4.

48. McPherson, *op. cit.*, p. 49.

49. David B. Truman, *The Congressional Party* (New York: Wiley, 1959), pp. 96–97.

CHAPTER TWELVE

Selections of Senate Majority Whips:
Long, 1965; Kennedy, 1969

What leadership abilities are hoped for in a party whip? Benjamin Disraeli, British Prime Minister from 1874 to 1880, once provided a most aspiring statement: the position demanded "consummate knowledge of human nature, the most amiable flexibility, and complete self-control." [1] The duties of contemporary House and Senate party whips can be said to incorporate many of the responsibilities of their nineteenth century House of Commons' counterparts. But it was probably as difficult then, as it is now, to locate and reelect party whips who fully measure up to Disraeli's exacting standards.

This chapter and Chapter 13 tell the tale of three Senate majority whips: Russell B. Long of Louisiana, Edward M. Kennedy of Massachusetts, and Robert C. Byrd of West Virginia. Senator Long was first elected whip in 1965 and served until his defeat by Senator Kennedy in January 1969. Two years later, Senator Byrd was to upset Kennedy with Long's enthusiastic assistance. All three Democrats continue to serve with distinction in the United States Senate: Long as chairman of the powerful Committee on Finance; Kennedy as a leading candidate for the Democratic presidential nomination, if not in 1976, then perhaps in 1980; and Byrd, as the incumbent majority whip and leading heir apparent to the majority leadership.

HISTORICAL BACKGROUND. From 1961 to 1964 the Senate was led by Majority Leader Mike Mansfield, assisted by Hubert H. Humphrey as majority whip. Although the Kennedy legislative program had been stalemated for most of the 87th Congress (1961–1962), by the first session of the 88th Congress it had begun to gain momentum. Then, on November 22, 1963, John Fitzgerald Kennedy, the 35th President of the United States, was assassinated in Dallas, Texas. Once Vice President Lyndon B. Johnson assumed the presidency, he moved quickly to grasp the reins of power and to implement the Kennedy legislative program. In terms of overall legislative output, the difference between the first and second sessions of the 88th Congress was dramatic. Banking on the wave of sympathy for the slain president, Johnson was able to put through such important legislation as the Civil Rights Act of 1964, a major tax cut, a program waging war on poverty, a federal pay bill, an urban mass transportation act, and a foreign aid program.

From early in 1964 it was apparent that President Johnson would be a strong favorite to win a full four-year term in his own right. Operating in a political climate which gave him almost complete freedom to choose his vice-presidential running mate, Johnson went to the Senate to select Hubert H. Humphrey, the Democratic whip. The Republican National Convention, meeting in San Francisco from July 13 to 16, opted for conservatives Senator Barry M. Goldwater of Arizona and William E. Miller of New York. Controlling the vital center of the American electorate, the Johnson-Humphrey ticket won handily.[2] President Johnson and Senator Humphrey led the Democratic party to its greatest national victory since 1936. They won by 61.4 percent of the popular vote.

Only an unusual degree of ticket-splitting saved the Republican party from complete disaster in Congress. Democrats gained but two seats in the Senate making the new balance 68 Democrats and 32 Republicans. The G.O.P. suffered a net loss of 38 seats in the House, reducing their total number of seats to the lowest figure since depression days, 140 Republican Representatives.

I

Competition for the majority whip's job vacated by Senator Humphrey got underway, if quietly, as soon as Senators returned from the August recess for the Democratic presidential nominating convention. Early speculation included the possible candidacies of Senator John O. Pastore of Rhode Island, the Democratic keynoter at the convention; Senator George A. Smathers of Florida, the secretary of the Democratic Conference; and Senator Thomas Dodd of Connecticut. Pastore was to emerge as the leading liberal candidate; Smathers was to decide against running in part because of what he termed the "confining" and rather mechanical nature of the job. Dodd's possible candidacy never really went beyond his brief moment in the limelight as a possible vice-presidential candidate when he accompanied Humphrey on the plane which flew down from Atlantic City to the White House during the 1964 Democratic Convention.[3]

THE CONTESTANTS. By November 1964, the field narrowed to three contenders, Russell B. Long of Louisiana, A. S. "Mike" Monroney of Oklahoma, and John O. Pastore of Rhode Island.[4] Of the three, Long was youngest at 46 but, more important, the candidate with the greatest seniority. Heir to the Huey Long dynasty, he was first elected to the Senate on November 2, 1948, one day before his 30th birthday (and the minimum constitutional age for a Senator). Pastore, 57, and Monroney, 62, had both been elected to the Senate for the first time in 1950.

The possible candidacies of two more junior Senate Democrats, Phillip A. Hart of Michigan and Edmund S. Muskie of Maine, briefly surfaced in late December. Neither seemed to have the requisite seniority, and the candidacy of either would have further diluted whatever chance northern liberals had to maintain the position in the hands of one of their own.

John Pastore, the fiery and aggressive legislator from Rhode Island, became the prime liberal hope for the job. Born March 17, 1907 to poor Italian immigrants, Pastore had helped to support his family and worked his way through Providence schools until he finally secured a law degree from Northeastern University in 1931. From his first successful race for the Rhode Island House of Representatives in 1934, through the governorship (1946–1950), and successive elections to the United States Senate beginning in 1950, Pastore had never lost an election.

Pastore's 5 ft. 4 in. height and his frequently caustic debating techniques quickly earned him the label of the Senate's "bantam rooster." "In 1957, walking and gesturing rapidly amid the semicircular rows of Senate desks, he gave the most powerful civil rights speech Congress heard in the decade." [5] His skill in debating and parliamentary tactics was unquestioned, but his aggressiveness (which has taken him across the floor to shout his arguments into the face of an opponent) has not endeared him to some of his more mild-mannered or conservative colleagues.

Early appointments to the Senate Commerce Committee and the

Joint Atomic Energy Committee launched Pastore toward a widely-acknowledged expertise in communications policy and atomic energy legislation. As a result of his debating skills he has frequently been called upon to speak in behalf of other legislation, such as foreign aid, which had fallen outside of his committee jurisdictions. As floor manager of such controversial legislation as the 1962 nuclear test ban treaty, the communications satellite bill, and wheat sales to Russia, he had earned the plaudits of some, but the animosity of others.

By 1965, Pastore also served as tenth-ranking member of the Senate Appropriations Committee and chairman of its Deficiencies and Supplementals Subcommittee. The wide scope of this subcommittee's jurisdiction gave Pastore frequent opportunities to support the needs of friendly Senators or make life more complicated for enemies.

Pastore's principal opponent and the eventual winner of the whip contest was likeable, ebullient Russell Long of Louisiana. Born in November 1918, the same month that his father, Huey Long, won his first political office, Russell Long was raised in the kind of penultimate political family that warrants both comparison and contrast with the Kennedys, the Tafts, or the Roosevelts.[6] Besides the election of both the legendary "Kingfish" and his brother Earl as governors of Louisiana, the Long family had sent no less than six of its members to Congress over the past three decades.

With a medium build inclined to plumpness, small feet and hands constantly in motion, full-faced with unruly brown hair, the younger Long closely resembled his father. Perhaps the son has never equalled his father's famous Senate oration on the virtues of "potlikker and cornpone," but few leave the floor or the galleries when Russell Long rises to urge the passage of a bill or defend the merits of a particular amendment.

Russell Long first came to the Senate as part of the extraordinary class of 1948 (it included, in addition to Long, such eventual Senate powerhouses as Lyndon B. Johnson of Texas, Hubert H. Humphrey of Minnesota, Robert Kerr of Oklahoma, Paul Douglas of Illinois, and Clinton Anderson of New Mexico). By 1964 Long had reached the near-pinnacle of power, ranking member of the Senate Finance Committee. He also served as fifth-ranking member on Foreign Relations, a seat he would relinquish to Senator Gale McGee of Wyoming in exchange for a seat on the Commerce Committee (McGee would later side with Long against Kennedy).

One reason that Long decided to run for the majority whip post was because he felt somewhat restricted operating under long-time Finance Committee Chairman Harry Flood Byrd of Virginia. Still, as ranking member, Long had floor-managed the Johnson Administration's 1964 tax bill when Byrd had opposed the legislation.

Long was never a bourbon aristocrat in the traditional southern sense, but he was conservative enough on matters of cold-war politics, military security, and the pervasive question of race relations to find common bond with most of his southern colleagues. On the other hand, his populist stance on questions such as increased social security benefits, improved welfare measures, and tax policy provided Long with a natural bridge to northern and western moderates and liberals.

Long once summed up his general approach to legislation by announcing that "what is good for Louisiana is good for the nation." His constant championing of the economic interests of his state—oil and gas production, sulphur mining, sugar-cane refining, rice, cotton, lumbering and fishing — has been reflected in Senate legislation more often passed than defeated. Following in the footsteps of his father, Long was a self-styled "economic populist," long before the term was rediscovered.

The third principal candidate, A. S. "Mike" Monroney of Oklahoma, entered the contest as a compromise possibility. Neither as conservative as Long nor as liberal as Pastore, Monroney was best known for management of the Legislative Reorganization Act of 1946 while still a member of the House of Representatives. First elected to the House in 1938, Monroney, like Pastore and Long, had never lost an election. A former Oklahoma newspaperman, he lacked the aggressiveness and color of either of his two opponents.[7] Monroney had, nevertheless, left his mark on national legislation, principally in the fields of aviation, post office and civil service, and legislative reform. By 1965 Monroney was second-ranking on Post Office and Civil Service, third-ranking on Commerce, and eleventh-ranking on Appropriations. In common with other southwestern Senators he was a staunch defender of the oil interests. Much more than Pastore or even Long Monroney epitomized the "inner club" stereotype of a Senator — "a workhorse not a showhorse." [8]

CONTRASTING CAMPAIGNS. There is little need to recount in detail the campaigns waged by the three main contenders — each Senator seemed to adopt a campaign effort representative of his own personal style and reflecting to some extent his interest in the job.

Russell Long was off early and running hard. As he later recalled his decision to go after the whip's job: "It was up for grabs and I'd just as soon run." More than most politicians, Long seemed to thrive on the give-and-take of a heated political contest, especially one in which his own reputation was at stake. He took initial soundings in August 1964 immediately following the Senate's return from its recess for the Democratic Convention. By mid-September he had secretly sought and obtained commitments from nearly all of the Senate's southern Democrats. So quietly and efficiently had he set about his task that *Congressional Quarterly*, the unofficial chronicler of Capitol Hill activities, did not even include Long in its speculation about possible successors to Humphrey.

As a highly influential member of the Senate Finance Committee, Long was in a position to do the kinds of favors for members on tax or reciprocal trade legislation which would be beneficial to a Senator's home state constituents. In his search for commitments he took advantage of past favors rendered and was quick to promise future assistance in exchange for support in the whip's race. Coming out of a more wide-open, "rough and tumble" political environment than most of his colleagues,[9] Long was not hesitant to tap into the friendship, camaraderie, and good will that characterizes a legislative body, or to resort to more specific *quid-pro-quos*. A national lobbyist with a Louisiana background summed it up: "You know Russell — he loves to deal, he loves to horse-trade."

From Long's viewpoint, "for a leadership job you think about the kind of person he is, how he does his business. You want a fellow to treat you fairly. You wonder how a person will conduct himself in the job *with particular reference to you*." [10]

In contrast, Pastore's campaign efforts were conducted in a removed, if almost desultory, way. On November 6, 1964, after Congress had adjourned, the Rhode Island Senator sent each of his Democratic colleagues a short and rather formal letter requesting their "consideration" of his candidacy. From all accounts most of Pastore's time, prior to the Democratic conference in January, was spent at home in Rhode Island. Pastore apparently made little effort to follow his letter with telephone calls until the week preceding the vote. Several of his colleagues (not necessarily supporters) implied that Pastore, having made a brilliant keynote address at the Democratic Convention in August, assumed that the job would automatically be his. Another colleague put it with more sensitivity: "John is a proud man; his aloofness hides a certain shyness — perhaps he was afraid to ask for votes for fear he would be turned down." One Senate intimate believes strongly that "Pastore just didn't want to be tied down to the job." Whatever the correct interpretation, most observers concurred that Pastore's campaign was a model of how *not* to seek a Senate leadership position.

Monroney seems never to have really been in the contest. His sole hope lay in Long and Pastore knocking each other out, with neither able to obtain the necessary 35 votes out of the 68 Democratic Senators who would make up the majority in the 89th Congress. Monroney's campaign was relaxed and low-keyed. A press-aide reported that by December 9 Monroney had telephoned nearly all of his Democratic colleagues. However, by that late date, the Louisiana front-runner had aligned most of the southerners and was making strong inroads among northerners and westerners. In the final analysis, Monroney's bid, like Pastore's, was a classic case of too little, too late.

THE DEMOCRATIC CONFERENCE ELECTS LONG. On January 4, 1965, the Democratic Conference, which met just before the opening of the 89th Congress, selected Russell B. Long of Louisiana as the party's new whip. Mansfield had intervened only to the extent of setting the ground rules. If no candidate received a majority on the first ballot, the low man would be eliminated and a new ballot would be held until, finally, one candidate received a majority. In tradition, the voting would be by secret ballot.

On the first ballot Long received just one vote short of victory, 34 votes. Pastore was second with 20 votes; Monroney, low man with 14 votes, was dropped out. Fully half of his votes appear to have gone to Long as the second and final ballot indicates:

Long (La.)	41
Pastore (R.I.)	25
Hart (Mich.)	2
Total	68

Two liberals, apparently not satisfied with either Long or Pastore, voiced a last-minute protest by casting ballots for Phillip Hart, the junior senator from Michigan.

Why did Russell Long, a southern conservative on most questions, win the number two post in the Democratic party hierarchy in a Senate which was dominated by nearly 40 moderate-to-liberal, northern and western Democrats? The answer to that question is neither difficult nor subtle. The decision was not fought on ideological grounds but rather on personal likes and dislikes. Moreover, Long was the first to seek support and the more aggressive at obtaining commitments.[11] He began with a solid regional base of 15 to 18 votes. Perhaps another dozen senators, many of them westerners, were more attracted to Long's easygoing manner and his solid commitment to looking after the resources of their respective states (especially oil, mining, and agricultural interests). Long's populism found common ground with still other Senators, for example Paul H. Douglas of Illinois. This respected liberal maverick was quick to support his friend from the class of 1948. Other Senators, such as the esteemed Clinton Anderson of New Mexico, endorsed Long partly from admiration for his drive, but also, perhaps, from appreciation for Long's role in a House-Senate conference committee action late in the 86th Congress.[12] On this and numerous other legislative issues, Long had established himself as a man of flexibility and reason, open to listening to his colleagues, even if he could not always assent to their viewpoints.

President Johnson, like Mansfield, took a hands-off position in the choice of the new whip. Few Presidents have run the risk of intervening in a question which is considered an internal Senate matter.[13] After his election Long indicated that, for his part, he would work for the passage of "Great Society" measures to the extent that he could. He also observed that he would reserve the right to take an independent line when he did not agree with administration proposals. He further noted that he was not an obstructionist and that he considered himself a liberal on economic matters, "which I believe is the way liberalism ought to be defined." [14]

II

If 1965 was a high point in the turbulent Senate career of Russell Long, then the next three years were something of a retroversion. At 46, the redoubtable, self-confident Long was elected whip. Within ten months Harry F. Byrd, the chairman of the Senate Finance Committee, announced his decision to retire because of ailing health.[15] For the next three years even a man with the seemingly unbounded energy of Long was to find himself cross-pressured. He was at once the chairman of the Senate's most powerful committee, the assistant leader of the majority party, and in 1968 a Senator from Louisiana facing what seemed likely to be a tough primary challenge from popular Louisiana Governor John McKeithen.

Throwing most of his energies into his prime love, the chairmanship of the Finance Committee, Long managed over the next three years to (1) incur the increasing displeasure of his majority leader, (2) please few of his colleagues with his performance as majority whip, (3) tie up the entire Senate for six weeks in an attempt to promote a presidential election campaign fund, (4) defend the unpopular cause of Senator Thomas Dodd, (5) antagonize a number of liberals with rather heavy-handed and arbitrary floor maneuvering, (6) aggravate a drinking problem, and (7) neutralize the backing of several of the most important senior southern oligarchs in the Senate.

Perhaps this indictment is too harsh. It is uneven in that it singles out most of what went wrong and understates what went right during those three years. To the extent that the analysis is accurate, however, the wonder is not that Long would lose his whip's position to Senator Edward F. Kennedy in 1969, but that he came as close as he did to retaining the job.[16]

Majority Leader Mansfield remained neutral in the 1965 whip contest, and for that matter, in the 1969 and 1971 challenges to incumbent whips. In complete character with his conception of his role as Majority Leader, a servant to the needs of other Senators, Mansfield expected his assistant majority leader to perform in a similar manner. The main responsibility of the whip in Mansfield's words was "to fill in for the leader when he's not there."

Russell Long was an astute parliamentarian, he liked the conviviality of the floor and cloakroom, and he thrived on the give-and-take of a heated legislative debate. Unfortunately, much of the floor activity of the Senate is characterized by just the opposite: routine procedures, few Senators present, dull speeches, and only desultory discussion. Long abhorred sitting around waiting to adjourn the Senate. For him, the whip's job was too much

> . . . one of not giving orders, but taking work. It's seldom that the whip is left in control. Usually he is carrying out orders somebody else has left — unanimous consent requests, the Senator from New Mexico wants 15 minutes, that sort of thing . . . Just a grueling, day-to-day, thankless, time-consuming job of being around when nobody else cares to be.

Even before Long was elected chairman of the Finance Committee the novelty of the whip's job had worn off and he was spending correspondingly less time on the floor. Complaints from Mansfield and other Senators brought only temporary relief. Finally, out of desperation, Mansfield, with Long's consent, activated a third level in the floor coverage. The members of the Democratic Legislative Review Committee, whose function heretofore had been to keep track of minor bills and screen out those objected to by fellow Democrats, found themselves elevated to the status of assistant whips. All four of these senators, Daniel Brewster of Maryland, Phillip Hart of Michigan, Daniel Inouye of Hawaii, and Edmund Muskie of Maine, were relatively junior and moderate-to-liberal in their philosophies. Their new assignment included taking turns covering the floor in the absence of Mansfield or Long.

When Senator George Smathers decided to resign as secretary of the conference in 1966 as a step toward not running for reelection to the Senate, a further complication was added to floor coverage. Smathers' eventual replacement as the third-ranking party leader, Robert C. Byrd of West Virginia, had little difficulty defeating ultraliberal Joe Clark of Pennsylvania in a January 1967 conference contest.[17] Unlike Long, whom Byrd greatly admired, the hard-working conservative Senator from West Virginia thrived on floor duties, including the mundane chores that went with them. As a protegé of both Richard Russell and Lyndon Johnson, Byrd was aware that there was no substitute for long periods of floor observation and involvement as a means of mastering parliamentary procedure. And he had watched Bobby Baker, first Johnson's and then Mansfield's secretary to the majority, develop an independent base of power through the performance of countless small favors for Senators.[18] With Long's encouragement, Byrd gradually assumed most of the responsibilities, although not the title of assistant floor leader. In the process he all but did away with the need for the assistant whips.

Meanwhile Long was off on a series of maneuvers which, in one form or another, antagonized first members from one wing of the party and then those from another. To Long's credit he was the first Senator to propose and secure passage of a tax check-off plan for financing the spiraling costs of electing presidential candidates. In 1967, however, when Senators like Mansfield, Albert Gore (D., Tenn.), and John Williams (R., Del.) attempted and ultimately succeeded in gutting his legislation, Long proceeded to hold up the work of the Senate in a protracted, bitter, almost irrational struggle. When the Senate was ready to censure Thomas Dodd of Connecticut for financial chicanery, Long stepped forward as the self-appointed attorney for the defense. In the evaluation of a former Long staff assistant, "It was not so much what he did, but how he went about it." In effect, he told the rest of the Senate, "he who is without sin, let him cast the first stone." As the staff member elaborated: "That's pretty hard on people like Mike Mansfield or John Stennis." On the final censure resolution, Long was on the losing side of the 92–5 vote.

More than once, Long would use his leadership position (and the right of first recognition) to deter liberals in their legislative efforts. On an aid-to-dependent-children amendment, which Senator Robert Kennedy strongly favored, the New York liberal had left Senator Joseph Tydings of Maryland on the floor to protect their right to a roll call vote. A staff member of Long's recalled:

> Tydings had dropped his guard for a moment. Long just whipped the bill through and was on the plane to Shreveport before Tydings knew what had happened. When Kennedy found out about it he was so mad I think he would have hit Long if he could have found him.

It took the intervention of Mansfield to call the bill up again so that the liberals could have a vote.

Long's stance on legislation was not made easier by the threat of a primary challenge from Louisiana Governor John McKeithen. It became increasingly difficult for Long, in his role as a national leader for the White House and a majority of the Democrats to be, at the same time, responsive to his more conservative Louisiana constituency. As one of his assistants commented, "every time Long voted with Johnson or did something for the President, there was a great outcry in Louisiana. The President just wasn't very popular there."

As if these problems were not enough, or perhaps because of them, Long's fondness for a "belt or two" after and even during Senate working hours began to be more noticeable.[19] Several times he wandered onto the Senate floor in his stocking feet. More than once he made speeches without his usual clarity and coherence. As one Senate observer summed up the situation:

> Heavy drinking is not the exception in the Congress, not in the Senate, nor in the House for that matter. In general, there's a tolerance by others. But [in this situation] I'm sure it caused some guys to ask: "What kind of leader is this?"

Long may have survived all of theses misfortunes or handicaps save one. When the challenge came from Senator Edward Kennedy, over the 1968 Christmas holiday, Long apparently suffered from the lack of solid backing from the South's senior patriarchs, men like Richard Russell of Georgia, John Stennis of Mississippi, and John McClellan of Arkansas. These men cared greatly about the Senate as an institution. They revered its decorum and its traditions. Russell Long may not have been "light years away from senators like Stennis and Russell" in terms of love and respect for the Senate, but his erratic behavior was proving to be an embarrassment to some of them. Quite likely almost all southerners ended up voting for one of their own against a junior senator from New England. It seems equally likely that few went strongly to Long's defense in his confrontation with Kennedy.[20]

Ironically, Senator Russell Long seriously considered giving up the whip position in the early fall of 1968. The challenge from Governor McKeithen had not materialized; Long had received only a minor primary challenge and no Republican opposition in his successful bid for a fourth complete term in the Senate. By 1968 he had accumulated 20 years of seniority, he had the chairmanship of the Finance Committee as a power base, and he had youth on his side. Did he want to bide his time and hope to become majority leader or should he follow the alternative path of Richard Russell, a behind-the-scenes power-wielder who had dominated the Senate for most of the 1950's and into the 1960's? In the words of one of Long's key advisers:

> It was a question of the wisdom of which route to take. Russell Long was not wild about being whip. He didn't intend to contest the incumbent majority leader and he had no driving ambition to be majority leader. So why not take the other course — attempt to take Richard Russell's place and be ready in the wings when he moved on. Russell Long would be much more comfortable in that position of informal leadership.

By the fall of 1968, from most accounts, Long had all but decided not to run again for the whip's job. After discussing the situation with Robert Byrd, Long had advised him that he would support Byrd as his successor. All these arrangements would be laid aside after November, however, when Senator Long heard about a possible challenge. It came, initially, not from Kennedy, but from another liberal Catholic New Englander, Edmund S. Muskie of Maine.

III

Once state and national election results are in and analyzed from
every possible perspective, a natural slowdown occurs. Most Representatives and Senators flee the nation's Capitol for warmer climates
or home-state hideaways. For the Hill's political reporters, who seek
ways to pass through the doldrums, it is often a time for speculation
about forthcoming congressional leadership change. If none is likely,
it is not beyond the enterprising reporter to foment some conflict.
There are always some outspoken members of a wing of each of the
four congressional parties — Senate and House Democrats, Senate and
House Republicans — unhappy with one or more of their leaders and
ripe to promote dissent. Under such conditions one or two critical
quotes usually can produce a counter-reaction. The press can never create a leadership contest out of whole cloth, but they can greatly enhance the likelihood of a challenge if other necessary conditions exist.
And, of course, the relationship between the press and potential challengers is symbiotic. Whether strategy calls for the launching of a trial
balloon or an all-out attack, it is the contestant who attempts to use the
press and not the other way around. The benefits are likely to be
mutual; a good story for one, the appropriate amount of "surfacing"
or exposure for the other.

What was the impetus for Senator Edmund S. Muskie's exploration
of a possible challenge to the incumbent whip in mid-November of
1968? In part, it stemmed from the strong upsurge of favorable reaction to his vice-presidential candidacy on the 1968 Democratic ticket.
Although Humphrey and Muskie lost the election to Nixon and Agnew, the gap in the last weeks of the campaign had closed to within
510,000 popular votes out of more than 73 million cast. At 54 years
of age, much of the Maine Senator's political career appeared to lie
before him. His name, together with Kennedy's, were the two most
prominent mentioned for the Democratic presidential nomination in
1972. In part, talk of a challenge was promoted by Senate corre-
pondents, confronted as always by a post-election dry spell in the
news. In part, this speculation was fanned by a group of bright liberal
Senate staff assistants, dissatisfied with the hesitancy with which their
Senators' legislative plans had been dispatched in the previous Congress. As administrative and legislative assistants from the offices of
Senators like Muskie, Kennedy, Hart, and Tydings congregated, a
recurring question became "Who can we get to run against Long, and
win?"

The question seemed all the more imperative because a Republican President would be in the White House in January. Richard M. Nixon would be the first successful G.O.P. presidential contender, since the 1920's, strongly identified with partisan causes, with the will to attempt realignment of the traditional one-sided dominance of Congress which Democrats have enjoyed since 1932. Further, Republicans had made a net gain of five Senate and four House seats. Their 42 Senate seats in the 91st Congress would represent the largest number they had held since 1956.

As one of the participants in those November–December meetings of liberal Democratic Senate staffers recalls:

> You have to remember that in late 1968 — those were bumptious times: the anti-Vietnam movement, the youth movement moving very fast toward its demise, calls for reform in the party, reform in Congress. The liberal members in the Senate needed a spokesman in the party leadership so the feeling was to make the whip more complete by electing an activist — someone who would be interested in these matters and doing something about them.

Reacting to many of these same political realities and feelings, Muskie cautiously began to sound out fellow moderate and liberal Senators in late November. According to one veteran Senate-watcher, *Newsweek*'s Sam Shaffer, Muskie was to get as many as 23 commitments, a figure 6 votes shy of a needed majority.[21] Other observers agree that the potential for over 20 votes was there, but that Muskie never formalized them, indeed, could not, until he actually declared himself a candidate.

In any event, such speculation is academic. While Muskie tried to make up his mind whether or not to run, Russell Long got wind of a possible challenge. All thoughts of stepping aside and supporting Byrd as a whip candidate were quickly abandoned. As one of Long's assistant recalls the decision:

> Long's reaction was "OK, I'm going to run." And for reasons as old as time I would imagine — the thrill of the chase, the excitement of running. Long had been challenged and he had to contest it.

Thus, Long began to counter the possible Muskie bid with an intensive telephone poll of his own. Within days he had more than 40 commitments and Muskie backed off from his challenge.

BURKE: "THE CONSENSUS IS IT'S A BAD IDEA"; KENNEDY: "LET'S GO ANYWAY." Senator Kennedy's first reaction to Senator Muskie's inquiry for support in case of a possible challenge had been positive and enthusiastic. He first heard of Muskie's decision *not* to run in a story written by John Averill of the Los Angeles Times Bureau and carried in a Miami newspaper. Following a visit to his invalid father in Palm Beach, Senator Kennedy flew to Chicago just before Christmas en route to a Sun Valley skiing vacation with his family.

In Chicago, Kennedy called David Burke, his administrative assistant in Washington, D.C. Burke took quick soundings from some other staff members and a few close Kennedy associates. Most argued that there would be a lot to lose and not much to gain. Kennedy, only 36, had made a positive legislative record in his six years in the Senate. Considered the front-runner for the Democratic nomination in 1972, why should he wish to be tied down to a mundane job like the whip? And what if he should lose? As Kennedy said of his decision:

> I asked Burke to check out the idea of my going . . . Most of the advice I got said not to go, but I decided the other way.

In the last analysis perhaps only Kennedy himself knows the reasons he decided to run. Several speculations can be advanced. Edward Kennedy's brother, Robert, had been tragically assassinated less than six months before. Edward Kennedy, tempted by both a presidential draft and a vice-presidential nomination offer in August, turned them down. By December of 1968, the youngest Kennedy brother seemed to feel it was time to move again. No matter what his decision, it would be interpreted in the context of a bid for the 1972 nomination.

Perhaps Burke has captured best the main thrust and rationale of their thinking:

> The decision to go pretty much took place in one day. It was a brand new idea . . . but rather surprising and rather exciting. We would be going all the way against the grain . . . but Long had been quiescent and he was vulnerable.

Kennedy arrived at Sun Valley on December 25 and began to make telephone calls the next day. The story has circulated that he launched his campaign because he had somehow gotten separated from his skis en route. Apocryphal as this may be (you can always rent skis), over the next two days Kennedy had been in touch with more than half of his 57 Democratic senatorial colleagues. His first several calls went to Senator Muskie, Hubert Humphrey, the defeated presidential candidate, and Majority Leader Mansfield. Muskie assured Kennedy that he did not intend to run and offered his support. Humphrey also was enthusiastic. He would have no vote but he agreed to make telephone calls on Kennedy's behalf if he were to become a candidate. Mansfield made no effort to encourage or discourage the young Massachusetts senator.[22]

Most of the initial calls did not seek a commitment; they were designed to sound out other Senators about the probability of Kennedy's success. Not surprisingly, Kennedy began with those Senators he felt most likely to be sympathetic to his candidacy — Birch Bayh of Indiana, Phillip A. Hart of Michigan, Joseph Tydings of Maryland, and George McGovern of South Dakota, Bobby Kennedy's old friend and supporter. Only later did he begin to sound out more senior Senators, southerners, and other likely Long backers.[23] Kennedy remembers: "For a while all we had were 15 to 18 commitments, the kind of base you'd expect. But the first responses were reasonably encouraging, so we kept on."

On Friday, December 27, Kennedy finally decided to call Long at his Baton Rouge farm and notify him of a prospective challenge. Both parties to the call recollect an amiable conversation. Kennedy remembers Long's general optimism, a welcoming of the contest, and his own surprise that Long had apparently not yet heard of the challenge.[24]

The gauntlet having been thrown down, Kennedy flew to Baltimore on Sunday evening, December 29, where two Senate aides met him at the airport a little after midnight and drove him to his home in McLean, Virginia. Here, a command post was set up which was to operate until the vote in the Democratic conference on Friday morning, January 3, 1969. When he returned to the Old Senate Office Building, Kennedy's tactics shifted from Senator-to-Senator contacts to the generation of support from home-state constituents. Aides such as Dick Drayne, his press secretary, drifted in and out. So did a number of close family associates, such as Milton Gwirtzman, an adviser and speechwriter for several of the Kennedys.

It is agreed that staff can provide very little assistance in leadership contests, with the important exception of information. Unlike House contests in which sheer numbers are a problem, a Senator or his administrative assistant can easily call the offices of other Senators and find out where that Senator may be reached, even when the Senate is not in session. Some staff members, especially those with considerable floor exposure, may be somewhat more helpful. They may, in the words of an aide, "know how to reach a member, who he's friendly with, who might be able to get to him." But for the most part, leadership contests consist of Senator-to-Senator communications. In the words of another Hill veteran:

> It's an inside contest. AA's and LA's can do very little. It's different with legislation. There they can help their principals because they can talk substantively to their peers and they can also help the Senator relate to constituents. But in a struggle for power, an inside contest, it's confined almost entirely to personal efforts by the candidate.

Of course, staff can perform the traditional role of acting as a sounding board for the candidate. They can, to a degree, help to evaluate the slackness or firmness of a given commitment — and they can pray.

Staff assistance can be helpful in leadership contests in other ways — making indirect contacts in the home state of a Senator with a financial contributor, a party official, a labor union spokesman. Kennedy and his staff made efforts to generate pressure from what was left of the "Kennedy apparatus," supporters of the presidential campaigns of both John and Robert Kennedy. In the closing days of the contest Kennedy also received selective assistance from his natural allies — men like Andrew Biemiller of the AFL–CIO, Joseph Rauh of the Americans for Democratic Action, and Clarence Mitchell of the National Association for the Advancement of Colored People. In a number of northern and western states possible Senate fence-riders began to receive telephone calls from local supporters of both candidates.

Still, as Lewis A. Dexter has so concisely observed, "pressure is how you see it." [25] In a power struggle all Senators expect such telephone calls and ride with them. A Kennedy supporter observed:

> It got as hot as the dickens in 1969. There were people coming through on something else, but on the way out they'd say, "Hope you can help Russell [Long]." At that time, I kind of cast it off; I didn't say how I was going to vote . . . I didn't take it too seriously, that this fellow would contact me on Russell's behalf.

Unlike the visible roll call vote characteristic of most legislation, in leadership contests any Congressman can choose to repair to the protection offered by the secret ballot.

Staff can also be of assistance in one final arena — public relations. Press seems not to have figured heavily in this race nor in the whip contests of 1965 and 1971. The duration of the Kennedy-Long contest was too short. As one press assistant put it, "About all you can do is make sure everybody knows [your candidate] is running after he announces. If a Senator is back home in the state and he runs across favorable press, that can help." Thus, while a positive press may help to shore up a decision, it probably never converts a vote.

On December 30, with the conference decision but four days away, Kennedy issued a formal press release announcing his candidacy. His statement did not mention Long explicitly, but his argument was clear:

> With a new Administration, Mike Mansfield's responsibilities will be heightened. He will need the devotion and energy of an assistant who can involve himself more fully in presenting the Democratic attitudes on the issues that come before Congress.
>
> Not bearing the heavy responsibilities of a chairmanship of a major Senate committee, I will be able to devote whatever time may be necessary to help make the work of the Senate more effective and efficient, and to make the Majority Whip a better instrument of the will of the Democratic membership.

Telephone calls were made from his office or his home throughout the remaining days. There was little time to write letters and few Senators were in town available for face-to-face encounters. "The telephone was not very satisfactory," Kennedy recalled, "but it was the only way." In conversations with his colleagues, he stressed the same themes developed in his press release:[26]

> It was that I felt the job of majority whip was important, that it could be effective, that although the job was not clearly defined, I would try if I won to make it important to the nation, the Senate and the party.

A largely unspoken inducement probably effective with more than one Senator (25 would be up for reelection in 1970) was that a commitment now might well insure the presence of Senator Kennedy, the likely Democratic nominee in 1972, at a campaign fund-raising dinner or a trip through their state during the next two years. Long had no way of matching this tempting, if unvoiced, appeal.

One measure of how well Kennedy was doing was the consistency with which his phone calls were returned. In Senate and in House races alike, this may well be the single best indicator, short of *firm* commitments, of how well a candidate is doing. Conversely, if telephone messages are not returned promptly or at all, then the candidate can consider himself in deep trouble.

Although cautiously optimistic after the initial round of telephone calls, it wasn't until the day before the vote that Kennedy felt he was going to win. He recalled,[27]

> On Thursday I went around to see several Senators, personally — four or five that were back in town by then. I figured I needed two out of the five Senators to win. I think I ended up getting all but one.

As he entered the Democratic Conference, Friday morning, Kennedy felt he had 30 firm commitments and several probables. A majority of 29 votes would be required for victory.

IV

LONG: "I LIKE TO WIN; I FIGHT VERY HARD TO WIN." What thoughts were likely to have crossed Senator Long's mind after he and Kennedy had talked with each other the week before the conference vote? He must have recollected his early fall leanings against running at all; he must have felt a sense of optimism given the ease with which he had disposed of a possible Muskie challenge, a Senator who had four more years of seniority than Kennedy.[28]

Now 50 years old and with 20 years of Senate experience behind him, Long was not about to step aside in the face of a contest from a 36-year-old, half-fledged Senator, even if that Senator was a Kennedy. As he often told associates, "Any bit of power you get, you never give up willingly."

Initially at a disadvantage because of the several days' head-start that Kennedy had, and because Senators were scattered around the world — their home states, the Virgin Islands, Europe — Long's main recourse, like his opponent's was to the telephone.

By nature, Long was a man who liked people, enjoyed "pressing the flesh" and throwing his arm around the colleague he was talking to.[29] Compared to Kennedy, Long was even less effective at vote counting when he couldn't react to "eye-ball to eye-ball contact," the shrug of shoulders, and the other nonverbal cues of a respondent.

When Long was asked how he went about aligning support he replied:

> You talk to Senators. Every politician knows that there is no substitute for talking to people, personally. You say to them, "I'm running; I'd appreciate it if you could vote for me." If on some occasion, you'd befriended [a Senator], you remind him. You tell him as a leader you are interested in him and what he is trying to achieve for his state. You are trying to help him achieve what he is trying to do.

In 1964–1965, Long had been able to talk directly to his colleagues; in 1968–1969, he encountered more of the evasion that seemed endemic to a challenged incumbent.

Because Long would remain in a position of power, nobody wanted to cross one of the Senate's most influential men. Regardless of the outcome of the whip's race, Long would retain his chairmanship of the Finance Committee. Thus, he would remain in a position to help or hurt another Senator. In November, Long had been able to obtain the commitment of several incoming freshmen's votes, even before a contest appeared likely. For example, Senator-elect Mike Gravel of Alaska had flown to Washington, D.C. to seek assignment to the Commerce and Interior Committees, committees which had jurisdiction over a number of issues important to his state, especially environmental protection and Alaskan native land claims. One of his first stops was to see Long, a member of the Commerce Committee, but more important an automatic member by virtue of his leadership position of the Democratic Steering Committee, which makes committee assignments. As Gravel subsequently recalled their meeting:

> He was very courteous to me as a freshman Senator. I was asking him to help me get an assignment on the Commerce Committee. He was helpful. And then as I was going out the door, he said, "I'm running for whip. Nobody's opposing me."
>
> I was asking him for help. What was I going to do? Say "no"?

Later, when Kennedy approached the outspoken freshman liberal for a commitment, Gravel had to refuse him; he had already given his word to support the incumbent whip.

As chairman of the Senate Finance Committee, which automatically made him chairman (or vice-chairman to his House counterpart) of the Joint Committee on Internal Revenue Taxation, Long was in a better position than almost any other Senator to follow up on his promises.[30] Tax matters, debt limitations, reciprocal trade legislation, oil and gas regulations, insurance, customs, tariffs and import quotas, social security, pensions, compensation of veterans — all came within this committee's jurisdiction. Further, two of the South's leading influentials, Richard Russell of Georgia and Allen J. Ellender from Long's home state, were due to become chairman and ranking Democratic member, respectively, of the Senate Appropriations Committee. With more than two-thirds of the Senate's older, more establishment members on his side, many of them long-time personal friends, Long had reason for confidence.

Well aware that Kennedy was activating any outside forces he could, Long wasted no time generating his own external support. If he could count on few northern governors or national party spokesmen, Long's contacts with private industry were widespread and long-standing. Self-admittedly he was "the darling of the oil and gas industry." He had no hesitation about bringing influence to bear on Senator Fred R. Harris of Oklahoma and other oil state Senators. Not all the pressures succeeded, however. Long was unable to reverse the liberal Harris' prior commitment to Senator Kennedy.[31] Past, and presumably future, campaign contributions, which Long was able to direct to one campaign or another, would seem to have played a role. However, observers differ greatly as to the extent that financial contributions were used and the impact which they might have had.[32]

The weekend before the vote Long flew back to Washington for an eleventh-hour blitz. By Tuesday, December 31, the incumbent leader felt confident enough to fly home to New Orleans to take in the Sugar Bowl football game. He remained in New Orleans to make a final round of telephone calls. On the eve of the vote, mainly for press consumption, he announced he had 34 votes and would score a "solid victory." [33] Less than 48 hours later, as he walked from his offices to the Old Senate Caucus Room, Long was privately convinced he had 29 firm votes, just enough to win.

V

The first Democratic Conference of the 91st Congress was called to order several minutes after 9 A.M. on Friday, January 3, 1969. In common with its Republican counterpart the Democratic Conference met in closed session. In addition to the 53 returning members and 5 incoming freshmen, only a handful of pages and several Senate functionaries were allowed in the room. Outside in the corridors newspapermen, magazine correspondents, and television crews mingled with Senate staff assistants, a scattering of lobbyists, and other onlookers. Last-minute rumors and indiscretions were exchanged as they waited for results.

Long was nominated for reelection by his colleague, 78-year-old Allen J. Ellender, a former floor leader and Speaker in the Louisiana state legislature under his father, and a U.S. Senator since January 3, 1937. Long's nomination was seconded by 76-year-old Spessard Lindsey Holland of Florida, another veteran Senator beginning his twenty-third year in the Senate.

Kennedy's name was placed in nomination by Muskie and seconded by Washington's Henry M. Jackson and Tennessee's Albert Gore.[34] Muskie was four years into his second term; Jackson and Gore had first come to the Senate in January 1953.

Balloting in a Democratic Conference is a simple process. The secretary to the majority, or one of his assistants, passes out a printed paper ballot to each Senator. They write or print their preferred choice and the slips are folded and deposited in a ballot box. Tally clerks are chosen from the ranks of the entering freshmen Senators. One of them opens the ballots and reads them out loud — Long, Kennedy, Kennedy, and so on — while the other freshmen Senators keep track of votes by hatch marks on a pad.[35] The result of this election, Kennedy, 31, Long, 26, was announced. Moments later word of the upset filtered out to the waiting crowd. The Democratic majority in the Senate had a new whip — Edward M. Kennedy of Massachusetts.

In theory, voting was by secret ballot; in practice, most Senators' votes became known. Many announced their preferences as a way of indicating support for their candidate; others let their choice be known, in the words of one Senator, because "if you don't announce how you stand, you may end up getting flak from both sides." Still, more than one Senator had recourse to Montana Senator Lee Met-

Table 12.1
Senator Kennedy Defeats Senator Long, 31–26

For Kennedy, 31 votes	For Long, 26 votes
Bayh (Ind.)	Allen (Ala.)
Burdick (N.D.)	Anderson (N.M.)
Church (Idaho)	Bible (Nev.)
Cranston (Cal.)	Byrd (Va.)
Eagleton (Mo.)	Byrd (W. Va.)
Fulbright (Ark.)	Cannon (Nev.)
Gore (Tenn.)	Dodd (Conn.)
Harris (Okla.)	Eastland (Mass.)
Hart (Mich.)	Ellender (La.)
Hughes (Iowa)	Ervin (N.C.)
Inouye (Hawaii)	Gravel (Alaska)
Jackson (Wash.)	Hartke (Ind.)
Kennedy (Mass.)	Holland (Fla.)
Magnuson (Wash.)	Hollings (S.C.)
Mansfield (Mont.)	Jordan (N.C.)
McGovern (S.D.)	Long (La.)
McIntyre (N.H.)	McCarthy (Minn.)
Metcalf (Mont.)	McClellan (Ark.)
Mondale (Minn.)	McGee (Wyo.)
Moss (Utah)	Montoya (N.M.)
Muskie (Maine)	Nelson (Wis.)
Pastore (R.I.)	Randolph (W. Va.)
Pell (R.I.)	Russell (Ga.)
Proxmire (Wis.)	Sparkman (Ala.)
Ribicoff (Conn.)	Stennis (Miss.)
Spong (Va.)	Talmadge (Ga.)
Symington (Mo.)	
Tydings (Md.)	
Williams (N.J.)	
Yarborough (Tex.)	
Young (Ohio)	

SOURCE: This is Senator Long's unofficial tally as revealed to the *Washington Post*, January 5, 1969, p. A-3. Both sides (principals and staff) generally agree that the tally is accurate within one or possibly two pairs of switches (or four votes in all). For example, to this day, neither side is sure how Majority Leader Mansfield voted.

calf's protective strategy: "I will know and God will know how I vote. But I will try to keep the man on my left and right in the caucus from knowing."

Other Senate Democratic leadership posts were uncontested. Mike Mansfield began his ninth year as majority leader; Robert C. Byrd was reelected secretary to the Democratic Conference and Richard B. Russell was nominated to succeed the retiring Carl Hayden of Arizona as President pro tempore of the Senate.

Kennedy was calm without, jubilant within, as he strode from the conference to confront TV cameras and reporters:[36]

> The winds of change, so evident this year, have expressed themselves. Rather than a personal victory, the significance of this action was much broader. I think it means a positive, constructive legislative program in this session.

At the same time, Kennedy also discounted his victory as the first step toward the Democratic presidential nomination in 1972.

Senator Long, hurt and disgruntled, placed a different interpretation on the outcome. By implication, it was the Kennedy name — "I don't think I could have been beaten by anybody else in the Senate." He also had words of warning for the new Republican President: "I would suggest that Mr. Nixon ought to be very careful and watch himself in the future." [37]

Although Mansfield would not reveal how he voted, he told reporters that he was delighted with the outcome. "Kennedy," he said, was "a link with the younger generation." When the 91st Congress got under way at noon, the young New Englander moved from a seat at the rear of the chamber to a desk in the front row, adjacent to the majority leader.

VI

LONG: "HE CAUGHT ME AT A LOW EBB, WHEN HE WAS AT A HIGH POINT." It remains to summarize why Long lost and Kennedy won in this, the first instance of a challenger getting the better of an incumbent Democratic leader in the contemporary Senate.

Long was defeated for a deceptively simple reason — his erratic behavior over the past four years made him vulnerable. There is no need to restate the personal and political difficulties which brought Long to a "low ebb" in the late fall of 1968. However, as the Louisiana Senator correctly observed following his upset, only one possible challenger in the Senate, Edward M. Kennedy, could have beaten him. "My guess is that I would have taken any other opponent by about a 2-to-1 margin," observed Long.[38] And he was probably right.

The day following the contest, Long was more philosophical and no longer bitter. "When I lose a fight, if I have any regret at all it is that maybe I should have worked harder and started sooner." [39]

The significance of Kennedy's early, aggressive start should not be minimized. No challenge to an incumbent can hope to succeed without an early drive for commitments. But it was much more the nature of Kennedy, the man, his legacy, and his potential, that resulted in his election as the youngest whip in the history of the United States Senate.

Born in Boston, Massachusetts on February 22, 1932, Edward Moore Kennedy was the youngest in a family of ten, the fourth son of Joseph Patrick and Rose Fitzgerald Kennedy. Like Russell Long before him, Kennedy had barely achieved the constitutional age requirement of 30 before he entered the Senate in 1962. Much more than his brothers, John and Robert,[40] Edward had quietly adapted to the fading folkways of the Senate; most notably, he worked hard and he was seen but seldom heard. Moreover he deferred to his elders and did his legislative homework. After his recovery from a near-fatal airplane crash in June 1964, the young Kennedy began to emerge as one of the more creative and successful of the new breed of liberal Senators making their marks in a post-*Citadel* Senate. One secret of his success, as it is with most potential leaders, was his ability to attract and motivate bright ambitious staff assistants. And, like his brothers, he had a capacity to utilize academic talent and the nation's richest pool to draw upon.

By the time of his second brother's assassination in 1968, Kennedy had much more going for him than his good looks, his father's money, and the Kennedy name. Following Kennedy's election as whip, the majority leader went out of his way to confirm this assessment: "Of all the Kennedys," said Mansfield, "the Senator is the only one who was and is a real Senate man . . ." [41]

The importance of the Kennedy legend should not be underestimated, however, not in January 1969 or beyond. He was and is the inheritor of the Kennedy charisma, developed not just in history books, but in folk songs, and in the sense of shared experiences that surrounded the deaths of Kennedy family members. No dynasty in American political history has come close to encountering the cumulative success and tragedy of the Kennedy's — John was elected President in November 1960, only to be assassinated in Dallas in November 1963. Robert was elected and seeming to be on his way to the 1968 presidential nomination, only to be shot down in Los Angeles after winning the California primary. Edward Kennedy had contributed to his brothers' victories; he also suffered the grief and agony of their assassinations in a crucible made all the more difficult because of its public nature. Weaker men (or men with a different kind of strength) might have chosen to leave politics altogether. This Senator chose to dramatize his return to active politics, not by acquiescing to a possible draft from Chicago in August 1968, or even by waiting for what seemed for a time to be a near-certain Democratic presidential nomination in 1972. Instead, he launched an audacious challenge to the incumbent majority whip in December 1968. The question of why he did this is still not adequately answered.

Confronted almost incessantly with the family legacy from the time of his first bid for the Senate,[42] Kennedy quite probably found persuasive the kind of argument put forth by one Senate staff member:

> I told him he needed to establish a track record. If he wished to become a candidate in 1972, people would say, "Well, what has he done — what leadership has he provided on his own?" Election by his peers would answer those arguments.

An associate of the Kennedy family attributes the outcome of the whip contest to a reservoir of "emotional feelings," a response spilling over from Robert Kennedy's assassination:

> People wanted to do something out of sympathy for Ted Kennedy, whose brother had been killed. They wouldn't have done it otherwise . . . It was a small thing they were asking, it was a relatively insignificant job.

> A lot of people didn't know why he wanted it. They said, "If this is what Teddy wants, let's do it for him."

Perhaps such "residual sympathy" motivated many people who helped Kennedy from the field, former supporters of Robert Kennedy calling in to urge the Senators to support the last of the Kennedys. However, sympathy alone seldom moves politicians. In the tough, and frequently harsh, world of the United States Senate, such sympathy may have received lip-service, but probably not much more.

What seems to have moved many Senators was Kennedy's political

potential. In December 1968 he appeared to be the odds-on favorite
to win the Democratic presidential nomination in 1972. More important, he seemed likely to be the one Democrat with a good opportunity to defeat incumbent President Richard M. Nixon should he
choose to run again. As one Senator recalls the mood:

> A number of Senators felt, "Sure, Teddy Kennedy is going to
> be around for a long, long time. It would be a good thing to
> deal with him, a kind of 'follow-the-leader' syndrome." Plus,
> there was the Kennedy magic which was significant inside the
> Senate as well as outside.

> But it was the potential of the presidency that set it off. A
> Senator could see himself being part of a future movement,
> being one of the 'chosen few,' in at the beginnings.

Sentiments such as these appear to have been widespread at the
beginning of the 91st Congress. They were intensified by an even
more pressing need — 25 of the 57 incumbent Democratic Senators
would be up for reelection in 1970. Kennedy, as a likely presidential
nominee, could do a great deal for many of these Senators through
fund-raising appeals and personal appearances. Positive inducements
were less important, in the view of one Kennedy aide, than negative
sanctions:

> It wasn't so much a case of "Let's vote for Kennedy, because
> then he'll campaign for me." It was more, "If I don't vote for
> him, then he may refuse to come to my chicken dinner in
> Peoria . . ."

Given his head-start on the presidential nomination, Kennedy had far
more "clout" nationally than Long could hope to offer, even with his
strong ties to the oil industry and other sources of campaign contributions. In Long's own words:[43]

> This happens to have been a race where it was a nationwide
> proposition, and while I had Senator Kennedy outgunned in
> the United States Senate, he had me outgunned in the United
> States.

In *Time* magazine's view, Long's statement was "more candid —
and accurate" than the Kennedy interpretation: "I view it as expressing a sense of the Democratic Senators in favor of an aggressive and
creative program in the upcoming Congress." [44] But from another

perspective, Long's *realpolitik* view may be as distorting as Kennedy's issue-oriented rhetoric. A Kennedy aide provides a partial antidote to Long's justication for his loss:

> He was saying by implication that although he had the pressure as a Senator, that we had a great deal of power "out there," some sort of fantastic machine. Just like drafts at a convention, they are not the real thing.
>
> Some calls were made on Kennedy's behalf, of course. We would call friends of Kennedy in a particular area, but that doesn't mean they were influential with the Senator in that state. If there was one vote that was changed — hell, that would be impressive... It's my belief that there wasn't any call made to promote Kennedy from constituents in states that brought in any votes at all.

Later, this same aide concluded: "That's not to say I don't understand Long's statement, however. It gave him an out and from our point of view it made us look good, looking to 1972."

The crucial point, here, is that no congressional leadership contest can ever be won from *outside* with the possible and rare exception of direct presidential intervention. What counts is not how many newspaper editorials are written, or how many important constituents call in, or even how much campaign money is spread around. What does count is what each Senator or House member sees the prospective winner *doing for him* or sometimes against him. This is not to de-emphasize the role that ideology, region, and personal friendships plays. It is only to stress the importance of the internal perspective and the considerable flexibility that almost every Senator and the vast majority of House members retain in leadership contests.

Kennedy believed in 1969, and he continues to believe, that by infusing the whip's job with greater importance he would be able "to help make the work of the Senate more effective and efficient." He hoped to transform a heretofore mundane job into an instrument for developing policy, not merely for carrying out the wishes of others. As he recalled his reasons for running in 1968–1969:

> Before, the whip position had been neither of great significance nor import. But in the wake of the 1968 presidential campaign, it seemed like an opportunity to make it more important. The system was opening up. I would bring new

views, new ideas, and a fresh attitude to it. That seemed very welcome to a majority of the Senators — my energy and my ideas. Most members sensed that generally.

To search for a simple explanation or a single common denominator to explain the outcome would be misleading. Certainly these themes predominate: the Kennedy view stressing issues and the need to breathe new life into a stagnant leadership; the Long perspective emphasizing a defeat only at the hands of a "future President" and his inherited national machine. Both perspectives need to be broadened to incorporate the Kennedy legend, and the possibility of some residual sympathy for Jack and Bobby cannot be ignored completely. The answer as to why the Senate had a new whip in 1969 lies somewhere between the necessary condition — Long's vulnerability — and the sufficient reasons — Kennedy, his promise as a Senator, as an aspiring presidential nominee, and as the "brother of the brother of the brother."

NOTES

1. Norman Wilding and Philip Laundy, *An Encyclopedia of Parliament* (1958), p. 659, as quoted in Walter J. Oleszek, "Majority and Minority Whip of the Senate," 92nd Cong., 2d Sess., Senate Document 92-86 (Washington, D.C.: U.S. Government Printing Office, 1972), p. 3.
2. Richard M. Scammon and Ben J. Wattenberg, *The Real Majority* (New York: Coward-McCann, 1970), pp. 36–37.
3. *Congressional Quarterly Weekly Report* **22** (September 25, 1964), pp. 2251–2252.
4. For detailed profiles, including voting patterns, of the three contestants, see "Whip Candidates," *Congressional Quarterly Weekly Review* **22** (December 18, 1964), pp. 2819–2827.
5. Harry McPherson, *A Political Education* (Boston: Little, Brown, 1972), p. 53.
6. The legend of the remarkable Huey P. Long is best chronicled in his own book, *My First Days in the White House* (Harrisburg, Pa.: Telegraph Press, 1935) and the definitive biography by T. Harry Williams, *Huey Long* (New York: Knopf, 1969). For comparisons with other American political dynasties, see Stephen Hess, *America's Political Dynasties from Adams to Kennedy* (Garden City, N.Y.: Doubleday, 1966).
7. "He could feel strongly about issues, and he was a witty and informed debater who conveyed, like Russell Long, a sense of actuality, of the real stakes at issue. Yet he was not a Senate power; one could not imagine Mike Monroney doing anything out of vindictiveness or obsession or self-aggrandizment. Hence it was rarely necessary to defer to him, to cope with him." McPherson, *op. cit.*, p. 46.
8. Donald R. Matthews, *U.S. Senators and Their World* (Chapel Hill: University of North Carolina Press, 1960), ch. 5, "The Folkways of the Senate,"

esp. pp. 94–95. The inner-club hypothesis was first set forth by William S. White, *The Citadel* (New York: Harper & Row, 1956), chs. 5–10. Cf. Ralph K. Huitt, "The Outsider in the Senate: An Alternative Role," *Am. Pol. Sci. Rev.* **55** (1961), 566–575.

9. In 1965 when the author was interning with House Majority Whip Hale Boggs and attending a leadership meeting in the Speaker's office, Senator Long's name came up in connection with a conference committee action. One participant in the meeting, which included a number of White House liaison staff, observed that "Senator Long was flexible." Whereupon some 20 of the highly politicized participants broke into spontaneous (but not derisive) laughter.

10. "In all societies there are "anchored relations" (or "pegged" ones) such that each end identifies the other personally, knows the other does likewise, and openly acknowledges to the other that an irrevocable starting has been made between them — the establishment of a framework of mutual knowing, which retains, organizes, and applies the experiences the ends [individuals] have of one another." Erving Goffman, *Relations in Public* (New York: Basic Books, 1971), p. 189.

11. One example colorfully illustrates the extent to which Long was willing to go to obtain a commitment. The only southern vote that he feared he might lose was Olin D. Johnston of South Carolina. Johnston had strong labor connections and labor was generally opposing Long because of his record of opposition to civil rights and medicare.

    It happened that the desk in the Senate chamber occupied by Russell Long had formerly been used by Huey P. Long, and even longer back in Senate history by the legendary John C. Calhoun of South Carolina. Saying to himself, "Please forgive me, Daddy, but this time I'm going for broke," Long offered the seat to Senator Johnston when the 89th Congress convened. In the whip election, Johnston ended up voting for Long. Tom Wicker, "The Son of the Kingfish," *The New York Times Magazine*, April 4, 1965, pp. 76 ff. at 89.

12. By helping to deadlock the passage of a Social Security bill in the 88th Congress, Long was influential in preserving the principle of medicare (even though he personally opposed it) until the full package could be passed by a Congress of more liberal persuasion. E. W. Kenworthy of the *New York Times* cites this action as the likely reason for Anderson's decision to throw his support to Long, "Party Picks Long as Senate Whip," *New York Times*, January 5, 1965, pp. 1, 18.

13. One major exception was Franklin Delano Roosevelt's intervention on Alben W. Barkley's behalf in the 1937 contest for Senate majority leader. Alben W. Barkley, *That Reminds Me* (Garden City, N.Y.: Doubleday, 1954); George H. Haynes, *The Senate of the United States: Its History and Practice* (Boston: Houghton Mifflin, 1938), I, p. 481, n. 1.

14. *New York Times*, January 5, 1965, p. 18.

15. *New York Times*, November 12, 1965, pp. 1, 33.

16. A further disclaimer seems in order. The next several pages can hardly do justice to Senator Long's performance from 1965–1968, or is it intended to do so. Rather, the attempt is to outline the concatenation of events that made Senator Long vulnerable to a challenge from Senator Kennedy.

17. The reported vote was 38 to 28. *Congressional Quarterly Weekly Report* **25** (January 12, 1967), p. 4.

18. Baker's meteoric rise from a poor boy from Pickens, South Carolina, to Senate page, to Lyndon Johnson's protegé, to secretary to the Senate Demo-

cratic majority, to independent entrepreneur was cut short in 1967. After a Senate investigation and a court trial he was sentenced to one-to-three years in the federal penitentiary for larceny, fraud, and tax evasion.

19. Alcohol is one of the taboo subjects on Capitol Hill; sex is another. If there were a way to write about Long's problems without reference to drinking, I would have preferred to have done so. However, clearly, drinking figured in Long's defeat, so much so that many a Senator and staff assistant I interviewed spontaneously mentioned that he was "on the sauce," "had a bottle problem," or a more polite euphemism such as "had personal difficulties." Most were quick to add that after Long's remarriage the problem appeared to have been overcome.

20. When John Stennis went to talk to a younger southern Senator on Long's behalf, the younger Senator raised the question of his uneasiness about Long's behavior on the floor. Stennis is said to have shook his head and remained silent.

21. *Newsweek*, January 13, 1969, p. 15.

22. As one Kennedy staffer surmised: "He was neutral. You know Mansfield — he's always very, very correct in his behavior. He knows that after the dust has settled he'll still be majority leader. Sure, you would call him early . . . , but you would get no encouragement from him. He would say, 'Well, Ted, uh, if that is what you think you should do . . .' Hell, if the newest freshman wanted to run, Mike wouldn't discourage him."

23. When Kennedy got around to calling Senator James Eastland of Mississippi, essentially out of courtesy, for a time he was mistaken by Eastland for a neighboring farmer. After that confusion was cleared up and Kennedy stated that he was going to offer himself for the whip's job, Eastland is said to have replied, "Boy, that job is taken."

24. Kennedy's aides seem to read more into this than may have been warranted. That is, by implication, Long was in trouble if he hadn't heard from other Senators that Kennedy was about to take the plunge.

25. Lewis Anthony Dexter, "The Representative and His District," *Human Organization* **16** (1957), pp. 2–13. Reprinted in Robert L. Peabody and Nelson W. Polsby, eds., *New Perspectives on the House of Representatives*, 2d ed. (Chicago: Rand McNally, 1969), pp. 3–29 at 24.

26. "The Ascent of Ted Kennedy," *Time*, January 10, 1969, p. 16.

27. The exception was Minnesota's Eugene McCarthy, a Catholic and the leading anti-Vietnam candidate for the Democratic presidential nomination in 1968. Reminded that after the previous summer's Democratic convention he had said that he would vote for Ted Kennedy on a presidential ballot, McCarthy was quoted as replying, "I can think of a lot of people I would like to see as Pope but would not like to see as my pastor." *Time*, January 10, 1969, p. 14.

28. In retrospect, it would appear that Muskie's abortive effort had hurt Long more than it helped him. If anything, the ease with which he obtained commitments against the Senator from Maine had made Long overconfident. And he may have read more of a blanket endorsement into the commitments that he received.

29. In these traits as well as others, Long shared common ground with Lyndon Johnson. Both were members of the Senate class of 1948; Long was one of a number of southern Senators who endorsed Johnson's presidential ambitions as early as 1956. Johnson consulted frequently with Long both in the Senate and later in the White House. Rowland Evans and Robert Novak,

Lyndon B. Johnson: The Exercise of Power (New York: New American Library, 1966), pp. 41, 130, 231, 356; McPherson, *op. cit.*, p. 43.

30. Still, of ten returning Finance Committee members, Chairman Long apparently lost five: Albert Gore (Tenn.), J. W. Fulbright (Ark.), Abraham Ribicoff (Conn.), Lee Metcalf (Mont.), and Fred Harris (Okla.).

31. Harris, at 38, was one of the Senate's most liberal and vocal young Turks. Co-chairman of Humphrey's election campaign, he withstood aggressive demands by the oil interests in his state and instead voted for Kennedy. Harris declined to run for reelection in 1972 in the face of strong primary and general election opposition.

32. They do agree, however, that contributions are likely to loom much larger in the scarcely populated Rocky Mountain states, where, as one cynic put it, "A $5000 contribution would be like discovering an oil well."

33. "Long Predicts 'Solid Victory' Over Kennedy in Whip Race," *Washington Post*, January 2, 1969, p. A-2.

34. Nominating speeches almost never change votes but the symbolic strength of the Kennedy line-up, compared to Long's, is rather striking. Kennedy was nominated by the previous year's Democratic vice-presidential candidate, supported by an influential western chairman, and a liberal southerner from Long's own Finance Committee. Although Ellender and Holland were well regarded senior southerners, neither was held in the esteem accorded Richard Russell or John Stennis, both of whom presumably voted for Long, yet neither of whom spoke out for him in the conference.

35. Most of the Senators keep their own tallies as the vote proceeds. Even as the initial announcement is made the count is verified. In order to preserve the secret ballot, votes are burned immediately.

36. "Kennedy Defeats Long for Senate Whip's Job," *Washington Post*, January 4, 1969, p. A-1.

37. "Kennedy, Scott to be Whips," *Washington Evening Star*, January 3, 1969, p. A-3.

38. *Time*, January 10, 1969, p. 13.

39. In a remarkably candid interview the day following his defeat, Long details at length for Morton Mintz some of the reasons he felt led a number of Senators, including 12 non-southerners, to vote for him. A sampling of Long's comments: On Dodd of Connecticut — "I stood by him when no one else would." On McCarthy of Minnesota — He is a member of Senate Finance whom "I helped every time I could honorably do so . . . Kennedy had a right to claim McCarthy's vote, but on a personal basis, I had a better right to it . . ." On McGee of Wyoming — McGee wanted to join the Senate Foreign Relations Committee and got to do so when, Long recalled, he swapped his seat to take McGee's place on the less prestigious Commerce Committee. On Anderson and Montoya of New Mexico — Anderson "has been practically a father to me from the very first day I came here . . ." and "Montoya's ambition is to serve on the Appropriations Committee." Wishing him luck, Long noted that Sen. Richard B. Russell of Georgia, "my dear friend," is destined to be chairman, and that Senator Allen J. Ellender, "my colleague" from Louisiana, is the ranking member . . . [Montoya made it]. "Long Denies Bitterness Over Defeat by Kennedy," *Washington Post*, January 5, 1969, pp. A-1, A-5.

40. Joseph Kennedy, Jr., the oldest Kennedy brother, was killed in a wartime airplane crash.

41. *Washington Post*, January 4, 1969, p. A-1.

42. Kennedy's first direct confrontation with the charge that he was riding along on the family name came during his dramatic television debate with Edward McCormack in the Massachusetts senatorial primary in 1962. Kennedy, in his initial bid for public office, was attempting to win the unexpired term of his brother, John. As McCormack, the state's Attorney General and the nephew of House Speaker John W. McCormack, lashed out: ". . . with your qualifications, Teddy, if it was Edward Moore [instead of Edward Moore Kennedy], your candidacy would be a joke . . ." The Massachusetts electorate thought otherwise. Kennedy defeated McCormack by better than two-to-one and went on to overcome his Republican opponent, George Cabot Lodge, by almost 300,000 votes in the general election.
43. *Time*, January 10, 1969, p. 13.
44. *Ibid.*

CHAPTER THIRTEEN

Kennedy vs. Byrd, 1969–1971

The 91st Congress was under way. The excitement of the upset victory for Kennedy had begun to fade. It was time to put the new leadership theories to test. Could the office of the Senate majority whip be made "a better instrument of the will of the Democratic membership"? The initial step would be to claim part of the "spoils," to take over the majority whip's office in the Capitol building, about to be vacated by Long. The second, more crucial, step would be to recruit an administrative assistant with sufficient intelligence, insight, and political experience to do the job.

Under Humphrey and Long, Senators with no mean talent for accruing office space and acquiring new staff, the emoluments of the majority whip's office had expanded. In addition to his regular office on the fourth floor of the Old Senate Office Building, Kennedy would now control an additional three-room suite located at the southwestern front of the Capitol. Ironically, S-148-150 with its splendid view down the Mall to the Washington Monument was once occupied by Bobby Baker, when he was secretary to the majority. Over the next two years Kennedy would take a wry delight in pointing this out to his visitors.

Although Kennedy considered a number of "Hill types" in his search for a whip's office administrative assistant, he ended up choosing a relative outsider, one with little initial familiarity with the intricacies of Senate rules and parliamentary maneuvers. He selected 32-year-old Wayne Owens, an astute and experienced field representative for Senator Frank Moss of Utah. Owens had spent little time in Washington, but he had proven his political skills in a number of Mountain State campaigns.

One strong factor in his selection was Owens' proven loyalty to the Kennedy family. Since the mid-1960's he had accompanied the Kennedys on camping and river trips in the West. Increasingly attached to Bobby Kennedy, he had served as Rocky Mountain States coordinator for the New York Senator's ill-fated presidential bid in 1968.[1]

When asked how he came to work in the whip's office, Owens' response was part serious and part in jest: "He, Ted, was heir apparent. He wanted somebody to run the whip's office who didn't have a Massachusetts accent." As the man in charge of Senator Moss' Utah political affairs for almost a decade, Owens brought with him numerous contacts with political leaders throughout the western states. Thus, his appointment could also be interpreted as a gesture of support toward the West, a sign of appreciation to the more than half-dozen western Senators who appeared to have backed Kennedy in the whip contest.

The week after the whip election, Kennedy's administrative assistant, Dave Burke, was in touch with Owens in Utah to ask him if he were interested in the job. Several days later Kennedy called Owens to confirm the offer and told him, in effect, "We don't know what the job description is — it's whatever we make of it." Kennedy had some broad, philosophical, educational, and communication goals in mind, the kinds of changes implied by, if not yet made specific in, his press statements during and following the whip contest.

When Kennedy, Burke, and Owens finally met in Washington in mid-January to confer about the scope of Owens' new duties, they were not unaware that the whip position had seldom served as anything more than an appendage to the majority leader. What finally evolved from their discussions, as Burke recalls, was "an attempt to develop a 'substantive' as distinct from a 'procedural' whip."

> We wanted someone who would make policy and attempt to apply pressures on issues, rather than merely seeing that the Senators would be on the floor. We would spend less time getting cabs for the airport after a roll call vote — the kind of thing that was traditional with the office.

And, as Owens remembers: "Kennedy wanted me to come up with a program, one aimed at shedding light on the operations of the Senate — and then doing something about them."

I

Owens began rather slowly, at first with education and communications improvements. A series of seminars were launched for the legislative assistants of the newly arriving Senators. A regular weekly whip notice was instituted. Floor-to-office communications were substantially improved by a recorded tape-telephone alert system.

Another innovation was to arrange systematically for speakers to be brought in to address the Democratic Policy Committee — tax and economic policy experts like Harvard Law School Professor Stanley Surrey, ex-Director of the Bureau of the Budget Charles Schultze, and New York banker David Rockefeller. Sometimes these appearances had a direct impact on policy; for example, in shaping Mansfield's 1969 statement that the tax surcharge would not be extended unless it was coupled with basic tax reforms. Moreover, it was Kennedy who brought the intellectual resources of Harvard, M.I.T., and other academic institutions to bear in the Senate fight against the Safeguard anti-ballistic missile system.

But for the most part, Kennedy and Owens encountered more resistance than they initially expected. As one Kennedy aide observed:

> It was an uphill job. There was a lot of disinterest on the part of a hell of a lot of guys. We had hoped to move immediately and realize some of the substantive changes we had in mind, but the Senate is in many ways like an Irish family. It hates to see one member of the family get [more] out in front than any other member.

The implementation of some of these programs was not made easier by the increasing pressures on Kennedy to respond to his national constituency. As a result, too often the routine aspects of being a whip were neglected. Rather soon Kennedy discovered that his tolerance for floor duty was not much better than Long's. As one Senate aide observed, "He enjoyed getting a debate started, but then he wasn't there." Senators began to complain that some of their traditional prerogatives of being protected on a vote or transported to and from the airports were not available. In short, Kennedy was finding that his prospective mantle as the next likely presidential nominee was not very compatible with service as a party functionary.

Kennedy was learning, like his predecessors, that the whip has little independently endowed power. As one experienced Senate staff member commented:

> You don't get any power by saying that you have it. If you are willing to do the minutiae, and the housekeeping chores, that's a way of assuming an independent role and some power can accrue. But Kennedy was not willing to make that sacrifice. He was not willing to work himself into a position where being on the floor would lead to improved channels of communication.

At first, Kennedy's relationship with Mansfield was superb. But Mansfield had always found it difficult to delegate responsibility. He would seldom say, "Ted, you take the floor from 3 to 6 P.M. today." When the majority leader came to the floor and did not find Kennedy there it increasingly irritated him. Seldom, if ever, did he admonish Kennedy for his absences, but he began to let other Senators know of his uneasiness. Meanwhile, the slack was beginning to be taken up by Senator Robert Byrd of West Virginia, secretary to the conference and number three man in the Democratic hierarchy.

In the late spring of 1969, it began to appear to Kennedy's staff, other Senators, and to Hill correspondents that the Massachusetts Senator was spreading himself too thin. There just didn't appear to be enough time to discharge all the burdens Kennedy bore and, at the same time, to operate as second in command of the Democratic majority in the Senate. Kennedy's many burdens included being head of all the Kennedy families, being a husband and a father to his own family, fulfilling the needs of his home state with his own reelection forthcoming in 1970, and continuing to participate in his Judiciary, Labor, and Public Welfare Committees activities. With almost every action of his interpreted in terms of presidential politics it is little wonder that Kennedy began to show signs of stress.

Staff could lighten some of these tasks for Kennedy, but most difficult decisions usually had to be made by him. One warning sign of the strain he was under came out of a hastily organized trip to Alaska in mid-April 1969 to investigate the problems of Indians in that state (after Robert Kennedy's assassination, Edward Kennedy had reluctantly taken over the chairmanship of the Special Subcommittee on Indian Education). Animosities that sprang from Alaskan Democratic Senator Mike Gravel's non-support in the whip contest, and Kennedy's subsequent blockage of Gravel's hopes to achieve a Commerce

Committee assignment, resulted in the failure of Gravel's office to coordinate the trip. Midway through the tundra-hopping expedition, three Republican Senators deserted the investigation charging that it was turning into a stage-managed "Roman circus." In Fairbanks, and on the commercial jet flight back, Kennedy apparently chagrined even some of the most case-hardened newspaper reporters with his heavy drinking.[2]

Then came Chappaquiddick.[3] The consequences of that fateful night of July 18, 1969 are still unfolding. The death of Miss Mary Jo Kopechne was tragic enough.[4] But it was the context of the situation, and even more important, the way in which Edward Kennedy responded or failed to respond to the crisis, which was to have the most far-reaching political effects.[5]

First, and for a time, it was not clear that Kennedy would stay in politics. The wound was grave, politically and also personally, in terms of self-esteem, his view of how others saw him, and indeed, his sense of commitment to public service.[6] On July 25, 1969, he made a 12-minute television statement to his Massachusetts constituents (also carried live on national networks) and asked for their advice, opinion, and prayers in helping him to decide whether or not he should seek reelection in 1970. Although a number of national commentators criticized the speech for its bathos as well as what was left unsaid, the response from his constituents was overwhelmingly in Kennedy's favor. Five days later a press release from his Boston office indicated that he would compete for his second complete term in the Senate.

A second consequence of this tragic event was that it all but precluded Kennedy from making a bid for the Democratic presidential nomination in 1972. In his statement announcing his Senate bid in 1970, he promised, if successful, to serve out the entire six-year term.[7]

A third consequence was aptly summarized by William H. Honen, writing in the *New York Times Magazine* some ten months after Chappaquiddick. His analysis may have overstated Kennedy's power, if not prestige, before the accident. But there is no question of the combined impact on Kennedy's Senate standing of the accident, followed by his withdrawal from the 1972 presidential sweepstakes:[8]

> He suffered a sort of instant political decompression. His enormous power and prestige in the Senate, supported by the reluctance of his colleagues to oppose a young man so likely to occupy the White House sooner or later, and by their eager-

ness to curry favor with one who could so readily lend glamour
and attract money to their personal causes, collapsed over-
night.

A fourth and closely related consequence was the drastic retarda-
tion of Kennedy's ability to function as an effective legislator. No
longer were other Senators quick to co-sponsor the bills he introduced. His amendments largely went unheeded or what was worse,
were voted down by embarrassingly large margins. Defeats of his
amendments on gun control, draft reform, tax legislation and the
administration's crime bill were cases in point.

Other complications followed from his loss of stature. Majority
Leader Mansfield took over a Kennedy-proposed measure advocating
the vote for 18-year-olds. In addition, because Kennedy's own case was
entangled in the Massachusetts courts, he had to abstain from leadership on the drive to block the Supreme Court nominations of
Clement Haynsworth and G. Harrold Carswell. Birch Bayh, Kennedy's junior Judiciary Committee colleague, took over the main
thrust of the challenges.

It is difficult to argue with Honen's overall assessment, that "Kennedy's record of non-accomplishment in the Senate over the next ten
months [July 1969 to May 1970] [was] truly astonishing." [9]

This same loss of stature drastically set back, if not eliminated,
whatever opportunity Kennedy and Owens might have had to reform
the whip's office and make it a more viable instrument of the Democratic majority in the Senate. His staff continued to labor in behalf
of change, but as another Kennedy associate recalled: "From the beginning, we encountered a hell of a lot more resistance than we
thought we would get. Then came Chappaquiddick and we were on
the down side after that."

In part, because of the cumulative effect these various incidents had
on Kennedy's effectiveness in the Senate, in part because of a series
of further complications which kept Kennedy away from the floor, a
final consequence of Chappaquiddick was to put Kennedy's whip position in ultimate jeopardy. Caught up in a period of agonizing self-
examination following the accident, he did not return to the Senate
until July 31, 1969. In November 1969, his father died after a prolonged illness. In February 1970, the young Massachusetts Senator,
who was rarely ill, missed additional days in the Senate because of
pneumonia.

As the fall of 1969 wore on and during the first 10 months Kennedy was increasingly preoccupied with his own Senate reelection campaign. He could hardly avoid extensive travel to Massachusetts, since the election results would be interpreted both as a possible reaffirmation of faith from his Massachusetts constituents and an opportunity to partially restore his national political stature.[10]

The inevitable costs were numerous days absent from the floor and multiple opportunities for other Senators to step in and assume leadership responsibilities. Through this combination of events, Kennedy was to become as vulnerable as his predecessor. Ironically, it began to appear that if Kennedy could be beaten, there was only one challenger who seemed to possess the requisite assets. No liberal would be inclined to take him on; the one or two with the greatest stature — Muskie or Bayh, for examples — were friends and/or already maneuvering for the 1972 presidential nomination. A challenge, if it came, would be launched from the right; the one man likely to make it was Robert C. Byrd of West Virginia.

II

"THE BOB BYRD STORY: FROM ORPHAN BOY TO U.S. SENATOR." Robert Carlyle Byrd was born January 15, 1918 in Wilkes County, North Carolina. Originally christened Robert C. Sale, he was sent to live with his aunt and uncle, the Titus Dalton Byrds, at the age of 10 months following the death of his mother.[11] He saw his father only once after he learned of his adoption at the age of 16. To this day Byrd has only rare contact with his three older brothers and one sister. Byrd's foster father lived on a farm and worked briefly for a brewery, but spent most of his life attempting to eke out an existence in the coal mines of West Virginia. As Byrd recalls his upbringing: "Maybe it was only pinto beans and cornbread, but we never existed in hunger ... I always worked to put food on the table. My foster father bought pigs every year and I went from house to house to gather scraps to feed them."[12]

Graduating from high school at 16 as class valedictorian, Byrd was not to resume his formal education for more than a decade. After leaving high school he worked as a filling station attendant, got married, and took a job as a produce boy in the company commissary. Four years later he advanced to the position of head butcher. Then, as now, he was powerfully motivated to get ahead: "It was my ambition to become the best meat-cutter in the business," he recalls.[13] For more than a decade he followed his profession with a year or so off to work in the shipyards of Baltimore and Tampa during World War II.

By 1946, Byrd owned his own general store, was the father of two daughters, and began to look for other challenges. He decided to put up his $10 filing fee and run for the West Virginia state legislature. His credentials were practically non-existent — he had only a high school education, he was not a veteran, and he was not especially well known.

Still he had a willingness to campaign hard and a talent for playing the fiddle. A Republican lawyer friend was said to have taken him aside and advised him: "Bob, you're not known. Your father wasn't a judge or politician. You don't have any money and you're going to have to get known, so I would suggest you make that violin your briefcase and where you go take it along." [14] Byrd followed the advice. Since he had not yet learned to drive, a friend took him to the isolated mountain homes and county social gatherings. The fiddle-playing and hard campaigning paid off. Byrd was elected twice to the House of Delegates, once to the West Virginia State Senate, and by 1952 was running hard for the U.S. House of Representatives.

It was not until this 1952 congressional primary that Byrd's earlier membership in the Ku Klux Klan became an issue, one that has periodically haunted him ever since. One of his primary opponents brought the charge, and Byrd met it head on. He admitted belonging in 1942–1943 — "those were my dues-paying years," he explained — "and after that I lost interest." Byrd won the primary (the Ku Klux Klan had not been that unpopular in West Virginia), but then someone turned up an embarrassing letter which Byrd had written to the Imperial Wizard in Alabama in 1946. In it, Byrd, as a former kleagle in Raleigh County, was urging the rebirth of Klan activity in West Virginia. Despite the plea by the incumbent Democratic governor that he withdraw from the ticket, Byrd took his case to the people. Borrowing $500 and raising additional money — a dollar here, fifty cents there from "the little crick and holler people" — Byrd appeared on television to denounce his critics for trying to divert attention from "the real dangers of communism, organized crime, the moral values and the degeneration of religious life." [15]

Byrd won the general election by 55.6 percent of the total vote, a margin he was to exceed in two subsequent bids for reelection to the U.S. House of Representatives. In 1958, he defeated the Republican incumbent, Senator Chapman C. Revercomb, by 59 percent of the vote. Reelected by 68 percent of the vote in 1964, in 1970 Byrd set a new record for a contested general election in West Virginia, carrying all 55 counties and amassing 78 percent of the total vote. Byrd could claim that from 1946 through 1972 he has held more legislative elective offices than any other individual in the history of West Virginia — and he does.

Hand-in-hand with his political advancement, Byrd worked on a university education. He began with college correspondence courses and eventually attended seven schools on his way to earning a B.A. and LL.D. The culmination came in 1963, when Byrd, at age 45, won a law degree *cum laude* from American University. On hand at the ceremony to congratulate him was President John F. Kennedy.[16]

Quick to identify with such Senate influentials as Lyndon B. Johnson and Richard Russell (and already known to them from his service in the House), Byrd received unusually prestigious committee assignments for a freshman — Appropriations and Banking and Currency. He was to remain on Appropriations (eighth ranking by 1970), but exchange his other assignments for the Judiciary Committee and Rules and Administration. Although low ranking on each, by 1971 Byrd had become chairman of the important Subcommittee on the Standing Rules of the Senate, through which virtually all rules changes must come.

For eight years, Byrd worked hard as chairman of the Senate Appropriations Subcommittee for the District of Columbia. It was in this role, especially his relentless crusade against unqualified welfare recipients including unwed mothers, that Byrd earned national fame if not notoriety.

At the opening of the 90th Congress in 1967, Byrd made his first move toward the Senate leadership ladder when he ran for the office of secretary to the Democratic Conference, a position made vacant by George Smathers' announced plans to retire. To almost no one's surprise, save possibly his opponent, Joseph Clark of Pennsylvania, Byrd won handily, 38 to 28. Offsetting the presence of more moderates and liberals than conservatives in the Senate was Byrd's status as a near-member of whatever passes as an "inner club." Clark, on the other hand, a millionaire doctrinaire liberal epitomized the Senate "outsider." [17]

The personal traits that paid off in Byrd's rise from poverty to formal leadership stood him in good stead in the Senate. "Loyal," "hard-working," "diligent," "resourceful" — these adjectives his colleagues used to describe him. His critics are likely to add "humorless" and "power-hungry." In Byrd's own terms: "I am an intense, driving person, a perfectionist — who falls far short of perfection. I am always trying to improve myself." [18]

His intense drive to succeed, his six- to seven-day workweeks, his concern for detail have taken their toll (Byrd has been plagued by ulcers for more than a decade). As to the violin that launched his political career, Byrd says he is "too busy to play any more." He and his wife, Erma, have almost never taken vacations longer than a weekend. Byrd seldom travels beyond Washington and West Virginia.

Not especially impressive physically, Byrd is a man of medium height and of rather compact features: intense eyes, a sharp nose, thin lips, and neatly parted, swept-back black hair, now tending to grey, with not a hint of sideburns. He dresses inconspicuously — dark blues and browns. Only lately has he switched to colored shirts and wider ties.

A devout Baptist who can quote the Bible with ease, Byrd is capable of giving a hand-clapping, fundamentalist sermon, and occasionally does. He does not drink, although he does at times indulge in the luxury of long, thick "El Producto" cigar. He and his wife live modestly in Alexandria, Virginia, about a 20-minute drive from the Capitol. Their two daughters, both married, live nearby.

A typical work-day finds Byrd rising by 8 A.M., then on his way to the office driving his own Buick sedan. In the office before 9 A.M., he reviews the mail and confers with his staff in the morning. Most of the balance of the day will be spent in his Capitol office or on the floor. When the Senate comes in earlier, as it does more and more during the later months of a session, then Byrd arrives earlier, too. Regardless of when the Senate adjourns, Byrd seldom goes home for dinner before 9 or 10 P.M. And it is more usual than not for Byrd to come into work part or all of Saturday and Sunday.

In terms of loyalty, hard work, and devotion to duty, Byrd expects "no more, if not much less" from his staff than he does from himself. His professional staff members are expected to be available in order to confer with Byrd no matter how late the Senate adjourns for the day. While this is not an uncommon practice, Byrd has instituted several staff patterns which have become Capitol Hill legends. His clerical staff works a typical five-day, 40-hour week with one further requirement; constituency mail which comes in during the week must be answered and sent out before Friday evening. Staff members, all of them, do not leave for the weekend until all mail has been cleared. Byrd extends his attention to detail to constituency mail. Unlike most Senators, he sees and signs all of it. Letters with mistakes or mis-wordings go back until they are perfect.

Another example of Byrd's thoroughness is a color-coded card file containing the names, addresses, and telephone numbers of more than 2500 West Virginia constituents — newspaper editors, television man-agers, ministers, union spokesmen, and party leaders, but also miners, taxicab drivers, and housewives — in short, people who have helped Byrd get elected and stay in the Senate. Byrd makes a special point of attempting to telephone everyone in the file at least once a year.

Byrd's personal embodiment of the puritan ethic is extended to his relations with his peers. With other Senators, Byrd is workmanlike, cordial, and in most cases, scrupulously fair. As the secretary of the Senate Democratic Conference he performed favors for liberals and conservatives alike. No detail seemed too small to attend to and Byrd apparently went out of his way to seek opportunities to render services.

On the telephone Byrd is likely to preface his calls to other Senators with a "Hello, chief," or reply with a "Yes, boss," but the tone is more cordial than servile. Such language seems merely to symbolize the at-titude he shares with Majority Leader Mansfield — party leaders exist to serve the needs of other Senators.

Within a year of becoming secretary to the Democratic Conference, Byrd had converted little more than a perfunctory position into one of considerable scope. By personal temperament he was better suited for the housekeeping aspects of floor leadership; he also understood, far better than Long or Kennedy, how small personal favors performed for other Senators might build a credit balance that could be put to other uses at a later date. Moreover, he welcomed the long hours on the floor, in part because it provided a further opportunity to perfect his knowledge of parliamentary procedure.[19]

What Kennedy could not and seemed not to want to compete with was Senator Byrd's great facility in dealing with details. Byrd saw that members were not downtown or out of town when a critical vote was pending, arranged for transportation after a roll call vote, provided Senators with "live pairs," and seldom missed an opportunity to re-mind his colleagues of the favors he had rendered. Byrd denies that he ever recorded the favors in a "black book." For a time he had his staff clip from the *Congressional Record* and send to individual Sen-

ators the portions of the *Record* that supported something he had
done for that Senator, but he discontinued the practice after several
press stories appeared commenting on it.

> About the only time I'd write a letter_to a Senator would be
> if I'd arranged for a live pair. If Senator X is going to be out
> of town and he wants a pair, I go to Senator Y or Z or maybe
> Senator A, and A says he will give him a pair. That means
> he loses his vote . . . I'll write to Senator A after the vote and
> thank him or I'll write to Senator X that Senator A gave him
> a live pair and send a carbon to Senator A so that he'll know
> too . . . Why do I do that? Because I may want to go back
> to Senator X sometime and say Senator A needs a pair. This
> way he knows that he's been noticed and appreciated.

When Long was whip he had welcomed Byrd's assistance on the
floor; Kennedy, however, resented it. Gradually a personal distrust —
at least as long standing as 1960, when Byrd had supported Hubert
Humphrey in the West Virginia primaries against John Kennedy —
broke into an open feud. On occasion, Byrd would be covering the
floor when the time would come for the Senate to adjourn for the
day. Wayne Owens would telephone Kennedy and then walk over to
Byrd and request a quorum call. A few minutes later Kennedy would
stroll in and adjourn the Senate.

From the Kennedy perspective, the feud seemed to be blown out
of proportion, more important to Byrd than to Kennedy or his staff.
A Kennedy aide would recall: "Bobby Byrd didn't get aggressive until
after Chappaquiddick; before that he was completely deferential." Perhaps the seeds of an unwillingness to take Byrd's possible challenge
with the seriousness it deserved are reflected in such an attitude.

Whatever the merits of the respective viewpoints, the controversy
boiled mainly behind the scenes for most of 1969 and 1970, with only
an occasional flareup. Although he was never to make a public announcement of his challenge, Byrd had become convinced by the
middle of 1970 that he deserved the position: "I've been doing the
work all along, why shouldn't I have the title, too?"

III

"If you ever get ready to take him on, count on me." Biding
his time, Senator Byrd was not to announce formally his challenge
to Senator Kennedy until the Democratic Conference on January

21, 1971. But he had decided to make the race at least a year earlier, providing he could align the necessary *firm* support. Years of watching Russell, Johnson, and Long had instilled in him an appreciation for the personal and philosophical vagaries which motivate people and the interests, both direct and more subtle, which might help to convert them. As he recalled the factors that led to his decision to run:

> First, a man must make up his mind that that is what he wants to do. I had served as secretary of the Democratic Conference... I had tried to assist the majority leader as needed... I was on very friendly terms with Senator Long; I never would have run against Senator Long...

> After Senator Kennedy became whip, naturally I was disappointed. I had been standing in line for the position... Someone had leapfrogged over me but the only thing I could complain about was fate.

Byrd began his campaign with the nearly solid support of the South and most of the 20 to 25 Democratic conservatives who had previously backed Long and were thus predisposed if not already solidly in his camp. The former majority whip, not one to lightly forget an affront, was an early and hard-working supporter, willing to commit the full resources of his position as chairman of the Finance Committee. Was it such a small distortion of the Golden Rule to do unto others as they have done unto you?

Through quietly arranged *quid-pro-quos*, through an expanding reservoir of good will based on small and not-so-small favors, Byrd was quickly picking up a promise of support here, a tentative commitment there. His method of aligning support was low-pressured, steady, and incremental:

> I began by talking to others. At about the same time [the summer of 1970], other Senators began to approach me — "If you ever get ready to take him on, count on me." I went to a certain southern Senator... I talked to a Senator from the Midwest on the telephone. He said, "I don't know if you should make the contest. You'd have a 50–50 chance to win, but I hope you run," — that was a message.

> I didn't make an open campaign, but every time the subject came up, I made some headway. As the time went on encouragement became commitment and commitments became more and more firm.

What was not clear was whether the myriad of small and sometimes larger services that Byrd had performed for other Senators could
offset the basic dominance of his party by moderate-to-liberal Democratic Senators. Winner over Long by a vote of 31–26, Kennedy could
normally expect better than a five-to-four liberal-to-conservative advantage among his colleagues. (This ratio would only marginally be
altered by the election results of 1970.)

Still, Byrd could rightfully claim to be an "economic liberal" — he
had voted for most poverty legislation, public works, manpower training, increases in food stamp appropriations, and most federal health
and safety programs, including medicare. Although Kennedy would
command strong support from organized labor, Byrd's voting record
was generally sympathetic to labor.[20] On most other legislative matters
Byrd could be said to have carved his own self-assessment as a "moderate conservative." [21] A hawk on Vietnam, with a mixed voting record
on economic regulations and environmental matters, what made Byrd
an anathema to many liberals was his anti-civil rights record. He had
voted against the Civil Rights Act of 1964, and had gone on record
against the Voting Rights Act of 1965. Overtly and repeatedly critical
of the Warren Court and most of its landmark decisions, Byrd broke
with a majority of his party and voted to confirm Nixon appointees,
Harrold Carswell of Florida and Clement Haynsworth of South
Carolina, to the Supreme Court in 1970. Both were defeated by close,
hard-fought, embittering votes. While such votes found common
ground with his southern base of support, a number of his northern
colleagues, civil rights groups, and labor unions felt that they should
disqualify him from becoming a party spokesman for majority Democrats.

Undaunted by the odds against him and largely ignoring a generally
hostile press, the West Virginia conservative continued to seek ways
to chip away at Kennedy's largely northern and western base of support. By mid-November 1970, as the lame-duck session of the 91st
Congress got under way, Byrd felt he was within striking distance of
the 28 votes he would need for a majority in the January conference.
In a November 15 UPI interview with Drew Von Bergen, Byrd refused to unveil his intentions. It was just too early to speculate
whether he would enter the contest or not. He maintained that he
wouldn't make a final decision "before the end of the session, if
then." [22]

IV

Both Kennedy and Byrd won their Senate reelection bids by large margins — Kennedy by a respectable 62 percent; Byrd by an overwhelming 78 percent of the vote. If the Massachusetts Senator had not repeated his 1964 landslide, at least he had duplicated the electoral margin run up by Senator Edmund S. Muskie of Maine, now widely perceived as the most likely prospect for the Democratic presidential nomination in 1972.

Despite an intensive and widespread election blitz by President Richard M. Nixon and Vice President Spiro T. Agnew, Democratic Senate defeats had been held to a net loss of two seats. Although the Senate would be slightly more conservative, House Democrats had made a net gain of eight. On the whole, prospects for 1972 appeared to be looking up for the Democratic party.

Kennedy's chances to retain his majority whip post in the 92d Congress seemed quite positive. Most of his possible liberal opponents were already engrossed in presidential pre-primary maneuvering. Kennedy had lost the support of defeated Senators like Joseph Tydings of Maryland and Albert Gore of Tennessee, but surely he would pick up the pledges of liberal newcomers like Adlai Stevenson III of Illinois and John V. Tunney of California, the latter a long-time personal friend from University of Virginia Law School days.

On November 11, 1972, a week after the election, Spencer Rich wrote a story for the *Washington Post* based on an interview with Kennedy. "I intend to stay on as whip," said the Senator. "I expect to be on the floor much more." Discounting Byrd as "probably too conservative to beat Kennedy in any head-to-head contest," Rich concluded his story with a prediction: "At present, a successful challenger for Kennedy's assistant leader does not appear in sight." [23]

Even before the post-election session began on November 16, 1970, animosity broke out anew between Kennedy and Byrd, a tension that was to build throughout the lame-duck session. Kennedy wanted to fly to Europe to attend a NATO Interparliamentary Union meeting. He telephoned Byrd after the election and after minimal mutual congratulations, he asked Byrd point-blank whether or not he intended to become a candidate for the majority whip. Byrd replied rather brusquely that he hadn't yet made up his mind, whereupon Kennedy hung up the phone and went off to the NATO meetings anyway.

For the balance of November and throughout December, with the Senate threatened by more than a half-dozen filibusters, the members, staff, and a bemused press were treated to one of the most peculiar sparring matches to preoccupy Capitol Hill in many a year. Attempting to reassert his leadership, Kennedy was present on the floor almost continuously, especially at the beginning and close of each session. Through many of the long hours of debate and especially at critical votes, Byrd would be in the chair, quick to display his mastery of parliamentary procedure. On one occasion, Kennedy was anxious to catch a plane to Boston while Byrd was still speaking. Finally, Kennedy had to leave, whereupon Byrd concluded his remarks, and allowed liberal California Senator Alan Cranston the privilege of adjourning the Senate.[24]

Byrd's general deftness and parliamentary skills received not a little aid from southerners and even Republicans, quick to take advantage of every opportunity to embarrass a Senator who still might become a presidential candidate, if not in 1972, then possibly in 1976. Kennedy was on the floor demonstrating his debating skills and quick grasp of legislation. More important, he seldom overlooked any opportunities to reassure his supporters and seek new converts. As Wayne Owens, his administrative assistant, recalled:

> We would be sitting on the floor and there would go Senator _____ into the cloakroom. Teddy would follow him and talk to him and then he would come back and tell me what happened. I would keep track of those Senators that Teddy had talked to and where they stood.

Both candidates found themselves in an increasing bind as to how their personal votes would be interpreted in the closing days of the 91st Congress. With their colleagues scrutinizing their actions with greater intensity, each tried to maintain the support of their normal allies without neglecting the rare opportunity to modify a position where it might soften up an as yet uncommitted Senator. Such opportunities were rare because of each Senator's own continuing ideological and constituency interests. Still, the latter constraints could be somewhat relaxed given the six years before either Senator would be called upon to confront an electorate.

In mid-December, however, Byrd found himself in a position to do a favor for two of the Senate's most powerful Democrats, Commerce Committee Chairman Warren Magnuson and Interior Committee Chairman Henry Jackson, both representing Washington state. Since the favor would require only a marginal variation from his normal voting proclivities, Byrd was able to help at little or no cost to himself. At stake were $290 million in appropriations for development of two prototype supersonic transports (SSTs). The Boeing Aircraft Company, with headquarters in Seattle, Washington was the prime contractor. Environmentalist forces, led by Senator William Proxmire of Wisconsin, were successful in deleting the funds from the Transportation Appropriations bill despite strong efforts by President Nixon and the two Washington Senators to keep the SST program alive. Byrd maintains that he was inclined to vote for the bill in any event, but his support and that of his fellow West Virginian, Jennings Randolph, combined with Kennedy's opposition on environmentalist grounds, apparently played a major role in shifting the support of Magnuson and Jackson away from Kennedy and toward Byrd. For them, the issue had become almost a question of economic survival for Seattle and their state. The two Washington Senators felt that Kennedy had made a commitment to help them; from Kennedy's view he had merely urged a postponement of the vote after the election. He and his advisers could not conceive that the votes on a single issue would lose him the support of two powerful Senate moderates like Jackson and Magnuson.

By the end of December with still no public indication of Byrd's candidacy, the Kennedy forces began to breathe a little easier. Kennedy had canvassed nearly every Senator except Byrd, Long, and the several other Senators he calculated to be closest to them. Among the five newly elected Democratic Senators — Tunney of California, Chiles of Florida, Stevenson of Illinois, Humphrey of Minnesota, and Bentsen of Texas — Kennedy felt there would be a division along ideological and regional lines. He was considerably miffed, however, that Humphrey, the former presidential candidate who had asked him to become his vice-presidential running mate in 1968, would refuse to make a commitment to him for majority whip in 1970.[25]

The 91st Congress did not adjourn until its constitutional deadline on January 2, 1971. As Senators and Representatives headed for home, hideaways and vacation lands, the Kennedy forces were mostly optimistic. The new Congress would convene at noon on Thursday, January 21, 1971. The vote, if it was to come, would take place that same morning in the Democratic Conference.

Their confidence was based on "31 absolute commitments," not vague promises but Senator-to-Senator affirmations. Over the next two weeks Kennedy would continue to work on the soft spots — Humphrey, the two Washington Senators, Nevada's Alan Bible, the chairman of the Appropriations Subcommittee which had handled SST, and one or two others. On ideological grounds it seemed hard to believe that these Senators could bring themselves to vote for Byrd. Even beyond these "probables," one southern chairman had promised a vote for Kennedy and another had told the incumbent whip: "You know I'd do nothing to hurt you, Ted." In their more optimistic moments, Kennedy aides could see their Senator ending up with as many as 40 of the 55 Democratic votes.

The week before the vote Kennedy felt confident enough to fly to Montego Bay, Jamaica with his family. In his eyes there was little more that he could do in Washington. He was reluctant to make follow-up calls to Senators who were already committed for fear it might be interpreted as a sign of weakness. For similar reasons he rejected activating outside constituency or interest group activity on his behalf. Why create unnecessary pressure or possible ill will if his reelection seemed secure? It was by no means clear that there would even be a contest in the Democratic Conference.

Back in town for the last several day before the vote his final canvassing efforts were generally frustrating. There was still no word from Humphrey; Magnuson remained out of town because of his wife's illness, but had given his written proxy to Mansfield. As late as the morning of the conference, Kennedy had hopes of securing Jackson's vote, a powerful influence in the Senate, a moderate already being boomed for the presidential nomination, and a Senator who had seconded his nomination two years ago against Long. He and Wayne Owens walked to Senator Jackson's Old Senate Office Building suite about 10 minutes before the conference. As Owens remembers: "He kept us waiting for about seven of the ten minutes. It was embarrassing. We stood there drawing in the dust with our toes." After Kennedy finally got in to see Jackson, he came out shaking his head and reported, "Scoop's against us."

Despite these negative omens, Kennedy and Owens remained guardedly confident as the Senator entered the conference and his administrative assistant awaited the results from outside. Both felt they had done their homework, going over the list of Senators as many as three or four times a day during the post-election and January sessions. As Owens recalls: "He didn't let it go at 'Don't worry about me, Ted,' he'd asked them, 'But will you vote for me?'" Kennedy's other administrative assistant, David Burke, who had participated closely in both contests, insists that Kennedy canvassed the vote more thoroughly in 1970–1971 than he had during the rapidly developed challenge to Long. And in Senator Kennedy's own words:

> All of those stories of not counting, of poor staff work are simply wrong. I did more counting the second time around than the first.

V

When Senator Robert Byrd walked into the Democratic Conference at 10 A.M. on January 21, 1971, he remained uncertain that he would challenge Kennedy. His decision hinged on whether his 28th vote, a proxy from Senator Richard B. Russell of Georgia, was still operable. The 74-year-old President pro tempore of the Senate was in critical condition in Walter Reed Army Hospital. The previous week, at Byrd's request, Hermon Talmadge, the junior Senator from Georgia, had visited the dying Senator Russell and had obtained the proposed proxy. Allegedly, it was the last time Russell was to sign his name.[26] Addressed to Majority Leader Mansfield, Russell's proxy read:

> In the event it is not possible for me to be present when the Senate Democrats caucus for the opening of the 92nd Congress, I hereby tender my proxy in favor of Senator Robert C. Byrd of West Virginia if he is a candidate for position of Assistant Majority Leader.

If Russell were still living, his proxy vote for Byrd could be counted. Only with Russell's proxy was Senator Byrd convinced that he had the necessary majority to beat Kennedy.[27]

Byrd, as secretary, presided when the conference began. After the Democrats routinely reelected Mike Mansfield as majority leader and only moments before nominations for the whip were to begin, Byrd slipped out of the conference to confer with a Russell or Talmadge aide (Byrd could not recall which). At 10:53 A.M. he was told that Senator Russell's condition had not changed. Returning to the conference, Byrd gave Jennings Randolph a prearranged signal and his West Virginia colleague put his name into nomination. It was seconded by Alaska's Mike Gravel.[28]

The incumbent whip was nominated by popular moderate Daniel

K. Inouye of Hawaii and seconded by liberal Phillip A. Hart of
Michigan.

About 15 minutes later, after three freshman Senators had tallied
the secret ballot vote, the Democrats had elected a new whip.[29]
Robert C. Byrd had received three more votes than he had expected.
He had upset the incumbent whip, Edward M. Kennedy, by a vote
of 31 to 24.

Byrd greeted the television cameras and press in the company of a
beaming Russell Long. The former whip was shouting: "We did it,
we did it." Byrd announced: [30]

> My role will be that of a legislative tactician. I view the office
> of whip as one which expedites the flow of legislative busi-
> ness. I want to facilitate a condition in which every Senator
> can exercise his will in a climate of impartiality.
>
> A careful study of my voting record shows I will support both
> liberal and conservative positions, depending upon the issue.

Kennedy, looking wan and withdrawn, had words of praise for Byrd's
attentiveness to floor activity. Byrd, he added, would perform his new
job with "great diligence." Asked how he felt about losing, he concluded: "I learned a long time ago that as long as you don't know
how to lose, you don't deserve to win." [31]

Four hours after the conference vote, Senator Russell died. After
the caucus but before his death, Senator Byrd told reporters that "If
Senator Russell had not been alive, I would not have run." [32] In a
sense, then, a mere four hours at the end of a 74 year life span deprived Kennedy of his incumbency as majority whip.

The Democratic Conference completed one more significant action
before it adjourned in order that the new whip and the vanquished
former leader could confront the press. Senator Frank E. Moss of
Utah, a moderate just elected to his third term, was elected secretary
of the conference with no opposition. Moss had considered opposing
Byrd for the number three position in the party hierarchy two years
earlier but had backed off for lack of support. Given a prospective
challenge to Kennedy from Byrd, Moss had put out further feelers in
the post-election session of the 91st Congress. Finally, on January 7,
1971, Moss sent around a "Dear Colleague" letter that announced his
intention to seek the office of secretary, given "a projected shift of
leadership in the Democratic Conference this year."

After announcing his intentions, Moss did little more, since his candidacy was contingent upon whether or not Byrd ran for whip. The day before the caucus he approached Wyoming's Gale McGee about nominating him should Byrd vacate his position. Moss described Kennedy's defeat and his own selection:

> After the Kennedy loss the whole caucus was startled. If Jimmy the Greek had been offering betting odds, I think he would have given about 2 to 1 that Byrd would not succeed against Kennedy — but he did.

> So, for the secretary of the conference, a vacuum opened up. McGee stepped forward, nominated me, and then John Stennis got up. I thought he was going to nominate a southerner . . . but instead he seconded my nomination. I had not talked to him at all. I admire him. We are good friends. But our views are diametrically opposed.

> I don't know who could head you off with that kind of nomination and seconding speech, so I had no opposition.

VI

Other than Russell's having lived long enough for his proxy to count, there is no simple explanation for why Byrd won and Kennedy lost. Certainly that isolated event does not account for the decisiveness of the outcome.

To begin with the consequences of Chappaquiddick, for one or two Senators it might have been a question of morality. Kennedy had been tested and found wanting. But for many more Democrats it was the political consequences that stemmed from the tragic Chappaquiddick event, not the event itself or even Kennedy's response to it, that mattered. By the late fall of 1970, Kennedy was only beginning to recover from that catastrophe. No longer was he the likely Democratic presidential nominee; public reaction and his own decision not to run had all but removed him from consideration in 1972. As one of his colleagues observed, "He no longer had the strong bandwagon going. It wasn't the case that you'd better be with the guy who's going to be in the catbird seat." And as another colleague commented, "the bloom was off the rose."

Chappaquiddick kept Kennedy away from the floor, it greatly reduced his legislative effectiveness, and it took most of the drive away from making over the whip position into more than just a service function. Kennedy's ability to discharge the duties of the assistant majority leader with style and effectiveness were further hampered by absences following his father's death in November 1969, his own illness in February 1970, and the demands of his own reelection bid to the Senate throughout the spring, summer, and early fall of 1970.

Perhaps Kennedy never had an opportunity to find out if he could convert the whip's job to his own conception of it. As with his predecessor, Russell Long, he never liked spending long hours on the floor nor was he fascinated with the intricacies of parliamentary procedure. Above all, he resented the mundane chores of the position. In the words of one of his staff, "Kennedy disliked having to polish apples, shine shoes, and he refused to do so. He just didn't like to do favors for other Senators."

Robert C. Byrd, in contrast, liked being on the floor, thrived on his knowledge of the rules, loved detail, and missed very few opportunities to assist his fellow Senators. Although he was up for reelection in 1970 as well, his campaign was so assured that he needed to spend very little time away from the Senate. He could even take the $18,000 which he received from the Senate Campaign Committee and ask that it be redistributed among other Senators who were more in need.

Campaign contributions — the most tangible of all legislative assets save the vote — may not have turned around a single commitment in this leadership contest. But in the words of one Senator:

> If it were put around it would have an immense effect. It's a very tangible sort of help. There is an implied *quid-pro-quo*. It would be immensely valued by senators in close contests . . . A fellow comes up with $5,000 or $10,000 and you can't help but be grateful.
>
> It's a general thing — a kind of obligation implied. [No one] would be so crass as to remind you; it's not done that way. He'd depend upon implied persuasion.

Byrd, working in alliance with Russell Long, may have been able to direct oil money into some close races — both Senators would probably deny it — but in any case, there was little offsetting liberal money which Kennedy could have diverted, even if he chose to do so. Further, if there ever was a national "Kennedy apparatus," it was in limbo or disarray throughout most of 1969–1970.

Byrd took no chances of activating or reuniting the external Kennedy forces that might be brought to bear. His campaign was kept low-keyed and submerged. He hardly discussed it with his own staff. When he did talk about it, it was almost exclusively with Senators on a one-to-one basis. His discussions with the press were brusque and evasive, calculated so as to discount the possibility of a contest. Shortly before the vote, when Byrd was making his final count down in Washington, an aide was quoted as saying, "The Senator is out of town and unavailable for comment. To the best of my knowledge he has made no decision one way or another." [33] As Byrd later recalled:

> My main reason for keeping it quiet [was that] I didn't want to activate the Kennedy organization. Of course, too, I never reached a final decision until that morning. I was pretty sure I was going to go the day before, maybe the day before that, but I wanted to avoid . . . Senators coming to me and saying that they were beginning to feel the heat.
>
> I wanted to protect them from the heat so I kept it behind the scenes.

Could Senator Kennedy have generated enough "heat" or even persuasion to keep himself in office? Perhaps. Urged by Owens to hold several small dinner parties for his colleagues in the fall, he rejected the idea as a little too "pat" for an internal election. The idea of bringing pressure on Senators from the outside was also considered and, for the most part, rejected. Kennedy surmised that Senators would resent interest group and state party activity on behalf of an incumbent. They might even interpret such pressure as a lack of confidence in their pledges on Kennedy's part, a sense of "no confidence in them."

Underlying both of these decisions was an underassessment of Byrd's chances — neither Kennedy nor his aides could bring themselves to take his challenge seriously. In part, they were blinded by the contrast in ideology, in part by the previous invincibility of the Kennedys. As one Massachusetts aide summed it up, "There's a history of liberals voting for liberals, southerners for southerners. And the tradition of not turning out incumbents and Kennedy's strength nationally. We just didn't see how it could happen." The incumbent whip was further lulled into a false sense of security by the ease and apparent firmness with which he obtained commitments.

In Kennedy's case he allegedly had 31 absolute commitments, not counting such probables as Humphrey, Magnuson, Jackson, and Bible. He ended up with 24 votes.[34] A full accounting of whose votes were "misunderstood," "hedged," or given to both sides is neither possible nor would it serve much purpose here.[35] Only Kennedy and Byrd together could construct a reasonably accurate count, a cooperative venture which is hardly likely to occur. Nevertheless, it is possible to set forth a conjectural breakdown of the vote, compiled from newspaper and magazine accounts and interviews (Table 13.1).

The tentative reconstruction shown in the table is not of particular note because of its ideological, regional, or seniority breakdown. Kennedy's hard core of votes, as it was in 1969, came from the moderate-to-liberal northerners, all of the major contenders for the 1972 Democratic presidential nomination (save for Jackson),[36] a scattering of westerners, and with few exceptions, the more junior members of the party (men with 12 years or less of Senate service). In contrast, Byrd capitalized on southern support and, with some exceptions, the more senior members of the party.

What is striking about the vote is the reversal pattern compared to the 1969 election (Senators Jackson, Magnuson, Spong, and probably, Fulbright) and the moderate-to-liberal character of the Senators classified as "unknowns," Mansfield of Montana, McIntyre of New Hampshire, McGee of Wyoming, Pastore of Rhode Island, and Symington of Missouri. Because of his position as majority leader, Mansfield took a "hands-off" role and refused to declare his vote. He had, however, tended to back incumbents in matters of party leadership choice. The other four could normally be expected to vote for a liberal over a conservative and yet at least three of the five seem likely to have ended up voting for Byrd.

VII

What can be learned from a comparison of these two contests, the unseating of two influential, if vulnerable, incumbent whips by underdog opponents?

The first, and most obvious, comparison between the upsets of Senator Russell Long of Louisiana and Senator Edward M. Kennedy of Massachusetts was that both men had become beatable, although for quite different reasons. For Long, it was erratic behavior on and off the floor, generally attributed to the pressures of being floor whip, chairman of the Finance Committee, and domestic and personal difficulties. Kennedy also found himself spread too thin, especially the demands of being "the last of the brothers" and the most likely choice

Table 13.1
Senator Byrd Defeats Senator Kennedy, 31–24

For Byrd, 31 votes	Unknown	For Kennedy, 24 votes
Allen, Ala.		Bayh, Ind.
Anderson, N.M.		Burdick, N.D.
Bentsen, Texas		Church, Ida.
Bible, Nev.		Cranston, Cal.
Byrd, W. Va.		Eagleton, Mo.
Byrd, Va.		Harris, Okla.
Cannon, Nev.		Hart, Mich.
Chiles, Fla.		Hughes, Iowa
Eastland, Miss.		Humphrey, Minn.
Ellender, La.		Inouye, Ha.
Ervin, N.C.		Kennedy, Mass.
Fulbright, Ark.		McGovern, S.D.
Gravel, Alaska	Mansfield, Mont.	Metcalf, Mont.
Hartke, Ind.	McIntyre, N.H.	Mondale, Minn.
Hollings, S.C. ← (+3)	McGee, Wyo. (+2) →	Moss, Utah
Jackson, Wash.	Pastore, R.I.	Muskie, Me.
Jordan, N.C.	Symington, Mo.	Nelson, Wisc.
Long, La.		Pell, R.I.
McClellan, Ark.		Proxmire, Wisc.
Magnuson, Wash.		Ribicoff, Conn.
Montoya, N.M.		Stevenson, Ill.
Randolph, W. Va.		Tunney, Cal.
Russell, Ga.		
Sparkman, Ala.		
Spong, Va.		
Stennis, Miss.		
Talmadge, Ga.		
Williams, N.J.		
(28 + 3 = 31)		(22 + 2 = 24)

Source: This vote has been reconstructed from newspaper and magazine accounts and more than a dozen Senate interviews. Both sides (principals and staff) generally agree that the reconstruction is accurate within several pairs of switches (or four votes in all).

for the 1972 Democratic presidential nomination. Without Chappaquiddick, his problems probably would have worked themselves out. It was the incident and its political repercussions which made Kennedy open to challenge. The vulnerability of the two men was fed by another factor. Both Senators, so unalike in philosophy, regional background, and personality, nevertheless shared a common dislike for the everyday chores and burdens of the whip's office. Neither Senator was willing to engage in the minutiae and housekeeping chores in any way which might lead to an independent base of power for the whip. In contrast, Robert Byrd, the number three man in the Democratic party hierarchy, thrived upon the day-to-day floor operations. Other Senators, especially the majority leader, came to depend and rely upon him.

Both beaten incumbent whips seriously considered stepping down from the whip's job — Long in the early fall of 1968, Kennedy in the fall of 1970. Although they discussed all the possibilities with their staffs, neither could come up with a *modus operandi* to allow them to exit gracefully and still keep the office in the hands of a Senator of similar ideological persuasion. Long wanted Byrd to succeed him, but first the Muskie threat and then the Kennedy challenge forced abandonment of his plans. Kennedy hoped to run unopposed or win easily in 1971, and then resign in the early spring. Even in a Senate in which not all members desire to become party leaders, however, there are always enough challengers lurking in the wings to force the hand of almost any incumbent whip, once he becomes liable to defeat.[37]

Once Long and Kennedy were challenged — directly in the first case, indirectly in the second — the incumbents exhibited another reaction in common. Neither man appeared to take his challenger seriously enough until it was too late. Long's political sensitivity was dulled by the ease with which he had put down a possible Muskie challenge.[38] Kennedy, at 36 with but six years in the Senate, hardly seemed a greater threat. Two years later the young Massachusetts Senator fell into a related trap — it seemed unbelievable that a Byrd could beat a Kennedy. In addition to contrasting styles, there seemed to be too many Senators of moderate-to-liberal persuasions for Byrd to have a chance. Both incumbents made the mistake, Long more than Kennedy, of allowing the challenger to seize the early initiative. More important in House races than in the Senate, because of the far more complicated logistic problems, still a Senator also "likes to be asked." The candidate asking first may end up with an early commitment from those otherwise likely to straddle the fence.

A further lesson to be learned from these case studies of revolt — Kennedy–Long in 1969, Byrd–Kennedy in 1971 — is that both incumbents were misled by inflated vote counts.[39] On the eve of the first contest, possibly in an attempt to create a winner's psychology, the Louisiana Senator predicted a "solid victory," a projected vote of 34 being "just a minimum." Retrospectively, he admitted walking into the Democratic Conference with 29 votes, just enough to win. But the secret ballot vote was 31 to 26 in Kennedy's favor.

Kennedy's ability to count, as the incumbent, was no better. He issued no public statement as to his tally, in part because he was not sure there would be a contest. Entering the 1971 Democratic Conference he was convinced, along with his staff, that there were 31 firm commitments out of 55. Byrd had waited to announce his candidacy until the end, fearing a last-minute Kennedy blitz and wanting to insure his election with Senator Russell's proxy vote. Byrd ended up with three more than his firm count; Kennedy with seven fewer votes than he was led to expect.

The results of party leadership contests in the House of Representatives also seem to support this generalization — that incumbents are likely to receive a "softer" count than their challengers. Both Martin and Halleck had inflated counts before their minority leadership contests in 1959 and 1965. Perhaps it is more difficult to say "no" to a party leader than to his opponent, if for no other reason than the fact that the incumbent has been and is more likely to be in a position to reward or punish other members after the contest. Still, challengers must also guard against inflated counts as the 1971 House majority leadership contest clearly demonstrated.

Less for its objectivity than for its incisiveness, perhaps Senator Long should have the last word in this tale of three whips:

> I could have kept that job as long as I wanted it, except that the man who could have been President let his friends promote him for it.
>
> It wasn't that smart. It set a precedent for ousting the whip.
>
> He caught me at a low ebb, when he was at a high point. Two years later, after Chappaquiddick, he was in low stock.
>
> He set a precedent. He [Kennedy] was hoisted by his own petard.

NOTES

1. In 1972, Owens overcame an otherwise strong Nixon trend in his state and won Utah's Second District seat in the U.S. House of Representatives. In 1974, he lost a close contest for the Senate seat vacated by Republican retiree Wallace F. Bennett.

2. Burton Hersh, *The Education of Edward Kennedy* (New York: Morrow, 1972), pp. 378–380.

3. What "happened" has been detailed in at least three biographies, several books, numerous articles, hundreds of newspaper accounts, to say nothing of five volumes of courtroom investigations and proceedings. Little would be gained from one more attempt at a synopsis. Our focus, here, is upon the political consequences of Chappaquiddick.

4. Miss Kopechne was one of several "boiler-room girls" attending a cookout reunion following a sailboat regatta at Edgartown Harbor, Massachusetts. The girls, all staff members in Robert Kennedy's 1968 presidential campaign, had worked out of a windowless room at Kennedy's 20th and L St., N.W., head-quarters. Miss Kopechne was a victim of drowning when the car that Senator Edward Kennedy was driving failed to make a turn and landed upside down in a swiftly flowing tidal estuary beneath the Dike Bridge on Chappaquid-dick Island.

5. The issue was still having consequences years later. See, for example, Robert G. Sherrill, "Chappaquiddick," *New York Times Magazine*, July 14th, 1974, pp. 8–9 ff. It was, however, not mentioned as a reason for Senator Kennedy's "firm, final and unconditional" decision to take himself out of consideration for the Democratic presidential or vice presidential nominations in 1976. That decision was based on family obligations. "Kennedy's Announcement," *Congressional Quarterly Weekly Report* 32 (September 28, 1974), pp. 2609–2610.

6. As late as mid-1970, Kennedy would say: "I've thought about retirement, sure. And I've made up my mind that if my effectiveness is not there, if my effectiveness has been compromised, I won't stay in public life." William H. Honen, "Can Teddy Kennedy Survive His Reputation?" *The New York Times Magazine*, May 23, 1970, pp. 25 ff, at 75.

7. More than two years later speculation would mount as to Kennedy's availability, if not for a convention draft, then perhaps for the vice-presidential nomination. Despite pressures from Senator George McGovern, the eventual Democratic presidential candidate, Kennedy would remain true to his promise. Theodore H. White, *The Making of the President, 1972* (New York: Atheneum, 1973), pp. 196–197, 207–208.

8. Honen, *op. cit.*, p. 80.

9. *Ibid.*

10. As David Broder described the intensity of his campaign activities in the early fall: "Shuttling between his home state and his Senate duties, the Senator is trying to spend at least four days a week campaigning. The days run 14 hours or more — broken when possible by a rest stop and hot tub at his Boston home, to provide relief for the back he broke in a 1964 airplane crash." "Kennedy Campaigns Like Underdog," *Washington Post*, September 20, 1970, p. A-1.

11. The slogan — "The Bob Byrd Story: From Orphan Boy to U.S. Senator" — was featured in Byrd's campaign brochures in his bid for a third consecutive term in the U.S. Senate in 1970.

12. *Washington Star Sunday Magazine*, June 20, 1965, p. 14.

13. *Ibid.*
14. Robert Sherrill, "The Embodiment of Poor White Power," *The New York Times Magazine*, February 28, 1971, p. 51.
15. *Ibid.*
16. Three years earlier, Byrd, an avid supporter of then Majority Leader Lyndon B. Johnson, had delivered a speech harshly critical of his fellow Senator, John Kennedy, on the eve of the West Virginia primary. Despite Byrd's opposition, Kennedy was to win that decisive primary and go on to obtain the 1960 Democratic nomination and the presidency.
17. Not the least of Clark's problems was that he had written or edited three books highly critical of Senate organization, procedures, and outcomes: *The Senate Establishment* (New York: Hill and Wang, 1963); *Congress: The Sapless Branch* (New York: Harper & Row, 1964); and *Congressional Reform: Problems and Prospects* (New York: Crowell, 1965). Ralph K. Huitt has observed that the role of the outsider has a number of functional payoffs for the institution and the person — "The Outsider in the Senate: An Alternative Role," *Am. Pol. Sci. Rev.* **55** (1961), 566–575 — but becoming a leader is not one of them.
18. *Washington Star Sunday Magazine, op. cit.*, p. 14.
19. Acknowledged one Kennedy staffer: "[Byrd's] knowledge of the rules . . . is superb. Whenever there would be a parliamentary ruling, he would be sitting on the floor studying the rules. When the parliamentarian made a decision he didn't understand, he would sidle down to the podium. You could see them whispering to one another. Byrd would then check it out, cross-reference it a time or two, until he had mastered it." And then rather plaintively the Kennedy aide added, "I always wanted Teddy to do that . . . but I couldn't get him interested."
20. For example, on six selected Senate votes in 1970, the AFL–CIO Committee on Political Education (COPE) gave Kennedy a score of 100 percent, Byrd, a score of 50 percent. *Congressional Quarterly Weekly Report* **29** (April 16, 1971), p. 865.
21. For the 91st Congress Byrd had an overall presidential support score of 52 percent compared to 38 percent for Kennedy (based on 163 Nixon-issue roll calls in 1969 and 1970). For the same Congress, Byrd had a record of voting in agreement with the conservative coalition (a majority of Republicans voting with a majority of southern Democrats against a majority of northern Democrats) 50 percent of the time compared with Kennedy's three percent (based upon 176 conservative coalition roll calls in 1969 and 1970). *Congressional Quarterly Weekly Report* **29** (January 29, 1971), pp. 223, 245.
22. Drew Von Bergen, "Attempt to Unseat Kennedy as Whip is Weighed by Byrd," *Washington Post*, November 15, 1970, p. A-2.
23. Spencer Rich, "Kennedy Would Keep Post as Party Whip," *Washington Post*, November 11, 1970, p. A-2.
24. Vera Glaser and Malvina Stephenson, "Ted Kennedy vs. Robert Byrd: Greatest Show on Capitol Hill," *The Miami Herald*, January 3, 1971.
25. Humphrey may well have ended up voting for Kennedy on ideological grounds. But his unwillingness to make a commitment should have been strong evidence to Kennedy that he was in severe difficulty in his bid to retain the majority whip position.
26. The text and signature, now framed, hang in Senator Byrd's suite of offices in the Old Senate Office Building.
27. At the risk of partly compromising an otherwise dramatic event, Byrd's retrospective feeling is that he had 27 firm commitments with four or five lean-

ing, "any one of which I thought on balance would vote for me." Inclined
to downgrade the implication that he wouldn't have gone unless Senator
Russell had still been alive, he nevertheless was counting on his proxy for
the 28th and winning vote.

28. Gravel's seconding speech was not designed to change votes — few such
speeches do — but coming from a liberal it may have given a few other on-
the-fence liberals a rationale for voting for Byrd. His speech was "directed
toward the idea that we shouldn't pick a whip by ideology. We should pick
him for mechanistic reasons — getting the job done."

29. Ironically, one of Senator Kennedy's closest friends, freshman-elect Senator
John V. Tunney of California, was one of three freshmen picked to tally and
announce the results. As Tunney pulled the votes out of the ballot box, he
read them aloud — "Byrd, Kennedy, Byrd, Byrd, Kennedy . . ." The votes
were recorded on yellow pads by two other freshman senators, Lloyd M.
Bentsen of Texas and Lawton M. Chiles, Jr. of Florida. Two ballots, presumably cast by freshmen, misspelled Byrd's name as "Bird," but this had no
effect on the outcome.

30. "Senate Upset: Byrd Defeats Kennedy for Whip," *Congressional Quarterly
Weekly Report* **29** (January 22, 1971), pp. 180–181, at 180.

31. *Ibid.*

32. "Russell Proxy Kept Byrd in the Race," *New York Times*, January 22, 1971,
pp. 1, 12; "The Tortoise and the Hare," *Newsweek*, February 1, 1971, pp.
18–20.

33. "Senator Byrd May Not Challenge Kennedy," *Washington Evening Star*,
January 20, 1971, p. A-1.

34. Although he received only 24 votes, newspaper reporters claimed to have uncovered at least 27 Senators who vowed after the contest that they had voted
for Kennedy. While these stories were rife, no one ever published a list of the
27 or 28. Moreover, there were at least a half-dozen Senators such as Clinton
Anderson of New Mexico, Frank Moss of Utah, Stuart Symington of Missouri and the two Washington State Senators who declined to say how they
voted. James Doyle, "Kennedy Forces Try to Find Senators Who Switched
Sides," *Washington Star*, January 22, 1971, pp. A-1, A-7.

A Congressional Quarterly telephone survey of senatorial aides reported 12
Senators for Byrd, 21 for Kennedy, 7 declining to divulge their votes, and 15
saying they could not speak for their Senator. *Congressional Quarterly Weekly
Report* **29** (January 22, 1971), p. 180.

35. On March 13, 1971, two months after his defeat, Kennedy had occasion to
address Washington's prestigious Gridiron Club banquet: "I want to take this
opportunity to thank the 28 Democratic senators who pledged to vote for me
— and especially the 24 who actually did. According to a story in the *Washington Post*, the Secret Service says I receive more anonymous threatening
letters than anyone else on Capitol Hill. It wasn't until January that I realized
most of them came from my colleagues in the Senate. Since I lost the whip
fight, many people have asked me when I realized I was in trouble. Frankly,
it was the morning of the vote, when my staff told me that we had nailed
down Joe Tydings, Ralph Yarborough, Albert Gore — and Senator Sorenson
of New York. [The first three were defeated incumbents; Ted Sorenson, a
speech-writer for John Kennedy, ran third in the 1970 New York Democratic
Senate primary.]

36. McGovern, Muskie, Hughes, Bayh, and Humphrey, the most active and prospective Democratic hopefuls, all indicated to the press that they had voted for
Kennedy. Kennedy himself dismissed as "speculation" reports that he might

have been done in by rival presidential ambitions. David S. Broder, "Kennedy's Spanking Dims '72 Outlook," *Washington Post*, January 22, 1971, p. A-1.

37. A former whip summed up the ambition: "The only reason people become whip is in the hopes of getting a better job at a later date. It's an inducement to become majority leader. It offers little freedom, otherwise."

38. As a Long aide put it: "For most United States Senators their word is good. They will tell you, 'There's no way for me to be there' (for your opponent). When Long campaigned against Muskie he got ample commitments, more than a majority, but he got a commitment just against Muskie, not against Kennedy — and that may have been misinterpreted."

39. John McConnell, former whip office administrative assistant to Senator Russell Long, relates a story which illustrates the common trickiness of vote counting. After Long had been defeated, he had cooperated with Wayne Owens in helping to set up Kennedy's whip office, and the two men had later become friends: "After the Byrd-Kennedy contest was over, Owens came up to me with a puzzled look on his face and said, 'John, I can't understand it. We had counted down to the last man. I don't understand how we lost.' I said, 'Yes, Wayne, . . . I understand.' He gave me a long look and all of a sudden we both burst out laughing."

CHAPTER FOURTEEN

The Choice of a Senate Minority Leader:
Scott vs. Baker, 1969, 1971

Everett McKinley Dirksen, Republican leader in the Senate since 1959, died at 4:52 P.M., September 7, 1969. His death came as no great surprise to his family or his Senate colleagues. The minority leader's great leadership talent, legislative skills, and energy had been on the decline for several years. Seventy-three years old, he had been in and out of the hospital for a variety of ailments. For a time it looked as if he might recover from an operation for lung cancer, but finally, his more than 36-year career in Congress had come to an end.[1] First elected to the House of Representatives in the 73d Congress (1933–1934), Dirksen had retired after eight terms because of failing eyesight. Two years later he had recovered and ran for the Senate in 1950, defeating Scott Lucas, who was then the Democratic majority leader.

The death of a congressional leader in mid-session, Senate or House, majority or minority party, is seldom sudden or unexpected. In common with most elderly deaths, save those by suicide or accident, they almost invariably follow a period of illness, hospitalization, and physical symptoms apparent to all. The waning health of a party leader inevitably brings out the best and worst from his colleagues. Loyalty and friendship are heightened, ranks are closed behind the leader, especially by staff and close associates, and the ailing leader is sheltered as much as possible from external and internal pressures. But the ambitions of other men also come to the fore. There is increased activity, kept as secret as possible, by those who hope to take advantage of the likely forthcoming change in leadership.

Thus, it was inevitable that senior and not-so-senior Republicans in the Senate in 1969 would take notice of the ailing Dirksen and react in not uncharacteristic ways. Many would draw closer and assist the minority leader in every way that they could. Other Senators could not help but make plans for a change in power. The legislative plans of the Republican administration and the work of the Senate would have to be carried on.

I

Within a week following Dirksen's death, three Republican Senators announced for the office of minority leader: Hugh Scott of Pennsylvania, the incumbent party whip, a veteran of 11 years in the Senate and 16 years in the House of Representatives; Roman L. Hruska of Nebraska, Dirksen's closest associate in the Senate with over 15 years of service; and a relative dark horse, youthful Howard H. Baker, Jr., of Tennessee, Dirksen's son-in-law and a member of the Senate for just two and one-half years.

With Richard M. Nixon in the White House, the position of Republican floor leader had taken on added importance. Whoever was elected would be responsible for guiding the administration's program through the Senate. Following Tuesday White House leadership meetings and every morning in the well of the Senate, the new minority leader would have multiple opportunities to initiate and shape issues of public policy. Further, Republicans were optimistic about winning enough seats in the 1970 elections — a net gain of eight would be needed — so as to control the Senate and earn the right to elect a majority leader and choose the committee chairmen. Having won the presidency and made a net gain of six Senate seats in the 1968 election there were grounds for some optimism.

Over the past two decades the office of floor leader has acquired considerable power, although much of it must be continually renewed and maintained by the incumbent. Dirksen had learned from watching the struggles of his predecessor, William Knowland, that an inflexible negotiator got all or nothing — and in the politics of the Senate minority party, that usually meant nothing.[2]

Dirksen was especially adept at uniting the bulk of his Republican colleagues so as to provide the balance of power on most of the far-reaching legislation passed during the 1960's. Much of the time he had worked with the natural allies of Republicans, the southern Democrats, on conservative vs. liberal issues. But he was also adept at cooperating with Presidents Kennedy and Johnson and the more liberal wing of the Democratic party on other issues, especially civil rights. One Republican Senator was to sum up Dirksen's strength in the Senate as follows:[3]

> If there are 41 Republicans in the Senate, Dirksen's power is absolute. At 37, the power is enormous. At 34, it is unstable. That is the tipping point. It can be formidable, but it can be overwhelmed.

How did Dirksen achieve his legislative successes? From his perspective, it was merely a matter of providing lubrication for the legislative machinery, a little here, some there. For Dirksen, "the oil can was mightier than the sword."

Until the Dirksen reign, leadership in the Senate G.O.P. tended to be more formal, limited and decentralized than it was in the Democratic party. The Democratic floor leader presided over meetings of all Democratic Senators in their Conference and supervised the formulation of party strategy and the scheduling of legislation as chairman of the Policy Committee. He also guided the appointment of Democrats to Senate committees as chairman of his party's Steering Committee. In contrast, in the Republican party, the counterparts of these positions were held by four different Senators.

Under Dirksen, leadership became more concentrated than these institutional arrangements would seem to allow. During his brief tenure as whip, from January to September 1969, Scott never did poll his fellow Republicans. It was Dirksen who authorized infrequent whip counts and these were compiled by a Senate minority employee. It was Dirksen and not the chairman of the Republican Policy Committee, Gordon Allott of Colorado, who after the Tuesday luncheon meetings of all the G.O.P. Senators would ride the elevator up to the Senate press gallery, sit cross-legged on a table, sip coffee and entertain enthralled members of the fourth estate with his famous dialogues.

But now Dirksen was dead. In his 10 years as minority leader he had become almost a national institution. No one would step easily or lightly into his position.

II

As the incumbent whip or assistant minority leader, Scott could be seen as the most logical successor to Dirksen, providing he could overcome what many of his colleagues seemed to regard as an overly liberal voting record. Earlier, on January 3, 1969, at the opening of the 91st Congress, Scott took a long step up the Republican leadership ladder when he upset Roman Hruska, 23–20, in a race for the vacated position of minority whip.

Most observers thought that Dirksen's endorsement of the conservative Nebraskan would be decisive. He had apparently gone so far as to warn the incoming Republican freshmen that their committee assignments, office space, and even their allotment of inauguration tickets would be dependent upon their support for Hruska. At midweek, before the vote, Dirksen was predicting that "Hugh Scott will be lucky to get fifteen votes." [4]

Scott, however, demonstrated his ability to put together a winning coalition despite the minority leader's opposition. It combined the tacit support of President-elect Richard M. Nixon with Massachusetts Senator Edward Brooke's strong arguments for a geographical and ideological balance within the party. Newly elected Republicans played a decisive role — six out of ten of the incoming freshman Republican Senators were said to have voted for Scott. Thus, the incumbent whip would begin his campaign for minority leader with most of the same moderate-to-liberal coalition already in his camp.

Scott's predecessor as whip, Thomas Kuchel of California, had been defeated in a bitter primary battle in June 1968. One result was to make the senior Pennsylvania Senator the candidate of those moderate-to-liberal Republicans who wanted to maintain a tradition of balancing off a conservative floor leader with one of their own. Scott was able to inherit the Kuchel mantle in part because no other moderate-to-liberal Senate Republican combined the necessary party leadership experience with an interest in the rather thankless but demanding tasks of party whip.

Probably the most valuable asset that Scott had going for him in September was his eight months' incumbency as the number two leader in the Republican party. As the incumbent whip, Scott had been in a position to do some favors for other members — assisting with their legislative interests, covering for them on the floor, insuring that their rights were protected. Moreover, he consistently looked for ways to demonstrate his ability to function as a team player with President Nixon during the first session of the 91st Congress. His voting record in 1969 compared favorably with that of other loyal administration supporters. (For 1969 his presidential support score would be 78 percent compared to an average Republican support score of 64 percent.)[5]

His stand in support of the President's anti-ballistic missile (ABM) program was only one, if perhaps the most crucial, test of party loyalty that he passed during this period. In June 1968 Scott was one of 12 Republicans who voted against President Johnson's request for a $227.3 million authorization to begin building Sentinel ABM sites around some of the nation's cities. But on August 6, 1969, after one of the longest and hardest fought legislative battles in recent Senate history, Scott joined the majority of his Republican colleagues and 21 Democrats (all but six of them southerners) in upholding President Nixon's Safeguard ABM system by climactic 50–50 and 49–51 votes.

Scott explained his reasons for voting against the Sentinel program but committing himself in favor of the Safeguard program in an April 1969 telecast beamed to his Pennsylvania constituents. While he "had many doubts," he did "not want to leave the President without the immensely important bargaining power of a continuance in the preparation for the defense of the United States." Later in the program, Scott commented on his feelings of obligation to the President. "He asked me if I would support him and I said, 'Yes, sir.' He knows that this is a hard one for me. He knows that the leadership post [minority whip] could cause me to do what I pledged I would do, support the President wherever I could . . . He asked me if I would support him. I said, 'Yes, sir — horse, foot, and dragoon; hook, line, and sinker.' "

The opportunity to serve as the number two man in the Republican hierarchy was important for Scott's campaign, but it was Scott's loyal performance as whip that proved crucial to his victory. One of his more conservative supporters later commented, "He did not conduct himself as an eastern establishment liberal. First and foremost he was a Republican Senator and a loyal supporter of the President's program."

A final advantage of being the incumbent whip was clear: unless Scott advanced to minority leader he was in the way of those who sought his job. If anything, Scott encouraged a proliferation of whip candidates who might succeed him, including Robert Griffin of Michigan, James Pearson of Kansas, and Jack Miller of Iowa — and this did him no harm. All these potential candidates for whip either worked actively in Scott's behalf or remained uncommitted. In effect, Scott had a position to offer without ever having to commit it to any one prospective whip candidate.

III

Dirksen had died on a Sunday. Nine days later on September 16, 1969, Senator Margaret Chase Smith, the chairman of the Senate Republican Conference, announced that his successor would be chosen on Wednesday morning, September 24, 1969. The 43 incumbent Republican Senators would meet to vote by secret ballot for the minority leader. The availability of this potentially powerful position opened up anew all of the divisions that characterize a legislative party — ideology, seniority, regional differences, and personal loyalties and antagonisms. These splits are apparent in the Senate Democratic party as well, but the frustrations of more than a decade of minority status seemed to make the divisions all the more acute among Senate Republicans.

By tradition, the G.O.P. almost uniformly has selected a senior conservative as its floor leader — Kenneth Wherry of Nebraska, Styles Bridges of New Hampshire, Robert A. Taft of Ohio, William Knowland of California, and Dirksen. Moderates and liberals, always a minority within Republican ranks, have had to settle for lesser party positions, such as the party whip.

If party unity scores, alone, were definitive criteria for selecting Republican leaders, Scott's moderate-to-liberal voting pattern would have seemed to make his chances rather slim. According to *Congressional Quarterly* on issues which divided a majority of Republicans from a majority of Democrats, Scott sided with his party less than half the time in both the 89th and 90th Congresses.[6] Only a handful of Republican Senators, headed by New York's Jacob Javits and New Jersey's Clifford Case, had more liberal voting records prior to 1969 than the senior Senator from Pennsylvania.

Experience and skill at party infighting, both within Congress and at national party conventions, could generally be counted as something of an offsetting Scott asset. Perhaps no Senator, save for the late Everett Dirksen, had been as intimately involved in the choice of Republican presidential candidates since 1940. Scott's service as a former party national chairman in 1948–1949 and, more recently, his willingness to travel and make speeches for his colleagues as vice-chairman of the Senate Republican Campaign Committee, all contributed to his understanding of the personal characteristics of his colleagues and the kinds of problems they faced in representing their respective states. His reputation as a national party leader was not without its liabilities, however. For a number of conservative colleagues, Scott, "a supporter of Dewey and Eisenhower," was just too closely associated with the eastern establishment.

The selection of Dirksen's successor was more than just a renewal of the perennial struggle for power among the conservative and liberal wings of the Republican party. With Baker's entrance into the race, the contest came to symbolize as well the restlessness of comparative newcomers chafing under the restraints of seniority and lingering traditions of apprenticeship. Underlying the struggle between conservatives vs. liberals and younger vs. older members was the further cross-cutting factor of regionalism. Would the election of a midwestern conservative like Hruska or even a relative moderate conservative from Tennessee be interpreted as further support for the implementation of a "heartland and southern strategy" on the part of the G.O.P.? Conversely, would a Scott victory help to offset those Republicans who seemed prepared to write off the Northeast, ignore the big cities and the black vote, and concentrate instead on wooing and holding the South, the Midwest, and the West? [7]

IV

The logistics of a Senate leadership contest are fairly simple compared to its House counterpart. For Scott, as well as the other declared candidates, Baker and Hruska, it would merely require being in touch with as many of their some 40 colleagues as possible, preferably face-to-face. As the campaign got under way, one of Scott's first decisions was to appoint as his campaign manager, Richard S. Schweiker, his junior colleague from Pennsylvania. After serving four terms in the House, Schweiker had upset Democratic incumbent Joseph S. Clark in 1968.

Within a week Scott and Schweiker contacted all but a half-dozen of their fellow Republican Senators. For the most part Schweiker concentrated on freshmen and sophomore members; he deferred to Scott and other older Republicans, such as Delaware's Caleb Boggs, to make overtures to their peers. A week's careful canvassing yielded 20 firm commitments. A majority of 22 votes would be necessary for victory.

Initially Scott surmised that his principal challenge would come from 65-year-old conservative Roman L. Hruska of Nebraska, the man he had narrowly defeated in January. A lawyer and former county commissioner from Omaha, Hruska had served for one term in the House of Representatives before running for and winning the unexpired term of the late Senator Hugh A. Butler in November 1954. Two elections later and by 1969, Hruska was the ranking Republican on the Judiciary Committee and the fourth ranking G.O.P. member on the Appropriations Committee. Only six Senate Republicans exceeded him in overall seniority. A dour, rather unimaginative man, Hruska's strongest claims to leadership were his avowed midwestern conservatism and his prior close association with the late Senate minority leader.

Another senior conservative, 62-year-old Gordon Allott of Colorado, briefly considered running for minority leader but decided he could better serve his party in his position as chairman of the Republican Policy Committee. In January, Allott had held off the last minute challenge of Michigan's junior Senator, Robert Griffin, by a vote of 25–18 as both men sought to take the place of retired Senator Bourke Hickenlooper of Iowa. Although somewhat more diplomatic than Hruska, Allott also smacked a little too much of the "old guard" to suit some of the younger members. In any event, he would have had to compete for approximately the same bloc of votes for which Hruska and Baker supporters were already scrambling.

V

Of the several possible conservative candidates opposing Scott, Baker's voting record was most closely in accord with Dirksen's right-of-center ideology. Allott and Hruska were somewhat more conservative. For example, for the 90th Congress, Baker had a conservative coalition support score of 73 percent compared to Dirksen's 60 percent, Scott's 35 percent, Hruska's 83 percent and Allott's 76 percent. (A conservative coalition occurs when a majority of Republicans join a majority of southern Democrats in opposition to a majority of northern Democrats.) [8]

Over the past 50 years no Republican has served as his party's principal leader without at least one term of six years behind him.

Scott, Hruska, and Allott met this qualification easily, but fully three-fourths of the Republican Senators had as much or more seniority than Baker. One factor pushing the 43-year-old Tennessean forward in the consideration was the relatively junior composition of Republican Senators. Five new members, including Baker, had been elected in 1966; 12 more had been added either by appointment or election in 1968.

Other, more personal, assets were working in Baker's behalf to off-set his relative juniority. He was no stranger to politics or to Washington. His father had represented the second congressional district of Tennessee from 1950 until his death in 1963. His wife, Joy, was the daughter of the late Senator and Mrs. Dirksen. From his first appearance on the floor of the Senate, the boyish-looking, smooth-talking Baker made a positive impression on most of his colleagues and the press. Assigned to the Committees on Public Works and Government Operations (and later, Commerce), Baker rather quickly demonstrated his independence of Dirksen on a number of environmental issues as well as legislation treating of "one man, one vote" congressional redistricting. By the summer of 1968, Baker was being mentioned as a possible vice presidential candidate on either a prospective Nixon ticket or Rockefeller ticket.

One of Baker's contemporaries in the Senate, who nevertheless ended up supporting Scott, summed up his assets: "He has a great deal of charisma. He's an eloquent speaker — there isn't a member here who wouldn't welcome Baker coming into his state to speak for him at a fund-raising dinner or political rally. He handles himself well on the floor."

On Monday morning shortly after 9:00 A.M., the day after Dirksen died, Baker's administrative assistant, Hugh Branson, showed up at the office of freshman Senator Robert W. Packwood of Oregon. Acting mainly on his own initiative, he wanted to raise the question of Baker's seeking the top leadership position. Enthused by such a possibility, Packwood made several telephone calls to other younger Senators that morning and was encouraged by the favorable reaction. Later that afternoon, following eulogies to Dirksen on the Senate floor, Packwood met with four other Republican freshmen — Henry Bellmon of Oklahoma, Robert Dole of Kansas, Edward Gurney of Florida, and Theodore Stevens of Alaska — to discuss possible "centrist" candidates. Baker's name figured most prominently among possible candidates who might head off Scott. Baker, preoccupied with comforting his wife and mother-in-law and looking after funeral arrangements, did not involve himself in these efforts. However, he did nothing to discourage them either.

Later in the week Packwood came to Baker with a list of nearly a dozen Senators who favored the Tennessee Senator, about half of whom had sided with Scott in the January whip vote. "It was far short of the necessary number," said Baker, "but a right impressive base." He began to sound out other Senators on his own behalf. Hounded by reporters all week, Baker finally announced his candidacy for minority leader in a hurried corridor press conference on Friday, September 12, 1969. Later that day, Minority Whip Scott formally declared his own candidacy.[9] Hruska entered the race for minority leader a day later.

VI

Several days before the vote Scott once again reviewed the entire list of Republican Senators with Schweiker, his campaign manager and junior colleague from Pennsylvania. By this time Scott had personally talked to more than 30 of the 43 members — "everyone except those who were absolutely locked in concrete for one of the other candidates." So confident was Scott of victory that he spent Friday, September 19, in New York City where he found time to add a small jade figure to his extensive collection of Japanese and Chinese art objects. He spent most of Saturday, the weekend before the vote, in his Old Senate Office Building suite, room 260, going over his tallies but taking time out to leisurely rearrange some of the pieces of rare Asian sculpture, pottery, bronze, and jade which crowd his personal office.

That same Saturday, his two opponents conferred privately one floor above in Senator Hruska's office. Baker had telephoned his senior colleague because (as he later recalled): "the race was getting close and I felt we ought to get together and talk about it." Following some 10 minutes of discussion of their respective chances, Hruska told the younger Senator that he would bow out in favor of Baker. Several of Hruska's conservative colleagues, among them Paul Fannin and Barry Goldwater of Arizona, had convinced the conservative Nebraskan that his withdrawal would deliver more votes to Baker than the other way around.

Heartened by Hruska's withdrawal, Baker increased his efforts to obtain more support from moderate-to-liberal Republicans, especially younger members. "I'm a liberal on some issues and a conservative on others," he argued. "I let the center of gravity take care of itself."

In a September 23 press release on the eve of the Conference vote Senator Goldwater made a strong statement on behalf of Baker: ". . . the generation represented by men like Senator Hugh Scott and me must come to realize that the future of the United States and of the entire free world depends on the young leaders who are coming up today."

Not all of Goldwater's senior colleagues, however, would go along with this reasoning. On Monday evening, September 22, a senior Senator (who personally preferred Hruska) telephoned Scott and told him that he could count on his support. As Scott later recalled: "I believed for several days I would win, but this was decisive."

VII

On Wednesday morning at the Republican conference the 68-year-old Scott defeated the 43-year-old Baker by a secret ballot vote of 24–19 (see Table 14.1). In an institution supposedly dominated by norms of seniority, why did Baker, a junior Senator with less than three years of tenure, emerge as Scott's final opponent? Why was the relatively liberal easterner able to defeat any candidate that the conservative majority of the Republican Senators could settle upon?

Some answers to these questions have already been suggested. Neither Hruska, Allott, nor any other senior conservative seemed to have much appeal to junior Republican Senators of any ideological hue. As Dirksen's son-in-law, Baker had gained early prominence in the national press. Within his first two years of office he had demonstrated his independence, his legislative talents, and a skill for public oratory. His conservative-to-moderate voting record made him ideologically acceptable to almost every shade of Republican in the Senate. But his lack of tenure and experience continued to bother a number of more senior Republican Senators.

Why did Hruska defer to Baker? At first, those who preferred a conservative candidate felt the senior Nebraskan would have the best chance. But after a week's canvassing it became clear that Hruska would lose the votes of too many moderates and younger members. Another factor working against the crusty Nebraska conservative was his prior loss to Scott in January 1969. A Senator active in both camps summed up the developing consensus: "Those against Scott became

Table 14.1
Minority Leadership Vote Breakdown, 1969:
Scott Defeats Baker, 24–19

For Scott, 24 votes	For Baker, 19 votes
Aiken (Vt.)	Baker (Tenn.)
Allott (Colo.)	Bellmon (Okla.)
Boggs (Del.)	Bennett (Utah)
Brooke (Mass.)	Cook (Ky.)
Case (N.J.)	Curtis (Neb.)
Cooper (Ky.)	Dole (Kan.)
Cotton (N.H.)	Dominick (Colo.)
Fong (Ha.)	Fannin (Ariz.)
Goodell (N.Y.)	Goldwater (Ariz.)
Griffin (Mich.)	Gurney (Fla.)
Hatfield (Ore.)	Hansen (Wyo.)
Javits (N.Y.)	Hruska (Neb.)
Jordan (Idaho)	Mundt (S.D.)
Mathias (Md.)	Murphy (Cal.)
Miller (Iowa)	Packwood (Ore.)
Pearson (Kan.)	Smith (Ill.)
Percy (Ill.)	Stevens (Alaska)
Prouty (Vt.)	Thurmond (S.C.)
Saxbe (Ohio)	Tower (Texas)
Schweiker (Pa.)	
Scott (Pa.)	
Smith (Me.)	
Williams (Del.)	
Young (N.D.)	

SOURCE: This is an unofficial recapitulation of the vote adapted from the *National Observer, Congressional Quarterly Weekly Report* **28** (September 26, 1969), p. 1762, and information from some 20 interviews with Republican Senators and staff. Both sides are in agreement as to the correctness of the vote within one or two paired switches from one column to the other.

convinced that Roman couldn't win. If there was going to be any chance, it would have to be with Howard." A further problem for Hruska was that his campaign got under way much slower than the other two, perhaps a hesitation out of respect for Dirksen's memory, but which nevertheless seemed to have cost him some early commitments.

In the final analysis, seniority proved more decisive than ideology.

If Baker (or Hruska) had been able to hold all the conservatives in line, Scott would have lost his bid for the minority leadership. Unofficial tabulations of the secret ballot vote suggest the crucial assistance that Scott received from six or seven senior conservatives — members like Milton Young of North Dakota, John Williams of Delaware, Norris Cotton of New Hampshire, Gordon Allott of Colorado, Jack Miller of Iowa, and Len B. Jordan of Idaho. A senior conservative, who remained uncommitted until the day of the conference and then apparently voted for Scott, makes the point: "There was just a feeling that people who had been here longer should be chosen before opening up the position to a freshman Senator." Of 14 Republicans with longer Senate service than Scott (first elected in 1958), only five — Karl Mundt of South Dakota, Wallace F. Bennett of Utah, Hruska and Carl Curtis of Nebraska, and Strom Thurmond of South Carolina — are said to have voted for Baker.

Conversely, among junior Senators, those with less than six years of service, Baker carried the vote by approximately 11 to 8. Here, perhaps, some of the senior conservatives overcalculated the appeal that Baker would have among the younger members. Seven or eight moderates and liberals among the first termers — Senators like William Saxbe of Ohio, Charles Goodell of New York, and Mark Hatfield of Oregon — stayed with Scott. Their votes, coupled with Scott's 2-to-1 ratio of support among members with more than one term of service made the final outcome as decisive as it was. Overall, Scott lost the votes of only two Republican Senators who considered themselves moderates or liberals. One of these was freshman Marlow Cook from Baker's neighboring state of Kentucky. The other was Robert Packwood of Oregon, who acted as Baker's unofficial campaign manager in the early stages of the contest.

According to Packwood, "We had most of those who were philosophically tuned to Howard, and we had many of the younger members who wanted newer, more dynamic leadership. But there were just enough older members who couldn't bring themselves to vote for a guy who had only been here two and one-half years." Senator Charles Mathias of Maryland, a Scott supporter, offered a different interpretation: "It was the cumulative result of all the things that Hugh Scott has done and been in politics, his experience as a former national chairman, his survival in the 1964 Republican blood-bath, his long legislative experience in both the House and the Senate. Scott just offered the kind of successful experience that had to prevail on the weight of its own merit."

Although agreeing on the importance of seniority as a key factor in his victory, Scott also took note of a sectional awareness: "There was a sense that the party and the President would be a lot better off if they had an *apertura oeste* — an opening to the East." A regional breakdown of the vote appears to substantiate this interpretation. The Pennsylvania Senator apparently won the votes of all 13 eastern Republican Senators, split almost evenly the votes of 23 Senators from the West and Midwest and lost 6 of 7 southern votes to his Tennessee rival. Put another way, Baker failed to pick up the vote of a single Senator from the states that Nixon lost in 1968; almost all of his votes came from the "heartland, sunbelt, and South."

VIII

Three hours later, following a luncheon recess, Baker suffered a second setback. After losing to Scott, he had been nominated for party whip, a position made vacant by Scott's elevation to minority leader. Four other candidates were also nominated: liberal Charles H. Percy of Illinois, moderates Robert P. Griffin of Michigan and James B. Pearson of Kansas, and conservative John G. Tower of Texas. Tower and Pearson had the greatest seniority, eight and seven years, respectively. The other three had either been appointed or elected to the Senate in 1966.

After some intensive discussion in a Senator's office, Percy was to withdraw from the contest, reasoning that his candidacy could only hurt the chances of moderates Pearson and Griffin.

On the first ballot Griffin led with 14 votes, Baker and Pearson were tied with 13 votes, and Tower, another last-minute candidate ended up with only three. With low man out, the second ballot showed Baker, 18; Griffin, 16; and Pearson, 9.

On the final ballot Griffin surged to the front, apparently picking up all but two of Pearson's supporters. He won by 23 to 20.[10]

The 45-year-old Griffin was no stranger to Republican congressional party infighting. Together with Charles Goodell of New York he had co-managed Gerald R. Ford's successful challenge to House Minority Leader Charles Halleck in 1965. Although defeated by Gordon Allott, 25 to 18, for the position of chairman of the Policy Committee in

January 1969, Griffin had nonetheless made a creditable showing. The 45-year-old Griffin had first gained national prominence as co-author of the 1959 Landrum-Griffin labor relations act. As a freshman Senator he was to lead a successful floor fight against President Johnson's nomination of Abraham Fortas for Chief Justice of the Supreme Court.

In September 1969, while Baker was seeking votes for the minority leadership, Griffin had publicly announced for whip and quietly set about securing the necessary commitments, including the votes of several younger conservatives who had preferred Baker over Scott. In retrospect, many members seem to agree that had Baker gone for the whip position directly he would have won. As a Griffin supporter acknowledged: "If Baker had gone for whip, there wouldn't have been the resentment about his moving too fast, too soon."

Baker claimed that his decision to run for minority leader was a conscious choice about which he had no regrets. "I gambled all my chips on the leadership race and lost it. If I had to do it all over again, I would do the same thing. As far as the whip position, if I had left the door open I'd have been dead for minority leader."

IX

Immediately after his election as minority leader, Scott was called to the telephone to receive congratulations from President Richard Nixon. The White House had stayed completely neutral in the contest. "There is no bitterness that I can detect at all," Scott told Nixon. The President apparently raised the possibility of gaining control of the Senate in 1970. Replied Scott, "No one can want to be the leader of the majority more than I do." But it was not to be, not in 1971, not in 1973 and, after Watergate, perhaps not for years to come.

EPILOGUE

Two years later, on January 21, 1971, Senate Republican leader Hugh Scott once again encountered a challenge from Howard Baker, Jr. Deferring his announced candidacy until the morning of the Republican Conference, the 45-year-old senior Senator from Tennessee would pick up one vote, but still lose, this time by 24 to 20.

Senator J. Caleb Boggs (Del.) nominated Scott for reelection as Republican floor leader. His nomination was seconded by George D.

Aiken (Vt.), the dean of Senate Republicans, Edward W. Brooke (Mass.), Theodore F. Stevens (Alaska), and freshman Lowell P. Weicker (Conn.). Baker was nominated by Senator Roman L. Hruska (Neb.) and seconded by Tennessee freshman William E. Brock III.

The interesting question is not so much "Why did Baker lose?" If anything, the composition of the Senate minority party in the 92d Congress (1971–1972) appeared more favorable for reelecting Scott than it had been for his initial selections as whip in January 1969 and minority leader in September 1969, following Dirksen's death. The more intriguing question would seem to be — "Why did Baker engage in a second losing effort?"

There seems little doubt that Scott faced a relatively favorable climate for reelection. He had the advantage of having been the incumbent minority leader for 15 months. If the White House and a number of Senate Republicans had been critical of his leadership during the early months — for example, Scott's vote against the Haynsworth Supreme Court nomination, his opposition to the administration's voting rights amendments — by the summer of 1970, a rapprochement seemed to have taken place. Counselor to the President Bryce N. Harlow went to considerable lengths to defend Scott in his June 22, 1970 introductory remarks before the National Coal Association:[11]

> The word is around town that he welshes on the President . . . Well, that's nuts . . . he has about the best supporting record for Nixon in just about the whole Senate. I can vouch for that. Anyway, never forget this — the best leaders are Senators, not ciphers. I have never known a congressional leader worth listening to who jumped through the hoop every time the administration spoke . . .
>
> So while this very distinguished man has not been with the President 100 percent, by golly, he has been with him almost that. That's good enough for us.

A White House spokesman subsequently reaffirmed Harlow's statement as "an expression of the President's feelings." More importantly, in a campaign speech in Lancaster, Pennsylvania on October 17, 1970, President Nixon endorsed Scott as a man "who has been our leader and I know will continue to be our leader in the years ahead." [12]

The results of the fall 1970 Senate elections seemed to further guarantee Scott's reelection as minority leader. A big infusion of conservative Republican freshman congressmen sought by President Nixon and Vice President Agnew as they campaigned across the land had not materialized. Republicans had hoped to pick up four or more Senate seats; they had to settle for a net gain of two. (The G.O.P. lost nine seats, net, in the House of Representatives.) Of five incoming Republican Senators — J. Glenn Beall (Md.), William Brock (Tenn.), William Roth (Del.), Robert Taft, Jr. (Ohio), and Lowell Weicker, Jr. (Conn.) — only one, Brock, could be expected to back Baker against Scott. Baker probably picked up another vote from New York Conservative James L. Buckley, who was allowed to participate in the Republican Conference.[13] Conservative Republican Senate candidates in 1970 who might have favored Baker — such as Lawrence Burton (Utah), George Bush (Texas), Anderson Carter (N.M.), William Cramer (Fla.), Thomas Kleppe (N.D.), and Richard Roudebush (Ind.) — were defeated. Discarding the votes of the four incumbent G.O.P. Senators who lost — Charles Goodell (N.Y.), George Murphy (Cal.), Ralph Smith (Ill.), and John J. Williams (Del.) — had little or no impact, since two had apparently voted for Scott and two for Baker in the September 1969 contest.

Why, then, did Baker run? No simple answer is forthcoming, especially given Baker's reputation as a competent legislator with a sure sense of timing and an ability to assess votes. He must have been aware that his chances were, at best, uphill.

A rematch, of course, had been anticipated, at least until the results of the November 1970 elections. All through the balance of the 91st Congress, Baker had missed few opportunities to criticize Scott's leadership when he felt it was warranted. He had been polite, even cordial, in his personal relationships with Scott, yet he had maintained an aloofness too. In November 1970, after the elections, Baker had gone so far as to seek an appointment with President Richard M. Nixon to ask his support in ousting Scott. But the President, increasingly needing Scott's leadership of a wing of the party he needed most, remained neutral.[14]

Although he had campaigned for several weeks prior to the Republican Conference, Baker acknowledged after his loss that his decision to run had been a last-minute one. Baker believed that he had uncovered enough uncertainty among a sizeable group of Republican Senators to warrant the challenge.

Further hopes for an upset had come about in mid-January when his as-yet unannounced candidacy had received a strong boost from the public endorsements of two senior Republicans, moderate John Sherman Cooper of Kentucky and conservative Milton R. Young of North Dakota. Both Senators had voted for Scott over Baker in the September 1969 balloting. In a January 1971 letter to his colleagues, Cooper had called Baker "philosophically and politically" open-minded, "not wedded to any particular group in the Senate or the country," and the right age to be "attractive to the young people of the country." [15]

Perhaps a combination of motives finally tipped Baker's hand. He was undoubtedly frustrated by the lack of strong conservative voice in the leadership. It seems clear in hindsight that he overestimated the degree of uncertainty about the leadership existing in the G.O.P. senatorial ranks. He must have discounted the apparent portent of the fall elections. Several Senators felt, in retrospect, that Baker had been overly encouraged by staff and close associates. After his loss, Baker maintained that he would continue to work for the passage of

The winner consoles the challenger: Minority Leader Hugh Scott with his arm around Senator Howard Baker of Tennessee after their second contest, January 1971.

(U.S. Senate Republican Policy Committee Photo)

President Nixon's legislative programs in the Senate and that he would cooperate with Scott on matters of mutual concern and interest. Asked if he thought the vote could be interpreted as a repudiation of the conservative wing of the Republican party in the Senate, Baker replied that he did not think so "because I had support from all segments of the party." Perhaps the losing candidate provided the most convincing rationale for his second challenge to Scott: "I ran because it was the only way to find out exactly how much support I had." [16]

For Baker, then, his second challenge to Scott appears to have been a calculated risk. Barring major Senate Republican setbacks in future elections, Baker may have seen this as his last chance to challenge Scott for some time to come.[17] Even if he lost, he felt confident he could make a strong showing — and he did. The 70-year-old Pennsylvanian appeared to be in good health. He had just been reelected for six more years. Meanwhile, Michigan's Robert Griffin, just two years older than Baker, was entrenching himself as minority whip and would quite likely be a strong contender for the minority leadership in the future. Lest conjecture about a future minority leadership contest carry us too far afield, it should be remembered that "politics is generally played in the present tense." Should Scott decide to retire in 1976, however, a Baker-Griffin contest for minority leader might well be in the offing.

NOTES

1. Neil MacNeil, *Dirksen: Portrait of a Public Man* (New York: World, 1970); Jean Torcom Cronin, "Minority Leadership in the United States Senate: The Role and Style of Everett Dirksen," Ph.D. dissertation, Johns Hopkins University, 1973; Charles O. Jones, *The Minority Party in Congress* (Boston: Little, Brown, 1970), pp. 167–170.
2. Ben H. Bagdikian, " 'The Oil Can Is Mightier Than the Sword,' " *The New York Times Magazine*, March 14, 1965, pp. 30–31 ff at p. 84.
3. *Ibid.*
4. *Newsweek*, January 13, 1969, p. 16.
5. *Congressional Quarterly Weekly Report* **28** (January 16, 1970), p. 149.
6. *Congressional Quarterly Weekly Report* **27** (September 12, 1969), pp. 1670–1671.
7. Kevin P. Phillips, *The Emerging Republican Majority* (New Rochelle, N.Y.: Arlington House, 1969).
8. *Congressional Quarterly Weekly Report* **27** (September 27, 1969), p. 1671.
9. *New York Times*, September 13, 1969, p. 12.
10. *New York Times*, September 25, 1969, p. 1.
11. Spencer Rich, "Nixon Reported Satisfied with Scott's Leadership," *Washington Post*, July 27, 1970, p. A-2.

12. Spencer Rich, "Scott Seen Sure of Keeping Post," *Washington Post*, November 13, 1970, p. A-2.
13. *New York Times*, January 22, 1971, p. 12.
14. Jack Anderson would conjecture that the reason Nixon had backed off was because he had attempted to intervene in several backstage House leadership battles while still Vice President, only to be "badly burned." *Washington Post*, November 24, 1970, p. C-9.
15. Spencer Rich, "Cooper to Back Baker Bid Against Scott," *Washington Post*, January 9, 1971, p. A-2.
16. *Congressional Quarterly Weekly Report* **29** (January 22, 1971), p. 182.
17. "I would not have challenged if I felt his incumbency had set in," Baker later recalled. He also acknowledged that he would not challenge him again. "Scott's leadership has been established and his incumbency has set in; and it would be foolish of me to attempt to uproot him." 'Interview with Howard H. Baker, Jr.,' *Ralph Nader Congress Project*, August 25, 1972 (Washington: Grossman, 1972), p. 12.

CHAPTER FIFTEEN

Senate Leadership Change: 1955–1974

Five contests illustrating U.S. Senate party leadership change — the election of Russell Long as majority whip in 1965, Edward Kennedy's upset of Long in 1969, and Robert Byrd's successful challenge to Kennedy in 1971; and two contests for the office of minority leader, Hugh Scott's successive defeats of Howard Baker in 1969 and 1971 — have been chronicled and analyzed in some detail (Chapters 12–14). How typical are these case studies of Senate leadership change, in general? What have been the patterns of leadership succession in the Democratic majority and Republican minority parties over the past two decades? How do these patterns compare and contrast with their counterpart leadership selection patterns in the House of Representatives?

Both intensive case studies and the examination of longer range trends are necessary for a deeper understanding of how the congressional parties select, and sometimes, dispose of their leaders. Leadership contests lay bare the personal strengths and weaknesses of the individual candidates, the networks of personal, regional, and ideological ties that are engendered within, and fed by, the close proximities and day-to-day interactions characteristic of legislative life. Unlike a major legislative issue, leadership contests involve only one party's members, interest groups generally play a secondary role, the duration is likely to be shorter, and the final outcome is usually resolved by a secret ballot vote in the party conference rather than a series of roll call votes on the floor. Nevertheless, major leadership contests, as measured by the intensity of candidate aspirations, the breadth of membership involvement, and their long-range consequences, would seem to approach, if not rival, all but the most important legislative and constitutional questions which face a given Congress. The leaders who are selected help to establish the timing if not virtually control much of the legislative agenda; they contribute greatly to the temper, tone, and pace of their party's activities within their legislative chambers; they act as spokesmen for their colleagues at the White House and represent their party to the media.

For a more complete understanding of how leaders are selected and with what consequences, the focus must, of course, go beyond individual contests, no matter how important any one outcome might be. Contests are, of course, the exception rather than the rule. Most Congresses are characterized by the reelection in incumbent leaders. Given the limited number of cases of contested leadership change — seldom more than four or five among top party positions in either Senate party over a decade — attempts to develop verified general propositions are inherently hazardous. Still, one does not generalize from a sample; these cases are a nearly complete universe for the 20-year period under analysis here. Precisely because research on leadership change forces attempts at generalizations over a series of Congresses, it should prove more fruitful than isolated case studies and help to complement in-depth analyses of the roles of particular congressional leaders over time.[1]

This analysis of Senate leadership change is, in the main, limited to ten Congresses, the 84th through the 93d (1955–1974). Some attention is also paid to the immediately preceding Congress, the 83d, since several leaders who served in the 1950's, most notably Lyndon B. Johnson and William F. Knowland, were initially elected floor leaders in 1953. But for purposes of making comparisons with prior research on the House of Representatives,[2] the period from 1955 to 1974 has been isolated. This time frame encompasses the ten Congresses since the last election bringing about a change in the control of Congress, the mid-term election of 1954. Since that election, Democrats have maintained a majority in both the House and Senate; Republicans have remained in the minority. Although this has some obvious advantages in generalizing about the Democratic majority as compared with the Republican minority in one or both Houses, there is also a disadvantage. It makes it impossible to prove or disprove any hypotheses relating leadership change to majority-minority status as over and against party differences, Democrat and Republican. For such interpretations longer range historical refinement will be required.[3]

Chapters 9 and 10 presented an analytical scheme for classifying intra-party leadership change in the House of Representatives. In order to facilitate comparisons between the House and Senate, three similar variables — (1) vacancy or non-vacancy; (2) the presence or absence of an established pattern of succession; and (3) the extent to which a change is contested — have been dichotomized to yield a comparable sixfold classification scheme (Table 15.1).

The several strictures advanced earlier regarding the interpretation of this analytical scheme need not be repeated here. However, it should be noted that the Senate has yet to develop as firm a pattern of succession as the House practice of selecting its Speakers from either the incumbent majority leader, or following party turnover, from the former incumbent minority leader. The closest approximation to this pattern in the Senate is one of elevating party whips to the position of floor leader, a pattern which began in the late 1940's, but could not be said to be fairly firmly established until the 1960's. As Chapter 11 has already indicated, the last three Democratic whips with the opportunity to advance to floor leader — Lucas (1949), Johnson (1953), and Mansfield (1961) — did so, as have three of the last four Republican whips confronted with that opportunity — Wherry (1949), Dirksen (1959), and Scott (1969). Only Leverett Saltonstall of Massachusetts, Republican whip from 1949 to 1957 was passed over.[4]

The upper left-hand cell of Table 15.1, the *status quo*, covers, of course, what typically happens at the beginning of each new Congress. All or most of the Senate leadership continues in office or has re-

Table 15.1
Types of Intra-Party Leadership Change

	NO CONTEST	CONTEST
NO VACANCY	*Status quo*	(5) Revolt or its aftermath
VACANCY Established pattern of succession	(1) Routine advancement	(4) Challenge to the heir apparent
No established pattern of succession	(2) Appointment or emergence of a consensus choice	(3) Open competition

cently been reelected. No vacancy in a leadership position exists and no contest takes place; hence, no change occurs. The remaining five types — (1) routine advancement, (2) appointment or emergence of a consensus choice, (3) open competition, (4) challenge to the heir apparent, and (5) revolt — are ordered, as in the House analysis, in terms of the amount of credit expenditure (time, energy, number of members involved, intensity of involvement, bargaining and resource trading, and so on) which each type of contest generally calls forth.

I

In the contemporary Senate as in the House, the predominant pattern of leadership selection is retention of incumbents rather than frequent leadership turnover. Table 15.2 lists the Democratic Senators who have occupied the positions of floor leader, whip, and secretary of the Democratic Conference for the past 10 Congresses, the 84th (1955–1956) through the 93d Congress (1973–1974). Two men — Lyndon Johnson of Texas and Mike Mansfield of Montana — have served as majority leader over this 20-year period; six Democratic Senators have shared the majority whip's duties; and four men have held the third ranking position in the party hierarchy, secretary to the Conference.

Table 15.3 sets forth the Republican Senators who have occupied the three top leadership positions in the minority party — floor leader, whip, and chairman of the Republican Policy Committee — over the past 10 Congresses. Over this same 20-year period three Republican Senators served as floor leader — William Knowland (Cal.), Everett Dirksen (Ill.), and Hugh Scott (Pa.) — five men have held the party whip's position, and four Senators have operated as chairman of the Republican Policy Committee, the third most prestigious position in the minority party hierarchy.

This analysis of Senate leadership change has been restricted to three positions in both parties (as compared to five in the House) for rather obvious reasons. Democratic party leadership in the Senate is largely concentrated in one man — the floor leader who is at the same time the chairman of the Democratic Conference, Policy Committee, and Steering Committee (Committee on Committees). In addition to the floor whip or assistant leader, the largely honorary position of President pro tempore,[5] and the chairman of the Senatorial Campaign Committee,[6] the only other Democratic leadership po-

Table 15.2
Democratic (Majority) Party Leaders, U. S. Senate, 84th–93d Congresses (1955–1974)

Congress	Floor Leader	Whip	Secretary to the Conference
84th 1955–1956	Lyndon Johnson, Texas (1-2-53)[a]	Earle Clements, Ky. (1-2-53)	Thomas Hennings, Mo. (1-2-53)
85th 1957–1958	"	Michael Mansfield, Mont. (1-3-57)	"
86th 1959–1960	"	"	"
87th 1961–1962	Mansfield (1-3-61)	Hubert Humphrey, Minn. (1-3-61)	George Smathers, Fla. (1-3-61)
88th 1963–1964	"	"	"
89th 1965–1966	"	Russell Long, La. (1-4-65)	"
90th 1967–1968	"	"	Robert Byrd, W. Va. (1-10-67)
91st 1969–1970	"	Edward Kennedy, Mass. (1-3-69)	"
92d 1971–1972	"	Byrd (1-21-71)	Frank Moss, Utah (1-21-71)
93d 1973–1974	"	"	"

[a] Dates in parentheses indicate when a Senator was first elected to his party leadership position by the Democratic Conference.

Table 15.3

Republican (Minority) Party Leaders, U. S. Senate, 84th–93d Congresses (1955–1974)

Congress	Floor Leader	Whip	Policy Committee Chairman
84th 1955–1956	William Knowland, Cal. (8-4-53)[a]	Leverett Saltonstall, Mass. (1-3-49)	Styles Bridges, N.H. (1-4-55)
85th 1957–1958	"	Everett Dirksen, Ill. (1-3-57)	"
86th 1959–1960	Dirksen (1-7-59)	Thomas Kuchel, Cal. (1-7-59)	"
87th 1961–1962	"	"	"
88th 1963–1964	"	"	Bourke Hickenlooper, Iowa (1-10-62)
89th 1965–1966	"	"	"
90th 1967–1968	"	"	"
91st 1969–1970	Scott (9-24-69)	Hugh Scott, Pa. (1-3-69) / Robert Griffin, Mich. (9-24-69)	Gordon Allott, Colo. (1-3-69)
92d 1971–1972	"	"	"
93d 1973–1974	"	"	John Tower, Texas (1-3-73)

[a] Dates in parentheses indicate when a Senator was first elected to his party leadership position by the Republican Conference.

sition of any significance is the position of secretary to the Conference. Up until the 1960's, this position had little import. It was mainly awarded to a middle ranking party loyalist as a means of providing geographical or ideological balance in the party hierarchy. But with the election of Senator George Smathers in 1961, and especially after the election of Senator Robert Byrd in 1967, the position began to gain some stature. Byrd is the first Democratic Senator to use the position as a stepping-stone to higher office, but under Majority Leader Mansfield the secretary has become an ex officio member of the Democratic Policy and Steering Committees, and its incumbent has also taken on broader floor responsibilities.

Although not strictly comparable in prestige or resources to the chairmanship of the Republican Policy Committee, the position of secretary to the Democratic Conference can be expected to grow in stature over coming decades and have the potential, at least, of becoming a training ground for higher leadership.

In contrast to the Senate Democrats, the Republicans diversify their leadership over six principal offices: floor leader, whip and the chairmen of its Policy Committee, Committee on Committees, Senatorial Campaign Committee, and the Republican Conference. The position of chairman of the Policy Committee has been selected as the third leadership position for our comparative analysis for two principal reasons. First, the position taps into considerable resources, including a staff of more than 20 professionals. Under the Legislative Reorganization Act of 1946 this committee receives more than $250,000 a year for research and policy analysis.

Second, incumbents of this position have twice advanced to the floor leadership, although both instances occurred before 1955. Both Robert Taft and William Knowland held this position immediately prior to their selections as majority leader in January and August of 1953. Taft, a member of the Senate since 1938, was first elected chairman of the nine-member Steering (later Policy) Committee in 1944. For a long time the Senate minority was run by a triumvirate consisting of Taft, floor leader Wallace White of Maine, and Arthur Vandenberg of Michigan, chairman of the Conference. But gradually Taft's legislative competence, his forceful personality, and stature as a leading presidential aspirant, led to assumption of de facto leadership among Senate Republicans.[7] With the election of a Republican President in 1952, Taft made himself available for the post of majority leader and was elected without opposition.

Taft's successor as Policy Committee chairman was William Knowland of California. When the senior Ohioan's health began to fail in the summer of 1953, be appointed Knowland as acting floor leader. Taft died of cancer on July 31. Four days later the 45-year-old Californian was unanimously elected majority leader. Knowland reigned for more than five years, sometimes helping Eisenhower get his legislative program through, but frequently following his own more conservative predilections. In 1958 he resigned from the Senate to launch an unsuccessful bid for the governorship of California, an effort which he hoped, eventually, would earn him his party's nomination for the presidency.[8]

Of the 30 changes in each party which hypothetically could be expected (a change in each of three positions over 10 Congresses) Republicans have made 11, Democrats but 9. As will become more apparent, the way in which change manifests itself, especially the extent of contested change, has more important consequences for individual career development and party fortunes than sheer frequency of change. Each of the five types of intra-party leadership change can be illustrated by one or more of the 20 instances which took place in the Senate from 1955 to 1974 (Table 15.4).

(1) ROUTINE ADVANCEMENT. This first type of intra-party leadership change takes place when a vacancy occurs in top leadership position (usually as a result of retirement, election defeat, or death), an established pattern of succession exists, and the next ranking member in the party hierarchy is elevated without challenge.

Mike Mansfield's selection as majority leader in January 1961, after four years' service as majority whip, is an appropriate illustration. First elected to the House of Representatives in 1942, Mansfield won his first term in the United States Senate in 1952. He became Majority Leader Johnson's compromise choice for whip when opposition to his first choice, George Smathers of Florida, materialized. After Senators Kennedy and Johnson had won the 1960 presidential election, they approached the Montana Senator and prevailed upon him to accept Johnson's vacated position of floor leader. Recalled Mansfield: "I didn't seek either job. I suppose they were looking for a man in the middle." Liberals, moderates, and conservatives alike had found Mansfield easy to work with as whip; he was to prove to be an accessible and accommodating floor leader as well.

The routineness of Mansfield's selection, while it by no means guaranteed that the choice of his successor would go uncontested, could be seen as one index of an increasing institutionalization of

Table 15.4

Types of Intra-Party Leadership Change, U. S. Senate, 84th–93d Congresses (1955–1974)

	NO CONTEST		CONTEST [a]	
	Democratic Majority	Republican Minority	Democratic Majority	Republican Minority
NO VACANCY	*Status quo*		(5) *Revolt*	
			Whip Kennedy vs. Long, 1969 Byrd vs. Kennedy, 1971	Floor Leader Scott vs. Baker, 1971
VACANCY Established pattern of succession	(1) *Routine advancement* Whip to Floor Leader Mansfield, 1961		(4) *Challenge to heir apparent* 	Whip to Floor Leader Dirksen vs. Cooper, 1959 Scott vs. Baker, 9-1969

No established pattern of succession	(2) Appointment or the emergence of a consensus choice		(3) Open competition	
	Whip Mansfield, 1957 Humphrey, 1961	Whip Dirksen, 1957	Whip Long vs. Pastore, Monroney, 1965	Whip Kuchel vs. Mundt, 1959 Scott vs. Hruska, 1-1969 Griffin vs. Baker, Miller, 9-1969
	Secretary, Conference Smathers, 1961 Moss, 1971	Policy Committee Chairman Bridges, 1955	Secretary, Conference Byrd vs. Clark, 1967	Policy Committee Chairman Hickenlooper vs. Saltonstall, 1962 Allott vs. Griffin, 1-1969 Tower vs. Taft, 1973
Total number of changes	5	2	4	9

[a] In cases of contest, the winning candidate is listed first.

Senate leadership.[9] As already noted, the practice of moving up the ladder from party whip to floor leader is essentially a post-World War II development. Scott Lucas (D., Ill.) served as whip in the 90th Congress and then was routinely advanced to floor leader in the 81st Congress when his predecessor, Alben Barkley (D., Ky.) became Vice President under Truman. After the defeat of both Lucas and Whip Francis Myers (D., Pa.) in the 1950 elections, Richard Russell, the leading Senate oligarch, prevailed upon Ernest McFarland of Arizona to become majority leader. Senator Robert Kerr of Oklahoma persuaded Russell to take Lyndon B. Johnson of Texas as whip, despite a seeming lack of regional balance. Two years later when McFarland was defeated by Barry Goldwater, the 44-year-old Johnson emerged as the heir apparent to the floor leadership. Yet, Johnson's elevation to minority leader in the 83d Congress could not be classified as routine advancement for two reasons. In the first place the young Texan had token opposition from Democratic liberals. Second, the practice of elevating the party whip to floor leader was only partially established. However, Johnson's near unanimous selection went a considerable way toward institutionalizing the practice. Eight years later when Senators Kennedy and Johnson moved on to head up the executive branch, their choice for majority leader, Mike Mansfield, was unopposed.

(2) Appointment or the Emergence of a Consensus Choice. The second type of leadership change is illustrated by a number of unchallenged elections at lower levels of the party hierarchy for which patterns of succession are not yet established. The selections of Democratic whips Earle Clements (Ky.) in 1953, Mansfield (Mont.) in 1957, and Hubert H. Humphrey (Minn.) in 1961, as well as the choices of secretaries to the Democratic Conference, Thomas Hennings (Mo.) in 1953, George Smathers (Fla.) in 1961, and Frank Moss (Utah) in 1971 are all illustrative.

In most instances, a floor leader, working closely with the senior oligarchs of his party, and taking geographical and ideological balance into account, chooses those Senators he feels will best complement his leadership. Through a process of consultation and clearance, most of whatever opposition that might arise can usually be eliminated. If a selected Senator arouses too much opposition, an alternative candidate may be substituted. Election in the Conference then becomes a mere formality.

Although Clements was first elected to party leadership in 1953, two years before Democrats resumed control of the Senate, his hand-picked choice by Johnson illustrates the "appointment" type of leadership selection quite well. Both men had served in the House of Representatives during World War II, Clements in the 79th and 80th Congresses (1945–1948). Subsequently elected governor of his home state, Clements resigned in 1950 to run for the vacated Senate seat of Alben W. Barkley. Johnson found Clements a loyal lieutenant, moderate in philosophy, with considerable legislative skills, and an able assistant floor leader. At Johnson's initiative the whip, for the first time, was provided with staff assistance and an office off the Senate floor.

Thomas C. Hennings, Jr., Johnson's choice for secretary to the Conference in 1953, also served in the House (74th to 76th Congresses: 1935–1940), but was not to enter the Senate until 1950. Personally popular with other members, Hennings was a natural choice to head off a threatened bid for the position by defeated presidential candidate, Estes Kefauver of Tennessee. Resented for the anti-southern stance he had taken at the 1952 national convention, Kefauver never was nominated and ended up seconding Hennings.[10]

After Clements was defeated for reelection in 1956, Johnson's first choice was George Smathers of Florida. Although Smathers was moderate by southern standards, he was opposed by more liberal elements in the party including some who disliked his aggressive campaign tactics against New Deal Senator Claude Pepper in the bitter Florida Democratic primary of 1950. One strong source of opposition was alleged to have been Johnson's old mentor, Speaker Sam Rayburn of Texas. Another possible candidate, Hubert Humphrey, was considered to be too much of an anathema to southerners, especially on the eve of a major civil rights battle. By process of elimination, Johnson finally settled on Mansfield.

Four years later, the competent but self-effacing Senator from Montana moved up the ladder from whip to majority leader. Humphrey, first elected to the Senate in 1948, became majority whip without opposition. Like Mansfield, he had the strong support of the newly elected President and Vice President. His liberal credentials were as solid as ever; but over the years Humphrey had also developed the friendship and respect of a number of southern conservatives. As the choice of Humphrey could be viewed as a move to placate liberals, so the selection of George Smathers to become the secretary to the

Democratic Conference was seen as a bid to help align southern support behind the Kennedy-Johnson legislative programs. Smathers filled a post left vacant by Hennings' death on September 13, 1960.

As Chapter 11 developed at some length, Majority Leader Mansfield has taken a much less active, if not quiescent, role in the selection of his supporting leadership than his predecessor. One result has been more frequent contests, but from time to time consensus choices have emerged. For example, Frank Moss of Utah, first elected to the Senate in 1958, appeared to be acceptable to all wings of the party when he ran unopposed for the position of secretary to the Conference in 1971.

Two further examples of the emergence of a consensus choice, both within the Republican party, were the selection of Styles Bridges, unanimous choice as chairman of the Republican Policy Committee in January 1955 and Everett McKinley Dirksen's unopposed selection as minority whip in January 1957. Bridges, who had served briefly as minority floor leader in 1952, and as President pro tempore of the Senate in 1953–1954 (creating an opening for Taft), was a logical choice for chairman of the Policy Committee. He succeeded Homer Ferguson of Michigan who had been defeated for reelection in 1954.

A vacancy in the whip's position was created in 1957 when Leverett Saltonstall opted for chairman of the Republican Conference. The whip job had always been a position of limited opportunity for the liberal Saltonstall. For the Illinois conservative, in contrast, it was to become a springboard to higher leadership. Dirksen had served eight terms in the House before he retired because of failing eyesight in 1948. Regaining his health he challenged and beat Scott Lucas, the Senate majority leader, in 1950. In 1957, Dirksen was regarded as about as conservative as Knowland and somewhat to the right of President Eisenhower. Two years after his uncontested election as whip, Dirksen had to overcome liberal opposition in his successful quest for the minority leadership.

(3) OPEN COMPETITION. The most prevalent type of leadership change in the U.S. Senate is open competition — a vacancy occurs in a party leadership position, no pattern of succession has been established, and no single candidate emerges as a consensus choice. Two or more candidates announce, work actively to obtain support, and the contest usually is resolved by a secret ballot vote in the party Conference. The election of Russell Long of Louisiana as whip over several other Democratic Senators in January 1965 was a clear illustration

(Chapter 12). Another example of open competition took place on January 10, 1967, when Robert C. Byrd of West Virginia rather decisively defeated Joseph S. Clark of Pennsylvania for the position of secretary to the Democratic Conference. George A. Smathers, who had served in that capacity since 1961, had announced in early December that he would not seek reelection to that post and planned to retire from the Senate in 1968.

All three of the past elections for Republican whip or assistant floor leader have been even more hotly contested. In January 1959, when conservative G.O.P. Whip Dirksen advanced to floor leader, his choice for party whip was liberal Thomas Kuchel of California. Kuchel defeated South Dakota conservative Karl Mundt by about the same three-to-two margin that Dirksen had won by over his more liberal opponent, John Sherman Cooper. The objective was to unite the party by providing a representative from both wings of the party in the leadership. With Dirksen's continued backing, Kuchel was able to survive recurring threats of a challenge to his incumbency over the next decade. But he was finally defeated by a conservative opponent in a bitter California primary battle in June 1968. Congressional veteran Hugh Scott of Pennsylvania became the leading candidate of those moderate-to-liberal Senate Republicans who wanted to maintain the practice of countering a conservative floor leader with a whip of liberal persuasion.

On January 3, 1969, at the opening of the 91st Congress, Scott moved into top Republican leadership contention when he upset Roman Hruska of Nebraska, 23 to 20, in a contest for the vacated position of minority whip. In the process Scott overcame Dirksen's endorsement of the conservative Nebraskan.

Dirksen, minority leader since January 1959, died on September 7, 1969, following an operation for lung cancer. Scott was able to survive a challenge from Dirksen's son-in-law, 43-year-old Howard H. Baker, Jr. of Tennessee. The same day that Scott was elevated to floor leader, Baker lost another contest, that one for whip. Robert P. Griffin of Michigan defeated Baker on a third ballot vote, 23 to 20 (Chapter 14).

Republicans have also resorted to open competition to fill their past three openings for the chairmanship of their Policy Committee. Following the death of Styles Bridges in November 1960, Leverett Saltonstall, the chairman of the Republican Conference since 1957, took over as acting chairman of the 24-member Policy Committee. For a time it appeared as if he would have no opposition, but then the conservative wing of the party got behind one of their own, Bourke B. Hickenlooper of Iowa. On January 10, 1962, Hickenlooper, with Dirksen's backing, overcame Saltonstall's initial lead and won by 21 votes to 14.

After Hickenlooper retired in 1968, the leading conservative candidate became Gordon L. Allott of Colorado. First elected in 1954, Allott easily defeated a last-minute challenge from Michigan moderate Robert Griffin at the opening Republican Conference of the 91st Congress, January 3, 1969. The vote was 25 to 18. Four years later, in 1973, Allott was upset by Floyd Haskell in the Colorado senatorial election. Once again Senate Republicans resorted to open competition to fill the vacancy. Conservative John G. Tower of Texas edged out Ohio moderate Robert Taft, Jr. by a vote of 22 to 19. Tower, the immediate past chairman of the Republican Senatorial Campaign Committee, had the advantage of more than 11 years of past Senatorial experience; Taft had only two years' service behind him. Had Taft effected the upset, he would have occupied the leadership position held by his father some 20 years earlier.

(4) CHALLENGE TO THE HEIR APPARENT. This fourth type of intraparty leadership change takes place when a vacancy occurs in a top leadership position, but the apparent heir's claim (generally that of a party whip) is contested. As Table 15.4 indicates, two challenges of this type have occurred in the Senate during the 84th to 93d Congresses. Both Republican whips — Dirksen in January 1959, and Scott in September 1969 — were able to overcome these challenges, the former with relative ease, the latter with some difficulty.

Although Dirksen represented the dominant conservative wing of his party, he was more than willing to make overtures to the liberal wing by earmarking the whip's position for them. As already noted, he defeated liberal John Sherman Cooper of Kentucky by a conference vote of 20 to 14. Republicans had suffered a net loss of 13 Senate seats in the election of 1958, but these could hardly be attributed to their party whip's activities or inactivities. (On the House side, however, Republicans replaced their ailing minority leader Joseph Martin of Massachusetts with Charles Halleck of Indiana.)

When Dirksen died 10 years later, Scott had been serving as whip for but seven months. His youthful conservative challenger, Howard Baker of Tennessee, had been a member of the Senate for only two and one-half years. His only other likely challenger, Roman Hruska of Nebraska, had already been defeated by Scott in the January 1969 whip contest. As Chapter 14 recounts in detail, Scott's support of Nixon, his acceptable conduct in the whip's office, and his senority were able to offset whatever other perceived weakness Scott had in the eyes of the party's conservative majority.

The closest Democratic parallel to these two Republican instances of a challenge to an heir apparent predates our 20-year period of analysis by one Congress. At the opening of the 83d Congress, Lyndon Johnson's bid to move from majority whip to minority floor leader generated scattered liberal opposition. The liberal's choice for floor leader was aging millionaire, cattle rancher, Senator James E. Murray of Montana. But when the January 3, 1953, Conference votes were tabulated, Johnson won so overwhelmingly that Murray's vote was not even announced in order to spare him any further humiliation.[11]

(5) REVOLT. This last type of leadership change is usually the most costly in terms of credit expenditure. A party leader, with all of the resources of his office at his command wishes to remain in power. If he cannot be persuaded to step aside, his challenger must not only start from a substantial base but convince fence-riders that he can win. Most members hesitate to move against established leaders without strong cause. Until 1969, challenges to incumbent leaders were without precedent in the contemporary Senate, and apparently no floor leader of either party had ever been ousted. Three revolts have occurred in recent Congresses: Edward Kennedy's upset of Majority Whip Russell Long in January 1969; (2) Robert Byrd's overthrow of Kennedy in January 1971, and (3) Howard Baker's second effort to become minority leader, also at the opening of the 92d Congress. For both series of contests, it seemed true that one conflict generated another — parallel cases occurred in the House.[12] Further, these several cases of revolt may be indicative of an increasing proclivity no longer to take incumbent leaders for granted in all four congressional parties.

The first case of revolt to preoccupy a contemporary Senate party came to a climax on January 3, 1969, when Senator Edward Kennedy of Massachusetts upset the incumbent whip, Russell Long, by a vote of 31 to 26. This race, pitting a junior northern liberal against a senior southern conservative, has already been described in depth (Chapter 12). Two years later Kennedy, in turn, was upset by Robert Byrd of West Virginia (Chapter 13). The Chappaquiddick incident and its aftermath had made Kennedy vulnerable not unlike Long before him. Committed to serving out his second full term in the Senate (1970–1976), he was no longer seen as the likely Democratic presidential nominee in 1972. For the second time in two years Senate Democrats had ousted their party whip.

In contrast, a Republican challenger has not yet unseated an incumbent party leader in the contemporary Senate. The closest attempt was Howard Baker's second bid to win the minority leader position, this time at the opening of the 92d Congress in January 1971. After losing to Scott in September 1969, by a vote of 24 to 19, Baker bided his time, figuring that one result of the 1970 elections would be to bring more conservatives into the Senate. Scott, incumbent floor leader, was able to hold off a second challenge from Baker, this time by a vote of 24 to 20, for reasons closely parallel to his first victory: (1) his performance as a leader, including enhanced credibility with the White House; and (2) maintenance of a near-solid base of moderate-to-liberal support, coupled with the continued loyalty of about a half dozen of the more senior Republican conservatives. Baker's hoped-for surge of new conservative votes coming out of 1970 election victories simply did not materialize.

II

From prior research on intra-party leadership change in the House of Representatives, it seemed reasonable to hypothesize that the Senate Republican minority party would resort more frequently to contested change than the Democratic majority party. The results presented in Table 15.4, although they show not quite as striking a contrast as in the House, would seem to support this hypothesis. Of 11 instances of change in the Republican party's top three leadership positions over a 20-year period, all but two were decided by contests. Only the selection of Styles Bridges as chairman of the Republican Policy Committee in 1955 and the choice of Everett Dirksen as minority whip in 1957 were uncontested. In contrast, the Democratic majority party resolved five out of nine of its choices for top party leaders — floor leader, whip, and secretary of the Democratic Conference — over these 10 Congresses by relatively harmonious means. The Democratic majority was able to make more frequent use of such types of leadership change as routine advancement, "appointment" from above, and the emergence of a consensus choice.

These patterns of Senate leadership change must be interpreted with caution, however. In the first place, the number of cases is small. Democrats selected only one floor leader during this period, the uncontested elevation of Majority Whip Mansfield in 1961. Republicans chose only two floor leaders, Dirksen and Scott, but both were challenged by candidates from the opposing ideological wing of their party. Secondly, Democrats were more prone to revolt than Republicans. In 1969 and 1971 Senate Democrats ousted their incumbent whips. The only instance of an attempted revolt against an incumbent leader by a Republican, at least since World War II, was Baker's rematch against Scott in 1971. Third, it should be reiterated that the position of secretary to the Conference, although considered the third ranking position in the Democratic party hierarchy, has been of lesser import than the chairmanship of the Republican Policy Committee. Discrepancies in the method of selecting the incumbents of these two offices have been quite pronounced (only one contest out of three for Democrats, three contests out of four for Republicans).

Closer examination of Table 15.4 suggests another reason for care in reading too much into party differences or even majority-minority status as principal causal factors in contested change. In Table 15.5 these 20 cases of leadership change are collapsed into three categories — C = Contest; ⓒ = Contested, but the incumbent retains his position; and NC = No contest — as controlled by party and position during the 10 Congresses. Although the differences between the two Senate parties are pronounced in the first 10 years (four uncontested changes for Democrats; three out of five contested for Republicans), there is almost no difference between the two parties in the final 10 years studied (1965–1974). All but one of 11 instances of change in the last five Congresses, Frank Moss's selection as secretary to the Democratic Conference, were contested (four out of five Democratic and all six Republican). In other words, *both* Senate parties have turned almost exclusively to *contested* means to choose their party leaders over the past decade.

Why did the Senate Democratic majority largely enjoy relatively orderly means of leadership change in the 1950's, but experience more stress in selecting incumbents for lesser party leadership offices in the late 1960's and early 1970's? Conversely — What caused the Republican minority to resort rather consistently to contested change in leadership throughout the 20-year period? The following chapter explores these questions and sets forth some contrasts and comparisons between the House and the Senate in their methods of party leadership selection.

Table 15.5

Contested and Non-Contested Change in Senate Party Leaders, Democratic and Republican, 84th–93d Congresses (1955–1974)

	84th 1955–56	85th 1957–58	86th 1959–60	87th 1961–62	88th 1963–64	89th 1965–66	90th 1967–68	91st 1969–70	92d 1971–72	93d 1973–74
Floor Leader										
Dem.									©	
Rep.			C	NC				C		
Whip										
Dem.		NC		NC		C		C	C	
Rep.		NC	C					C		
Number 3 Position[a]										
Dem.				NC			C	C	NC	
Rep.	NC			C						C

C = Contested; © = contested, but incumbent retains position; NC = Non-Contested.

[a] Secretary to the Democratic Conferences; Chairman of the Republican Policy Committee.

NOTES

1. For example, Ralph K. Huitt, "Democratic Party Leadership in the Senate," *Am. Pol. Sci. Rev.* **55** (June 1961), 331–344; Neil MacNeil, *Dirksen: Portrait of a Public Man* (New York: World, 1970); Jean Torcom Cronin, "Minority Leadership in the United States Senate: The Role and Style of Everett Dirksen," Ph.D. dissertation, Johns Hopkins University, 1973.
2. Robert L. Peabody, "Party Leadership Change in the House of Representatives," *Am. Pol. Sci. Rev.* **61** (September 1967), 675–693. (Cf. Chapters 9 and 10 of this book also.)
3. Garrison Nelson, "Party Control Periods of the U.S. House of Representatives and the Recruitment of Its Leaders, 1789–1971," Ph.D. dissertation, University of Iowa, 1973; G. Nelson, "Partisan Patterns of House Leadership Change, 1791–1973," paper delivered before the 1974 Annual Meeting of the American Political Science Association, Chicago, September 1, 1974.
4. Saltonstall was originally awarded the party whip post in 1949 as a consolation prize to the liberal wing of the party. In 1952, following the death of Minority Leader Kenneth Wherry, the Massachusetts liberal sought to advance only to be defeated by conservative Styles Bridges of New Hampshire, 26 to 15. Saltonstall continued to serve as whip until 1957 when he became chairman of the Republican Conference. In 1962, he lost another contest, this time for the chairmanship of the Republican Policy Committee.
5. Traditionally, since the 1920's, the position of President pro tempore of the Senate has gone automatically to that member of the Senate majority with the greatest seniority. The President pro tempore ranks third in terms of presidential succession behind the vice president and the Speaker of the House of Representatives. But the position holds little independent power.
6. The fourteen-member Democratic Senatorial Campaign Committee is not without importance, especially for Senators up for reelection. Its purpose, of course, is to raise funds and otherwise assist in the campaigns of incumbent Democratic Senators and promising freshman nominees. The chairmanship is rotated every two years. Typically, its incumbent is selected for speech-making and fund-raising abilities from among the class of Senators who will not be up for immediate reelection.
7. On Taft's leadership, see Charles O. Jones, *The Minority Party in Congress* (Boston: Little, Brown, 1970), pp. 147–148, 161–162; and Randall B. Ripley, *Majority Party Leadership in Congress* (Boston: Little, Brown, 1969), pp. 126–130, 153–155.
8. On Knowland's leadership, see Jones, *op. cit.*, pp. 95, 148; Ripley, *op. cit.*, pp. 126–127, 129–130, 134, 174.
9. Cf. Nelson W: Polsby, "The Institutionalization of the U.S. House of Representatives," *Am. Pol. Sci. Rev.* **62** (1968), pp. 144–168.
10. *New York Times*, January 3, 1953, p. 8.
11. William S. White was to report Johnson as "unanimous choice" for minority leader — *New York Times*, January 3, 1953, pp. 1, 8. Evans and Novak, however, make a convincing case for token opposition — *Lyndon B. Johnson: The Exercise of Power* (New York: New American Library, 1966), pp. 56–57.
12. The best examples are the House contests for minority leader in 1959 and 1965 (Chapter 4), and, to a lesser extent, Representative Morris K. Udall's bids for Speaker in 1969 and majority leader in 1971 (Chapters 5–7).

President Gerald Ford receives congratulations from House and Senate congressional leaders after his first address to a joint session of the Congress, August 12, 1974. John Rhodes, his successor as House Minority Leader is shaking Ford's hand; to his left is Majority Leader Thomas P. O'Neill, Jr. Second row, behind the President, l. to r.: John Tower, Senate Republican Policy Committee chairman; Robert Griffin, Senate Republican whip; Hugh Scott, Senate Minority Leader. Third row, l. to r.: Frank Moss, Secretary to the Democratic conference; Robert Byrd, Senate Majority whip; and Mike Mansfield, Senate Majority Leader.

(White House Photo)

PART IV

Conclusion

PART I

Conclusions

Congressional Leadership Stability and Change: Some House and Senate Comparisons

Members, staff, the press and other close observers of Congress are fond of contrasting the many differences between the Senate and the House of Representatives: size; length of tenure of members, their prestige, nature of the constituencies they represent, and extent of their legislative specialization; flexibility of rules, strength in conference committees, ideological differences, and so on.[1] Most students of Congress tend to downplay the common features, including similar overall institutional workloads, approximately parallel committee systems, relatively decentralized party structures, and shared political cultures and environments. Short of a full-scale examination of these and other comparable and contrasting features of the House and Senate, several further generalizations about trends in party leadership and causes of patterns of overall change are warranted. Once these overall patterns in the four congressional parties have been summarized, it then is possible to explore in some depth the underlying conditions which seem to account for one type of change taking place rather than another.

First, in terms of whether selection of leaders is made by contested or non-contested means, the two parties in each House exhibit remarkably parallel patterns. Table 16.1 compares the four congressional parties over the past 10 Congresses in terms of contested change. As previously summarized in Table 15.4, Senate Democrats resorted to contested means to resolve leadership selection in 4 of 9 instances (44.4 percent); Senate Republicans in 9 of 11 cases (81.8 percent). In terms of the selection of major House leaders, Democrats utilized contested means in 5 of 11 instances (45.4 percent). In contrast, Republicans resorted to contested change in 8 of 9 cases

Table 16.1
Contested and Non-Contested Party Leadership Change,
Senate and House of Representatives,
84th–93d Congresses (1955–1974)[a]

	NO CONTEST		CONTEST	
	Democratic Majority	Republican Minority	Democratic Majority	Republican Minority
SENATE	5	2	4	9
HOUSE	6	1	5	8

[a] See Tables 9.4 and 15.4 for complete categorization of the types of leadership change in the House and Senate during the 10 Congresses studied. In the Senate, positions include floor leaders, whips, the secretary to the Democratic Conference, and the chairman of the Republican Policy Committee; in the House of Representatives the positions include the Speaker, both floor leaders and whips, and the chairman of the Republican Conference.

(88.8 percent) over this 20-year period (1955–1974). For purposes of this comparison, House cases of leadership change have been restricted to the three top leadership positions in each party — Speaker, majority leader, and whip for the Democratic majority; floor leader, whip, and Conference chairman for the Republican minority (see Table 9.4).[2] In sum, the Democratic party over the 10 Congresses studied was more inclined to choose its leaders by relatively harmonious means in both Houses as compared to their Republican counterparts. However, as previously noted, since the late 1960's Democrats have increasingly turned to contested means to select leaders in the House and, especially, in the Senate.

Second, in terms of internecine warfare the House Republican minority emerges as the most conflict-prone of the four congressional parties. Over this 20-year period five out of its eight contested selections involved challenges to incumbent leaders: Halleck vs. Martin (1959), Ford vs. Hoeven (1963), Ford vs. Halleck (1965), Frelinghuysen vs. Arends (1965), and Devine vs. Anderson (1971). All but the last two challenges were successful. In contrast, no Senate floor leader has been deposed in the twentieth century, but one Republican leader (Scott, 1971) was challenged and two incumbent Democratic whips (Long in 1969 and Kennedy in 1971) were challenged and defeated. On balance, the Senate leadership environment has been somewhat more stable than the House, especially before 1969. Just why this is the case becomes clearer after we examine some of the underlying conditions which seem to inhibit or facilitate change in leadership in the two bodies.

I

In Chapter 1 some 20 factors or conditions were set forth in outline form as guidelines for exploring the several case studies of congressional leadership change which followed. Six of these factors — the personality and skill of the incumbent, patterns of leadership succession, the nature of accession to office, election results, majority-minority status, and differences in party hierarchy and structure — were singled out in Chapter 10 as contributing to differential rates of contested change between the House Democratic and Republican parties. Many of these same factors, especially the first, have an obvious bearing on dominant modes of leadership stability and change in the Senate. Instead of a restricted focus, here, on Senate patterns of leadership choice, these and other variables will be examined in terms of House-Senate comparisons.

The exploration of two decades of House and Senate leadership selection is a pursuit of continuing fascination, if not a little frustration. It is relatively simple to identify competitors for party leadership positions, but much more difficult to explain their motivations for running and why certain candidates win and others lose. Attempts to identify, let alone to demonstrate, patterns of survival, succession, and change among the four congressional parties are even more hazardous. Perhaps the most complicated problems of all are posed by efforts to isolate and relate the underlying conditions which seem to lead a congressional party to favor one predominant pattern of leadership selection rather than another.

Table 16.2 lists four clusters of conditions or variables — individual, positional, institutional, and external — which appear to influence the selection and also the subsequent survival of House and Senate party leaders. Although the relationships are more amorphous and indirect, many of the same variables would also seem to have an impact on leadership success in the broader sense of legislative achievements and electoral victories. But, here, our focus continues to be upon indi-

Table 16.2

Clusters of Variables Conditioning the Selection and Success of Congressional Leaders

Individual	Positional	Institutional	External
Personality and skill	Level of position	House-Senate differences	Election results
Party	Patterns of succession	Party strength and cohesion	Presidential involvement
Ideology	Nature of accession to office	Majority-minority status	Interest group activity
Constituency and region	Stage of leadership development	Differences in party hierarchy and structure	Media influences
Seniority	Degree of internal leadership involvement	Membership expectations	Temper of the times

vidual and aggregate leadership success in terms of winning, maintaining office, and sometimes advancing to higher leadership positions.

Most of these variables, if they are not already self-explanatory, will become clearer in their exposition. Some lend themselves better to operational definition than others. Thus, a candidate's "party," "constituency," and "seniority" are rather easily described: for example, "Democrat," "the Second Congressional District of Arizona," "five terms." One of the most important explanatory variables, "the personality and skill" of a candidate, remains much more difficult to isolate, define, and measure.[3] For purposes of this study I have mainly depended upon personal observations and characterizations derived from membership interviews. In general, in proceeding from individual and positional variables to institutional and external factors, I found that the problems of definition and measurement, let alone causal determination, intensified.

Moreover, not all the variables are necessarily limited to a single category of clusters. "Party," for example, can be used in both an individual ascriptive sense — "Carl Albert is a Democrat" — as well as an aggregate or institutional label — "House Democratic majority." The personal skills and characteristics of incumbents will have a direct bearing on certain positional variables, such as the "stage of leadership development" and the "degree of internal leadership involvement" in the selection of lesser party leaders.

Such obvious relationships tempt one to build more order and finality into Table 16.2 than perhaps is warranted at this stage of research on congressional leadership change. However, two rather simple assumptions can be made: (1) individual factors such as ideology, seniority, and personality operate so as to greatly restrict the opportunities which most members have to be selected as leaders; and (2) external variables also influence the individual career potentials, positional variables, and institutional forces already at work, although in a more marginal and indirect way. That is to say, leadership selection is primarily, although not exclusively, determined by individual competition played out within positional and institutional restraints.

No other attempt has been made to link variables within or across clusters except in a rather general expository way. The problem is, of course, that the real world of party leadership stability and change is immensely complex. In one context or another, as the intensive case studies illustrate, just about every variable appears to be an influence, albeit in varying strengths and sometimes at cross-purposes. At this stage of social science research and especially for this kind of problem, most of the variables do not lend themselves to clear-cut isolation, easy operationalization, assignment of weights, or sophisticated causal orderings.

Still, a number of generalizations, however tentative, can be teased from the eight intensive case studies and the more than 50 instances of leadership change that have taken place in the House and Senate during the 20-year period under study, 1955 to 1974.

II

Who runs for party leadership in the House of Representatives and the Senate? The minimum requirement, of course, is that the aspirant must be a member of good standing of one of the four congressional parties: House Democrats or Republicans, Senate Democrats or Republicans. Whether or not a potential leader is a Democrat or a Republican, obviously has a direct impact over time on his frequency of service in the majority or minority party. With the limited exceptions of the 80th and 83d Congresses, for example, no Republican could expect to be elected Speaker or the Senate majority leader. Other constraints, such as the member's ideology and voting record, the safeness of his seat, his possession of a minimal degree of seniority, act so as to drastically reduce the number of eligible competitors for House and Senate leadership positions.

With only a rare exception or two, a potential candidate cannot deviate far from the mainstream of his party's ideological orientation if he hopes to become a leader. This research complements the previous findings of Truman, Patterson, and others that party leaders are "middle-men," located well within the dominant wing of their party's general ideological orientation.[4] In both Houses, Democratic leaders are usually "moderate-to-liberal" or "national Democrats" but almost never "Americans for Democratic Action-type" liberals or southern conservatives. Republican leaders are almost universally selected from the conservative mainstream of their party. Not infrequently the leading candidates for House congressional party offices tend to mirror each other in ideology, for example, Albert vs. Bolling (Chapter 3) or Ford vs. Halleck (Chapter 4). Senate candidates more frequently reflect liberal vs. conservative ideological differences — Long vs. Kennedy (Chapter 12), Kennedy vs. Byrd (Chapter 13) or Scott vs. Baker (Chapter 14). If, by an unusual combination of circumstances an ideological exception is elected, for example, the relatively liberal Senate Minority Leader Hugh Scott of Pennsylvania, he generally shifts toward his party's center in his subsequent voting behavior.

Naturally, the characteristics of a particular House or Senate constituency affect the ideological voting pattern of the incumbent as well as his chances for successfully running for party leadership. A few seats are so liberal or conservative as to virtually preclude a member from that district or state from competing for party leadership. A congressional party leader has to be able to vote as a "national Democrat," or as a "mainstream Republican" most of the time. Democrats from the Deep South or Republicans from the urban Northeast would have less flexibility in departing from predominant constituency viewpoints than colleagues from other regions. But most congressional districts and states are heterogeneous enough to allow members from different ideological backgrounds to carve out their own "constituencies," varying considerably from one incumbent to the next.[5]

A much more severe requirement for an aspiring House leader is that he must represent a consistently "safe" seat. Although the standard designation in electoral analysis for a safe seat is assumed to be a winning margin of 55 percent of the two-party vote in congressional races, the requirements for potential House leaders are usually more stringent — at least in the high 50's and, preferably, 60 percent or better. These requirements are relaxed considerably for the generally more populous base of most Senate leaders, actual or aspiring. Lyndon Johnson was selected as his party's floor leader in January 1953, despite the narrowest of victories, an 89-vote edge, in the 1948 Texas Democratic primary elections. He had, however, defeated his Republican opponent in the general election by a two-to-one vote. Hugh Scott's margin of victory in the 1958, 1964, and 1970 Pennsylvania Senate races never exceeded 53 percent of the total popular vote. Moreover, two Senate floor leaders, Democrats Scott Lucas and Ernest McFarland, went down to defeat in the early 1950's, whereas no House floor leader of either party has suffered electoral defeat for over four decades.

Without a safe seat an aspiring leader can seldom acquire the necessary seniority for appointment or election to high office.[6] In the contemporary House, at least five terms would seem to be a minimal requirement for seeking elective party office. The last four House Democratic whips each had been elected to an average of seven terms before their *appointment* to the lowest run of their party's leadership ladder. On the other hand, Morris K. Udall's relatively low seniority clearly hurt him in his unsuccessful bids for party office (Chapters 5–7).

Seniority as a requirement for Senate leaders is generally less severe than in the other body, in part because their pool of potential leaders frequently includes former House members. For example, Johnson was elected floor leader after just four years in the Senate, but he had previously served five terms in the House.[7] Moreover, all four of the top ranking Senate leaders in the early 1970's — Mansfield and Byrd, Scott and Griffin — had experienced at least three terms in the House of Representatives before their election to the Senate. On the other hand, Howard Baker had no prior House service and less than three years seniority in the Senate when he failed in his bid for the Senate minority leadership (Chapter 14).

Members who satisfy the minimal requirements of party loyalty, a "middle-man" ideology, a safe seat, and seniority (approximately one term, or six years, in the Senate; five terms, or ten years, in the House) would still constitute roughly one-third of each congressional party's membership.

What winnows out most of the remaining members from possible competition for party leadership positions? Above all, it is a set of more or less intangible traits labeled "leadership potential." Members must believe they have the capacity to lead their colleagues and they must act on that belief in characteristic ways. They seek out leadership in class clubs; they take on extra-committee activities such as service as an assistant whip or membership on a policy or steering committee. They go out of their way to spend more time on the floor; parliamentary procedures become a subject of more than technical interest to them. Few opportunities to cultivate the friendship and sponsorship of existing leaders are overlooked. Familiarity with the names, personal habits, and district characteristics of colleagues become stock-in-trade.

An aspiring leader must guard against too openly expressing ambition or too aggressively making a quest. Representatives and Senators, alike, do not like to see any other member getting too far out in front of themselves. Exceptional ability must be exercised with caution; superior intellect must not be flaunted.

All these endeavors have but a minimal pay-off if the aspiring party leader is not also seen as possessing "leadership potential" by a growing majority of colleagues. By definition, election to the House or

Senate is proof of demonstrated political skills. But, the capability to lead one's peers requires something more.

The traits that members are likely to ascribe to colleagues they identify as actual or potential leaders are not easy to assemble or classify.[8] Interviews are replete with both task-related and affective words and phrases such as "he's a stand-up guy," "you can trust him," "he knows how to get the job done," "nobody can match him for shrewdness," "when he lays into the other side, he takes their skin off," "conscientious," "courageous," "he has integrity," "he's got guts," "an iron fist, but a glove of velvet." Conversely, most members seem to dislike "aloof," "stand-offish," "abrasive," or "overly aggressive" leaders. Still, from time to time, members do select men with some of these characteristics, for example, Lyndon Johnson in the Senate and John Nance Garner and Hale Boggs in the House of Representatives. Perhaps the main generalization worth making, lacking a systematic assessment of desired leadership traits in the House or Senate, is that the personal characteristics tolerated in a leader are rather wide-ranging. Members seem to welcome strong leadership, although they frequently settle for less.

A "self-selection out" process seems to take place in Congress as it does in any large, complex organization. Firm estimates are difficult to come by, but perhaps as many as three-fourths of a given House or Senate do not really see themselves as potential congressional party leaders. Most members of the House and Senate remain content to make their legislative contributions as members of committees. Status accrues to those who gain seniority and a steadily increasing rank as either the majority or minority members of influential committees. Ambition for other offices — for Representatives, opportunities to become governors or Senators; for Senators, a chance to run for the presidency or the vice presidency — also appear to siphon away the pool of potential congressional leaders.

Once members are elected to office, what accounts for their continuing survival? Why are most congressional leaders routinely reelected, term after term? In the Senate as in the House, perhaps the most important characteristics that account for both stability *and* change are the age, personality, style, and skill of the incumbent.

During the 20-year period of this study, the Senate Democratic majority was led by two strong floor leaders, Lyndon Johnson and Mike Mansfield, one man aggressive and domineering in style, the other more restrained and passive but nevertheless highly respected by his

colleagues (Chapter 11). On the Republican side, only Everett Dirksen could be said to have developed comparable skills at floor management. Moreover, Democratic floor leaders never quite achieved
Dirksen's effectivness as an external party spokesman. William Knowland, Dirksen's predecessor as floor leader, proved adequate but not
exceptional. His personality and his conservatism seemed to keep him
too isolated from his colleagues and rather estranged from the Republican President with whom he served. Having survived the one challenge to an incumbent minority leader in the twentieth century,
Hugh Scott's skills have generally been tested and accepted by most
of his colleagues. Overall, neither the Senate Democratic majority nor
the Republican minority has been confronted with a crisis in top
leadership of the magnitude that confronted House Republicans in
1959 or 1965.

Two successful revolts did take place at a secondary level in the
Democratic majority party in 1969 and 1971. The two party whips
who lost — Russell Long and Edward Kennedy — had both made
themselves vulnerable as a result of a combination of personal problems and sporadic inattention to the details of their leadership responsibilities.

Leadership contests in the Senate are highly individualized efforts.
The sizes of the two Senate parties — a majority party seldom larger
than 55 to 65 members; a minority party which rarely shrinks below
30–35 Senators — make it quite feasible for candidates to personally
contact each of their party colleagues save those absolutely "locked
in" for the other side. The object, of course, is to obtain a majority of
firm commitments. Unless a contest takes place when most Senators
are out of town, candidates seek "eyeball-to-eyeball" commitments —
not tentative votes or reported leanings over the telephone — but actual commitments made face-to-face, one Senator to another. While
the greatest commitment in time and effort must come from the candidates themselves, a cadre of loyal supporters can be helpful in the
Senate (more critical in the House) to cross-check support or shore
up waverers.

Every congressional candidate begins with an established identity,
a defined ideological stance, a regional base. Given six-year terms of
office and a relatively high frequency of committee and floor interaction, almost every Senator is sensitized to the strengths and weaknesses of almost all of his party associates. House contests are fought

out at a greater psychological distance; few candidates have much more than a speaking acquaintance with most of their colleagues. Thus, respect, trust, affection, and a sense of a common purpose, seem somewhat more important in leadership contests in the Senate than in the House.

On the other hand, bargains based on what incumbent or prospective leaders can do for their backers, now or in the future, appear less important in the Senate. Prospective favors, especially influence over committee assignments, generally loom larger in the House. Morris K. Udall's 1969 challenge to Speaker McCormack had limited chance from the beginning because he had little to counter the resources available to the incumbent of the most powerful position in the House. Two years later, in the 1971 majority leadership contest, one strong asset Hale Boggs used to his advantage was his ranking position in the Ways and Means Committee. As every incoming freshman was quickly made aware, its members would make the committee assignments, but only after the majority leader had been selected. None of the other candidates for majority leader could offer pledges of possible assistance on committee assignments — only Boggs.

Still, even in this contest, the most decisive issue remained how members evaluated the personality and skill of the candidates. Had not charges of "instability" been raised against Boggs, a contest involving four other candidates would have been much less likely (Chapters 5-7). The relative ease with which Thomas O'Neill advanced to the majority leadership in 1973 following Boggs' death, only serves to reinforce this interpretation. Still, one cannot discount the importance of positional variables. As a direct result of their prior whip service, both Boggs and O'Neill were already identified in the eyes of many of their colleagues as an integral part of the Democratic party hierarchy and, as such, "entitled" to advancement.

III

Increasingly, in both parties and in both Houses, party leaders have served an apprenticeship, in terms both of years of experience and, more generally, occupancy of lesser party positions. Hence, the rise in importance of a hierarchy of party offices, which, in turn, has led to emerging or established patterns of leadership succession.

Among House Democrats, as Chapters 3 and 5-10 discuss in detail, a clear-cut pattern of succession from the appointive whip to floor leader to Speaker has become increasingly institutionalized. Speaker Albert was the first to travel the complete route, but Boggs, before his death, and O'Neill were or are on that ladder. In contrast, for House Republicans, no such easily identifiable pattern has developed (Chapters 4, 9, and 10). Instead, minority leaders have been selected from a pool of lesser leaders — Campaign Committee chairmen (Martin, 1939 and Halleck, 1947), Conference chairman (Ford, 1965), and Policy Committee chairman (Rhodes, 1973). On the other hand, Leslie Arends, the party whip since 1943, has been bypassed for floor leader at four critical junctures: 1947, 1959, 1965, and 1973.

Both Senate parties have increasingly adopted a two-step party leadership selection process: whip to floor leader. As Chapters 11 and 15 review in some detail, the last three Democratic whips who had that option, Lucas in 1949, Johnson in 1953, and Mansfield in 1961, were elevated to floor leader. Moreover, Majority Whip Robert Byrd of West Virginia must be considered the likely heir apparent when and if Mansfield should retire — possibly after 1976.

Three of the last four Republican whips presented with an opening — Wherry in 1949, Dirksen in 1959, Scott in 1969, but not Saltonstall — advanced to floor leader. (The latter was generally considered too liberal by his colleagues.) When a vacancy presents itself in the top position, perhaps in 1977 or even before, it remains to be seen whether Minority Whip Robert Griffin of Michigan will be elevated or whether his colleagues will turn to Scott's principal challenger in past contests, Howard Baker of Tennessee. Republicans have a third option, that of turning to incumbents of other leadership positions such as the Policy Committee chairman. Their decentralized party hierarchy facilitates these options more readily than in the Senate Democratic Party.

All four congressional parties have developed three or more levels in their formal party hierarchies, although the level of any given position beyond the Speaker and floor leaders is likely to fluctuate with the prestige and strength of the given incumbent. From earlier detailed analyses (Chapters 9 and 10 for the House, Chapter 15 for the Senate), it is possible to generate a set of hypotheses that involves levels of positions and patterns of leadership succession in the four congressional parties:[9]

1. *House Democratic majority:*

    a. The Democratic majority is more likely than the Republican minority to resolve questions of leadership change by non-contested elections and appointments.

    b. An established pattern of succession from majority leader to Speaker is being supplemented by an emerging pattern of succession from whip to majority leader.

    c. Dissatisfaction with the emerging pattern may lead to the creation of an elective rather than an appointive whip.

2. *House Republican minority:*

    a. The Republican minority is more prone to intra-party leadership change by contested means.

    b. Floor leaders are selected from a pool of senior leaders. There is no one established pattern of succession.

    c. Long periods of minority status coupled with a vulnerable leader and decisive election defeats (the net loss of 30 or more seats) promote leadership change through revolt.

3. *Senate Democratic majority:*

    a. The Senate majority party is less prone to leadership selection by contested means than the Republican minority.

    b. The dominant pattern of succession is one from whip to floor leader.

    c. Competition for lesser party offices varies inversely with the degree of involvement of the floor leader.

4. *Senate Republican minority:*

    a. The Republican minority almost inevitably selects its party leaders by contested means.

    b. The nearly dominant pattern of succession is one from whip to floor leader.

Even in the face of a fairly established pattern of succession, the impact of additional variables, such as the nature of the accession to office (harmonious, contested, or otherwise), and the stage of leadership development at which a particular incumbent finds himself, can complicate the outcome of any particular contest. A leader who comes to office by conflictful means, especially revolt against an incumbent, quite obviously is confronted with a different environment and set of constraints than one who advances up a leadership ladder and wins office against little or no opposition. Thus, it is not too far-reaching to compare the kind of climate that Charles Halleck faced after his overthrow of Minority Leader Martin in 1959 with that confronting Edward Kennedy in 1969 after he had successfully challenged and defeated the Democratic whip, Russell Long. Each would find their initial attempts at organizational reform and legislative initiatives at least partially stymied by the enmities and animosities left over from the conflict. Both contests led to subsequent revolts, six years and two years later, respectively. And both Martin and Long stayed around to vote and campaign on behalf of the eventual victors, Ford (1965) and Byrd (1971).

Furthermore, it is obvious that, symbolic challenges aside (Udall vs. McCormack, 1969 or Conyers vs. Albert, 1973), the opportunity costs of challenging a party leader in his prime are far greater than taking on an elderly, ailing, or otherwise vulnerable party leader. Indeed, the history of party leadership contests over the 20 years of this study suggests that realistic challengers to an incumbent leader, even a near heir apparent, are seldom initiated *unless* the leader is highly vulnerable. For one reason or another, Martin, Halleck, Boggs, Long, Kennedy, and even Scott to a degree, had all laid themselves open to challenge.

Thus, the stage of a particular leader's development can be crucial in postponing or bringing on a challenge. Has the leader just assumed office? Is he moving with relative caution? Is much of his supporting alliance still to be anchored in? After several terms in office has he consolidated authority, developed a coterie of loyal followers, strengthened his bargaining powers with committee leaders, the other body, and the executive branch? Or has the leader reached the end of his career — his effectiveness on the wane, his personal faculties less keen, some of his long-time supporters departed from Congress? Obviously, congressional leaders, like all executives, progress through stages of growth and risk a possible decline if they overstay their time and competence. But, unlike most other organizations, Congress has no mandatory retirement plans when a member reaches age 65 or 70. The case of House Minority Leader Joseph Martin, deposed in 1959, was the most notable recent example of a leader who outlived his prime, although the reputations and personal powers of both Speaker John McCormack and Senate Minority Leader Everett Dirksen were on the decline in the closing years of their leadership.

A final positional variable — the degree of internal leadership involvement in lesser party positions — also relates back to the personality and skills of the top party leaders. The starkest contrasts in contemporary Congresses have been provided by the strong intervention of Democratic Majority Leader Johnson, as compared with Mansfield's relative non-involvement in the selection of Democratic whips and secretaries to the Conference (Chapters 12, 13, and 15). For Johnson not to have been actively involved in the choice of his party whip or secretary to the Conference would have been unthinkable — these men were his lieutenants; he needed and demanded their allegiance, their loyalty, their outright devotion. Clement, Hennings, and, to a lesser extent, Mansfield, were cases in point. Johnson went out of his way to clear his selection of lieutenants with other senior Senators, abandoning an initial preference only if substantial opposition developed. His objective was to arrive at a consensus choice, a person who would be confirmed in Conference without opposition.

In contrast, Mansfield as majority leader appeared content to work with whomever the Democratic Conference selected. Unlike Johnson, he never seemed to have actively lifted a hand, for or against, in the selection of any of his whips — Humphrey, Long, Kennedy, or Byrd. Under his conception of leadership, such office-holders were to be considered servants of all the Democratic Senators. When leadership contests developed, as they almost inevitably would under such a *laissez-faire* outlook, Mansfield deliberately stayed neutral: "It's been my policy not to take a stand ahead of time, to let the caucus decide, and to lean toward those who had been in office. That's been my consistent pattern." To highlight the contrasting roles of these two floor leaders in party whip selection is only to stress, once again, the importance of personality in Senate leadership.

The degree of Republican top leadership involvement in the selection of their successors or lesser party leaders has been mixed. Policy Committee Chairman William Knowland appeared to have been the direct choice of ailing Majority Leader Robert Taft, who died in 1953. Everett Dirksen went out of his way attempting to unite the two wings of his party when he supported liberal Thomas Kuchel for whip in 1959. Moderate Hugh Scott followed a more neutral policy in the September 1969 whip contest. He needed the support of most, if not all, of the several whip candidates in his own bid to move up to the floor leadership. Again, the fact that the office of Democratic leader combines most of the important elective party leadership positions, while the Republicans decentralize their leadership among several men, makes strict comparison difficult. In general, however, it would appear that Republican floor leaders have maintained some control over the choice of their party whips, but less influence over other party leadership positions.

Party differences in terms of leadership grooming of lesser party positions are, if anything, more striking in the House of Representatives than in the Senate. A major reason is, of course, that the whip position, third ranking in the House Democratic hierarchy, is *appointive*. Speakers and majority leaders have almost complete control over this position, and as a result of an increasingly established pattern of succession, may well determine their successors for years to come. A crucial test may come when a vacancy occurs in either the Speakership or the majority leader position and if the current whip, John McFall, or a successor attempts to climb the ladder. Alternatively, there may come a renewed effort to make the whip an *elective* position. Phillip Burton of California, successor to Conference Chairman Olin Teague, who retired in 1974, may be in a crucial position to advance to higher office.

House Republicans, have, as yet, established no ongoing pattern of leadership succession. The one contemporary attempt by a Republican floor leader to select his own whip — Ford's effort to replace Arends in 1965 — failed. With the retirement of the veteran Illinois whip in 1974, John Rhodes, the Republican minority leader, had an opportunity to influence the choice of the new whip. In the wake of substantial House Republican losses in the November 1974 elections, Rhodes seemed primarily content to allow the decision to be made through open competition.

IV

Large scale institutional differences between the two chambers, such as size, length of term of members, and the nature of the constituencies represented, have multiple consequences for party organizations, committee structures, and legislative outcomes. These differences probably have greater impact upon the party leaders' effectiveness rather than on the method of their selection.

Take size, for example. A number of consequences for party leadership and committee operations flow from the simple fact that the House of Representatives is more than four times as large as the Senate. First, there is a much clearer separation of formal party leadership from committee leadership. Of the four top elective leaders of the House in the 93d Congress — Speaker and majority leader, minority leader and minority whip — only the Republican whip, Leslie Arends of Illinois, served on a committee (Armed Services) and acted as a ranking minority member on a subcommittee (the Special Subcommittee on Investigation). His counterpart, Majority Whip John McFall (D., Cal.) retained his chairmanship of the Appropriations Subcommittee on Transportation, but McFall was an appointed, not an elected, whip. The remaining top three leaders — Speaker Carl Albert of Oklahoma, Majority Leader Thomas P. O'Neill, Jr. of Massachusetts, and Minority Leader John J. Rhodes of Arizona — were full-time party leaders in that they served on no committees and indeed relinquished senior positions on important standing committees when they assumed top leadership.

In prior decades House party leaders, even Speakers, had occasionally served on committees. A major consequence of the 1910 revolt against Speaker Cannon was, of course, the successful effort to remove him as chairman of a powerful five-member Committee on Rules. Before 1919, the chairman of the House Ways and Means Committee frequently held the position of majority leader as well. In recent years both House parties seem to have concluded that the responsibilities of their principal leaders are too burdensome to also allow service as committee members and, further, that such powerful positions should be distributed among a wider set of members. An exception was made, however, to allow a member from the majority and minority party leadership to serve on the newly created Budget Committee.

In contrast to their House counterparts, all four principal Senate leaders — majority leader, majority whip, minority leader and minority whip — play active roles on two or more standing committees, and indeed average four or more subcommittee chairmanships or ranking minority positions per leader. By tradition, the top party leaders seldom hold a committee chairmanship simultaneously, but as recently as 1966–1968, Senator Russell Long of Louisiana was both chairman of the Finance Committee *and* majority whip. (His concentration on the former role to the neglect of the latter contributed to his loss of the whip's position to Senator Edward Kennedy in January 1969.)

It would be misleading to conclude from the number of subcommittee positions held by a leader in the Senate that his responsibilities are any less demanding than those of his counterparts in the House.

But it seems clear that the smaller size and more collegial atmosphere of the Senate allows leaders more time to pursue their own legislative interests and committee activities. On occasion, a leader like Mike Mansfield can combine that role with pursuance of a prime interest, for example, Mansfield's concern with foreign policy questions. Overall, committee activities remain more peripheral than central for most Senate leaders.

It follows that a second distinguishing characteristic between the two bodies is that the potential for conflict between the elective leaders and the committee leaders is much more pronounced in the House than it is in the Senate. This is not alone because Senate leaders are more immersed in the committee phase of the legislative process, but rather because the crystallization of legislation seems to take place at a much later stage in the Senate — on the floor rather than in the relatively small and typically unrepresentative Senate subcommittees or even the full committees. With every Senator serving on at least two, and usually three, committees, usually rushing from one subcommittee meeting to another, the atmosphere is scarcely conducive to legislative craftsmanship in the mark-up sessions. That it does occur from time to time is more a tribute to the skills of individual Senators and the dedication of staffs than it is to the process itself.

House subcommittees and committees, in contrast, are more truly "little legislatures," larger and more balanced geographically and ideologically.[10] Sharp adversary procedures, close questioning of witnesses, full participation in mark-ups, the search for accommodation is more likely to occur at these stages. When bills reach the floor they are more carefully drafted, less subject to amendment or even wholesale "rewriting." The latter practice is far more commonplace on the Senate floor.

Coupled with the size differential between the two bodies, it also follows that House committees are more likely to come to the floor in an adversary relationship to the rest of the body. Especially with regard to major legislations, committee leaders tend to be preoccupied with protecting their bills before the onslaught of their colleagues, Democrats as well as Republicans. Senate committee leaders appear more tolerant of floor amendments; distinctions between committee members and non-committee members are blurred. As Fenno concludes in his masterful comparative study of *Congressmen in Committees*:[11]

Since the House and Senate are different institutions, it should not be surprising that their committees are also different. Senate committees are less important as a source of chamber influence, less preoccupied with success on the chamber floor, less autonomous within the chamber, less personally expert, less strongly led, and more individualistic in decision making than are House committees.

Since the institutions are different and their committee structure and operations differ, it can hardly be surprising, either, that overall leadership roles and patterns of selection vary.

Thus, a third major distinction between House and Senate leadership is that power is more widely shared in the smaller body. Size is a contributing factor as are the spread of committee assignments and the relationship of committee to the parent body. Shared power has also been encouraged in recent years by the leadership styles of both Majority Leader Mansfield and Minority Leader Scott. Their styles contrast with those of their predecessors, Johnson and Dirksen, both of whom sought and, to some extent, succeeded, in centralizing power. Yet one wonders whether either Johnson or Dirksen widely acknowledged as the strongest floor leaders in the post-World War II era, began to approach the power concentration of Speaker Cannon, Longworth, and Rayburn. Even at the height of his powers, Johnson had to contend with Russell, Kerr, and other senior influential Senators. Senators, far more than Representatives, believe in demonstrating that theirs is a body of equals. Although Rayburn was occasionally at odds with his committee oligarchs, he had been able during his 50 years in the House, the last 25 as a party leader, to build up a great reservoir of personal influence. Coupled with his still imposing formal powers, "he often commanded decisive support in the House on major issues," [12] or at least until his health began to fail in 1960. House leaders, in general, have greater resources to set them apart from their colleagues, especially relatively junior members.

Leadership must be shared not only between formal leaders, committee leaders, and rank-and-file membership of the same party, but also across party lines. Bipartisan cooperation is much more apparent in the Senate than in the House both between leaders — one recalls the close working relations between Johnson and Dirksen, Mansfield and Dirksen, and Mansfield and Scott — and in the everyday playing out of the legislative process. From time to time similar bipartisan relationships develop in the House — one thinks of Rayburn and

Martin, Albert and Ford — but, in general, the communications between Speakers and minority leaders are more formal, partisan, and distant than they are in the Senate.

Senate leadership tasks appear to be more sharply defined, if no less difficult, than those of their House counterparts. It is more apparent, in part because of the fewer votes to be counted and evaluated. A former House member, now a Senate leader, comments:

> Here in the Senate, for example, if you want to spend your time actively going around and talking to Senators on the floor, or maybe calling their office, you can, in a relatively short period of time, make quite an impact . . . I think it's much harder to do that in the House. You have a pretty good idea of how votes are going in the House but there you can only come within a certain range. Here, because of the size of the body — it's smaller — we many times know right on the nose what the vote is going to be.

On the other hand, the tasks of leadership may be as difficult because Senators have greater autonomy and thus are less dependent upon party and administration pressures or other influences. In the words of this same Senate leader:

> Over here, we're more "managing the store," scheduling the legislation and trying to bring some order into what is otherwise a chaotic situation — and trying to effect the vote. But you know, Senators are much more individualistic than [members] are in the House. They are not so likely to go along with a position just because it's a party position or because the administration wants it.

Somewhat paradoxically, Senators seem to expect less from their leaders while at the same time providing them with an environment of greater flexibility within which to perform their roles. Their organizational hierarchy is "flatter," the psychological distance between members not so great. House leaders work in a more constraining environment, characterized by greater perceived distances between leaders, mid-career committee influentials, and rank-and-file members. Theirs is a more concentrated, pyramidal-type hierarchy with attendant problems of size, complexity, and a greater likelihood of communication distortions and breakdown. House members are both more dependent upon strong leadership and more frustrated if it fails to occur.

The Speaker must continuously balance a dual role of impartial presiding officer, yet partisan leader. Senate floor leaders, even if they must cooperate with one another, are under much less severe restraints. And they appear to retain greater flexibility when compared with House floor leaders. If the job is more flexible, then direct challenges to Senate leaders should come less frequently. Still, many of these institutional differences operate most directly upon leadership effectiveness and only indirectly upon their initial selection.

Other institutional variables such as party strength and majority-minority status appear to have a more direct impact on patterns of party leadership stability and change. The most dramatic of all shifts in party strength is one which converts a minority into the majority. Inter-party leadership change in the House usually finds the former minority leader being elevated to Speaker. The whip may advance to majority leader, or a possbile contest may take place at that level, depending upon alternative candidate options. Meanwhile, the former Speaker and majority leader typically drop back to minority leader and whip, respectively. Inter-party leadership change in the Senate usually requires less shuffling — a shift in titles from majority to minority leader and whip — but the consequences in terms of enhanced party resources are no less far-reaching.

When Republicans gained control of the House and Senate in the 80th (1947–1948) and 83d (1953–1954) Congresses they generally elevated their existing leaders, with at least two important exceptions. In 1947, Charles Halleck won a contest for majority leadership from a field of contenders that included Everett McKinley Dirksen, then a Representative from Illinois. In 1953, Robert Taft took over as majority floor leader from Styles Bridges, who become President pro tempore of the Senate. Although one might have anticipated several contests when Republicans dropped back to minority status in 1949 and 1955, none materialized.[13]

It would seem obvious that increased party strength would enhance leadership stability — and this has generally been the case in all four congressional parties.[14] Riding the crest of an election tide, perhaps swept into office with an activist President, members are apt to be less concerned with infusing their leadership with new blood than they are with securing the best possible committee assignments and getting on with the passage of legislation. Challenges to incumbent leaders in such a climate would generally be viewed as counterproductive.

Party strength is, of course, directly convertible into majority control or minority status. Given a strong, two-party system, all that is normally required for control of the House or Senate is 50 percent of the membership plus one, that is 218 House or 51 Senate members of one party. Over the past two decades House Democrats have fluctuated between 232 and 295 seats, Senate Democrats between 49 (in a 96-member Senate) and 67 seats.[15] A number of consequences of being in the House majority or minority were developed at some length in Chapter 10. Many of the same arguments that impacted upon Democrats and Republicans there, can also be applied to the two Senate parties.

The Democratic party in the Senate has benefited from greater leadership stability in part due to control over superior resources, both tangible and intangible. Since 1955, Majority Leaders Lyndon Johnson and Mike Mansfield generally operated in a climate of expanding rather than contracting credit. Majority leaders receive first recognition on the floor. They have substantial control over the legislative agenda. Members of their party chair the committees and subcommittees, hire the bulk of the staffs, decide how investigatory funds will be allocated. A higher proportion of majority party members' bills introduced, 25 compared to those of minority members, will be reported out of committee. When legislation is passed it is usually identified by its majority sponsors. Since there are more benefits to go around, Senate majority members, like their House counterparts, are likely to be more satisfied with and less critical of their leadership.

In contrast, Senate Minority Leaders Knowland, Dirksen, and Scott have operated, in general, in an environment of restrained opportunities and restricted credit. They must confer with the majority as to when legislation will be scheduled. Their senior associates enjoy less than a third of the committee staff support and funds allocated to their majority counterparts. Although opportunities of constructive participation in the drafting and implementation of legislation vary from committee to committee, they are inhererently more restrictive for the minority party. Limited resources, insufficient recognition, unlikely prospects for victory in committee or on the floor, contracting credit overall — these conditions are likely to foster internal unrest in a minority party, a dissension which may promote future leadership contests.

Two conditions help to mitigate the harshness of their restrictive environment. Although Republicans have not organized the Congress since the 83d Congress (1953–1954), they have controlled the White House and the executive branch for 15 of the past 23 years. By assisting in the sponsorship of Eisenhower, Nixon, and Ford legislative programs, by elevating their own staff to key administrative positions, by benefiting from executive branch largesse, minority membership disadvantages in the legislative branch have been considerably alleviated.

Moreover, a Senate minority member is never as isolated and seldom as frustrated as his House counterpart. He operates from a position of considerable autonomy. The legislative process in the Senate is less partisan, more cooperative. A Senator's seat is not up for reelection every two years. For all these reasons, it would seem that minority status has had less volatile impact on leadership change in the Senate than in the House of Representatives.

Party strength and majority-minority status can help to set a climate or tone which, at least marginally, can inhibit or promote leadership change. Every two years elections occur which not only affect party strength, and more rarely, majority-minority status, but also have a direct bearing upon the proportion of junior to senior members and the ideological and geographical balance or imbalance of a congressional party. Throughout most of the past two decades, Senate Republicans seem not to have had a disproportionate number of junior members (less than one complete term of six years) compared with more senior members.[16] From the 84th to the 90th Congress this proportion averaged about one-third junior to two-thirds senior members, a ratio quite comparable to the Senate Democratic party save for the impact of the large incoming class of 1958. Over the 86th to 88th Congresses (1959–1964), junior members of the Senate Democratic party made up over 40 percent of their party's 64-to-68 members.

However, beginning with the results of the election of 1968 and particularly following the 1970 and 1972 elections, the number of junior Republican Senators underwent a marked increase. In the 93d Congress almost half of the 43 Senate Republicans had not yet served a full term in the Senate. By comparison, the ranks of junior Democratic Senators numbered only about one-fourth of their 57 members.

If one accepts the premise that disproportionate numbers of junior members help create a climate for leadership change, as seemed to be the case among House Republicans on the eve of the Ford-Halleck contest, then Senate Republicans continue to remain in a potentially volatile situation. Younger members want more of "what there is to get," and backing a successful challenger may materially assist those needs. However, disparities between junior and senior members in the Senate in terms of committee assignments, staff assistance, and other valued legislative resources are not as great as in the House. Put simply, complaints against seniority are just not the problem in the Senate that they are in the House of Representatives.

Other characteristics of Senate party structure, such as geographical dispersion and ideological balance, also tend to mitigate against radical leadership change. At some risk of oversimplification and ignoring variations from one Congress to the next, the Senate Democratic majority has been composed of three groups of approximately equal strength: about 30 percent conservatives, mainly from the Deep South (like Russell of Georgia, Eastland of Mississippi, Allen of Alabama); about 30 percent moderates, mainly from the western, border, and mountain states (like Anderson of New Mexico, Jackson of Washington, Bentsen of Texas); and about 40 percent liberals, mainly from the Midwest and East (like Pastore of Rhode Island, Douglas of Illinois, Kennedy of Massachusetts). Liberals are somewhat stronger in numbers, but because of their heretofore limited seniority, they have tended to occupy fewer committee chairmanships than moderates and southerners.[17] As in the House of Representatives (see Chapter 10) no single faction of the Democratic party can organize the Senate nor reap the benefits of majority status without the support of the other ideological groupings. Thus, tendencies to come to agreement over leadership and legislative programs are inevitably stronger than proclivities to fly apart.

One further implication of this three-way split has been to concentrate party leadership almost exclusively from among border, southwestern, or mountain state moderate Democrats. Given their limited numbers, southern conservatives in the Democratic party have been content to mount the seniority ladder, moving slowly but steadily toward committee chairmanships. On rare occasions an unusually adept southerner will dominate the Senate from behind the scenes as apparently Russell of Georgia did in the late 1940's and early 1950's. Infrequently, a southerner with more moderate ideological leanings, such as Russell Long of Louisiana, has been able to put together a conservative-to-moderate coalition and win a position within the leadership. But one must go back three decades or more to Joseph T. Robinson of Arkansas (1923–1937) and Oscar W. Underwood of Alabama (1920–1923) to uncover a Democratic floor leader from the Deep South. Southerners formed a consistently larger and more durable bloc among Democratic Senators in those earlier decades.[18]

Senate Republicans, like their House counterparts, have divided more sharply into two wings over the past two decades: conservatives (such as Knowland of California, Hruska of Nebraska, Goldwater of Arizona) and liberals (such as Case of New Jersey, Kuchel of California, Javits of New York). Moderates like Thruston B. Morton of Kentucky or Robert Griffin of Michigan have been more the exception than the rule, although their ranks have increased in recent Congresses. Even if one combines moderates with liberals, Senate Republican conservatives have generally enjoyed at least a 3:2 advantage within their party throughout much of the 1950's and into the 1960's. In more recent Congresses (90th–93d) the moderate-to-liberal wing of the Senate Republican party has narrowed the ratio to about 5:4. One direct result has been the selection of two of its own, Scott and Griffin, as floor leader and whip, respectively.

The ideological polarization characteristic of the Senate Republican party seems to have been a contributing factor to their high proportion of contested elections. For most of the past two decades, liberals have sponsored candidates, only to lose out to the leading conservative choice. Until the Scott defeat of Baker in 1969, the liberal wing of the party has had to mainly content itself with the consolation prize of the whip's position.

One final institutional variable, membership expectations about leaders, needs but brief recapitulation here. As developed at some length in Chapters 2 and 11, the great majority of House and Senate members do not find themselves overly preoccupied with questions of leadership change. For most of their legislative careers, each Representative and Senator is more concerned with cultivating his own constituency, improving his chances for reelection, attending to his committee business, pursuing varied legislative interests. A few House members will seek outside offices, a senatorial or gubernatorial nomination. Not a few Senators have hopes of winning their party's presidential or vice-presidential nomination. Only a half-dozen officeholders in each party, plus a small coterie of associates are actively engaged in congressional leadership functions. Probably not more than another three or four Senators and, at most, a dozen Representatives in each party are contemplating or actively aspiring to House or Senate leadership. The cloakrooms of each party and even the floors of both chambers may periodically echo with grumblings about leadership ineffectiveness or complaints about specific shortcomings. But these criticisms usually amount to little more than a letting off of steam, a release of tensions endemic to legislative bodies.

Every two years, customarily at the opening of a new Congress, Representatives and Senators have an opportunity to ratify the selection of their existing leaders, or more rarely, choose between competing candidates for party office. Most frequently, especially in the House and Senate Democratic caucuses, conditions combine to reinforce stability in leadership. The resources held by incumbent leaders, the definite risks for rebels attempting to bring about alternative choices, the combined weights of inertia stemming from most members pursuing their own, largely isolated, career plans are generally powerful enough to offset all the strongest forces working for change.

V

Who the President is and which party has control of the executive branch — these are central questions for the governance of the country and the introduction, modification, and passage of legislative programs. But answers to such questions are far less critical for congressional party leadership change except as they transmit themselves through and affect periodic congressional election results.

As analyzed in Chapter 10, severe election setbacks — a net loss of 30 or more seats in the House of Representatives — can create a ripe climate for change, especially within the minority party. Successful revolts against Minority Leaders Martin and Halleck directly followed from 41- and 38-seat net losses by House Republicans in the elections of 1958 and 1964. Despite equally severe election losses in the 1974 congressional election, House Republicans did not move against John Rhodes, their new minority leader. Other factors must also be present, namely, an incumbent leader who is perceived as vulnerable by a near or actual majority of his colleagues and a challenger behind whom dissident party groupings can coalesce. Ironically, severe election losses among House majority Democrats generally result in the entrenchment of its establishment leadership. Those marginal-seat Democrats most likely to suffer large-scale election defeats preponder-

Table 16.3
Party Line-Ups, Senate and President, 1954–1974

Election Year	Congress	Senators Elected Dem.	Rep.	Misc.	Gains/Losses[a] Dem.	Rep.	President
1954	84th	48	47	1[b]	+1	−1	Eisenhower (R)
1956	85th	49	47		+1	0	
1958	86th	66	34		+17	−13	
1960	87th	64	36		−2	+2	Kennedy (D)
1962	88th	68	32		+4	−4	
1964	89th	67	33		−1	+1	Johnson (D)
1966	90th	64	36		−3	+3	
1968	91st	58	42		−6	+6	Nixon (R)
1970	92d	55	45		−3	+3	
1972	93d	57	43		+2	−2	
1974	94th	61	38	1[c]	+4	−4	Ford (R)

Source: Adapted from *Congress and the Nation*, Vol. III, 1969–1972 (Washington, D.C.: Congressional Quarterly Service, 1973), p. 30; *Congressional Quarterly Weekly Report*, 33 (January 18, 1975), p. 111.

[a] Net gains or losses are calculated on the basis of the total shift in party strength from one election to the next. They do not reflect minor shifts within a Congress due to deaths, resignations or special election outcomes. Gains and losses may not always balance as a result of the factors, plus the admission of Alaska and Hawaii to statehood.

[b] Sen. Wayne Morse (Ind., Oregon).

[c] The result of the New Hampshire senatorial contest was undecided as of June, 1975.

antly come from its more liberal, change-oriented, and junior members.

Unlike the House of Representatives, leadership change in the Senate seems only indirectly or slightly related to election outcomes. The most obvious reason, as Table 16.3 demonstrates, is that most Senate elections are characterized by relatively low net turnover. Over the past 10 Congresses, from the elections of 1954 to 1972, the average net gain or loss for the Republican party was 3.5 seats. In part, this low net turnover results from the constitutional requirement that only one-third of its members are up for reelection every two years. Moreover, Senators are less likely to be swept from office by the coat-tail effects of presidential elections. Only rarely does a violent swing take place, a net shift of 10 or more seats, which might lead to a possible scape-goating effect and promote attempts at Senate leadership change.

Over the past two decades just one election, that of 1958, resulted in a radical shift of strength from one party to the other. In that year an economic depression and general dissatisfaction with Eisenhower Administration policies brought on a net G.O.P. loss in the Senate of 13 seats. However, whatever animosity might have accrued against the Senate Republican leadership was largely dissipated because Minority Leader Knowland had retired from the Senate. This landmark election converted a hitherto closely divided Senate into one which was to be dominated for the next eight years by two-to-one Democratic majorities. Republicans failed to make inroads six years later with conservative Senator Barry Goldwater at the head of their presidential ticket. Not until the election of 1968 were Republicans able to stage a moderate comeback and win at least a 40-seat share of the Senate.

Yet election results and their impact on Senate leadership cannot be minimized altogether. For example, the failure of several conservative Republican senatorial candidates in 1970 to win expected seats played a significant role in thwarting conservative Howard Baker's hoped-for upset of moderate Minority Leader Hugh Scott in January 1971. Moreover, the chances of Majority Whip Robert Byrd to step up to floor leader following Mansfield's possible retirement in 1976 may turn on the size and ideological and regional composition of the class of Senate Democrats entering the 95th Congress.

What if a Democratic Muskie- or Kennedy-type liberal is elected as President in 1976? Would he be likely to involve himself in support of the candidacy of a more liberal Senate majority leader? In the light of historical perspective, it seems unlikely.

Presidents and their principal staff associates, regardless of party, seldom intervene in Senate or House leadership contests for at least one theoretical and several practical reasons. For a President to take an active hand in such an important internal congressional decision would appear to be, at least in theory, a violation of the separation of powers doctrine. And this principle is frequently invoked as the rationale for Presidents staying out of House and Senate leadership contests.

However, a number of practical and political reasons also mitigate against White House involvement. The first and foremost reason is that of limited opportunities. Congressional leaders, with their lengthy seniority, may have assumed office before a President's term begins and continue in office even after the end of a President's second term. The two-decade domination of House leadership offices by Sam Rayburn and Joseph Martin are only the most extreme cases. Majority Leader Mansfield has held office under four Presidents. Further, a President can hope to intervene with any effectiveness only in leadership contests of his own party. Finally, a President may decide against intervention because he believes he can work with either candidate regardless of the outcome.[19]

If a President decides to intervene, the occasions must be selected with care. There is little advantage in bringing White House pressure to bear when the outcome largely is predetermined. In those contests for top leadership positions for which the influence of the White House might be decisive, the danger of the President ending up on the losing side can be ignored only at great peril. The consequences of a major breakdown of communication between the President and one chamber of Congress would be severe and perhaps jeopardize the success of his legislative program. Even if a President comes in on the winning side, which is more likely, he still may succeed in alienating a large bloc in one of his congressional parties. Sometimes a President is better off working with a leader who serves as a spokesman for the opposing wing of his own party, as long as the relationship can be kept reasonably open and cordial. Thus a liberal Democratic President, might get more legislation from Congress working with a moderate-to-conservative Senate floor leader with strong southern ties than with a leader closer to his own ideological persuasion.

Presidents, then, for the most part, affect leadership contests mainly to the extent that they stay neutral. Candidates are usually free to fight out the struggle on their home grounds. More rarely, Presidents may condone a challenge to an incumbent by their refusal to take sides on his behalf. Thus, President Eisenhower is said to have staved off a possible Halleck challenge to House Republican Minority Leader Martin after the 1954 and 1956 elections, only to give tacit consent for a challenge in 1959 because of Martin's age, ailing health, and increasing ineffectiveness.

Examples of presidential intervention in senatorial leadership contests appear to be even more rare than these several House examples. No President, Democratic or Republican, appears to have figured in a major Senate leadership contest since President Franklin Delano Roosevelt's celebrated and "successful" intervention in 1937 on behalf of Democratic majority leader candidate, Alben W. Barkley of Kentucky.[20] Despite his former Senate service, President Harry Truman seems not to have played a role in the selection of Scott Lucas or Ernest McFarland.[21] One underlying reason might well be the relative autonomy and freedom to ignore pressure that Senators enjoy as compared with House members.

President Eisenhower may have played a small part in persuading Robert Taft to accept the Senate majority leadership in 1953, but he appeared not to have influenced the subsequent selections of Minority Leaders Knowland and Dirksen. President-elect Kennedy and Vice President-elect Johnson strongly urged Mike Mansfield to accept the majority leadership in 1961 but it seems unlikely that Mansfield's elevation from whip would have been challenged in any event.

Although he took no active role in either of the Scott-Baker contests for minority leader in 1969 and 1971, President Nixon apparently gave quiescent approval to Scott's challenge to Roman Hruska, Dirksen's preferred choice for party whip in 1969. Overall, the historical record reveals remarkably little direct intervention by Presidents in the choices of those who were largely accountable for the success or failure of their legislative programs in the Senate or the House.

If Presidents appear to have only marginal influence on congressional leadership choice, what about the influence of other external forces? Polsby's insightful case study of "Two Strategies of Influence: Choosing a Majority Leader, 1962," reprinted in this book as Chapter 3, outlines the inherent limitations of any leadership candidate's strategy based extensively upon outside or indirect appeals. The media and interest groups may be active and even marginally useful, but a final outcome decided by a secret ballot vote in caucus or conference all but precludes either set of forces from having a decisive or even very direct bearing on leadership contests. None of the subsequent case studies presented here provide much evidence which would contradict these basic observations.

The reasons for lack of media impact are fairly simple and straightforward. Newspaper columns and endorsements, magazine essays, and television commentaries are rather fleeting and fragmentary in their impact. Even if a candidate goes to the trouble to reproduce and circulate to his colleagues an especially laudatory column or editorial, there is little guarantee that other members will read it, let alone act upon it. Members, used to being bombarded by press and television commentary on the eve of an important legislative vote, have developed considerable immunity to all but what they want to read or hear. Thus the major benefits of an external media campaign are mainly the reinforcement of existing preferences, as well as the maintenance of the viability of a candidate and his campaign, rather than conversion. The use made of friendly and even neutral columnists by Hale Boggs in his 1970–1971 campaign for House majority leader (Chapter 6) further illustrates this theme.

Behind-the-scene interest group activities in leadership contests remain more nebulous and difficult than media influences to fully assess in terms of impact. Polsby notes that both Richard Bolling and Frank Thompson of New Jersey, a principal backer in Bolling's 1962 majority leadership campaign, were adept at "pulling strings." That is, both men knew their colleagues, their districts, and could conceive how interest groups favorable to Bolling's candidacy might, for various reasons, be able to reach and, perhaps, persuade other House Democrats on his behalf. Similarly, various candidates for the Senate majority whip, Long, Kennedy, and Byrd, were not averse to generating external interest group pressures on members.

The central problem posed by such efforts is twofold: the indirect nature of the contact, and the difficulty of checking on the outcome, given secret-ballot voting. Even if a candidate succeeds in obtaining labor, business, or other interest group support in his behalf, he cannot easily monitor their efforts. Representatives and Senators are well versed at listening sympathetically to interest group requests, but then proceeding to vote their own conscience, district, or state interests. Moreover, leadership contests are viewed by practically all members as internal affairs. Unlike legislative issues which sooner or later come to public votes, a member's vote in his party conference is by secret ballot and can seldom be identified. Hence, sanctions for noncompliance are all but impossible to apply.

The six-year term of office and the greater overall autonomy of Senators compared to Representatives make their leadership contests even more immune to external forces — White House, interest groups, state or local party influentials, and the media. They listen to outside spokesmen, especially campaign contributors. They keep abreast of editorial opinion in their home states. But they remain relatively free to make up their own minds about whom they support. Still, Senate candidates cannot ignore attempts to arouse external support any more than House candidates. Aside from reinforcing the viability of a candidate and his campaign, outside efforts can convert a marginal number of undecided votes, perhaps as many as one or two Senators or five to ten Representatives, in any given contest.[22] Unless the outside strategies of the opposing candidate or candidates neutralized these effects, even a few switches could well determine the outcome of a close contest.

One final factor — the temper of the times — can sometimes help to explain leadership stability or change when other factors seem to be operating at cross-purposes. In attempting to account for complex phenomena, social scientists sometimes fall back on what they term a "residual variable," or those nebulous factors left over when all other independent variables have been exhausted. In somewhat analogous fashion, the temper of the times refers to those broad historical and political forces which set a climate or mood for an era — war, depression, civil strife, or the aftermath of a major political scandal. Congressional leaders and followers are responsive to such forces. Much of the landmark legislation over the decades can be traced back to such forces. The urgency of the first 100 days of President Roosevelt's Administration and the 73d Congress (1933–1934), the mounting pressures to terminate the Vietnam War from the 90th to the 92nd Congress, the response of Democratically controlled Congresses to President Nixon's use of the veto powers in the 93d Congress — exceptional circumstances — illustrate the potential import of external events upon congressional leadership and their opportunities for accomplishments, vacillation, or immobility.

The direct impact of political, social, and economic crises upon leadership *selection* is both more tenuous and arduous to establish.

Perhaps an example or two can illustrate their possible impact. The election of freshman Speaker William Pennington just before the outbreak of the Civil War was earlier cited as one instance of the "temper of the times" at work. It may be that one of the secondary effects of the consensus politics of World War II was to enhance the myth and reality of Speaker Rayburn's effectiveness as a leader at the same time it contributed to his prolonged tenure. Moreover, it seems that all the events that culminated in the Watergate crisis, including Vice President Spiro Agnew's resignation, had a profound bearing and will continue to influence Republican congressional leadership selection patterns for some time to come. Most directly, of course these events led to Gerald Ford's appointment as Vice President and the selection of John Rhodes as the new House minority leader. Following President Richard M. Nixon's resignation in August 1974, under threats of House impeachment and Senate conviction, Ford was elevated to the presidency. The consequences of Ford's pardon of former President Nixon and other political crises of the new administration are unfolding now. The long-range impact of the Watergate incident on Republican congressional fortunes is not easy to project. At a minimum, it probably will handicap, if not postpone indefinitely, Republican hopes of becoming a majority in either the House or Senate for some time to come.

VI

Four major clusters of variables — individual, positional, institutional, and external — condition, if not determine, leadership selection, continuity, and change in the contemporary United States Senate and House of Representatives. This study has primarily focused upon the first three clusters, the *internal* conditions, which seem mainly to inhibit but sometimes facilitate congressional party leadership change. Only one *external* variable — congressional election results — has been singled out as especially critical for leadership selection. But even its impact has mainly been limited to the House minority party.

If there is one overall theme of this study which needs stressing, it is that *internal* conditions are primarily determinative in deciding who is to lead the House and Senate, Democrats and Republicans. Other external forces, such as presidential intervention or the role of the media and interest groups, are almost always indirect and marginal in their influence. Most often, internal and external conditions have combined to reinforce stability of leadership in all four congressional parties.

Of the 20 variables highlighted in this analysis, the most pervasive and continuing influence upon leadership selection for party office has been exerted by the personality and skill of the candidates and, especially, of the incumbent. Every leader in Congress, as in other organizations, brings to office a unique set of characteristics: age, ambition, education, health, personal skills, prior political and professional experience — in sum, a personality. Not only does this personality effect the opportunities he may have to obtain a leadership position, they also, in part, influence the extent to which he can maintain office and perhaps even alter the scope and potential of a given party position. A leader's personality, his strengths and liabilities, also is the single most important variable that affects his ability to withstand or succumb to a challenge.[23]

I make no ultimate claims to the exhaustiveness of the variables used in this study to attempt to explain congressional leadership selection processes. Some may prefer to collapse two or more variables into a single factor; other research may yield additional variables. Nevertheless, these 20 factors — usually present in most leadership contests and often working at cross-purposes — can be used to account for or explain the outcomes of nearly every major and minor case of leadership selection in the House and Senate over the past two decades.

Further historical research is needed to determine the degree to which the findings of this book are limited to the ten Congresses studied, the 84th to 93d (1955–1974), or, perhaps, have a broader applicability.[24] One major question raised by this study, but not yet answered, is the extent to which differential rates of contested change among the two parties in both chambers can be attributed to party differences — Democratic and Republican — or to extended majority or minority status. Clarification might come through detailed examination of the periods 1894 to 1930 and 1931 to 1954. During the earlier period the Republican party was in the majority save for a Democratic interlude from 1911 until 1918 in the House and 1913 to 1918 in the Senate. Since 1931, Democrats have controlled all but the 80th (1947–1948) and 83d (1953–1954) Congresses. A number of questions are central: did *majority* Republicans have proportionately fewer contested changes in the earlier period and if so, why? To what extent were the House revolt against Speaker Cannon (which stopped short of leadership change) and the Gillett-Mann (1919) and Snell-Tilson (1931) contests the exceptions among House Republicans rather than the rule? Conversely, to what extent did the *minority* Democrats of the pre-1930 Congresses resolve their party leadership selections through relatively harmonious means? How was the House Democratic party in the 1920's, fluctuating in size from 131 to 205 members, mainly able to avoid leadership contests? Were the series of party struggles which preoccupied House Democrats in the 1930's a spilling-over of the frustrations of prolonged minority status or a reflection of its new and relatively unwieldy party structure, or both? What explanatory factors were central to House leadership change, and which were of lesser importance in these earlier periods as compared to the last two decades? Of course, many of the same kinds of questions can also be raised with respect to majority Republican and minority Democratic leaders in the Senate. Much of the data will be difficult to collect, especially for the earlier Congresses. Interpretation, comparisons, and generalizations must be made with great caution. The contemporary House of Representatives, the character of the two major parties, and the nature of party leadership have all undergone extensive change, especially since World War II. The early formative decades of modern congressional leadership, however, have only recently begun to be explored and analyzed in any depth.

VII

Although the opening of the 94th Congress (1975–1976) was characterized by decisive Democratic gains and a predominant reform mood, in general, party leadership change was restrained. Democrats made a net gain of four seats in the Senate, beginning the session with a 61 to 38 seat advantage (the contested seat of New Hampshire was vacant for most of 1975). A net gain of 43 seats in the House gave Democrats a two-to-one-margin — 291 seats to 144 held by the G.O.P. The main thrust of the reform efforts was felt not by party leaders but by senior, southern conservative, House committee chairmen. Three chairmen — Wright Patman (D., Texas) of Banking and Currency, F. Edward Hébert (D., La.) of Armed Services, and W. R. Poage (D., Texas) of Agriculture — were ousted from their positions by votes in the House Democratic caucus. In addition, Wilbur Mills of

Arkansas, the venerable leader of the House Ways and Means Committee, retired from his chairmanship because of a combination of personal scandal and poor health. These four men averaged 74 years in age; their combined House service totaled 154 years.

Only one incumbent party leader in either house, Democrat or Republican, was contested at the opening of the 94th Congress. John Anderson of Illinois, the chairman of the House Republican Conference and the lone moderate in his party's leadership, withstood a challenge from Charles E. Wiggins, a conservative from California at his party's pre-Congress Conference on December 2, 1974. Anderson won by a vote of 85 to 52, a much more decisive margin than his close call over another conservative challenger in 1971. Wiggins, first elected to the House in 1966, had come to prominence as a staunch defender of President Nixon at the House Judiciary committee's impeachment inquiry during the summer of 1974. Although his stance on Watergate-related issues may have hurt Wiggins among his badly-battered, but surviving colleagues, Anderson's winning margin more closely reflected the heavy losses suffered by conservative House Republicans in the 1974 congressional elections.

John J. Rhodes, the conservative House minority leader, was not threatened with a revolt, despite his party's substantial electoral setback. Almost all outside observers, and more important, his own colleagues, were inclined to attribute these defeats to matters largely beyond his control, the Watergate affair, President Nixon's resignation from office, and the unhealthy state of the economy. Nevertheless, an older, less able Republican leader might have been under heavy fire, but Rhodes was maintaining the respect and allegiance which had won him the minority leadership by unanimous agreement only a year before. New York Representative Barber Conable, who had succeeded Rhodes as chairman of the House Republican Policy Committee in December 1973, also was routinely reelected in December 1974 by the over 140 returning or newly-elected Republicans.

A three-way contest to decide who would take the place of retiring House Minority Whip Leslie Arends of Illinois yielded a predictable outcome. Robert H. Michel, a nine-term, conservative member from Illinois, easily defeated two more junior and moderate opponents, Jerry L. Pettis of California and John N. Erlenborn of Illinois. Michel, who had succeeded Bob Wilson of California as chairman of the Republican National Congressional (Campaign) Committee in 1973, received 75 votes to 38 for Pettis and 22 for Erlenborn. His former position as the principal House Republican campaign fund-raiser was subsequently taken by Guy Vander Jagt of Michigan.

True to earlier historical patterns, an upsurge of Democratic congressional victories led to concentration upon caucus and committee reforms rather than party leadership confrontations. House Democratic party leadership selection patterns in 1975 were strongly characterized by maintenance of the *status quo*. Speaker Carl Albert of Oklahoma and Thomas P. O'Neill, Jr. of Massachusetts were both unanimously reelected by a pre-94th House Democratic Caucus with some 290 participants on December 2, 1974. They, in turn, reappointed John J. McFall of California as majority whip.

The selection of Senate Democratic and Republican leaders was likewise characterized by equanimity and continuity. All four top party leaders — Majority Leader Mike Mansfield of Montana, Majority Whip Robert C. Byrd of West Virginia, Minority Leader Hugh Scott of Pennsylvania and Minority Whip Robert P. Griffin of Michigan — were reelected unanimously to their positions by the opening-day party conferences on January 14, 1975.

The only party leadership contests taking place at the opening of the 94th Congress, beyond the two within the House Republican party already mentioned, were two contests held to fill vacated party leadership positions. Olin E. Teague (D., Texas) had retired from the chairmanship of the House Democratic Caucus (although not from the House), honoring a traditional two-term limitation on Democratic Caucus chairmen. Norris Cotton (R., N.H.), the Senate Republican Conference chairman for two years, had not run for reelection to the 94th Congress.

The outcome of the race for Democratic Caucus chairman appears likely to have the most far-reaching implications. At one of a series of pre-Congress caucuses held December 2, 1974, Phillip Burton defeated his fellow Californian, B. F. Sisk, by a vote of 162 to 111. The 75 newly elected Democrats were credited with having played a key role in the liberal Burton's victory over his more senior and conservative colleague. The first former chairman of the Democratic Study Group to advance to an important party leadership position, Burton has been frequently mentioned as a possible candidate for higher leadership office, perhaps as soon as 1977.

A reinstatement of traditional conservative-liberal voting patterns characterized the contest for the chairmanship of the Senate Republican Conference. On January 14, 1975, conservative Carl T. Curtis of

Nebraska defeated liberal Jacob K. Javits of New York by a vote of 23 to 14. Javits was apparently unable to widen his base beyond the support of the liberal-leaning Senate Republican Wednesday Club.

Were there any outcomes or unusual factors in the 94th Congress which might lead one to modify or alter earlier generalizations about party leadership selection patterns over the previous 10 Congresses? Not really. Most leaders were routinely reelected; the contests that took place came about to fill vacated positions; open competition was the rule. Republicans, especially in the House, continued their predominant reliance upon contested change; the Burton-Sisk battle over the House Democratic Caucus chairmanship was in character with an increasingly contentious mode of leadership selection in the majority party.

VIII

Future leadership change in all four congressional parties will provide a further test of the tentative findings of this study as well as perhaps generate a need for subsequent modifications of its underlying theoretical assumptions. Given the number and complexity of conditioning factors and the high component of chance — what Machiavelli called fortune, and modern social scientists label exogenous variables — prediction in politics, especially in terms of leadership selection and revolt, will always be hazardous. Poor health, a tendency to drink too much, other personal foibles, and even the possibility of extensive, party-wide, election losses can, perhaps, be taken into calculations about political change. But who can foresee a party leader's crippling heart attack, a fatal airplane crash, or a sudden decision to retire?

What can one predict about leadership stability or change in forthcoming Congresses? Is it possible to state with any precision the specific Democratic and Republican congressional leaders who will retire, will continue in office, will be challenged, will be defeated? Assessments of probabilities come easier than specific predictions. Even in the more rigorous natural sciences, specific predictions are often difficult, if not impossible. Ernest Nagel has commented:[25]

> We cannot predict with much accuracy where a leaf just fallen from a tree will be carried by the wind in ten minutes; for, although available physical theory is in principle capable of answering the question provided that relevant factual data

> are supplied about the wind, the leaf, and the terrain, we rarely if ever have at our command knowledge of such initial conditions. Inability to forecast the indefinite future is thus not unique to the study of human affairs, and is not a certain sign that comprehensive laws have not been established or cannot be established about the phenomena.

And, of course, the validity of conclusions developed from social or political inquiry are made all the more complicated by the possibility of "self-fulfilling or self-denying prophecies." Research findings about political events may sometimes, however rarely, lead to modifications in the behaviors of the actors under study.

These caveats aside, a science of politics would seem to be as dependent upon its ability to predict as on its capacity for explanation. Moreover, as Abraham Kaplan has observed, "if we can predict successfully on the basis of a certain explanation we have good reason, and perhaps the best sort of reason, for accepting the explanation." [26]

When change comes about in the House Democratic majority, it is most likely to occur because of the retirement of Speaker Albert, perhaps as early as 1976. Incumbent Majority Leader O'Neill probably will advance to the Speakership, although unlike his predecessors, he may face more than a symbolic challenge to his "automatic" succession. A contest is likely to develop for the majority leadership whenever it is vacated, most probably between the incumbent Democratic Caucus chairman, Burton; one or both of the appointive whips, McFall or the chief deputy whip, John Brademas of Indiana; and possibly a southern candidate as well. The two external variables most likely to affect the outcomes of these possible contests, indeed, whether they occur at all, are the presence or absence of a Democrat in the White House and the rate of return of the 75 Democratic freshmen, predominantly liberal, who were first elected to the House of Representatives in 1974. If Massachusetts Senator Edward Kennedy, for example, should be elected President, then O'Neill's elevation to the Speakership would be materially enhanced.

Leadership stability or change in the House Republican minority party will also turn somewhat upon the outcomes of the presidential and congressional elections of 1976. Minority Leader Rhodes should be able to maintain his position without challenge *unless* President Gerald Ford, his close friend and former colleague, chooses not to run or is defeated and the House G.O.P. makes little or no gains in the 1976 congressional races. Rhodes, like Ford before him, is unlikely to want to remain "a minority leader in perpetuity." But given Rhodes' popularity, the structure and the reduced numbers of his party, the next major House Republican leadership contest is more likely to come about as a result of his retirement rather than through a direct challenge.

Both Senate parties face the possibility, if not the probability, that their floor leaders will retire in 1976. Mansfield will be 73 years old and Scott, 76. Both normally would be up for reelection, Mansfield to his fifth term, Scott to his fourth. Should one or both men retire, then a contest in one or both parties would be almost inevitable. Robert Byrd, the Democratic whip, has to be considered the odds-on favorite to succeed Mansfield, but his moderate-conservative ideology is likely to draw liberal Democratic opposition. The problem for his opponents will be to agree upon a candidate with sufficient moderateness, seniority, and popularity around which to form a majority. Much will depend upon which liberal Democratic Senators are lured into the presidential sweepstakes. Incumbent Minority Whip Robert Griffin, Howard Baker, and, perhaps, John Tower are the most likely Republican Senators to replace Scott, should he choose to retire. Again, one or both contests could be influenced by the outcome of the presidential nominations and election and, of course, the number and ideological leanings of the incoming Democratic and Republican freshmen.

IX

Studies in depth of past and future leadership continuity and change in the United States Senate and House of Representatives as well as modification of the conceptual framework and leading hypotheses so as to apply to other legislatures — for example, the British House of Commons or the French Parliament — should improve our understanding of party leadership stability, succession, and change. Such research will also provide an opportunity for more examination of such important explanatory variables as the personality and skill of candidates, ideology, stages of leadership development, majority and minority status, party hierarchy and structure, and the impact of election results on party leadership stability and change. Who the leaders are and by what means they survive or fail would seem to be crucial questions for the understanding of workings of legislatures and their fundamental role in representative democracies.

NOTES

1. See, for example, Lewis A. Froman's listing of House-Senate contrasts in *The Congressional Process: Strategies, Rules, and Procedures* (Boston: Little, Brown, 1967), p. 7.
2. The House Democratic whip is an appointed position, which, of course, virtually eliminates the possibility of a contested challenge. The closest approximation to a contest came in 1973 when a substantial minority of House Democrats tried to convert this position into an elective one (see Chapter 8).
3. For a general assessment of this literature, see Fred I. Greenstein, *Personality and Politics* (Chicago: Markham, 1969); Jeanne N. Knutson, ed., *Handbook of Political Psychology* (San Francisco: Jossey-Bass, 1973).
4. David B. Truman, *The Congressional Party* (New York: Wiley, 1959), pp. 106–107, 206–208; Samuel C. Patterson, "Legislative Leadership and Political Ideology," *Public Opinion Quarterly* **27** (1963), 399–410. For an important qualification of this theme, however, see William E. Sullivan, "Criteria for Selecting Party Leadership in Congress," *Am. Pol. Qtr.* **3** (January 1975), pp. 25–44.
5. For example, one New York Senate seat over the past decade has been consecutively represented by Republican liberal Kenneth B. Keating, Democratic liberal Robert F. Kennedy, Republican liberal Charles E. Goodell (a Rockefeller appointee), and conservative Republican James L. Buckley. One Washington congressional district, the Fifth, consistently reelected conservative Republican Walter Horan for 11 consecutive terms. Since 1964, substantially the same district has returned moderate Democrat Thomas S. Foley, the chairman of the Democratic Study Group in the 93d Congress. Multiple examples of this wide range of ideological and party tolerances for many House and Senate seats could be cited.
6. In the nearly 200-year history of the House of Representatives, only three men were elected Speaker in their first terms: Frederick Muhlenberg of Pennsylvania (1789–1791, 1793–1795), the first Speaker; former Senator Henry Clay of Kentucky (1811–1814, 1815–1820, 1823–1825), who served in the House only as Speaker; and William Pennington of New Jersey (1859–1861), who was chosen because it seemed "impossible to elect anyone with a definitely avowed policy." M. P. Follett, *The Speaker of the House of Representatives* (New York: Longmans, Green, 1896), p. 71; *Guide to the Congress of the United States* (Washington, D.C.: Congressional Quarterly Service, 1971), pp. 129–147. For the implications of seniority on party leaders, in general, see Barbara Hinckley, *The Seniority System in Congress* (Bloomington: Indiana University Press, 1971), pp. 94–107.
7. Only one other twentieth-century Senate floor leader, John Kern of Indiana (1913–1917), was elected to that position in his first term and he after only two years in the Senate. Floyd M. Riddick, "Majority and Minority Leaders of the Senate: History and Development of the Offices of Floor Leaders," Senate Doc. 92–42, 92d Cong., 1st Sess. (Washington, D.C.: U.S. Government Printing Office, 1971), p. 9.
8. In the process of conducting over 400 interviews with members of Congress and their staffs during the past decade, a number of leadership attributes were mentioned with some frequency. Since the responses were elicited by a number of questions in which the wording was varied, and since most were keyed to particular individuals in the context of specific contests, generalizations do not come easy and they cannot be considered "representative" in the strict sampling sense of the term.

9. A further word of caution is in order about these and earlier propositions (Chap. 9). My initial inclination was to project such findings in a linear fashion, that is, the longer the majority or minority status, the more likely the leadership selection patterns would continue or be strengthened. Subsequent observations over four more Congresses suggest the need for caution in terms of extended trends. Patterns of leadership selection may be linear in the short run, cyclical over a longer time period. Uninterrupted majority status, now extending for two decades for House and Senate Democrats, may result in a congressional party which becomes overly rigidified at the top, its leadership, almost exclusively selected from its most senior establishment ranks. If this leadership becomes too prone to protect the *status-quo*, a natural reaction may set in among younger, more junior members. Instead of increased acceptance of leadership selection patterns, including their extension to lower levels in the party hierarchy, long majority status may increase widespread frustration and possibly, generate more contests rather than fewer. If a substantial number of younger members come to share these feelings, one or more of them — such as Udall, Conyers, Gibbons, or Burton — may launch challenges or try to thwart the pattern of succession, even if their initial chances of success appear slim.

Conversely, within the minority party, the presence of an especially popular floor leader, such as Jerry Ford or John Rhodes, may sometimes offset otherwise strong tendencies toward leadership change.

10. George Goodwin, *Little Legislatures* (Amherst: University of Massachusetts Press, 1970).

11. Richard F. Fenno, Jr., *Congressmen in Committees* (Boston: Little, Brown, 1973), pp. 190–191.

12. Representative Richard Bolling (D., Mo.), one of his closest lieutenants in the House, argues that Rayburn's powers were too heavily dependent upon personal influence: "A strong man during his tenure as Speaker, Rayburn surely was first among legislators . . . His power was so personal, so immense that it masked the institutional frailties of the House in general, and the Speakership in particular." Bolling, *House Out of Order* (New York: Dutton, 1965), p. 65.

13. House Democratic leaders, making the simplest of all transitions, merely resumed their former majority leadership positions in both 1949 and 1955. With transitions eased by the resignations of the two Senate floor leaders in 1948, both Democrats and Republicans chose to elevate their whips in January 1949. Kenneth Wherry of Nebraska replaced Wallace White of Maine for the Republicans; Scott Lucas of Illinois succeeded Alben Barkley of Kentucky, who had resigned from the Senate to become Vice President. In 1955, Lyndon Johnson (D., Texas) and William Knowland (R., Cal.) merely traded titles as Johnson became the new majority leader and Knowland took over as minority leader. Perhaps the House Republican transitions posed the greatest potential danger of conflict. In both 1949 and 1955 Speaker Joseph Martin dropped back to minority leader, Whip Leslie Arends retained his position, and Halleck was left somewhat in limbo as the acting assistant floor leader.

14. However, an unusually large number of incoming freshmen — on the order of 60 or more House Democrats or Republicans, 15 or more Senate freshmen of either party — might actually dampen party cohesion and bring on trying times for their party leadership. One recalls the problems faced by House Democratic leaders following a large class of freshmen members in the 75th

(1937–1938) and 86th (1959–1960) Congresses, and the situation faced by Senate Majority Leader Johnson after the 1958 election. However, none of these situations proved severe enough to bring about contested leadership change.

15. The smallest Democratic majorities for both Houses were in the 84th Congress (1955–1966); the largest were in the 89th Congress (1965–1966), see Tables 10.1 and 16.3.

16. Compiled from Tables of Continuous Service of Senators, *Congressional Directories*, 84th to 93d Congresses (Washington, D.C.: U.S. Government Printing Office, 1955–1974).

17. Norman J. Ornstein and David W. Rohde, "Seniority and Future Power in Congress," in Ornstein, ed., *Congress in Change* (New York: Praeger, 1975).

18. From the 67th (1921–1923) to the 72nd (1931–1933) Congresses, Senate Democrats, consistently in the minority, ranged in size from 37 to 47 members. Thus, southern dominance of their party caucus and leadership selection was virtually assured.

19. As Nelson W. Polsby suggests in Chapter 3, this appeared to be a major factor in President John F. Kennedy's decision not to intervene in the Albert-Bolling contest for House majority leader in 1961–1962.

20. Joseph Robinson of Arkansas, Democratic floor leader since 1923, died on July 14, 1937. Within 48 hours, Roosevelt had written Barkley his famous "My dear Alben" letter, pointedly addressing him as "acting majority leader in the Senate." Subsequently, the President was to pull back, conferring with Barkley and his more experienced and conservative opponent, Pat Harrison of Mississippi, and assuring both of his impartiality. *New York Times*, July 21, 1937, p. 1. The following day Barkley upset Harrison by one vote in the Democratic Caucus, 38 to 37. George H. Haynes, *The Senate of the United States: Its History and Practice* (Boston: Houghton, Mifflin, 1938), I, p. 481, n. 1.

21. In President Truman's case, Lucas was unopposed in 1949, but McFarland had opposition in 1951 from a so-called "Fair Deal" challenger, Joseph C. O'Mahoney of Wyoming. McFarland won by a vote of 30–19. One can only conjecture, here as in other leadership contests, the extent to which Presidents may get involved in behind-the-scenes activities, a quiet conversation here, a telephone call or two there. Especially for Presidents with prior service in one or both Houses, the temptations must be high.

22. This is little more than a "ball-park" estimate based on extensive interview responses and an occasional newspaper account. The complexity of motivations underlying a member's decision to support one candidate rather than another would prevent much greater precision, even if all such motivations could be determined. Most members would be inclined to downplay their receptivity to external pressures.

23. To argue that personality is crucial to understanding congressional leadership change is not to subscribe to any simplistic "great men" or "heroic" interpretation of history. Charismatic leaders are rare in Congress for many of the reasons first set forth by Max Weber, in his discussion of the routinization of charisma, in *Theory of Economic and Social Organizations*, ed. by Talcott Parsons (Glencoe, Ill.: Free Press, 1947), p. 106, n. 30; pp. 358–373. Moreover, all leadership contests are played out in the context of other important variables, such as seniority, ideology, patterns of succession, majority-minority status, election results, and so on.

24. See, for example, Robert A. Waller, "The Selection of Henry T. Rainey as

Speaker of the House," *Capitol Studies*, III (Spring, 1973), pp. 37–47; and the promising historical analysis of Garrison Nelson, previously cited in Chapter 15, n. 3.

25. Ernest Nagel, *The Structure of Science* (London: Routledge & Kegan Paul, 1961), p. 461.

26. Abraham Kaplan, *The Conduct of Inquiry* (San Francisco: Chandler, 1964), p. 350.

Index

509